LEADERSHIP EDUCATION 1990

A SOURCE BOOK

LEADERSHIP EDUCATION 1990

A SOURCE BOOK

**FOR THOSE PLANNING PROGRAMS AND
TEACHING COURSES IN LEADERSHIP**

Edited by

Miriam B. Clark and Frank H. Freeman

Published by

CENTER FOR CREATIVE LEADERSHIP
Greensboro, North Carolina

and

LEADERSHIP LIBRARY OF AMERICA, INC.
West Orange, New Jersey

LIBRARY OF CONGRESS CATALOGING IN PUBLICATION DATA IS AVAILABLE:

LC CARD NUMBER 90-35188

© Copyright 1990 by **Center for Creative Leadership**
　　　　　　　　5000 Laurinda Drive
　　　　　　　　P.O. Box P-1
　　　　　　　　Greensboro, North Carolina 27402-1660

ISBN 1-878435-01-9

Published by **Leadership Library of America, Inc.**
　　　　　　　235 Watchung Avenue
　　　　　　　West Orange, NJ 07052

CONTENTS

I. COURSES AND PROGRAMS - A list of courses and programs in leadership studies and development with contact persons (arranged alphabetically by institution).

Section A
COURSES ON COLLEGE AND UNIVERSITY CAMPUSES

Course syllabi are not categorized as are the program descriptions. Almost all of the courses are offered by colleges and universities. Some focus on leadership theory, others on development of leaders. Departments offering them and disciplines sponsoring them vary. Not all are at the undergraduate level; some are taught by graduate schools or in professional schools, or in continuing education divisions, or in the community. A few are long-established; many are new or emergent. Academic credit is offered by many. Student affairs offices are the overseers of some, while others couple curricular and co-curricular bases by using committees.

Reading through them, whatever the level of educational intent, one can find similarities --in stated objectives, purposes and goals as well as in teaching techniques. Within general frameworks, one can find similar methods used for the same or different outcomes. For example, journals and logs serve numerous purposes; internships and mentorships are used widely; some courses are didactic in tone, others experiential or combinations of both; some take their orientation from traditional disciplines such as psychology, sociology, political science, history, literature, and philosophy; others are interdisciplinary. Courses differ in format, size, and use of faculty and teachers. Some are offered during the day or in the evening; some are offered semester-long or on weekends or for intense week-long intervals. In each the objectives are stated explicitly and the methods are defended as pedagogically sound.

COURSES ON COLLEGE AND UNIVERSITY CAMPUSES

TABLE OF CONTENTS

Ball State University
Dept. of Secondary, Higher,
  and Foundations of Education
Muncie, IN 47306

James Marine
Ass't. Dean for Student Programs
317/285-5036

Leadership and Development of Student Organizations - ED HI 401
3 Credit Hours

PURPOSE: The course has as its central focus leadership of student organizations. However, the carryover to other areas of leadership is not only intended, but it is attested to by many former students who have taken the course during the past seven years. Three quarter hours of credit are granted by the department through which the course is offered and in which the instructor has academic rank. The course is designed to facilitate leadership development, thereby improving the campus and community.

ORGANIZATION AND CONTENT: This credited undergraduate course is organized into four units, preceded by an introductory session during which course objectives, content, format and requirements are discussed and class members get acquainted with each other.

The first unit of the course consists of a basic orientation to higher education. A special emphasis is placed on the historical role of student organizations in shaping programs and policies of higher education to help students better understand their own institution; attention is given to its history, philosophy, organization and personnel.

The second unit deals with the student clientele. Research on interests, needs and concerns of contemporary college students is reviewed. Basic theory and research dealing with learning and development of young adults, the primary constituency of student groups, are drawn from the social and behavioral sciences and applied to work with student groups.

The content of the third unit includes topics related to the building of effective groups: characteristics of groups, functional roles of group members, interpersonal communication, decision making, and techniques of improving group process. A variety of activities is utilized to explore various facets of group process, including role playing, viewing of films, exercises, demonstrations, discussions, case studies, and listening to recordings.

The final unit of the course deals with the skill areas in which competency is needed by individuals in order for them to fulfill leadership functions effectively. The areas which are included are: utilization of group resources, time management, effective meetings, goal setting, program planning, motivation and evaluation. Since a major focus of student organization life is program development, several sessions are devoted to that topic. Students are required, as their term project, to draw up and present a plan for a program or activity which the student would propose to be carried out by a student or community organization.

EVALUATION: A formal written evaluation is conducted at the conclusion of each term in which the course is offered. Students complete anonymously a rating scale which covers course content, format, outcomes, and instruction.

The student evaluations of the course have been very positive with the students reporting that they gain a great deal from it. An indication of the favorable response by students is the fact that most who enroll in the course do so based upon recommendations of students who have previously taken the class.

COURSE OBJECTIVES: The course is designed to assist students in assuming leadership roles in student organizations by focusing on understandings and skills required for effective involvement in groups. Specific goals of the course are to: Develop in the student a basic understanding of the historical development of student organizations within the structure of higher education; Enhance the student's understanding of the current scene in higher education in general and the nature of Ball State University specifically; Examine processes of personality development among college students as they relate to work with student organizations; Assist the student with self-understanding and self-realization as an individual as the basis for his/her assuming leadership roles in student organizations; Develop in the student an appreciation for and improved understanding of group processes, including formation of groups, goal setting, leader and member roles, and dynamics of group functioning; Refine the student's knowledge of techniques and methods of effective work with groups and organizations; Provide opportunities for the student to learn and apply skills in the leadership of groups; Improve the quality of student programs and organizations at Ball State University through the development of well-prepared student leaders.

COURSE ORGANIZATION: Very practical in its orientation, this course is structured as a seminar to promote maximum student interaction and problem solving. Except for one individual project, all of the work in the course is completed in class. It includes: Introduction; Foundations of Student Organizations; Interests, needs and concerns of students and their growth and development; The Building of Effective Groups; Management Skills.

REQUIREMENTS: Reading and review of articles and materials; Class participation and discussion; Case study analyses--application of principles and practices to group leadership situations; Term project; Mid-term and final examinations.

GRADING: Class Participation, 25%; Project, 25%; Examinations, 50%.

Project Outline: Goal(s) and Objectives; Organization (chart of committees/areas with number of persons and responsibilities of each; Resource Needs (facilities, materials, personnel); Program Details (activities, location(s), time(s), admission or sale price(s), date(s). Attach copies of any rules, guidelines, or schedules to be utilized; Promotion/Publicity; Timetable (deadline for getting tasks accomplished); Budget (detailed income and expenditures); Evaluation (specify evaluation techniques). Include copies of evaluation instruments to be utilized.

6

Blackburn College
Carlinville, IL 62626

Sam T. Meredith
Professor, Political Science
217/854-3231, ext. 267

Approaches to Political Leadership - PS 325

PURPOSE: The purpose of this course is to develop at Blackburn the area of leadership development. We are able to do this because we have in-house leadership experiences in the student-managed Work Program and other more common on-campus leadership opportunities. The purpose is to link this experience with liberal arts education and discover ways to develop the full potential of the Blackburn experience.

PHILOSOPHY: It is the philosophy of the course that effective leadership education is built on three pillars: a broad liberal arts education, specialized training in leadership, and experience in a leadership position. Liberal Arts has been the education of leaders throughout most of the English speaking world for several centuries. A solid grounding in history, philosophy, behavioral science, and communications gives future leaders the skills, the vision, and the flexibility to adapt to the many roles that they must occupy in the future. From history they learn to see themselves and what they are doing in historical perspective and develop a vision that connects the past with the future. From philosophy they learn to understand the values upon which decisions are based. From this they can develop the values of their followers and build commitment to the general principles that bind together organizations and social systems. They are able to deal with others who have different values without losing their own sense of direction. From the behavioral sciences they learn how the social, political, and economic systems behave and interact and how to influence these systems to achieve their goals. In addition, specific training in leadership or management is necessary to focus and apply the skills derived from liberal arts to solve particular problems and get desired results. Liberal arts alone is unfocused, management training alone tends to create a narrow focus. Finally, academic training must be informed by actual experience for the ideas to come alive and a deep understanding to develop. A leader must be able to "see" the concepts at work all around him before he can use them to achieve results. The leadership experiences in the Work and Social Programs, mundane and frustrating though they may seem, provide an ideal experiential base for leadership development. The purpose of the course is to pull these three sources of information together into a coherent, integrated understanding of leadership.

Leadership ability developed through both action and study should yield individuals who can see the connections between the abstract world of academic disciplines and the chaotic, mundane world of everyday experience. A leader is one who sees patterns where others see isolated events and who connects them to the goals and aspirations of the community where others see only their personal needs and frustrations. A leader is one who is firm on goals and standards but flexible in her dealings with followers, sensitive to their fears and aspirations and able to link her goals and standards to their needs. A leader must be sensitive to changing circumstances, able to diagnose the situation and style her approach to constraints she faces. The goal of this course is to build the intellectual component of these leadership skills.

REQUIRED TEXTS: Barber, James David, <u>Politics by Humans</u>, 1988; Bennis, Warren, and Burt Nanus, <u>Leaders: The Strategies for Taking Charge</u>, 1985; Edelman, Murray, <u>Constructing the Political Spectacle</u>, 1988; Fisher, Roger and William Ury, <u>Getting to Yes: Negotiating Agreement Without Giving In</u>, 1981; Kellerman, Barbara (ed.), <u>Political Leadership: A Source Book</u>, 1986; Portnoy, Robert A., <u>Leadership! What Every Leader Should Know About People</u>, 1986.

GRADING: Grades will be computed according to the following formula: Papers #1 and #2 worth 20% each. Papers #3 and #4 worth 25% each; Class participation worth 10%.

CLASS PARTICIPATION: Role-playing simulations are an integral part of the learning experience and active participation by all members of the class is essential. Absenteeism during simulations reduces the number of roles included and lowers the value of the experience for participants. Class participation grade is calculated as follows: Begin with 6 points out of a possible 10; unexcused absences during a simulation leads to a one point reduction per absence; additional points up to 10 may be earned by a positive contribution to the simulations and class discussion.

Each student will write <u>4 papers</u> designed to link the readings with experiences. The pedagogical purpose of the papers is to achieve a synthesis of three sources of insight: structured experiences done in class (e.g. role-playing simulations), "real world" experiences encountered outside of class (e.g. the Work Program), and the theoretical literature read during the semester. Topics for each paper are open but must be written within the following constraints: (1) Clarify lessons drawn from some of the structured experiences. (2) Identify and explicate parallels between these experiences and "real world" experiences outside of class. (3) Analyze and explain the theoretical meaning of these experiences using the literature covered in that section, which <u>must</u> be properly footnoted. The writer should make an effort to integrate as much of the reading as possible and footnotes will be used as the measure of how much reading was done. Grading will be based on content, originality, documentation, clarity, and composition. Plagiarism and crimes against the English language will adversely affect the grade.

<u>Looking Glass, Inc.® Simulation</u>: At some point in the semester we will be participating in a major simulation jointly with the business management class. It simulates the behavior of decision-makers in a glass company. This package is used by the Center for Creative Leadership in Greensboro, NC as part of its (very expensive) leadership training for executives in major corporations. <u>Attendance</u> is very important but I feel it is the student's responsibility to decide whether or not to attend class. However, while there is no formal penalty for missing class except on days when role-playing simulations are used, it is only reasonable to think that a regular pattern of nonattendance will hurt the class participation grade.

<u>Disagreements with the professor</u>: Political attitudes and opinions tend to reflect one's social background and self-interest, and since we have different backgrounds and interests there is no reason why we should be expected to agree. A student does not have to agree with the professor to get a grade in this class. It is both legitimate and desirable for you

to disagree with me and independently and critically evaluate the material. I will exercise my academic freedom and say what I think is accurate about politics; you have the same right. Political Science is a way of thinking about politics, not a set of right answers. I am not an infallible source of right answers; I have often been wrong and changed my opinions and interpretations. Airing our disagreements is an excellent way to learn how to think. So please, if you feel I am wrong, challenge me. Former Speaker of the House Sam Rayburn had two bits of advice for new members: "Learn to disagree without being disagreeable" and "Don't turn political differences into personal differences."

SCHEDULE

Part I: Theories in Action--Learning from Experience

Class Meetings
    1   Syllabus, role-playing exercise

A. Micropolitics and Leadership: Interpersonal Communication
    2   Robert A. Portnoy, Ch. 1, "Training Leaders to Work With People," pp. 1-22
           Ibid, Ch. 2, "Mechanisms of Human Behavior," pp. 23-56
    3   Ibid, Ch. 3, "Emotional Stability in Leadership," pp. 57-80
    4   Ibid, Ch. 4, "Basic Communication Skills," pp. 81-100
           Ibid, Ch. 5, "Applied Communication: Directions and Policies," pp. 101-124
    5   Ibid, Ch. 6, "Case Studies: Problems and Solutions," pp. 125-156
           Ibid, Ch. 7, "Summary," pp. 157-174

B. Integrative Bargaining and Interpersonal Problem-solving
    6   Fisher and Ury, Ch. 1, "Don't Bargain Over Positions," pp. 3-16
    7   Ibid, Ch. 2, "Separate the People from the Problem," pp. 17-40
           Ibid, Ch. 3, "Focus on Interests, Not Positions," pp. 41-57
    8   Ibid, Ch. 4, "Invent Options for Mutual Gain," pp. 58-83
           Ibid, Ch. 5, "Insist on Using Objective Criteria," pp. 84-100
    9   Ibid, Ch. 6, "What If They Are More Powerful?" pp. 101-111
           Ibid, Ch. 7, "What If They Won't Play?" pp. 112-133
    10   Ibid, Ch. 8, "What if They Use Dirty Tricks?" pp. 134-150
           Paper #1 Due

C. Organizational Politics and Leadership: Putting it All Together
    11   Bennis and Nanus, "Mistaking Charge," pp. 1-18
           Ibid, "Leading Others, Managing Yourself," pp. 19-86
    12   Ibid, "Strategy I: Attention Through Vision," pp. 87-109
    13   Ibid, "Strategy II: Meaning Through Communication," pp. 110-153
    14   Ibid, "Strategy III: Trust Through Positioning," pp. 152-186
    15   Ibid, "Strategy IV: The Deployment of Self," pp. 187-214
           Ibid, "Taking Charge: Leadership and Empowerment," pp. 215-229

Part II: Developing an Interdisciplinary Theory of Leadership

A. The Classic Studies: Many Separate Approaches, Little Common Theory
1. The Impact of Leaders on History
      16   Sidney Hook. "The Eventful Man and the Event-Making Man," in Kellerman, Political Leadership, pp. 24-35

                Fred Greenstein, "Personality and Politics," in Kellerman, Political Leadership, pp. 36-48

2. The Psychology of Leaders: Why Do They Lead?
      17   Alexander L. George, "Power as a Compensatory Value," in Kellerman, Political Leadership, pp. 70-91

                E. Victor Wolfenstein, "The Revolutionary Personality," in Kellerman, Political Leadership, pp. 92-100

                Paper #2 Due

3. The Psychology of Followers: Why Do They Follow?
      18   T. W. Adorno et al., "The 'Authoritarian' Syndrome," in Kellerman, Political Leadership, pp. 118-122

                Stanley, Milgrim, "The Dilemma of Obedience," in Kellerman, Political Leadership, pp. 129-138

      19   Fred H. Willhoite, Jr., "Primates and Political Authority," in Kellerman, Political Leadership, pp. 139-169

4. Types of Leaders: Is it the Person or the Situation?
      20   a. Democratic Leadership; Joseph A. Schumpeter, Democracy as Competition for Leadership," in Kellerman, Political Leadership, pp. 199-205

                b. Totalitarian Leadership; Hannah Arendt, "The Totalitarian Leader," in Kellerman, Political Leadership, pp. 211-220

                c. Revolutionary Leadership; Crane Brinton, "The Accession of the Extremists," in Kellerman, Political Leadership, pp. 221-231

      21   d. Charismatic Leadership; Ann Ruth Willner, "Charismatic Leadership," in Kellerman, Political Leadership, pp. 245-249

                e. Entrepreneurial Leadership; Eugene Lewis, "Political Leader as Entrepreneur," in Kellerman, Political Leadership, pp. 250-264

                f. Nonconstituted Leadership; Robert C. Tucker, "Nonconstituted Leaders," in Kellerman, Political Leadership, pp. 265-268

5. Leader-Follower Interactions: The Chemistry of Leadership
      22   J. R. P. French, Jr., and B. Raven, "The Bases of Social Power," in Kellerman, Political Leadership, pp. 300-318

                Niccolo Machiavelli, "The Prince," in Kellerman, Political Leadership, pp. 376-387

                Kurt Lewin, "Authoritarianism and Democratic Leadership," in Kellerman, Political Leadership, pp. 388-395

      23   Irving L. Janis, "Groupthink," in Kellerman, Political Leadership, pp. 327-346

6. What is a Leader?
      24   James MacGregor Burns, "The Difference Between Power Wielders and Leaders," in Kellerman, Political Leadership, pp. 287-299

Ibid, "Leadership," in Kellerman, <u>Political Leadership</u>, pp. 419-424

Leadership: The Human Dynamic

OBJECTIVES: The objectives of this course are to: 1. provide a basic understanding of the theories of leadership and group dynamics; 2. assist students in developing a personal philosophy of leadership, an awareness of the moral and ethical responsibilities of leadership, and an awareness of one's own ability and style of leadership; 3. provide the opportunity to develop essential leadership skills through study and observation of the application of those skills; 4. encourage students to develop their leadership potential and to engage in productive leadership on campus.

An outline of the major sections of this course, and the skills and values to be developed within each, is presented at the end of this syllabus.

TEXTS: Johnson, David W., Johnson, Frank P., Joining Together. Prentice-Hall, Inc.; Gardner, John W., Leadership Papers, 1-6. The Independent Sector; McConagha, Glenn L., Blackburn College, 1837-1987: An Anecdotal and Analytical History of The Private College. Ovid Bell Press; Assigned readings

READING ASSIGNMENTS: These assignments should be read for discussion in class on the day for which they are listed in the syllabus. G-1, etc. refers to the Leadership Papers by John W. Gardner. Ch-1, etc. refers to the corresponding chapter in Joining Together. McC 1-6, etc. refers to the corresponding sections in Blackburn College, 1837-1987. In addition to these texts, articles will be distributed in class, and one autobiography or biography will be read.

WRITTEN ASSIGNMENTS: Two 5-page (typed, double-spaced) papers will be written. The first paper will address a topic of particular interest to the student's leadership development. The second paper will be an assessment of the leadership style of a well-known person (determined from an autobiography or biography and current events, if appropriate). Both the topic for the first paper and the book for the second paper may be chosen by the student and approved by the instructor.

Students will also work in small groups to interview campus constituents and present a 2-page group report on the political realities of campus decision-making.

CLASS PARTICIPATION: Regular attendance and participation in class discussions and activities is expected. Students with two or fewer unexcused absences, and who have contributed to the classes, may receive up to 50 additional points for "class participation."

EXAMINATIONS: There will be two examinations in this course: a mid-term and a final covering assigned readings and class discussions.

Components of the Final Grade: Mid-term, 100; Papers I & II, 200 (100 pts. each); Group Report, 50; Final, 150; Total, 500.

SYLLABUS

<u>Leadership Theory and Styles</u>
Class Meeting
1   Introduction: The Study of Leadership
2   The Nature of Leadership, G-1
3   The Tasks of Leadership, G-2
<u>Understanding Self</u>
4   Styles of Leadership, Ch. 2
5   Myers-Briggs Type Indicator, Ch. 1
6   Assessment of MBTI, Handout
7   Values Clarification, Ch. 6
<u>Understanding Groups</u>
8   Communication Process, Ch. 5
9   Active Listening and Emotional Literacy, Handout
10   Reading A Meeting, Ch. 5, Handout
11   Group Decision-Making, Ch. 3
12   Conflict Resolution, Ch. 7
13   Mid-term, **Paper I Proposal**
14   Power: What Is It?, G-4, Ch. 8
15   Power: Use and Abuse, **Paper I Due**, G-4, Ch. 8
16   Moral Aspect; The Leader As Servant, G-5
17   Motivation and Volunteers, **Paper II Proposal**, Ch. 11
18   Effective Meetings: Parliamentary Procedure, Handout
19   Goal Setting in Groups, Ch. 4
20   The "Life" of a Group, Ch. 12
<u>Understanding The Context</u>
21   The Life and Mission of B. U., McC 1-6
22   The Life and Mission of B. U., McC 7-10
23   A History of Student Involvement, McC 11-14
24   Analysis of Political Realities, McC 15-18
25   Analysis of Political Realities, McC 19-22
26   Analysis of Political Realities, **Paper II Due**, McC 23-26
27   Identification of Campus Issues, McC 27-30
28   Effective Advocacy: Gameplan, McC 31-34
29   Traits of Leadership, G-6
30   Free Day
31   Final Exam

13

STAGE	SKILL	VALUE

Self	active listening
	speaking
	feedback--accurate
	  reflection
	recognition of one's
	  own/other's feelings
	appropriate assertiveness
	recognition of one's
	  personal profile and
	  interests
		acceptance of diversity
		understanding of feelings/compassion
		self-esteem/positive regard

Groups	situational leadership
	innovative problem
	  solving
	managing conflict
	motivating others
	identifying needs
	group process analysis
	  and "life"
	communication analysis
	active listening
	parliamentary procedure
	goal setting
	understanding of
	  organizational culture
		developing servanthood
		empathy with other's views
		ethical concerns in leading others
		finding positive dimensions
		  in anger, conflict, adversity
		ethics of power

Context	discernment of
	  Blackburn's unique
	  mission and history
	administrative
	  functioning
	effective campus advocacy
	recognition of the
	  political realities
	  of a situation
		goals of higher education (esp.
		  Liberal Arts)
		concern for the development of
		  the "whole person"
		involvement
		positive dimensions of change
		  and tradition
		servanthood
		commitment

(Based on the Elliot Fellows Program)

Black Hills State College
1200 University, Spearfish, SD 57783

Doug Wessel
Assoc. Professor/Education & Psychology
605/642-6550

Leadership: Theory and Practice - Ed 452, PE 291/491, Pols 292/492, Soc 294/494, Comm 291/491, BAd 487

PURPOSES: A. An interdisciplinary survey of leadership behavior; B. An opportunity to observe and/or practice leadership behavior outside of the classroom.

OBJECTIVES: A. Cognitive: Understanding leadership in a historical perspective; Knowledge of leadership theory and research; Awareness of the philosophical and ethical issues in leadership; Familiarity with the contributions of several disciplines to the understanding of leadership; Understanding the application of various leadership styles in different settings. **B. Process - Skills:** Continued development of reading and oral skills based on critical thinking; Enhancement of writing skills; Development of skills that will increase the student's ability to be an effective leader. **C. Affective:** Increased insight into personal leadership style and its effects on other people; Enhancement of a personal sense of civic responsibility; Creation of the desire to serve as an effective leader.

TEXTBOOKS AND READINGS: In Search of Excellence, Thomas J. Peters and Robert H. Waterman, Jr., 1982; The Nature of Leadership and The Tasks of Leadership, John W. Gardner, 1986; Handouts provided in class.

EVALUATION:

A. Involvement: This class is designed to encourage discussion and student participation in reacting to the ideas presented by the faculty and the readings. 25% of the final grade will be based on involvement as assessed by the coordinator; attendance will be one factor considered in this component.

B. Applied Component: This may be fulfilled by either involvement in a leadership position in a campus or noncampus organization during the semester or a one week observation of a leader during spring break. 20% of the final grade will be based on oral and written analysis of this experience. If you elect the observation option, the coordinator and other faculty will assist you in arranging the placement.

C. Written Assignments: 9 short (2-4 pages) written essays and reaction papers assigned by various faculty members during the course and evaluated by the respective faculty member, the grade reported to the coordinator. 45% of the final grade will be derived from these assignments.

D. Final Exam: An essay written during the final exam period to synthesize the course material. 10% of the final grade.

REMARKS: This course is an exciting opportunity to explore the topic of leadership from an interdisciplinary perspective. If you have any problems or questions regarding the course, please visit with the coordinator or other faculty. Suggestions for improving the course are welcome.

TENTATIVE COURSE OUTLINE:

I. What is Leadership?

Sessions
1   Introduction
2   History of Leadership Study
3   Leadership: General Concepts and Qualities
4   Transactional or Transformational Leadership
5   Creativity and Leadership
6   Parent Education and Leadership

II. Styles of Leadership

7   Classical Styles of Leadership
8   Leadership in the Public Sector
9   Presidential Leadership
10   Presidential Leadership
11   Leadership in the Private Sector
12   In Search of Excellence - Film
13   In Search of Excellence
14   Leadership in the American Indian Community
15   Leadership in the American Indian Community

III. How Do People Lead?

16   Preparation for Observations
17   Observations
18   Oral Reports on Observations
19   Oral Reports on Observations
20   Using Research on Principal Leadership
21   Assessment of Behavior Styles and Leadership
22   Assessment of Behavior Styles and Leadership
23   Leadership as Ethos/Credibility
24   Leadership as Deep Rhetoric
25   Stages of Small Group Development
26   Stages of Small Group Development
27   Leadership Through the Informal Organization
28   Leadership Assessment of Organizational Effectiveness
29   Understanding of Organizational Climate and Culture
30   Ethics in Leadership
31   Film "Citizen Kane"
32   Synthesis
33   Final Exam

Bryant College
450 Douglas Pike, Smithfield, RI 02917-1284

Ronald Deluga
Coordinator
Learning for Leadership Program
401/232-6279

Learning for Leadership Program
Education for Business Leadership

The Bryant College's Learning for Leadership Program is designed to prepare, challenge, and inspire students to meet the changing leadership needs of the national and international business climate.

The Learning for Leadership Program is organized into a two-semester course sequence.

PART I. ID 361 Learning for Leadership - 3 credit hours

REQUIRED READINGS: Clemens, J. K., & Mayer, D. F. (1987). The Classic Touch: Lessons in Leadership from Homer to Hemingway. Garfield, C. (1986). Peak Performers: New Heroes of American Business. Yukl, G. (1981). Leadership and Organizations. Outside readings, handouts, etc. as assigned.

DESCRIPTION: A classroom action-oriented intensive examination of aspects of "leadership" viewed from multidisciplinary and international perspectives. Related issues applied are: why study leadership; leadership lessons learned from history; sources, theories, and styles of leadership; characteristics of peak performing and high achieving leaders; power and politics of leadership; ethical decisions; values clarification; gender issues; leader effectiveness; leader-follower dynamics; followership; leadership in groups; costs of leadership, stress; wellness/physical fitness; creativity; decision making, analyzing and solving problems.

The course facilitates student/professor learning and is built on student's individual strengths. Whether your personal strengths involve: verbal communication skills (class contributions); writing abilities; and/or objective test-taking skills (objective/subjective test), you will have opportunity to "shine." The course will provide each student occasions to practice undeveloped strengths in the relatively safe environment of the classroom.

OBJECTIVES: A. Discriminate basic theoretical constructs. Given objective questions/ essays, you will demonstrate an ability to identify and discriminate leadership issues. (Method: Final Exam.) B. Develop familiarity with relevant leadership issues and literature. (Method: By written analysis and discussion of: Leadership Profile paper [10 pages]; Three Reaction Papers to Guest Lecturers [3-5 pages each]; Success/Failure Paper [7 pages]). C. Increase skills in testing and communication of ideas. (Method: Through enthusiastic class contributions, participation in guest lecture series, class debates, & experiential exercises). D. Learning about yourself as a future leader. (Method: Through self-assessment, class exercises, and assignments).

GRADING: 1. Leadership Profile (100 pts.) 2. Final Exam (comprehensive) (100 pts.)
3. First Reaction Paper (25 pts.) 4. Second Reaction Paper (25 pts.) 5. Third Reaction
Paper (25 pts.) 6. Class contributions (50 pts.) 7. Strengths/Weaknesses Paper (75 pts.)
Total possible = 400 pts.

PART II. ID 497 Mentorship Program - 3 credit hours - Prerequisite: ID 361

As an optional second course, advanced leadership students are exposed to professional
leadership activity through an arranged mentoring relationship. Mentors are recognized and
experienced area leaders who have expressed a desire to assist student leadership
development. Advanced leadership students serve as mentors to lower level undergraduate
students. The course enables the student to utilize and test what was learned in ID 361
with an established leader and his/her leadership situation. Course objectives are to:
enhance the leadership development of both students and mentors; provide experiences in
relationships needed for personal, career, and organizational success; expose participants
to ideas and thinking of different generations; develop a Bryant College leadership network.

The Learning for Leadership Program addresses the applied-practice leadership education
spectrum through the enactment of three converging areas: leadership theory, self-
assessment, and applied experiences.

1. **Theory** - A multidisciplinary perspective is used: why study leadership; leadership
lessons learned from history; sources, theories, and styles of leadership; characteristics of
peak performing and high achieving leaders; power and politics of leadership; ethical
decisions; values clarification; gender issues; leader effectiveness; leader-follower dynamics;
followership; leadership in groups; costs of leadership, stress; wellness/physical fitness;
creativity; decision making, analyzing and solving problems; application of these issues.
2. **Self-Assessment** - Students learn about their own strengths, weaknesses, attitudes, and
behavior patterns through extensive feedback obtained from: leadership workshops; videotaped group and individual exercises; paper and pencil instruments; class assignments;
mentoring relationships.
3. **Applied Experiences** - ID 361 Learning for Leadership class exercises and assignments;
ID 497 Mentorship; Leadership Speakers Forum; Linkages with area leadership professional
groups; Student campus, employment, and community leadership activities; Participation in
the ongoing evaluation and improvement of all components of the Program.

A variety of learning techniques to stimulate student leadership development include
experiential exercises, case studies, issue debates, Leadership Speakers Forum, lectures,
group activities, written assignments, exams, and the joint sharing of leadership experiences.
The aim is to have students experience success and discover that the study and exercise of
leadership is an exciting and demanding endeavor. Successful leadership practitioners and
prominent scholars are invited to campus as "a guest leader for the day." The Forum
enables students to interact informally with them. ID 361 and ID 497 meet College
requirements for Social Science, Liberal Arts, and unrestricted electives.

California State University
Sacramento, CA 95819

Pauline Guinther
916/278-6192

Leadership and Communication - PE 139

Leadership and Communication is a three-unit course that meets in a two-hour-block of time once a week with 15 hours arranged. Because this course is based on the experiential model of teaching/learning, the experiences are specifically designed to run from 1.5 to 2 hours, including the debriefing.

Students are placed in a structured experience setting based on concepts listed in Course Content of the course outline. In that setting, students act and interact, problem solve and are debriefed. As a result of the debriefing, the knowledge bridge between theory and reality are gapped and a set of generalizations are derived which are then applied to the situation or similar situations.

As a basis for these events, students are required to complete a project, based on all of the required readings, in the form of a series of in-depth conceptual questions related to leadership and communication. This "forces" them to do all of the wide reading required in advance and use their interpretations to answer the questions posed. This knowledge is then used as the basis of the interactions in the structured experiences as well as the subsequent debriefing sessions. They then have information to generalize from and to make applications to real life situations. They do this in the form of a required reaction paper which is due after participation in each of the structured experiences.

When projects are turned back to students, they may add to, delete from, modify and turn them back in as many times as possible until the final deadline. They will spend considerable time in consultation with the instructor during each phase of the project. (Projected time for project completion is from 18 to 25 hours, which is part of the 15 additional hours arranged.) Projects are revised every semester.

At present, Leadership and Communication is an elective in the Physical Education program and is open to non-majors. It is required for Biodynamics students moving into the services area of corporate fitness and other related programs. It is essential that students learn (hands-on) how to deal effectively with people at all levels of the business and corporate as well as educational hierarchy.

COURSE OBJECTIVES: Students shall: Investigate and implement the theories of group dynamics; Participate in small and large group interaction; Demonstrate ability to communicate effectively orally and in written form; Demonstrate ability to effect problem-solving techniques; Write acceptable critiques related to structured experiences; Write an in-depth research project related to leadership and communication literature; Actualize a personal approach to the process of leadership and communication based on an ethical format.

COURSE CONTENT: The communication process (written and verbal); Non-verbal communication; Listening; Group dynamics; Cooperation; Competition; Conflict resolution;

Consensus seeking and decision making; Negotiation; Leadership; Problem solving; Personal ethics; Synthesizing the literature; Putting it all together.

COURSE REQUIREMENTS, ASSIGNMENTS AND GRADING PLAN:

Written Literature Search	100
Role Play	25
Reaction Papers to Structured Experiences	
(8 to 10 points each)	80
Non-verbal Communication Reaction Paper	10
Verbal Presentation (arranged)	25
TOTAL	240

A - 92% of total or 220 points
B - 83% of total or 199 points
C - 77% of total or 184 points

EQUIPMENT NEEDED:

Overhead Projector; Filmstrip Projector; Tinker Toys; Lego Blocks; Cooperation Squares Puzzle; Paper, Pencils, Felt Pens, Planning Sheets; Tables; Structured Experience Master Sheets

METHODOLOGY:

Discussion (large and small group); Tape Recordings (student); Filmstrips (student); Simulation and Interaction Games (student); Problem Solving; Student Demonstrations; Role Playing (student); Special Communication Presentation.

BASIC READING LIST:

Ackoff, R. L. (1978). The Art of Problem-Solving. New York: John Wiley; Adams, J. D. (Ed.). (1980). Understanding and Managing Stress: A Book of Readings. San Diego, CA: University Associates; Argyris, C. (1982). Reasoning, Learning and Action. San Francisco: Jossey-Bass; Arnold, H. J. and Feldman, D. C. (1986). Organizational Behavior. New York: McGraw-Hill; Bass, B. M. (1985). Leadership & Performance Beyond Expectations. New York: Free Press; Benne, K. D., Bradford, L. P., Gibb, J. R. and Lippitt, R. D. (Eds.). (1975). The Laboratory Method of Changing and Learning. Palo Alto, CA: Science and Behavior Books; Bennis, W. and Nanus, B. (1985). Leaders: The Strategies for Taking Charge. New York: Harper & Row; Blake, R. R. and Mouton, J. S. (1984). Solving Costly Organizational Conflicts. San Francisco, CA: Jossey-Bass; Blake, R. R. and Mouton, J. S. (1983, June). Developing a Positive Union-Management Relationship. Personnel Administrator, pp. 23-32; Blake, R. R. and Mouton, J. S. (1984). Managerial Grid III (3rd Ed.). Houston, TX: Gulf; Bradford, L. P. (1976). Making Meetings Work. San Diego, CA: University Associates; Brown, L. D. (1983). Managing

Conflict at Organizational Interfaces. Reading, MA: Addison-Wesley; Burke, W. U. (1983). Organization Development. Boston, MA: Little, Brown; Burley-Allen, M. (1983). Managing Assertively. New York: John Wiley; Duncan, P. K. (1983). Current Topics in Organizational Behavior Management. New York: Haworth; Fisher, R. and Urg, W. (1983). Getting To Yes. New York: Penguin; Francis, D. and Young, D. (1979). Improving Work Groups: A Practical Manual for Team Building. San Diego, CA: University Associates; Goodstein, L. D. and Pfeiffer, J. W. (Eds.). (1985). The 1985 Annual: Developing Human Resources. San Diego, CA: University Associates; Gordon, T. (1977). Leader Effectiveness Training. New York: Wyden; Harvey, D. F. and Brown, D. R. (1982). An Experiential Approach To Organization Development (2nd Ed.). Englewood Cliffs, NJ: Prentice-Hall; Hersey, P. (1985). The Situational Leader: The Other 59 Minutes. New York: Warner Books; Hersey, P. and Blanchard, K. (1982). Management of Organizational Behavior (4th Ed.). Englewood Cliffs, NJ: Prentice-Hall; Horn, R. E. (1978). The Guide to Simulation Games for Education and Training. Lexington, MA: Information Source; Johnson, D. W. and Johnson, F. P. (1982). Joining Together: Group Theory and Group Skills. Englewood Cliffs, NJ: Prentice-Hall; Kaufman, R. (1982). Identifying and Solving Problems: A System Approach (3rd Ed.). San Diego: University Associates; Kaufman, R. A. (1983). Planning for Organizational Success: A Practical Guide. New York: John Wiley; Kolb, D. and Fry, R. (1981). Experiential Learning Theory and Learning Experience in Liberal Arts Education: New Directions for Experiential Learning. San Francisco: Jossey-Bass; Kolb, D. A., Rubin, I. M., and McIntyre, J. M. (1984). Organizational Psychology: An Experiential Approach to Organizational Behavior (4th Ed.). Englewood Cliffs, NJ: Prentice-Hall; Lassey, W. R. and Sashkin, M. (1983). Leadership and Social Change (3rd Ed.). San Diego, CA: University Associates; Likert, R. and Likert, J. G. (1976). New Ways of Managing Conflict. New York: McGraw-Hill; Locke, E. and Latham. G. P. (1984). Goal Setting: A Motivational Technique That Works. Englewood Cliffs, NJ: Prentice-Hall; Maccoby, M. (1976). The Gamesman: The New Corporate Leaders. New York: Simon & Schuster; McConkey, D. D. (1983). How to Manage by Results (4th Ed.). New York: AMACOM; Ouchi, W. (1981). Theory Z. Reading, MA: Addison-Wesley; Nierenberg, G. (1968, 1982). Fundamentals of Negotiating. New York: Hawthorne; Pascale, R. T. and Athos, A. G. (1981). The Art of Japanese Management. New York: Simon & Schuster; Peters, T. and Austin, A. (1985). A Passion for Excellence: The Leadership Difference. New York: Random House; Peters, T. and Waterman, R. H. Jr. (1982). In Search of Excellence: Lessons from America's Best-Run Companies. New York: Warner Books; Pfeiffer, J. W., Goodstein, L. D., and Nolan, T. M. (1986). Applied Strategic Planning: A How To Do It Guide. San Diego, CA: University Associates; Pfeiffer, J. W. and Goodstein, L. D. (Eds.). (1984, 1986). The Annual: Developing Human Resources. San Diego, CA: University Associates; Pneuman, R. and Bruehl, M. (1982). Managing Conflict: A Complete Process-Centered Handbook. Englewood Cliffs, NJ: Prentice-Hall; Robert, M. (1982). Managing Conflict From Inside Out. San Diego, CA: University Associates; Schorer, J. J. (1984). The Pinch Package: For Renewing Relationships at Home and at Work. San Diego, CA: University Associates; Shea, G. F. (1983). Creative Negotiating. Boston, MA: CBI; Simmons, J. and Maris, W. T. (1983). Working Together. New York: Alfred A. Knopf; Zuher, E. (1983). Assertiveness

Training for Managers. New York: AMACOM.

Journals: California Management Review; Group and Organization Studies; Harvard Business Review; Human Systems Management; Journal of Applied Behavioral Science; Journal of Applied Psychology; Journal of Creative Behavior; Journal of Instructional Development; Journal of Organizational Behavior Management; Management Science; Organizational Behavior and Human Performance; Organizational Dynamics; Performance and Instruction Journal; Personnel Journal; Personnel Psychology; Psychology Today; Psychological Bulletin; Training; Training and Development Journal.

Supplemental Reading List:

Bass, B. M. (1985). Leadership and Performance Beyond Expectations New York: Free Press; Clemens, J. K. and D. F. Mayer (1987). The Classic Touch: Lessons in Leadership from Homer to Hemingway. Homewood, IL: Dow Jones-Irwin; Cribbin, J. J. (1982). Leadership: Strategies for Organizational Effectiveness. New York: AMACOM; Crosby, P. B. (1987). Running Things: The Art of Making Things Happen. New American Library; Geneen, H. S. and Moscow, A. (1984). Managing. New York: Doubleday; Guest, R. H., Hersey, P. and Blanchard, K. (1986). Organizational Change Through Effective Leadership. 2nd Ed. Englewood Cliffs, NJ: Prentice-Hall; Hein, E. C. (1986). Contemporary Leadership Behavior: Selected Readings. 2nd Ed. Boston: Little, Brown; Heller, T. (1986). Leaders and Followers: Challenges for the Future. JAI Press; Hoferek, M. J. (1986). Going Forth: Woman's Leadership Issues for Women in Higher Education and Physical Education. Princeton, NJ: Princeton Book Company; Johnston, J. S., Jr. et al. (1986). Educating Managers: Executive Effectiveness Through Liberal Learning. San Francisco, CA: Jossey-Bass; Kellerman, B. (Ed.). (1984). Leadership: Multidisciplinary Perspectives. Englewood Cliffs, NJ: Prentice-Hall; Kennedy, D. M. and Parrish, M. E. (Eds.). (1986). Power and Responsibility Case Studies. San Diego, CA: Harcourt Brace Jovanovich; Lasoncy, L. (1985). The Motivating Leader. Englewood Cliffs, NJ: Prentice-Hall; Portnoy, R. A. (1986). Leadership: What Every Leader Should Know About People. Englewood Cliffs, NJ: Prentice-Hall; Rosenbach, W. E. and Taylor, R. L. (Eds.). (1984). Contemporary Issues in Leadership. Boulder, CO: Westview; Schaller, L. E. (1986). Getting Things Done: Concepts and Skills For Leaders. Abingdon.

Carson-Newman College
Box 1925, Jefferson City, TN 37760

Bernard F. Bull
Director of Student Teaching
615/475-9061 ext. 319

Teacher as Leader - Education 538

DESCRIPTION: Assists the teacher in developing skills to use appropriate leadership styles for various situations. The teacher will demonstrate practical applications of these leadership roles.

TEXT: Clifton Williams, Leadership Quest; Developing Leadership Skills, Enhancing Your Power to Influence, Leadership Press, Inc. 1986.

OBJECTIVES:
- gain a broad overview of leadership styles and situations for using different approaches;
- become aware of one's self and how one's values influence ethics, decision making and self-confidence;
- develop skills for better organizational planning and ways and means for creativity and risk taking;
- plan for better time management;
- learn the relationship between personality and leadership and to develop proper assertiveness;
- learn how to maintain a high level of motivation;
- learn to delegate responsibility and to elicit participation;
- improve skills of conducting meetings, establishing agendas;
- learn to be more effective in making decisions;
- establish ways for motivating others to voluntarily follow;
- learn how to organize one's position on a professional issue and present it effectively to an audience of peers, parents and/or supervisors;
- establish professional goals and implement effective strategies for goal attainment;
- develop meritorship qualities and supervisory skills needed for the teacher as a leader.

OUTLINE:
Module I   Leadership: A Bias for Action
Module II Personal Dimensions of Leadership Development
Module III Developing Your Leadership Skills

ASSIGNMENTS:
- Study text and participate in discussion on each section; lead the class in discussion of a section of the text.
- Read a book approved by the professor related to the topic; report on it.
- Develop a personal Leadership Development Plan, to include goals, objectives and projected dates for accomplishing each goal (include personality, behaviors, and projects).
- Prepare an annotated bibliography of five journal articles on leadership (preferably related to your topic of discussion).

GRADING:

25% - Leadership in class discussion, both content and ability to motivate participants. Annotated Bibliography and book report.

50% - Leadership Development Plan

25% - Tests

GRADING SCALE
93-100 = A; 85-92 = B; 78-84 = C; 77 & below = F

BIBLIOGRAPHY:

Listed at the conclusion of each section of the text also:

Bass, Bernard. Leadership and Performance Beyond Expectations. New York, N.Y.: The Free Press, 1985.
Bennis, Warren and Nancy Burt. Leaders: The Strategies for Taking Charge. New York, N.Y.: Harper & Row, Publishers, 1985.
Hendrix, Olan. Management for the Christian Leader. Milford, MA: Mott Media, 1981.
Hollander, Edwin. Leadership Dynamics: A Practical Guide to Effective Relationships. New York, N.Y.: The Free Press, 1978.

Chadron State College
10th & Main Street - Crites 109, Chadron, NE 69337

Edwin C. Nelson
President Emeritus
308/432-6259

Creative Leadership
Three courses taught by Edwin C. Nelson

OVERVIEW: A course designed for those who are now in leadership positions, for those who aspire to leadership posts, and for those who may be interested in the study of this subject. Persons serving in the professions, business, agriculture, and the home should benefit from the study of creative leadership.

> One of the most universal cravings of our time is a hunger for compelling and creative leadership. . . . The crisis of leadership today is the mediocrity or irresponsibility of so many of the men and women in power, but leadership rarely rises to the full need for it. . . . If we know all too much about our leaders, we know far too little about leadership. . . . Leadership is one of the most observed and least understood phenomena on earth.
> James MacGregor Burns, <u>Leadership</u>, Harper & Row Publishers: New York, 1978, pages 1 and 2.

Many definitions of leadership, management, and administration can be found in literature prepared through the decades but the subject of leadership has not yet been well structured.

PURPOSE: The purpose of this course is to offer involvement in the study of selected topics relating to the definitions, concepts, styles, and roles of creative leaders. It is proposed that this course will contribute toward the orderliness of the study of this subject while serving to assist the students in their pursuit of knowledge about leadership. The course provides: Opportunities for interaction and communication in identifying areas of particular interest as they relate to leadership; Access to rich resources from college and private holdings of visual and audio materials on leadership; Privileges of listening to experienced leaders in various fields and careers; Environment and encouragement to promote a better understanding of the importance of creative leadership as it applies to education, business, government, and social organizations; Opportunities to enjoy working and associating with congenial people.

By the close of the course, students will be able, verbally, in writing, or in practice, to: review various definitions of leadership; formulate their own definition of leadership as it relates to career choices; name and describe various leadership styles and their effectiveness; analyze organizational structures which fit with certain styles of leadership; describe the role of the leader in promoting change; understand the resistance to change; formulate proposals for promoting innovation and change; describe models of decision making; discuss the importance of communication; discuss the importance of goal setting; describe management by objectives; examine more critically the apparent characteristics of quality leadership; identify one's own characteristics of leadership behavior; recommend systems of time management; participate in goal setting; understand one's own philosophy of leadership and followership; be a positive member of the change makers; view the projections of the futurists; appreciate the place of ethics in leadership; understand the importance of teams and support groups; appreciate the importance of innovation, change, and growth; understand the dynamics of personal leadership; appreciate the value of creative thinking; describe the work load of a leader.

CONTENT: The course will focus on Leadership Styles, Ethics, and Characteristics as well as Leadership and Planning, Change, Creativity, Power, Communications, Politics and Supervision.

TEXT: Leaders by Warren Bennis and Burt Nanus (New York: Harper & Row, 1985). A list of supplementary books, articles, audio cassettes and video cassettes will be furnished to the class.

COURSE DESIGN: Class meets Thurs. evenings from 7-10 p.m. Lectures from the instructor will be supplemented by presentations from outstanding leaders in business, government, education, agriculture, and community groups. These leaders, while delivering their observations and advice, will serve as leadership models. Some presentations will be live and others will be via videotape and audio materials.

Students enrolled for graduate credit will be expected to prepare a paper on an appropriate topic approved by the instructor. Periodic quizzes and a final examination will be administered. Evaluations will be based on these activities plus class participation.

Strengthening the Rural Community by Using the Basic Keys to Effective Creative Leadership

A six-hour seminar packed with information, activities, and ideas for improving personal leadership and enhancing community leadership. It is designed to preserve and to further strengthen the many positive characteristics of the rural community.

WHO SHOULD ATTEND? No one is excluded from this seminar. It should be attended by men and women, couples, high school students, the elderly, those in agriculture, business, government, and the professions. A variety of backgrounds will help to produce long-lasting and effective results from this seminar.

OBJECTIVE: To stir the excitement and re-affirm the enthusiasm and the interests of the community in focusing on its vision for the future. Guidelines will be furnished for continuous creative thinking in pursuit of opportunities for thriving in changing times in Rural America. The future of a community does not depend on the geography or the climate. It depends on leadership of its people. Every community is filled with creative persons. Every person has the ability and the responsibility to serve as a leader. The basic keys to effective leadership can be learned. The rural communities are hungry for new expressions of creative leadership. These are times of opportunities for diversified ventures in rural communities.

The Seminar will provide opportunities for experiencing, enjoying, and discussing creative thinking as it applies to the development of dreams, ideas, and visions for the future of the community. There will be a review of examples of successful projects in many very small communities where great happenings are helping to overcome adversities. Economic development can happen in any community. ConAgra is one of the promoters and sponsors of this seminar--Strengthening the Rural Community--because of the interest of this Omaha-based company in promoting the welfare of Rural America. ConAgra, in partnership with local establishments, is supporting this program offered free of charge to interested individuals.

Community Revitalization Through the Schools - A Workshop

OVERVIEW: The workshop supports the belief that schools and communities must be strong partners in assisting youth to appreciate the characteristics of Rural America and to develop entrepreneurial skills appropriate for the times. Following is a statement from Noteworthy, a production of the Mid-continent Regional Education Laboratory, Aurora, Colorado:

> Rural schools and communities are linked together symbiotically; the health of one is dependent on the well-being of the other. In many rural communities, the school district boundaries are the psychological borders of the community. Suggestions to consolidate a smaller school into a larger are countered by local beliefs that, "If you take our school, this town will die." Conversely, the school suffers when a community can't provide jobs for families and they move where there are jobs, taking with them their taxes and students.

There will be a review of practices and thoughts for the revitalization of the rural communities. The workshop will draw upon the experiences of the Rural School and Community Development Project of western South Dakota and it will entertain ideas from the entrepreneurs, government officials, and leaders from various fields of endeavor. The workshop is expected to produce suggested guides for practical projects for the benefit of the community, the school, and the youth of Rural America.

PURPOSE: To provide the opportunity for teachers, school administrators, economic developers, and community leaders to plan together as change makers in enhancing the future for rural communities and their schools. It will provide: Opportunities to assess conditions in Rural America; Privileges of listening to experienced leaders in education and community development; Information about Nebraska's planning for the future; Knowledge about the entrepreneurial efforts in the small communities; Understanding of the importance of community leadership; Appreciation for sources of assistance; Opportunities for interaction and communication in designing plans; Access to rich resource materials; Experience in participating as leaders in community revitalization; Opportunities to enjoy working and associating with congenial people.

Enrollee qualifications are a genuine interest and willingness to serve as a member of the workforce in studying and proposing solutions in the revitalizing of the small communities.

Those who are interested in earning three semester hours of credit may enroll in EdCI 536, BE 460/560, or VE 440/540. Others may enroll simply to audit the course without credit or specific assignments.

WORKSHOP DESIGN: Since there are only ten working days for completing the course, the credit-earning participants will be expected to devote full-time efforts to the workshop. The class will meet each day from 9 a.m. until noon and from 1 p.m. until 3 p.m. for announcements, lectures, reports, and special presentations. Some of the afternoons will be devoted to individual or small group sessions of study, research, and development of selected projects. After an orientation and a review of the course, the credit-earning participants will develop units which might be incorporated into certain parts of a school curriculum. The individuals or the groups will prepare written reports and oral presentations for the full membership. These will serve as practical guides for the local communities so they will vary with conditions and areas of interest.

No single textbook will be required. The class will be furnished with various materials and with samples of books, brochures, video-cassettes, and audio tapes.

Credit-seeking participants will be evaluated on the quality of the individual and/or group reports, class participation, and other assignments as prescribed by the director.

SCHEDULE:

Day 1
9:00 a.m.   Introduction to the workshop and its participants (Nelson)
               How and Why the Workshop Developed (Dr. William Taylor, Dean, Center for Regional Services)
               Welcome (Dr. Sam Rankin, President, Chadron State College)
10:30 a.m.   Rural School and Community Development (Jim Doolittle, Black Hills Special Services Cooperative, Sturgis, SD)
1:00 p.m.   Presentations on Rural Education (Paul Nachtigal and/or Toni Haas, MidContinent Regional Educational Laboratory, Denver, CO)

Day 2
9:00 a.m.   The South Dakota Rural School and Community Development Project; Teachers and students from high schools in communities like Belle Foruche, Hot Springs, Harding County, Custer, Lyman, and Edgemont will review experiences
1:00 p.m.   Continuation of morning program.

Day 3
9:00 a.m.   Community Leadership (Nelson)
10:30 a.m.   Nebraska Futures (John Gottschalk, President Omaha World-Herald, Omaha, NE)
1:00 p.m.   Center for Economic Education (Dr. Ron Burke, Director)
2:00 p.m.   Project Designing

Day 4
9:00 p.m.   New Horizons for Nebraska (Rod Armstrong, Legislative Research Division, Lincoln, NE)
10:00 a.m.   Ideas from a State Senator (Senator Sandra Scofield, 49 Legislative District)
11:00 a.m.   The Help of the Extension Services (Dr. Duane Olsen, Nebraska Cooperative Extension Services, Lincoln, NE)
1:00 p.m.   Reports from Entrepreneurs (Ralph and Linda Byerly, Phoenix, AZ)

Day 5
9:00 a.m.   Report from Entrepreneur (Charles [Mike] Harper, Chairman and CEO, ConAgra, Omaha, NE)
11:00 a.m.   The Nebraska Community Improvement Program (Dave Miller, Dept. of Economic Development, Lincoln, NE)
1:00 p.m.   Experiences of an Entrepreneur (Beth Tielke, Tielke's, O'Neill, NE)
2:00 p.m.   Food Processing (Dr. Steve Taylor, Dir., Food Processing Center, UNL, Lincoln, NE)

Day 6 (optional)
8:30 a.m.   Breakfast with the Governor, The Honorable Kay Orr, Governor of Nebraska

Day 7
9:00 a.m.   The Nebraska Business Development Center (Cliff Hanson, Chairman, Dawes County Economic Development Corporation, Chadron, NE)
10:30 a.m.   Economic Development in Small Communities (Lee Peterson, Dir. of Economic Development, Chadron, NE)
1:00 p.m.   Entrepreneurial Experiences (Norman and Marsha Keller, St. Paul, NE)

Day 8
9:00 a.m.   Workshop Discussions
1:00 p.m.   Entrepreneurial Experiences (L. B. Pearson, Pearson Livestock Equipment, Thedford, NE)

Day 9
9:00 a.m.   Workshop Activities
10:00 a.m.   Roger Christianson, Dir. of Nebraska Dept. of Economic Development, Lincoln, NE
1:00 p.m.   Workshop Project Reports

Day 10
9:00 a.m.   Workshop Project Reports
to 3:00 p.m.

Day 11
9:00 a.m.   Workshop Summary
to Noon
Noon   Luncheon and Adjournment

Concordia College
Department of Business Adm. & Economics
Moorhead, MN 56560

Clifford E. Harrison
Professor and Chairman
218/299-3476

Leadership - Bus Ad 462

OBJECTIVES: Broadly speaking, the course is designed to help you gain an introduction to and comprehensive understanding of leadership--theory, research and practice. It will help you to examine your own leadership ability and style and to identify ways that your leadership potential can be enhanced. Objectives of the course are as follows: To introduce and examine historical, philosophical and theoretical aspects of leadership; To explore and evaluate the ethical and influence dimensions of leadership; To provide small group experiential exercises which will permit you to experiment with and evaluate various leader behaviors and skills; To examine critically the apparent characteristics of effective leadership and to encourage you to consider ways to shape your own future leadership style, goals and values.

FORMAT: Based on the belief that active involvement in the learning process stimulates interest and facilitates learning, a number of methods will be used in the class sessions. The course content will be presented through lectures, class discussion, small group assignments, case studies and experiential exercises. Visiting lecturers will be invited into the classroom, including professors from other disciplines.

COURSE REQUIREMENTS AND EVALUATION

1. A major research project or paper   25% of grade
    In-class presentation of paper   10% of grade
2. A reflective journal with entries made   20% of grade
    weekly, handed in 3 times during semester
3. Three examinations   <u>45%</u> of grade
                                                     100%

Notes: 1. Please be aware of "due dates" for assignments. Since follow-through on commitments and deadlines is an important dimension of effective leadership which we need to practice, no reminders will be given to you about those deadlines. It is up to you to meet them. Assignments are due in the class period on the given dates. Missed deadlines will result in grade penalties, unless there are compelling reasons for the lateness. 2. You will have considerable flexibility in selecting the topic for your paper or your research project. You may choose a subject relevant to the course, study an historic or current leader, or do a field project. Be creative! 3. You are expected to do considerable reading beyond the assignments in the two texts. This will provide much more background and material for your reflective journals. Read in journals, newspapers and other library materials. Selected books will be on reserve in the library and many others available in the regular stacks.

TEXTS: Rosenbach and Taylor. <u>Contemporary Issues in Leadership</u>. Boulder, CO, Westview Press, 1984. Yukl. <u>Leadership in Organizations</u>. Englewood Cliffs, NJ, Prentice-Hall, Inc., 1981. Other materials to be provided as course progresses.

COURSE SCHEDULE

Class meetings	Topic	Assignments
1	The Nature of Leadership	R&T 1, 3
2	Personal Profile	Yukl 1
3	Philosophical and Historical Foundations	
4	(continued)	
5	(continued)	Paper topic due
6	Theories of Leadership	Yukl 5, 6
7	(continued)	R&T 5, 12
8	(continued)	Journal due
9	Examination I	
10	Leadership and Motivation	Yukl 4
11	Power and Influence	Yukl 2, 3
12	(continued)	
13	Ethics and Values	Paper outline due
14	(continued)	
15	(continued)	
	Mid-Semester Break	
16	Political Leadership	Journal due
17	Leadership vs. Followership	R&T: Ch 13, 14
18	Female/Minority Issues	R&T: Ch 16, 19
19	Leadership vs. Management	R&T: Ch 7, 8, 10
20	Examination II	
21	Planning	
22	Communications	Completed paper due
23	Decision Making/Problem Solving	Yukl 8
24	Participative Leadership	Yukl 9
	Thanksgiving Vacation	
25	Conflict Management	
26	Organization Development	
27	Meeting Leadership	
28	Leadership in Other Cultures	Journal due
29	Leadership for and in the Future	R&T 25, 26, 28
30	(continued)	Yukl 10
31	Final Examination	

Creighton University
2500 California Street, Omaha, NE 68178

Martha Brown
Associate Dean of Students
Student Services
402/280-2718

Leadership: Theories, Styles, and Skills - EDU 320

OBJECTIVES: Students in this course will have an opportunity to: gain a working knowledge of leadership theories and group dynamics; develop and improve leadership skills; apply leadership knowledge and skills in a practical setting; assess their leadership skills and develop a plan to improve those skills; learn about themselves and the way they function in groups.

REQUIRED TEXT: Contemporary Issues in Leadership, edited by William E. Rosenbach and Robert L. Taylor, 1984, Westview Press. Other readings as assigned.

Components of Final Grade	Due	% of Final Grade
1. Article reviews/Reaction papers	Bi-weekly	15%
2. Take Myers-Briggs Type Indicator at Counseling Center	by 1/25	N/A
3. Book review & short reaction paper	2/11	20%
4. Summary of interviews with community leader	3/24	25%
5. Final exam - take home	4/28	40%
		100%

COURSE REQUIREMENTS

1.   Participation/attendance: This course relies on the active involvement of each student. Therefore attendance is expected at each class session. Absences will affect your total points in the class. More than six absences will affect the final course grade, lowering it by one letter grade per absence over six. Active participation is also expected so students should read all assignments and come to each class session prepared to discuss the day's topic.

2.   Article reviews/reaction papers: Those articles reviewed must pertain to the content of the course, and must be taken from one of the periodicals listed in this syllabus unless prior approval has been obtained from the instructor. Only one article per periodical may be submitted. Reviews should summarize the content of the article, followed by your reaction to it. Submit a copy of the article with your review. Come to class prepared to discuss your articles. You may be called upon. Reaction papers reflect your reaction to ideas presented in class. They should not be summaries or reactions to class procedures, but rather should be reactions to class content, especially concepts that intrigue, trouble, and/or interest you. Length of each review or reaction paper should be one to one and a half pages typed (double-spaced). A combination of five papers are required, including at least 2 article reviews and 2 reaction papers. Each paper counts 3 points for a total of 15 points. These are due as scheduled. One point will be subtracted for each class day a review or reaction paper is turned in late.

3.   <u>Book review and short reaction paper</u>: Choose a famous leader to study. If you would like to choose a famous leader that is not included on the attached list, you need to obtain the consent of the instructor. Each class participant should choose a different leader to study.

Read at least one biography or autobiography of your leader. Summarize the reading you have done in 2 pages typed (double-spaced). The reaction paper should address the following questions: 1. Why was this person a leader? 2. What preparation did he/she have for leadership? 3. Describe this person's leadership style. 4. What leadership strengths and weaknesses did he/she possess? 5. What values did he/she believe to be important in leading? 6. Who or what influenced this person? The reaction paper should be 3-5 pages typed (double-spaced). Points will be subtracted for each class day the review and reaction paper are turned in late.

4.   <u>Community leader interviews</u>: Choose a community leader from the list distributed in class. Contact your leader. Explain your project and arrange for an interview time. Ideally, you should be able to spend some time observing your leader in his/her work setting and talk to co-workers, supervisors, subordinates. These observations should be included in your paper. In this project, your goal is to interview a current leader to attempt to determine what factors or characteristics distinguish this person as a leader. Try to learn as much about this person's leadership style as you can. The questions below are only tools that may assist you in your interviews. You are encouraged to ask about other topics you feel are relevant to the study of leadership. A successful interview should reflect your own interests rather than consisting of the use of a list of standard questions. 1. Tell me about your career path and career decisions. 2. What is your background, in terms of education and experience? 3. What is your definition of leadership? 4. What does a leader do that distinguishes him or her from others? What is your personal philosophy of leadership? 6. When you think of your own characteristics as a leader, what would you describe as skills you have gained and what would you consider as traits you have always possessed? 7. How would you characterize your style of leadership? How has your style changed over the years? Does your style change in different settings or situations? If so, how? 8. Who do you consider to be great leaders? Why? 9. Who have been influential people for you in terms of leadership? 10. How did you learn leadership? 11. What are some of the most important lessons about leadership you have learned? 12. What are some of the personal rewards you experience as a leader? What are some of the personal frustrations or pain caused by leadership? 13. What is the most difficult aspect of being a leader for you? 14. What are your goals and ambitions? 15. What advice do you have for today's young leaders?

Remember, you are representing Creighton University so we expect you to be professional in your manner and dress. The paper you write to summarize your interviews and your reactions to them should be 4-6 pages typed (double-spaced). Two points will be subtracted for each class day the paper is turned in late.

5.   <u>Final Exam</u>: Take-home due two weeks later. One letter grade will be subtracted for

every day the exam is late.

6.   Grading   90 - 100 = A
         Article Reviews = 15 points   80 - 90   = B
         Book review & paper = 20 points   75 - 80   = C+
         Community ldr. interviews = 25 points   70 - 75   = C
         Final exam = 40 points   60 - 70   = D
         Total = 100 points   Below 60 = F

Study of a Famous Leader

Susan B. Anthony	Saint Ignatius
Omar Bradley	Abraham Lincoln
Jimmy Carter	Martin Luther
Rosalynn Carter	Douglas MacArthur
Fidel Castro	Mary, Queen of Scots
Oliver Cromwell	Mao Tse-tung
Jefferson Davis	Golda Meir
Dwight D. Eisenhower	Bertoldi Mussolini
Queen Elizabeth I	Richard Nixon
Geraldine Ferraro	Peter the Great
Mahatma Gandhi	George Patton
Adolph Hitler	Ronald Reagan
Lee Iacocca	Eleanor Roosevelt
Thomas Jefferson	Franklin D. Roosevelt
Jesus	Theodore Roosevelt
Lyndon Johnson	Albert Schweitzer
John F. Kennedy	Joseph Stalin
Robert Kennedy	Margaret Thatcher
Martin Luther King	Henry Truman
Henry Kissinger	Queen Victoria
Edward Koch	Booker T. Washington

Periodical List

Academy of Management Journal, Academy of Management Review, Administrative, Science Quarterly, Campus Activities Programming - Brandeis 107, Change, Chronicle of Higher Education, Educational Administration Quarterly, Harvard Business Review, Journal of Applied Behavioral Science, Journal of Applied Psychology, Journal of College Student Personnel, Journal of Counseling and Development, Journal for Specialists in Group Work, Management Review, Organizational Dynamics, Phi Delta Kappan, Psychology Today, Training, Training and Development Journal, Wall Street Journal.

COURSE OUTLINE

By class
<u>meeting</u>
1	Course introduction
2	Goal setting; Read: Chapter 1
3	Leadership theories; Guest: Dr. Andy Vinchur, Psychology, Due: Choice of famous leader to study
4	Myers-Briggs interpretation; Guest: Dr. Tom Grandy, Counseling Center; Due: 1st article review
5	Lecture discussion; Read: Chapters 4, 5
6	Lecture discussion, Leadership Styles; Read: Chapters 8, 9
7	Situational Leadership; Choose community leader
8	Beliefs about Leadership; Read Chapters 10, 13, 14; Due: Book review and short reaction paper
9	Leadership assessment exercise; Guest: Dr. Ron Slepitza, Student Services
10	No class - make individual appointments with instructor to discuss assessment
11	Discussion of assessment; Guest: Dr. Ron Slepitza, Student Services
12	Delegation; Read: Chapter 15; Due: 2nd article review
13	Effective listening; Guest: Dr. Don Yoder, English and Speech
14	Lecture discussion, Motivation and morale; Read: Chapters 16, 17
15	Group communication; Guest: Dr. Jim Dickel, Education
16	Lecture Discussion, Conflict management; Read: Chapters 19, 20; Due: 3rd article review
17	The art of persuasion; Guest: Dr. Don Yoder, English and Speech
18	Small group dynamics; Guest: Dr. Andy Hoh, Management; Due: Summary of interviews with community leader
19	Qualities of leadership
20	Translating skills to the world of work; Read: Chapter 21; Due: 4th article review
21	The influence of gender and race on Leadership; Guest: Dr. Shirley Scritchfield, Sociology
22	Lecture discussion; Read: Chapters 22, 23, 24
23	Group decision making/change strategies; Guest: Karen Thurber, Student Services; Read: Chapters 25, 26
24	Studying leadership from a historical perspective; Guest: Dr. Stephanie Wernig, Student Services Lecture discussion; Due: 5th article review
25	Values/ethics of leadership
26	Values/ethics of leadership (continued); Guest: Sr. Maryanne Stevens, Theology
27	Personal leadership philosophies; Read: Chapters 27, 28
28	Evaluation; Due: Final Exam
Exam Week	Make an appointment with instructor to return and discuss exam

Cypress College
9200 Valley View Street, Cypress CA 90630

Karen Bergher
Director, Student Activities
714/826-3360

Leadership Course - #135

___

OBJECTIVE: Learn to identify, classify and analyze the components essential to the development of those who assume leadership roles. Lecture, simulation games and activities, group interplay, role play and discussion will be used to help students learn leadership concepts in this 3 unit course that meets one day a week.

TEXTS: Primary Required: Whetten, David A., Developing Management Skills. Illinois: Scott, Foresman and Company, 1984. Bennis, W., Leaders: The Strategies for Taking Charge. New York: Harper and Row, 1985. **Supplemental:** Morrison, Emily Kittle, Skills for Leadership, Working with Volunteers, Volume I. Arizona: Jordan Press, 1983. **Excerpts From:** Rose, Twelve Angry Men (to be provided in class).

Grading: Components: A) 11 weekly quizzes at 10 points each (110 points). B) 15 weekly assignments at 10 points each (150 points). C) Term Paper on Leadership (refer to guidelines) up to 100 points. D) Involvement in class discussion will be noted based on attendance and participation, 10 points per class (150 points). E) 10 extra credit assignments at 10 points each (100 points). It might be in the students' best interest to do extra credit to help improve grade status.

Course Grading Scale: 510-490 A; 489-469 B; 468-448 C; 447-427 D; 426 F

WEEKLY REQUIRED ASSIGNMENTS

	Topic	Assignment
1	Course Overview	
2	Individual Approaches to Leadership	Read Whetten pp. 34-84; Discussion Questions pg. 65 "Brainwashing"; Discussion Questions pg. 67 "The Boy, the Girl, the Ferryboat Captain, and the Hermits"; *#1 EC Due
3	Personal Considerations in Leadership	Read Whetten pp. 86-138; Management Problem in Whetten pp. 21-33 "The Tampa Pump & Valve Company"; #2, #3 EC Due
4	Solving Problems Creatively	Read Whetten pp. 139-191; Discussion Questions pg. 183 "Admiral Kimmel's Failure at Pearl Harbor"; #4 EC Due
5	Establishing Supportive Communication	Read Whetten pp. 192-242; Response Inventory Problems 1-8 pp. 193-196 Whetten; Skill Practice - United Chemical Company pp. 236-238 Whetten; Reflective Listening Exercise pg. 241 Whetten; #5 EC Due
6	Gaining Power and Influence Profile	Read Whetten pp. 243-300; Exercise Empowerment Whetten pp. 244-245; Preferred Influence Strategies Whetten pg. 246; Skill Practice pg. 294 Whetten Repairing Power Failures In Management Circuits - Task 1; #6 EC Due
7	Improving Performance	Read Whetten pp. 301-347; Discussion Questions pg.

	Through Motivation	344 for "Elizabeth Steinberg & Judith Greene" exercise; #7 EC Due
8	Delegating and Decision Making	Read Whetten pp. 348-398; Inclinations Toward Delegation Exercise pp. 351-352 Whetten; Discussion Questions pg. 388 for "The Finance Case" Whetten; #8 EC Due
9	Conflict Management	Read Whetten pp. 399-448; Discussion Questions pg. 441 for "The Harried Supervisor" and "Webster Arsenal" Whetten; #9 EC Due
10	Conducting Effective Group Meetings	Read Whetten pp. 449-498; Discussion Questions pg. 488 for "It Wasn't Just Another Dull Meeting" Whetten; #10 EC Due
11	Group Dynamics	Read Twelve Angry Men
12	Leadership, Management & Ambiguity	Read Bennis pp. 1-86
13	Ethics in Leadership	Leadership Term Paper Due
14	Evaluating the Organization	
15	Final Review	

Note: Quizzes or assignments missed due to absences recorded as zeros. Ordinarily, no make-ups or extensions. Excuses will be accepted in writing for unavoidable absence.

EVALUATION CRITERIA: Term Paper; Class Participation; Weekly Quizzes; Weekly Required Assignments; Extra Credit Assignments.

REQUIRED: "What is Leadership" - Paper - 100 Maximum Points.

You will have the opportunity to experience several workshops providing insight into the concept of leadership dynamics. Based on your observations your paper would include: 1. Your definition of leadership. 2. Qualities you admire most in a leader and why? i.e., communication skills, decision making, people skills--combination of any and/or other examples provided in lectures. 3. How you perceive yourself as a leader. Support your comments by 4 references applicable to leadership development. References may be obtained from handouts, lecture notes, or library research. References must be noted.

Keep in mind: 1. Term paper must be double-spaced, typewritten. 2. Each day the paper is late will be a loss of 5 points per day. 3. Turn in an original and one copy.

Grading: Maximum of 20 Points Per Area: 1. Expression of Ideas (originality and quality of ideas) 2. Support (references; quality, quantity) 3. Organization (logical narrative sequence; appropriate logical placement of statements and references) 4. Fluency (sentence structure; clear syntax, position progression) and Editing (spelling, punctuation, capitalization, grammar) 5. Depth of Analysis (analysis of research, synthesis of ideas).

Genesee Community College
College Road, Batavia, NY 14020

Alan Williams
[New position - Director of Guidance
Oakfield-Alabama School
7001 Lewiston Rd., Oakfield, NY 14125
716/948-5211]

Psychology of Leadership - Psych. 193
3 Credits

INTRODUCTION: The aim of this course is to study leadership and its practical applications. Our experiences and the experiences of historical and contemporary leaders will provide the framework for discussion and reflection.

The success of this course depends on the opportunity to share and experience. The seminar method will give us an opportunity to practice leadership capabilities and shape future styles and qualities.

Class attendance and participation in discussions and structured exercises are important elements of this course. We will be stretching our thinking, organizational and expressive skills.

This course will help clarify the tenets of effective leadership, identify the dilemmas we face, help us to evaluate positions of leaders past and present, and help us formulate personal philosophies.

OBJECTIVES: The objectives include the following: (1) To examine the phenomenon of leadership functions, (2) To review followership and its implications for leader succession, (3) To examine historical, philosophical, theoretical and practical perspectives and applications of leadership development, (4) To help enhance self-confidence and self-worth, (5) To broaden leadership potential for current and future leadership roles and (6) To take time out for reflection and fun.

COURSE FORMAT: A 3-ring binder will serve as the major reference and notebook. Sections will include: Course Description, Class Handouts, Class Assignments, Miscellaneous and Class Notes. There will be no specific text assigned.

Materials will be presented in lecture form, handouts and guided discussions on selected topics. There will be simulated skill building exercises, in-class and out-of-class written assignments, observations of leaders in a variety of situations and a mid-term and final examination.

GRADING: The criteria for grading includes the following: (a) attendance and participation, (b) evaluation of written work, (c) extent which papers and understanding grow from the reading and experiences, and (d) grades obtained on the mid-term and final examinations.

MAJOR SOURCES: The issues of <u>Campus Activities Programming</u> (National Association for Campus Activities, P.O. Box 6828, Columbia, SC 29260) and <u>Developing Human Resources</u> (Annuals); <u>Structured Experiences for Human Relations Training</u> (Series) from University Associates, Inc., 8517 Production Avenue, San Diego, CA 92121 will be the major references.

REQUIREMENTS: In addition to attendance, the following are requirements for this course. Due dates and examination dates will be announced during the first week of classes.

1. Attend a meeting on or off campus. Write a short paper on your impressions of whether or not it was a well-run meeting. Be prepared to defend your statements.
2. Choose a leader that has made a significant impact on the United States or world. On paper, describe his or her leadership style and why the person plays, or played, such a significant part in history--focusing on this as a reason for prominence, success or failure. This paper must be properly documented and the topic must be approved in advance.
3. Each class participant will be responsible for presenting an oral report on the significant leader. Be as creative as possible. Make your leader re-live his or her most significant moments.
4. You are responsible for 5 talking point papers dealing with leadership. Read and review recent magazine, journal or newspaper articles and respond to the following: What is the single most important thing said about leadership in this article? Do you agree or disagree? Explain your answer. Papers are to be properly documented and students should be prepared to defend or explain their articles on due dates.
5. Show how differences in the media affect leaders and help make or break them. Provide 3 examples; summarize and document. Be creative and imaginative.
6. Choose an interpersonal communication variable to observe at a meeting. Write a short paper describing what you observed and provide conclusions about the variable as it relates to the group.
7. Prepare a 1-2 page Case Study which may serve as a focus for group discussion. The study should consider a leadership situation and include: (a) The Problem, (b) Possible Alternatives, (c) Recommendations and (d) Justification.
8. Students will be expected to complete the mid-term and final examination on the dates assigned.

CLASS TOPICS: Some of the topics for discussion will include: Leadership and Leadership Functions; Factors in Succession and Transition; Self-Esteem and Motivation; Hierarchies of Needs; The Psychology of Winning; Star Power; Agenda Development; Team Building; Retention of Volunteers; Working With Impossible People; Marketing Volunteer Experiences; Sex, Gender Roles and Power; Leadership Styles; Historical and Contemporary Leaders and Their Impact; Assessing and Validating Skills; Conflict Resolution; Interpersonal Communication Skills; Perceptions; Visibility and Credibility Factors; Left-Right Brain Orientations; Delegating Skills; Theory X and Y; Self-Concept; Group Attractiveness; Achievers and Non-Achievers; Self Image; Behavioral Styles; Styles of Communication and Leadership Practices.

Note: A course outline (topics and exercises) will be distributed during the first week of classes.

Harvard University
John F. Kennedy School of Government
79 John F. Kennedy St., Cambridge, MA 02138

Ronald A. Heifetz
Lecturer in Public Policy
617/495-7867

A paper pertinent to the courses described below appeared in the Journal of Policy Analysis and Management Vol. 8 No. 3., 536-562 (1989) entitled "Teaching and Assessing Leadership Courses at the John F. Kennedy School of Government." The authors were Ronald A. Heifetz, Riley M. Sinder, Alice Jones, Lynn M. Hodge, and Keith A. Rowley. It was written to answer the questions: "How useful do students find the course materials for analyzing their past professional experience? How relevant and effective do students find the courses for understanding and intervening into politics and organizations after rejoining professional life? In the article, a summary is provided of the setting, theory, and methods for these courses, as well as the results of a survey of students after they had resumed their careers. The authors conclude with a brief discussion of the risks involved in teaching leadership" (quotation is taken from the Abstract to the article).

Leadership and the Mobilization of Group Resources - M-698   Ronald Heifetz

This course gives students a fundamental understanding of leadership. It is designed for people from various backgrounds and cultures, those who have had experience exercising leadership and those who have not. It aims to increase one's ability to sustain the demands of leadership and develop further one's capacity to exercise leadership and authority.

Drawing from several disciplines, the course develops an analytical framework for intervening in political and organizational systems to get work done. Philosophy provides the groundwork for understanding the concepts of paradigm and change. Political science and business management offer perspectives for examining the functions of authority and distinguishing these from the exercise of leadership. Social psychology gives insight into the workings of social systems and provides an approach to diagnosing what goes wrong in them. Music suggests a language for working with elusive qualities like harmony, inspiration, timing, conducting, creativity, listening, and resolution.

SCHEDULE: Lectures: Once weekly 2:30-4:30 p.m. Group Study: One hour per week. Debriefing for designated authorities and case presenters (twice during semester): 9:00 a.m.-12:00 noon.

GROUP STUDY SESSION: The class is randomly divided into small groups (8-10) to meet one hour a week in laboratory session to: apply what they are learning in class and in readings to their past and current experience; investigate ways they manage the roles and functions of leadership and authority; discover and analyze properties of leadership and dynamics of how groups work.

Each student is designated to exercise authority in his or her group once during the semester on a rotating basis. A different student each week will prepare and present a case study (preferably from their own experience) to serve as a focus of work for the group. A guide to preparing the case will be distributed. A debriefing seminar is held weekly for designated authorities and the case presenters from each group.

REQUIREMENTS: Complete and prompt attendance. Completion of a weekly questionnaire to analyze the group study sessions (2-3 pages). Completion of two or three short written assignments (1-5 pages). Preparation of a case study based on one's own experience or taken from history. A major paper, which can be based on the case study, analyzing aspects of leadership (20-25 pages). No exam.

GRADING: Classroom work, 30%; Weekly papers, 30%; Major paper, 40%.

SYLLABUS:

Week
1   Introduction: What does it mean to be a leader?
2   Leadership and the Process of Educating Groups; Readings: Kuhn, The Structure of Scientific Revolutions, pp. 1-22, 23-25, 35-42; Plato, "The Philosopher-King," from The Republic, pp. 175-263; Burns, Leadership, pp. 9-28, 228-240, 444-462. Orientation to group study sessions.
3   Leadership and the Nature of Work; Readings: Fisher, Small Group Decision Making, pp. 1-8, 13-68, 69-91, 92-93, 99-115 (optional: pp. 115-125, 133-142); Argyris and Schon, Organizational Learning: A Theory of Action Perspective, pp. 1-29 (optional: pp. 30-44); Pascale, "Zen and the Art of Management," from Harvard Business Review--On Human Relations, pp. 125-139; Tucker, Politics as Leadership, pp. 1-30; Meir, "Two Nations in Israel," from This is Our Strength: The Selected Papers of Golda Meir, pp. 49-52.
4   Group Dynamics; Readings: Freud, Group Psychology and the Analysis of the Ego, pp. 1-36, 49-60; Fisher, Small Group Decision Making, pp. 142-180 (esp. p. 170), 201-207, 215-223, 228-295 (optional: 180-201); Rogers and Roethlisberger, "Barriers and Gateways to Communication," from Harvard Business Review--On Human Relations, pp. 294-305.
5   Leadership and Creativity; Readings: Kuhn, The Structure of Scientific Revolutions, pp. 77-91, 92-97, 109-110, 111-115, 160-173; May, The Courage to Create, Chs. 1-4 (pp. 1-109); Kuhn, "The Essential Tension: Tradition and Innovation in Scientific Research," from The Essential Tension--Selected Studies in Scientific Tradition and Change, pp. 225-239; Weber, from Gerth and Mills, Essays from Max Weber: Essays in Sociology, pp. 245-252, 253-255; Friedan, The Second Stage, pp. 15-18, 23-31, 38-41; Deutsch, "Discovery is the Cutting Edge of Learning," from MacIver, The Hour of Insight, pp. 71-84; Perkins, The Mind's Best Work (optional).
6   Leadership and Authority; Readings: Selznick, Leadership in Administration, pp. 22-28, 134-154; May, The Courage to Create, Chs. 6-7 (pp. 133-169); Gandhi, Indira, My Truth, pp. 161-173; Tucker, Politics as Leadership, pp. 59-67, 77-97; Kellerman, Leadership: Multidisciplinary Perspectives, Chs. 2 and 7; Barnard, The Functions of the Executive, pp. 215-234; Zaleznik, "Managers and Leaders: Are They Different?", from Harvard Business Review--On Human Relations, pp. 162-179; Machiavelli, The Prince (optional).
7   Assassination; Readings: Neustadt, Presidential Power, pp. 3-10 (optional: 10-25), 44-79 (esp. 78-79), 133-135 (esp. 135), 140 (top)-143, 155-156; Musashi, A

       Book of Five Rings, pp. 33-50, p. 95, skim 1-32; James, "Expiation and Atonement," from Sacrifice and Sacrament, pp. 104-128; Freud, Totem and Taboo, pp. 100-161 (esp. 132-161); Clausewitz, "On Military Genius," from On War, pp. 100-114.

8   Purpose, Task and Work Avoidance Mechanisms; Readings: Kellerman, Leadership: Multidisciplinary Perspectives, Ch. 10; Fisher, Small Group Decision Making, go over pp. 60-68; Neustadt, Presidential Power, pp. 150-152; Exercise: Small group analysis of "Excalibur" (film).

9   Intervention: Managing Chaos and Conflict; Readings: Fisher, Small Group Decision Making, go over pp. 228-259; Kellerman, Leadership: Multidisciplinary Perspectives, Ch. 12; Burns, Leadership, go over pp. 234-240 (on Mao); Case Study: "Freezing the Arms Race: The Genesis of a Mass Movement," excerpts; Collier, "Business Leadership and a Creative Society," from Harvard Business Review--On Human Relations, pp. 418-435; Rukeyser, "Ann Burlak," and "Kathe Kollwitz," from The Collected Poems of Muriel Rukeyser, pp. 196-199, 479-484.

10   Leadership and Listening (Sensing the Environment); Readings: Rice, Selections from: Learning for Leadership, from Coleman and Bexton, Group Relations Reader, pp. 71-121 [On Reserve Only]; Neustadt, Presidential Power, pp. 112-118; Wrapp, "Good Managers Don't Make Policy Decisions," from Harvard Business Review--On Human Relations, pp. 74-85; Neruda, Pablo, "To Acario Cotapos," from Fully Empowered, pp. 68-75; Whitman, "Proud Music of the Storm," from The Portable Walt Whitman, pp. 255-261.

11   Inspiration and Persuasion; Readings: Neustadt, Presidential Power, pp. 26-43; Fischer, The Life of Mahatma Gandhi, pp. 420-505; Gandhi, Indira, My Truth, pp. 179-186, 190-192; Emerson, "Self-Reliance"; Film.

12   Partnership in Leadership; Readings: Schlesinger, The Coming of the New Deal, pp. 511-588; Walker, The Color Purple.

13   Summary and Thoughts about the Future; Readings: Plato, "The Philosopher-King," from The Republic, re-read pp. 175-263.

Burns, James MacGregor, Leadership, Harper Colophon, 1978; Fischer, Louis, The Life of Mahatma Gandhi, Harper Colophon, 1950; Fisher, B. Aubrey, Small Group Decision Making, 2nd ed., McGraw-Hill, 1980; Freud, Sigmund, Group Psychology and the Analysis of the Ego (1921), Strachey translation, Norton, 1959; Freud, Sigmund, Totem and Taboo, (1913), Strachey translation, Norton, 1950; Harvard Business Review--On Human Relations, Harper and Row, 1979; Kellerman, Barbara (ed.), Leadership: Multidisciplinary Perspectives, Prentice-Hall, 1984; Kuhn, Thomas, The Structure of Scientific Revolutions, 2nd ed., University of Chicago, 1970; May, Rollo, The Courage to Create, Bantam, 1975; Morris, E. (ed.), The American Heritage Dictionary, 1st ed. (large format edition), Houghton Mifflin, 1969; Musashi, A Book of Five Rings, Overlook, 1982; Neustadt, Richard, Presidential Power, Wiley, 1980; Plato, The Republic, Cornford translation, Oxford, 1941; Selznick, Philip, Leadership in Administration, Harper and Row, 1957; Tucker, Robert C., Politics as Leadership, University of Missouri Press, 1981; Walker, Alice, The Color Purple, Washington Square Press, 1982.

Research Seminar in Leadership - M-699   **Ronald A. Heifetz**

A BRIEF COURSE DESCRIPTION:

1.   This course is a clinical training in leadership in which you will be investigating the determinants of your own efficacy as a leader.

2.   Your research will require a field setting or laboratory in which to formulate and test hypotheses about diagnosis and intervention into social/political systems.   The setting should be a task-oriented group or organization, probably in the community.

3.   Examples of settings: political groups or organizations;   private companies;   community action organizations (abortion, NRA, environment, nuclear, voting, race relations, discrimination, etc.);   church groups;   school organizations;   group or organizational projects;   Tavistock Conference.

4.   You should select a group which is personally important to you.   Don't approach the project in a detached, uninvolved manner as if you were the consultant and the organization or group were the client.

5.   The seminar will meet 3 hours a week during which students will present their research findings for supervision and discussion.

6.   The readings for the course will be determined primarily by the students.

7.   The class will be limited to 16 students.   <u>M-698: Leadership and the Mobilization of Group Resources</u> is a prerequisite.

8.   Selection for the class will be based on your ability to find a field setting, as well as the degree to which you are willing to tackle what it will mean for you to be a leader to people.

9.   A final report (25-35 pages) analyzing your research experience will be due at the end of the course.

Political Leadership - M603   **Marty Linsky**
Tue. & Thurs., 8:30-10:00   617/495-1163

Designed for students who have run for office, are thinking about running for office, or are at least thinking about thinking about running for office. The purpose is to explore the electoral option: what does it mean in a democratic society to be in elective office? What distinguishes it from holding other positions in public or private life? What skills, personal qualities, and commitments are required? What are your own assets and liabilities? In what ways does holding elective office provide resources and constraints on leadership? It assumes that like the policy analyst and public manager, the elected official plays an important, professional, legitimate, and distinct role in governance.

This course combines some ideas explored in **Running for Office (M626)**, with some ideas explored in **Leadership and the Mobilization of Group Resources (M698).** It complements M698 in applying some ideas about leadership from M698 to the specific environment of elective office. M698 is neither a prerequisite for nor a bar to taking M603. It is new, part of a broader effort at the Kennedy School to focus more attention within the curriculum on elective office. Two-thirds of the course addresses two questions: why run for office, and what does it take to run? Issues are more personal qualities and the nature of the commitment than campaign strategy. The last third addresses the question, what are the resources and constraints of elective office in exercising leadership?

While this is not a hands-on course in how to run a campaign, it is intended to provide insight and experience about running for office. In that sense it is a hands-on course in being a candidate. When it is over, if the course is successful, you will understand considerably more than you did before about whether you want to run for office or for higher office, what it will require of you, and what are your strengths and vulnerabilities in doing so.

There will be short writing assignments, a final paper, no exam. Class time will be split between discussion of issues raised in readings and exercises simulating the experiences of candidacy. Also, we will use the class as a case in point to observe how leadership is exercised and to give each of us experience to think about whether this is a path to pursue. One exercise, an election for M603 Class President, begins about one-third of the way through the semester and continues, running parallel to the course, until the last class.

Since this is a course in political leadership, it is not surprising that active participation is expected, both in the discussions and in the exercises. Your own experience in the course will give you data to use as you consider whether and how to pursue elective office.

Grades will be based 50% on participation in class, 30% on written work, and 20% on work in the exercises.

SYLLABUS AND CLASS SCHEDULE: Note: All students are expected to see the movie, The Seduction of Joe Tynan, before the first class.

I.   Gaining Political Authority

Session

1   Issues and Purpose. What themes of the movie are important to you and why? What is your idea of a good elected official? What expectations and assumptions are reflected in your ideal? What is your purpose? Why seek political authority? Why run for office?

2   Personal and Public. Read: Jeff Greenfield, Playing to Win, Ch. 1; Edmund P. Willis, ed., Fame and the Founding Fathers, Ch. 1, Douglass Adair's paper presented to the March Conference on Early American History at Moravian College in 1966; Goffman, The Presentation of Self in Everyday Life, excerpts. Where are you in your thinking about running for office? What are your considerations? What does it mean to you to be a public person?

3   Roots. Read: Edward Koch, Mayor, Ch. 1
Who are you, politically speaking? What do you stand for already? Where do you live? Where do you come from? What is your heritage? Your ideology? Do you need one? (M603 election briefing.) Due in class: In a two-page letter to your mentor, preferably your real mentor but imagined is acceptable, describe where you are in the process of thinking about running for office. Why would you do it? Why not? What are the considerations that seem most important to you? What are the assets which you think you would bring to the quest? To the service? What are the liabilities?

4   Reading and discussion of letters to mentors in small groups and discussion of themes in large group.

5   Who Runs? Read: James David Barber, The Lawmakers, Ch. 6, "The Development of Political Personalities." Note: This reading is based on a study which is over two decades old. Some of the findings and language are dated and even offensive in 1980s terms. On the other hand, the typology Barber develops provides some insights about political personalities which have stood the test of time; James MacGregor Burns, Leadership, Ch. 5, "The Crucible of Political Leadership." What qualities does it take to run for office? What personal needs might running for office fulfill? How will you decide? In class we will show a videotape of a conversation among some people who share both a Kennedy School background and experience in running for office.

6   Candidacy and Diversity. What are the special considerations faced by candidates who embody issues of sexual, racial or other diversities? Read: Three articles about State Representative Marjorie Clapprood; "Schroeder and Politics: The Problems of Gender," by Nadine Brozan, NYT, 11/23/87, p. B12; "The Right Image," In the Running, Ch. 2, by Ruth B. Mandel; My Life, by Golda Meir, pp. 106-113.

7   Campaign Announcements. Some members of the class will tape campaign announcements, to be reviewed by the entire class.

8   Pressing the Flesh. <u>Read</u>: Mario Cuomo, <u>Diaries of Mario Cuomo</u>, March 2-21, and September 6-25, 1982. What are the differences in goals and techniques of making a speech to a large group of supporters, making a speech to a large group of uncommitted people, working the crowd at a cocktail party, or trying to convince twenty people at a coffee party to give you some help?

9   Pressing the Flesh (cont'd). Simulation of some of these environments.

10   Conveying the Message. <u>Read</u>: Greenfield, Ch. VII, VIII, and IX; Hunter S. Thompson, <u>Fear and Loathing on the Campaign Trail</u>, Introduction, pp. 15-21. What do you want from the press? What does the press want from you? The newspaper story, television news, a paid ad in one or the other, a radio spot, a brochure: how do the differences in the media affect the presentation and the message? What is it that you want people to know? How do you want them to understand you? <u>Due in class</u>: Write your campaign slogan. Design a simple brochure for your campaign. You may write it as if you were running for office now, or some time in the future.

11   Analyzing the Brochures.

12   Paying the Piper. <u>Read</u>: <u>Joe Kennedy's Dilemma</u> What would you have done? Why? What qualities does it take to raise money for yourself? What would be your guidelines?

13   Asking for Money. Simulation of several fund-raising environments.

14   Confrontation. <u>Case</u>: The Helms-Hunt Senate Race (selected excerpts); <u>Case</u>: The 1969 Election Debate Among Candidates for Mayor in NYC. When and how do you attack your opponent? What should Lindsay have done in '69?

15   An Exercise in Confrontation.

II. Exercising Leadership From Elective Office: Resources and Constraints

16   Leadership <u>and</u> Elective Office? <u>Read</u>: Ronald L. Heifetz and Riley M. Sinder, "Political Leadership: Managing the Public's Problem Solving," draft chapter for <u>The Power of Public Ideas</u>, Robert Reich (ed.), Ballinger, 1987; William Riker, <u>The Art of Political Manipulation</u>, Preface, Chs. 1, 2, 3, & 6; J. Anthony Lukas, <u>Common Ground</u>, Chs. 9 & 28.
What is leadership for an elected official? What is the difference between leadership and manipulation? What forces does an elected official attract? What qualities are required for effective leadership?
<u>Note 1</u>: This is a heavy assignment, but these readings will form the foundation for much of our discussion for the remainder of the semester.
<u>Note 2</u>: At 9:30 we will begin an exercise, called the Institutional Event, designed to give you a further opportunity to experience and to study the nature of political leadership in a group context.

17   Institutional Event, 7:00-10:00 p.m.

18   Institutional Event, 8:30-9:15; Debriefing, 9:15-10:00.

19   Further Debriefing on Institutional Event. <u>Due in class</u>: Each student will write a brief memo, not more than five pages, analyzing the issues and his or her experience in the Institutional Event.

20   Setting the Agenda and Framing the Issue.

21   Listening, Managing Attention, and Getting Work Done. How do you hear what someone is saying? How do you hear what a group is saying? How do you hear the song behind the words? How do you know what to do with what you hear? <u>Cases</u>: The decision of Senator McGrail; Ruckelshaus and Arasco.

22   Exercises in Hearing.

23   Political and Policy Stands as Heuristic Devices. What difference does it make whether alcoholism is identified as a health problem or a criminal problem? Analyze a law from the perspective of whether and in what ways it affects the way people deal with one another, public deliberation, and public learning.

24   Election, Post-election Analysis, and Victory Party.
<u>Final Paper</u>: An opportunity to think about and bring some coherence to your learning in the course. The learning that will be the subject of this paper takes place first by observing one's own participation, its nature and quality, in the election exercise, the simulations and the class discussions. What did you learn about yourself, and your interest and capacity for seeking political authority and exercising political leadership? and second identifying and integrating into your own framework the ideas in the course which were most important to you. The final paper will consist of your reflections on these two aspects of your learning, in not more than five pages each. In the first include some reflection on your experience in the election exercise. The paper will be due a week after last class.

Leadership, Politics, and Democracy - M604   **Marty Linsky**
Mon. and Wed., 3:00-4:30

This course is designed for students who aspire to exercise leadership in public affairs. What does it mean to exercise leadership? With whom? For what purpose? What skills, personal qualities, and commitments are required? What are your own assets and liabilities? What is a leadership opportunity? What is the relationship between position and leadership, power and leadership, vision and leadership, authority and leadership? And what is the relationship among leadership, politics and democracy?

We will draw on the literature in the field and our own experience, engaging in exercises designed to provide us with more data, and using the class itself as a leadership case in point. We will explore ideas as well as technique.

This course is new, building on the experience of some of the leadership courses offered at the School. If it is successful, you will come away with a richer understanding of what it means to exercise leadership in public affairs, how you exercise leadership, and your potential for doing so.

There will be short writing assignments, a final paper, no exam. We will work in small groups as well as the class as a whole. In addition to discussions and role-playing exercises, we will use the class to observe how leadership is exercised and to give each of us some more experience to use in thinking about whether leadership is a path to pursue. There is a political exercise, an election for M604 Class President, which will begin about one-third of the way through the semester and will continue, running parallel to the course, until the election on December 7.

Since this is a course in leadership, it is not surprising that active participation is expected, both in the discussions and in the exercises. Your own experience in the course, or lack of it for that matter, will give you data to use as you consider whether and how to pursue leadership opportunities. Grades will be based 25% on participation in class, 50% on written work, and 25% on work in the exercises.

SYLLABUS AND CLASS SCHEDULE: Note: All students in the course are expected to see the movie, Twelve O'Clock High, before the first class.

Session
1   Issues in Leadership: What themes of the movie are important to you and why? What is your idea of a good leader? What expectations and assumptions are reflected in your ideal? What is your purpose? Why seek to lead?

2   Leadership and Authority. Read: Ronald L. Heifetz and Riley M. Sinder, "Political Leadership: Managing the Public's Problem Solving," in The Power of Public Ideas, Robert Reich (ed.), Ballinger, 1988.
    What is the difference between leadership and authority? What is the relationship of leadership and position? Due in class: In a two-page letter to your mentor, preferably your real mentor but an imagined mentor is acceptable, describe where you are in the process of thinking aspiring to exercise leadership. Why would you do it? Why not? What are the considerations that seem most important to you? What are the assets which you think you would bring to the aspiration? To the exercise of leadership itself? What are the liabilities?

3   Work, Social Systems, and Work Avoidance. Read: Sigmund Freud, Group Psychology and the Analysis of the Ego, W.W. Norton, 1959, Introduction, Chs. 2-6 and 9-11; Aubrey Fisher, Small Group Decision Making, Introduction, Chs. 1, 2, 5 (pp. 142-164), and 6.

4   Small Groups I. Discussion of mentor letters.

5   Management and Manipulation. Read: William Riker. The Art of Political Manipulation, Preface, Chs. 1, 2, 3, & 6. Due in class: In no more than four pages, please write a succinct personal case history of a leadership opportunity which was presented to you sometime in the past. It could have occurred in a professional situation, in a family situation, among friends or whatever. It could have taken place when you were a child or an adult. Most important, it should be one in which you have doubts about whether you were effective. It should be one about which you would be willing to hear some consultation from colleagues. And it should be one about which you are willing to reconsider your existing assumptions, analysis and interpretation.

6   Defining the Problem and Framing the Issue. J. Anthony Lukas, Common Ground, Chs. 9 & 28.

7   Managing Creativity, Chaos and Conflict. Fisher, Ch. 8.
    What do conflict and chaos indicate about how the work is going? Are people

competing for leadership, authority or both? How do you manage the creative process so that it is productive?

8   Small Groups II. Personal Case.
9   Confrontation Exercises.
10   Small Groups III. Personal Case.
11   Issues of Role and Self. Goffman, <u>The Presentation of Self in Everyday Life</u>, excerpts.
12   Videotaping Exercise.
13   Small Groups IV. Personal Case.
14   Alliances for Consultation, Advice and Feedback. Assessing 604 at midstream. What have you learned in the small groups? How effective has our feedback been in the confrontation and videotaping exercises? How well have you used the rest of us? How well have we used you?
15   Roots. Who are you? What are your roots? How do your roots affect your potential for leadership? <u>Note</u>: At 3:45 we will begin an exercise, called the Institutional Event, designed to give you a further opportunity to experience and to study the nature of political leadership in a group context.
16   Institutional Event, 7:00-10:00 p.m.
17   Institutional Event (cont'd), 3:00-4:00; Debriefing, 4:00-4:30.
18   Institutional Event Debriefing (cont'd). <u>Due in class</u>: Each student will write a brief memo, not more than five pages, analyzing the leadership issues and his or her experience in the Institutional Event.
19   Small Groups V. Personal Case.
20   Gender and Race. What are the special considerations faced by candidates who embody issues of sexual, racial or other diversities? <u>Read</u>: Three articles about state Representative Marjorie Clapprood. <u>Note</u>: Preliminary election will be held at the end of this class.
21   Small Groups VI. Personal Case.
22   Leader as Teacher and Learner. <u>Read</u>: Ruckelshaus and Asarco
23   Small Group Experience Debriefing and Election of 604 President. <u>Note</u>: Each of the small groups will have a brief opportunity to share their learning with the large group, both their learning about leadership issues from discussion of the personal cases and their learning about group processes from the workings of their own group. There will be no allocated time within the formal structure of the course for the groups to prepare for their presentation. Groups are encouraged to schedule some outside time to do this work.
24   Student as Leader I.
25   Student as Leader II. Closure. <u>Final Paper</u>: In no more than five pages--an opportunity to think about and bring some coherence to your learning in the course first by observing your own participation, its nature and quality, in the election exercise, the simulations and the class discussions. What did you learn about yourself, and your interest and capacity for exercising leadership? and second by identifying and integrating into your own framework the ideas in the course which were most important to you. You may want to return to your personal case for part of this section of the paper. In the first of these, you must include some reflection on your experience in the election exercise.

Metropolitan State College
1006 11th Street, Box 33, Denver, CO 80204

Mary A. Miller
Prof., Dept. of Nursing & Health
303/556-3136

Leadership - NUR 355
2:00 - 3:15 p.m.

OBJECTIVES: A course designed to develop the leadership roles of the nurse in working with individuals, families, groups and communities striving for high-level wellness, also extending to professionals and paraprofessionals in health care settings. Leadership roles are examined through the theoretical formulations of perception, communication, adaptation, systems, decision and role. Emphasis is placed on leadership theory, role theory, group dynamics, decision theory, change process and communications, recognizing that the leadership role is influenced by the biological, psychological, sociological, and cultural background of all members of a group.

Various aspects of the course include: role theory in utilizing the nursing process; decision theory used in making discriminatory judgments; the leadership role of teacher, collaborator, resource person and change agent in working with individuals, families, groups, and communities in achieving high-level wellness; concepts of group dynamics in collaborating with clients and members of the interdisciplinary health team; descriptions of how perception, communication, adaptation and roles of the nurse, the client, and co-workers are interrelated in the process of change; strategies for implementing change; the role of the nurse in resolving leadership problems in health care settings; and through self-examination, illuminates the need for development of leadership roles.

COURSE READING: Sullivan, E. and Decker, P. (1988). Effective Management in Nursing. California: Addison-Wesley Publishing Co.

ASSIGNMENTS: Grading will be by contract; standards are as follows:
A = all of B and C; completion of mid-term and final examinations; or completion of mid-term and final paper
B = all of C; completion of one of the following: group proposal for change or other agreed upon project/activity
C = Active participation in discussion and activities. Read required reading assignments. Regular class attendance. Five absences are considered excessive.
F = failure to meet the standards of grades A, B, or C.

The quality of performance on the project and papers must be deemed Satisfactory by the instructor in order to earn the grade for which the student is contracting. See the Guidelines for Writing the Mid-term and Final Paper and Characteristics of Satisfactory/Unsatisfactory Papers. A combined average score of 90% must be earned on the mid-term and final examinations in order to be acceptable for the A grade. If the student's work does not meet the standards for the grade for which s/he has contracted, the grade will be lowered according to the above grade requirements. The instructor will issue the grade that represents the quantity and quality of the student's work in the course.

The grade will be lowered for excessive absences. Four absences are acceptable; 5-6 absences lowers the grade by one letter; 7+ absences lowers the grade by two letters.

50

Excessive tardiness/leaving early will count as absences (4 = 1 absence).

Guidelines for the Proposal for Change

The purpose of developing a proposal for change is two-fold. The primary purpose is to experience the process involved in bringing about planned change by applying a problem-solving model to a nursing situation. Secondly, by working as a group on the proposal, many of the theories taught in the course are demonstrated, for example leadership, behavior, group process, group decision making, role behaviors, group communication, perception and adaptation.

PROCESS: The purpose of the group project is to apply a problem-solving model of change to a Nursing Situation which occurs in any setting in which there is interaction between a nurse and a client resulting in a set of behaviors which assist the client in reaching his highest level of wellness. Learners will work in groups of not more than four individuals. The nursing situation may be hypothetical or actual. It cannot be a critique of an on-going or a past institutional change. The proposed change topic must be approved by the instructor. Several class periods will be set aside for the development of the group project; it is expected that groups will meet outside of class as necessary to complete the project. The project will be presented to the instructor in term paper format. The group will present an oral report to the class for discussion. A late penalty may be assessed if the paper is turned in late. The paper will be evaluated as follows: A. Form - 10%; The paper may be written according to any acceptable form; Approximately twelve typewritten pages in length excluding the title page; Turn in the original copy; it may or may not be returned. B. Content - 90%; Assessment, 20%; Planning, 20%; Implementation, 30%; Evaluation - 20%.

Outline of the Proposal for Change

Assessment: Assess interest--is anyone dissatisfied with the present situation? What is the motivation of the change agent/s? Assess motivation using Maslow's hierarchy of needs; Assess the organizational environment. How receptive is it to change? Is there an awareness that a problem exists? Is there an emphasis on problem solving? Diagram and discuss your assessment of the situation using Lewin's driving and restraining forces; Diagnosis of the problem--state it concisely. How large is the discrepancy between what is and what should be? Identify the change you want to bring about.

Planning: From which category(ies) will you select a change strategy (empirical-rational, power-coercive, normative-reeducative)? What assumptions are you making about the target population? Based upon the diagram of driving and restraining forces, conceptualize the strategies for bringing about the change. Will you add a driving force, weaken a restraining force, etc.? State specific goals. The long-term goal is the change itself; short-term goals are significant points along the way. Goals should be realistic, appropriate to the change, achievable within the specified time frame and measurable; What sources of power are available? This may be an individual and/or interested groups. How many people support the change? What are their assets--skills, credibility, status, contacts, finances, etc.? How will others be involved? Anticipate the most likely sources of resistance to the change. Consider psychological (insecurity, attitudes, beliefs) and structural (finances, equipment, facilities) sources. How will the change affect the target system and individuals within it? Address cost effectiveness. Why should this change be adopted--will it save time, money, energy? Will it enhance quality care? What documentation is available in the literature?

<u>Implementation</u>: Develop a time line or PERT network that shows the plan for implementation. What are the significant events (points) in the change itself? What can people expect? Who is involved and when? Identify the roles individuals are expected to perform. Since the sources of resistance have been anticipated, specify how the impact of the change can be minimized; What recognition and reward systems will you implement for those individuals whose actions are furthering the change? What is the role of the change agent/s? Illustrate how the following MSC leadership roles apply to implementing the change: teacher, collaborator, resource person; How will you communicate the change and minimize perceptual difficulties?

<u>Evaluation</u>: Plan evaluation activities based upon the long- and short-term goals. How will the goals be measured? How will you know the goals have been achieved? Specify appropriate evaluation points along the way; How will evaluation feedback be obtained --direct observation, questionnaire, cost reductions, patient responses, group feedback sessions, etc.? Develop a sample evaluation tool; At what point will you be satisfied that the change will maintain itself (refreezing)?

Metropolitan State University
Dayton's Bluff, A Bldg.
203 Maria, St. Paul, MN 55408

Gerri Perreault
612/624-5701

Leadership/Management - Followership Ethics

COURSE: Designed to increase knowledge and understanding of ethical and unethical behavior.

SAMPLE COMPETENCE: Knows and understands the cognitive, social, and psychological factors involved in leadership/followership and management/subordinate ethics well enough to analyze the ethical or unethical behavior of a leader/manager (individual or organization).

OUTCOMES FOR STUDENTS: To increase "ethical sensitivity," the ability to identify/recognize ethical issues, including the ability to see "the emperor's new clothes"; To clarify their own ethical assumptions and values; To gain ability to identify, analyze, and evaluate the cognitive, social, and psychological factors involved in ethical and unethical leader/manager and follower/subordinate behavior; To affirm one's ethical inclinations in the face of pressures to the contrary; To appreciate the difficulty of behaving ethically; To sustain hope for the future.

COURSE DESCRIPTION: Why do leaders/followers and managers/subordinates behave ethically or unethically or both? Are these just "bad" people? The course introduces some of the cognitive/philosophical and social-psychological factors involved.

BULLETIN COPY: Bring to first session an ethical case (or cases) you would like to see discussed at some point; can be personal, work-related, from newspaper, hypothetical, etc. Note: You can remain anonymous in submitting these.

SCHEDULE OF SESSIONS: Readings with asterisk (*) are required.

Week
1   Covers instructor and student introductions, instructor assumptions about ethics, overview of four components of an ethical act, and an exercise on ethical sensitivity.
2   Topic A: <u>Ethical Leadership and Ethical Followership Characteristics</u>; Topic B: <u>Why Unethical Acts Occur: A Beginning Exploration</u>; Will discuss student views of the characteristics of ethical leaders and followers: students will review their own experiences as well as propose what they consider to be ideal qualities; Will discuss student views of the barriers to and facilitators of ethical and unethical behavior (At the end of the seminar, students will be asked to state their views about the above again.); Will do a preliminary analysis of the factors involved in ethical behavior in three cases: Dalkon Shield, Challenger Disaster, and Lake Hospital. These cases will be revisited from time to time in the light of new theories, principles, and information.)
Readings: Hills book <u>Corporate Violence</u>; "The Dalkon Shield" by Morton Mintz, pp. 30-40; "A Plea for Corporate Conscience" by Judge Miles W. Lord,

pp. 41-46.

Handouts: <u>Star Tribune</u> article, "The Tangled Saga of the Dalkon Shield"; One-page news article on Dalkon Shield; "Ethics in Organizations: The Challenger Explosion"; One-page news article on the NASA panel; (Recommended "Outsider's Inside View of the Challenger Inquiry" by Richard Feyneman; (Recommended) "The Dreamless Society" by Warren Bennis

3   <u>Social-Psychological Factors</u>;   We will review the studies on obedience to authority (Milgram) and conformity (Asch, Zimbardo, and Janis) for their relevance and compare them to student views shared in the previous session. In a later session, we will discuss the relationship of people's ethical beliefs, principles, and levels of moral reasoning ability to pressures to conform;

Readings: Handouts: *"On Killing the Innocent with a Clear Conscience" by Sabini and Silver (covers Milgram, Asch, & Zimbardo's prisoners study); *"Groupthink in the Corporate World" by Goleman; *"DC 10" by Mokhiber (the DC-10 is the type of airline involved in the Iowa crash); Hills book <u>Corporate Violence</u>: *"Introduction," pp. 1-10; *"Epilogue: Corporate Violence and the Banality of Evil," pp. 187-206; *"Why Should My Conscience Bother Me," Kermit Vandivier, pp. 145-162;

Cases: Government contract with B. F. Goodrich Co. (Vandivier reading above);   Review Dalkon Shield and Challenger cases in light of these readings.

4   <u>Lying, Secrets, and Deceptions (to self and other)</u>, including rationalizations;

Readings: Bok book <u>Secrets</u>: *Ch. V: "Secrecy & Self Deception," pp. 59-72; *Ch. VIII: "Secrecy, Power and Accountability," pp. 102-115;

Handouts: *"Lies for the Public Good" by Sissela Bok from her other book, <u>Lying</u>; *"What Would You Do? . . .Like the Suffocating Smoke of a Blazing Room" by Doug Wallace; *"Asbestos injury suit vs. Conwed settled out of court"; *"Manville" by Russell Mokhiber (This asbestos case is similar to the Ford Pinto one; rationalizations and coverup. Recall last week's discussion in Hills book in the "Epilogue," pp. 187-191, of German corporations under the Nazis;

Cases: Thunderbolt Defense Co. (Wallace reading);   Manville and asbestos (Mokhiber reading).

5   <u>Ethical Courage and Whistleblowing</u>;   Types of courage (physical, social, intellectual, creative, ethical) and discussion "What is ethical courage?" and "How does it differ from courage in general?" The steps involved in dissenting from an individual or organization's practice will be outlined and discussed with a special focus on whistleblowing, the last step in that process. Examples of ethically courageous people will also be discussed.

Readings: Bok book <u>Secrets</u>: *Ch. XIV "Whistleblowing & Leaking," pp. 210-229; Hills book <u>Corporate Violence</u>: *"Exposing Risks of Nuclear Disaster (Confessions of a Whistle-Blower)," pp. 170-184;

Handouts: *Summary of Rolla May on courage, by Gerri Perrault; "That Dirty War," transcript of a "60 Minutes" interview with the Mothers of the Disappeared who kept a public vigil in Argentina; *"Whistleblowing" by Glazer and Glazer; *"When Corporate Courage Counts" by Harvey Hornstein; Summary of Vernon Jensen on "Whistleblowing" by Gerri Perrault (not distributed); *"J'Accuse" by Donald Soeken; *"What Happens When an Ordinary Woman Blows the Whistle on Her Boss?" by Gloria Steinem (Based on book <u>Marie</u>, about Marie Ragghianti and the State of Tennessee's government); "Examples of Ethical Courage"; "Pair of 'whistleblowers' awarded millions in Ashland Oil Trial"; *"Engineers' transfers prompt NASA inquiry"; *"Why I Blew the Whistle on NASA's O-Ring Woes";

Recommended reading: "Moral Courage" included in later session's readings

Cases: Mothers of the Disappeared (Argentina); Marie; Nuclear plant whistleblower; Martin Luther King

VHS: "I Have a Dream" by Martin Luther King

6   Topic A: <u>Ethical Principles, Self-Perceptions & Assumptions, Reasoning, and Judgment</u>; Topic B: <u>Criteria for Judging Leaders (individuals and organizations)</u>; Covers ethical principles and values used in ethical decision making, different models of ethical decision making (classical ethics, Kew Gardens, Rest, Josephson, Perreault), issues in professional ethics, and the interaction of ethical principles with social-psychological pressures to behave unethically. Examples provided of leaders who express different principles. Also, examination of ethical criteria being developed for reviewing corporate policies and practices (and return to these in later sessions).

Readings: Handouts: (Note: you will be sent a reading from our speaker for today.); *"Letter from a Birmingham Jail" by Martin Luther King; *Quotes from <u>The Prince</u> by Machiavelli (not distributed yet); *"Vision and the Emerging World View: From Separation to Connectedness" by Gerri Perreault; "Why Should a Woman Be More Like A Man?" by Carol Gilligan; "Emerging: 'the caretaking gap'" (Goodman); "The clout of women's conviction" (Goodman); "Do women, men differ on judging right/wrong?"; *"Leadership, Followership, and the State" by Kegan & Lahey; *"Professionalism and the Human Services" (Perreault); *"What Issues Seem to Arise in Your Profession" by Alverno College; *"Car that exploded linked to defects"; *"Pinto" by Mokhiber; Hills book <u>Corporate Violence</u>: *Review the speech from Judge Lord; *"Pinto Madness," by Mark Dowie, pp. 13-29.

Recommended reading (not distributed): "Living in Moral Pain" by Peter Marin; "Looking in the Mirror: A Response to Jonestown," by Carter Heyward. She says Jonestown was us. We will see on VHS, King's speech: "I Have A Dream."

7   <u>Views on Government Ethics</u>;

Readings: Handout: *"Deaver, capital's ethical fabric to be questioned" by Star Tribune, 1986; "Morality Among the Supply Siders" by Richard Stengel; "What's Wrong" by Walter Shapiro; *(Handout to be distributed by the speaker, Mary Turck); Bok book <u>Secrets</u>: *Ch. VIII "Military Secrecy," pp. 191-209; *Ch. XII "Secrets of State," pp. 171-190; *Ch. XVIII "Conclusion," pp. 281-285.

Recommended reading: (not distributed) Bly: "Bad government and Silly Literature" (see me for copy); <u>The Secret Government</u> by Bill Moyers (in paperback in bookstores).

Case: Iran-Contra

In class: VHS: "The Secret Government" by Bill Moyers

8   <u>Views on Business Ethics</u>; **Readings:** (Required vs. optional <u>to be determined</u>.); Book <u>Corporate Violence</u>: Review "Epilogue: Corporate Violence and the

Banality of Evil," pp. 187-206; "A Slap on the Wrist for The Kepone Mob," by Christopher D. Stone, pp. 121-132 (This and the next article covers government-business-community collusion.); "Benton Harbor: Distributors of Unsafe Drugs," James T. Carey, pp. 163-169;

Recommended reading: "The Dumping of Hazardous Products on Foreign Markets," by Mark Dowie and Mother Jones, pp. 47-59.

Handouts: *"Oil," by Russell Mokhiber, pp. 318-328; "Teapot Dome revisited: U.S. trying to sell oil fields"; *"Do Businesses Have to Cheat to Win?" Blanchard and Peale; *"The Ethical Roots of the Business System," Douglas S. Sherwin; *"Ethics in Business: An Overview," Michael Josephson; *"Inventory of Ethical Issues in Business"; "Ethical Managers Make Their Own Rules" by Sir Adrian Cadbury.

Cases: Exxon, if I can get material.   (Revisit earlier cases.)   LBOs? Incinerators?

9   Topic A: <u>Ethical organizations/people</u>; Topic B: <u>Hope for the Future: What's Being Done. What Can Be Done. Useful Resources</u>; Topic C: <u>Tips on Living Ethically</u>;

Readings: Handouts: *"Ethical Investing" (I will do a 2-page summary); *"Rating America's corporations"; *"Building Integrity in Organizations" by Wallace and White; *"Hands on, Values Driven"; *"Moral Courage: The 'Sine Qua Non' of Greatness," by O'Toole; *"Corporate Crimes and Violence" by Mokhiber; Read pp. 38-65 on "What to do: A 50-point law and order program to curb corporate crime."

10   ???

11   Topic A: <u>Wrap-up</u>; Topic B: <u>Student Evaluations</u>.

ASSIGNMENTS: 1. Attend class. 2. Read all "required" material. Try to read some of "recommended" (optional) reading. The readings will be selections from the books required for the course (<u>Corporate Violence</u> by Hills and <u>Secrets</u> by Bok) and articles selected from journals, newspapers, and other books. 2. Prepare responses to study questions for discussion. (These are for your own use; they do not have to be turned in.) 3. Complete midquarter and final. For each, one portion will be a series of questions asking your analysis of either the Dalkon Shield or Challenger Disaster (your choice). 4. Participate in class discussions. 5. Complete competence statement, self-evaluation, & course evaluation. (Guidelines will be provided for the first two.)

(Ed. notes) Available from Gerri Perrault are: An extensive bibliography, exercises, and notes on the exams, all of which are accessible to the students.

Miami University
Dept. of Political Science
Oxford, OH 45056

Distinguished Professor
513/529-4394

Political Leadership - POL 626

The course is an examination of theoretical, comparative, empirical, and experimental studies of leaders and leadership in subnational, national, and global contexts. Following the initial meeting, each week the seminar will focus on one of the topics indicated on the course outline. Certain readings dealing with various aspects of a topic will be the subject of class presentations by individual seminar members, who are expected to "lead" us through a subject, an issue, or a problem. See Assignment Sheets and Selected Bibliography. The instruction shall articulate the overall framework of the course, establish the parameters for the treatment of each topic, highlight the principal issues in connection with each topic, coordinate the discussion of each topic, summarize and synthesize each topic, relate each topic to preceding and succeeding topics, and generally keep the course on track. Given this format, a "successful" course is dependent entirely on timely and effective contributions from all seminar members.

Seminar members will have three responsibilities:
  • class contributions on a week-to-week basis,
  • class presentations based on assigned materials,
  • final examination.
The conventional requirement of a seminar paper is waived for this course in order to allow concentration of energies on a very large and demanding topic. Regular attendance is assumed.

Course grade will be based on class contributions (10%), class presentations (45%), final examination (45%).

TEXTS: Burns, J. M., Leadership, New York: Harper Colophon, 1978; Kellerman, B., ed., Political Leadership: A Source Book, Pittsburgh: Univ. of Pittsburgh Press, 1986.

TOPICAL COURSE OUTLINE

Session	Topic
1	Introduction: Substance and Procedure
2	Defining Political Leadership: Great-Man and Social Forces Approaches
3	Defining Political Leadership: Synthetic Approaches
4	Defining Political Leadership: Critique and Controversy
5	Defining Political Leadership: Power, Management, and Domination
6	Leaders, Followers, and Skills
7	Types of Political Leaders: Transactional and Transforming Leaders
8	Types of Political Leaders: Symbolic, Entrepreneurial, and Manufactured Leaders
9	Motivations of Political Leaders
10	Functions of Political Leaders
11	Comparative Studies of Leaders: Elites and Power in America

57

12 Comparative Studies of Leaders: Global Elites
13 Women Leaders
14 Lacunae in the Study of Political Leaders
15 (Either final examination or continuation of any topic that may require attention. In the latter case, final exam will occur during finals week.)

The above topics are detailed on nine pages of Assignment Sheets (Topics I-IX) and a 23-page course bibliography. These two documents should be studied in tandem as they have been constructed in such a way as to parallel one another.

Miami University
Oxford, OH 45056

Richard L. Nault
Director, Honors Program
513/529-3398

Thelma Flanery Reeder Leadership Seminar
The Analysis of Leadership - EDL 380.A
Instructors: Peter Magolda, Richard Nault and Sally Sharp
T. & Th. 3:45 - 5:15 p.m.

OVERVIEW: The purpose of this seminar is to help you better understand how leadership is effectively exercised and to enhance your leadership abilities. The course will help you: 1. strengthen your leadership skills; 2. enhance your ability to analyze and critique the leadership approaches others take; 3. become more clear about your career goals and the settings in which you'd like to exert leadership; 4. develop associations with the other class members that will support you in taking leadership on this campus.

REQUIREMENTS: We ask that you contribute effectively to class discussions, both by presenting your ideas and by facilitating the participation of others. You also will be asked to complete three short analysis papers and a ten-page analysis of an interview with a leader. All participants in the class are expected to take part in the class leadership trip scheduled for four days between semesters.

Grades for the course are credit/no credit. This is a two-credit seminar. Half your grade will be based on your written assignments; half on your class participation.

RECOMMENDED TEXTS: David Campbell, If I'm In Charge Here, Why is Everybody Laughing? Greensboro, North Carolina: Center for Creative Leadership, 1984.

Series of six leadership essays published by John Gardner (Independent Sector, 1828 L Street, N.W., Washington, D.C. 20036): The Nature of Leadership. The Tasks of Leadership. The Heart of the Matter. Leadership and Power. The Moral Aspect of Leadership. Attributes and Context.

Additional readings and handouts for the class are collected in a packet which can be purchased. A few references are on reserve.

I. The Analysis of Leadership

Session I Overview of the course. Assignment: In groups of five you are asked to prepare a fifteen-minute presentation for the class that responds to the question, "Has Ronald Reagan been an effective leader?" Your arguments should be well-substantiated and interestingly presented. Your group presentation will be scheduled either for Session X or XI. Background reading: Time, May 23, 1988, 14-16, "Why He's a Target."

Session II Leadership Retreat. The retreat will allow you to become more comfortable working with the other members of the class, become more effective giving feedback to others, and to analyze your approach to participating in groups. The retreat begins at 4:00 p.m. on Friday and ends at 3:00 p.m. on Saturday.

Session III The Definition of Leadership. Assignment: From your reading of the two biographies over the summer, please submit a five-page double-spaced paper in which you argue the traits that most allowed the leaders to be successful, the ways in which they differed in their approaches to leadership, and the factors that might have accounted for these differences. Please type your paper. Due Session VII.

Session IV The Dimensions of Leadership. John W. Gardner, The Nature of Leadership; David Campbell, If I'm In Charge Here, Why is Everybody Laughing? Assignment: Interview a student leader to learn what motivates them to take leadership positions. Due Session V.

Session V Other Ways of Conceptualizing the Task of Leadership. Robert Greenleaf, Servant Leadership. Ramsey, N.J.: Paulist Press, 1977. 7-14; James MacGregor Burns, Leadership. New York: Harper & Row, 1978. 18-23, 241-254.

Session VI Movie: Patton, 6:30 p.m.

Session VII Traits of Leaders. John W. Gardner, Attributes and Context.

Session VIII Tasks of Leadership. John W. Gardner, The Tasks of Leadership.

Session IX Self-Diagnosis of Leadership Effectiveness.

Session X Group Presentations on Reagan's Effectiveness as Leader.

Session XI Discussions of Reagan's Leadership Effectiveness continued; Analysis of the Functioning of the Working Groups.

II. Identification of Career Goals

Session XII Identification of Your Transferrable Skills. Gail Sheehey, Passages: Predictable Crises of Adult Life. New York: Dutton, 1976. 20-32. Assignment: Complete Your "Goals for Personal Development" inventory. Due Session XIII.

Session XIII Identification of Preferred Working Conditions. Assignment: Complete "Career Goals Summary" form. Develop a career lifeline based on your transferrable skills, preferred working conditions, and your goals for personal development. Due Session XIV.

Session XIV Report to the Group on Career Paths.

Session XV Reports continue.

III. Components of Effective Leadership

Session XVI Power, Influence and Authority. Gary Yukl, Leadership in Organizations. Englewood Cliffs: Prentice-Hall, 1981. 38-39; Morgan McCall, Jr., "Power, Influence and

Authority: The Hazards of Carrying A Sword." (Closed Reserve); Richard H. Hall, Organizations: Structure and Process. Englewood Cliffs: Prentice-Hall, 1977. 197-236; Dennis C. King and John C. Glidewell, "Power."

Movie: Norma Rae, 7:00 p.m.

During this week we will meet with you in individual conferences to discuss your participation in the class and how we can make this seminar a more effective experience for you.

Session XVII Power and Organizational Conflict. Daniel Katz and Robert Kahn, The Social-Psychology of Organizations. New York: John Wiley, 1978. 612-621; Udai Pareek, "Preventing and Resolving Conflict"; John Gardner, "Leadership and Power." Assignment: As your major paper for this course you are asked to interview a person who has taken leadership in some community. Using the perspectives of this course and referring to course readings, analyze that person's approach to leadership. Please type your paper and keep it under ten pages. Papers due Session XXX.

Session XVIII Conflict, cont. Simulation: "Win as Much as You Can."

Session XVIX Influencing Organizational Change. Richard Hall, Organizations: Structure and Process, 293-300; A Case Study of the Effects of the Women's Protests on Miami. Assignment: Write a two- to four-page paper analyzing an organization of which you were a member or leader using the analytic perspectives of power, conflict, change, creativity or motivation as a basis for your analysis. Due Session XXI.

Session XX Use of Creativity to Increase Organizational Effectiveness: Creative Problem Solving Simulation. David Campbell, Take the Road to Creativity and Get Off Your Dead End. (Closed Reserve); Morgan W. McCall, Jr., "Conjecturing About Creative Leaders," in Contemporary Issues in Leadership, edited by William E. Rosenbach and Robert L. Taylor. London: Westview Press, 1984. 271-280.

Session XXI Components of Effective Leadership; Starpower Simulation. Assignment: Observe the behaviors of men and women in mixed-sex task groups and note the differences in their behaviors. Look at your behavior in relation to men and women in mixed-sex groups. Do you treat men and women differently? Do you behave differently in single-sex groups? What implications does this have for who becomes the leader of the group? At a meeting of a group of which you are a part, pretend you are a member of the opposite sex and behave accordingly. How is your behavior different than usual? Prepare this information for sharing in class Session XXII. This does not have to be written up, but should be information you are ready to share with the class. Organizational analysis papers due.

IV. Leadership in Context

Session XXII Women in Leadership. Marilyn Loden, "A Machismo That Drives Women Out," New York Times, February 9, 1986; "Why Women Execs Stop Before the Top," U.S. News and World Report, December 29, 1986, 72-73; Ann Morrison, Randall P. White, and Ellen Van Velsor, Breaking the Glass Ceiling. Reading, MA: Addison-Wesley, 1987, 99-137; (Optional) - Stephanie Riger and Pat Gilligan, "Women in Management: An Explanation of Competing Paradigms," American Psychologist, October 1980, 902-910.

Session XXIII Women in Leadership. Seminar Speaker: Karen Schilling, Coordinator, Women's Studies; Edwin P. Hollander and Sam Yoder, "Some Issues in Comparing Women and Men as Leaders." From Contemporary Issues in Leadership, edited by William E. Rosenbach and Robert L. Taylor. 234-248.

Session XXIV No class. Time available for trip planning.

Session XXV Minority Leadership. King E. Davis, "The Status of Black Leadership: Implications for Black Followers in the 1980s." From Contemporary Issues in Leadership, edited by William E. Rosenbach and Robert L. Taylor. 192-208; Brent Staples, "The Dwindling Black Presence on Campus," New York Times Magazine, April 27, 1986, 46-54, 62; William Julius Wilson, "The Hidden Agenda," The University of Chicago Magazine, Fall, 1987, 2-11. Material excerpted from The Truly Disadvantaged: The Inner City, The Underclass, and Public Policy, University of Chicago Press, 1987.

Session XXVI Ethics and Leadership. John Gardner, The Moral Aspects of Leadership.

Session XXVII No class. Time available for trip planning.

Session XXVIII Leadership in Context. President Pearson.

Session XXIX Ethics and Leadership. Harvard Business School's Duke Power Plant Case Study.

Session XXX Analysis of interview with leaders due.

Session XXXI Discussion of papers and your involvement in the seminar.

Nebraska Wesleyan University
5000 St. Paul, Lincoln, NE 68504

Richard B. Artman
Vice-President, Student Affairs
402/465-2153

Creative Leadership - Speech/Theatre 190, #7709

OBJECTIVES: To provide the opportunity for students to explore various components of leadership theory and skills and organizational behavior. Students will gain knowledge about leadership theories and their own leadership style, practice their leadership skills and develop attitudes about what makes one an effective leader.

CONTENT: Among the concepts to be examined are: leadership theories, followership, leadership styles, leadership and management, gender issues in leadership, delegation, motivating others, the ethics of leadership, the concepts of power and authority, group dynamics, goal setting, conflict management, running effective meetings, assertiveness, communication skills, small group process and observation, and decision making.

Various instructional methodologies will be employed including lecture, class simulation, case study, film and video, self-assessments and field experiences.

REQUIRED TEXT: Bennis, W. and Nanus, B. Leaders: The Strategies for Taking Charge, Harper & Row, NY, 1985.

REQUIREMENTS: A. Class attendance/participation - Required! Because the class meets only once a week, you are expected to attend. Valuable learning experiences will occur through classroom activities; therefore, attendance and participation will influence your grade. You are expected to be on time, every time. It is your responsibility to inform me in advance of any absences and to obtain assignments, notes, etc., from your classmates if you miss class. (0-10 points); B. Quizzes and exams - I believe there should be frequent opportunities to assess our mutual efforts of teaching and learning. Therefore, unannounced quizzes are possible and there will be established dates for exams. Missed exams or quizzes cannot be made-up except through extra credit. (Quizzes 0-5 points) (Exams 0-30 points); C. Personal journals - You are expected to maintain a personal journal which will chronicle your experiences in the course. A three-ring notebook is recommended for ease in arranging the journals and other course readings, handouts, etc. The journals will be collected three times (see syllabus) and I will read them and react to your entries. Journals are not graded but will be recorded as credit or no credit based upon your effort. Journals received late result in only partial credit. (0-15 points, 5 points each); D. Biography of a leader - You must select and read a biography (or autobiography) of a leader (past or present) who has had a significant impact on her/his field, community, nation. You must prepare a paper based on the biography and it must be submitted as scheduled on the syllabus. (0-20 points); E. Leader interview - You are required to interview a person who currently holds a leadership position in industry, government, church, community, school or other profession. Names will be available through the Career Assistance Network or you may select an individual on your own. You will be assigned to ask specific questions about leadership issues and to deliver a report (oral and written) summarizing your interchange. (0-15 points); F. Group observation - You are required to observe an actual meeting of a campus or community group in action and to report on various aspects of group dynamics and communication patterns of the group (0-5 points);

G. <u>Extra credit</u> - Opportunities can be arranged and negotiated for earning extra credit provided they are agreed upon between us before the deadline indicated on the syllabus; H.   <u>Summary of evaluation opportunities</u> - Class attendance/participation, 0-10 pts.; Quizzes, 0-5 pts.; Personal journals (5 each), 0-15 pts.; Biography of a leader, 0-20 pts.; Leader interview report, 0-15 pts.; Exams, 0-30 pts.; Group observation report, 0-5 pts.; Extra credit, 0-10 pts. A+ = 98-100; A = 95-97; A- = 90-94; B+ = 87-89; B = 84-86; B- = 80-83; C+ = 77-79; C = 74-76; C- = 70-73; D+ = 67-69; D = 64-66; D- = 60-63; F = 59 or below.

BIBLIOGRAPHY

Bennis, Warren and Nanus, B. <u>Leaders: The Strategies For Taking Charge</u>. Harper & Row, NY, 1985;

Blanchard, Kenneth and Johnson, Spencer. <u>The One Minute Manager</u>. Berkley Books, NY, 1981;

Blanchard, K. and Peale, N. V. <u>The Power of Ethical Management</u>. William Morrow and Company, Inc., NY, 1988;

Bradford, Teland P. <u>Making Meetings Work</u>. University Associates, La Jolla, CA, 1976;

Deal, Terrance E. and Kennedy, Allan A. <u>Corporate Cultures</u>. Addison - Wesley Publishing Co., Reading, MA, 1982;

Dodge, Golen. <u>Priceless People</u>. Nebraska Human Resources Research Foundation, Lincoln, NE, 1986;

Garfield, Charles. <u>Peak Performers</u>. Avon, NY, 1986;

Kanter, Rosabeth Moss. <u>The Change Masters</u>. Simon and Schuster, NY, 1983;

Kerr, Barbara A. <u>Smart Girls, Gifted Women</u>. Ohio Psychology Publishing Co., Columbus, OH, 1985;

Korda, Michael. <u>Power: How To Get It. How To Use It</u>. Ballentine Books, NY, 1975;

McCormack, Mark H. <u>What They Don't Teach You At The Harvard Business School</u>. Bantam Books, NY, 1984;

Peters, Thomas J. and Waterman, Robert H. <u>In Search of Excellence</u>. Harper & Row, NY, 1982;

Rosenbach, W. E. and Taylor, R. L. <u>Contemporary Issues in Leadership</u>. Westview Press, Boulder, CO, 1984;

Schaef, Anne Wilson. <u>Women's Reality</u>. Harper & Row, NY, 1981.

TENTATIVE SYLLABUS

<u>Topics and Activities</u>

<u>Session</u>

1   <u>Introduction to Course, Mechanics, Logistics, Get Acquainted</u>; Video - Peak Performance

2   <u>Leadership Issues and Topics</u>; Text 1-86, 222-225; Leadership Cases, Leadership Myths; Text 19-25, 58-79
     <u>The Self and Its Relationship to Leadership</u>; Text 187-213; Lecturette: <u>Priceless</u>

<u>People</u> (Dodge), Leadership Skills Assessment Inventory; Values Handout:
Lecturette: <u>Peak Performers</u> (Garfield)

3   <u>Approaches to Goal Setting</u>; Text 87-229; The Visionary Leader; Text 141-145;
The Manager - Lecturette: <u>One Minute Manager</u> (Blanchard & Johnson);
Leadership Goals Exercise

4   <u>Assertiveness</u>; Assertiveness Quotient Inventory; Handout: Philosophy of
Thinking/Personal Freedoms; Role Playing: "How to Say No"; <u>Getting Things
Done</u> - Time Management and Goals

5   <u>Interpersonal Communication</u>; Text 74-75, 96; Feedback, Openness, Verbal and
Non-verbal, Cross Cultural, Listening Skills; Biography Sources Due; Exam 1;
Communication Exercises: One Way Two Way Broken Squares

6   Board Retreat; <u>Leading Effective Meetings</u>; Journal Collection; Basic
Parliamentary Procedure, Agendas, Meeting Tips, Time Wasters; <u>Dynamics and
Group Observation Skill</u>; Roles of Group Members; Lecturette: <u>Making
Meetings Work</u> (Bradford)

7   <u>Leadership Styles</u>; Take Home Inventories; MBTI, TP, RAT, SIT, Formal and
Informal, Followership, Mirroring; Trust; Text 151-154

8   <u>Motivating Others</u>; Motivation Inventory; Text 126; Motivation Theories (Maslow,
Herzberg, McGregor); Volunteer Organizations (handout)

9   <u>Competition and Cooperation</u>; Exercise, Prisoners Dilemma, Teambuilding,
Gilligan, Dollar Bill Auction; Lecturette: <u>Women's Reality</u> (Schaef)

10   <u>Gender Issues in Leadership</u>; Panel; Cinderella Factor; Lecturette: <u>Smart
Girls, Gifted Women</u> (Kerr); Sexual Harassment Issues - Role Playing

11   TBA; Group Observation Reports Due

12   <u>Power or Empowerment</u>; Text 15-18, 79-86, 138, 217-229; Lecturette: <u>Power:
How to Get It, How to Use It</u> (Korda); Personal Power Stages, Star Power,
Negotiations and Compromise, Conflict Management (skills, strategies, exercise,
dyads, fantasy); Transformative Leadership; Journal Collection; Exam 2; Text
217-229

13   <u>Decision Making</u>; Participative Mgt., Japanese Mgt., Brainstorming Techniques,
Group Decision-making Exercise, Abilene Paradox; Biographies Due; <u>Principles
of Delegation</u>

14   <u>Organizational Leadership</u>; Open and Closed Systems; Text 50-53, 118-142, 138,
209-214; Lecturette: <u>What They Don't Teach You at Harvard Business School</u>
(McCormick); <u>In Search of Excellence</u> (Peters and Waterman)

15   <u>Ethics and Leadership</u>; Leader Reports Due; Lecturette: <u>Power of Ethical
Management</u> (Blanchard and Peale); Moral Development, Ethical Decision-
making Hierarchies, Ethical Dilemma Exercise; Text 152-154

16   <u>Creating Change and Organizational Learning</u>; Resistance to Change; Journal
Collection; Text 146-151, 185-186, 187-214; Lecturette: <u>The Change Masters</u>
(Kanter)

17   Final Exam to be Announced

Southeast Missouri State University
900 Normal, 2nd Floor, Cape Girardeau, MO 63701

Bob Beodeker
Ass't. Dir., Student Activities
314/651-2953

Leadership and Group Management - GC210
Tues. and Thurs. 2:00 - 3:15 p.m.

COURSE OVERVIEW: Success as a leader may be determined by many variables such as: the type of group; the personality of the leader; the environment within which the group exists; and the present condition of the group. However, success also depends on whether that leader possesses the skills required for that moment in the group's life. Leadership skills, although enhanced by certain personal characteristics, can be developed by any person who wishes to learn them.

This course is for those individuals who wish to develop their leadership skills. It is designed to aid students in increasing their understanding of themselves, of the theories and techniques of leadership, of group processes, and managerial skills. The course will attempt to integrate theoretical concepts with the reality of application within the group setting.

COURSE MODEL: This course will be taught using an experiential model. The emphasis is on your experiences as the learner, rather than vicarious experiences garnered through such teaching methods as traditional lectures. For such an approach to be viable, each individual is ultimately responsible for his or her learning. In addition to numerous in-class discussion exercises, involvement in an organization or group serves as a secondary learning laboratory. The instructor is committed to the course as a learning process and will serve as a group leader.

COURSE OBJECTIVES: 1. To help participants grow as persons, to add to their self-knowledge and to improve their effectiveness in interpersonal relations. 2. To provide opportunities for participants to develop skills and knowledge which will allow them to function as leaders in a group setting. 3. To assist participants in learning to communicate effectively. 4. To learn more about human growth and development, particularly in the college years. 5. To increase understanding of the dynamics of groups so as to be sensitive to the effects of roles, power, and varying leadership styles.

COURSE OUTLINE:

Unit One: Leadership and Groups - This unit will establish a common set of assumptions about leadership and groups to provide a foundation for the rest of the course. Some of the areas covered will include: What is a group? What are some of the general characteristics of groups? Why is leadership important? What are the key tasks and roles of leaders? Who are leaders? What are their characteristics and attributes? What are the styles of leadership?

Unit Two: The Role of Personality and Maturity in Leadership - One attribute of highly effective leaders is self-understanding. This unit will provide personal feedback to each class member about key personality characteristics affecting their leadership comfort or approach in one way or another. Theories of human growth and development will be discussed in terms of how they can provide insight into interpersonal relationships. Models

66

like the Myers-Briggs Type Indicator will be used to assist students in learning more about themselves.

Unit Three: Communication skills are directly linked to success as a leader. This unit will focus on the improvement of interpersonal communication skills including active listening, assertiveness, conflict resolution and non-verbal communication. Written communication skills will also be discussed.

Unit Four: Organizational Development - Building Effective Working Groups - An understanding of group development is essential to be an effective leader. This unit will explore roles within groups, the development levels of groups, decision making in groups, and the effects of power and influence on groups. Motivation for involvement will also be explored and tips will be given on group facilitation/management.

Unit Five: Values and Ethics as Leaders - Personal values have a strong impact on a leader's interpersonal relationships and interaction with a group. This unit will allow participants the opportunity to explore their own values and gain insight into the way these values impact them as leaders. Gender issues in leadership will be explored, as well as the issues of accountability and professionalism.

COURSE REQUIREMENTS:

Participation: Because this class is an experience oriented learning process, participation is imperative. Students are expected to attend all classes and participate fully in discussion exercises. Students will be evaluated on the value of their participation.

Readings: There is no text; selected articles/handouts will be distributed. A reading list will be supplied to students at the end of the second class meeting. Students are required to read two books during the course of the semester that relate to leadership/group development and submit a typed two-page paper focusing on personal reactions to each book. You can read two books from the reading list or select your own reading material.

Exams: A take-home mid-term and final exam with questions requiring synthesis of information presented during the semester and practical applications of the course material.

Project: A case analysis/organizational assessment will be done by each student (may be done in pairs) attending to as many components skills learned in the course as possible, critiquing the group based on information gained in the classroom setting as well as your personal experience. After reviewing the group you should write a paper summarizing the findings and providing insights regarding organization strengths, weaknesses, leadership, development, and possible recommendations for improvement. A student organization, business, educational institution, agency or political entity may be used for this purpose. Your paper should be 7-10 pages typed.

GRADING: A contract grading system will be used. Certain minimum requirements are set with the completion of additional personal learning projects required to earn a higher grade. A final course grade will be determined by an accumulation of points awarded for each of the following:

Participation - Both quality and quantity will be noted, 250 points.
Book Discussions (each book worth 100 points), 200 points.
Mid-Term Exam, 150 points. Final Exam, 150 points.
Course Project, 250 points.
Personal Learning Projects, 200 points.
Total Points: 1200 points.

Final Grading Chart:

1200-1020	points	= A
1019-840	points	= B
839-660	points	= C
659-500	points	= D
499-0	points	= F

PERSONAL LEARNING PROJECTS:

To maximize the individualism of this learning experience, students participate in developing their own projects and selecting appropriate learning experiences and methods of evaluation. To receive credit for personal learning projects, it must be a part of the learning contract and completed satisfactorily as reviewed by the instructor. Projects can include independent study experiences, class projects, etc. The minimum standard and point values will be decided by mutual agreement of the student and instructor. All projects must be typed. Some suggested projects are:

Book Review Read an additional book on leadership/group development. Review it focusing on your reactions to the information presented by the author(s). (75 points)

Personal Leadership Style Paper Based on the different leadership theories learned in class, come up with a personal leadership style that suits you as a leader. Explain why you feel this style best suits you as a leader. (3-5 pages typed) (75 points)

Leader Profile Select a contemporary or historical "leader" who has had a significant impact on the United States and/or the world. Analyze his/her leadership style/skills focusing on this as a reason for prominence and success or failure. Autobiographies, biographies, and other resource materials should be used to support your analysis. (5-7 pages typed) (150 points)

Development Seminars Attend a development seminar pre-approved by the instructor to receive credit. Write a short summary of what you learned. (Limit of 2) (50 points)

Self-Portrait Write a self-portrait reflecting your personal development/growth. Describe any significant experiences that affected your growth and development and influenced your values, attitudes, ambitions and relationships. (5-7 pages typed) (150 points)

Stanford University
Graduate School of Business
Stanford, CA 94305

James G. March
Professor of Management
415/723-2105

Organizational Leadership - Business 379, Political Science 108, Sociology 165

Issues In Thinking About Leadership

This course considers some central issues in thinking about organizational leadership. The ones outlined here are not exhaustive, and a proper list at the end of the course would undoubtedly be somewhat different. These issues do, however, give some idea of the kinds of discussions that are likely to be pursued:

1. <u>Private lives and public duties</u>. Leaders have private lives from which they draw emotional balance and human sustenance, though they often find their public lives systematically more rewarding. Leadership tends to destroy both the privacy and the quality of personal lives. Importance and conspicuousness lead to loss of authenticity in personal relations. They also lead to curiosity and gossip. Followers claim a right to knowledge about a leader's private life on grounds of its relevance to assessing character and establishing rapport. At the same time, private lives tend to corrupt public responsibilities. Personal motives and relations affect the actions of leaders to the detriment of the organization. Personal jealousies and loyalties bend a leader's judgment. What are the possibilities for combining a rich personal life with a life as an organizational leader?

2. <u>Cleverness, innocence, and virtue</u>. The literature on leadership is ambivalent about sophistication and cleverness. On the one hand, leaders are often portrayed as astute manipulators of resources and people, praised for their use of superior knowledge and adroitness. And they are frequently described as intelligently devious, secretive. On the other hand, they are often pictured not as sophisticated but as possessing an elemental innocence that overcomes the fatuous sophistication of clever people and goes instinctively to the essentials. And they are often praised for their openness, the trust they extend to others. What is the place of cleverness, innocence, intelligence, and ignorance in descriptions of, or prescriptions for, leadership?

3. <u>Genius, heresy, and madness</u>. Great leaders are often portrayed as geniuses. They see further and more accurately than others and are able to transform an organization through that ability. Leadership genius, however, is in conflict with the establishment, which prefers safer, more reliable behavior. The preference is not perverse. Though deviants occasionally show unusual genius and creativity, they are more frequently simply crazy. Thus, great leaders are characteristically heretics who overcome the orthodoxy of the organizational establishment, but most heretics (for good reason) do not become great leaders. What is the relation between genius and madness? How do we recognize great leaders among the crazies? How do we nurture genius if we cannot recognize it?

4. <u>Great actions and great expectations</u>. Leadership ideology emphasizes reason more than foolishness, strategy more than opportunism, thinking more than imitation. Action is seen as driven by expectations with respect to its consequences. We ask whether this is an

adequate description of leadership behavior or an adequate moral foundation for it. In particular, we examine the consequences of justifying great actions by great hopes in a world in which causality is complex and effectiveness problematic. In an ethic of consequentiality, how do you sustain commitment in the face of adverse or ambiguous outcomes? How does an organization sustain illusions of efficacy in its leaders? What are the consequences? Are there alternatives?

5. <u>Power, domination, and subordination</u>. Many of our ideologies treat inequalities in power as illegitimate. Yet, we pursue power and have a fascination with it. We write history and describe progress in terms of changing patterns of domination and subordination. We equate personal power with personal self-worth and powerlessness with a loss of identity. Thus, there is a stress in organizations between hierarchy and participation, between power and equality, between control and autonomy. Power is often said to corrupt the holder of it, to transform normally virtuous people into monsters. It is also said to condemn, to undermine the ordinary pleasures of honesty in interpersonal relations. Leaders have power, some more than others. How do they use it? What are its limits? What are its costs? How does a person with little power function in a power-based institution? What are the moral dilemmas of power?

6. <u>Gender and sexuality</u>. Leadership in contemporary western society has strong links to questions of sexual identity. Most leaders are men; the rhetoric of leadership is closely related to the rhetoric of manliness; being a leader and being seen as having power are components of sexual appeal. Changes in gender stereotypes with respect to leadership are affected by, and affect, the ways women and men are interpreted to have (or not have) distinctive styles, characters, positions, beliefs, or behaviors, as well as by our understandings of their relations, not only outside hierarchical organizations but also within them. With or without such changes, the manifest elements of sexuality in leadership are probably relevant to understanding leaders and being one.

7. <u>Ambiguity and coherence</u>. Leadership is generally seen as a force for coherence. Thus, it is pictured as resolving conflicts, eliminating contradictions, and preventing confusions. Much leadership training emphasizes ways to bring conflicting groups together through persuasion, bargaining, and incentives; and to remove inconsistencies, ambiguities, and complexities through clear objectives and well-conceived plans. The persistence of ambiguity, conflict, contradiction, and confusion in organizations suggests that the compulsion toward harmony, coherence, and control could be a misleading basis for understanding or improving leadership and life, as do some recent efforts to understand the role of conflict and ambiguity in change, development, and adaptation.

8. <u>Visions and reality</u>. Leadership is often described as involving the transformation of visions into reality. Thus, it implies an ability to live in at least two worlds--the world of imagination, fantasy, and dreams and the world of pragmatic action. The talents required to see events, people, and situations in multiple "realities" simultaneously, to see the humor in tragedy and the pathos in comedy, to transform an ordinary organizational event into a phantasmagoria of impressions, sensations, delights, and outrages, while retaining

70

consciousness of its commonplace representation, seem likely to be related to literary and poetic imagination in a way that might be relevant to understanding and improving leadership.

9.   Evaluating leadership. The "bottom line" of leadership is a reputation for having done the job well, a judgment by history (or by God). The formation of that reputation involves accountants, stock analysts, newspaper reporters, academics, and school children. Understanding leadership as a phenomenon involves recognizing the processes by which reputations are developed and maintained. Of even greater interest, perhaps, are the appropriate criteria for reputation. What should we value in the leadership role and in an individual leader? What are the ethics and aesthetics of leadership? What makes it beautiful or just? How can we attach evaluative meaning to the mundane features of organizational life?

It is possible that some of these issues will not be fully resolved by the end of the quarter.

COURSE CONTENT: This course is about leadership in organizations such as business firms, schools, public agencies, armies, and churches. Although it is intended for people who expect to be organizational leaders or to deal with them, no claims of practicality or relevance are made or implied. The course is not intended to be useful in the usual sense. The focus is on understanding and interpreting the leadership role in contemporary organizations and on the complications of becoming or being a leader, or confronting one. The primary texts are drawn from classical literature.

COURSE FORMAT: The course provides some reading, some opportunities for commentary, and some lectures:

Reading: Four works are required reading (or rereading) during the quarter: Miguel de Cervantes, Don Quixote; William Shakespeare, Othello; George Bernard Shaw, Saint Joan; Leo Tolstoy, War and Peace.

These are classic exercises in comprehending life, and therefore leadership. If you have not read them, the course should be viewed primarily as an opportunity to do so. If you have already read them, the course should be viewed primarily as an opportunity to reread them. If you have already reread them, the course should be viewed as an opportunity to reread them again. If you have already . . .

Commentary: At the end of each lecture, a "query" is posed by the instructor for discussion at the end of the following lecture. Opportunities for commenting on the queries (and other material in the course) are provided in the discussion period after each lecture, in the discussion sections, in written essays on one or more of the queries, and in a special "happening."

The discussion period occupies about 30-45 minutes after each lecture. The focus is on the query posed at the end of the previous day's lecture. The <u>discussion sections</u> are optional. They meet for one hour once a week and provide an opportunity for further discussion of the issues raised in the class. The <u>written essays</u> are optional. Each essay should cover one of the queries. An essay can be of any length but should be precise, careful, and articulate; a finished piece of work. You may submit as many (or as few) essays as you wish. The <u>"happening"</u> may or may not occur. Participation is optional. It is tentatively scheduled for November 24.

Lectures: The instructor gives some lectures during the quarter. The general issues to which the lectures are addressed are indicated in the attached list, but their main point is to encourage you to read the books and think about their implications for leadership. Each lecture is self-contained. Students are invited to attend, but there is no presumption that absence is incontrovertible evidence of moral decay.

LECTURES:

1	Leadership appreciation
2	Private lives and public duties
3	<u>Othello</u>
4	Cleverness, innocence, and virtue
5	<u>Othello</u>
6	Genius, heresy, and madness
7	<u>St. Joan</u>
8	Great actions and great expectations
9	<u>War and Peace</u>
10	Power, domination, and subordination
11	<u>War and Peace</u>
12	Gender and sexuality
13	<u>War and Peace</u>
14	Ambiguity and coherence
15	<u>Don Quixote</u>
16	("Happening" tentatively scheduled)
17	Visions and reality
18	<u>Don Quixote</u>
19	Leaders as poets and plumbers

GRADING: The course may be taken on either a graded or a pass/no credit basis. The rules for recording the pass/no credit option are the rules of the school in which the course is being taken. Please note that the rules of the Graduate School of Business differ from the rules of the School of Humanities and Sciences.

The grade depends on two things: 1. <u>Commentary</u>. The wisdom of class commentary is evaluated in terms of its pertinence, clarity, and perceptiveness. Opportunities for comments are provided in the post-lecture discussion periods, in the optional Friday discussion sections, in optional written essays on the queries, and in contributions to the "happening" if it occurs. 2. <u>Final examination</u>. A three-hour final examination is given at the regularly scheduled time for examinations.

Each student determines the weights to be assigned to the two components in determining his or her grade. Individual weighting schemes may be filed or revised in writing (using the attached form or a copy of it) at any time up to and including the last day of class. Weights must sum to 100% and satisfy the following constraints:

Commentary: 10%, 20%, 30%, 40%, or 50%
Final examination: 90%, 80%, 70%, 60%, or 50%

Grades for students taking the course as Business 379 use Graduate School of Business notation (H,P, etc.) and standards. Grades for other students use Stanford standard notation (A,B, etc.) and standards. Students enrolled in Business 379 on a pass/no credit basis must earn a grade of at least "P-" to pass. For all others, "D" is a passing grade.

State University College at Buffalo
1300 Elmwood Ave., Buffalo, NY 14222-1095

Scott G. Isaksen
Director
Center for Studies in Creativity
716/878-6223

CRS 303: Creative Leadership through Effective Facilitation

This course provides a grasp of leadership principles in creative problem-solving groups and an awareness of the approaches to the study of creativity and leadership and how these two areas inter-relate.

Since the emphasis of this course is on creative leadership and facilitation, students who have some context within which to apply the concepts and skills will find the course highly relevant. An attempt will be made to blend theory and research with practical applications and skill-building. Creative Studies students will find the course helpful in preparing to facilitate Creative Problem Solving. Students of business or management may find it more applicable to planning, decision making and dealing with personnel matters. Education, Social Work and other majors may find the course useful in identifying appropriate use of a facilitative style in working with others and conducting effective meetings. Resident Assistants and Public Safety Aids may be able to increase their effectiveness by integrating leadership style information with student and group development theory.

MAJOR GOALS: The student will: A. Demonstrate a greater knowledge of definitions, theories, and approaches to the study of creativity and leadership; B. Increase awareness of a variety of skill areas associated with creative leadership including: Identification and interpretation of personal style through feedback from various assessments; Communication skills; Conflict resolution; and through understanding the dynamics of Situational Leadership II; C. Apply the information from readings, course activities and presentations, assessment and discussions to a personal project.

REQUIREMENTS: Students are expected to be present, prepared for and participate in all class meetings. More than two class absences will result in the lowering of course grade by one full letter. (Worth 140 points.)

Reading Assignments: You will read the materials assigned on the course schedule (and those assigned during class) and be prepared to take quizzes on the content of these materials. (Worth 50 points toward your grade.) We will be using a series of papers written by John Gardner: The Nature of Leadership: Introductory Considerations (1986); The Tasks of Leadership (1986); The Heart of the Matter: Leader-Constituent Interaction (1986); Leadership and Power (1986); The Moral Aspect of Leadership (1987).

Reading the literature of creativity and leadership and writing a paper. Your paper will use the course text, supplementary texts, and other readings of your choice which focus on a topic area of your choice related to creative leadership. See the course handouts: "What is a paper?" and "Some helpful ideas and questions. . ." for more information. (Worth 50 points.) The course text is: Campbell, David (1980). If I'm in charge here, why is everybody laughing? Greensboro, North Carolina: Center for Creative Leadership. (164 pp.)

74

Supplementary texts include: Bass, B. M. (1985). <u>Leadership and performance beyond expectations</u>. New York: The Free Press; Bennis, W. & Nanus, B. (1985). <u>Leaders: The strategies for taking charge</u>. New York: Harper & Row; Gordon, T. (1977). <u>Leader effectiveness training</u>. New York: Wyden Books; Kellerman, B. (1984). (Eds.). <u>Leadership: Multidisciplinary perspectives</u>. Englewood Cliffs, New Jersey: Prentice-Hall; Rosenbach, W. E. & Taylor, R. L. (1984). (Eds.). <u>Contemporary issues in leadership</u>. Boulder, CO: Westview; Yukl, Gary A. (1981). <u>Leadership in organizations</u>. Englewood Cliffs, New Jersey: Prentice-Hall.

Final examination: An essay-type exam will focus on your internalization of the major concepts presented in class. (Worth 50 points.)

Application of course content: You will be required to make application or transfer of course content (information from class presentations, videotapes, readings, activities, etc.) to an out-of-class area of your own choice and interest. (Worth 80 points.) This may be accomplished through: A. <u>Facilitation observations</u>. For those students who have had CRS 205 and CRS 302, involvement in the introductory classes as a facilitator is an option. This becomes a project in that you will join a class for at least eight sessions; work with the instructor to define your role, keep a facilitator journal and meet with Scott to discuss your involvement and outcomes. See the course handout:* "Facilitation Application Guidelines" for more information. B. <u>Completing a project</u>. This can be an internship opportunity that you create for yourself; working in a leadership role with a student organization; exploring some concept or idea more thoroughly; or some other option developed by you to apply the course content outside of class. You will need to negotiate this project by working closely with an instructor to maintain agreement on **what** is to be done and **how well** the task or product is accomplished. You must complete a tentative description of your proposed project following the guidelines described in the course handout:* "Project Planning Form." You will be evaluated on the eight criteria indicated in the handout.

* These forms (reduced in size) follow the course schedule.

Evaluation: You will be evaluated on the attainment of course requirements through the use of a point system. There are **370 total points** available for the course. You are required to earn a minimum of 280 points for a grade of "C". Any student who does not meet the minimum requirements of the course may be assigned a grade of "E" or "F" at the discretion of the instructor(s).

> **"C" Grade** - 280-314 points from Attendance, Reading and papers, Exam and application of course content.
> **"B" Grade** - 315-341 points (85% of 370 points).
> **"A" Grade** - 342-370 points (95% of 370 points).

It is the policy of this instructor that no incomplete grade will be given for failure to complete course requirements unless there is evidence of severe illness. Please consider completion a challenge!

COURSE SCHEDULE

<u>Class</u>

1   **Introduction to Course; Definitions of Leadership:** Course requirements handout; Students fill out biographical information cards; Questions and answers on requirements; Leadership definitions activity; Newspaper Tower Exercise; Assignment: Gardner's <u>The Nature of Leadership: Introductory Considerations</u> (Reading #1)

2   **Approaches to Studying Leadership:** New students to fill out cards; Questions & answers on course requirements; Quiz on Gardner reading assignment #1; Discussion of Quiz on the Nature of Leadership; Presentation on history and approaches to leadership studies (focus on one and two dimensional approaches); X&Y assessment; Assignment: Read Gardner's <u>The Tasks of Leadership</u> (Reading #2) and <u>The Definitions of Leadership</u> Handout

3   **The Tasks of Leadership:** Quiz on Gardner reading assignment #2; Discussion on The Tasks of Leadership and scoring of quiz; Qualities of effective leadership activity 1) Generate all the qualities of an effective leader, 2) Small groups to select three "hits", 3) discussion results; Paired Comparison Analysis Activity on tasks of leadership (finish this activity for homework); Discuss (Q&A) on project planning form and facilitation application guidelines; Assignment: Gardner's <u>Leadership and Power</u> (Reading #3)

4   **Leadership and Power:** Quiz on Reading Assignment #3; Discussion & correct quiz on Leadership and Power; Starpower Simulation; Discussion of "Power"; Assignment: Write brief paragraph description of application projects and Read Gardner's <u>The Heart of the Matter: Leader-Constituent Interactions</u> (Reading #4)

5   **Conceptions of Creative Leadership:** Collect project description paragraphs; Quiz on Reading Assignment #4; Discussion and correct quiz; Conceptions of Creative Leadership Presentation; Collect PCA on tasks; Assignment: Read <u>SLII: A Situational Approach to Managing People</u> and complete Leader Behavior Analysis II (LBAII) Form

6   **Understanding Situational Leadership:** Projects discussion; Overview of Situational Leadership Models; Score LBAII; discuss style flexibility and effectiveness scores; Video on Matching Leadership Style to the Situation and completion of class handout; Assignment; Complete Kirton-Adaption Innovation Inventory (KAI) & Myers-Briggs Type Inventory (MBTI)

7   **Group Development:**   Collect MBTI and KAI; Video: Flowers are Red; Presentation on Models of Group Development (Tuckman, Jones, etc.); Discussion

8   **Leadership and Communication:**   Collect remaining MBTI & KAI; Communication lecture; Feedback exercise; Role playing; Assignment: Students must make appointments to discuss project applications

9   **Change Agents: Adaption-Innovation Theory:** View video **Discovering the Future: The Business of Paradigms**; Discuss KAI theory; Personal feedback on the KAI; Assets & Liabilities of A's and I's in leadership roles; Assignment: Complete the Project Planning Form

10   **Valuing Diversity:**   A matter of personal style: Johari Window and the need for feedback; Presentation on the MBTI;   Personal feedback from the MBTI; Small groups - the implications of the MBTI & KAI to leadership; Assignment: Finish papers and Read Gardner's **The Moral Aspect of Leadership** (Reading #5)

11   **Moral Aspects of Leadership:**   Collect Project planning forms and Papers; Quiz on Reading Assignment #5; Discussion on Moral Aspects of Leadership; Personal "hero or heroine" Activity 1) Write down five qualities or characteristics of your own hero or heroine, 2) Dyads: discussion of similarities/differences

12   **Utilizing Group Resources:**   Discussion on Climate: person/group/environment; Leadership Characteristics: Examining Values in Personnel Selection Simulation (University Associates Structured Experience: Could use Blizzard or other suitable substitute)

13   **Conflict Resolution Strategies:**   Dr. Murdock guest presentation on conflict resolution; Personal Conflicts and their causes; Roleplay A's and I's; Begin Project Presentations

14   **Final Class: CEP Week:**   Finish project presentation; Class final exam; Course & Instructor Evaluations

(Ed. Note)   This is one course in a leadership studies program.   Since we are not repeating material printed in Source Book '87, you are referred to that edition or to Scott C. Isaksen for further information.

FACILITATION APPLICATION GUIDELINES

CRS 303: Creative Leadership through Effective Facilitation

Name _____ Date _____

One of the options you have as a student enrolled in CRS 303, if you have successfully completed CRS 205 and CRS 302, is visiting a section of the Introductory Creative Studies courses. Students elect this option to learn more about various aspects of creative leadership and view the unique experience of the Creative Studies classroom from a new perspective. **Should you choose to observe and participate in the introductory courses (CRS 205) as your application area, you should read and carefully consider the following guidelines:**

• You should make plans early in the semester to visit a few classes before making a final decision regarding which one you will "join." Make this decision based on what you hope to learn from this experience rather than on what class fits your schedule best.

• Write out your personal goals for observing and participating in the class sections before actually deciding on which section you will become involved. Discuss these goals with Scott early in the semester!

• Another reason for preparing to become involved early in the semester is the importance of seeing the class become a group. Previous students who elected this experience indicated that this was very helpful.

• Preparation for class visitations should include:

A.   Reading and learning about various observational and other facilitation techniques. (You may focus on these topics for one of your papers.)

B.   Arranging some time following the class to "debrief" with the instructional team. Following class, you need to briefly discuss your observations, raise questions and attain clarification from the instructor.

C.   Review the introductory course syllabus and plan for the semester to avoid visiting classes which do not meet your needs or interests. Some classes may not involve the type of interaction you wish to observe.

• You need to schedule yourself for at least eight observations. You are free to negotiate more with Scott and your class instructor based on your own needs and interests.
• Have the instructor "sign-off" on this form after completing the "debriefing" of each class.
• Keep a journal of your experiences to record ideas, observations, questions and reactions. This will provide data for the conference you will schedule with Scott and for the presentation you will plan with others who elected this facilitation option. Your presentation will be made as a group (if more than one person elected this option) and will be provided during the presentation of projects at the end of the semester.

FACILITATION / CLASS OBSERVATION / PARTICIPATION RECORD

• **Record each date, briefly describe the class you observed.**
• **Have the instructor sign your facilitation log.**
• **This log should be contained within your facilitation journal and should be reviewed with Scott during your meeting.**
• **This log is in addition to your ongoing A-L-U from your experiences.**

© **Center for Studies in Creativity. Prepared by Scott G. Isaksen, 1988.**

PROJECT PLANNING FORM

CRS 303: Creative Leadership through Effective Facilitation

Name _____ Date _____

What is a project?

As a part of your involvement in this course, you are expected to apply what you have learned (or in the process of learning) from the course. You may choose between observing Creative Studies Classes (if you have the necessary prerequisites) or completing a project. Projects can be actual finished products or events; they can be like a small-scale independent study; or they can be self-designed internships. Examples have ranged from students starting or developing their own businesses to leaders in student organizations developing a leadership team. There is no single correct approach to choosing or developing a project.

YOUR INITIAL PLAN (Due _____)

Although you cannot be expected to begin the course with a complete or "finished" idea for what you will accomplish for your project, you will be asked to provide a brief statement of what you are interested in doing by the fifth class meeting. Your separate one-page **"Tentative Description of Project"** should cover the following points:

1. **How am I going to demonstrate preplanning?** Be sure to state your goals of the project in your description. What do you hope to accomplish? What do you wish you could do? In addition, you should have a tentative idea regarding how you plan to accomplish these hopes, wishes or goals. State some specific ways you might do what you plan.

2. **How am I going to show some outcome?** Outcomes can be products, processes (like running meetings a certain way or organizing activities), practicing skills, making presentations, designing visual aids, forming an organization, participating in some type of internship opportunity, conducting interviews of community leaders or any of a wide variety of other options. Whatever the type of outcome you choose, you need to plan for providing some type of evidence that your project was accomplished. Some projects may be easier to document than others. In any case, provide some idea regarding how you will provide some evidence of your work (pictures, videotapes, reports, newspaper coverage, artifacts, etc.).

3. **How am I going to show that I was successful?** You should have some ideas about how you will be able to evaluate progress regarding your project. What should be seen or learned as a result of your project? What worked well and what didn't (and why)? What did others say or think about your project?

How do I decide what to do?

Given the opportunity to do a project can be viewed as a challenge. At first, however, being given such wide choice can be frustrating. Just remember that you are doing the project for you. Of course you must meet certain requirements, but basically the project is yours. You might think about the following:

• What would I like to learn more about?
• What skills or abilities would I like to strengthen?
• Brainstorm with your friends for some ideas.
• Finding some themes in your idea systems.
• Extending some reading I've done for a paper.
• Were any insights gained from the inventories used in class?
• Does my style preference suggest any activities for development?
• What does the group I lead need to accomplish?
• What really interests me about creative leadership?

In general, you should choose a project area for which you have some degree of influence, for which you have a large amount of interest, and which can benefit from new and useful development or activity. Your project should clearly relate to your definition of leadership and your leadership role.

YOUR FINAL PLAN

Do not submit this until you have received preliminary approval from your one-page "Tentative Description of Project."

Title of project _____

___ **Brief description** _____

_____

___ **What do you plan to accomplish? (What have you accomplished?)** _____

_____

___ **What do you expect to learn? (What have you learned?)** _____

_____

___ **How does your project relate to Creative Leadership?** _____

_____

___ **How does your project relate to what you learned in class?** _____

_____

___ **My plan (outline) for my presentation (Presentations will last no more than 10-15 minutes) is attached.**

Submitted for approval by:

Student's Signature _____
                                                              DATE

___ **Final plan approved. Be ready to present.**

___ **Final plan tentatively approved. Make appointment to see me.**

___ **Provide a supplementary explanation of any item checked (including criterion #8) and resubmit for approval.**

___ **Not approved. We need to discuss this.**

Faculty Signature _____ _____
                                                              DATE

State University College at Buffalo   **Scott G. Isaksen**

CRITERIA

The following criteria will be applied by the instructor(s) in evaluating your final project. (You may wish to be certain that these items are specifically covered during your presentation.)

1. To what extent did the project relate to Creative Leadership?

      1   2   3   4   5   6   7   8   9   10

2. The project clearly related to h/her leadership role.

      1   2   3   4   5   6   7   8   9   10

3. The project planning form gave a clear presentation about the project.

      1   2   3   4   5   6   7   8   9   10

4. To what extent did the project demonstrate evidence of pre-planning?

      1   2   3   4   5   6   7   8   9   10

5. Did the project have high quality results? (Were the objectives met well even if the project may not have been totally complete?)

      1   2   3   4   5   6   7   8   9   10

6. The student's presentation was well-planned and shared?

      1   2   3   4   5   6   7   8   9   10

7. Did the student evaluate h/her progress?

      1   2   3   4   5   6   7   8   9   10

Total points awarded for project   _____

Please return this form before you make your presentation so that the points can be recorded. After points are recorded you will be able to have this form returned.

Comments:

© **Center for Studies in Creativity. Prepared by Scott G. Isaksen, 1988.**

State University of New York at Buffalo
60 Grotton Drive, Williamsville, NY 14221

Fred Dansereau
School of Management
716/636-3236

Leadership and Motivation - MGB 607

OVERVIEW: This course focuses on Leadership and Motivation in organizations. After an introduction, basic managerial concepts and tools in motivation and leadership will be presented. Class sessions and in class exercises focus on these concepts and tools. The last part of the course focuses on the use of multiple concepts and tools in dealing with key management issues. Provided the number of students is not large (less than 35), students will select a project of the type listed below and report to the class. Various formats will be used for presentation purposes (see attached student project material).

ASSIGNMENTS: 1) Final Exam or Paper (70% of grade) Comprehensive, integrative, take-home, covers all readings and class materials. A paper on an approved topic may be substituted. However, it must be comprehensive and directly related to the course material. 2) Student Projects (30% of grade) A student will select a presentation format and a set of topics for consideration in a project and work alone or with others on the project. A student will: a) Present the results of a project in one half class session; the remaining half will include a discussion on the project led by the instructor. b) Submit a written report; each group member may present a complete report for the project.

REQUIRED TEXTS: Yukl, G. Leadership in Organizations. Englewood Cliffs, New Jersey: Prentice Hall, 1981. (Y) Steers, R., Porter, L. Motivation and Work Behavior. New York: McGraw-Hill, 1988. (S & P)

COURSE OUTLINE

Introduction First 3 weeks - Motivation (S&P) Ch. 1; Leadership (Y) Ch. 1.

Basic Movational Tools Second 3 weeks - Need Approaches* (S&P) Ch. 2; Reinforcement Approaches* (S&P) Ch. 4; Cognitive Approaches* (S&P) Ch. 3; Equity Approaches (S&P) Ch. 3; Social Motivation* (S&P) Chs. 3 and 4.

Basic Leadership Tools Week 7 - Team Building Approaches* (Y), Chs. 4, 5 and 6; Week 8 - Dyadic Approaches*, Dansereau, Alutto, and Yammarino, Ch. 4 (Y) Chs. 2 and 3; Week 9 - Structural Approaches*, Ch. 7; Transformational Approaches*, Handout; Other issues, Chs. 8 and 9.

Eight Approved Topics for Student Projects Dates will depend on selection of topics. A schedule for weeks ten through fifteen will be provided once topics are selected. (Final exam will require knowledge of at least six of the eight topics.)

1) Popular Management Approaches; Abodaher, D. Iacocca, New York: Kensington Publishing Corp., 1982. (Copies in bookstore.) Peter, T. and Austin, N. A Passion for

<u>Excellence: The Leadership Difference</u>. New York: Warner Books, 1986. (Copies in bookstore.)
2) Job Design and Structural Factors and Leadership (S&P), Ch. 10, (Y) Ch. 7.
3) Employees Absenteeism and Turnover (S&P), Ch. 8.
4) Careers (S&P), Ch. 7.
5) Marginal Performance (S&P), Ch. 9.
6) Group and Dyad Processes with Special Emphasis on Leadership (S&P), Ch. 6 and (Y), Ch. 9.
7) Reward Systems (S&P), Ch. 5.
8) Participative Management and Other Issues (S&P), Ch. 6, (Y), Ch. 8. Other topics may be constructed based on student interests and instructor's approval.

*Indicates one of eight basic approaches for which handouts will be given.

Illustrative Integrative Final Exam Questions

Construct a specific performance problem in an organization. Describe it briefly at the beginning of your exam, using it to answer the last portions of questions 1 and 2.
1. Motivation - Present an integrated approach to the motivation tools and illustrate how each alone and then all in combination could be used to solve your problem.
2. Leadership - Do the same as for Part I but do so for the leadership tools.
3. For at least five of the seven topics explain how your approach, developed in parts 1 and 2, allows solutions in the particular problem areas. (For list of topics see List of Reports.)

OPTIONAL Supplementary Material for MGB 607: Dansereau, F. Alutto, J., and Yammarino, F., <u>Theory Testing in Organizational Behavior: The Varient Approach</u>. Englewood Cliffs, NJ: Prentice Hall, 1984: <u>Ch. 1</u>, pp. 11-13 - explains different units of analysis in OB; pp. 13-16 - explains multiple levels of analysis in OB; pp. 17-21 - explains different ways variables can be combined in OB; pp. 21-24 - explains the difference between contingent and non-contingent relationships in OB. <u>Ch. 2</u>, pp. 38-41 - explains difference between parts and wholes in OB (the remainder of the chapter is research oriented). <u>Ch. 3</u>, pp. 67-70 - explains the perspective taken on levels of analysis in OB; p. 71 - provides a simple example of multiple levels of analysis in one organization; pp. 72-78 - describes the difference between the person and dyad levels of analysis in one organization.
<u>Ch. 4</u>, pp. 88-95 - gives a theory of collectives; pp. 95-104 - gives a theory of dyads; pp. 104-109 - compares the previous two theories. <u>Ch. 5 to 8</u> - Explains mathematical basis of testing theories. These chapters have a research orientation. <u>Ch. 9</u> - Provides a test of the collectivity theory described in Ch. 4. <u>Ch. 10</u> - Provides a test of the dyad theory described in Ch. 4. <u>Ch. 11</u> - Combines the results present in Ch. 9 and 10. <u>Ch. 12 to 15</u> - These chapters have a research orientation.

<u>Types of Student Projects</u> (See attached illustrations)
1. A report to the class suggesting a solution to a set of problems faced by a specific organization. Use the basic tools, as well as one or some combination of the topics listed at the end of the course outline. (Requires at least 2 persons.)

2. A speculative model attempting to integrate some of the basic tools into an approach for dealing with one or some combination of the topics listed at the end of the course outline. (Should be applied as well as theoretical.)

3. Interviews or observations of a leader or leaders that illustrate the basic tools and various topics listed at the end of the course outline.

4. A review of previous empirical research on some set of tools that attempts to integrate previous studies of leadership and motivation in a new way that touches on one or some combination of the topics listed at the end of the course outline.

5. Other projects of interest to students. NOTE: You cannot simply illustrate how to motivate and lead in your own job, but you can work with at least one other person with a similar job or interest to develop such a topic (see Items 1 and 3 above). In addition, all projects should include the basic tools from class plus at least one topic from list of student project topics. You may, however, suggest an additional topic for approval by the class as a substitute for the approved topics.

Illustration of Type 1 Project Presentations Purpose: To illustrate the use of the concepts and tools in this course to solve managerial problems; Focus: Assume the instructor serves as the president and chairman of the board of a company and the class serves as his vice presidents and board members. Structure: 1) give background about the (hypothetical) company you are describing. 2) list the problems you are attempting to solve. 3) present an analysis of the problems which demonstrates your ability to use the concepts of the course. 4) present your recommendations. (Exercises will be used during the first part of the course to illustrate these steps). Illustrative Topics - General Applications of Concepts: This project illustrates how the concepts and tools covered in this course should be used to explicate and understand "popular" descriptions of management (Iacocca and A Passion for Excellence). The project should assume it has been asked to: (1) draw out key concepts and tools illustrated in Iacocca. (2) criticize and evaluate the ideas presented in A Passion for Excellence relative to the concepts and tools presented in the course. This presentation serves as a summary of the concepts and tools in the course. Job Design and Structural Factors in Leadership: This panel focuses on the way jobs should be designed for effective output in an organization (once you identify problems you will need to think through how jobs might be designed to overcome problems) and on the consequences of alternative collective level designs for groups, dyads and persons as well as problems in terms of implementing proposed designs. Team Building and Interpersonal Dynamics: This panel focuses on how a person should function in groups and in one on one situations and how to react to and create groups to obtain outcomes. Problems are: group meetings that seem to accomplish nothing, groups that are hostile to each other, poorly conducted group meetings. You should be concerned about collective and person issues as well. Turnover and Absenteeism: Problems involving turnover, absenteeism, too much or too little commitment to poor or good solutions to problems, stress and dissatisfaction and satisfaction of individuals are appropriate here. Include considerations of collectives, groups and dyads. Reward and Punishment (and/or Managing Ineffective Performance) Systems: Focus on problems that arise in the design of reward and punishment systems and propose how to design such systems appropriately for an organization. Include salary, fringe benefits, withholding pay, seniority and performance based needs, docking of pay, paid holidays, suspensions, etc.). <u>Participative Management</u>: There are multiple ways to view participation (this is, at different levels of analysis). Propose when to use and when not to use such approaches to management. In many ways this is the most difficult panel because it focuses on complex multiple-level issues.

Illustration of Type 2 and 4 Projects <u>Purpose</u>: To develop your own approach to leadership and motivation in organizations based on the material in the course, and/or on previous research. <u>Focus</u>: Assume the instructor serves as an academic consultant, and/or researcher and the class contains a mixture of consultants, practitioners and researchers. <u>Structure</u>: Indicate the topics from the course that make up your focus; the degree to which your approach is speculative (based on your own creative activities) and/or grounded in previous research. Present your approach; illustrate how you would use it to solve specific problems in an organization (i.e., explain what your approach predicts). <u>Illustrative Topics</u>: <u>Type 2</u>. A. You may try to create a "grand" large scale approach to leadership and motivation and illustrate its implications for predicting, for example, turnover, absenteeism, and/or performance. (Topics in the list for student projects.) B. You may create a less "Grand" approach to a specific topic (such as only job design) and focus on modifying existing approaches to job design. In this option, you need to be sure to include the basic tools, as well as the approaches to the topic in the texts. For example, a student might use expectancy approaches to explain the careers materials, and leadership approaches to explain "mentoring" in one's career. <u>Type 4</u>. You may review previous empirical studies to ascertain the degree of empirical support for a particular approach. For example, you might review the set of studies cited in the text for one approach to leadership and/or participation and give us an idea of the empirical support for the effectiveness of participation, etc.

Illustration of Type 3 Project <u>Purpose</u>: To illustrate the use of the concepts and tools in this course to understand the behavior of leaders. <u>Focus</u>: Assume the instructor and class serve as individuals interested in key motivating actions used by leaders. <u>Structure</u>: Indicate the source of your information about one or several leaders; explain what was observed and how these observations relate to a set of motivational and leadership basic concepts and additional student project topics; integrate the observations into speculations about motivating leading behaviors; use the observations to raise questions about the approaches to leadership and motivation discussed in the course. <u>Illustrative Topics</u>: You might simply observe yourself and another individual. (If you chose this option you need another person to do the same project so that you can compare notes.) You might analyze and/or collect data (archival or some other type of data). These observations should be aimed at understanding individuals' motivation and relationships with others. You might then show how these observations explain job design, turnover, performance, or group processes, etc., as well as the basic concepts in the course.

The Colorado College
Colorado Springs, CO 80903

Thomas E. Cronin
Professor
303/473-2233

Leadership and Governance (with emphasis on writing) - Political Science 213

PURPOSE: The purpose of this course is to explore what leadership and governing are all about. We will read at least six books on different aspects of leadership. We will view an equal number of films and have an equal number of guest speakers. In addition, this course will emphasize writing, revising and rewriting.

COMMON READINGS: Saul D. Alinsky, <u>Rules for Radicals</u> (Vintage); Perry Smith, <u>Taking Charge</u> (Avery); Warren Bennis and Burt Nanus, <u>Leaders: Strategies for Taking Charge</u> (Harper and Row); Paul Hawken, <u>Growing a Business</u> (Simon and Schuster); John Gardner, <u>Self-Renewal</u> (Norton); Robert Fisher and William Ury, <u>Getting to Yes: Negotiating Agreement Without Giving In</u> (Houghton, Mifflin).

RECOMMENDED READINGS: Bernard M. Bass, <u>Leadership and Performance Beyond Expectations</u> (Free Press); William Glasser, <u>Positive Addiction</u> (Perennial Library); James Kouzes and Barry Posner, <u>The Leadership Challenge</u> (Jossey-Bass); James MacGregor Burns, <u>Leadership</u> (Harper and Row); Richard Neustadt, <u>Presidential Power</u> (Wiley); Richard Neustadt and Ernest R. May, <u>Thinking In Time: The Use of History for Decision Makers</u> (Free Press); Tom Peters, <u>Thriving on Chaos</u> (Knopf); John Keegan, <u>The Mask of Command</u>; W. Rosenbach and R. Taylor, <u>Contemporary Issues in Leadership</u>, 2nd edition (Westview, 1989).

FILMS: Twelve O'Clock High; The Man Who Shot Liberty Valence; Norma Rae; The Huey Long Story; Paradigm Shifts; The Pygmalion Factor; Bolero; In Search of Excellence; Caine Mutiny; Lord of the Flies.

SPECIAL GUESTS: Alex S. Yankovich, Bank of Montreal, Class of '64; Ed Marsten, Editor and Publisher, <u>High Country News</u>; Steve Sundstrom, IBM, Class of '86; David Lowland, Coordinator--CC Leadership Program; Speeches at CC by David Brower, former president, Sierra Club, and Paul Watson, Greenpeace & Sea Shepherd Leader; CC Coaches.

ASSIGNMENTS: A careful reading of all common readings; high quality participation and contribution to class discussions and class readings.

SCHEDULE:

<u>Session</u>

1	Introductions; Course overview; The Write Stuff
2	David Brown Talk
3	Discuss Brown Stories; Cronin Theories on Leadership
	Greenpeace Founder, Paul Watson
4	Read and Write on Alinsky Book
5	Read and Write on Smith Book

6	Publisher Ed Marsten of <u>High Country News</u> will visit class; Smith Paper, IBM Junior Executive Steve Sundstrom will talk
7	Bank Executive Alex Yankovich will join us in our discussion of Bennis; Head Hockey Coach Brad Beutow will talk about his coaching philosophy
8	Read Hawken book
9	Business Leadership - Yankovich and Hawken
10	Reading revised papers Rewrite Day
11	Read Gardner Book, paper
12,13,14,15	<u>Baca</u> - Leadership Film Festival and review writing Leadership Debates; Writing and Class Readings
16,17	Read Fisher and Ury on Negotiating; Workshop on Conflict Management and Negotiating, Cronin and Lowland
18	Final Paper

University of California - Santa Cruz
203 Palo Verde Terrace, Santa Cruz, CA 95060

Pamela Roby
Professor
408/429-2587

Sociology of Leadership - Soc. 189

DESCRIPTION AND PURPOSE: We will examine biographies, research and theories about the exercise of leadership in relation to contemporary social organizations and social change. The primary definition of leadership to be used in the class will be thinking and communicating about a group as a whole to achieve shared goals. Following this definition, leadership may be exercised with or without title, and a single group may have multiple leaders who are responsible for different activities. The central goals of the class are to understand and interpret the leadership role in contemporary organizations and social change efforts, and to examine factors involved in becoming or being a leader and/or of working with one. The class meets for an hour and a quarter twice a week for ten weeks. It is an elective 5 credit (per quarter) course in the Sociology Department. Generally undergraduate junior and senior level students are drawn from Economics, Psychology, Political Science and Sociology. The average class size is 32.

TENTATIVE OUTLINE: (The Required Reading List is numbered; Further Reading is alphabetically lettered - Both follow the course description.)

Day 1: Introduction to the Course
Day 2: Conceptions and Definitions of Leadership; Readings 5, 9
Day 3: The Necessity of Leadership; Readings 19, 26, A6, A23
Day 4: Class, Race, Gender and Leadership; Readings 3, 4, 17, 29, A5, A7, A9, A12, A14, A21, A25, A26, A27, A32, A36, A51, A52, A57, A58 *Comment Due (see assignment 2)
Day 5: Leadership and Power; Readings 10, 27, A4, A29
Day 6: Changing Theories of Leadership; Readings 2, 38, A62
Day 7: Feminist Perspectives on Leadership and Power; Readings 12, 22, 31, A11, A50
Day 8: Leadership in Complex Organizations; Readings 24, 25, A2, A13, A22, A33, A39, A40, A41, A45, A47, A54, A59, A62
Day 9: Leadership and Social Change; Readings 18, 23, A24
Day 10: Leaders and Leadership: Karl Marx, Vladimir Lenin, Jane Addams, Mao Tsetung, Martin Luther King, Anne Moody, Shirley Chisholm, Akio Morita: Film: "Martin Luther King, Jr.: From Montgomery to Memphis," (26m, 16mm/VT, BFA Educational Media).
*Assignment 3 due:
Day 11: Human Agency and Social Structure; Readings 20, 39, A8, A42, A61
Day 12: Leadership Styles and Functions: Film "You," (4m, 16mm/VT, dist. Calley Curtis, 213-467-1101); Readings 16, A28
Day 13: Leadership Development; Readings 28, 33, 35, A17, A38, A46, A48 *Comment Due (see assignment 2).
Day 14: Assessing Leadership Effectiveness; Readings 1, 6, A35, A43, A44, A53
Day 15: Improving Leadership Effectiveness; Readings 7, 41, A1
Day 16: Leadership, Influence and the Communication of Important Information; Readings 14, 15, 21 *Comment Due (see assignment 2).

Day 17: Leaders and Followers: Video excerpts: "Eyes on the Prize"; Readings 11, 30, 32, 34, 40, A3, A10, A15, A16, A18, A19, A20, A30, A31, A34, A37, A49, A55, A56, A60

Day 18: The Meaning and Satisfactions of Leadership; Readings 13, 36 *Assignment 4 due.

Day 19: The Future of Leadership; Readings 8, 37

Day 20: Summary and Conclusions

ASSIGNMENTS: 1. Preparation for and class participation in discussion of readings. Readings are to be completed by the date they are assigned. The required readings, listed above, are in the Sociology of Leadership Reader.

2. As part of preparation for class discussions, you are encouraged to keep a journal of notes on each reading including: questions you wish to raise for discussion, an outline of the basic ideas of the reading and your reactions to these ideas, the author's perspectives on leadership, and the key implications of the article for the understanding and practice of leadership. On dates assigned class members are to submit a one-page comment on two or more articles which are part of the class reading for that day and/or any of the days from that date up to the next "comment" due date. These "comments" are intended to stimulate thinking and discussion concerning the readings. They are to be read by other members of the class and are to be submitted but not graded.

3. On a date assigned, a five-to seven-page review of one of the following biographies or autobiographies in which you describe the main concepts you learned about leadership and analyze the person's leadership from the perspective of the concepts and/or theories of leadership contained in four or more class readings of your choosing (cite the concepts and the course readings which you are using specifically).

Isaiah Berlin, Karl Marx: His Life and Environment, Second Edition, New York: Oxford University Press, 1948; Nadezhda Krupskaya, Reminiscences of Lenin, New York: International Publishers, 1930; Jane Addams, Twenty Years At Hull House, New York: New American Library, 1960; Han Suyin, The Morning Deluge: Mao Tsetung and the Chinese Revolution, Boston: Little, Brown and Company, 1976. Han Suyin, Wind in The Tower: Mao Tsetung and the Chinese Revolution, 1949-1975, Boston: Little, Brown and Company, 1976; Stephen B. Oates, Let The Trumpet Sound: The Life of Martin Luther King, Jr., New York: Mentor Books, 1982; Anne Moody, Coming of Age in Mississippi, New York: Dial Press, 1968; Shirley Chisholm, Unbought and Unbossed, Boston: Houghton Mifflin, 1970; Akio Morita with Edwin M. Reingold and Mitsuko Shimomura, Made in Japan: Ako Morita and Sony, New York: E. P. Dutton, 1986.

4. On a date assigned a five-to eight-page paper in which you describe the history of your own experience of leadership, and analyze your experiences from the perspectives of a) at least five course readings (cite the course readings and the concepts which you are using specifically), and b) the impact of social (family birth order, gender, race, class, religion, etc.), economic and historical factors on your leadership.

5. Final exam covering the required class readings and lectures.

REQUIRED READING:

1. Bartol, K. M., and D. A. Butterfield, "Sex Effects in Evaluating Leaders," Journal of Applied Psychology, Vol. 61, 1976, pp. 446-54;

2. Bass, Bernard M., "An Introduction to Theories and Models of Leadership," in Bernard M. Bass (Ed.), Stogdill's Handbook of Leadership: A Survey of Theory and Research, New York: The Free Press, 1981;

3. Bass, Bernard, "Women and Leadership," Bernard Bass (Ed.), Stogdill's Handbook of Leadership: A Survey of Theory and Research, New York: The Free Press, 1981;

4. Bass, Bernard, "Blacks and Leadership," from Bernard Bass (Ed.), Stogdill's Handbook of Leadership: A Survey of Theory and Research, New York: The Free Press, 1981;

5. Bass, Bernard M., "Concepts of Leadership," from Bernard Bass (Ed.), Stogdill's Handbook of Leadership: A Survey of Theory and Research, New York: The Free Press, 1981;

6. Bennis, Warren, and Bert Nanus, "Mistaking Charge," and "Leading Others, Managing Yourself," Leaders: Strategies for Taking Charge, New York: Harper & Row, Publishers, 1985, 1-86;

7. Bennis, Warren, and Bert Nanus, "Taking Charge: Leadership and Empowerment," Leaders, pp. 215-229;

8. Bunch, Charlotte, and Beverly Fisher, "What Future for Leadership?," Quest, Vol. 2, Spring 1976, pp. 2-13;

9. Burns, James MacGregor, Leadership, New York: Harper & Row, Publishers, 1978, pp. 1-5;

10. Burns, James MacGregor, "The Power of Leadership," Leadership, New York: Harper & Row, Publishers, 1978, pp. 9-17;

11. Burns, James MacGregor, "Leadership and Followership," Leadership, New York: Harper Colophon Books, 1978, pp. 18-23;

12. Carroll, Susan J., "Feminist Perspectives on Political Leadership," in Barbara Kellerman (Ed.), Leadership: Multidisciplinary Perspectives, Englewood Cliffs, NJ: Prentice-Hall, 1984;

13. Chusmir, Leondard H., and Barbara Parker, "Dimensions of Need for Power: Personalized vs. Socialized Power in Female and Male Managers," Sex Roles, Vol. 11, Nos. 9/10, 1984, pp. 759-769;

14. Costanzo, Mark, Dane Archer, Elliot Aronson, and Thomas Pettigrew, "The Behavior of Energy Conservation: The Difficult Path from Information to Action," The American Psychologist, Vol. 41, No. 5, pp. 521-528, May 1986;

15. Daniels, Arlene Kaplan, "Good Work and Good Times: The Place of Sociability in the Work of Women Volunteers," Social Problems, Vol. 32, No. 4, April 1985;

16. Denmark, Florence, "Styles of Leadership," Psychology of Women Quarterly, Vol. 2, No. 2, Winter 1977, pp. 99-113;

17. Dumas, Rhetaugh Graves, "Dilemmas of Black Females in Leadership," in La Frances Rodgers-Rose (Ed.), The Black Woman, Beverly Hills: Sage Publishers, 1980;

18. Eichler, Margrit, "Leadership in Social Movements," in William R. Lassey and Marshall Sashkin (Eds.), Leadership and Social Change, Third Edition, San Diego: University Associates, 1983;

19. Freeman, Jo, "The Tyranny of Structuralessness," Berkeley Journal of Sociology, Vol.

17, 1972-3, pp. 151-164;

20. Giddens, Anthony, "Agency, Structure," <u>Central Problems in Social Theory: Action, Structure and Contradiction in Social Analysis</u>, Berkeley: University of California Press, 1979, pp. 49-53, 71-73;

21. Green, Ben, "Building The Ranks: One on One: The On-the-Job Canvass in Florida," in <u>Labor Research Review</u>, No. 8;

22. Hartsock, Nancy, "Political Change: Two Perspectives on Power," <u>Feminist Theory</u>, New York: Longman, 1981;

23. Kahn, Si, "Chapter 2: Leaders," <u>Organizing: A Guide for Grassroots Leaders</u>, New York: McGraw-Hill, 1982;

24. Kanter, Rosabeth Moss, Chapter 7, "Power," <u>Men and Women of the Corporation</u>, New York: Basic Books, 1977;

25. Katz, Daniel, and Robert L. Kahn, "Leadership," Chapter 6 of <u>The Social Psychology of Organizations</u>, New York: John Wiley and Sons, 1978;

26. Kellerman, Barbara, "Leadership As A Political Act," Chapter 4 in <u>Leadership: Multidisciplinary Perspectives</u>, Englewood Cliffs, NJ: Prentice-Hall, 1984;

27. Lerner, Michael, "Surplus Powerlessness," <u>Social Policy</u>, Vol. 9, No. 4;

28. Maccoby, Michael, "Chapter 10: The Development of Leadership," <u>The Leader</u>, New York: Ballantine, 1981;

29. Matza, David and David Wellman, "The Ordeal of Consciousness," <u>Theory and Society</u>, Vol. 9, 1980, pp. 1-27;

30. Michels, Robert, "Chapter Two: Mechanical and Technical Impossibility of Direct Government by the Masses," <u>Political Parties</u>, New York: The Free Press, 1962;

31. Miller, Jean Baker, "Women and Power," <u>Social Policy</u>, Vol. 13, No. 4, Spring 1983;

32. Morris, Aldon, <u>The Origins of the Civil Rights Movement: Black Communities Organizing for Change</u>, New York: The Free Press, 1984, excerpts;

33. Roby, Pamela, "Becoming Effective Leaders," <u>SWS Network</u>, Vol. 9, No. 2, October, 1979;

34. Roby, Pamela, "Leaders and Constituents," an excerpt from "Women and Unions: The Experience of Rank-And-File Leadership," a paper presented to the SUNY-Albany Conference on Ingredients for a Women's Employment Strategy, April, 1985;

35. Roby, Pamela, "Paths to Rank-And-File Trade Union Leadership: Gender Similarities and Differences," a paper presented to the Eleventh World Congress of Sociology, New Delhi, India, August 1986;

36. Roby, Pamela, "The Experience of Leadership: Gender Similarities and Differences Among Trade Union Stewards," a paper presented to the Third International Interdisciplinary Congress on Women, Dublin, Ireland, July, 1987;

37. Rosener, Lynn, and Peter Schwartz, "Women, Leadership and the 1980s: What Kind of Leaders Do We Need?" in <u>New Leadership in the Public Interest</u>, A Report of the Round Table on New Leadership in the Public Interest, New York: NOW Legal Defense and Education Fund, 1980;

38. Sashkin, Marshall, and William R. Lassey, "Theories of Leadership," in Sashkin and Lassey (Eds.), <u>Leadership and Social Change</u>, Third Edition, San Diego: University Associates, 1983;

39. Spencer, Herbert, "The Great Man Theory Breaks Down," <u>The Study of Sociology</u>, New York: D. A. Appleton, 1884, pp. 30-37;

40. Weber, Max, "The Three Types of Legitimate Authority," Talcott Parsons (Ed.), <u>The Theory of Social and Economic Organization</u>, New York: The Free Press, 1947, pp. 324-392;
41. Yukl, Gary A., "Implications for Improving Leadership," <u>Leadership in Organizations</u>, pp. 278-288;

FURTHER READING:

A1. Argyris, Chris, <u>Increasing Leader Effectiveness</u>, New York: Wiley Interscience, 1976;
A2. Baldridge, J. Victor, David V. Curtis, George Ecker, and Gary L. Riley, <u>Policy Making and Effective Leadership: A National Study of Academic Management</u>, San Francisco: Jossey-Bass Publishers, 1978;
A3. Bass, Bernard, "Part 4: Leader-Follower Interaction," in Bernard M. Bass (Ed.), <u>Stogdill's Handbook of Leadership: A Survey of Theory and Research</u>, New York: The Free Press, 1981;
A4. Bass, Bernard M., "Chapter 11: Power and Leadership" and "Chapter 12: Power Distribution and Leadership," in Bernard M. Bass (Ed.). <u>Stogdill's Handbook of Leadership: A Survey of Theory and Research</u>, New York: The Free Press, 1981;
A5. Brown, Stephen M., "Male Versus Female Leaders: A Comparison of Empirical Studies," <u>Sex Roles</u>, Vol. 5, No. 5, 1979;
A6. Bunch, Charlotte, "Womanpower: The Courage to Lead, The Strength to Follow and The Sense to Know the Difference," <u>Ms.</u>, Vol. 9, No. 1, July 1980;
A7. Cann, Arnie, and William D. Siegfried, Jr., "Sex Stereotypes and the Leadership Role," <u>Sex Roles</u>, Vol. 17, Nos. 7/8, 1987, pp. 401-408;
A8. Chemers, Martin M., "The Social Organizational and Cultural Context of Effective Leadership," in Barbara Kellerman (Ed.), <u>Leadership: Multidisciplinary Perspectives</u>, Englewood Cliffs, NJ: Prentice-Hall, 1984;
A9. Constantini, Edmond, and Kenneth H. Craik, "Women as Politicians: The Social Background, Personality and Political Careers of Female Party Leaders," <u>Journal of Social Issues</u>, Vol. 28, No. 2, 1972;
A10. Davis, King E., "The Status of Black Leadership: Implications for Black Followers in the 1980s," <u>Journal of Applied Behavioral Science</u>, Vol. 18, No. 3, 1982, pp. 309-322;
A11. Denmark, Florence, and J. C. Diggory, "Sex Differences in Attitudes Toward Leaders' Display of Authoritarian Behavior," <u>Psychological Reports</u>, Vol. 18, 1966, pp. 863-872;
A12. Derber, Charles, "Hidden Privileges of Class," <u>The Pursuit of Attention: Power and Individualism in Everyday Life</u>, Cambridge: Schenkman, 1979;
A13. Dubofsky, Melvyn, and Warren Van Tine (Eds.), <u>Labor Leaders in America</u>, Urbana, Illinois: University of Illinois Press, 1987;
A14. Epstein, Cynthia Fuchs, and Rose Laub Coser (Eds.), <u>Access to Power: Cross-National Studies of Women and Elites</u>, London: George Allen and Unwin, 1981;
A15. Etzioni, Amitai, "Dual Leadership in Complex Organizations," <u>American Sociological Review</u>, Vol. 30, 1965, pp. 688-99;
A16. Fagan, Richard, "Charismatic Authority and the Leadership of Fidel Castro," <u>Western Political Quarterly</u>, Vol. 18, 1965, pp. 275-84;

A17. Freeman, Frank H., Robert A. Gregory, and Miriam B. Clark (Eds.), Leadership Education: A Source Book, Greensboro, North Carolina: Center for Creative Leadership, 1986;

A18. Friedland, William H., "For a Sociological Concept of Charisma," Social Forces, Vol. 43, 1964, pp. 18-26;

A19. Friedrich, Carl J., "Political Leadership and the Problem of Charismatic Power," The Journal of Politics, Vol. 23, 1961, pp. 3-24;

A20. Gerth, Hans, "The Nazi Party: Its Leadership and Composition," American Journal of Sociology, Vol. 45, 1940, pp. 517-41;

A21. Greer, Scott, Last Man In: Social Access to Union Power, New York: The Free Press, 1959, excerpts;

A22. Gross, Neal, and R. E. Harrott, Staff Leadership in Public Schools, New York: Wiley, 1963;

A23. Gross, Edward, "Dimensions of Leadership," Personnel Journal, Vol. 40, 1961, pp. 213-218;

A24. Gusfield, Joseph R., "Functional Areas of Leadership in Social Movements," The Sociological Quarterly, Vol. 7, No. 2, Spring 1966;

A25. Heller, Trudy, Women and Men as Leaders: In Business, Educational and Social Service Organizations, New York: Praeger, 1982;

A26. Henley, Nancy M., "Power, Sex, and Nonverbal Communication," in Barrie Thorne and Nancy Henley (Eds.), Language and Sex: Difference and Dominance, Rowley, Mass.: Newbury House Publishers, 1975;

A27. Hennig, Margaret, and Anne Jardim, The Managerial Woman, New York: Doubleday, 1977;

A28. Inderlied, Sheila Davis, and Gary Powell, "Sex-Role Identity and Leadership Style: Different Labels for the Same Concept?," Sex Roles, Vol. 5, No. 5, 1979, pp. 613-625;

A29. Janda, Kenneth F., "Towards The Explication of the Concept of Leadership in Terms of the Concept of Power," in Glenn Paige (Ed.), Political Leadership, New York: The Free Press, 1972, pp. 45-68;

A30. Jenkins, L. Craig, "The Transformation of a Constituency into a Movement: Farmworker Organizing in California," in Jo Freeman, Social Movements of the Sixties and Seventies, New York: Longman, 1983;

A31. Joreen, "Trashing: The Dark Side of Sisterhood," Ms., Vol. 4, No. 10, April, 1976;

A32. Kanter, Rosabeth Moss, Men and Women of the Corporation, New York: Basic Books, 1977, Appendix II: "Some Observations of Women's Leadership in Organizations," pp. 299-303;

A33. Kanter, Rosabeth Moss, The Change Masters: Innovation for Productivity in The American Corporation, New York: Simon and Schuster, 1983;

A34. Katz, Daniel, and Robert L. Kahn, The Social Psychology of Organizations, Second Edition, New York: Wiley, 1978, p. 571;

A35. Kushell, Elliott, and Rae Newton, "Gender, Leadership Style, and Subordinate Satisfaction," Sex Roles, Vol. 14, Nos. 3/4, 1986, pp. 203-209;

A36. Lamm, Roger, Black Union Leaders at the Local Level, Industrial Relations, Vol. 14, No. 2, May 1975;

A37. Lipset, Seymour Martin, Martin Trow and James Coleman, "Democracy and Oligarchy in Trade Unions," in Union Democracy: The Internal Politics of the International

Typographical Union, New York: Doubleday and Company, Inc., 1956;

A38. Lockheed, Marlaine, and Katherine Patterson Hall, "Conceptualizing Sex as a Status Characteristic: Applications to Leadership Training Strategies," Journal of Social Issues, Vol. 32, No. 3, 1976;

A39. Maccoby, Michael, The Leader: A New Face for American Management, New York: Ballantine, 1981;

A40. March, James G. (Ed.), Handbook of Organizations, Chapter 1, Chicago: Rand McNally, 1965;

A41. Marine Corps Development and Education Command, Challenges in Leadership: A Text For U. S. Marine Corps Junior ROTC, Washington, D.C.: U.S. Government Printing Office, 1974;

A42. Merton, Robert K., "Bureaucratic Structure and Personality," Social Forces, Vol. 18, May 1940, pp. 560-568;

A43. Offermann, Lynn R., "Visibility and Evaluation of Female and Male Leaders," Sex Roles, Vol. 14, Nos. 9/10, 1986, pp. 533-543;

A44. Porter, Natalie, Florence Lindauer Gein, and Joyce Jennings, "Are Women Invisible as Leaders?," Sex Roles, Vol. 9, No. 10, 1983, pp. 1035-1049;

A45. Richman, B. M., and R. N. Farmer, Leadership, Goals and Power in Higher Education, San Francisco: Jossey-Bass, 1974;

A46. Russ, Joanna, "Power and Helplessness in the Women's Movement," Women's Studies Quarterly, Vol. 10, No. 1, Spring 1982, pp. 7-10;

A47. Selznick, Philip, Leadership in Administration: A Sociological Interpretation, New York: Harper & Row, Publishers, 1957;

A48. Sherover-Marcuse, Erica, "Marx's Two Perspectives on Emancipatory Consciousness," Emancipation and Consciousness: Dogmatic and Dialectical Perspectives in the Early Marx, New York: Basil Blackwell, 1986, pp. 4-7;

A49. Spencer, M. E., "What Is Charisma?" British Journal of Sociology, Vol. 24, 1973, pp. 341-54;

A50. St. Joan, Jackie, "Female Leaders: Who Was Rembrandt's Mother?" in Charlotte Bunch et al., Building Feminist Theory, New York: Longman, 1981;

A51. Statham, Anne, "The Gender Model Revisited: Differences in the Management Styles of Men and Women," Sex Roles, Vol. 16, Nos. 7/8, 1987, pp. 409-429;

A52. Stevens, Gwendolyn, and Sheldon Gardner, "But Can She Command a Ship? Acceptance of Women by Peers at the Coast Guard Academy," Sex Roles, Vol. 16, Nos. 3/4, 1987, pp. 181-188;

A53. Stitt, Christopher, Stuart Schmidt, and Karl Price, "Sex of Leader, Leader Behavior and Subordinate Satisfaction," Sex Roles, Vol. 9, No. 1, 1983, pp. 31-42;

A54. Tannenbaum, Robert, I. R. Wechsler, and Fred Massarik, Leadership and Organization, New York: McGraw-Hill Book Company, 1961;

A55. Tse-Tung, Mao, Reform Our Study, Peking: Foreign Languages Press, 1965;

A56. Tucker, R. C., "Personality and Political Leadership," Political Science Quarterly, Vol. 92, 1977, pp. 383-93;

A57. Wentworth, Diane Keyser, and Lynn R. Anderson, "Emergent Leadership as a Function of Sex and Task Type," Sex Roles, Vol. 11, Nos. 5/6, 1984, pp. 513-524;

A58. Winther, Dorothy A., and Samuel B. Green, "Another Look at Gender-Related Differences in Leadership Behavior," Sex Roles, Vol. 16, Nos. 1/2, 1987, pp. 41-56;

A59. Wood, James, <u>Leadership in Voluntary Organizations: The Controversy Over Social Action in Protestant Churches</u>, New Brunswick, New Jersey: Rutgers University Press, 1981;

A60. Wood, James R., "Chapter One: The Bases of Legitimate Leadership," <u>Leadership in Voluntary Organizations: The Controversy Over Social Action in Protestant Churches,</u> New Brunswick, New Jersey: Rutgers University Press, 1981;

A61. Yukl, Gary A., "Chapter Seven: Situational Determinants of Leader Behavior," <u>Leadership in Organizations</u>, Englewood Cliffs, New Jersey: Prentice-Hall, 1981;

A62. Yukl, Gary A., <u>Leadership in Organizations</u>, Englewood Cliffs, NJ: Prentice-Hall, 1981, chapters 1-8.

University of Detroit
Department of Psychology
4001 West McNichols, Detroit, MI 48221

Joseph Lapides
Adjunct Professor
313/569-3219

Psychology of Leadership and Supervision - Psychology 437

PURPOSE: To explore issues related to the psychology of leadership and supervision.

TEXT: Lassey, W. R., & Sashkin, M. (Eds.). (1983). Leadership and Social Change (3rd Edition). Calif.: University Associates.

Additional readings by students in journals available at the Library or given as handouts.

REQUIREMENTS: Read assignments. Participate in class activities and exercises, serve as recorder for minutes at group discussions. Attend 90% of sessions (12). Engage the instructor in discussions regarding issues of leadership. Submit 4 papers of up to 750 words each (the shorter the better) based on research and readings related to the psychology of leadership and supervision. For an "A" grade students must submit a well organized paper that is written in a concise style. The paper must include an introduction or statement of the problem, the thesis and conclusion. It is expected that the writer will be either expository or persuasive. The paper should begin with a firm statement, make a presentation that is clear, assertive and unified and conclude with a restatement of the thesis statement, summary of the major idea(s) and a drawn conclusion from the facts (based on research).

For a "B" paper students may utilize a sentence outline format that has an introduction, mainpoints of the thesis (referenced to research) and conclusion drawn from the thesis. The instructor will suggest topics for the papers. Pass 4 short quizzes that will be announced and based on the assigned readings. Pass a take-home final examination that will include application and analysis questions. All written assignments and take-home final must be typed and prepared according to the Publication Manual of the American Psychological Association (APA).

EVALUATION: Class Participation (90% attendance), 15%; Papers (4), 40%; Short examinations (4 quizzes), 20%; Final examination (take home), 25%.

CLASS SCHEDULE:

Class Meetings

1   Climate setting; Human Resource Development; Course expectations and outline; Presentation: Leadership.

2   Assignment: Read: Part I in text Basic Concepts pp. 5-106; Write: A good leader is. . ., The best leader is one who. . ., The characteristics of a good leader are. . .; Presentation: Sources of Power and Influence; Activity: The Power Game; Discussion: Debriefing on power game.

3   Assignment: Read: "The nature of managerial work" in Yukl, G. A. (1989). Leadership in Organizations. (2nd ed.). NJ: Prentice-Hall. Handout, also in text, Part 4, pp. 233-259; Presentation: The nature of managerial work in the private and public sector; Activity: A comparison of decision-making approaches #429 (1987); Discussion: Debriefing activity.

4   Quiz I, on Part 4 in text; Assignment: Read: In text Part 2: Leadership styles from different theoretical points of view; Activity: 1. Are you X or Y? 2. Are you a 9,9 or 1,1? 3. Lead 4. Contingency Model; Discussion: Consistency in leadership styles.

5   Assignment: Write: How can leadership style affect productivity?; or Productivity declined in your organization; Based on readings and research advise your CEO on leadership style for the supervisors in the organization; or Your company is being merged. What are the attributes of the transformational leader?; Read: In text "Leadership in Social Movements," pp. 286-305 and pp. 319-324; Presentation: Charismatic and transformational leadership; Activity: Leadership Dimensions: Dividing the loot (GE 60, Volume III); Discussion: Leadership.

6   Assignment: Read "Employee motivation and morale in industry" (handout) and Notz W. W. (1975) Work motivation and the negative effects of extrinsic rewards. American Psychologist, 30, 884-891 (handout) or Nord W. R. (1977) Job satisfaction reconsidered. American Psychologist, 32, 1026-1035 (on your own). Write III: Motivating American workers toward higher productivity or write a research based memo to your boss on how to motivate workers to get better quality and more effort from the workers; Presentation: "Motivation the driving forces"; Activity: What do people want from their job? Motivation experiences (Games, p. 115).

7   Quiz 2: Knowledge and comprehension questions on readings; Assignment: Read "The individual and groups" and "Norms conformity and deviance" in Bonoma and Zaltman (1981) Psychology for Management, Boston: Kent Publishing Co. (handout); Presentation: Group processes and norms; Activity: 1. Developing group commitment (SE Vol. I, p. 74) 2. Souogram (SE Vol. II, p. 99); Discussion: Debriefing.

8   Assignment: Read in text "Dynamics of Educational Leadership" pp. 181-202. Bring $1.00 for Myers-Briggs Type Inventory (MBTI); Activity: MBTI, all students; Presentation: Different drums for different drummers; Activities: What kind of leaders are we? Discussion: On MBTI Leadership.

9   Quiz 3: On norms and group process and MBTI; Read: "Community Leadership" Part 4, pp. 233-269; Presentation: Looking Glass; Activity: Looking Glass assignment. Separate agenda will be provided.

10   <u>Continue</u> Looking Glass assignment; <u>Discussion</u>: The lessons of Looking Glass.

11   <u>Assignment</u>: Read: "Status, esteem, charisma and leadership" in Bass, B. M. (1981). <u>Stogdill's handbook on leadership: A survey of theory and research</u>. New York: The Free Press and "Leadership under stress," ibid, (handouts); <u>Write IV</u>: "Stress management for leaders." or Management issues in a multicultural diverse organization or Issues related to women and/or minorities in management; <u>Presentation</u>: Leadership and stress--The Challenges of life; <u>Activity</u>: Stress assessment and stress reduction techniques.

12   <u>Quiz 4</u>: related to Looking Glass issues and stress; <u>Assignment</u>: Read: Yankelovich "Work value and new breed" xerox handout; <u>Video Presentation</u>: What you are is where you see; <u>Discussion</u>: Implications for leadership.

13   <u>Assignment</u>: Read: Yukl, G. A. "Managerial Traits and Skills" Ch. 9 handout; <u>Presentation</u>: Overview of findings on leadership; <u>Discussion</u>: How important is leadership? Students provided with Final Examination.

14   Final examination to be returned; Synthesis; Celebration!!

Power Exercise, a simulation

This exercise requires that the class be the central committee of a political party with the task of nominating several members and electing one of them to be the chairperson.

The elected chairperson will have great power and control. Specifically, the chairperson will have 100 units of patronage to assign to deserving members.

Each member of the class will be assigned a different amount of power that they can exercise as they wish in electing the chairperson. The power consists of different number of units of 100 votes. Thus, the most powerful member in a 12-person class would be assigned 1200 votes and the least powerful would have 100 votes. The basis for assigning votes consists of each person in the class drawing a slip of paper on which the number of votes is indicated.

<u>Time Schedule</u>

10 minutes   Instructions, draw lots, list number of votes each member has on newsprint.

15 minutes   First note writing period
                          • <u>no</u> verbal communication
                          • <u>no</u> limits to number of target notes
                          • notes <u>must</u> contain name of sender and receiver
                          • notes <u>cannot</u> be read until end of period

15 minutes   Second note writing period
                          • only change, notes can be read as soon as they are received

15 minutes   Free negotiation period
                          During this period, members may go to speak to various people to try
                          and get the nomination or to ask for their help in getting someone
                          nominated.

5 minutes   Test readiness for Election
                          • Instructor asks, "Are you ready to vote?"
                          • Members write "yes" on slip of paper if they feel they are ready to
                          hold the election and "no" if they do not feel they are ready to hold the
                          election
                          • In this test of readiness <u>each member has only one vote</u>
                          • Simple majority carries

15 minutes   Either additional free negotiation period (in case readiness test yielded
                          a majority "no" vote) followed by retest for readiness for election

OR

15 minutes   Hold Election
                          • Each member has different assigned number of votes which they drew
                          in the lottery. They assign these votes any way they wish
                          • Simple majority carries
                          • Each member signs the slip of paper on which they indicate how they
                          cast their votes
                          • If no one gets the majority, renegotiate and vote again

15 minutes   In group, analyze what happened--How was power used?

University of Illinois at Chicago

Seminar on Leadership - 319

V. Jon Bentz
201 Willow Rd.
Elmhurst, IL 60126
312/833-7149

This course was taught Winter Quarter - 1988-89 at the University of Illinois at Chicago by V. Jon Bentz who was Visiting Professor in the Dept. of Psychology. Questions concerning an overall evaluation of the course and student papers and research may be directed in writing to V. Jon Bentz.

Leadership is a significant topic within I/O psychology. It is of interest to other psychological domains because it deals with the interrelationships among cognitive, personality and social variables. It looms large in terms of societal concerns.

While the seminar will develop a framework for understanding leadership in its broader context, the major focus will be on research dealing with high-level leaders. The positions held by high-level leaders are marked by complexity, diversity, uncertainty and ambiguity. Such leaders deal with diversity in the service of achieving organizational unity. That's among the many reasons that they are interesting to study.

Within the past decade leadership research has made marked progress. This seminar will tie into that progress by capturing work at the cutting edge of the field. Sources functioning at the forefront of the field have provided yet unpublished papers. We have permission to use previously classified government studies dealing with the identification and development of military general officers. Other substantive material has been provided by prominent leadership researchers. These will be placed within the context of current theory. Consequently students will deal with the most recent products of thinkers and scholars.

Sources from the bibliography will be selected from an in-depth study. While the reading list will be extensive, the seminar's format will allow us to range over a great deal of material without overloading individual students. This will be accomplished by forming teams of participants. Each team will be responsible for presenting a module of content. In this way students will have an opportunity to develop presentation skills in addition to learning about the field of leadership.

CONTENT AREAS TO BE EXAMINED

1. **Overview of the Leadership Domain:** Three sources will provide a framework for viewing material to be studied during the course of the seminar. Clark's paper places the study of leadership within the broader context of psychological research, indicates reasons why greater progress has not been made and looks to the future. Part I of Measures of Leadership by K. Clark and M. Clark, available early 1990, Leadership Library of America, provides an overview of leading concepts, types, functions and theories. Finally we will read a thoughtful review of what has gone on in leadership research and practice in recent years. The sources are as follows: Clark, Kenneth, (1988). Leadership. The introductory paper for the recent San Antonio Conference on Psychological Measures and Leadership. Clark is the recently retired president of the Center for Creative Leadership. Bass, B. M. (1981).

Stogdill's Handbook of Leadership, Part I, pp. 3-41. Revised and Expanded. New York: Free Press. Hollander, E. P., Offermann, Lynn (1988). Power and Leadership in Organizations. A pre-publication paper. Hollander is University Distinguished Professor of Psychology, CUNY I/O Psychology Doctoral Program, Baruch College & University Graduate Center. Offermann is at George Washington University. Yukl, G. A. (1981). Leadership in Organizations. Englewood Cliffs, NJ: Prentice Hall.

2.   **Themes That Inform Various Areas of Leadership Research:** The seminal works should be examined since reference to these writings continuously surface in the literature. One cannot be literate in the area of leadership research without an awareness of these contributions: Fiedler, F. (1967). The Theory of Leadership Effectiveness. New York: McGraw Hill. Fischer, K. W. (1980). A Theory of Cognitive Development: The Control and Construction of Hierarchies of Skill. Psych. Rev., 87, 477-531. Mintzberg, H. (1973). The Nature of Managerial Work. New York: Harper & Row. Isenberg, D. J. (1984). How Senior Managers Think. Harvard Business Review, Nov-Dec., 81-90. Jaques, E. (1986). The Development of Intellectual Capacity: A Stratified Systems Theory. Journal of Applied Behavioral Science, 22, 361-383.

3.   **A View of the Top: Sears Research Concerning High-Level Executive Leadership:** A series of interrelated studies that begins with (a) delineating job elements characterizing high-level positions, then (b) proceeds to define and describe the nature of high-level performance, (c) examines critical career experiences that contribute to later effectiveness in high-level positions, (d) isolates characteristics that make for successful performance, (e) isolates characteristics that cause high-level failures and examines organizational practices that contribute to such failure, (f) looks at the process by which information derived from the study of high-level success and failure is converted into a criteria for assessing performance, and finally, (g) examines validity data that resulted from relating psychological test data to criterion measures. These studies provide a comprehensive example of one researcher's efforts to discover, describe and predict high-level leader behavior. These findings will be related to major themes in the leadership research literature.

4.   **High-Level Military Leadership:** For this seminar, T. O. Jacobs (Chief, Executive Development Research Group, Army Research Institute, Arlington, VA) has given special permission to use unpublished papers relevant to the identification and development of general officers. These will be supplemented by other recently available documents. Cognitive complexity is a major theme in these papers. Jaques, Elliott - General Theory of Bureaucracy. New York: Heineman Books. Jaques, Elliott, & Jacobs, T. O. (1988). Military Executive Leadership: A Study of Three and Four Star Generals. Army Research Institute, Arlington, VA. Paper prepared for San Antonio Conference on Psychological Measures and Leadership. Jaques, Elliott, & Jacobs, T. O. (1987). Leadership in Complex Systems. In Zeidner (Ed.), Human Productivity Enhancement. New York: Praeger. Jaques, E., Clement, S., Rigby, C., & Jacobs, T. O., (1985). Senior Leadership Performance Requirements at the Executive Level. Research Report 1420, U. S. Army Research Institute for Behavioral and Social Science, Arlington, VA. Executive Leadership

(1987). DA Pam XXX-X, U. S. Army Research Institute for Behavioral and Social Sciences, Arlington, VA. Campbell, David P. (April 1984). The Personality Profiles of General Officers. Campbell is a Senior Research Fellow at the Center for Creative Leadership. This paper was delivered to the Department of Defense Psychologists Conference. Air Force Academy, Colorado Springs, Colorado.

5. **Transformational Leadership:** Transformational Leadership is practically a "movement" within the leadership domain. Bass is currently re-editing the monumental Handbook of Leadership Research. He has figured in furthering both theory and training/development practices. Recently Posner has made significant contributions to the field. The seminar will concentrate on the following recent writings: Bass, B. M. (1985). Leadership and Performance Beyond Expectations. New York: Free Press. Bass, B. M., & Yammarino, F. J. (1988). Long Term Forecasting of Transformational Leadership and Its Effect Among Naval Officers. Paper prepared for San Antonio Conference on Psychological Measures and Leadership. Posner, B. Z., & Kouzes, J. M. (1988). Development and Validation of the Leadership Practices Inventory. San Antonio Conference on Psychological Measures and Leadership. Gibbons, T. G. (1988). Revisiting the Question of Born vs Made: A Theory of Development of Transformational Leaders. San Antonio Conference on Psychological Measures and Leadership. Sashkin, M., & Fulmer. R. M. (1987). Toward An Organizational Leadership Theory. In J. C. Hunt, B. R. Balizaslt, P. Dachleg, and C. A. Schriesheim (Eds.)., Emerging Leadership Vistas. Boston, Lexington. Sashkin, M. (1988). The Visionary Leader. In Charismatic Leadership: The Elusive Factor in Organizational Effectiveness. San Francisco, Jossey-Bass.

6. **AT&T Longitudinal Studies - The Bray-Howard Studies:** While Assessment Centers have been around for some time, Bray is their modern father. His AT&T work stands as a landmark in I/O psychology. It earned Bray the APA Gold Medal for outstanding contribution to applied psychology. These are the seminal studies: Bray, D. W., Campbell, R. J., & Grant, D. L. (1974). Formative Years in Business. New York: Wiley. Howard, A., & Bray, D. (1988). Predictions of Managerial Success Over Long Periods of Time: Lessons from the Management Progress Study. San Antonio Conference on Psychological Measures and Leadership. Howard, A., & Bray, D. (1986). Cool at the Top. Paper prepared for the Pepsico Leadership Conference. Howard, A., & Bray, D. (1988). Managerial Lives in Transition. New York: Dorsey Press.

7. **Focus on High-Level Leadership:** Several recent contributions to understanding high-level leadership have ranged from sound research to the distillation of thoughtful experience. These sources pop up in most references as major sources: Kotter, John (1982). The General Managers. New York: Free Press. Kotter, John (1988). The Leadership Factor. New York: Free Press. Kotter, J. (1982). What Effective Managers Really Do. Harvard Business Review, 60 (No. 6) Nov-Dec., 175-87. Bennis, Warren & Nanus, Bert (1985). Leaders: The Strategy for Taking Charge. New York: Harper & Row. Bennis, Warren (1985). Four Traits of leadership. USC Paper. Boyatzis, R. E. (1982). The Competent Manager. New York: Wiley. Steiner, G. A. (1983). The New

CEO. New York: MacMillan. Luthans, F., Hodgetts, R. M., & Rosenkrautz, S. A. (1988). Real Managers. Cambridge, Ballentines.

8.   **The Derailment Studies:** At the Center for Creative Leadership, McCall and Lombardo launched a series of creative investigations about why successful executives did not achieve what was expected of them: McCall, M. W., & Lombardo, M. M. (Jan. 1983). Off the Track: Why and How Successful Executives Get Derailed. Tech Report 21, Center for Creative Leadership, Greensboro, N. C. Lombardo, M. M., Ruderman, M. N., & McCauley, C. D. (1986). Success and Derailment in Upper-level Management Positions. Center for Creative Leadership, Greensboro, N. C. McCauley, C. D. & Lombardo, M. M. (1987). Why Managers Derail. Center for Creative Leadership, Greensboro, N. C. Eichinger, R. W., & Lombardo, M. M. (1989). Preventing Derailment: What to do Before It's Too Late. Center for Creative Leadership, Greensboro, N.C.

9.   **Personality Theorists' Contribution To Leadership Studies:** Prominent personality researchers have recently begun to look for systematic relationships between personality and leader competence. Their writings bring a fresh perspective to the literature: Hogan, R., Raskin, R., & Fazzini. (1988). The Dark Side of Charisma. Tulsa Institute of Behavioral Science. Paper prepared for San Antonio Conference on Psychological Measures and Leadership. Gough, Harrison. Testing for Leadership with the California Psychological Inventory. Institute of Personality Assessment and Research, University of California, Berkeley, CA. Paper prepared for San Antonio Conference on Psychological Measures and Leadership.

10.   **Observations Concerning Leader Competence:** Byham, President of Development Dimensions, has written a brief monograph capturing observations from his extensive work with Assessment Center Technology: Byham, W. C. Dimensions of Managerial Competence, Mongraph VI. Development Dimensions, International, Pittsburgh, PA. Personnel Decisions, Inc., Minneapolis, MN, has a series of executive assessment and development programs and have distilled their experiences with thousands of executives and many companies into the PDI Wheel that lists factors and dimensions of executive competence.

11.   **Wrap Up - Putting It All Together:** Throughout the seminar we will extract salient behaviors from the examined literature and identify consistent themes in the literature. We will try to isolate those things that are generic and organize them into a model representing what we know (found) about effective leadership.

Leadership - Management 680

This seminar explores leadership from a practical point of view. It is limited to 16 students who interact directly with the teacher, with each other, and with successful leaders. Students will have the opportunity to develop and practice the skills needed for effective leadership, especially communicating and interacting with others. We will stress thinking, learning, and creating, focusing on the manager and leader as human beings. We will examine and discuss ethics in business--from the viewpoints of the individual and the organization. Students will meet and interact with successful executives from Louisville area organizations.

OBJECTIVES:
1. To give you a better understanding of the manager and leader--what they do and the skills they need.
2. To help you become more effective by developing the skills a successful manager or leader needs: a. To think clearly; b. To communicate clearly; c. To interact effectively with others.
3. To improve your skills in communicating--speaking, writing, listening, reading.
4. To give you the chance to interact with successful leaders (managers/executives).
5. To increase your self-knowledge.

The following books will be required reading (in the order listed):

The Elements of Style by Strunk and White
How to Get Your Point Across in 30 Seconds--Or Less by Milo Frank
"I Hear You" by Eastwood Atwater
The Effective Executive by Peter Drucker
The One Minute Manager by Blanchard & Johnson
The Prince by Niccolo Machiavelli (Penguin)
Management & Machiavelli by Antony Jay
A Whack on the Side of the Head by Roger von Oech
The Tao Jones Averages by Bennett W. Goodspeed
What They Don't Teach You at Harvard Business School by Mark H. McCormack

Students will also be required to read articles that can be purchased in a special packet. We will discuss the main ideas of these books and articles in class, with emphasis on how the students can apply these ideas to their own careers.

A one-page paper--in the form of a business memo--will be required each week, and students should be prepared to make oral reports to the class. We will use videotape to help students improve their oral presentations.

Two special projects will take the place of the weekly memo. In one project, each student will prepare a business letter and resume and then have a private job interview with the teacher. The other will be a team project where students will be given an assignment and then make a formal presentation to the rest of the class (tentatively, King Lear, Macbeth, Antigone, and The Tao of Pooh by Benjamin Hoff).

Students will also work on an informal project. They will prepare a genogram and a "lifeline." In the genogram they research their own family history, and in the lifeline they draw an autobiographical graph. The object is to gain greater insight into themselves by understanding the patterns and values in their family heritage and in their own lives.

Students will be held accountable for completing all assignments on time. Class attendance is expected. Any absence must be cleared with the teacher in advance.

Two-thirds of the academic grade will be based on written assignments. One-third of the grade will be based on oral presentations and responsiveness in the class. Students will have at least five required individual meetings with the teacher. They will frequently be given feedback on how they are doing. A primary goal of the course is for each student to gain self-knowledge.

There will be no exams.

"All authorities get nervous when learning is conducted without a syllabus" -- Neil Postman & Charles Weingartner, Teaching As a Subversive Activity.

University of Michigan
1220 Student Activities Bldg.
Ann Arbor, MI 48109-1316

Sherryl Ann Fletcher
Ass't. Director of Admissions
313/764-7433

**Regional Alumni Recruiting Coordinator/Alumni/Alumnae Club
President Leadership Training Workshops**
Staff is Sherryl A. Fletcher and Glen R. Williams, Director of Alumni Clubs, University of
Michigan Alumni Association

Ed. Note: This is the description of a training workshop with a specific goal--to train
alumni leaders to recruit students for a particular University. Although its purpose and
time requirements are not broad-ranging, it suggests a model for working with volunteers
to achieve a desired end. Adapting it to a given local need should not be too difficult.
For general purposes, the "how" here is nearly as important as the content.

PURPOSE:

The RARC/Alumni/Alumnae Club President Leadership Training Workshops are an
outreach leadership educational effort jointly implemented by the Office of Undergraduate
Admissions and the Alumni Association. The eight instate regional workshops were
planned throughout the 1988-1989 academic year.

LEADERSHIP TRAINING OBJECTIVES:

The workshops are designed as a pilot program to meet three objectives:

- to present an Undergraduate Admissions policy/philosophy outline to instate alumni
  leaders
- to sponsor cooperative efforts between the RARC network and Alumni/Alumnae
  Club Presidents
- to test market a set of specific admitted student recruitment tools

TRAINING RESOURCES:

The workshop packets contain University resource materials from the following academic
and student services offices: Undergraduate Admissions, Campus Information Center,
Financial Aid, Housing, Orientation and Career Planning and Placement.

WORKSHOP DESCRIPTION:

The three-hour workshop is designed to be succinct and pragmatic. The outline is designed
to teach the volunteers from a general to specific informational objective orientation.
Topics to cover include: purpose of the workshop, review of instate Admissions
philosophy/policy/programs, the function of the Regional Alumni Recruiting Coordinator
program, how to recruit admitted students to enroll, when/how to refer students to other
University offices, how to develop club participation in the student recruitment process and
how to design a club network of regional alumni recruiters.

EXPECTED LEARNING OUTCOMES:

We expect that the volunteer alumni participants will be able to:

- understand and describe the Undergraduate Admissions general policies and commitments
- refer students to appropriate University offices
- motivate admitted students to pursue enrollment at The University of Michigan
- lead other local alumni in the recruitment process of underrepresented minority students, top scholars and young scholars
- lead and develop local club involvement and commitment to positive prospective student campus visitation programs
- apply recruitment leadership skills to the development and implementation of new club programs for local students and parents to create a positive and accurate image of The University of Michigan

EVALUATION TOOLS:

Workshop participants receive an evaluation questionnaire and letter of appreciation for their involvement in the training workshop. The questionnaire identifies workshop learning outcomes and assesses future educational or follow-up needs. The individual or club needs are personally addressed within the week following the workshop.

University of Minnesota
College of Liberal Arts
215 Johnston Hall, 101 Pleasant St., S.E.
Minneapolis, MN 55455

George Shapiro
Professor, Speech Communication
612/624-3309/5800
Gerri Perreault
Curriculum Coordinator
612/624-5701

Ethical Leadership-Followership
Thurs. 12:15-2:00

This 4-credit seminar is an overview of different perspectives on leadership-followership, ethical leadership-followership, the characteristics of ethical leader-followers, and the individual, social/psychological, and environmental factors that hinder or facilitate ethical action.

PREREQUISITES: An interest in ethics, leadership, and followership.

Students will be able to:
A. Understand and discuss different perspectives on leadership-followership and ethical leadership-followership.
　1. List and describe different perspectives on leadership and ethical leadership.
　2. Compare and contrast leadership approaches on the following dimensions: Leadership-followership relationships; Basic assumptions about human nature, ethics, and values; Definitions of leadership and of ethical leadership; Decision-making process (implicit and explicit); Attention to factors of race, sex, and class; Individual-environment continuum.
　3. Evaluate the characteristics of leaders prescribed by different authors.
　4. Analyze a leader on the above dimensions, and evaluate her/him for her/his ethical leadership views and actions.
B. Understand and evaluate the factors influencing ethical leadership-followership.
　1. Describe and discuss the components of an ethical act.
　　a. Know the factors involved in recognizing an ethical issue exists.
　　b. Outline a continuum (worst to least harmful) of unethical behavior.
　　c. Know the factors involved in making ethical judgments about a problem.
　　d. Know the social-psychological factors influencing (hindering or facilitating) ethical behavior, including the role of courage.
　　e. Evaluate a person (or organization) for factors shaping her/his/its ethical leadership-followership views and actions.
　2. Be knowledgeable about the scholarship on what makes an ethical leader-follower (descriptive and prescriptive literature).
　3. Analyze the relationship between the ethical environment of a social unit (organization, family, society in general) and ethical behavior.
　　a. Identify the goals (both espoused and implicit) and analyze them for their ethics and values.
　　b. Analyze the gap between the goals and behavior or between goals and unit functioning.
　　c. Identify possible reasons for the gap.
　　d. Compare the differences between one corporation's ethical action and another's unethical action.
　4. Appreciate the difficulty of behaving ethically.

C. Develop an awareness of one's leadership views and behaviors.
   1. Explore the leadership-followership skills and characteristics one has and those one wants to develop.
   2. Formulate and justify a list of characteristics of ethical leadership-followership.
   3. Reflect upon and analyze the factors hindering and facilitating one's own ethical behavior.
   4. Appreciate the difficulty of behaving ethically.

READINGS: 4 or 5 chapters from <u>Leadership</u> by James MacGregor Burns. Articles and selections from books and journals. Your suggestions for readings for the class are welcome. If you find articles that you think would interest the class, please make them available for copy for the class.

COURSE REQUIREMENTS:
A. Attend class. If for some reason you are unable to attend, you are still responsible for any additional material distributed.
B. Participate in class discussion. Class participation will generally not be counted as part of the grade except in borderline cases. People should feel free to participate without the pressure and anxiety of being graded.
C. Complete all required readings.
D. Complete Weekly Response Sheets. (Typed or clearly printed, these replace a second paper.) To be turned in at the beginning of the class session. Make a copy for yourself before turning it in. No late submissions accepted. Quotation marks must be used for direct quotes of authors. Each Weekly Response Sheet should follow this outline:
   1. Perspective of author.
      a. What are the key points?
      b. What is the author's view of followers and followership? (Skip if you have already answered this in "a".)
      c. Ethics--What does s/he say about the ethics of leaders-followers-organization behavior? If ethics is not addressed directly, what are the implicit ethics?
      d. Values--What are the values, implicit or explicit, underlying her/his views?
      e. Are the views of different cultures represented? (Or are men and white males treated as the norm?)
   2. Research.
      a. What important questions would one ask from this perspective?
      b. How would you answer the questions (research method)?
   3. Your questions--what questions does this generate for you?
   4. General comments: What is your general reaction? For example, like, dislike, strongly agree or disagree, illuminates a particular situation, new insight into..., etc.
E. A paper (with abstract) on an ethical leader or follower. (This can be a person or a corporation or organization). You have the option to do this as research with real (that is, in person) individuals and corporations or as a library research project. If you are an accomplished library researcher, then you may wish to try a field study

approach. In addition to providing a paper, you will be asked to make a 10-minute presentation to the class (plus 5 minutes for discussion). This presentation should include a one-page abstract for class members to keep.

GRADING: The Weekly Response Sheets count as 60% of the grade; the paper counts as 40%. In borderline cases class participation will be counted. Students who turn in late papers will not qualify for an A grade, unless lateness is considered valid.

COURSE OUTLINE AND READINGS:

Session
1   Overview: Introductions. Overview of syllabus and assignments. Overview of Maslow and Kohlberg/Rest stages. Definitions of ethical leadership and ethical followership, unethical leadership and unethical followership.
2   Perspectives: Burns' views
      Readings: Burns' book, ch. 1, 2, 16, 17
3   Perspectives: Machiavelli's views. Lying and deception. Components of ethical action.
      Readings: Selections from Machiavelli's The Prince; Bok, "Lies for the Public Good"; Sabini and Silver, "On Destroying the Innocent with a Clear Conscience"; Kegan and Lakey: "Leadership, Followership, and the State"
4   Perspectives: Hagberg's views; Greenleaf's views
      Readings: Hagberg: "True Leadership"; Greenleaf: selections from book Servant Leadership.
5   Perspectives: Bennis' views; Gardner's views
      Readings: Bennis: "The 4 Competencies of Leadership," "The Dreamless Society"; Gardner: "Leadership: An Overview" (paper #12); "The Changing Nature of Leadership" (paper #11); "The Moral Nature of Leadership" (paper #5); "The Tasks of Leadership" (paper #2); "Leadership and Power" (paper #4).
6   Moral Courage: Readings: May: "The Courage to Create"; Hornstein: "When Corporate Courage Counts"; Glazer and Glazer: "Whistleblowing"; Soeken: "J'accuse" (See also O'Toole's "Moral Courage" from session 8.)
7   Ethical Leadership research report - by George Shapiro
8   Ethical Organization/Corporations: Speaker: Julie Belle White, Director, Masters in Organizational Leadership, College of St. Catherine
      Readings: O'Toole: "Moral Courage"; Kanter: "The Trials of an O in a World of X's"; "Structuring the Inside: The Impact of Organizations on Sex Differences"; Wallace and White: "Building Integrity in Organizations"; Tuchman: "Pursuit of Policy Contrary to Self Interest"; "Epilogue" (from The March of Folly); Peters and Waterman: "Hands on, Value Driven"; "Ethics in Organizations: The Challenger Explosion"
9   Student Presentations: Note: All papers are due today with one-page abstracts (enough abstract copies for class distribution).
10   Student Presentations
11   Student Presentations

University of Minnesota
College of Liberal Arts
225 Johnston Hall, 101 Pleasant St., S.E., Minneapolis, MN 55455

Gerri Perreault
612/624-5701

Leadership-Followership - Concepts and Issues
8:30 a.m. - 12:30 p.m.

COURSE DESCRIPTION: This course is an introduction of approaches to leadership-followership, including ethical leadership-followership. It examines and evaluates diverse perspectives on the topic. The focus is on analyzing, comparing, and contrasting the different authors on a number of variables, including definition and purpose of leadership, basic assumptions (explicit and implicit), values and ethics, attention to women and people of color and class, definition of power, desired characteristics of leaders, the relationship of leaders to followers, and decision-making processes.

Since the course is a survey course to introduce students to a variety of approaches and issues, this means it will not delve into depth in any one topic. However, the paper each student writes will allow for exploration in depth of a topic related to leadership-followership; and these will be shared with the class the last session.

Note that this is _not_ a course on "How to be a leader." The focus is on how one thinks about leadership. My assumption, however, is if we can change how we think about the nature of leadership, we can create a different view and practice of leadership-followership. I don't think leadership can be taught but I think we can create the education and the conditions that facilitate the development of leaders-followers, particularly ethical leaders-followers. In the long run, my hope is that the creation of a different view/practice of leadership and followership will contribute to the creation of a more humane world.

I want to say also that all of you have been (are now?) leaders-followers at some time and will be in the future. The course is to contribute to your development as an effective and ethical leader-follower.

COURSE OBJECTIVES: Students will be able to: Understand and discuss different perspectives on leadership-followership (LF) and ethical leadership-followership (ELF); Understand and evaluate the factors influencing ethical leadership-followership; Ask critical questions of material read on LF and ELF; Develop an awareness of different feminist approaches to leadership; Appreciate the difficulty of behaving ethically, as a leader and as a follower; Develop an awareness of one's own views and behaviors; Be able to discuss factors and issues related to women and people of color as leaders and followers.

SCHEDULE WITH READINGS:

1st meeting Introduction and Overview

2nd meeting Topic 1: Context of Leadership
Topic 2: Approaches to Management/Leadership (early history and classical approaches)

Required readings: Gardner: "The Nature of Leadership";   Bennis: "The Dreamless Society"; Cleveland: "Control: The Twilight of Hierarchy"; Gardner: "The Moral Aspect of Leadership"; Maccoby: "Leadership Needs of the 1980s"; Sashkin and Lassey: "Theories of Leadership: A Review of Useful Research"; Lassey and Sashkin: "Dimensions of Leadership"; McGregor, Douglas: "Theory Y: The Integration of Individual and Organizational Goals"; Blanchard: "Theory Y Managers Can Fail without Careful Assessment"; Argyris: "Increasing Interpersonal Competence"; Blake and Mouton: "An Overview of the Grid"

Situational leadership: LEAD Self; Questionnaire (Leader Effectiveness and Adaptability Description); Answers and Explanations; Hersey, et al.: excerpt from "The Impact of Situational Leadership in an Educational Setting"; What is Situational Leadership?"; Blanchard: "Usefulness of Different Styles of Managing Varies with Setting"; Scoring the Questionnaire"; "Power Perception Profile" (self-assessment instrument)

Assignments: Complete readings and Weekly Response Sheet; Complete LEAD Self and bring in for scoring; Complete "Power Perception Profile."

3rd meeting   Topic 3: Approaches to Followership
                            Topic 4: Power, Authority, and Legitimacy

Required readings: Heller and Van Til: "Leadership and Followership: Some Summary Propositions"; Litzinger and Schaefer: "Leadership through Followership"; Janeway: "The View from Below"; Handy: "On Power and Influence"; Sprunger and Bergquist: "Authority and Accountability"; Kipnis & Schmidt, "The Language of Persuasion"; Machiavelli: The Prince (some excerpts); Tavris: "What's Your P.Q.?"

Recommended readings: McClelland: Power: The Inner Experience; Kanter: chapter on "Power" in Men and Women of the Corporation; Janeway: Powers of the Weak; Hartsock: Money, Sex, and Power

Review: Lassey & Sashkin: "Dimensions of Leadership" pp. 18-20; See also Hagberg on "Leadership and Power"
Optional: Complete "What's Your P.Q.?"
Complete: Required readings and Weekly Response Sheet

4th meeting   Topic 5: Characteristics of Leadership
                            Topic 6: Approaches to Leadership--Stage Models, Servant Leadership, Japanese Management and Theory Z

Required readings: Bennis: "The 4 Competencies of Leadership"; McCall and Lombardo: "What Makes a Top Executive?"; Cleveland: "Learning the Art of Leadership"; Korda: "How to be a Leader"; Hagberg: "Leadership and Power"; Pearson: The Hero Within: Six Archetypes We Live By (selected chapters); Greenleaf: Servant Leadership (3 chapters)

Recommended readings: Burns, Chapter 6: "Intellectual Leadership" (book, pp. 141-168) Review earlier works, if you can. See also Burns, next week's readings.

5th meeting   Topic 6: Approaches to Leadership: Transforming Leadership

Required readings: Burns book: chapters 1, 2, 16, 17
Due today: Topic choices
Complete: Readings and Weekly Response Sheet

6th meeting   Topic 7: Women, Feminism, and Leadership
                  Topic 8: People of Color and Leadership

Required readings: Kanter: "The Trials of an O in a World of X's"; Kanter: "Structuring the Inside: The Impact of Organizations on Sex Differences"; Bennis: "False Grit"; Marshall: chapters from Women Travellers in a Male World; Davis: "The Status of Black Leadership: Implications for Black Followers in the 1980s"

Recommended readings: Favia: "Think like a man, dress like a doll, and work like a horse: Advising the woman manager"; Mayes: "Women in positions of authority: A study of changing sex roles"; Bunch: "Woman Power: The Courage to Lead, the Strength to Follow, and the Sense to Know the Difference"

7th meeting   Continuation of Above

Due today: Final choice of topic with brief description

8th meeting   Topic 9: Ethical Leadership

Required readings: Jackson: "Jackson, Jacob, and the Jews"; Heyward: "Looking in the Mirror: A Response to Jonestown"; Sabini and Silver: "On Destroying the Innocent with a Clear Conscience: A Sociopsychology of the Holocaust"; Perreault: "Vision and the Emerging World View: From Separation to Connectedness"; Gilligan: "Why Should a Woman be More Like a Man?"; Lorde: "The Master's Tools Will Never Dismantle the Master's House"; Bok: "Lies for the Public Good"

Recommended readings: Hahn: "Being Awake"; McCall and Lombardo: "What Makes a Top Executive?"; Riddle: "Politics, Spirituality, and Models of Change"; Kegan and Lahey: "Leadership, Followership, and the State"; Capra: "National Insecurity"

Review: Burns' concept of a transforming leader

Complete: Readings and Weekly Response Sheet

9th meeting Topic 10: Courage

Required readings: May: "The Courage to Create"; Hornstein: "When Corporate Courage Counts"; Glazer and Glazer: "Whistleblowing"; Soeken: "J'Accuse"; Steinem: "What happens when an ordinary woman blows the whistle on her boss?"

10th meeting No assignments: Time to finish paper

11th meeting Student Presentations
        (Bring a one-page summary of your paper to distribute to class. And present a 5-minute summary of your paper to the class. Turn in paper to instructor.)

COURSE REQUIREMENTS AND EVALUATION:
Note: Students may negotiate different requirements and bases for evaluation.

Requirements: Read all the "required" material. Try to read some of the "recommended" material, if possible.

About the readings: You should purchase Leadership (in paperback) by James MacGregor Burns. The remaining readings will be xeroxed and distributed to you. Although the reading list looks lengthy, it won't be as bad as you think because (a) some of the articles are brief, even 1 page; (b) all are very readable except for Burns and one other article; thus you will not have to plow through torturous academic jargon or dense research studies; (c) there is redundancy among the readings; and (d) at the end of each session, I will review the readings assigned for the next session.

I strongly encourage your suggestion of articles for the class also.

Complete the following: Weekly Response Sheets

Student Self-Evaluation Guidelines: Each student must write a competence statement and self-evaluation.
1. Competence Statement: Write a competence statement that reflects your learning in the course.
2. Self-Evaluation: Provide statements evaluating your work in the course.

Indicate whether or not you want me to comment on both (a) the content and (b) writing and organization of your paper. If I have time, I will do both, BUT ONLY for those who want such feedback. Otherwise, I will comment only on the content.

Note: Perreault has developed detailed Weekly Response Sheets for students that outline questions to be resolved; worksheets that present guidelines for completing assignments, writing papers, conducting interviews and surveys, selecting topics for consideration, and samples of competency statements. She also uses an extensive bibliography.

University of Missouri
5100 Rock Hill Road, Kansas City, MO 64110

Joseph Caliguri
Chair, Div. of Educational Admin.
816/276-2716

Leadership in Public Education - 513R

OBJECTIVES: To increase knowledge and judgment about leadership-communication and group processes behaviors. To increase knowledge and skills in problem-solution behaviors.

COMPETENCY AREAS: Leadership Behaviors; Communication Behaviors; Group Processes Behaviors.

OUTCOMES: Ability to use problem-solving skill models in developing a self or school problem plan for implementation.

SCHEDULE:
Leadership
  Session 1
    30 min.   Orientation
    45 min.   Self-Leadership Questionnaire
    1 hr.   Leadership - Definitions; Leadership in Context; Administrative Assessment Centers - Skills
    45 min.   Administrative Styles; Questionnaire
    1 hr.   Course Assignment Choices: Self-Leadership Project; Case Record Project; Action Learning Project

  Session 2
    1 hr.   Motivation and Growth
    45 min.   Small Group Discussion
    1 1/2 hrs.   Problem Solving Exercise; Small Group Interaction on Exercise
    45 min.   Assignment Choices - Review

  Session 3
Communication Behaviors
    1 hr.   Basic Concepts and Johari Model
    30 min.   Listening Actively
    1 1/2 hrs.   Communication Barriers - Anger Tape
    1 hr.   Summary - Assignments: Saturday Assignment - Field Trip

  Session 4
Assignments

                   Trust Assignment; Decision Assignment - Best/Worst Decisions

Session 5
Antioch Field Trip
1 hr.	Team Conference; Breakfast
1 hr.	Observation and Descriptive Note-Taking on Jerk Typology and Employee/Customer Behaviors: Listening; Assertive/Aggressive/Passive; Muted Language
2 hrs.	Assessment and Closure

Session 6
Group Processes
1 hr.	Feedback on Trust & Decision Assignments
1 hr.	Managing Conflict - Sources of Organizational Tensions
30 min.	Conflict Tape - Class Discussion
1 1/4 hrs.	Conflict and Thomas Kuhlman Questionnaires

Session 7
Problem-Solution Skill Building - Concepts & Application
1 hr.	Decision Models
45 min.	Value Systems
45 min.	End Game
1 1/4 hrs.	Organizational Decision Making in Situational Contexts

Session 8
1 hr.	Teaching Evaluation - Exercise
45 min.	Small Group Discussion
45 min.	Analysis of Problem Solving Groups - Cohesive Characteristics
1 3/4 hrs.	One to One Conferences

Session 9
30 min.	Review
45 min.	Course Assignment Plan and Submission Dates
1 1/4 hrs.	Career Planning
30 min.	Course Evaluation

University of Nebraska
200 Nebraska Union, Lincoln, NE 68588-0453

Sara A. Boatman
Dir., Campus Activities & Programs
402/472-2454

Emerging Leader Program - Educ. Psych. 496 One instructor, a teaching assistant, two group facilitators, and three faculty consultants. Class meets once each week for 3 1/2 hrs.

PHILOSOPHY/OBJECTIVES: To provide leadership information, build skills, allow students to gain experience in leadership, apply their new learning on campus and enable new students to expedite their involvement as leaders at UNL. Throughout the semester each student will assess his/her personal strengths and weaknesses as well as leadership abilities and work to create a plan to develop both personally and as leaders throughout the college career.

The success of the course and its benefits will depend on opportunities provided to experience and share with each other during class. Since the class meets only once a week attendance is necessary for constant and effective feedback. Everyone is expected to be prepared (reading assignments) and to participate in class. Absence from class must be arranged.

Weekly assignments, given at each class involving a variety of ways to build skills while gaining more understanding of each leadership topic, will include short reaction papers (max. 3 pages), group work with one's small group, interviews with community leaders and observing student organizations and leaders.

Each student taking the course for 2 or 3 credits will keep a journal to integrate lecture information, class discussions, class assignments and readings applied personally as an emerging leader. Although the journal will not be graded, completion of the journal, at an acceptable level, will be a percentage of the final grade.

Two 30 minute meetings with the primary instructor will be required of all students for planning and assessment.

Students taking the course for 3 credits will integrate all course materials in a final paper (10-15 pages) on a leadership topic. Sample topics will be provided and there will be opportunity to discuss topics with the instructors throughout the semester.

CREDIT OPTIONS: Students may select from three options:
No-credit option: Must do all class assignments and attend class. Attend two instructor meetings. (Each student taking the no-credit option who completes work at an acceptable level will receive a certificate of recognition in the Emerging Leader Program.)
Two-credit option: Must do all class assignments and attend class. Attend two instructor meetings. Complete journal.
Three-credit option: Must do all class assignments and attend class. Attend two instructor meetings. Complete journal. Final paper (10-15 pages).

Grades will be determined as follows: 1. Requirements that will not be graded but must be completed are two instructor meetings and journal; 2. Class Participation/Attendance: (will be recorded for each session) A-present, asking/answering questions, discussing; B-present, actively engaged; C-present, listening but not sharing ideas; D-present, minimal engagement; F-unexcused absence; 3. Class Assignments: (each will be given points using the following criteria):

> A, Truly Outstanding - 100 points; B+, Very Good - 90 points; B, Good -85 points; C+, Above Average - 80 points; C, Average - 75 points; D+, Below Average - 70 points; D, Poor - 60 points; F, Unacceptable - 50 points

4. Final Paper (third credit for 3-credit option): a. Development of content to demonstrate understanding of concepts: 40 points; b. Organizational scheme and use of evidence: 30 points; c. Clear written communication: 30 points.

Meetings

1 Topic: Introduction, "Building a Team"; ASAP Involvement Checklist; Paragraph Completion Test.
Assignment:"Team Building" by Paul

2 Topic: "Leadership," Guest Lecturer: Dr. Sara Boatman, Dir., Campus Activities and Programs
Assignment:"The Nature of Leadership," Paper 1 by Gardner

3 Topic: "You as a Leader"; Strength Deployment Inventory by Porter
Assignment:"Situational Leadership" by Protzman

4 Topic: "From Vision to Reality"; Guest Presenter: John Beacon, Director of Financial Aid & Admissions
Assignment:"Motivating Volunteers" by Christensen & Myers; "Organizing Committees & Evaluating Members" by Finney; "Goal Implementation" by K. Allen

5 Topic: "The Essential Leadership Skill: Communication"; Defining Issues; Test
Assignment:"Defensive/Supportive Communication" by Lauber; "Responding to Others"

6 Topic: "Making Decisions/Solving Problems"; Guest Presenter: Dr. James Griesen, Vice Chancellor for Student Affairs & Prof. of Educational Administration
Assignment:"Searching for Solutions" by English; "Decisions: They are Better Made Together" by Anderson

7 Topic: "Responsibilities of Leadership"; Ethical Leadership; Guest Presenter: Dr. Lyn Jakobsen, Asst. Director of Housing/Residential Education
Assignment:"Ethical Leadership" by Boatman; "Leadership Education Overview" by Bennis; "Moral Aspect of Leadership," Paper 5 by Gardner

8 Topic: "Responsibilities of Leadership Part II"; Understanding and Appreciating Differences
Assignment:"Dragon Dancers & Desert Directions" by Stern; "Awareness and Sensitivity: First Steps" by Green

9 Topic: "Leader as a Role Model"; "Peer Leader Mentoring Program"
Assignment:"Planning for Wellness" Chapt. 1 by Ardell & Tager

10 Topic: "Leadership for a Global Society"; Guest Presenter Dr. Robert Oberst, Assoc. Prof. of Political Science, Nebraska Wesleyan University; Panel of Guest Presenters
Assignment:"The Attitude & Capacities Required of Successful Leadership" by Jaworski; "Leadership Development," Paper 7 by Gardner

11 Topic: Evaluation
Assignment:"Preparing to Choose a Leadership Position" by Anderson

University of South Carolina
College of Education, Dept. of Educational
  Leadership & Policies
Columbia, SC 29208

Kenneth L. Schwab
Executive Vice-President
803/777-3101

Leadership in Higher Education
Interns in College Teaching: Katie Brondino and Terri Marshall

---

PURPOSE: The course will provide an opportunity for students to explore the leadership role of administrators in American higher education. The seminar will examine different leadership theories and styles while affording students the opportunity to assess their own leadership skills. An examination of the research in the area of leadership behavior will focus on the identification of the necessary support systems required for improving academic management and performance. Attention will be given to examining the role of leaders in a variety of positions and settings within higher education.

OBJECTIVES: To examine the literature concerning leadership in higher education; To analyze leadership theories and how individual theories can be applied in the educational setting; To develop an understanding of the skills and competencies identified as essential to effective leaders in higher education and how such skills and competencies could be developed; To gain increased understanding of one's own leadership abilities and explore how to further develop effective administrative behavior; To provide opportunities for examination of specific leadership positions in a variety of institutional settings; To develop an awareness of administrative style congruent with one's personal attributes, the social context, and the organizational setting in which administration may be studied or practiced; To increase ability in analyzing complex problems and issues which administrators face.

CONDUCT OF COURSE: All students are expected to participate actively in every part of the course. Students will be expected to be involved in the teaching of the course through formal presentations of projects and research, engaging in class discussions, and leading discussions of reading assignments. Guest speakers will present and stimulate discussions on specific topics.

REQUIREMENTS: Each student will be expected to:
1. Attend all class sessions and participate actively in class discussion.
2. Complete all reading assignments and lead class discussions as assigned on particular articles, reports, and books. Each class presentation should be supported by appropriate handouts summarizing pertinent information from the reading(s) utilized. Additionally, each student will be responsible for presenting a review of an assigned book. These reviews will be scheduled to coincide with weekly class topics.
3. Prepare for and take the mid-term exam.
4. Identify a leader in a higher education setting that will serve as mentor during the course. Each student will be expected to spend a minimum of 15 hours observing and discussing leadership issues with this mentor during the semester. A journal recording observations and insights gained from this experience will be expected at the end of the course.
5. Prepare a seminar paper that examines and develops a personal theory of leadership drawn from the readings and the observations made during the course and mentor

experience using personal experiences with their mentor, guest speakers, and classroom presentations and discussions. A literature review should also be conducted to support the personal leadership theory developed. This paper should be ten to fifteen pages in length and will be presented to the class at an assigned time.

COURSE GRADING: The students' final grade in the seminar will be based on the following criteria:
1. Participation in Class, 20%, 20 points; 2. Class presentation of assigned book and other readings, 25%, 25 points; 3. Mid-Term Exam, 25%, 25 points; 4. Seminar Paper, 30%, 30 points.

GRADE RANGE: Each of the four areas listed above will be given up to the maximum designated points and at the end of the semester all the points received by the student will be totaled. Grades will be assigned as follows: 93 and above - A; 85-92 - B; 75-84 - C; 65-74 - D.

REQUIRED TEXT: Bass, Bernard M. (1981) Stogdill's Handbook of Leadership (rev. ed.) New York. Free Press

Texts To Be Used For Book Reviews:

Class Two:	The Art of Administration, K. Ebel (presented by teaching intern)
Class Four:	The Effective College President, Fisher, Tack & Wheeler
Class Five:	The Effective Administrator, D. Walker (two students reporting)
Class Six:	Power of the Presidency, J. Fisher (two students reporting)
Class Seven:	Academic Strategy, Keller; New Directions for Higher Education: Institutional Revival: Case Histories, D. Steeples, editor
Class Nine:	Passion for Excellence, Peters & Austin (part three); Take the Road to Creativity and Get Off Your Dead End, D. Campbell
Class Ten:	Beyond the Ivory Tower, Bok (part one); New Directions for Higher Education: Professional Ethics in University Administration, Stein & Baca, editors
Class Eleven:	Leaders for a New Era, M. Green (part 2); Contemporary Issues in Leadership
Class Twelve:	Beyond the Ivory Tower, Bok (two students reporting part two and part three)

SUPPLEMENTAL TEXTS: Bennett, J. B. & Peltason, J. W. (1985). Contemporary issues in higher education. New York: Macmillan and American Council on Education; Bok, D. C. (1987). Beyond the ivory tower. Cambridge, MA: Harvard University Press; Brown, D. G. (Ed.). (1984). Leadership roles of chief academic officers. New Directions for Higher Education, 47; Campbell, D. P. (1984). If I'm in charge here why is everybody laughing? Greensboro, NC: Center for Creative Leadership; Campbell, D. P. (1985). Take the road to creativity and get off your dead end. Greensboro, NC: Center for Creative Leadership; Campbell, D. P. & Van Velsor, E. (1985). The use of personality measures in the leadership development program. Greensboro, NC: Center for Creative Leadership; Cohen, M. D. & March L. G. (1974). Leadership and ambiguity. New York:

McGraw-Hill and the Carnegie Commission on Higher Education; Davis, R. M. (Ed.). (1985). Leadership and institutional renewal. New Directions for Higher Education, 49; Eble, K. E. (1988). The art of administration. San Francisco: Jossey-Bass; Fisher, J. L. (1984). Power of the presidency. New York: Macmillan and the American Council on Education; Fisher, J. L. & Tack, M. W. (Eds.). (1988). Leaders on Leadership: The College Presidency. New Directions for Higher Education, 61; Fisher, J. L., Tack, M. W., & Wheeler, K. J. (1988). The effective college president. New York: Macmillan and the American Council on Education; Green, M. F. (1988). Leaders for a new era: Strategies for higher education. New York: American Council on Education and Macmillan; Hampton, D. R., Summer, C. E., & Webber, R. A. (1978). Organizational behavior and the practice of management. Glenview, IL: Scott, Foresman, & Co.; Hersey, P. (1984). The situational leader. Escondido, CA: Center for Leadership Studies; Jennings, E. E. (1960). An anatomy of leadership: Princes, heroes, and superman. New York: McGraw-Hill; Keller, G. (1983). Academic strategy. Baltimore: Johns Hopkins University Press; Kotter, J. P. (1988). The leadership factor. New York: Free Press; Kouzes, J. M. & Posner, B. Z. (1987). The leadership challenge: How to get extraordinary things done in organizations. San Francisco: Jossey-Bass; Lassey, W. R. & Fernandez, R. R. (1976). Leadership & social change. La Jolla, CA: University Associates; Lombardo, M. M. (1978). Looking at leadership: Some neglected issues (Technical Report No. 6). Greensboro, NC: Center for Creative Leadership; McCall, M. W. (1977). Leaders and leadership: Of substance and shadow (Technical Report No. 2). Greensboro, NC: Center for Creative Leadership; McCall, M. W. (1978). Power, influence, and authority: The hazards of carrying a sword (Technical Report No. 10). Greensboro, NC: Center for Creative Leadership; McCall, M. W. & Lombardo, M. M. (Eds.). (1978). Leadership-- where else can we go? Durham, NC: Duke University Press; McCall, M. W. (1980). In pursuit of the manager's job: Building on Mintzberg (Technical Report No. 14). Greensboro, NC: Center for Creative Leadership; Peters, T. & Austin, N. (1985). A passion for excellence. New York: Random House; Plante, P. R. (1987). The art of decision making, New York: American Council on Education and Macmillan; Rosenbach, W. E. & Taylor, R. L. (1984). Contemporary issues in leadership. Boulder, CO: Westview Press; Stein, R. H. & Baca, M. C. (Eds.) (1981). Professional Ethics in University Administration. New Directions for Higher Education, 33; Steeples, D. W. (Ed.). (1986). Institutional revival: Case histories. New Directions for Higher Education, 54; Walker, D. E. (1986). The effective administrator. San Francisco: Jossey-Bass.

CLASS SCHEDULE:

Class One: Topic: Introduction and Orientation to Course
Activities: 1. Introductions. 2. Distribution and discussion of syllabus. 3. Discuss class schedule and projects. 4. Discuss class presentations for leadership theories. 5. Discuss book review schedule and reading list. 6. Begin discussion on the assessment of leadership; complete Myers-Briggs. 7. Discuss self-assessment project due next week.

Class Two: Topic: Assessing Yourself as a Leader
Activities: 1. Guest lecturer: Dr. Larry Salters, Director of Career Planning 2. Discussion of self-assessment assignment: What did students learn, who were their role models, what

was their impact, what issues and skills do they need to address? Does higher education have an impact on one's style/definition of leadership or are students in the field of higher education because their definitions seem to mesh with higher education? 3. Begin discussion of leadership definition and its difference and/or similarity to management and administration; 4. Discuss and schedule book review choices; book review on The Art of Administration.

Readings and Assignments: Bass Ch. 1 and 2; "Academic Leadership"; "On Leadership"; Personnel Administrator, "Personality Clash"; "The Role of Mentors in Developing Leaders for Academe"; "Leadership in an Organized Anarchy"; Self-assessment paper due: A 3-4 page paper consisting of the student's self-assessment of his/her personal leadership style and skills. Students can explore the impact of their personal values, beliefs, role model/mentors, experiences, and the setting of higher education on the development of their leadership framework using this exercise to identify issues and skills needed to improve leadership foundation and actions. Students are encouraged to identify great literature and authors (i.e., Plato, Machiavelli, Hess, Faulkner, Perssick (Zen)) which have had a significant impact on their understanding of and approach to leadership. Students should also include their personal definition of leadership. In doing so, they should consider "what is leadership?" What are some examples of extraordinary leaders?; Book review choices prepared.

Class Three: Topic: Leadership Theories
Activities: 1. Students will present a summary (no longer than 20 minutes per theory) of theories as presented in Bass chapter 3. State the historical context and development, characteristics and constructs, strengths and weaknesses, and an example of an issue resolved within the confines of the theory. Theories under discussion will be Great-Man theories, Environmental theories, Psychoanalytic theory, Interaction-Expectation theories, Humanistic theories, and Perceptual-Cognitive theories. 2. Case study distributed. Review and discuss the leadership approach used in resolving the issue.

Readings and Assignments: Bass, Ch. 3, 4, 5 and Bass leadership theory presentations.

Class Four: Topic: Leadership Theories, cont.
Activities: 1. Students will present a summary (no longer than 20 minutes per theory) of theories as presented in Terry's "Six Views of Leadership." State the historical context and development, characteristics and constructs, strengths and weaknesses, and an issue resolved within the confines of the theory. Theories under study for this class are: Trait theory, Situational theory, Organizational theory, Power theories, Vision theory, and Ethical Assessment theory. 2. Case study distributed. Review and discuss the leadership approach used in resolving the issue; Discuss how these theories differ and/or parallel those presented in class 3. 4. Discuss integrating the theories and if higher educations requires a different perspective not found in the examined theories. 5. Discuss how and whether the theories presented affected student's personal theory or concept of leadership. 6. Book review presentation: The Effective College President.

Readings and Assignments: Bass, Ch. 6, 7, 8; Terry, "Reflective Leadership Program; Leadership--A Preview of a Seventh View"; Terry leadership theory presentations.

Class Five: Topic: Skills and Competencies of Leaders
Activities: 1. Guest speaker: Mr. Fred Sheheen, South Carolina Commissioner of Higher Education. 2. Discuss self-evaluative exercises as means of assessing strengths and weaknesses. Use the CCL's Leadership Styles Indicator as an example. 3. Book reviews: The Effective Administrator (two reports). 4. Discuss what are the skills and competencies necessary for leaders in higher education and whether/if these differ from those of non-educational leaders. 5. Film: "Productivity and the Self-Fulfilling Prophecy."

Readings and Assignments: Bass Ch. 9, 10, 11, 12; "Skills and Knowledge Necessary for Administrators"; "Seven Keys to Business Leadership."

Class Six: Topic: The Context of Leadership
Activities: 1. Guest Speaker: Dr. James B. Holderman, USC President. 2. Discuss the following: a) how do power and authority tie into leadership, b) group dynamics and the importance of mediation and conflict resolution, c) building an administrative team, d) how to handle the media, e) how many masters do leaders/administrators serve--trustees, students, alumni, parents, accrediting agencies, state and federal policy-makers, press, private and public funding sources, fiscal responsibilities. 3. Book reviews: Power of the President (two reports).

Readings and Assignments: Bass, Ch. 13, 14, 15, 16; "The Team Effectiveness Critique"; "On the Front Lines: Presidents Build Institutional Image"; "Out of Context--Why the Media Doesn't Tell Your Story"; "In Praise of Followers."

Class Seven: Topic: Dynamics of Leadership Styles
Activities: 1. Panel presentation of speakers illustrating the types and approaches to leadership in an institution's various contexts: Dr. Jim Rex, Senior Vice President for Development, USC; Mr. Johnny Gregory, Legislative Liaison, USC; Dr. Paul Hurray, Senior Vice President for Research, USC. 2. Class presentations of leadership styles as organized in Bass chapters 18, 19, 20, 22: a) Democratic vs. Autocratic Leadership, b) Participative vs. Directive Leadership, c) Relations Oriented vs. Task Oriented Leadership, d) Laissez-faire Leadership vs. Motivation to Manage. 3. Book reviews: Academic Strategy; New Directions for Higher Education: Institutional Revival: Case Histories.

Readings and Assignments: Bass Ch. 17 (Also review chapters 18, 19, 20, and 22 in preparation for class presentations); Class presentations of leadership styles as organized by Bass in chapters 18, 19, 20, 22.

Class Eight: Mid-Term Examination

Class Nine: Topic: Vision, Creativity, Change and Risk Taking
Activities: 1. Guest Speakers: Mr. Michael Mungo, Chairman of the Board of Trustees, and Mr. Thomas Stepp, Secretary to the Board of Trustees. 2. Discuss examples of and

cases involving risk taking, change and creativity in higher education administration. 3. Book reviews: <u>Passion for Excellence</u>, part 3; <u>Take the Road to Creativity and Get Off Your Dead End</u>. 4. Assign case study on values and ethics. 5. Creativity exercise. <u>Readings and Assignments:</u> Bass Ch. 26 and 29; "Should College Presidents be Educators?"; "Taking the Risk and Making the Difference."

Class Ten: <u>Topic:</u> The Values and Ethics of Leaders
<u>Activities:</u> 1. Guest speakers: Dr. David Bell and Dr. Nora Bell. 2. Values clarifications exercise. 3. Case study discussion. 4. Book reviews: <u>Beyond the Ivory Tower</u>, part 1; <u>New Directions in Higher Education: Professional Ethics in University Administration</u>.

<u>Readings and Assignments:</u> Prepared to discuss case study; Complete related readings.

Class Eleven: <u>Topic:</u> Dealing with Diverse Constituencies; Cultural Differences
<u>Activities:</u> 1. Guest speaker: Dr. Sue Rosser. 2. Discuss topics such as a) women in leadership positions, b) minorities in leadership positions, c) cross-cultural leadership issues in a global economy, d) leading diverse constituents, e) helping the university community appreciate differences, f) assumptions that block and facilitate cross-cultural relations. 3. Book review: <u>Leaders for a New Era</u>, part 2; <u>Contemporary Issues in Leadership</u>.

<u>Readings and Assignments:</u> Bass Ch. 30, 31, 32; <u>One Third of a Nation</u>; "The Status of Black Leadership: Implications for Black Followers in the 1980s"; "Careers in College and University Administration: How are Women Affected"; "Career Mapping and the Professional Development Process"; "Interpersonal Effectiveness in Organizations: The Cross-Cultural Dimension"; "The New Agenda of Women for Higher Education."

Class Twelve: <u>Topic:</u> Leadership and Society; Leadership into the Nineties
<u>Activities:</u> 1. Guest Speaker: Dr. Jim Hudgins, Pres., Midland Technical College. 2. Book reviews: <u>Beyond the Ivory Tower</u>, parts 1 and 2. 3. Discuss the importance of planning for the future. 4. Class discussion of "What now?" "What does the future hold?" "How can leaders prepare themselves for that future?" 5. Turn in Seminar Papers!!!

<u>Readings and Assignments:</u> Seminar papers due! "The Role of the Academy in the Nuclear Age"; "2001: Formulation of a Vision"; "Leading-Edge Leadership"; "Reflections on Revolution and Leadership by Surprise."

Class Thirteen: Class presentations of final seminar paper/project: oral reports on the students' projects should include how their leadership perspective and definition have changed as a result of the experiences in this course.

Class Fourteen: Class presentations of final seminar paper/project: oral reports on the students' projects should include how their leadership perspective and definition have changed as a result of the experiences in this course; Tying up loose ends from course discussions; Course Evaluation.

Virginia Commonwealth University
P. O. Box 2031, Richmond, VA 23284

Gil Fairholm
Dept. of Public Administration
804/367-1046

COURSE DESCRIPTION

In this seminar you will critically review and analyze some of the major current ideas about leadership theory and practices from both academic and operational perspectives. While your input will provide a final agenda for action, the focus will be on research and presentation of findings before peers in a conference format. The course will also emphasize leadership skills and knowledge needed in the last part of the 20th century.

Insofar as is possible specific examples from current experience in Virginia will be used. Professionals dealing with these issues will be asked to interact with you to provide practical and operational perspectives on issues discussed.

The seminar will be divided into three parts.

Part one will focus on development of a course objective and an agenda for research. You and your colleagues will explore your own ideas about what leadership is, develop a working agenda, "validate" that definition from current literature, and otherwise become acquainted with the dimensions of the leadership phenomena in 20th century America. The class will develop a preliminary research action agenda and through interactive methods of negotiation and consensus building, will develop a specific research, discussion, and presentation plan to guide the seminar in planning and conducting a leadership conference later in the semester.

Part two will focus on general research to describe, delimit, and place in context major ideas (1) about leadership research approaches, (2) styles, (3) theories, and (4) practice. In accomplishing these objectives, you will prepare descriptive materials to define, explain, and place in relevant context to modern leadership styles and current theoretical models.

As part of this phase, selected leaders will be asked to make presentations on their perceptions/ practice of leadership in today's organizations. As assigned we will invite high-level practitioners from the Virginia government scene to make presentations and participate in discussions to help interpret specific leadership issues in practical and theoretical terms.

Part three will conclude the seminar and will constitute a conference on Current Issues in Leadership in Government at which you will make formal presentation of your individual research. Each participant will make a major presentation reporting on his/her research to identify, describe, analyze, evaluate, and recommend further actions regarding a specific leadership issue facing government leaders in Virginia (and the nation). Colleagues will criticize and comment on these presentations. Presentations should be of publishable quality and may be submitted for publication or for consideration in the Department's contemplated public affairs papers series.

A fully professional conference paper is required. This 3000-6000 word paper should explore fully one critical issue in leadership and provide insight on theory and practical aspects of the issue. You will be asked to present central findings of your research to the class in a 30-45 minute presentation along with a 2-3 page precis (in sufficient copies for each class member) on your assigned day.

Two copies of the final written paper will be provided to the instructor at the end of the semester. All conventions of academic term papers should be observed.

The grade for the course will be based on the following factors:

Summaries	10%	
Extended Outlines	15% (5% oral; 10% written)	
Monitoring of Guest Speaker Presentations	5%	
Precis	5%	
Research Paper	45%	
Oral Presentation	10%	
Critical Class Involvement	10%	(performance on panel/class involvement generally)
Total	100%	

Note: Failure to meet any assigned delivery schedule will result in a loss of credit of 5 percent for each occurrence.

<u>Texts and readings:</u> William E. Rosenbach and Robert L. Taylor (eds.). <u>Contemporary Issues in Leadership</u>. (Boulder, Colo.: Westview Press) 1984. A reference work is also recommended: Bernard M. Bass. <u>Stogdill's Handbook of Leadership</u>. (New York: The Free Press) 1981. This is a definitive reference work and should be in the library of serious professionals.

You will be asked to read extensively in the field, prepare a selected bibliography for use by your colleagues and yourself in your research and use relevant materials in your descriptive (part two) paper and in the (part three) conference paper and presentation. This course will be conducted in all respects in accordance with the provisions of the University Academic Integrity Policy on file in the Department and elsewhere within the University. You are encouraged to make appointments at your convenience to discuss the course or other matters with me. Normally papers will be returned at the next class following their submission for grading. If you want papers mailed to you, please include a stamped, addressed envelope.

Virginia Cooperative Extension Service   **Delwyn A. Dyer**
Center for Volunteer Development   Director
Donaldson Brown CEC, CVD Suite, Blacksburg, VA 24061-0150   703/231-7966

Leadership in Groups and Organizations

The Virginia Cooperative Extension Service has available a 150-page correspondence course--Publication 301-005--dated April 1984 that was prepared by: Community Resource Development in cooperation with the Center for Volunteer Development.

*The publication is in response to the demands facing persons who occupy positions of leadership in committees, clubs, associations, groups, and organizations. It responds to the need for knowledge of leadership styles and mores, knowing why people join organizations and what they expect in return, knowing how to organize and run effective meetings, as well as displaying a competent understanding of the dynamics of group decision making, communication, motivation, and team building. It points out the irony in the fact that most persons who aspire to be leaders or who occupy leadership positions do so without the benefit of any training. Few organizations, groups, or associations take the time to train persons for leadership positions. In like fashion, few organizations orient or train persons already in leadership positions. It is assumed leaders know what to do.

In light of this reality, the Virginia Cooperative Extension Service prepared the "Leadership in Groups and Organizations" correspondence course. The goal of the course is to provide the reader with practical and useful information about leadership and the responsibilities leaders have in groups and organizations. Group and organizational leadership literature are reviewed; mini-exercises are used throughout the course.

TOPICS COVERED ARE:

Organizations and Leadership:
> Organizations: Why Organizations; Organization Characteristics and Functions; People and Organizations; A Working Definition for Organization; You in Organizations.
> Leadership: Nature of Leadership; Leadership Research; The Emerging Synthesis; Leadership in Organizations; Bibliography and Recommended Readings.

The Leadership Function:
> The Subject is Meetings: What Meetings Provide; Why Meetings Sometimes Fail; Meeting Characteristics; Meeting Management: The Leader's Role; Tools for Meeting Management; Leading Discussions; A Guide for Meeting Management.
> Decision Making: Why Groups Have Trouble Making Decisions; Improving Decision Making in Groups.
> Conflict and Its Management: Nature and Value of Conflict; How We Handle Conflict; Ground Rules for Conflict Resolution; Bibliography and Recommended Readings.
> Motivation: Nature and Process of Motivation; Motivation Theories; Motivation and the Organization Leader.

Communication: The Communication Process; Elements of the Process; Types of Organizational Communication; Why Communication Fails; Improving Communication; Listening and Communication.

Team Building: Defining Team Building; Assessing the Need for Team Building; Doing Team Building; Creating a Climate for Team Building; Bibliography and Recommended Readings.

Applying Leadership in the Community:

Concept of Community: How Things Get Done in the Community; Role of Organizations in the Community.

The Concept of Change: Reactions to Change; Leadership for Change; Determining Community Needs; Selecting a Needs Assessment Technique; Needs Assessment Techniques; Getting Things Done: A Final Word; Bibliography and Recommended Readings.

*Taken from the Preface and Table of Contents

Westmont College
955 La Paz Road, Santa Barbara, CA 93108

Joel Kruggel
Associate Chaplain
Carol Lundberg
Instructor
805/969-3108

Leadership Seminar I - IS 065 A, B

This course will explore Biblical foundations for leadership studies and theories of leadership. Attention will also be given to the assessment of student leadership styles and effective management of self.

OBJECTIVES: The student will: develop a continuing theology of leadership within a Christian world view; develop a conceptualization of effective servant leadership; demonstrate knowledge of his/her leadership styles and the appropriate use of them; develop an understanding of the principles of self-management (goal setting, time management, and stress management); understand the issues of power and ethics in leadership.

TEXTS: Bennis, Warren. "Four Traits of Leadership" from Taking Charge. San Francisco: Harper and Row, 1983; Dayton, Edward and Engstrom, Ted. Strategy for Living. Ventura: Regal Books, 1976; Gardner, John. Leadership Papers (1-6,8,11). Washington, D.C.: Independent Sector, 1987; Greenleaf, Robert. Servant Leadership. New York: Paulist Press, 1977, pp. 1-48; Hersey, Paul and Blanchard, Kenneth. Management of Organizational Behavior. Englewood Cliffs, New Jersey: Prentice-Hall, 1982; Horner, Matina. "Toward an Understanding of Achievement-Related Conflicts in Women," Journal of Social Issues, 1972, (pp. 157-175); Kellerman, Barbara, editor. Political Leadership: A Resource Book. Pittsburgh: University of Pittsburgh Press, 1986; McCauley, Cynthia. "Stress and the Eye of the Beholder." Center for Creative Leadership, 1987.

REQUIREMENTS: Read assigned texts and articles before class. A weekly quiz will cover the material. Meet with one of the instructors or T. A. once during the semester to personalize the course by building relationships and discussing the course's impact on the student's life. Interview a student leader regarding his or her approach to leadership and accompany that leader to a meeting or event for which the leader has leadership responsibilities. A two-page, typed report of the interviews is required. Write a two-page, typed leadership analysis of either Bush or Dukakis. Complete a three-day "time-tracking" profile. Participate in a 13-hour project which offers opportunity to serve in a campus or community organization. An analysis of followership and leadership within that organization is required. Attendance at two seminars of the Leadership Conference will allow you to take an automatic 100% for three quizzes of your choice.

GRADING will be determined by the following allocation of points:

Grade Scale

Weekly Quizzes (12 at 10 pts ea)	120	A	= 372-400	(93-100%)
Mid-Term	50	A-	= 360-371	(90-92%)
Leadership Interview	30	B+	= 352-359	(88-89%)
Presidential Candidate Analysis	30	B	= 329-351	(83-87%)
		B-	= 320-328	(80-82%)

Time-Tracking Profile	30		C+	=	312-319	(78-79%)
Project Reflection Paper	40		C	=	292-311	(73-77%)
Final Exam	100		C-	=	288-291	(70-72%)
			D+	=	272-287	(68-69%)
Possible Points	400		D	=	252-271	(63-67%)
			D-	=	240-251	(60-62%)
			F	=	239 and below	(below 60%)

Class Meetings

1   Orientation to the Leadership Program

2   Course Overview, Definitions of Leadership, T/P Inventory. Read: Gardner Paper #1, "Nature of Leadership"; Gardner Paper #2, "Tasks of Leadership"

3   Nehemiah: Case Study in Biblical Leadership. Read: Excellence in Leadership

4   Jesus: Case Study in Servant-Leadership. Read: Gospel of Mark; Greenleaf, Servant Leadership, pp. 1-48

5   Approaches to Understanding Leadership. Read: "Leader as Hero," Thomas Carlyle in Political Leadership, pp. 5-9; "Great Men," Wm. James in Political Leadership, pp. 16-23; Gardner #6, "Attributes and Context"

6   Situational Leadership. Read: Hersey and Blanchard, "Leader Behavior," pp. 82-103; Hersey and Blanchard, "Situational Leadership," pp. 149-167. Due: "Leadership Interview" (2 pages, typed)

7   Power and Leadership. Read: "Power Wielders and Leaders," James MacGregor Burns in Political Leadership, pp. 287-299; "Mein Kampf," Adolph Hitler in Political Leadership, pp. 438-443; "Satyagraha," Gandhi in Political Leadership, pp. 449-452; "The Prince," Machiavelli in Political Leadership, pp. 376-387; Gardner #4, "Leadership and Power"

8   Followers and Mid-Term Exam. Read: Gardner #3, "The Heart of the Matter"; Gardner #8, "Followers"

9   Case Study of Current Leaders. Read: Bennis, "Four Traits of Leadership"; Bush and Dukakis readings to be announced; Due: "Analysis of Presidential Candidate"

10   Ethics and Leadership. Read: Gardner #5, "Moral Aspects of Leadership"; "Leadership," James MacGregor Burns in Political Leadership, pp. 419-424.

11   Leadership and Personality: Myers-Briggs Inventory. Read: begin Strategy for Living, pp. 1-90

12   Leadership of Self: Goals, Priorities, Planning. Read: Strategy for Living, pp. 91-187; Due: Time-Tracking Profile

13   Leadership of Self: Achievement & Failure. Read: Horner, "Achievement-Related Conflicts," pp. 157-175

14   Leadership of Self: Managing Stress/Final Review. Read: McCauley, "Stress and the Eye of the Beholder"; Due: Project Reflection Paper

15   Cumulative Final Exam

Leadership Seminar II

This course explores the skills and competencies required for effective leadership. Emphasis will be given to the process of change, team leadership, planning, problem-solving, decision-making, negotiation, and communication. Prerequisite: Leadership Seminar I or approval of instructor.

OBJECTIVES: The student will: develop leadership skills in team building, empowering others, communicating vision, planning, decision-making, problem-solving, negotiating, marketing, and evaluating; gain an understanding of the college administrative structure; apply leadership skills through a group project which focuses upon Westmont College.

TEXTS: Kouzes, James and Posner, Barry. The Leadership Challenge. San Francisco: Jossey-Bass, 1987; Fisher, R., and Ury, W. Getting to Yes. Boston: Houghton-Mifflin, 1981; Gardner, John. "The Moral Aspect of Leadership." Leadership Paper 5, Washington, D. C.: Independent Sector, 1987; Hersey, Paul and Blanchard, Kenneth. Management of Organizational Behavior. Prentice-Hall, 1982. Selections; Yukl, Gary. Leadership in Organizations. Prentice-Hall, 1981. Ch. 8, 9; Rood, Raymond. "The Politics of Visionary Thinking"; Handout on Planning.

REQUIREMENTS: Read assigned texts before class. Discussion in classes will be based upon that assumption; There will be four quizzes, a group project, and a cumulative final exam to evaluate students' learning from texts and class sessions; Group Project: Each team will assess the college community to determine needs not currently being addressed. On basis of the assessment, each team will plan, implement, and evaluate a project. The project may be either initiating a campus activity which meets a need or a proposal for a policy change on campus which would result in meeting a particular need. Proposals will be presented to the President's Administrative staff; Personal Reflection on A Group Project: Each student will submit a 2-3 page typed evaluation of his or her contributions to the project, assessment of personal leadership growth through the project, and significant learnings about team leadership; Team Meetings with Instructors: Each team will meet with the instructors for a progress report.

GRADING will be determined by the following allocation of points:

		Grade Scale		
		A	= 372-400	(93-100%)
Quiz 1	50	A-	= 360-371	(90-92%)
Quiz 2	50	B+	= 352-359	(88-89%)
Quiz 3	50	B	= 329-351	(83-87%)
Quiz 4	50	B-	= 320-328	(80-82%)
Final Exam	100	C+	= 312-319	(78-79%)
Group Project	50	C	= 292-311	(73-77%)
Personal Reflection on		C-	= 288-291	(70-72%)
Group Project	50	D+	= 272-287	(68-69%)

		D	= 252-271	(63-67%)
Possible Points	400	D-	= 240-251	(60-62%)
		F	= 239 and	(below 60%)
			below	

Class Meetings

1   "Introduction and Overview of Course" - Self-Assessment of mastery of skills - Leadership and a Kingdom Vision. Read: Leadership Challenge, Ch. 1

2   "Leadership for a Change" - Looking at the dynamics of bringing change - Case Study: Corazon Aquino. Read: Hersey and Blanchard, pp. 266-285, Leadership Challenge, Ch. 3

3   "Implementing Change as a Leader" - Development of leadership vision - Understanding the culture. Read: Leadership Challenge, Ch. 5, "The Politics of Visionary Thinking"; Quiz: Challenge, Ch. 1, 3, 5; Hersey and Blanchard, pp. 266-285; lectures. *Preliminary proposal for project and group design due.

4   Leadership Week - Some of the team from Washington, D.C. will join us for discussion of "Leadership and the Reality of Jesus Christ"; Team Leadership/Team Building. Read: Challenge, Ch. 7, 8

5   "Decision-Making/Ethics" - Individual vs. Group Decisions - Principles of Good Decision-Making - Christian Ethics and Decision-Making. Read: Gardner, Paper 5 "Moral Aspects of Leadership"; Yukl. Ch. 8, "Participation and Delegation"; Quiz: Challenge, Ch. 7, 8; Gardner #5, Yukl and lectures

6   "Problem-Solving" - Paradigms for Effective Problem-Solving. Read: Yukl, Ch. 9 "Leadership in Decision-Making Groups"

7   "Planning Process" - Critique survey of needs by teams - Weigh alternative through cost analysis - Paradigms of Strategic planning. Read: Challenge, Ch. 10; Planning Handout

8   "Communication and Encouragement Skills." Read: Challenge, Ch. 11, "Recognize Contributions," Hersey and Blanchard, Ch. 10, "Discipline"; Quiz: Yukl, Ch. 9; Challenge Ch. 10, 11, Planning Handout; Hersey and Blanchard, Ch. 10; lectures

9   "Managing Conflict/Successful Meetings" - Conflict Style Assessment - Making Group Meetings Successful. Read: Hersey and Blanchard, pp. 285-293; Begin Getting to Yes

10   "Negotiation." Read: Getting to Yes (all). Quiz: Hersey and Blanchard, 285-293, Getting to Yes

11   "Proposal for Change" - students present proposals to class for analysis and refinement - force-field analysis of proposals. Read: Challenge, Ch. 9

12   Session with President's Administrative Staff

13   Evaluation. Read: Challenge, Ch. 13

14   Final Examination (cumulative)

Forms for stating objectives, detailing projects, and stating expectations from mentors have been designed for students. Leadership scholarships, projects, and certification have been devised.

Section B
PROGRAMS ON COLLEGE AND UNIVERSITY CAMPUSES

Although a leadership course or two in an academic institution can inspire a given number of students profoundly, the incorporation of a course or several into an overall plan can influence the entire institution and all the student body in many ways. In this section are described programs that are in position, others that are on the planning board with some or most components already tested or in the works.

The range is broad. Examples include: Institutes--both within and between disciplines; degree programs--both major and minor; A School of Leadership offering degrees and other educational opportunities; programs that encompass not only the college or university itself, but also the community of which it is a part; a model designed by an inter-college committee that can be adapted and implemented at any number of institutions; modules that can be put into place in other programs and with other persons; ways to design and implement a plan; programs that go beyond single colleges and universities to select students for summer or year-long leadership development; methods for recognizing and rewarding students such as scholarships and ceremonies and transcripts; and ways of incorporating leadership education into more technical and business areas.

The reader is encouraged to pluck out those good ideas that fulfill the potential need of a program and appear to fit the environment. Some plans and programs and even organizations are educational resource mines that can be called upon to customize a match to a particular requirement. In most programs there is clear intent to insure learning about leadership as well as offerings of opportunities for developing leaders. The methods for skill-building and encouraging better citizenship are plentiful. Since residential colleges and universities are appropriate and ready sites for leadership education, they are good places to study as models for replication.

PROGRAMS ON COLLEGE AND UNIVERSITY CAMPUSES

TABLE OF CONTENTS

Alverno College
Effective Citizenship Dept.
3401 S. 39th St., Milwaukee, WI 53215-2040

Leadership Education at Alverno College

Greta Salem
Coordinator
Assoc. Prof. of Social Science
414/382-6245

The educational program helps students develop multiple abilities, orientations and dispositions required for living in a complex world. These personal qualities are the outcomes of a liberal arts education and are important for the exercise of leadership within the framework of leadership education. This integrated liberal arts/professional education enables graduates to live personal, professional and civic lives of value to themselves and others.

Abilities, such as communication, group interaction, and self-assessment are designed as specific learning experiences. Orientation toward thinking in terms of long and short term goals, a tolerance for conflict and ambiguity, and an appreciation for individual/community relationships and the diverse perspectives inherent in them are developed in a series of learning environments. Opportunities are provided curricularly and extra-curricularly for students to accept the initiative and responsibility to conceptualize tasks to achieve specific goals and structure activities and groups to accomplish them.

Integrating learning experiences relevant to leadership education across the curriculum for all students assumes that some will take on formal positions of authority and others will exercise leadership in a number of different settings, but all will need to understand and practice analytic and interpersonal orientations and behaviors that characterize exercise of leadership. How abilities contribute to student leadership potential and how pedagogical strategies and educational environment specifically address the learning goals identified in the leadership education literature are cited below. To meet Alverno's graduation requirements students must demonstrate the achievement of eight abilities which they develop in sequential fashion over time. These abilities--Communication, Analysis, Problem Solving, Valuing, Social Interaction, Responsibility for the Global Environment, Effective Citizenship and Aesthetic Responsiveness--have been defined developmentally by the faculty as broadly agreed upon criteria assessed variously within and across the academic departments.

COMMUNICATION: Leadership literature cites the importance of effective communication, especially speaking and interactive communication. Many sources emphasize listening as an unrecognized and thus underdeveloped ability. At Alverno, communication includes writing, speaking, reading, listening, and the use of media and computers. Social interaction encompasses interpersonal communication and group problem solving. Students work on communicating knowledge and understanding in areas of study and professional areas. Aware of skills already developed and those needing attention, they move to increasingly refined communication as subject matter becomes more complex.

Students begin work on communication upon entrance. In speaking, for example, they make a short presentation recorded on video and, with appropriate guidance, they analyze their strengths and weaknesses in speaking and set personal goals for developing that ability. Initially in a required course and laboratory, and later in diverse content area courses like biology and history, they continue to work on speaking skills and develop the abilities and confidence required for effective presentations. Because faculty have identified specific criteria for effective demonstration in speaking, as in all the abilities, students are able to assess their performance relative to objectively defined standards. They have available a documented history of the speeches they have videotaped as they work to strengthen their skills; this approach is used in helping students develop other communication abilities, writing or using media as a strategy for forceful transmission of their message.

The interactional nature of leadership is addressed in the social interaction ability. In a required course on small group behavior, students learn about several models of social interaction which they then use to evaluate their own participation in groups. Later in other discipline-based courses, students engage in group work to practice, develop and assess their ability to work effectively in groups using video taping which serves as an important assessment tool. Students observe their behavior and faculty view videotaped group interactions to assess and provide feedback. Also, external assessors, men and women from the local community who volunteer their time, are trained for specific interaction assessments and to provide feedback.

Group projects require not only that students work together to accomplish a task, but also to identify the tasks, determine how they are to be accomplished, allocate responsibilities, motivate group members and take responsibility for seeing that all the requisite work is done. Whether these are collaborative projects in writing courses, business simulations or team research, these experiences foster tolerance for ambiguity, exercise of interdependence, need to clarify values, building of motivation, acceptance and management of conflict, and the persistence required to keep a group focused on its goals.

Students socialized in an information transmission model of education find such projects difficult and frustrating in their early years at Alverno. By the time they graduate, however, they have experienced significant growth in abilities and orientations required for effective group participation and have developed a conviction regarding their importance.

INTERDEPENDENCE AND COMMUNITY RESPONSIBILITY: Abilities related to Responsibility for Global Environment and Effective Citizenship focus on wider civic and community participation. Faculty have designed learning experiences to assist students to understand themselves as participants in interdependent systems ranging from intimate to more global relationships. They take courses to acquire substantive knowledge about the operation of national and global systems to foster understanding of the impact of varying perspectives on the analysis of political and social issues. Faculty assist students to view themselves as actors in the public arena with responsibility to take on civic as well as professional roles.

All students take introductory general education courses to become familiar with frameworks for analyzing social and political institutions that foster understanding of complex interrelationships between the person and the environment. This focus is emphasized in science courses examining pollution, acid rain and toxic waste, and in social science courses dealing with poverty, international trade, and social stratification. Students become familiar with a wide range of social and political institutions and learn to appreciate varying perspectives associated with diverse roles, status positions and institutional affiliations, as well as those related to one's own position in the social system.

An explicitly stated component of these abilities is the capacity to understand the impact of various perspectives on judgments made in evaluating events and information. Specific efforts are made to help students understand analysis of issues, how to ask relevant questions, how information is examined, how to offer interpretations and recommend appropriate action. As they advance, all students are required to take at least three courses in which these relationships are central. Students are required to take one of a series of courses that provides an in-depth exploration of a global issue and consideration of actions related to that issue at the local level. A world hunger course, for example, may involve students in assessing the efforts of local hunger task forces or in considering how our consumption habits affect the world-wide resource distribution system.

INTERNSHIPS AND COMMUNITY SERVICE: All Alverno students are required to participate in internships or field experiences associated with their majors. This provides an opportunity for them to apply both the substantive knowledge they have acquired in their major area of study and the communication and social interaction abilities they have developed in the general education program. These learning experiences are relevant to civic and leadership education. Since most civic efforts are communal, it is important for students to learn to analyze formal organizations and function effectively within them. Students involved in an internship take a weekly seminar to share and process what they have learned and assist them to analyze their organizations and their specific roles.

Internships designed for advanced students focusing on leadership abilities include: 1) Advanced internships and field experiences in professional programs such as Education, Nursing, Business and Management, and Professional Communications; 2) participation in a community service project and in an associated Leadership Seminar; or 3) participation in a class with a specific leadership focus and/or a community service project.

Students in advanced seminars or field placements assume roles to exercise responsibility and initiative. In the associated class or seminar, they analyze their experience by focusing on issues related to the practice of leadership and organizational effectiveness. A Business and Management major, for example, is asked to assess her leadership potential, using the leadership frameworks learned in her business courses. She also receives new information on what leadership "looks" like in different organizational settings.

Students work on development of leadership abilities by participating in a community service project based on two goals: 1) to exercise personal initiative in identifying issues that they would like to address and in carving out a role for themselves that would allow them to do so; 2) to make new community connections through volunteer work either on or off campus. Since civic activity of this sort is learned through a socialization process, for those with previous experience, civic activity becomes a means for addressing social problems. Those with no such experience rarely consider civic action as an option. The first step is always the hardest; therefore it is frequently not taken at all; this volunteer service option offers a foundation on which students can build a life of civic involvement.

Students in this volunteer involvement also attend a six session leadership seminar to process their experiences and identify and develop strategies to achieve their personal goals as well as those set by the organization with which they have affiliated. This seminar is also designed to help students understand and develop some of the orientations, abilities, and dispositions identified in the leadership literature, becoming familiar with some of the literature; participating in a conflict management training workshop, and working on nurturing their social imagination, the ability to motivate and organize others and the persistence required to bring projects to a successful resolution. Students are also required to identify a leader with whom they can discuss issues related to leadership styles and experience.

Leadership is also addressed within a number of disciplinary courses many of which include community service components. The following are currently established in the curriculum: 1) An advanced Nursing course required students to devote some time during the course of one semester in volunteer work with a community health service agency. Student logs are required in which they record and analyze their experiences as a basis for class discussion. 2) In a course offered by the Professional Communications Department students serve as consultants to local social service agencies. They work with agency personnel to identify communication needs and negotiate an agreement to provide specific services such as newsletters, slide-tape productions, etc. This experience connects students with community organizations and gives them an opportunity to apply abilities specific to their major. Class time is spent analyzing strategies and organizational and interpersonal challenges confronted in these projects. 3) The Social Science Department requires students to take an Applied Research course in which they apply their research abilities in projects designed to meet the information needs of local community groups and service agencies. They must also negotiate with a client to identify specific information needs and how they can assist in meeting these needs. 4) The Business and Management Division offers a seminar on Women and Leadership. Students read selections from the leadership literature and focus specifically on works dealing with women in leadership positions. Since each student has been assessing her own growing leadership potential as she has moved through the curriculum, a particular goal of this seminar is to engage the student in considering the roles she might take after she graduates. Students are also asked to take on some leadership responsibilities which are monitored and analyzed during the course.

EXTRA-CURRICULAR ACTIVITIES AND STUDENT SERVICE: Here students develop leadership ability by participating in extra-curricular activities, taking on formal leadership roles in the residence halls or as Peer Advisors for new students. They serve as student representatives for the college in meetings with college leaders and with visitors from other institutions. The Student Services Department provides special training as well as ongoing support for those who take on these responsibilities and for those taking the formal leadership roles in student organizations.

Finally, the leadership abilities and a civic orientation are nurtured in Alverno's Travelship Program which provides funding support for students wishing to participate in educational opportunities outside the Milwaukee area but who are financially unable to do so. Students receiving these Travelships attend professional meetings, workshops and seminars, as well as summer or semester long programs in Washington or abroad. Students receiving Travelship support are obligated to take a leading role in the fund raising activities of the Student Services Department which sustains the Travelship Fund. They must also share their experiences either in articles for the school newspapers or in presentations at our annual Student Conference Day. While this program creates an environment to encourage students the exercise of individual initiative and responsibility in gaining support for their educational goals, the criteria for participation also stimulate the development of an enhanced sense of community membership and obligation. In this respect the members of the Alverno community as well as the individual recipients are enriched.

CONCLUSION: In designing the outcome-oriented curriculum and the pedagogical environment in which students learn, Alverno faculty have focused not only on the transmission and application of knowledge, but also on the development of attitudes supportive of life-long learning, a sense of community membership and the development of self-knowledge and self-esteem. These orientations will enable students to meet the challenges of the complex society in which they live and work. Consequently the curriculum is infused with opportunities for students to develop abilities related to judgment-in-action, initiative, leading meetings, communicating group goals and mediating conflicts. We do not promise to graduate "leaders." We do, however, promise that our graduates will have developed some of the necessary attitudes and abilities that make for effective leadership at all levels of society and that contribute to a more meaningful life.

Arizona State University
Alumni Association
Tempe, AZ 85287

Neil G. Giuliano
Director, Constituent Programs
602/965-3566

Insuring Tomorrow - a national leadership network and enrichment program for college and university students

---

The Vision for Insuring Tomorrow

The growing success of the Insuring Tomorrow program at ASU has led Associated Students and the Sun Angel Foundation to the concept of building a national network of student leaders to plan and implement the Insuring Tomorrow program for their campus community. As a national leadership network and enrichment program, Insuring Tomorrow will focus on the important issues of the day and recognize student leaders from across the nation who have made outstanding contributions to their organization, campus and community. As of this writing fifteen colleges and universities have joined the network insuring the program for their communities.

The Insuring Tomorrow program is comprised of the following:

- A recognition program honoring the Outstanding Student leaders on your campus.
- A one-day Issues Conference which brings together selected student leaders and members of the professional organization you select to be the co-sponsor of the program for your campus, i.e.: a booster group, alumni association, faculty association, local civic group. This conference will cover the topics your planning committee determines to be of interest for your campus and community. Group interaction is stressed using the Insuring Tomorrow Issues Conference format.
- A recognition banquet or luncheon, as part of the Issues Conference, features the Outstanding Student Leader Award recipients and a Keynote Speaker who is well known. This event should be the highlight of the program on your campus, with administrators and community leaders in attendance.

What You Receive as a Member of the Insuring Tomorrow National Leadership Network and Enrichment Program

- The Insuring Tomorrow Program Planning Guide: a three-ring binder contains all the details, guidelines, sample correspondence, budgets, agendas, programs and information necessary to successfully plan and implement the program.

- Four (4) subscriptions to the Insuring Tomorrow National Newsletter: containing information on Insuring Tomorrow programs across the country, features on student leaders, program suggestions and hints and articles written by members.

- The Insuring Tomorrow National Directory: a comprehensive listing of the students and campuses involved with Insuring Tomorrow by name and interest area or major. A members-only registration rate for the Insuring Tomorrow National Issues Conference: with national issues, speakers and recognizing the national outstanding

142

leader award recipients.

CED 498 ST: Personal Leadership Development   Neil G. Giuliano
3 cr. hrs.

<u>Purpose of the course and proposed outcomes are to develop students'</u>: understanding of leadership in a variety of situations; awareness of their own skills, interests and abilities; communication skills in group settings; awareness of leadership theory; change, conflict, time, and stress management skills; meeting and project planning skills; self-discovery and potential.

<u>By completion of the course you will have learned or experienced</u>: a sense of accomplishment in learning about yourself and others; cooperative atmosphere among students and instructor; increased awareness of your style of relating to others; expanded awareness of your creative potential.

<u>Factual Outcomes</u>: greater knowledge of the role and impact of a leader; strategies for broadening your leadership potential; ways to organize, motivate, confront and apply people and projects; processes for handling various leadership situations.

<u>Skill Outcomes</u>: skills will be developed in each topical area covered in the course.

Weekly Class Sessions will cover the following topics and assignments:

1. <u>"So You Want To Be A Leader"</u> - Welcome, course review, expectations.

2. <u>"Preparing To Study Leadership"</u> - What is it? Who is a leader? Am I ready to lead? Values in leadership.

3. <u>"Qualities of a Leader"</u> - The leadership profile.

4. <u>Special Guests</u>: the ASU Vice-President for Student Affairs and the President of Associated Students. Self-analysis paper due. Group projects information.

5. <u>"The Latest Style May Not Be Yours"</u> - Leadership styles and theories.

6. <u>"Personal Leadership Expansion"</u> - Expanding your power base.

7. <u>Group Presentations (two)</u> - Review for Exam I.

8. <u>Exam I</u>.

9. <u>Group Presentations (two)</u> - "When the Best of Me Brings Out the Best In You" Teamwork.

10.   "Student Foundation Leadership Seminars" (4 hours). Ten points extra credit for attendance and a one-page written summary. $12.00 includes materials and luncheon.

11.   "When You Wish Upon a Star, Don't Count on Anything Happening" - Goal Setting. Building Action plans.

12.   Group Presentations (two) - "I know I explained it to them." Communicating what you mean.

13.   Paper #2 is Due - "Problems, Problems, Problems, Decisions, Decisions, Decisions, Decisions." Strategic decision making.

14.   Group Presentations (two) - "The Art of Confrontation." How do you handle conflict?

15.   Group Presentations (two) - "Being a 'Charitable' Chair." Agenda building and running a meeting.

16.   "It Ain't Over Till It's Over" - End of semester party, review for Exam II.

17.   Exam II.

PERFORMANCE EVALUATION AND GRADING: Exams - 200 points total - There are two and they are short answer, short essay type, worth 100 points each. Papers - 150 points total - Your first paper is an in-depth self-analysis of your strengths and weaknesses. The other will be a reaction paper to the book The Choice by Og Mandino. Leadership in Action - 100 points total - Each class member will be a team member for a project to implement a community service project for the campus. This is an opportunity to demonstrate vision and skill. Teams will meet with the instructor on the project development. Group Project - 100 points total - Groups of 5 students will each be responsible for a short (30-40 minute) class presentation on a leadership topic. Criteria for grading will be explained. Each group participant gets the same number of points. 100 points available. Attendance - 75 points total - You've got to be here and participate to fully understand the information presented. So, 5 points will be awarded for attendance at each class session. (15 sessions at 5 points = 75 points). Participation - 75 points total - Your class involvement, attitude, effort, contributions, assignments and overall performance as a student in the course will be reviewed, and points awarded, at the discretion of the instructor for an excellent, good, average, or below average scale. MAXIMUM POINTS = 700: A = 630-700 points; B - 560-629 points; C = 490-559 points. Note: The 700 points does not include the extra credit for the Student Foundation Leadership Seminar or other extra credit opportunities.

Evaluation

Total Respondents: 36   Subgroup Respondents: 36

Response Set: A - Very descriptive   Response Weight: A - 05
                        B -   B - 04
                        C -   C - 03
                        D -   D - 02
                        E - Not descriptive   E - 01

	A	B	C	D	E	Miss.	N	Mean	SD	MDN

1) Has command of the subject, . . .

	A	B	C				N	Mean	SD	MDN
Total f:	34	1	1				36	4.92	0.37	5.0
Total %:	94.4	2.8	2.8							

2) Presents material in a clear and organized manner, . . .

	A	B					N	Mean	SD	MDN
Total f:	34	2					36	4.94	0.23	5.0
Total %:	94.4	5.6								

3) Is sensitive to the response of the class, . . .

	A	B					N	Mean	SD	MDN
Total f:	34	2					36	4.94	0.23	5.0
Total %:	94.4	5.6								

4) Is available to and friendly toward students, . . .

	A	B	C				N	Mean	SD	MDN
Total f:	29	5	2				36	4.75	0.55	5.0
Total %:	80.6	13.9	5.6							

5) Enjoys teaching, is enthusiastic about the subject, . . .

	A	B					N	Mean	SD	MDN
Total f:	33	3					36	4.92	0.28	5.0
Total %:	91.7	8.3								

Response Set: A - Among the very best   Response Weight: A - 05
                        B -   B - 04
                        C -   C - 03
                        D -   D - 02
                        E - Among the very worst   E - 01

	A	B	C	D	E	Miss.	N	Mean	SD	MDN

6) How does the instructor of this course compare, . . .

	A	B	C	D			N	Mean	SD	MDN
Total f:	33	1	1	1			36	4.83	0.61	5.0
Total %:	91.7	2.8	2.8	2.8						

Leadership Scholarship Program   Gabriel Vasquez

The Arizona State University Student Leadership Scholarship Program recognizes 15 outstanding Arizona high school graduating seniors who have achieved excellence in leadership. Students selected for the program will have demonstrated leadership abilities and responsibilities. Serious consideration is also given to academic performance as well as community service.

The award will be renewed each year the recipient attends Arizona State University as an undergraduate. Renewal criteria include: continued involvement in the leadership program and successful academic progress.

The award includes a fee waiver valued at $1220, a $1200 scholarship for the first year, and a $700 scholarship the sophomore through senior years. The scholarship currently carries a four-year total value of $8180; however, any increase in University fees will be covered by the waiver.

In addition to the financial award, the students participate in the following activities: leadership development training; academic and career counseling; seminars with community/national leaders; social recreational events.

Two awards are granted annually to non-Arizona residents who have achieved leadership excellence in Key Club International, a high school service and leadership organization sponsored by Kiwanis International. The four-year tuition and fee waiving is valued at over $20,000.

College of Wooster
Classical Studies & History
Wooster, OH 44691

Vivian L. Holliday
Professor
216/263-2488

Leadership and Liberal Learning

At The College of Wooster, the study of leadership is placed within the context of a liberal arts curriculum.

Wooster's program, **Leadership and Liberal Learning**, has been recognized as a model for the balanced investigation of leadership and the exploration of both its theoretical and practical aspects. Established in 1984, Wooster's program combines an interdisciplinary, team-taught, semester-long seminar and a field experience emphasizing the direct observation of leaders in a variety of contexts which include government, industry, education, the arts, and foundations.

The third component of the Leadership Program is an annual symposium which serves as a stimulus to the further examination of leadership and its development in the context of the concerns of the invited guests.

Leadership: Theory and Practice - Interdepartmental 390
T, Th: 2:30-3:50

Description: The Leadership Seminar focuses on significant theories of leadership and their applicability to accounts of leaders, past and present. The major objectives of the Seminar are: to investigate major theories of the art and science of leadership; to read, view, reflect upon and discuss nonfictional and fictional accounts of leaders in diverse cultural and temporal contexts, with special emphasis on the global interdependence and consequences of contemporary acts of leadership; to provide through theoretical and case studies a foundation upon which to build a better understanding of leadership; to prepare for the intensive field experience of interaction with leaders participating in the Acquaintanceship and with senior scholars participating in the Symposium; to scrutinize, evaluate, and contribute to multidisciplinary scholarship on leadership.

Methods: Each topic is introduced through selected readings and occasionally viewing films or videos to be announced at least one class session prior to viewing. Class discussions and visiting lecturers complement individual student's analysis of theoretical concepts, issues, and situations of leadership addressed in the readings and/or viewing.

Participants are responsible for producing for each topic a one- to two-page critique (or "Talking-Paper") on some aspect of the topic treated in the assigned reading or viewing (see Topics A-J under **"Description"**). Appendices are helpful in framing some questions and topics you wish to raise in your Talking-Paper and discussions.

Visiting faculty discussants will join us after the second week of the Seminar. While they will introduce and guide the discussion, it will be our responsibility to focus on topics and questions germane to our program of inquiry into leadership. We will have opportunities during the Symposium to raise questions with the presenters (see tentative program in the Appendices).

Reading, Viewing, Symposium Participation, and Final Essays: Under each topic are listed required reading and viewing. In addition to those listed, brief selections may be assigned or suggested from the works listed in the Appendix: "Bibliography" and from the publications of the Symposium speakers.

Full participation in all sessions, including the Symposium, is assumed. In addition to the sessions scheduled, we will gather informally from time to time. Informal social gatherings are optional.

There will be a Final Essay (12-15 pages double-spaced), a draft of which will be due on date noted with the completed Final Essay due no later than 4:00 p.m. two weeks later. Select for the Final Essay one (or more) leadership issue(s) from those studied and discuss the issue(s) in light of your study and experiences in the Acquaintanceship. What impact does your current understanding of the issue have on your views of the act of leadership? Your perception of leaders and followers? Of the feasibility of educating for leadership without cultural hegemony?

Evaluation: 40% of the grade is based on the quality and quantity of participation in the Seminar. In determining this portion of your grade, I will weigh heavily evidence of careful and thorough reading, viewing, reflection upon, and analysis of the assigned material. I will also consider the degree to which you explored during the Acquaintanceship experience and the Symposium the issues raised in the Seminar; 40% of your grade will be based on the quality of your "Talking-Point Papers" for each topic; 20% of your grade will be based on your work in the Final Essay.

SYLLABUS

A. **What is Leadership? Theory X, Theory Y, Theory. . ./Multidisciplinary Views**
Class Sessions 1-4.

Introduction to the course/Exploration of the basic theories and literature of leadership/Consideration of "permutations of the question, 'What is Leadership?': Do leaders require followers? Does the concept of leadership have different meanings in different institutional, national, or historical settings? Does the role of leader assume authority? Does this authority require consent? How do power and authority relate in the concept of leadership? How do leaders actually lead? How do we assess how well they lead?" [Irving J. Spitzberg, Jr., "Paths of Inquiry into Leadership," Liberal Education, March/April 1987, p. 24.]

Reading/Viewing [See Appendices for full bibliography.]
Required: Bennis and Nanus, Leaders; Cronin, "Thinking and Learning About Leadership"

[**handout**]; Sophocles, <u>Antigone</u>; Plato, "The Philosopher-King" from <u>The Republic</u>, Cornford translation (1941), pp. 175-263 [**handout**]; Thucydides, <u>The Peloponnesian War</u>, Rex Warner translation, selections announced in class [**reserve**].
<u>Recommended</u>: Burns, <u>Leadership</u> (Harper Colophon, 1978), pp. 9-28, 228-240, 444-462 [**reserve**].

B. Leadership: Style and Power

Reading/Viewing - Sessions 5, 6
<u>Required</u>: Shakespeare, <u>Julius Caesar</u>, edited by William and Barbara Rosen, including selections from Plutarch (in Signet Classics edition, pp. 139-182 or in a more recent translation). Visiting Discussion Leader, Professor Peter Havholm, English.

Reading/Viewing - Sessions 7, 8
<u>Required</u>: Machiavelli, <u>The Prince</u> (in <u>The Portable Machiavelli</u> translated and edited by Bondanella and Musa) and selections to be announced. Visiting Discussion Leader, Professor Mark Weaver, Political Science.

C. Leadership in the Japanese Context

Reading/Viewing - Sessions 9, 10
<u>Required</u>: Vogel, <u>Japan as Number One</u>; Nakane, <u>Japanese Society</u>;
Taichi Sakaiya, "The Japanese Company's Fatal Flaw," <u>Intersect</u>, October 1988, pp. 14-16; Sano Yoki, "Seven Mysteries of Long Working Hours," <u>Japan Quarterly</u>, July-September 1988, pp. 248-252. Visiting Discussion Leader, Professor Frank Miller, Political Science.

D. Leadership: Organizations and Corporations

Reading/Viewing - Sessions 11, 12
<u>Required:</u> Geneen and Moscow, <u>Managing</u> (Doubleday, 1984) or Iacocca and Novak, <u>Iacocca</u> (Bantam, 1984); Lee Bolman and Terence Deal, chs. 14, 15, 16 and Epilogue in <u>Modern Approaches to Understanding in Managing Organizations</u> [**reserve**]; Rosabeth M. Kanter, "Power Skills in Use: Corporate Entrepreneurs in Action" (in <u>The Change Masters</u>) [**handout**].

<u>Recommended Viewing:</u> <u>Iacocca: An American Profile</u>.

Visiting Discussion Leaders, Professors John Sell, Business Economics, Session 11, and Charles Hurst, Sociology, Session 12.

E. Military Leadership

Reading/Viewing - Sessions 13, 14
<u>Required</u>: Josiah Bunting III, "George C. Marshall: A Study in Character [**handout**]; Martin Blumenson, "Leadership and the Art of Command: Together With Some Thoughts

on George S. Patton, Jr." [**handout**]; Selections from Cornelius Ryan, The Longest Day [**handout**]; Selections from David Donovan, Once A Warrior King [**handout**]; Fred Downs, "Death and the Dark Side of Command" [**handout**]; John M. Gates, "American Military Leadership in the Vietnam War" [**handout**].

Viewing: film Patton.

We will meet with Professor John Gates, History, at my home, Session 14.

F.   **Leadership and the American Presidency/Politics, Leadership and Character**

Reading/Viewing - Sessions 15, 16, 17
Required: Selections from Barbara Kellerman, The Political Presidency; David Stockman, "The Triumph of Politics," Newsweek (April 21, 1986), pp. 40-59, and Newsweek (April 28, 1986), pp. 50-64; and The Tower Commission Report, pp. 462-487 [**handout**].

Visiting Discussion Leader, Professor Eric Moskowitz, Political Science, Session 15; Symposium, 7:00 p.m., Session 16; Panel Response to Symposium led by Professor James Hodges, History, Session 17.

SPRING BREAK AND ACQUAINTANCESHIP - Next Several Sessions

G.   **Leadership, Social Conscience and Ethics** - Next 6 Sessions

Required: Oates, Let The Trumpet Sound; Selections from Simone Weil, An Anthology, edited by Sian Miles.

Viewing: to be announced.

Acquaintanceship Debriefing, 2 sessions; Symposium, next session; Professor Terry Kershaw, Sociology, Visiting Discussion Leader, 2 sessions; Professor Richard Bell, Philosophy, Visiting Discussion Leader, 1 session.

H.   **Leadership and Gender**

Reading/Viewing - Two Sessions
Required: Virginia Woolf, Three Guineas; Selections from Sarah Hardesty and Nehama Jacobs, Success and Betrayal [**reserve**]. Visiting Discussion Leaders, Professor Joanne Frye, Women's Studies and English and Professor Barbara Burnell, Economics.

I.   **Leadership and Communication**

Reading/Viewing - Two Sessions
Required: Jameson/Campbell, The Interplay of Influence, Chapters 4 and 11 [**handout**];

Garber, <u>Mass Media</u>, and <u>American Politics</u>, Chapters 7 and 8 [**handout**].

<u>Viewing</u>: Selected Political TV Advertisements 1950s-1980s and other video selections.

Visiting Discussion Leader, Professor Amos Kiewe, Speech Communications.

J.   Educating for Leadership without Cultural Hegemony - Two Sessions

We will discuss with one another and a number of visitors the appropriate education for creative responses to diverse voices, agendas, and contexts of leadership. Among those invited to join us if their schedules permit are Mr. Henry Luce III, Mr. Stanley Gault, and the following Wooster administrators: Henry Copeland, President; Donald Harward, Vice President of Academic Affairs; Glenn Bucher, Dean of the Faculty.

APPENDIX: BIBLIOGRAPHY

<u>Leadership Education '87: A Source Book</u>, edited by Clark, Freeman, and Britt, contains on pages 329-389 an extensive annotated bibliography of possible sources for research and study of leadership. For the sake of convenience, I include below some of the brief descriptions provided in <u>A Source Book</u> on the pages noted above (herein deleted).

Required reading of considerable length is listed without annotation while shorter selections are usually omitted from the bibliography.

Bennis, W. G. (1985). <u>Leaders: The strategies for taking charge</u>. New York: Harper & Row.; Burns, J. M. (1978). <u>Leadership</u>. Harper & Row; Campbell, C. (1986). <u>Managing the presidency: Carter, Reagan, and the search for executive harmony</u>. Pittsburgh, PA: University of Pittsburgh Press; Clemens, J. K. & Mayer, D. F. (1987). <u>The classic touch: Lessons in leadership from Homer to Hemingway</u>. Homewood, IL: Dow Jones-Irwin; Cohen, M. D., & March, J. G. (1986). <u>Leadership and ambiguity</u>. 2nd ed. Boston, MA: Harvard Business School Press; Cronin, T. E. (1980). <u>The State of the Presidency</u>. Boston: Little, Brown; Cronin, T. E., "Thinking and Learning About Leadership," <u>Presidential Studies Quarterly</u>, Vol. XIV, Number 1, Winter 1984; Erikson, E. H. (1970). <u>Gandhi's truth: On the origins of militant nonviolence</u>. New York: Norton; Freidl, E., <u>Vasilika, A Village in Modern Greece</u>. (1962); Gardner, J. W., <u>Leadership Papers</u> 1-7 (1964-1987). [The seven papers are as follows: 1. "The Nature of Leadership: Introductory Considerations"; 2. "The Tasks of Leadership"; 3. "The Heart of the Matter: Leader-Constituent Interaction"; 4. "Leadership and Power"; 5. "The Moral Aspect of Leadership"; 6. "Attributes and Context"; 7. "Leadership Development." All 7 papers were prepared for the Leadership Studies Program sponsored by Independent Sector]; Geneen, H. S., & Moscow, A. (1984). <u>Managing</u>. New York: Doubleday; Greenleaf, R. K. (1977).

Servant leadership: A journey into the nature of legitimate power and greatness. New York: Paulist Press; Hartsock, N. C., Money, Sex, and Power (1983). Northwestern University Press; Iacocca, L. and Novak, W. (1984). Iacocca: An autobiography. New York: Bantam Books; Kanter, R. M. (1983). The change masters: Innovation for productivity in the American corporation. New York: Simon & Schuster; Kanter, R. M. (1977). Men and women of the corporation. New York: Basic Books; Kellerman, B. (Ed.). (1986). The Political Presidency. Oxford University Press; Kellerman, B. (Ed.). (1986). Political leadership. Pittsburgh, PA: University of Pittsburgh Press; Keegan, J. The Mask of Command; Kellerman, B. (Ed.). (1984). Leadership: Multidisciplinary perspectives. Englewood Cliffs, NJ: Prentice-Hall; Little, M., & Haley, A. (1965). The autobiography of Malcolm X. New York: Grove Press; Lipman-Blumen, J. (1984). Gender roles and power. Englewood Cliffs, NJ: Prentice-Hall; Machiavelli, N. The Portable Machiavelli, edited and translated by P. Bondonella and Mark Musa. Penguin; Morrison, A., White, R., and Van Velsor, E., Breaking the Glass Ceiling: Can Women Make it to the Top in America's Largest Corporations? (1987). Addison-Wesley; Nakane, Chie, Japanese Society. (1970). University of California Press; Neustadt, R. (1980) Presidential Power: The politics of Leadership from FDR to Carter. New York: Wiley; Neustadt, R. E., & May, E. R. (1986). Thinking in time. New York: Free Press; Oates, S. B. (1983). Let the Trumpet sound: The life of Martin Luther King, Jr. New York: New American Library; Ouchi, W. (1981). Theory Z. Reading, MA: Addison-Wesley; Rubenstein, Richard E. Alchemists of Revolution: Terrorism in the Modern World. (1987). Basic Books; Shakespeare. Julius Caesar. Signet Classics; Sophocles. Antigone; Smith, Robert C. Black Leadership: A Survey of Theory and Research. Howard University; Thucydides. The Peloponnesian War, Rex Warner translator. Penguin; Vogel, Ezra F. Japan as Number One. (1979). Harper Torchbooks; Woolf, Virginia. Three Guineas. Harvest; Yukl, G. A. (1981). Leadership in organizations. Englewood Cliffs, NJ: Prentice-Hall.

APPENDIX: SHAPIRO RESEARCH ON LEADERSHIP AND ETHICS

During the summer of 1987, George Shapiro presented at the Leadership Education Conference (see "Special Report, Leadership Education Conference, 1987," compiled and edited by Miriam B. Clark) an updated report on his continuing research on "ethical leadership." Professor Shapiro of the University of Minnesota in his small sample research (for details on selection of interviewees, see "Special Report") asked the following questions:

(1) Name the most ethical leader you have interacted with in the past seven years.
(2) Why did you select her/him? (3) What additional attributes are important?
(4) How would you evaluate yourself on the attributes you have listed? (5) What must be done to improve your lowest scores? (6) What causes your "Dark Moments" . . . your "Moments of Despair"? (7) What do you do at those times?

(8) Given Freedom, Justice, Order and Caring, which one do you value most highly and why? (9) How would people who watch you lead describe your highest priority? (10) What were the experiences that had the greatest impact on your ethical behavior? (11) What do you want from Ethical Followers? (12) What do you do to encourage Ethical Followers? (13) What would you do if it was your responsibility to develop ethical leaders and ethical followers? --from George Shapiro in "Special Report," Leadership Education Conference, 1987, p. 80.

Professor Shapiro summarized the results of his interviews as follows:

1. Ethical leaders express a strong commitment to the mission; 2. Ethical leaders express a strong respect for and caring about the individual person; 3. Ethical leaders are seen to be competent informed people; 4. Ethical leaders express the belief that bad means cannot result in good ends; 5. Ethical leaders report that they experience extremely lonely times; 6. Ethical leaders express, as their core value, their belief in the right to dignity of all persons; 7. Ethical leaders express a willingness to laugh at themselves; 8. Ethical leaders report having early models; 9. Ethical leaders report that intercultural experiences were important in shaping their ethical perspective; 10. Ethical leaders appear to be androgynous; 11. Ethical leaders appear to be committed relativists. --from George Shapiro in "Special Report," Leadership Education Conference, 1987, p. 201.

You may find Shapiro's questions and summary helpful. As we discuss ethics and leadership, I will share other details of the study with you.

APPENDIX: "Some Views of Leadership" compiled by Professor James Hodges on pages 1-10 of the syllabus for "Leadership: Theory and Practice" 1986.

I. Some Views of Leadership

Leadership is a word on everyone's lips. The young attack it and the old grow wistful for it. Parents have lost it and police seek it. Experts claim it and artists spurn it, while scholars want it. Philosophers reconcile it (as authority) with liberty and theologians demonstrate its compatibility with conscience. If bureaucrats pretend they have it, politicians wish they did. Everybody agrees that there is less of it than there used to be. . . . If there was ever a moment in history when a comprehensive strategic view of leadership was needed, not just by a few leaders in high office but by large numbers of leaders in every job, from the factory floor to the executive suite, from a McDonald's fast-food franchise to a law firm, this is certainly it. --from Warren Bennis and Burt Nanus, Leaders: The Strategies for Taking Charge (1985).

The Fremont [Calif.] plant is a classic example. It was so bad, we closed it. The problem was supposed to be "labor relations," a term I just hate. We decided to do a joint venture with Toyota. Toyota reopened Fremont and hired the same "recalcitrant" people. Today the highest-quality cars built by General Motors in the United States are built in the Fremont plant by the same people who were so bad we closed the plant. What's the difference? Japanese-style management: the philosophy that every employee is a brother. Is it possible to save our big companies? Sure, it's the easiest thing in the world. <u>All we've got to have is a little leadership. Absolutely, there is a vacuum in corporate America now, a horrible leadership vacuum</u>. We're turning out very bright, very able people who could have been incredible leaders, but they are manipulators, numbers guys, merger-and-acquisitions guys. They destroy tens of thousands of jobs. Now we've got to change the emphasis, which we can do, and put it on leadership and building and making our companies competitive. --from Ross Perot, late of General Motors Board.

Leadership has an elusive, mysterious quality about it. It is easy to recognize, hard to describe, difficult to practice, and almost impossible to create in others on demand. Perhaps no other topic has attracted as much attention from observers, participants, and philosophers--with so little agreement as to basic facts. --from David Campbell in William E. Rosenbach & Robert L. Taylor, <u>Contemporary Issues in Leadership</u>.

I think the very best leaders are those who, when things go well and the job is done, nobody really knows who the leader was. --from Marty Schottenheimer, Cleveland Browns Head Coach.

Leaders differ not only in terms of their official role, but also according to the values and attitudes they promote and defend. Leaders succeed only when they embody and express, for better or worse, values rooted in the social character of group, class, or nation. --from Michael Maccoby, <u>The Leader</u>. See Maccoby who for his study of leaders developed the leadership interview. You might want to answer the questions and decide what kind of leader you are.

One of the most universal cravings of our time is a hunger for compelling and creative leadership. . . The crisis of leadership today is the mediocrity or irresponsibility of so many men and women in power. . . We know far too little about <u>Leadership</u>. . . Leadership is one of the most observed and least understood phenomena on earth. . . There is, in short, no school of leadership, intellectual or practical. --from James MacGregor Burns, <u>Leadership</u>.

Leadership is one of the most widely talked about subjects and at the same time one of the most elusive and puzzling. Americans often yearn for great, transcending leadership for their communities, companies, the military, unions, universities, sports teams, and for the nation. However, we have an almost love-hate ambivalence about power wielders. And we especially dislike anyone who tries to boss us around. Yes, we admire the Washingtons and Churchills, but Hitler and Al Capone were leaders too--and that points up a fundamental problem. Leadership can be exercised in the service of noble, liberating, enriching ends, but it can also serve to manipulate, mislead and repress. --from Thomas

E. Cronin, "Thinking and Learning About Leadership."

Characteristics of Leaders: Appropriately bright, mentally alert; Seek out responsibility, like to control; Skilled in the organization's core activities; Energetic; Good communicators; Resilient, can withstand stress; Free from pathological quirks; Can learn from experience; Perhaps a little lonely. --from David Campbell, his scientifically reduced Trait List, Center for Creative Leadership.

A definition should do more than identify leaders and indicate the means by which they acquire their position. It should account also for the maintenance and continuation of leadership. Thus, few groups engage in interaction merely for the purpose of creating leaders and dropping them as soon as they emerge. For the purposes of this Handbook, leadership must be defined broadly. Leadership is an interaction between members of a group. Leaders are agents of change, persons whose acts affect other people more than other people's acts affect them. Leadership occurs when one group member modifies the motivation or competencies of others in the group. Research in the 1970s often expressed this as the directing of attention of other members to goals and the paths to achieve them. It should be clear that with this definition, any member of the group can exhibit some amount of leadership. Members will vary in the extent they do so.

Four decades of research on leadership have produced a bewildering mass of findings. . . The endless accumulation of empirical data has not produced an integrated understanding of leadership. --from Bernard M. Bass, Stogdill's Handbook of Leadership (Behavioral Science research on leadership--856 pp., costing $47.95).

In summary, the effective leader must have a desire for impact, for being strong and influential [by which he means power]. Moreover, this need must be stronger than either the need for personal achievement or the need to be liked by others." --from James L. Fisher, Power of the Presidency.

A leader must know how to use power (that's what leadership is all about). . . --from Michael Korda.

But as long as anyone in a leadership role operates with reward-punishment assumptions about motivation, he is implicitly assuming that he has (or should have) control over others and that they are in a jackass position with respect to him. Such a relationship is inevitably one of condescending contempt whose most blatant mask is paternalism. The result of that psychological position is a continuing battle between those who seek to wield power and those who are subject to it, as reflected in the Harmon study referred to earlier, and in the history of labor-management relations. The consequences are increased inefficiency, lowered productivity, heightened absenteeism, and other modes of withdrawal from engagement in a combative struggle. --from Harry Levinson, The Great Jackass Fallacy.

Eight Leadership Principles for Modern Corporations

1. A bias for action: a preference for doing something--anything--rather than sending a question through cycles and cycles of analyses and committee reports.
2. Staying close to the customer--learning his preferences and catering to them.
3. Autonomy and entrepreneurship--breaking the corporation into small companies and encouraging them to think independently and competitively.
4. Productivity through people--creating in **all** employees the awareness that their best efforts are essential and that they will share in the rewards of the company's success.
5. Hands-on, value driven--insisting that executives keep in touch with the firm's essential business.
6. Stick to the knitting--remaining with the business the company knows best.
7. Simple form, lean staff--few administrative layers, few people at the upper levels.
8. Simultaneous loose-tight properties--fostering a climate where there is dedication to the central values of the company combined with tolerance for all employees who accept those values. --from Thomas J. Peters and Robert H. Waterman, Jr., In Search of Excellence.

Knowing more about leadership will enable us to better understand our past and present, and, hopefully, to better manage the future. --from Barbara Kellerman (ed.), Leadership: Multidisciplinary Perspectives.

The problem is that no field of study calls for a more difficult and daring crossing of disciplinary borders than does the study of Leadership, and no field suffers more from narrow specialization. --from James MacGregor Burns in Kellerman (ed.), Leadership: Multidisciplinary Perspectives.

Much of the traditional literature on leadership and political elites has overlooked women or portrayed them in a distorted manner. When women have appeared in leadership positions, they frequently have been treated as though they were invisible, or barely visible and insignificant. Moreover, statements about women often have been undocumented with empirical evidence and frequently reflected an underlying assumption that males are naturally suited for leadership while females and female traits are incompatible with the idea of leadership. --from Susan J. Carroll, "Feminist Scholarship of Political Leadership" in Kellerman (ed.), Leadership: Multidisciplinary Perspectives.

Leadership [in colleges and universities] seems to be less a matter of straightforward instrumental action and hierarchical control than is anticipated by classical descriptions. In examining those decision processes and the president's role in them, we picture college presidents as generally more powerful than others in the college but as having less power than casual observers or participants frequently believe they do, or than they often expect to have on entering office. In a world that is difficult to predict and control, we commend an approach to leadership that recognizes, even encourages, ambiguity. --from Michael D. Cohen and James G. March, Leadership and Ambiguity.

Where is Outrage?

It is my belief that in our time institutions, and each of us individually, face a real test of moral leadership. We are bound together by commitments each of us made long ago to live by constitutional principles, religious convictions, and our inherent desire for justice, decency and fair play.

[He reminded his audience--presidents, administrators and deans of North Carolina colleges and universities--that among their responsibilities was the training of] courageous leaders committed to serving the public good. Our country has no greater need than that of generations of graduates who through useful and constructive lives will advance the ongoing cause of human freedom at home and abroad. . . What greater and more rewarding opportunity might we possess? --from William Friday, President, University of North Carolina, from an editorial, The Charlotte Observer.

The fact is that the institutions which portray themselves as producing "tomorrow's leaders" do not systematically explore the significance and implications of understanding leadership. Moreover, even if the conceptual work were accomplished, the relation between understanding and practice is not cultivated in our colleges. Neither the conceptual nor the pragmatic dimensions appear as explicit objectives of liberal arts programs, and students are not encouraged explicitly in the curriculum to believe that their creative potential can be developed or that they can become better leaders. However, without both concept and practice, developing leaders will continue to be "accidental." --from Donald Harward, Vice President/Academic Affairs, The College of Wooster.

The 1989 symposium encourages your participation in this effort to understand "the diverse voices and agendas of leadership."

LEADERSHIP'S DIVERSE
VOICES AND AGENDAS

Wednesday, March 1

7:30 p.m.   **WELCOME: Vivian Holliday**, Professor of Classical Studies, History and the Leadership Seminar, The College of Wooster

7:15 p.m.   **POLITICS, LEADERSHIP AND CHARACTER**
Mary F. Berry, Geraldine R. Segal Professor of American Social Thought, University of Pennsylvania. Former U. S. Assistant Secretary for Education in the Department of Health, Education and Welfare. Commissioner, U. S. Commission on Civil Rights.

William Mayer, Department of Government, Harvard University

Tuesday, March 28

2:00 p.m.   **WELCOME: Vivian Holliday**

2:15 p.m.   **LEADERSHIP AND THE NATION'S SOCIAL AGENDA**
                 Charles Murray, Social and research scientist, Manhattan Institute for
                 Policy Research

                 Molly Yard, President, National Organization of Women

7:00 p.m.   **LEADERSHIP, INDIVIDUAL RIGHTS, AND THE COMMON GOOD**
                 Daniel Schorr, Senior Analyst, National Public Radio. Former
                 correspondent, The New York Times, Christian Science Monitor, London
                 Daily Mail, and "CBS News"

We are pleased to recognize that the Leadership and Liberal Learning Program at The
College of Wooster is made possible by support from The Henry Luce Foundation.

Danielson Associates
411 S. Sangamon, Ste. 5A
Chicago, IL 60607

Doris K. Danielson
Public Relations
312/243-7890

Inroads, Inc.

Inroads develops and places talented minority youth in business and industry and prepares them for corporate and community leadership. Blacks, Hispanics and Native Americans are eligible. Preference goes to high school and college students with 3.0 or better grade averages.

Since Inroads started in Chicago in 1970 with 25 college student interns and 17 sponsoring corporations, the organization has grown to 34 affiliates, some 3,600 high school and college students, and over 1,000 sponsoring corporations. More than 1,400 graduates are pursuing professional and managerial careers.

For college students, Inroads four-year internships combine summer work experience at a local sponsoring corporation with year-round academic instruction, training, and guidance from Inroads counselors. For high school students, it combines intensive instruction in basic academic skills (math, science, English) with career counseling. The Pre-College Component works with 27 host universities.

Inroads is tough, requiring a long-term commitment from both interns and sponsoring corporations. College interns must complete their job assignments to the sponsors' satisfaction; they must remain in good academic standing, participate in Inroads training and counseling, and set goals for their career, education, social development, and community service. Unsatisfactory performance in any area leads to dismissal.

Sponsoring corporations pledge to develop a career opportunity for each intern, provide two performance evaluations each summer, and designate a coordinator/liaison to Inroads, as well as an advisor or mentor for each student sponsored. The company pays an annual sponsorship fee to Inroads and the intern's summer salary.

On average, two-thirds of each year's graduates are offered and accept full-time positions with Inroads sponsors. More than 9 in 10 sponsors recommend participation to other companies, and alumni unanimously recommend Inroads to minority youth. Both alumni and parents have organized nationally to support the organization and students.

Inroads is privately funded through corporate sponsorship fees, foundation grants, and contributions; no government funds are involved. Inroads has 34 affiliates from coast to coast, with plans to add two in 1989.

Duke University
Institute of Policy Sciences and Public Affairs
Box 4875, Duke Station, Durham, NC 27706

Bob Braverman
Director
919/684-5475

The Leadership Program at Duke University

A Statement of Mission: Objectives and Strategy

INTRODUCTION: A belief that the country has urgent needs for abler and more ethical leadership, and that students might become better leaders through more active, imaginative, and experiential kinds of learning, led in 1985 to the establishment of the Leadership Program at Duke. The program is part of Duke's Institute of Policy Sciences and Public Affairs, which has sponsored our courses and appointed faculty in support of our activities.

The Leadership Program has developed innovative courses, and sought out unusual adjunct and volunteer teachers. It has sent students off the campus and into community service, arranging internships and mentor relationships in several cities and towns. It has brought national and community leaders to the campus for discussion. It has offered support and learning opportunities to student groups seeking change at Duke and in Durham, and it has assisted in the growth of national efforts for leadership studies and development, and for student community service.

Our mission centers on the needs of students who want to live more useful lives and the program is unusual, in some ways unique. Its purposes and strategic vision, however, respond to the best that American students have to offer: energy, hope, intelligence, and earnest desires to do something of value for others.

OBJECTIVES: Like other teachers, we mean to deepen the knowledge and enlarge the capacities that students bring with them. We try to help them develop their characters and to find ways to greater awareness of the people and the processes around them. Hoping that they will be more effective, more thoughtful, and more able to act supportively with others, we emphasize these more specific aims:

Democratic and Civic Values. These core values of our society set limits to personal and organizational self-interest, and shape our notions of the public good and of the social ideals toward which we strive. In courses and activities, students discover for themselves the meanings and the importance of these values.

Conscience. Internalized community standards, felt strongly and steadily enough, can check or correct moral errors. But our conscientious feelings also fight against irresponsible passivity, inspiring action toward decent ends. When time is short and the stakes are high, conscience may be a leader's most important guide.

Confidence. The psychological abilities of an individual to tolerate ambiguity, risk, delayed reward, and failure are crucial to an active and constructive role in organizations and institutions. While confidence grows primarily from nurtured and comprehended experiences of success, insight and reflection can build confidence even from choices that bring suffering and failure.

160

Consciousness. An awareness of individual motives and drives, of needs for mastery and the claims of security, needs to be matched with the recognition that the achievement of an individual's best hopes depends on the existence of the community, on the shared values and obligations that undergird social life.

Character. The concept combines psychological and moral dimensions; at best, it indicates some harmony of conscience, confidence, and consciousness. Character is both tested and developed in action, especially in difficult and uncertain circumstances.

Skill. No person has all the skills a community needs. But those involved in making changes, in motivating others, or in maintaining a community's values and capacities when these are threatened, are likely to find certain skills especially valuable: communication (reading, writing, listening, speaking); negotiation; the analysis of group problems and processes, and of the values and interests at stake in common choices.

Passion and Commitment. Energy comes from passion, which needs more to be discovered and channeled than to be forgotten or repressed. Commitment is an active willingness to invest sufficient energy over sufficient time to produce a desired outcome. It implies the ability to connect with others, to make promises and to keep them.

A Strategic Vision: Students arrive with different hopes and intentions, and at different stages in the development of leadership capacities. They learn in different ways. Our multifarious array of courses and experiences is meant to challenge students to find more active ways of educating themselves and helping each other. Our approach is experimental and partly opportunistic, but certain common elements inform our vision:

1. The central role of experience in learning and in teaching.

The major elements of the program are based in experience. This is not to say that there are no texts and no resort to the opinions of experts, but rather that the objective is for each student to construct an individual leadership commitment and style out of his or her own strengths and weaknesses, needs, contexts, and opportunities. The elements of experience with which we deal include students' personal histories; the classroom processes of interaction between themselves and with the faculty; individual and group projects students undertake in the courses and activities of the program.

We believe there is an essential connection between thought and action, that experience demands dialogue with others and individual pondering. Every off-campus activity ought to be matched by on-campus discussions and opportunities for thoughtful writing.

Leadership and teaching are similar, sometimes identical. The faculty of the program needs to include people who care about and in some measure reflect its aims, and who have experience in getting things done, in working with groups and organizations, in developing communities, in facing difficulties. In addition to those in the program with faculty appointments, students can learn from mentors and advisors affiliated with the program, and from each other. Teaching in the program takes students seriously as individuals. Classes

161

encourage discussion: most are seminars.

2. Working with others.

Individuals are connected to communities by shared values, by love, and by the experience of working together for common ends. We try to create an experience of what community means, of how it can nourish and support each member's aims while not diminishing others' possibilities. The classroom is a prime opportunity for the creation of community. It can also be a good place for developing students' own capacities for authority, especially when they can question and come to terms with the authorities of texts and teachers.

Many students lack deep experience of organization or knowledge of group processes. Most activities and projects of the program encourage or require work with others, and provide opportunities to consider the resulting relationships.

3. Sources and assumptions: the intellectual background.

History and literature are the great resources for those who would think about responsibility and failure, about the passions (pity, terror, love, and others), or about the experience of triumph or catastrophe. Biographies, dramas and novels can help in understanding why leadership so often has tragic dimensions, and they can prompt analyses of ethical dilemmas, the nature of charisma, or the aesthetic dimensions of leadership and power. Such works play a central role in the courses of the program.

Competing responsibilities and opposing conceptions of the public good are the common dilemmas of leaders in many fields. Our sense is that any study of leadership that ignores the central moral problems can hardly be a serious enterprise. Dialogue, serious talk about difficult cases, is a constant feature of what we do.

4. The world beyond the campus.

Our structure has plenty of space for student-initiated activities (not necessarily for credit, and not necessarily formally part of the program). Faculty and others associated with the program attempt to be available to students when they are ready to discuss whatever they have been attempting or inventing. In time, we offer such blessings, praise, and criticism as seem appropriate.

We sponsor and encourage a variety of connections to business and nonprofit organizations, and to agencies and branches of government at several levels. People from outside the academic world who join our projects and activities can help students to believe more fully in the importance of their present experiences. They can also assist students in finding internships and other off-campus opportunities. Contact with these various worlds provides intellectual cross-fertilization for our thinking. More important, friends and supporters from all these areas assist the program in providing the kind of depth of teaching and advising that is impossible within the resources of the regular faculty.

The Leadership Program aims at helping a broad range of students to become more thoughtful, energetic, and ethically aware, more alert to pressing human needs, and more committed to effective and democratic government. It challenges students to learn about the harm even good leaders can do, to experience some of the satisfactions and costs of leadership, and to learn the skills of working productively and compassionately with others.

Since its beginning in 1985, the program has involved well over five hundred students in demanding courses, community service activities, and internships. It has sponsored a broad range of visitors to the campus: corporate and governmental leaders, community organizers, leaders in voluntary organizations and churches, student leaders from other campuses, educators and journalists.

COURSES: The program's introductory course, "Leadership, Policy, and Change," open to undergraduates in any field, introduces students to dilemmas of leadership. It examines the lives and experiences of significant leaders, better ones and worse, and uses dramas, psychological, political and philosophical works in studying ethical and organizational problems. Beyond the twice a week class meetings, students are expected to spend ten or more hours each week working in one of Durham's voluntary organizations, and to write seriously about the kinds of leadership they see and the effectiveness of their own work as supporters, followers, or constituents. A seminar version was taught by Bruce Payne in Spring 1989.

John Ott teaches a seminar, "Leadership and Judgment," which explores particular questions about leadership, about ways of seeing, about power and community, and about empathy and failure. The class itself becomes a laboratory for leadership, as each session is guided by students who both prepare and evaluate their session with the professor. Other components of the class include ten hours each week in community leadership projects and outdoor experiential exercises.

What does leading mean in a world threatened by faltering health care, decaying educational institutions, and nuclear annihilation? Ed O'Neil's seminar, "Civic Life and Leadership," moves from a political and historical framework to articulate new conceptions of the public space and citizenship, and to explore ways citizens can exert influence over the pressing issues of the day.

Bob Braverman explores the nature and meaning of work in his seminar, "Leadership and Influence." Students examine differences between craft and careerism, particular strategies for achieving influence within large corporate structures, and probe deeply and personally the conflicts and opportunities inherent in becoming part of such structures. His seminar, "Humanistic Perspectives on Leadership and Politics," works with novels by Dostoyevsky, Stendhal, Greene, Gordimer, and others to reveal the relationship between public and private responsibility.

Other courses that regular and adjunct faculty have offered include "The Mind of South Africa," "Corporate Leadership," "Leadership and Social Conscience," "Women and Leadership," "Power and Freedom."

LEADERSHIP PROJECTS: Students in many of the Program's courses are required to participate in substantial leadership projects, most often in the Durham community, though expansive and creative projects affecting Duke have also been approved. Examples of these projects are as varied as the students in the program. They include the Duke Africa Initiative, a project created by four leadership students that has sponsored over thirty internships in famine stricken countries in Africa. Several students initiated the Food Salvation program to move all of the food not used by Duke Food Services to the Community Soup Kitchen. A group of students organized the Coalition for a Women's Center on campus, that in the last two years has accomplished what no previous efforts could: a commitment of resources and space and staff for such a center, to open later this year. Students have provided literally thousands of volunteer hours for the homeless shelters and soup kitchen in Durham. The Duke Homeless Project has sponsored several campus-wide symposia on this growing crisis. One student organized an a cappella choir; another a soccer league for middle school students. The list goes on and on.

THE INTERNSHIPS: During the last three summers, through the Interns in Conscience Program, over 100 students have been involved in some of our country's toughest social problems, and with some of its most powerless people: families in New York who are homeless and without hope; children and teenagers in D.C. who are in trouble, with drugs, with the courts, with their families and themselves; Haitian and Guatemalan migrant workers and refugees in southern Florida. They prepare thoroughly for the summer, volunteering with organizations in Durham that confront problems similar to those they would encounter over the summer, and dissecting intellectually the many dimensions of these problems in seminars they design and lead at Duke.

Throughout the summer, they meet with journalists, public officials, and others who helped them understand the broader context of their efforts. And they work--hard--often 60 or more hours a week, helping out and making a difference, both in individual lives and within their sponsoring organizations.

Experiences over the last two summers, particularly in Florida, have led to two new initiatives for next summer. 1) Working closely with the North Carolina Student Rural Health Coalition to explore the potential for internships in rural North Carolina next summer; 2) Exploring an initiative to begin a leadership school during the summer in Durham, targeting some of this city's most disadvantaged families. John Ott met with parents, teachers, community leaders, and children in Durham to plan this project.

Leadership, Policy, and Change - PPS 145
Instructor: Bruce L. Payne
Taught 3 hrs. each week in seminar.

REQUIRED READING: Keeping up with the reading is essential. Be prepared to discuss the readings and/or films on the day for which they have been assigned. The first week's readings should, if possible, be prepared in advance.

Items marked (*) should be purchased, others are available as a Course-Pak from Copytron.

<u>Session</u>

1   Intentions, assumptions, reservations: O'Connor, Flannery "The Lame Shall Enter First" in *The Complete Stories of Flannery O'Connor*; Gardner, John W. "The Heart of the Matter," "Leadership and Power," "The Moral Aspect of Leadership," and "The Changing Nature of Leadership"; Sharansky, Natan *Fear No Evil*, pp. 359-363; Payne, Bruce "Service, Leadership, and University Students."

2   Case histories of conflict and charisma: I & II Samuel, I Kings, ch. 1 to 11 (*The Oxford Annotated Bible*, Revised Standard Version, has useful notes and introductions).

3   Power and authority, women and men, this world and the next: *Sophocles *Antigone* (tr. Elizabeth Wyckoff) in *Sophocles I: Three Tragedies* (a volume of *The Complete Greek Tragedies* edited by David Grene and Richmond Lattimore).

4   Power and freedom, teaching and taking risks: *Plato *The Apology* and *Crito* in *The Last Days of Socrates.*

5   Political and military power--strategy and tactics: Leuchtenburg, William E. "Franklin D. Roosevelt: The First Modern President" in Fred I. Greenstein, ed. *Leadership in the Modern Presidency* (pp. 7-40); *Larrabee, Eric *Commander-in-Chief: Franklin Delano Roosevelt, his Lieutenants, and their War* (pp. 1-353).

6   American organizational processes: Larrabee, Eric *Commander-in-Chief* (pp. 355-648); *Rosie the Riveter* (film).

7   War stories, leadership and moral judgment: *12 O'Clock High* (film); *Keegan, John *The Mask of Command*, ch. 4 "False Heroic: Hitler as Supreme Commander," pp. 235-310; Walzer, Michael "Moral Judgment in Time of War" in Richard A. Wasserstrom, ed. *War and Morality.*

8   Leadership, gender, power, and social change: *Nies, Judith *Seven Women: Portraits from the American Radical Tradition.*

9   Individuals and organizations; acting with others: *Garrow, David *Bearing the Cross: Martin Luther King, Jr., and the Southern Christian Leadership Conference* (pp. 11-286, 527-624).

10 Power and social change--the group as protagonist: *Matewan* (film); Sayles, John *Thinking in Pictures*, pp. 1-34.

11 Power and social change--men and women: *Norma Rae* (film).

12 Good intentions, self-understanding, and the problem of failure: *Ibsen, Henrik *An Enemy of the People.*

13 Leadership and tragedy: *Shakespeare, William *King Lear.*

14 The sense of an ending: Shakespeare, William *King Lear.*

WEEKLY EXAMS: A short exam at the beginning of class each Tuesday, questions coming from the list of study questions for the week's assignments. Although no exam grade will be dropped when calculating exam average, there is the option of substituting a reflection paper for an exam, up to a maximum of two exams, on subjects chosen by the instructor. These papers, graded in place of the exams, should be at least four typed double-spaced pages and are due at the beginning of class one week after the date of the missed exam.

LEADERSHIP PROJECTS: Each student will be asked to write regularly about someone who is making a difference in the lives of people in Durham. To do this, you may want to work as a volunteer in one of the local social service organizations, or with some other program or group. I will expect some writing every other week, which can be informal (as journal entries, for example), but which should capture some of your subject's actual words, and offer portraits of what she or he does.

By Session 10 I would like to have the first draft of a publishable article on your subject. After an editorial response from me, a final version will be due Session 13.

VISITORS: Several times during the semester, you will be expected to join with visiting leaders, journalists, and scholars in seminar discussions. Some preparation--usually reading about forty pages of material--will be required for participation in these discussions. You will be asked to prepare questions in advance and to write one-page reaction papers afterwards.

OPTIONAL GROUP PROJECTS: I will be interested to talk with you and to read your reflections about any groups with which you are involved. If you have time, organizing community service activities with others (especially others in the class) would be especially rewarding. A substantial paper relating these activities to the course is expected, or some alternative kind of negotiated report on the group's work.

Groups of up to seven students might be formed out of the class to do a study of a significant woman who played an important role in 20th century public life, the aim being to prepare a study guide, an oral presentation, and a publishable article based on the biography of a significant woman leader.

CLASS PARTICIPATION: The class will be small enough for everyone to join in the discussion, and you are expected to do that. But it will often be the case that there is not time enough even for those things that seem most significant to you. Let me encourage you to add brief (or even lengthy) notes to me, or to the class as a whole, based on your reflections following our discussions.

I am eager for each of you to be seriously involved in the class. If things are not going to your liking, it is your responsibility to let the rest of us know that.

GRADING: Course grade will be based on the following relative weights: weekly exams and reflection papers, 65%; leadership project, 15%; class participation (including after-class memos, and participation in meetings with visitors), 20%. (For those who do optional projects, the grading scheme will be 55% for exams and reflection papers, 15% each for the leadership project, class participation, and the group project.)

International Leadership Center
1600 Two Turtle Creek Village, Dallas, TX 75219-5419

Stan Altschuler
Executive Director
214/526-2953

Leadership America

OVERVIEW: Leadership America is a unique leadership education opportunity for collegiate undergraduates. Each year 50 students are selected through an intense national competition and are invited to participate in its ten-week summer session. They take part in a wide range of activities, all focused on leadership.

The purpose of the program is to help encourage leadership development among college students. It intends to achieve this objective by: 1) helping to prepare 50 of today's outstanding undergraduates for the leadership challenges of their generation; 2) promoting awareness of leadership issues to each of the applicants for the program; 3) serving as a national recognition of those students who have committed a portion of their undergraduate careers to leadership responsibilities; and 4) sharing the insights it learns about leadership education with those institutions and organizations interested in expanding or developing their programs.

To be eligible the student must be in the junior year of a four (or more) year undergraduate program at an accredited college or university. Students participate in the summer between their junior and senior years. Selection is based on a written application, a copy of which may be obtained from a designated individual on the campus or directly from Leadership America if no such campus representative has been designated by the institution.

COMPONENTS: Leadership America's ten-week session encompasses seven distinct components. The first is a weekend orientation, the purposes of which are to help students become familiar with one another and to establish the expectations for the summer.

The second component is the Leadership Development Program at the Center for Creative Leadership in Greensboro, NC. This six-day session concentrates on self-assessment. During the fifth day, each student meets for three hours with a skilled psychologist who assists the student to better understand his or her strengths, weaknesses, and interests. This week serves as an important building block for the self-understanding that is gained during the remainder of the program.

The next component is the Executive Development Program of Colorado Outward Bound and takes place in Leadville, CO. This week has two major objectives, building self-confidence and supporting team bonding. Physical activities such as rock climbing and the ropes course are ideal individual confidence-builders, while the team involvement in these activities as well as on the peak climb helps enhance understanding of group functioning.

While Leadership America makes no claim to teach "leadership vision," one of its key tenets is that vision can be a by-product of enhanced understanding of one's environment. Consequently, during the program's three-week classroom component, the emphasis is on the global environment, change in technology, and miscellaneous issues of leadership. Using classroom sessions that combine lecture, question-and-answer, and role-playing or

167

simulation, the students expand their understanding of the global issues, opportunities and challenges confronting their generation. Changes in technology are addressed in field trips to corporations and institutions at the forefront of such change. Miscellaneous issues include topics such as the role of the media, community service and minority leadership. Ethics and values are studied in separate sessions and underlie all other discussions.

At this mid-point of the program, the students separate into individual, self-selected internships to provide each student access to a true-world perspective of leadership in a position of specific interest to the student. Most of the internships involve a mentor who works closely with the student and attempts to demonstrate the interrelationship of career, community service, and family. Internships take place throughout the United States and around the world.

The final week of the program provides an opportunity for the students to review their internships with each other, critique the overall summer session, and share plans for the future. In addition, they make oral presentations on their team projects to the rest of their class and to invited experts in their field of study.

The seventh component of Leadership America is the team project. Each student is assigned to one of five ten-person teams, each of which is asked to study a topical issue and prepare both a written and an oral presentation. The issues studied are community-related (e.g., the homeless, AIDS, child abuse, teenage pregnancy) or environmental (e.g., ozone depletion, water resources, waste management). The team project gives each student a better appreciation of the group process and a greater awareness of the importance of community service.

GENERAL DETAIL: Application deadline for Leadership America is the last weekday in January. Applications are available through local campus representatives or by contacting Leadership America. Selection committees meet throughout February and invitations are extended in mid-March.

Funding for the administrative and operating costs of the program are provided by corporate, foundation and individual gifts. Student costs are limited to some personal aspects of the internship. Stipends to offset the loss of summer income are not offered, and scholarship aid is limited.

Academic credit has been offered by many schools. Such credit generally involves the student arranging the details with a local faculty sponsor. The staff of Leadership America will provide the information necessary to assist in establishing academic credit.

Marietta College
McDonough Center, Marietta, OH 45750-3031

Stephen W. Schwartz
Assoc. Dir.
614/374-4760

McDonough Center for Leadership and Business

As an academic, primarily undergraduate unit, the Center and its programs allow students to study leadership in general and with reference to one of leadership's primary environments--the world of business. In the process students learn to characterize, analyze and criticize leadership. They are given opportunities to develop their own potential for leadership in the relatively risk-free environment of the academy and to begin making decisions about their responsibilities as citizen-leaders.

From a philosophical/pedagogical point of view, the method for achieving the Center's goals is consistent with the liberal arts nature of Marietta College and can be viewed as two horizontal bands sweeping across a series of vertical bands representing the traditional academic disciplines constituting the curriculum of Marietta College. Leadership and business (either as separate or related entities) cut across the curriculum and become part of the skills and knowledge base of a variety of disciplinary courses as they are taught at Marietta College.

The primary means for achieving these goals, to date, is the McDonough Leadership Program. Students can participate in this 18-hour program regardless of their academic major. On completion of the Program, candidates are graduated as McDonough Scholars, and this distinction is noted on their diplomas and transcripts.

Admission to the McDonough Leadership Program. The Program is open to all students regularly accepted as members of the freshman class. Interested students complete an application and two letters of recommendation intended to demonstrate their curiosity, perseverance, faith in personal convictions, and positive attitude toward academic work.

Candidacy is also available to those students who were admitted to the College provisionally or others who simply did not apply prior to arrival on campus. At the end of the freshman year these students can apply to begin the program as sophomores.

The Program begins with a special orientation including an "out-of-door" experience intended to provide a sense of group identification. Candidates take a required two-semester Seminar on Leadership. The only other course required by the Program is a senior seminar designed to synthesize the students' experiences both within and outside of the Program.

In addition to these three courses, students are required to take a minimum of 9 hours of designated leadership courses. <u>It must be pointed out, however, that these courses are open to all students, regardless of whether or not they are candidates in the McDonough Leadership Program</u>. Some of these carry the LEAD prefix and are offered by the McDonough Center. Others have departmental prefixes and are offered within the framework of the department. To date, for example, the following courses have been offered under the Lead prefix: Lead 221--Seminar in Leadership Behavior; Lead 307--

Industrial Leadership Dialogues. Leadership courses offered or to be offered by departments include: Hist 302--History and Change: Studies in Historical Biography; Hist 314--Leaders in Protest; English 210--The Novel and Politics; Computer Science 494--Managing Technological Change; Arth 373--Women in the Visual Arts; Mngt 451--Small Business Institute/ Entrepreneurial Mentors; Mass 393--Film Directors as Leaders; Pols 210--The Presidency and Executive Leadership.

One further requirement is the completion of a special internship/project to be pursued during the junior year and completed in the first semester of the senior year.

Augmented Program: The McDonough Leadership Program is only part of the mission of the Center. Other activities include promoting, enhancing and supporting the students, faculty, staff, community and business community-at-large. Some of these goals are encouraged by the physical presence of the Center itself (the Center is housed in a newly constructed $2.5 million building) and by the general atmosphere created by the Center. It is expected that co- and extra-curricular life will be enhanced by the Center and its programs.

Campus-wide leadership activities outside the Center will be supported by Center-sponsored programs or personnel. For example, with the help of Practicum students from neighboring Ohio University's graduate program in student personnel, the Center and Student Affairs staff help to provide leadership opportunities in the area of students activities and residential life. Moreover, brown-bag lunch series on practical issues, such as the management of clubs and activities, are sponsored by both groups.

An example of outreach to the community is the inclusion of Marietta College's Business Resource Center (a small business development center) as a service within the McDonough Center. The BRC provides consulting services to local businesses as well as seminars and workshops (e.g., microcomputer applications, desktop publishing, etc.). Other outreach projects currently under consideration include conferences (e.g., corporate leadership environments; women, leadership and business; leadership environments for minorities, etc.); roundtables (e.g., leadership in commerce, in government, in education, etc.); musical recitals and art exhibitions.

Following are syllabi of courses currently within the framework of the McDonough Leadership Program. Some have been designed especially for inclusion in the Program; others are restructured courses in the curriculum. Some are in the process of trial and review.

Leadership Dialogues: Business and Industry* - Leadership 294
J. Douglas McGrew

TEXTS: <u>Endurance</u> by Alfred Lansing and <u>Great Writings in Management and Organizational Behavior</u> by Boone and Bowen.

PURPOSE: To hear recognized, experienced, and established business and industrial leaders give their personal opinions on what it takes to be a leader in today's world. To compare each individual's opinions on this subject with those of the other speakers and with the conventional and accepted writings on business and industrial leadership and with recognized leadership behavior in the text.

DIALOGUES: Every Friday if possible we will have a business person present as a guest lecturer. A written review with regard to the leadership qualities of each speaker will be submitted by each student.

TERM PAPER: On the leadership qualities of a business leader selected from a prepared list including both living leaders and leaders from the past.

BOOK REPORT: From a selected list of books.

ATTENDANCE: Voluntary, not required; It is hoped that the class will be interesting enough so that you will want, rather than be forced, to attend. Speakers are scheduled for Friday. Fridays, especially before holidays, are sometimes days of poor attendance. It will be embarrassing to invite a speaker, have the speaker take the time and trouble to come to class, and have only a few members of the class show up to hear the speaker.

GRADING: Two exams (a mid-term and a final). Scores based on: Mid-term = 100 pts; Final = 200 pts; Term paper = 100 pts; Book Report = 100 pts; Speaker Evaluations = Approx. 150 (ten pts. each); Class participation = 100 pts; Total = Approx. 750 pts.

A - 675 to 750; B - 600 to 674; C - 525 to 599; D - 450 to 524; F - below 450

*The title of the course may vary according to the focus of the speakers invited; for example, it may be titled Leadership Dialogues: Science and Technology.

Leaders in Protest - History 314
Wm. C. Hartel

GOALS: To examine some of the aspects of leadership in the United States since the turn of the century. The following topics will be touched upon through lectures, special readings, videos, and through taking of three examinations: (1) is history "made" by the actions of determined individuals, by actions of groups, by impersonal forces, or by a combination of factors; (2) what might legitimately be termed "protest" in the United States; (3) are protest leaders in the American society doomed to failure? if so, why? (4) are there cause and effect links between the generations of protest leaders? and (5) is there something special about protest leaders? At the conclusion of the semester, it is hoped that you have a better understanding of how your civilization developed so that you will therefore become a more cultured individual. In addition, it is hoped that you have begun to look at the concept of leadership with a critical eye. Of equal importance you will sharpen some basic skills. You will improve your ability to learn basic information data, to compare and contrast, to show cause and effect, to recognize and construct analogies, and to see different points of view.

ASSIGNED BOOK AND READINGS: Dale Fetherling's <u>Mother Jones: The Miners' Angel, A Portrait</u> and numerous handouts. In addition to the readings, it is anticipated that several videos will be viewed outside the classroom.

STUDENT RESPONSIBILITIES: Complete the reading assignments on the date pre-announced; view the videos on the date pre-announced; prepare one question for each class. These questions must be written out possibly to be turned in and must refer to material/topics previously covered in class or in special assignments.

FORMAT OF THE CLASS: Lecture but with every opportunity for questions coming from either the students or the instructor. Such questioning will lead to occasional freewheeling discussions. Therefore, all students are responsible for taking notes, the written question referred to above, and any special materials specifically assigned for class discussion, as well as a willingness to get involved in the subject matter.

EXPECTATIONS:
1. Attendance: Absences will be recorded for each class session; penalty for absences will be self-imposed. The instructor reserves the right to question any student about excessive absences.

2. Academic behavior: Students are expected to be active learners, to ask questions and be involved in question answering and/or class discussions. Outside the classroom, students must read assignments on time and view assigned videos. This is an undergraduate course and while students are not expected to become experts in the field of American protest, they are expected to master enough to demonstrate a basic understanding of the discussed concepts and topics on the examinations. Also, students will demonstrate an ability to analyze using comparisons, logic and inter-relationships.

EXAMINATIONS: Three major essay-type examinations. The first two hour examinations count 30% each; the final 40%.

The examinations are essay in format. There will be a question, or questions, that every student must answer and then there will be a choice of two essays out of three for each of the three examinations. The examinations are not comprehensive but the necessity for retaining cumulative knowledge will be considered.

SBI/Entrepreneurial Mentors - Management 451
Stephen Schwartz

REQUIRED READINGS: No required textbooks but there will be reference to several textbooks and manuals for case analysis. Six articles on reserve in the library are required readings for the course. These articles deal with issues in Entrepreneurship/Small Business Management/Leadership and are useful for case analysis. Answers to questions on the required readings are due from each student at the end of the semester.

SEMINAR FORMAT: Deals exclusively with small businesses and each student is assigned to a consulting team for the semester. Each consulting team deals with one client company for the semester. The seminar meets at the beginning of each semester to explain the cases to the class. The class hears Dr. Ross speak on Interpersonal Relationships and Transactional Analysis and Dr. O'Donnell speaks on Interviewing Techniques before initial client visits.

Students then meet with clients and periodically with a faculty member and SCORE/ACE Advisor in private team conferences. Each student team must meet privately with Professor Mabry O'Donnell and Professor Charlie Pridgeon regarding oral and written communication skills before preparing written reports and oral presentations. After consulting reports are written and revised, the entire seminar meets at the end of the semester to hear oral presentations of each consulting team.

COURSE GRADES: On individual basis of work on consulting team, contribution to the written report, participation in seminar session, team member evaluations, and answers to the required readings. Heavy weight will be given to attendance and participation in the seminar session. Do not assume that all members of a consulting team will automatically receive the same grade.

ABSENCE POLICY: Students are expected to attend and <u>actively</u> participate in all sessions. Absences from client contacts, team meetings, and seminars will have a downward effect on course grades.

<u>Sessions</u>

1	Course explanation
2	Case assignments
3	MBTI Test and Interpretation, Dr. Margaret Ross (3 hrs.)
4	Interviewing Techniques, Dr. Mabry O'Donnell
5	Report Writing Techniques, Dr. Charles Pridgeon Then schedule initial client visitation with instructor. Periodic client meetings. Periodic team conferences with instructor and SCORE advisor.
6	Lecture and team training appointments with Professors O'Donnell and Pridgeon
7	*Written consulting report due - absolutely no exceptions (Make one copy before turning in to assist in preparing oral presentations.)
8	2 oral presentations (2 hours)
9	2 oral presentations (2 hours)
10	2 oral presentations (2 hours) Answers to required readings on reserve <u>Due</u>.

*Written reports will be read and corrected by the instructor. Reports may have to be rewritten before submission to the Small Business Administration. Final written reports must contain a statement of client satisfaction and a signed client acknowledgement. Clients will be contacted by telephone to insure written reports have been received before grades are issued.

REQUIRED READINGS:

Article 1. The Heart of Entrepreneurship: Discuss the differences in the decision-making process of "promoters" (entrepreneurs) and "trustees" (administrators). Describe some methods corporate officers can utilize to stimulate and encourage entrepreneurship in organizations.

Article 2. Entrepreneurship Reconsidered: The Team as Hero: Will the concept of "Collective Entrepreneurship" be included in future "Principles of Management" textbooks, or is it a passing fad? Defend your position and cite examples.

Article 3. The Dark Side of Entrepreneurship: Did your SBI client or Entrepreneurial Mentor exhibit any of the three personality traits discussed in the article? If so, which one(s)?

Article 4. Run Your Business or Build an Organization: Which management philosophy was most evident from your SBI client/Entrepreneurial Mentor--that of "commitment to building an organization" or that of "concentration on running the company"? Cite an example.

Article 5. Small Company Finance: What The Books Don't Say: Cite several reasons why textbook methods of financial analysis give unreliable results of small company performance.

Article 6. Is a Manager a Leader? Do you agree with the author's viewpoint that a leader's effectiveness is measured by the effectiveness of his/her organization? Why or why not? Can you have an "effective leader" in an "ineffective" organization?

Rules, Requirements, and Guidelines for the SBI Program

1. Each team coordinator must submit a 641-A SBA report by 4:00 p.m. each Friday to be mailed to SBA District Office.
2. The coordinator must call the client to arrange an appointment before each visit. On your first visit, you must bring a 641 Request for Counseling Form for your client's signature. Since most calls are toll calls, they should be kept as brief as possible, no more than four or five minutes to schedule an appointment.
3. All toll calls, other than those for an appointment with a client, must be approved.
4. Visits to the client should always be by all team members. This keeps everyone informed and saves the client time.
5. Always make an appointment to see your client. At least six client visitations is the benchmark for a good SBI report.
6. The coordinator must keep a log of all the time spent on each client visit or activity

to be able to submit a final report to the SBA. The instructor will inspect this log at each review session in his office.

7. The student coordinator is responsible for making an appointment with Professor O'Donnell and Professor Pridgeon to discuss oral presentation and written communication skills.

8. The student coordinator is responsible for delivering the _final_ written report to the client company.

9. Each team should have weekly-scheduled, private meetings until the case is completed.

10. SCORE persons should always be invited to all meetings with the instructor and to the final class report. Do not meet with a SCORE person at any other time; never take a SCORE person with you on a client visit.

11. The final report must be typewritten and written in the following format: Executive Summary (covering history of the company and owner's objectives); Detail of Problems/Opportunities; Detail of Solutions; Detail of Recommendations (Implemented and Not Implemented); Financial Information; Summary and Conclusions; Statement of Client Satisfaction (signed by client); Acknowledgement of Exit Interview (signed by client); Statement of SBA release; Copy of original 641 Form; Copy of 641-A Forms; Appendices.

12. Each client will be invited by and urged by the team coordinator to attend the class sessions when the SBI team reports their case.

13. All students are required to sign an "Oath of Confidentiality" before client contact can occur.

14. The team should use their own vehicle for transportation to the client. The Department will reimburse student drivers at the rate of 20 cents per mile. The coordinator must keep a careful record of all mileage for billing purposes. If the team does not have access to a private vehicle, the instructor will arrange for a college vehicle.

15. _Ten_ visits to the client's location will be the maximum allowed per semester. The SBI team coordinator will be responsible for turning in _one_ final travel voucher for the entire team for the entire semester. Travel vouchers _must_ be turned in before the end of final exams.

16. Absolutely no final grades will be released until the client has a copy of the final report for his/her files.

Checklist of Possible Areas of Concern

1. Goals and Objectives: Evidence of Planning; Short-Range; Long Range.
2. Management Functions: Planning: Organizing and Staffing; Directing and Controlling; Communications and Feedback; Public Relations.
3. Accounting Functions: Type of system; Cash controls and cash flow; Cost accounting; Billing system; Accounts receivable; Accounts payable; Inventory control; Pricing.
4. Financing Functions: Sources and uses of funds; Accounting ratios; Credit and collections; Trend analysis; Ratio analysis.
5. Personnel: Morale and working conditions; Salaries and benefits; Chain of

command; Hiring and firing policies; Personnel manuals.
6. <u>Operating Functions:</u> Location of office/plant/warehouse/building; Condition of buildings and equipment; Customer service-parking, friendliness, convenience; Work flows and layouts; Hours of operation; Purchasing and material availability; Research and development.
7. <u>Marketing Functions:</u> Place in overall operations of business; Determination of target market; Channels of distribution; Competitive analysis; Diversification, new products, etc.; Analysis of: product, price, place, promotion; Methods of research, information gathering; Marketing communications.

Film History: Great Directors - Mass Media 493 (Special Topics Course)
3 credits, one evening per week
Ronald Jacobson

The course is intended for students in Continuing Education, specifically those in the Leadership track of the graduate program.

DESCRIPTION: The study of American and foreign film directors and their films, with special emphasis on the directors' creative leadership, distinctive styles, and contributions to motion picture history.

TEXTBOOK: Mast, Gerald. <u>A Short History of the Movies</u>. Indianapolis: Bobbs-Merrill, 1986. (4th edition).

Students are expected to attend the lectures, view every film, participate in discussion, and read the assigned portions of the textbook. Each student will present an oral abstract of the major term paper (15-25 pages in length) on a topic chosen in consultation with the instructor. There will be two take-home exams.

GRADING: Mid-term examination - 25% of total grade; Term paper/oral presentation - 30%; Final examination - 30%; Attendance and participation - 15%.

Tentative Course Outline:
Week #
1   Introduction / Survey of library resources for studying film* / Film: The Inventors and the early pioneers / Focus on D. W. Griffith
2   The silent film and the beginning of the star system / Focus on Chaplin and Keaton
3   Sound comes to film / Leaders in the studio system / Focus on Howard Hawks
4   The independent director / Focus on King Vidor and Orson Welles
5   The Director as expressionistic artist / Focus on Luis Bunuel
6   The Director as social commentator / Focus on Vittorio DeSica
7   The Director who turns to the real world / Documentaries / Focus on Robert Flaherty
8   The relationship of film art and business / Focus on Walt Disney Productions

9	The relationship of the director and the State / Focus on Ingmar Bergman
10	The Director as theorist / The amateur theory of film / Focus on Francois Truffaut
11	The immigrant director / Focus on Fritz Lang
12	The Director as international ambassador / Focus on Akira Kurosawa
13	The Director today and tomorrow / Focus on Stanley Kubrick
14	Student Reports
15	Student Reports / Wrap-up

*Library resources on film are plentiful in our own Dawes Library. For instance, there are books about Bergman, Bunuel, Griffith, DeMille, Disney, Eisenstein, Renoir, Hitchcock, Welles, Vidor, Flaherty, and more. Students can also use Film Quarterly for their research.

Leadership and Change: Studies in Historical Biography - Leadership 200
James O'Donnell

Leadership and Change: Studies in Historical Biography is a one semester course in which the student will seek to identify those persons (both men and women) whose leadership practices have resulted in historical and social change. Each week the class will discuss assigned readings which treat the lives of various leaders. Every student will turn in a weekly six hundred word synopsis of his/her readings. These weekly written assignments will be counted as 20% of the final grade. Two one-hour exams and a final exam will be given based on the assigned reading materials. These tests will be counted as sixty percent (20% of the final grade). As part of their attempt to grasp certain characteristics which seem reflective of leaders and their styles, each student will research and write a ten-page leadership profile paper on some historical personage who has not been assigned for the class readings. This paper will constitute the final 20% of the grade. The papers will be completed in five stages: proposal of leader; working bibliography; outline of paper; rough draft; final paper.

Required readings for the course will be in the form of handouts or reserve readings in the library, save in those instances where it is assumed the student has a personal copy of a source such as The Bible.

Sessions
1	Xenophon, "On the Education of Cyrus"
2	Plutarch's Lives, selections on reserve
3	The Bible, Exodus 1.1-19.25; 2 Samuel
4	The Bible, Esther; Ruth
5	Sophocles, Oedipus the King. **Proposal Due**
6	Book VI and VII of The Republic
7	The Bible, Matthew, Mark, Luke, John
8	The Koran, readings on Mohammed
9	Machiavelli, The Prince, selections. Working Bibliography due
10	Leonardo da Vinci, Notebooks, selections

11	Erik Erikson, <u>Young Man Luther</u>, chapter II
12	Ignatius Loyola, selections
13	Shakespeare, selections from <u>Lear</u>, <u>Henry IV</u>, <u>Coriolanus</u>
14	Elizabeth I, selections
15	**Test. Outline Due**
16	Arthur Koestler, <u>The Sleepwalkers</u>, chs. on Copernicus & Newton
17	Fawn Brodie, <u>Thomas Jefferson: An Intimate Memoir</u>, selections
18	Napoleon, selections. **Rough draft Due**
19	Sir Charles Lyell, selections
20	Charles Darwin, <u>Evolution</u>, selections
21	Karl Marx, <u>Das Kapital</u> and other selections
22	<u>Simon Bolivar</u> by Madariaga, selections
23	Test
24	Elizabeth Cady Stanton and Susan B. Anthony, selections from <u>A History of Woman's Suffrage</u>
25	Margaret Sanger, selections
26	Eleanor Roosevelt, <u>Autobiography</u>, selections
27	Shirer, <u>Rise and Fall of the Third Reich</u>
28	C. P. Snow on Mao, selections. **Paper Due**
29	Coretta King, <u>My Life with Martin Luther King, Jr.</u>

Seminar in Leadership Behavior - Leadership 221
Margaret Ross
(limited to 20 students)

This seminar is an experiential workshop in which the participants will gain knowledge about themselves and how they interact with others as well as enhance their abilities to work with others. There are no prerequisites. The seminar will be held from 9 a.m. to 12 noon on six Saturday mornings for 1 hour credit. Class attendance and participation is mandatory and is a part of the course evaluation. In addition, students will keep journals.

The journal will incorporate two themes. The first will be termed "Intellectual" in which students will write their reactions to assigned readings. The second will be "Personal" in which the students will write a self-analysis of how each has incorporated what has been learned in the seminar. For example, after the session on assertiveness training there will be specific assignments. Individuals will be asked to keep a diary of when they were assertive (or not), what was going on, what their behavior was, what were the results, how they might modify their behavior in the future. This would be done for each of the seminar topics. Journals will be handed in at the following seminars.

Students will be assigned readings in the attached list. In addition each will be asked to purchase a relaxation tape. Materials will be prepared for each topic to be covered in the seminar. Students should purchase 3-ring binders and index dividers. Students will be required to take the Myers-Briggs Type Indicator.

As a result of this seminar, students will: Explore methods used to motivate; Have a better understanding of themselves; Become aware of their own communication style; Learn to express themselves in ways that will get tasks accomplished; Understand stress factors and how to better cope with them; Appreciate the value of time management skills; Gain an appreciation of problem-solving techniques.

LIBRARY RESERVE MATERIALS:

Assertiveness: Alberti & Emmons, Stand Up, Speak Out, Talk Back; Smith, When I Say No, I Feel Guilty

Stress Management: Braiker, The Type E Woman; Walker, Learning to Relax; Curtis & Detert, How to Relax

MBTI: Keirsey, Bates, Please Understand Me; Myers, Gifts Differing; Lawrence, People Types and Tiger Stripes

Communication: Bern, Games People Play; Oldenburg, What You Hear Isn't Always What You Get; Brammer, The Helping Relationship (esp. Chapter 6); Kanter, The Change Masters (esp. Chapter 6); James & Jongeward, Born to Win

Motivation: Mann, Triggers

Time Management: Time Magazine, Your Time

Problem Solving: Josefowitz, Paths to Power

Leadership Styles: Leman, The Birth Order Book; Toman, Family Constellations

----

The Presidency and Executive Leadership - Political Science 210
Credit 3 hours

This course focuses on the roles of the President, governors, mayors and other political executives in the American political system, emphasizing the possibilities and constraints for executive leadership. The Constitutional powers, historical development, and current responsibilities and problems of the presidency are examined. The President's relations with Congress, the courts, the bureaucracy, the press, and the public are also included. Similar issues are examined with respect to governors and local government executives, with emphasis on the variety of powers and approaches possible for state and local executives. Students will examine the career and contributions of one political executive as part of the course.

OBJECTIVES: By the end of the course the student will be able to: explain with examples the constitutional powers of and limitations on the President and be aware of the great variety of powers that may or may not be available to other political executives; identify characteristics important for executive leadership; explain current issues between Congress and the President in terms of the historical development of the relationship between the two branches; give examples of ways in which the President and Congress are required to work together to develop policy; describe the various models of relationships between the President (or governors, mayors) and their respective bureaucracies; explain the role that the press and public may play in the executive's conduct of his or her office; illustrate many of the above through detailed examination of one political executive's career.

SUGGESTED TOPIC OUTLINE: Constitutional Provisions about the President and Court Interpretation; Development of Presidential Powers and the Institutional Presidency; Evolution of Presidential-Congressional Relations; Political Executives and Bureaucracy; Political Executives, the Press and Voters; State Constitutions and Governors; Typical Responsibilities and Problems of Local Executives; Political Executives and Policy; Case Studies of Particular Executives.

SUGGESTED TEXTS: Pious, Richard M. The American Presidency, New York: Basic Books, 1979; Weinberg, Martha, Managing the State, Cambridge: M.I.T. Press, 1977; Royko, Mike, Boss, E. P. Dutton and Co., 1971.

GRADING POLICY: There will be two exams during the semester and a comprehensive final exam. Full participation in class discussions of readings and current events related to political executives is expected. Final grades will be determined as follows: In-term exams 40%; Research project (oral presentation and written report) 25%; Class participation 10%; Final exam 25%.

Monmouth College
West Long Branch, NJ 07764

Eugene J. Rosi
Provost/Senior Vice Pres. for Academic Affairs
201/571-3405

Leadership and Social Responsibility

Monmouth College has developed a comprehensive college-wide program of curriculum, co-curriculum and community outreach initiatives designed to promote leadership in the public interest. Programs are being built within the context of a general education reform that provides a multicultural, gender-balanced and global perspective.

COMPONENTS:

A multi-disciplinary B.A. degree program in Policy and Leadership Studies is now being developed. The disciplines of Sociology, Political Science, Management, Psychology, and Social Work are involved.

A Four-Year Leadership Program will accept the first group of 25 students per year in the fall 1990.

A series of curriculum and co-curriculum activities will engage the students in direct contact with leaders, with opportunities for leadership and with the study of leadership.

An Institute for the Study of Democratic Leadership sponsors public lectures, conferences, and seminars to join faculty, students and community representatives in the exploration of democratic leadership.

A Public Servants in Residence Program provides an opportunity to expose the campus and community to individuals dedicated to service in the public interest.

A Master Lecture Series will address questions of concern to leadership for the 21st century.

Students in the Community initiatives involve students in community-based courses, internships, and volunteer placements.

A Pre-College Leadership Program beginning in fall '89 will promote the development of leadership skills in minority students and will support their persistence through high school.

Mount St. Mary's College
12001 Chalon Road, Los Angeles, CA 90049

Cheryl Mabey
Dir., Women's Leadership Program
213/476-2237

Leadership Studies

The MSMC model of leadership studies is based on the assumptions that everyone is/can be a leader in some contexts, in fact that it is an important constituent of higher education that students be encouraged to be leaders, develop their leadership potentials (empowerment), understand how to empower others, and find appropriate arenas for their leadership. In addition, we assume that the goals of leadership are not givens but must be critically evaluated and creatively developed in a context of the best of moral analyses available and of a realistic assessment of the structures within which the person functions as a leader.

In light of these assumptions we understand leadership education to consist of the following three components. These are <u>not</u> to be understood as sequentially developed. They are basic constituents which should be taken into account in any courses which form the program of leadership studies, though some courses focus on one or more. The goal of leadership studies is that students will have a strong grounding in all of these when they have completed their course of study and that they will know where they need further study/development as a continuation of their education.

I.   **Descriptive Component:** focus on: who is the leader?
     A. In order to understand who leads, students must first have the opportunities to assess who they are in a variety of settings. This includes assessments of their personality, styles of learning and dealing with others, and their personal and professional goals. An understanding of the influences on them of family, education, friendships, etc. is essential as well as an assessment of why they have chosen their particular course of study and professional goals and the implications of these choices for their future leadership potential. In addition an understanding of their world, national, and local situation is essential to an understanding of their leadership potentials.
     B. Self-assessment cannot be separated from a study of models of leadership both successful and unsuccessful. Students will identify a variety of leaders and be guided to both understand and assess their leadership. This includes historical studies of leadership, biographies, literary models, and studies of contemporary group leaders.
     C. At a women's college with the ethnic diversity that MSMC presently possesses the question of the implications of sex-roles and ethnicity on leadership cannot be overlooked. This will mean that both self-assessment and the studies of leaders will be done in the context of an awareness that women and ethnic minorities have not been adequately represented in studies of persons and of social dynamics, let alone leadership. Thus different models/concepts of leadership must be considered and self-assessment must be done in a fashion that is true to the person's own self-understanding and reinforces the values that they bring from their sexual/ethnic perspectives. This means that what may be generally accepted as "deviant" may have to be re-conceptualized from a different perspective.

182

II.   **Functional/Operational Component**: focus on: how to lead more effectively.
    A. Skill-Building: includes critical thinking, group dynamics, public speaking, ability to analyze organizational structures.
    B. Leadership styles: includes a study of various styles and their appropriateness to various contexts, the openness to developing new forms, and the practice of flexibility in leadership style.
    C. Organizational behavior: includes a study of various forms of organizational behavior; the ability to assess and understand their inner workings, goals, and assumptions; the ability to see where they are flexible (adaptable) and where they are not; and practice in both organizing and working to change given organizations.

III.   **Policy Component**: focus on: how to create and assess policy directions, which includes awareness of substantive issues relevant to leadership, both those relevant to particularized situations and those that take into consideration more global concerns; how to assess these and to formulate leadership objectives that are realistic, practical, effective, and which promote the best in human and community life.
    A. This includes a study and assessment of the ideas, concepts, and assumptions related to: the goals of leadership, an understanding of human nature, and the nature/possibilities of societies of all forms (government, business, professions, family, Church, etc.).
    B. More specifically, students will study and practice analyzing policies of specific organizations in specific contexts to identify issues/problems and determine which can/should be the effective targets for change.
    C. This necessitates an understanding of social change theories and strategies in light of their relationship to leadership.

Note: Mount St. Mary's College has been developing its leadership program for some years. Cheryl Mabey is well-known in the United States for her efforts in this area. Previous editions of the Leadership Education Source Book have included course descriptions and other aspects of the college program; we have endeavored to include in this edition that which was not described previously. Details of programs noted but not described may be obtained by writing or calling Cheryl Mabey's office at the college.

Leadership Studies Minor Students arrange a plan of study with the Director of the Leadership Program

The Leadership Studies Minor is designed to provide students with an in-depth understanding and practice of leadership as it relates to women. The study of leadership must include the following components: 1. **Descriptive:** Focuses upon "who is a leader" in a variety of contexts; this component utilizes history, biographies, self-assessment, literary models, and cross-cultural studies to explore the dimension of leadership. 2. **Functional/Operational:** Focuses on "how one leads more effectively"; this component reviews leadership styles and organizational behavior while developing specific leadership skills in students. 3. **Policy:** Focuses upon social change theories and strategies, goals of leadership, and specific analysis of policies and issues affecting society.

RECOMMENDATIONS and PREPARATION: ENG 18 Studies in World Literature; ENG 25 Myth Making. The Quest for Meaning; ENG 54 Studies in American Literature; HIS 5 European Leaders and Ideas; HIS 171 US: Revolutionaries and Constitutionalists; HIS 173 US: Civil War and Reconstruction; PHI 21 Moral Values; POL 1 American Government; POL 171 Presidents and Personalities; POL 192 Plays and Politics; PSY 1 General Psychology. Each course is 3 units.

REQUIREMENTS: A minimum of 19 units taken from the following areas or approved substitutes. Number of units noted in ( ) following course title.
Leadership Theory and Skill Building (10 units): SSC 16A Introduction to Leadership (1); PSY 2 Psychology of Communication (2); SSC 16B Leadership Skill Building (1); SPE 11 Practicum: Oral Argumentation (1); SPE 12 Business and Professional Communication (1); SSC 100 Leadership Fieldwork (3); SSC 125 Leadership Studies Seminar (3).
Policy Analysis (3 units): BUS 192 Business Policy (3); ECO 107 Political Economics (3); PHI 170 Social and Political Philosophy (3); POL 135 Selected Problems in International Organization (3); SOC 112 Contemporary Social Issues (3); PTH 162 Administration and Supervision of Physical Therapy (3); SOC 161 Racial and Cultural Minorities (3).
Organizational Behavior/Social Change Theory (6 units): BUS 184 Organizational Behavior (3); or POL 187 Organizational Theory and Governmental Management (3); SOC 190 Social Change (3); NUR 182 Leadership/Management in Nursing (3).

Also required are: SSC 16A Leadership Seminar 1 (1). An introduction to the theory and issues of leadership, with particular emphasis on the application of these principles to women in higher education; SSC 16B Leadership Seminar 2 (1). An investigation of the concepts and techniques of leadership which enables the student to assess individual leadership skills. Particular attention is devoted to the study of building and participation in leadership skillbuilding workshops; SSC 16H Self and Innovative Society: Honors Leadership (1). Seminar exploring interconnections among self, creativity, and leadership from developmental and political perspectives. Team work and decision making skills emphasized through a leadership project; SSC 116C Advanced Leadership Seminar 3 (1). A seminar focusing upon problem solving through case studies with professionals in business, public service, law, and medicine. Particular attention is devoted to practical application of leadership skills; SSC 125 Leadership Studies Seminar (3). A critical examination of four themes of leadership: the leadership context, strategy for change, emerging styles of leadership, and future vision/current values of particular leaders. A special focus will be on role of women as leader and follower within organizations and society; SSC 190 Leadership Fieldwork (3). Experience-oriented course enabling the students' observation and application of the principles of leadership. Weekly seminar includes integrating fieldwork with theories and models of community leadership. Enrollment with consent of the Director of Women's Leadership Program.

Leadership Fieldwork - SS 100 (3 units)
Instructors: Gail Gresser and Cheryl Mabey

OBJECTIVES: This course combines weekly seminars with experiential learning to provide an opportunity to examine community leadership; To analyze concepts of community, community development, leadership, culture, power, participation within the context of southern California; provide opportunities to interact with community leaders both in the field and in the seminars; develop awareness and skills necessary to interact with varied peoples and organizations; provide a structure and process for student-initiated leadership projects within the community; share the needs, ideas, strategies, and vision of the southern California communities with the Mount community.

FIELDWORK EXPECTATIONS: Once a project is submitted and approved within the first month, students are expected to be in the field a minimum of 30 hours. Fieldwork is scheduled for six weeks, with an estimated 5-10 hours per week in the community site.

A fundamental tenet of the Mount's program is that leadership requires an active process of action <u>and</u> reflection. While the varied readings can provide a framework of reflection, the leadership projects provide an opportunity for action. Students enrolled are expected to identify a need or situation requiring leadership, and to play some role in providing or finding it beyond the short term of this semester. This does not mean that every student must lead a separate project. Some of the best leadership fieldwork requires students to be observers or followers. But even in those, the student must have a relationship with a leader, and be in a position to evaluate the leader's performance. As part of their fieldwork, students are required to meet with one of the instructors or a "community advisor" at least twice during the semester. During these meetings, the student and advisor will explore particular strategic questions about their observations and actions. Many of these conversations also will explore more personal questions about talents and fears, strengths and weaknesses. In short, just as the student will be present in a community, the advisor will be there for the student.

ASSIGNMENTS: Students are expected to read prior to the seminar and actively participate. Students will keep (1) a reflective reading journal and (2) fieldwork log. Students will complete a community needs assessment, proposal and report of fieldwork project. At the end of the semester, all students will present a synthesis of their fieldwork experience to "external experts" and interested Mount faculty, administrators and students.

READING ASSIGNMENTS: Saul D. Alinsky, <u>Rules for Radicals</u>. NY: Vintage Books, 1972; Harry Boyte, <u>Community is Possible</u>. Harper & Row, 1984; Notebook of selected articles specially prepared for Fieldwork course. James P. Spradley. <u>Participant Observation</u>. NY: Holt, Rinehart, Winston, 1980.

GRADING: The following is the grading scale to be used:
Reflective reading journal (due monthly), 100 points; Fieldwork log (due weekly), 200

points; Fieldwork project report, 200 points; Seminar participation, 200 points; Fieldwork presentation, 100 points.

FIELDWORK BREAKFASTS: Beginning the third week of the semester, guest speakers will join us at 7:30 a.m. for a continental breakfast and discussion of what they do and respond as expert listeners/supporters of what students are experiencing in the field. Breakfasts are <u>optional</u>. Opportunities to interact with community leaders such as Executive Director of Los Angeles United Way, Executive Director of the Council of Liberal Learning, and the author of the text will provide the context for experience as well as invaluable networking possibilities. Each community leader will then stay for the class discussion.

The following projects were identified, selected, and completed by students in the first Fieldwork class:

Needs assessment survey of elementary school parents through bilingual phone conversations presented to faculty/administration of school; Generation of extensive list of family/community volunteers matching skills/interests with needs; volunteer orientation and recognition sessions; Conversion of empty neighborhood lot into grass playing field for use of central Los Angeles elementary school children; Development of parent volunteers to open/staff school library; Collaboration and conducting of leadership training for young adult service organization; Introduction of Boy Scout troop into parish/school through identification/communication with parent/community scout leaders; Conducting of present needs assessment of neighborhood "safe harbors" project for SLOC membership--creation of materials for cooperation play games for multicultural K-2 graders.

Leadership Fieldwork Syllabus

<u>Session</u>

1	**Introduction:** Leadership and Community Development
	Alinsky, <u>Rules for Radicals</u>
2	**What is the Role of "Community Within American Culture?"**
	Pre: "Conversation with Robert Greenleaf on Servant Leader" (video)
	Readings: Notebook Selections; Boyte, pp. 1-36
3	**Community Needs Assessment:** Notebook Selections; Boyte, pp. 37-69
4	**Field Trip:** Meet community leaders and "see" different sites in central and south central Los Angeles
5	**Power: Resources and Organizations:** Fieldwork projects approved; Notebook selections; Boyte, pp. 70-89
6	**Leaders and Citizen Leaders:** Notebook selections; Boyte, pp. 90-124
7	**Group Development Through Team-Building and Problem-Solving:** Notebook selections
8	**Populism: Community Involvement and Citizen Participation:** Notebook selections; Boyte, pp. 125-159
9	**Political Process: Election '89**

10   **Community Conflict: Negotiating Skills:** Notebook selections; Boyte, pp. 160-184

11   **Evaluation: What Impact? Wrap-up Fieldwork Projects:** Notebook selections; Boyte, pp. 185-211

12   **Project Presentations with Response from Author/Community Activist, Harry Boyte:** Boyte, pp. 212-219

13   **Project Presentations--Open Forum** for college students, faculty and administrator

----

Leadership Studies Seminar - SS 125 (3 units)

This seminar focuses upon four variables which impact the exercise of effective leadership: 1) culture and diversity; 2) varied contexts of leadership; 3) values and ethics of leaders; and 4) change. Two additional threads will connect disparate disciplinary perspectives of the study of leadership--impact of gender on leadership and what are leaders like.

This course relies on the seminar method of report and discussion, including case studies and two simulations during the semester. Several guest facilitators representing different academic disciplines will interact, posit propositions, and give focused feedback to seminar participants. One unique feature of the seminar will be the opportunity for a "weeklong acquaintanceship" or "shadowing" experience with an important leader providing a lab linking theoretical learning with world of practice. Central to this seminar is a personalized synthesis of each student's skills and experiences connected to leadership during the past four years; a "leadership file" will be distributed to focus each participant on academic, co-curricular involvement, community service, professional networks relevant to leadership.

BASIC BOOK LIST: Rosabeth Kanter, <u>Tale of O</u>. NY: Harper & Row, 1980; Diane Koos Gentry, <u>Enduring Women</u>. College Station: Texas A&M University Press, 1988; Barbara Kellerman, <u>Leadership: Multidisciplinary Perspectives</u>. Englewood Cliffs, NJ: Prentice-Hall, 1984; Warren Bennis and Burt Nanus, <u>Leaders: Strategies for Taking Charge</u>. NY: Harper & Row, 1985; David Campbell, <u>If I'm In Charge Here, Why Is Everybody Laughing?</u> Greensboro, NC: Center for Creative Leadership, 1984.

GOALS: To understand some of the major questions, theories, and answers about Leadership; to develop reading and oral skills based upon critical thinking; to participate effectively in a small group to further its task; to develop the skill of oral persuasion and formal presentations; to refine your writing skills; to expand both personal and professional network of contacts; to integrate theoretical dimensions of leadership with practice of leadership.

EVALUATION AND WRITTEN ASSIGNMENTS: The seminar method relies on full participation by students; 50% of the credit for this course is based on the quality of such participation. Three criteria will guide the instructor in assessing credit: What does the student have to say? Does the student's participation connect to the reading? Has the student stretched critical analysis or insights to the limit given personality and communicative abilities?

TALKING POINT PAPERS OR POSITION PAPERS: This seminar is made up of busy, committed women. These papers then should be no longer than 500 words/(2) typewritten pages taking various informal directions: such as unrelated points that arise from the reading, expository arguments, questions for guest speakers or insight from personal experience. Position papers make up 30% of the course; oral and written report about the acquaintanceship accounts for the final 20%.

SEMINAR SYLLABUS AND COURSE ASSIGNMENTS:

Session

1   Presidential Inauguration and Leaders Transferring Power and Symbols

2   Introduction and Political Leadership: Rhetoric, Images and Actions; inaugural speech; Kellerman, Leadership, pp. 63-89

3   Leadership and Diversity: Tale of O; Enduring Women, introduction, pp. 220-244; **Talking Paper Due**

4   Cultural Implications of Leadership: Kellerman, Leadership, pp. 39-62; article, "Motivation, Leadership and Management: Do American Theories Apply Abroad?"; Enduring Women, select one profile (woman in different "culture" from own); guest facilitator: Gail Gresser, anthropologist; **Talking Paper Due**

5   The Upward Spiral: What Are Leaders Like?: If I'm In Charge Here Why Is Everybody Laughing?; Enduring Women, pp. 125-149; autobiography of Leader (students select with consultation with instructor); guest facilitator: Mary Williams, Director of Career Planning; **Talking Paper Due**

6   The Artistic or Intellectual Leader; Kellerman, pp. 179-198; LA Times article (distributed in class); guest lecturer: Dr. Mary Ann Bonino, KUSC/Director of Da Camera Society, musicologist; **Talking Paper Due**

7   Change and Continuity: College Presidential Candidates. Review resumes and meet both candidates; Bennis/Nanus, pp. 87-109; Kellerman, pp. 91-112; **Talking Paper Due**

8   Ethical Leadership; review/complete ethical organizational assessment; Kellerman, pp. 263-280; guest facilitator: Sr. Kathleen Mary McCarthy, Director, Center for Spirituality and Ministry; **Talking Paper Due**

9   Spirituality and Leadership; assigned readings; review Enduring Women for spiritual expression; guest facilitator: Sr. Kathleen Mary, Center of Spirituality and Ministry; luncheon guest: Lola McAlpin-Grant, J.D., attorney/former dean of law school; No Talking Paper due; Spring Break--Acquaintanceship Experiences

10   Alternative Leadership Styles: What Can a Leader Do?; Shadowing experiences update; Organizational Change Through Effective Leadership; Plant Y Revisited: Class Consensus vs. Theoretical Options; productivity in different groups; guest facilitator: Dr. Connie Whitney, management consultant

11   Case Analysis in Public Agencies; prepare 3 different case analyses as talking paper, including 1) identify issue(s), 2) Analyze what went wrong or how to improve situation. Golembiewski, Cases in Public Management; scan Kellerman, pp. 113-138; guest facilitator: Dr. Ronald Oard, historian/public administration; **Talking Paper Due**

12   What Makes For a Successful Executive?; What Makes For a Successful Female Executive?; simulation preparation; Bennis/Nanus, pp. 110-186; Fortune article, "What Makes Successful Business Leaders" (hand-out); guest facilitator: Dr. Connie Whitney, consultant; **Talking Paper Due**; Individual "file" assessment/appointments

13   Alternative Conceptions About Leadership; scan Kellerman, pp. 139-152; Bennis/Nanus, pp. 1-86; guest facilitator: Dr. James Delahanty, political science; **Talking Paper Due**; Individual assessments continued

14   Women and Leadership; Shadowing Experiences Presentations

15   Final Assessment/Celebration--open to faculty, alumnae and administration

LEADERSHIP FILE ON CAREER AND PERSONAL GROWTH

NAME_____DATE_____

Introduction: Within a few weeks, each of you will receive a "Leadership File" upon which you will include a complete inventory of activities, experiences related to leadership while you have been in college. Listed below is a sample of information so that you can begin to think and gather pertinent information.

Collegiate experiences: 1. Outline your employment history during college. Please include dates and level of responsibility. 2. List all student activities/roles you have assumed. (Please designate whether you were elected (E), appointed (A), or volunteered (V); whether you used communication skills (C) and/or organizational/productivity skills (O). 3. List any honors or awards you have received during college. 4. Describe community service activities you have participated in during college (include dates). 5. Any internships/practicums? 6. Participation in either Women and Public Policy Seminar (Washington D.C.), Sacramento Symposium in Public Policy or Model United Nations? Other experiences in public policy?

Self-knowledge: 1. What are your personality temperament preferences (Myers-Briggs)? 2. Situational leadership style range--Adaptability score. 3. Have you received a personal assessment of your effectiveness in: interpersonal communication, group dynamics, public speaking, organizational management skills, problem-solving skills, creativity/innovativeness, other? 4.Review the leadership activities and experiences you have had at Mount St. Mary's College. What have you learned about yourself? What have you learned about leadership?

Leadership networking/contacts: 1. If you could meet and talk with any leader in the United States, whom would you choose? Explain why. 2. Anyone in California or Southern California you would want to contact and observe them in action? 3. Estimate the number of leadership role-models you have met and observed during college. 4. List all names of members of Network whom you have met during college (graduates of leadership program).

Career/Network: 1. List any ideas you have for career options. 2. Any interest in advanced degrees? 3. How many career surveys have you completed with people in your interested field? 4. Estimate number of people --outside of the college--in your career network (i.e., family, friends, business cards contacts, etc.). 5. Estimate how comfortable you are with: writing a resume/job application, job interviewing, job search techniques, professional dress/image, other.

North Carolina State University
NCSU Fellows Program
Box 7316, Raleigh, NC 27695

Gerald G. Hawkins
Director
919/727-3151

The North Carolina Fellows Leadership Development Program
A Follow-up Study Related to Perceived Value of the Experience

---

INTRODUCTION: Since its inception in 1968, the North Carolina Fellows Program has been founded upon the belief that there is a continuing need in our society for the exercise of responsible leadership. Society traditionally looks to its institutions of higher education to provide the environment from which many new leaders will emerge. However, few colleges and universities have given a priority to this role of encouraging the development of leadership among its outstanding students. The North Carolina Fellows Program is designed to provide talented university students opportunities for accelerating their personal development and leadership potential during the four year undergraduate experience.

Originally called the Richardson Fellows Program, its primary goals were to: accelerate and support the development of highly motivated students with exceptional leadership potential; provide opportunity for increased self-development by exposing Fellows to a variety of individuals and experiences they would not ordinarily encounter until after graduation; encourage each Fellow to think about what leadership is and how to expand his/her own potential; produce graduates who will become involved in responsible, effective leadership early in their careers.

The program was well established at Davidson College, North Carolina State University and The University of North Carolina at Chapel Hill. Two other campuses, East Carolina University and North Carolina A&T University, had program grants but their efforts were short-lived. In the mid 70s, the program's name was changed to The North Carolina Fellows but the original goals and tradition of leadership development were maintained.

METHOD: With the approach of the program's twentieth anniversary, an alumni survey was conducted to determine past participants' perceptions of the value of the program. Over 500 questionnaires were mailed to alumni from all three campuses who had graduated since the program's orientation. The survey form was divided into five areas related to leadership development: 1) Personal Development; 2) Value of Program; 3) Community Involvement; 4) Internship Experience; 5) Program Activities. In each category, the respondent was to assign a perceived value rating. At the end of the survey, participants were asked to complete an open-ended question about the program.

Approximately 300 questionnaires were returned and the data in this report are based on those responses. The high degree of interest in the concept of leadership development and what proved to be an above-average undergraduate experience produced a response rate range of 45-65%.

RESULTS: The data are divided by campus for comparison of the differences among each university's program. The program goals are primarily the same at all three institutions.

Six areas of student development were identified as important to leadership development and priorities of the program. Alumni were asked to rate the personal growth value of the program to each of these areas (see Table 1).

Table 1

Question: To what extent did your participation in the Fellows Program assist in the following areas:

| | Key: | 1 = Not at all | 3 = Quite a bit |
| | | 2 = Somewhat | 4 = Very much |

	NCSU	Davidson	UNC	Total
Self-Awareness	**3.14(1)*	2.74(1)	2.68(2)	2.88(1)
Leadership	3.07(2)	2.65(3)	2.72(1)	2.84(2)
Relationships	2.78(3)	2.47(5)	2.68(3)	2.66(3)
Independence	2.78(4)	2.66(2)	2.42(5)	2.63(4)
Values/Ethics	2.78(5)	2.46(6)	2.58(4)	2.62(5)
Career Plans	2.67(6)	2.62(4)	2.33(6)	2.54(6)
Total	2.87	2.60	2.57	2.69

** Response Mean
* Rank Order

NCSU alumni rated their program experience of higher overall value than the other two universities. The program assisted the development of leadership and self-awareness more than the others areas of development and affected career plans less than the other areas.

Participants were asked how valuable the program was to their undergraduate education and leadership development skills. The results are displayed in Table 2.

Table 2

Question 1:   In comparison to other collegiate experiences, how valuable was the Fellows Program to your education?

Question 2:   In comparison to other collegiate experiences, how valuable was the Fellows Program in developing your leadership skills?

Key:	1 = Very little value	3 = Quite a bit of value
	2 = Some value	4 = Very much value

	NCSU	Davidson	UNC	Total
Question 1:	3.60	2.96	3.08	3.24
Question 2:	3.34	2.74	2.86	3.01

NCSU alumni rated their program having greater value to their education and leadership skills than the other two groups. All three university programs gave a higher value to the students' overall undergraduate education than to their leadership skills. Each activity of the Fellows Program was rated by the respondents with the results shown in Table 3.

Table 3

Question: Please rate the following activities

Key:	1 = Very little value	3 = Quite a bit of value
	2 = Some value	4 = Very much value

	NCSU	Davidson	UNC	Total
Internships	**3.85(1)*	3.85(1)	3.59(1)	3.76(1)
Self-development seminars	3.65(2)	3.24(4)	3.19(3)	3.36(2)
Interaction with Fellows	3.17(6)	3.01(7)	3.39(2)	3.19(3)
Selection as applicant	3.19(5)	3.26(3)	3.11(4)	3.19(3)
Dinners with leaders	3.15(7)	3.08(6)	3.02(5)	3.08(5)
Contact with director	3.45(3)	2.73(9)	2.96(8)	3.05(6)
Leadership course	2.77(11)	3.27(2)	3.04(6)	3.03(7)
Selection as interviewer	3.05(8)	2.91(8)	3.02(7)	2.99(8)
Individual projects	2.93(10)	3.20(5)	2.68(10)	2.94(9)
Orientation	2.97(9)	2.62(10)	2.81(9)	2.80(10)
Field trips/tours	3.24(4)	2.35(12)	2.62(11)	2.74(11)
Bi-monthly meetings	2.64(12)	2.44(11)	2.22(12)	2.43(12)
Other	2.27(13)	2.24(13)	2.18(13)	2.23(13)
Total	3.10	2.94	2.91	2.98

** Mean
* Rank Order

NCSU alumni gave a higher value rating to all of the events combined than the other two schools. The highest rated activities in order were: (1) internships, (2) self-development seminars and (3) interaction with Fellows. Orientation and bi-monthly meetings were rated as having the least overall value.

There were several significant differences among the three schools for certain activities. NCSU alumni rated contact with program director much higher than the other two schools' alumni; however, they rated the leadership course far below the average. Davidson College participants placed a much higher value on individual projects which were not a part of the program at the other two schools. As noted in Table 3, all participants rated internships as the most valuable component of the program. Respondents were asked to rate the quality of their internship experience. The results are shown in Table 4.

Table 4

Question: Rate the quality of your internship experience using the following scale.

Key: 1 = Poor   3 = Good
           2 = Satisfactory   4 = Excellent

	NCSU	Davidson	UNC	Total
Overall experience	3.32(1)	3.56(1)	3.29(1)	3.38(1)
Defining career goals	3.17(2)	3.15(3)	2.90(2)	3.09(2)
Your contribution	2.90(3)	2.89(4)	2.84(4)	2.88(4)
Responsibility	2.89(4)	3.23(2)	2.89(3)	2.99(3)
Degree of Supervision	2.72(5)	2.65(5)	2.47(5)	2.63(5)
Total	3.00	3.10	2.88	2.99

Davidson College alumni had the highest average value rating for the internship experience. All three schools, however, rated the internship supervision the lowest of the five aspects of this experience.

Participants were also asked to rate their degree of involvement in different kinds of community organizations. The results in Table 5 are divided into earlier graduates (before 1981) and recent graduates (in 1981 or after). There is no significant difference among the three universities or the age groups with respect to responses.

Table 5

Question: Listed below are a number of types of community, public service and special
              interest organizations. For each of these organizations, please tell us your
              degree of involvement using the key below.

              Key: 1 = Not very active
                       2 = Fairly active
                       3 = Very active

              (pre-1981 graduates/graduates from or after 1981)

Organization	NCSU	Davidson	UNC	Total
Political	*1.10/1.21	1.39/1.31	1.38/1.48	1.29/1.33
Civic	1.42/1.24	1.43/1.60	1.37/1.54	1.41/1.46
Professional	1.78/1.75	1.83/1.53	1.64/1.55	1.75/1.61
Business	1.41/1.30	1.22/1.14	1.37/1.24	1.33/1.23
Charitable	1.44/1.62	1.92/1.68	1.66/1.66	1.67/1.65
Educational	1.51/1.69	1.86/1.87	1.65/1.86	1.67/1.81
Religious	1.71/1.90	1.89/1.53	1.68/1.63	1.76/1.69

* Mean

At the end of the survey, respondents wrote how they felt the Fellows Program influenced their leadership and personal development. Many mentioned a boost in self-confidence as a major outcome in their leadership development ability. Some recalled certain experiences and activities from the program that greatly enhanced skills in decision making, communication skills, time management and self-motivation.

SUMMARY: The purpose of this follow-up study was to attempt to gauge the impact of the North Carolina Fellows concept on its participants. The inquiries focused on two main areas: the perceived value of the Fellows Program activities, and the perceived influence of the Fellows Program on personal and career development. Most aspects of the NCSU program were rated higher than the same aspects at the other schools, with a few exceptions. For instance, NCSU was rated significantly lower on the SOC 501 class (a leadership development course for Fellows) than at UNC or Davidson; however, NCSU ranked much higher than the other schools on self-development seminars, contact with the program director, and field trips and tours. It is noted however, that the activities listed on the questionnaire were not always a part of each campus Fellows program, for example, field trips and bi-weekly meetings. NCSU has had the benefit of greater continuity with the same program director for most of the twenty-year history on that campus. Data from all three schools ranked internships and self-development seminars the highest value.

The NCSU program was also ranked highest with regard to both education and leadership development; however, all three programs were considered to be more valuable toward education than toward leadership development. With regard to personal development, "Developing competence in leadership skills" and "Gaining an understanding of self" were ranked first by alumni of all three schools. "Clarifying career plans and aspirations" was ranked last.

At the end of the survey, respondents could express how they felt the Fellows Program influenced their leadership development. Many mentioned a boost in self-confidence, implying that self-confidence is an important factor in their leadership development ability.

Many of tomorrow's leaders can be found on college campuses today. Faced with life's challenges, they'll be called to lead, asked to lead, even forced to lead. They'll find themselves up against that "special moment" so poignantly described by Winston Churchill as the moment when a person is "figuratively tapped on the shoulder and offered the chance to do a very special thing, unique to him and fitted to his talent; what a tragedy if that moment finds him unprepared or unqualified for the work which would have been his finest hour."

According to the program alumni, this is what the North Carolina Fellows Program is about: leadership development for university students who want to meet this "special moment." Whether they are called to lead, asked to lead, or forced to lead--as a result of the North Carolina Fellows concept a greater number of these outstanding individuals might accept the responsibility, opportunity and challenge. This institutional commitment is well worth the time and resources required.

North Carolina State University
Univ. Student Center, Campus Box 7306
Raleigh, NC 27695-7306

Kathy Cleveland Bull
Assistant Director
919/737-2452

Leadership Development Series

The Student Leadership Center was created to meet the growing need for leadership training as a component of a total higher education. The center sponsors a variety of programs such as the Leadership Development Series, the Role Model Leaders' Forum and the G.T.E. Gold Scholarships. These programs are designed to give all NC State students the opportunity to explore the nature of leadership and to unleash their own leadership potential.

The Leadership Development Series consists of approximately 50 Leadership Learning Modules which focus on different aspects of leadership. Students identify topics of their own particular interest and register for the 3-hour modules offered on those topics. For ease of scheduling, most modules are offered from 6:30-9:30 p.m. on Monday and Tuesday evenings in the University Student Center. All modules are offered at least once each semester.

Module presenters are professionals in academic disciplines, business and/or student personnel. They have become involved in this project because of their own commitment to leadership development and have invested 6 months to one year preparing their module!

To insure quality interaction between the presenter and student, each module has an enrollment ceiling of 30 students. Therefore, students are encouraged to register early in the semester for greater module selection.

Any interested NCSU student may register for the Leadership Development Series by coming to the Student Leadership Center, 3111 University Student Center. A $5 per module fee is assessed. Students who are active members of a campus organization that has purchased an organizational membership are eligible to attend modules free of charge.

The most attractive aspect of participation in the Leadership Development Series for many students is the Descriptive Leadership Transcript. This official document describes each leadership module a student has taken as well as lists their leadership experiences and accomplishments while at NC State! The transcript informs employers of a student's sincere interest in leadership experiences and training. The transcript is designed to give students an edge in the competitive job market.

North Carolina State publishes a booklet each year that lists and describes leadership learning modules and provides other information about their leadership development offerings. Three modules are described here as examples. More complete information can be obtained by contacting Kathy Cleveland Bull as noted above.

**Role Models and Risk Takers: Blueprints
for Successful Leaders LDS 047**

<u>Presenter Profile</u>: George Richard Dixon, Director of Admissions, holds a bachelors, masters and doctorate from North Carolina State University. He was a Fulbright Scholar to the Federal Republic of Germany in 1984 and has been with the North Carolina State Admissions Office for thirteen years.

DESCRIPTION OF MODULE

Why do some people succeed in their careers while others fail? Are there common personal traits among "winners" that can be "learned" by those aspiring to become successful? Is it possible to glean from successful role models a formula for personal success--to develop a personal "blueprint" for success?

These questions are among those to be addressed *and answered* in this module designed to expose you to three successful "role models" through SyberVision's Profiles of Achievement video tape series. The video tapes plus group discussions of selected current literature will provide each participant with the knowledge for personal growth and development as leaders and as achievers in all endeavors.

THE KEY BENEFITS: You'll learn what common personal traits and characteristics are consistently found in successful leaders; You'll discover how to develop and refine those necessary personal traits and characteristics to fit your personality, your style, your ambitions; You'll develop insights about other people which will enable you to identify winners and those with the potential to become winners. Successful people surround themselves with winners--you'll learn how; You will develop your own personal "blueprint" for becoming a successful leader. You'll outline a step-by-step approach of self-improvement patterned after individuals who have achieved remarkable success in their lives--role models from which much can be learned.

TOPICS: HERE'S WHAT YOU WILL LEARN

- Risk Taking--When; how much; what's acceptable; cost vs. benefits
- Decision Making--How to get people behind decisions; how to make "hard" decisions palatable.
- Insight and wisdom gleaned from actually seeing successful people in action.
- The importance of identifying good role models and learning from their experiences.
- How to develop in yourself those personal traits and characteristics found in achievers.
- How to plan your own personal "blueprint" for becoming a successful leader, for becoming an achiever.

Nurturing the Leadership Image: Selling Yourself - LDS 054

Presenter Profiles: D. J. Señeres is a Junior in Civil Engineering with an A.A.S. in Mechanical Drafting and Design Technology from Wayne Community College. He is currently working with the Academic Skills Program as a Peer Tutor and Supplemental Instructor in Chemistry and is one of the 1988 GTE GOLD Scholarship winners. He completed 48 LDS Modules. John Allen Burke II is a Junior in Mechanical Engineering having received a 1988 GTE GOLD Scholarship for participation in the Leadership Development Series. He completed 41 LDS Modules.

DESCRIPTION OF MODULE

Every day, you interact with new people, whether by chance or through planning. How do you continue your interaction with these people beyond the first meeting?   IMAGE!! Continued interaction depends on the kind of image that you project.

This Leadership Learning Module is designed to explore what kind of image we project, how we can improve it, and how we can nurture it into growing and helping us become successful leaders.

Through the use of Brian Tracy's videotape "10 Keys to a More Powerful Personality" and group discussions and exercises, you will learn about the basic ingredients to personal and career success.

THE KEY BENEFITS:
- You will learn how to accomplish more in the next 30 days than you have in the past six months;
- You will learn about a "force field" that attracts everything you need to realize your dominant goals;
- You will learn to be 16 times more successful than your peers and thus open the "Red Sea" of opportunity;
- You will learn the only sure-fire way to measure your excellence at any point in your life.

TOPICS: HERE'S WHAT YOU WILL LEARN

- What is the effect of studying success?
- What are the 10 C's?
- Result Orientation
- Fun and Easy 'vs' Hard and Necessary

Taking Charge: The Magic of Personal Leadership - LDS 040

Presenter Profile: Robert E. Wenig has a PhD in Technology Education from The Ohio State University and a B.S. and M.Ed. in Industrial Arts Education from Bowling Green State University in Ohio. His major interest and study for the past 10 years has been personal and organizational leadership development. He is the graduate adviser of Industrial Arts Education and has been with North Carolina State University since 1978.

DESCRIPTION OF MODULE

Personal leadership skills are rarely taught in the classroom. Yet they are the skills required of individuals who want to achieve and experience life's well being. People who are in charge of their own lives control their destiny; they resist manipulation, exploitation, and/or dominance by others.

As you internalize the three skills of *positive self-control*, *positive self-assertion*, and *positive self-affirmation* your well being (self-esteem) will be enhanced. As a skilled take-charge person you will become more self-expressive and do things on self-initiative. Anxiety or tenseness in key situations will be reduced. The result is you will feel the joy of being in control of your world, hence an increased sense of self-worth. By gaining increased self-confidence and self-respect in your personal life you will begin to apply these same leadership skills at work/school.

THE KEY BENEFITS: You will learn how to exercise positive self-control over life situations by choosing an appropriate winning behavior; You will learn how to apply a positive self-assertive style in making life events thrilling and upbeat; You will learn selected self-motivational processes through an array of positive self-affirmation inputs.

TOPICS: HERE'S WHAT YOU WILL LEARN

- How to analyze what has been holding you back.
- How to deal with stressful situations.
- How to handle difficult situations.
- How to resolve personal conflict.
- How to overcome "put-downs."
- How to express assertiveness through positive action.
- How to determine your winning profile and successes.
- Impact of conscious and unconscious mind.
- How to use and improve self-affirmation.
- Music as a force to self-improvement.

Pennsylvania State University
217 Hub, University Park, PA 16802

Art Costantino
Director, Center for Student
Involvement and Leadership
814/863-3787

Leadership: Enrichment and Excellence Through Involvement

Reflecting its strong value on educating students for involvement as future community leaders, agents for change and effective employees, Penn State offers diverse opportunities to learn the skills, knowledge and attitudes of leadership.

The program consists of a series of workshops, provided at various levels of student growth ranging from preparing students for involvement in campus or community activities to strengthening skills as a student leader to in-depth study of certain skills critical to leadership (conflict management, ability to give constructive criticism, active listening, motivating and empowering others). These workshops are offered at varying times and are available to student organizations or to students regardless of affiliation with an organization. They are presented as single programs, usually two hours in duration, as part of a series of programs, or in a conference-type format and are designed and presented by a group of faculty, staff and students who have experience as workshop trainers. Last year, this aspect of the leadership education program was responsible for 121 programs consisting of a total of 240 hours of instruction, and reached 2700 students.

A three-credit course for student leaders is also offered each semester for thirty newly enrolled student leaders as a seminar on leadership and a support network for student leaders. Instructors are experienced human relations trainers and members of the student services staff at the university.

The Center for Student Involvement and Leadership is engaged in a new collaborative effort with the College of Engineering called WISE (Workplace Integration Skills for Engineers). Students majoring in engineering are provided with fifty hours of instruction about skills that will enhance their employability upon graduation. Student interest in the program has increased and the number of sections offered to students for the 1989 program will double. Recruiters support and encourage the effort and indicate that their companies now spend considerable time and other resources in training new employees to use the same set of skills included in the college-based program (i.e., conflict management, active listening, giving and receiving feedback, leadership style, group dynamics).

Undergraduate students are also expressing interest in learning to present leadership workshops to their peers. Those trained as trainers (approximately 45 students) have performed at a level equal to many full-time staff and faculty who also conduct workshops on similar topics. Students whose career goals include management and supervision activities seem especially motivated to learn the skills of a leadership educator.

The leadership education program provides private consultations with a full-time staff member about personal concerns or group concerns in the area of involvement and leadership development and serves approximately fifty students per year, mostly for presidents or other officers of a campus student organization seeking assistance with such problems as unclear goals, team building needs, low attendance at meetings, dealing with troublesome group members, image to the campus, involving members in activities.

The leadership education program has a resource library of over 2,000 items ranging from books and articles about a leadership topic to films, tapes, or simulations that can be used in workshops to full workshop outlines. Approximately 200 students and staff use this resource library each year. Faculty teaching several courses on such subjects as group dynamics and public speaking have discovered the resource library, and now routinely assign students a project involving the use of the library holdings.

Student Organization Management - CN ED 301 Dr. Craig Millar
Fall, 1988 - Three Credits Dr. Arthur Costantino

CLASS OUTLINE - READINGS
The course focuses on "hands-on" experiences to develop an understanding of how to be a more effective, self-aware, and knowledgeable student leader.

Class I	Information and Introduction to Leadership
Class II	Communication Skills; Listening and Feedback
Readings	"Interpersonal Communication," Warner Burke, <u>Behavioral Science and the Manager's Role</u>, William Eddy, 1969. "Conditions Which Hinder Effective Communications"; J. William Pfeiffer, <u>1973 Annual Handbook for Group Facilitators</u>, Univ. Assoc., 1973. <u>Leader Effectiveness Training</u>; Thomas Gordon, Ch. 5, "Making Everyday Use of Your Listening Skills," 1977. <u>Leadership Guide</u>; Arthur Costantino and Andrew Mozenter, Sect. 1, Communications, 1985. "Giving Feedback: An Interperson Skill"; <u>The 1975 Annual Handbook for Group Facilitators</u>, Univ. Assoc., 1975.
Class III	Conflict and Personal Goal Setting
Reading	<u>Leadership Guide</u> - Sect. II, Personal Goal Setting and Managing Time
Class IV	Understanding Group Dynamics; Quiz; First Paper Due
Reading	"What to Look For in Groups," <u>1972 Annual Handbook for Group Facilitators</u>, Univ. Assoc., 1972.
Class V	Understanding Power
Reading	"Power is," from <u>Power Management: A Three-Step Program For Successful Leadership</u>; James Brewer, J. Michael Ainsworth and George Wynne, Prentice Hall, 1984.

Class VI	Management Style
Reading	"Leadership; Management's Better Half"; John Zenger, <u>Trainer</u>, December 1985.

Class VII	Leadership Style
Readings	<u>Situational Leadership</u>; Paul Hersey and Ken Blanchard, 1984. <u>Leadership Guide</u>; Arthur Costantino and Andrew Mozenter, Sect. II, Motivation, Leadership Style, Developing Human Potential, Sharing Responsibility, 1985. "Leaders Are Made, Not Born"; <u>Leadership in Action</u>; Kenneth Benne, 1961. <u>Leaders</u>; Warren Bennis and Bert Nanus, Ch. 2, "Leading Others, Managing Yourself," 1985.

Class VIII	Diversity
Reading	"Racial Identity Development: Implications for Managing the Multiracial Work Place"; Bailey Jackson and Rita Hardiman, <u>The NTL Managers Handbook</u>, 1983.

Class IX	Goal Setting, Team Building and Decision Making
Readings	"Decisions...Decisions...Decisions"; Robert Blake and Leland Bradford from <u>Selected Readings One: Group Development</u>, National Training Laboratories, 1961. <u>Leadership Guide</u>, Arthur Costantino and Andrew Mozenter, Sect. III, Membership Recruitment, Team Building, Organizational Goal Setting, Organizational Decision Making, 1985. <u>A Passion for Excellence</u>; Tom Peters and Nancy Austin, Ch. 15, "Applause, Applause," 1985.

Class X	Programming and Running Meetings
Readings	"Thematic Programming"; Sara Boatman from <u>Perceptions</u>, 1984. <u>Leadership Guide</u>; Arthur Costantino and Andrew Mozenter, Sect. III, Meetings, Programming, Officer Training and Transition, Promotion and Publicity, 1985.

Class XI	"Back Home" Application

Class XII	Creativity

Class XIII	Review, Final Exam and Evaluation; Quiz; Third Paper Due

EVALUATION CRITERIA

You will be evaluated by the following criteria:
1. Three quizzes - 30 points (each counts 10 points)
2. Short papers: 1st - 5 points; 2nd - 10 points; 3rd - 15 points
3. Class participation - 40 points:
    a) Feedback; you must be able to receive and give constructive feedback.
    b) Listening; you must exhibit appropriate non-verbal attending behaviors as well as the ability to reflect both content and feeling.
    c) Cooperation; your willingness to join in exercises and assigned tasks.
    d) Self-disclosure; degree to which you share thoughts and feelings about yourself.
    e) Receptivity to ideas; you must exhibit openness to new ideas.
    f) Level of participation; the amount of participation exhibited in class discussions.
    g) Quality of participation; the degree to which you add positively to the class discussions.
    h) Application of learning; degree to which you integrate concepts and ideas from the course into the discussions.

Given the nature of the course, class attendance is required. One absence is permitted.
For each additional absence 5 points will be deducted from your point total.

Rensselaer Polytechnic Institute   **Marsha Paur Hall**
School of Management   Dir., Professional Leadership Program & External Affairs
Troy, NY 12180-3590   518/276-6586

The Professional Leadership Program

Some of the most pressing global challenges we face--from the elimination of world hunger to the prevention of world war--require the resolution of complex technical problems. The visionaries to whom the world will turn for answers will need a thorough grounding in technical issues, plus a perspective that takes them beyond the technical issues to considerations that are philosophical, historical, and global.

Preparing such leaders is the goal of the School of Management's Professional Leadership Program (PLP) at Rensselaer Polytechnic Institute. PLP is a participatory, dynamic, change-oriented leadership training ground; it focuses on the integration of disciplines and looks beyond academic concerns to create an environment where leadership can develop and flourish.

Believed to be the most comprehensive scientifically based academic leadership development program in the country, PLP is based upon a pioneering study called Early Identification of Management Talent (EIMT). Rensselaer's School of Management conducted EIMT in the early 1970s in cooperation with leading firms such as Colt Industries, General Electric and IBM. It is a system for identifying, early in a technical student's career, the skills necessary for a successful future as a leader in industry--forecasting and planning, salesmanship, technical competence, and influence and control. PLP uses the data developed through EIMT to select outstanding Rensselaer students to nurture the next generation of technical leadership.

Approximately 350 students have completed the PLP program since its inception in 1980. Feedback from graduates indicates that they are far better prepared than their peers for management responsibilities and enjoy a competitive advantage in the job market. Their confidence level is higher and they rise faster in their organizations. As might be expected, industry's response to PLP graduates has been uniformly enthusiastic.

Principal support for the PLP has come from the faculty and administration at Rensselaer, from dedicated executives and technical managers who contribute time and energy by advising and teaching in the classroom, and from business and philanthropic organizations that underwrite the program with financial commitments.

The Professional Leadership Program takes talented, technically oriented students beyond a narrow, grade-oriented environment and places them in circumstances where important discoveries can take place. It prepares them for the time when passive learning skills and competition for grades are irrelevant to success--when individual insight, creativity and ability to inspire others are the sole determinants in achieving goals. It prepares them for leadership.

Seminar Component - 2-3 hour weekly participation includes: Executive Speaker Series - Industry perspective and mentor interaction; Experts from Academia/Industry Series - communication skills; Experiential Sessions - including role playing, simulations, oral presentations, and creative problem solving.

Summer Internship Component - With a Pre-Internship of a two-day off-site pre-employment workshop to increase organizational awareness, self-assessment and goal setting, the Internship is a challenging work assignment requiring a high degree of responsibility and professionalism. It utilizes technical, communication, and interpersonal skills and includes exposure to the business environment and experience with the executive interview. A supervisor is appointed who acts as mentor, and an action plan diary is utilized.

Career Counseling Component - Individual counseling sessions are available to all participants with a focus on career path awareness, self-assessment, goal setting and attainment, and interview skill enhancement.

Research Component - Past research consisted of the Early Identification of Management Talent (EIMT), a collaborative effort with industry and RPI's School of Management for the purpose of developing methods for identifying management talent in a technical population. Research efforts led to the development of assessment tools and methods for identifying and selecting management talent in a technical college population and to the development of the Professional Leadership Program.

Present research consists of identification of managerial potential and success in a technical population, used in selection of program participants; greater understanding of the unique characteristics of a technically trained population; development of innovative training techniques to increase the "probability of trainability" in leadership dimensions such as "charisma and sensitivity"; industry-based research--collaborative efforts in areas such as: 1) the development of selection criteria for use in the recruitment of technical individuals; 2) the development of techniques to assess the needs of technically trained individuals with regard to training programs; 3) longitudinal study--assessing graduates' performance in industrial setting.

The Professional Leadership Program is very powerful and innovative in that it is uniquely designed to meet the needs of three participating groups: 1) students, by providing them with an intense innovative approach to management training and leadership enhancement which allows them to assess whether a management career and formal preparation for that career is appropriate for them as individuals, 2) Rensselaer's School of Management, by exploring and contributing to the research innovations for technological management, and, 3) industry, by offering an improved method of identifying individuals most likely to rise to positions of leadership, thus justifying the investment of early career training and support.

PLP graduates are attuned to an organizational perspective, are superior in technical competence, and possess well-developed interpersonal, communication, organizational, and planning skills and a professional orientation to technological leadership.

Ripon College
Campus Box 248, Ripon, WI 54971

Jack M. Christ
Director, Leadership Studies
414/748-8358

The Leadership Studies Program

The Leadership Studies Program at Ripon College was founded in 1979. It consists of two interdependent enterprises: an interdisciplinary academic program and a Leadership Institute devoted to research, production of educational materials, and communication with individual leaders and organizations.

The academic program features six courses within the Leadership Studies Department and supporting courses within the Departments of Anthropology, Sociology, Economics, History, Philosophy, Politics and Government, Psychology, and Speech Communication. A three-credit introductory course in Leadership Studies, "Leadership, Organizations, and Values," is a prerequisite to upper-level courses within the Department. Three-credit sophomore courses are offered on "Effective Organizations" and "Biographical Studies." Junior offerings include an independent-study or team-project internship ranging from two to five credits and a three-credit course on "Strategic Planning." A three-credit variable-topic senior seminar completes the curriculum of the Leadership Studies Department. Students can elect a minor in Leadership Studies comprised of courses from the eight participating departments or design a customized major in Leadership Studies in collaboration with the Program Director. Course enrollments within the Leadership Studies Department total 65 each semester, and fifteen students are enrolled as minors or self-designed majors at any given time.

The most significant projects of the Leadership Institute have been a development of an archive of in-depth tape-recorded autobiographical interviews with leaders in virtually all walks of life; production of the "Leadership Skills and Values" series of videotapes for distribution to secondary schools and colleges; and a series of conferences and visiting speakers. Students within the Program, particularly those enrolled in the junior-level internship, are significantly involved in the work of the Leadership Institute. They conduct research, interview prominent leaders for the archive of autobiographical interviews, and help to produce and edit videotaped materials for the "Leadership Skills and Values" series.

The "Leadership Skills and Values" series of videotapes includes sixteen programs completed or currently in production. Each program features interviews with prominent leaders, dramatizations, background footage shot on location in organizational settings, and special graphic or video effects.

LEADERSHIP STUDIES

Interdisciplinary courses in leadership studies are designed to introduce students to the dynamics of groups and organizations and to the roles and responsibilities of leadership in a variety of contexts. Since expertise in the relevant field of endeavor is one aspect of leadership, course offerings in leadership studies are meant to supplement the knowledge of a particular field provided by a student's major.

Some Courses Offered Are:

110. Leadership, Organizations, and Values. (Three Credits)
Introduction to leadership study in relation to considerations of human values. The course
will summarize leadership study in various disciplines such as psychology, sociology,
philosophy, economics, politics and government, management, and communication.
Historical and biographical case studies of organizations and individual leaders will relate
this material to questions of human values. Reciprocal roles and interdependencies
between leadership and followership will be stressed. Lectures, discussion, papers, and
group projects.

221. Effective Organizations. (Three Credits)
Group dynamics, innovation, change, and effectiveness in relation to leadership issues and
problems. Longitudinal and comparative case studies from a variety of historical eras and
cultural contexts, but mostly from contemporary American organizations, form the primary
substance of the course. Lectures, discussion, papers, and group projects. **Prerequisite:
Leadership Studies 110 or consent of the instructor.**

231. Biographical Studies. (Three Credits) (Offered in alternate years)
Traditional biographical and contemporary psychobiographical approaches to individual
leaders in various walks of life, historical eras, and cultural environments. The development
of character and personality will be stressed in order to investigate individual values and
goals as they are expressed through group action. Lectures, discussion, papers, and group
projects. **Prerequisite: Leadership Studies 110 or consent of the instructor.**

320. Internship. (Two to Five Credits)
Guided participation in a research project related to the Leadership Institute. Such projects
typically involve research, writing for publication, interviewing prominent leaders,
conference development, and management of institute enterprises. All students will submit
written reports at the conclusion of internship projects. **Prerequisite: Leadership Studies
110 or consent of the instructor.**

Rutgers University
LeaderStyle Associates, School of Business
New Brunswick, NJ 08903

Barbara E. Kovach
Professor of Management & Psychology
201/932-5756

The Leadership Program

OBJECTIVES: To provide a learning environment that facilitates the development of excellence and leadership potential in university students so that they graduate from the program with a greater understanding of themselves and organizations, with a greater recognition of their commitment to others, a greater willingness to assist others, and a higher degree of initiative in undertaking projects which make a positive difference in their work, university and community environments.

Guidelines for Developing Leadership: Reflect on experience both in and out of the classroom; Initiate activities in high-priority areas which matter; Work with and through other people in team and group settings; Accept difficulties and overcome obstacles; "Keep your head down, keep moving, and take care of your people"; "Make this world a better place to live in."

ONE-YEAR COURSE PLAN (Courses may be scheduled over one year or may be scheduled over a period of two and one-half years depending on the students' schedules and preferences.)
Fall - Introductory Seminar: **Leadership & Work** (3 credits); Concurrent Activities are **Leadership Applications** (1.5 credits)
Spring - Concluding Seminar: **Leadership Concepts** (3 credits); Concurrent Activities are **Leadership Applications** (1.5 credits)
Summer - Leadership Project: **Leadership Experience** (3 credits)

COURSE DESCRIPTIONS:
Introductory Seminar: Leadership and Work An interdisciplinary team-taught exploration of topics of contemporary interest related to leadership and work--organizational life, creativity, work/family integration--drawing upon conceptual frameworks and students' life experiences.

Concluding Seminar: Leadership Concepts An interdisciplinary team-taught study of concepts related to leadership and work requiring that students designate one area of their current life experience as a leadership internship and reflect on this experience in weekly journals and papers.

Concurrent Activities: Leadership Applications Related events sponsored by the Leadership Development Institute featuring noted corporate, professional and academic speakers on selected evenings throughout the year and in two major conferences in the fall and spring, a percentage of which students must attend and reflect upon in analytical papers.

Leadership Project: Leadership Experience Requires that students develop a detailed plan to effect change, working with and through people in one area of their school, work or community lives, that they implement this plan and report on the results to selected teams of academic, corporate and professional guides, coaches and mentors.

CONCURRENT ACTIVITIES:
Alternative Career Designs (six evenings a year): Outstanding speakers who have followed non-traditional career paths speak informally about their life and work with students and members of the larger community.

Major Executive Decisions: Creative and dynamic executives from the highest offices of America's biggest companies describe the processes by which they made significant organizational decisions, the consequences of these decisions, the mistakes they made and what they learned in the process.

Roadmaps for Leadership: Academics from universities around the country present papers describing institutional programs to develop student leadership potential. Discussions led by Senior and Instructional Council members of the Leadership Development Institute.

LEADERSHIP DEVELOPMENT INSTITUTE:
Senior Council: Senior officers from GM, AT&T, J&J, Rockwell meet with outstanding senior academics in management and leadership to establish and review guidelines for developing student leadership potential; **Instructional Council:** Managers from AT&T, IBM and J&J and Rutgers faculty design and implement curricula in college classrooms in accord with Senior Council guidelines; **Student Advisory Board:** Students in and alumni of the **Leadership Program** participate in clarification of guidelines and preparation of course outlines.

GENERAL COURSE INFORMATION: Courses are taught one evening a week, Monday to Thursday, from 6:10 to 8:50 p.m., preferably in a non-classroom atmosphere, i.e. chairs are placed in a circle rather than in rows, a coffee pot is available, students often come early to eat their dinner or to talk with each other before class begins. Classtime is organized so that presentations by the instructor and other members of the instructional staff will occur in the first hour and one-half of class. Following a break, students then meet in small groups (in which members of the Instructional Staff may be participants) to discuss reading material from the previous week working from student-generated discussion questions, to work through structured group and individual exercises, or to discuss specific issues raised by the presentation. Presentations are made by the six members of the Instructional Staff, generally one presentation each, and remaining presentations are made by the Instructor whose task is to provide the integrative theory which unites all of the presentations.

ASSIGNMENTS: Students have weekly reading assignments, either two or three articles, a relatively short book, or sometimes 1/2 of a longer book, and must turn in prior to class a 2-3 page, typed response to this reading. Generally, papers are graded on an S+, S, or S- basis by the instructor during the class presentation or within the following week and are returned immediately. All articles are copied in packets prior to the first class sessions and may be purchased by the students for a small duplicating fee. Books are ordered so that students may purchase them.

GRADING: Grades reflect students' degree of insight and organization in the final paper (or on essay examinations depending on instructor's preference), the quality of weekly papers and discussion questions, and quality of class participation. The paper or exam grades largely determine the final grade which may then be adjusted slightly in terms of the quality of the other work. Failing to turn in one of the weekly papers prior to the end of the semester, however, may lower the student's grade at least one-third of a grade for each paper that is missing.

Introductory Seminar: Leadership and Work I: Organizational Experience (Private)
Two instructors

Week
1   Introduction: Overview of Organizational Concepts
2   A Management Perspective
3   A Leadership Perspective
4   A Sociological Perspective
5   A Political Perspective
6   An Economic Perspective
7   A Strategic Perspective
8   Project Definition I
9   A Psychological Perspective: Individual Behavior
10   A Social Psychology Perspective: Group Behavior
11   A Psychological and Moral Perspective: Individual Behavior
12   An Anthropological Perspective: Corporate Culture
13   Methodology of the Social Sciences
14   Project Definition II and Conclusions

REQUIRED READING: Kovach, B., **The Flexible Organization**, Prentice-Hall, 1984; Frost, P.J. et al. (ed.), **Organizational Reality: Reports from the Firing Line**, Scott Foresman, 1986; Hai, D. M. (ed.), **Organizational Behavior: Experiences and Cases**, West, 1986; Pugh, D. S., (ed.), **Organization Theory**, Penguin, 1984.

Introductory Seminar: Leadership and Work II: Creativity, Art and Work
Two instructors

Week
1   Introduction: The Creative Process and the Creative Personality
2   A Psychologist's Perspective on Creativity and Development
3   An Artist's Perspective from the Visual Arts: A Split Pea in the Creative Soup
4   Project Definition: You and Creativity
5   Costume: A Creative Mode On Stage & Off
6   Music, Dance, Theater & Art Exhibitions
7   More About Creativity & Pea-Soup: The Artist in Commerce & Group Creativity
8   Art & The Corporate Culture: Giants of Commerce & Art

9   Creativity & Communication in the Media
10   Modern Dance, What Does It Mean? Movement, Anchored in the Soul
11   Creativity: Keeping the Child in the Adult
12   Modern Dance Interpretation
13   Artists Undercover: Creative Leadership in Organizations
14   Artists and the Corporate World
15   Conclusion

REQUIRED READING: Warren Bennis, **Leaders**; Joseph Kidder, **Soul of a New Machine**; Rollo May, **The Courage to Create**; Chaim Potok, **My Name is Asher Lev**; Lionel Trilling, **Sincerity and Authenticity**.

Introductory Seminar: Leadership and Work III: Work/Family Integration
One instructor, et al.

Week
1   Introduction: Life Priorities in the 1980s
2   Establishing Life Priorities I
3   Establishing Life Priorities II
4   How We Got This Way I: Culture and Biology
5   How We Got This Way II: Infancy and Development
6   Differences for Women and Men at Work
7   Differences for Men and Women at Home
8   Family Roles in the 1980s
9   Career Success in the 1980s
10   Coping with Multiple Responsibilities
11   Seeking Personal Fulfillment I
12   Seeking Personal Fulfillment II
13   Rethinking Life Priorities
14   Conclusion

REQUIRED READINGS: Baruch et al., **Lifeprints**; Kovach (Forisha), **Sex Roles & Personal Awareness**; Kovach (Forisha), **Power and Love**; Kovach (Forisha) & Goldman, **Outsiders on the Inside: Women & Organizations**; Kovach, B., **Survival on the Fast Track**; Hall and Hall, "The Dual-Career Family" (handout); Pleck, J., "Fathers and Work."

Senior Seminar: Leadership Concepts Two instructors, et al.

Week
1   Introduction: Functions of Leadership
2   The Leadership Experience I
3   The Leadership Experience II
4   Knowing Self & Personalities of Leaders
5   Finding Patterns & Creativity & Vision

6   Talking & Listening & Group Behavior
7   Evaluating Actions & Learning from Mistakes
8   Leadership, Power and Community
9   Planning for Contingencies
10   Management Frameworks
11   The Necessary Partnership: Business and Government
12   Personal Identity and Integrity
13   Telling Your Story: Passing the Baton
14   Telling Your Story: Passing the Baton II.

REQUIRED READING: Ackerman, L. "Transition Management: An In-Depth Look at Managing Complex Change," **Organizational Dynamics**, Summer, 1982, pp. 46-66; Bennis, W. "The 4 Competencies of Leadership," **Training and Development Journal**, August, 1984; Carew, D. K. et al. "Group Development and Situational Leadership: A Model for Managing Groups," **Training and Development Journal**, June 1986; Jerry Harvey, "The Abilene Paradox," **Organizational Dynamics**, 1974; Kovach, B. **Survival on the Fast Track**. NY: Dodd Mead, 1988 (selected chapters); Kovach, B. "Derailment of Fast-Track Managers," **Organizational Dynamics**, Autumn, 1986; Kovach, B. & Parish, J. "Managing Change in a Manufacturing Plant," **Training and Development Journal**, 1988; Kovach, B. **Organizational Sync**; Nadler, D. "Managing Transitions to Uncertain Future States." **Organizational Dynamics**, Summer 1982, pp. 37-45; Nadler, D. "Managing Organizational Change: An Integrative Perspective." **Journal of Applied Behavioral Science**, April-May-June 1981; Sashkin, M. "True Vision in Leadership." **Training and Development Journal**, May, 1986; Schein, E. "Interpersonal Communication, Group Solidarity, and Social Influence," **Sociometry**, 1960, 23, pp. 148-160; Vaill, P. "Purposing of High-Performance Systems," **Organizational Dynamics**, 1982.

Leadership Project: Leadership Experience

COURSE OBJECTIVES: 1. To identify a high-priority problem in one sector of one's regular life activities: (a) which is of sufficient personal interest to pursue over time; (b) the solution to which will benefit a **significant** number of people; and (c) the probability of arriving at this solution is **feasible** or possible within a few months given limited current resources. 2. To effectively develop a specific plan involving **working with and through people** which may provide a solution for this problem; 3. To implement this plan with the council and guidance of the Institute's Instructional Council; 4. To write up a report of the plan, the implementation process, and steps which might have improved this process, within a conceptual framework; and 5. To report on the results of this project to a faculty-corporate committee and to intelligently answer both conceptual and practical questions asked by the committee.

COURSE OUTLINE:

Week 1. Identifying Personal Interests: (a) Who you are and where you've been; (b) Goals and dreams. Identifying Important Topics: (a) Significant projects are ...; (b) "Worthwhile

212

projects I have considered . . ."   Week 2. Identifying Costs and Resources: (a) Feasible projects are . . .; (b) Closing the gap between significance and feasibility. Developing the Plan: (a) Stating goals and objectives; (b) Creating timelines and contingency plans.

*****

Week 13. Preparing the written report: (a) Stating the problem concisely; (b) Outlining the plan, action, and evaluation steps;   Week 14. Clarifying material for presentation: (a) Identifying key points; (b) Integrating theory and practice.

Leadership on the Fast Track (Summer Institute in Innovative Leadership)

People who love their work, give it their best, and face successive challenges and responsibilities are those on the fast-track--in whatever occupation and at whatever level. Leadership on the fast track is simply making this possible by (1) establishing clear priorities based on accurate knowledge of oneself and one's organization, and (2) working with and through others to achieve one's own priorities and organizational goals.

Each of the Institute's two seminars creates a learning environment in which participants can develop a conceptual understanding of and practice the skills associated with leadership on the fast track. The first seminar, **Leadership on the Fast Track I** ("Life is a group experience"), emphasizes self-awareness, priority-setting, and communication as a basis for moving onto the fast track. The second seminar, **Leadership on the Fast Track II** ("Doing what you say you will"), emphasizes the planning and implementation skills essential for carrying out one's priorities as well as an understanding of the responsibilities accompanying success. The first seminar is a prerequisite for the second.

Each session is taught by a team of experts from the academic, educational and corporate worlds, all of whom have worked with the Institute over the past two years, and been highly evaluated by participants. The opportunity to work with managers and executives from major corporations as well as outstanding faculty in a variety of disciplines provides an educational experience not found in any other setting.

Participants leave each session with an action plan tailored for their specific work environment, a network of new connections with others pursuing similar goals and visions, and a greater awareness of their own career potential. Those who have completed at least two sessions of Institute seminars almost invariably have achieved their goals in the workplace--independently receiving promotions and new responsibilities within their current organizational setting.

Seminars are taught in three different frameworks: (1) in all-day, one-week sessions in the New York metropolitan area during the last week of June and second and third weeks of July; (2) in fifteen one-evening-a-week session on the Rutgers University campus during the fall and spring terms of the academic year; and (3) in a mutually-agreed-upon format at another location when sponsored by an outside organization. Participants include managers of major organizations, vice-presidents of financial institutions, principals and superintendents in the public schools, and administrators in universities.

Southern Illinois University at Edwardsville
Student Leadership Development Center
Edwardsville, IL 62026-1168

Lori A. Schlosser
Coordinator
618/692-2686

Student Leadership Development Program

The Student Leadership Development Program, Building Your Leadership Potential, is designed to strengthen skills that focus on personal and career goals and assist individuals to serve effectively as informed citizens and community leaders. First offered in January 1988, the program provides opportunities to complement classroom experiences. Two components, a) University and Community Service and b) Active Citizenship, focus on civic awareness and appreciation for the intrinsic benefits of contributing to the world. The third component, c) Leadership Modules, acquaints students with business and community leaders, faculty, staff, alumni, and other students to share information about leadership on campus and in the community. To complete the program two of these three components are selected.

All enrolled SIUE students may participate in the program, regardless of academic major or class standing with no admission requirements or fees. A plan for involvement in accord with individual interests and time is designed and completed by the student.

A transcript is developed for participants who successfully complete at least two components of the program. Designed to accompany a student's resume, the transcript provides certification of citizenship experiences and service. It also documents module involvement.

Graduates of the program have benefited from:
- increased self-confidence;
- a clearer understanding of issues facing today's leaders;
- valuable contacts with peers, faculty, staff, and leaders in government, business, and service agencies;
- recognition for skills and service, enhanced employment and promotional potential;
- new insight into their own potential to improve the lives of others.

University and Community Service: The service component focuses on leadership experience available through non-paid service to the University or community. Attendance at two modules is required in addition to 36 service hours, 100% of which must be served in an agency external to the University. Students may volunteer for student organizations, campus advisory boards and committees, academic clubs, and a variety of University events to gain service credit. Off-campus experiences are also available.

UNIVERSITY AND COMMUNITY SERVICE

Required: Leadership Module #03, "Community Service: Opportunities and Responsibilities" and an elective module. Module 18, "Human Relations," is suggested, but any module may be selected. Module completion prior to service is advised.

University and Community Service is undertaken on a non-paid, non-academic-credit basis and may include activities completed through elective office, committee assignments that

214

are appointed or elective, or service to student organizations or honorary academic organizations. Community service includes volunteer opportunities at a broad range of service sites. The program coordinator: facilitates the match of placement requests with your interests, skills and qualifications; decides if program credit can be given for service hours completed while a student was enrolled in the University but had not yet enrolled in the program; approves additions to the published agency listing.

In order to receive credit toward the leadership transcript, service hours must be verified and a form detailing duties performed and skills acquired must be completed. An explanation of the service experience in relation to goals is also to be provided on the form, as is an assessment of the service as a learning opportunity. Professional objectives and interests in depth should be considered when selecting service sites. The program coordinator can assist in planning University and Community Service commitments and should be consulted early.

Active Citizenship: The citizenship component offers the opportunity to enhance understanding of law, democracy, the judicial system or public policy development. Participants are required to complete three modules and a civic awareness experience which includes an individually designed observation, proposal, and project. The experience reflects one's primary area of interest and is designed and completed with the assistance of a mentor.

Modules #02, "Understanding Freedom and Democracy," and #06, "Civic Responsibility" are required. An elective must also be selected from Modules #16, "Major Influences in the Political Process, #24, "International Affairs: What a Leader Needs to Know," and #27, "Law and Its Impact on Society."

A total of 10 hours of observation is required and may include attending seminars on public policy issues, city council meetings, political debates or courtroom sessions or interviews with government officials, lawyers or judges. This serves as the foundation for the proposal and project. Completion is documented on an Observation Form and verified by the mentor.

The citizenship proposal completed prior to undertaking the project outlines project specifics, including anticipated goals and outcomes. It is designed, completed and verified with the assistance of the mentor.

The citizenship project allows you to gain experience in your area of interest. The project requires a 25-hour commitment that is also monitored and verified by your mentor. Projects which may be considered include, but are not limited to, organization of a voter registration drive, assistance in a political campaign, advocacy activity for a public policy issue or research for judicial proceedings.

Leadership Modules Titles and Descriptions: The leadership modules are two-hour interactive sessions covering leadership, citizenship and service topics. Modules are offered at 2:30 p.m. and 7 p.m. on Tuesdays during fall, winter, and spring quarters. Presenters include University faculty, staff, students and community leaders. This schedule provides a long-range look at the modules to be presented this academic year. A complete listing of module dates, times, locations and presenters is available prior to the beginning of each quarter.

Specific modules are required for each component of the program. The following guidelines apply:

Modules Component: #01 through #10, Mandatory; #11 through #36, Elective (select 10); Total required = 20

Citizenship Component: #02, #06, Mandatory; #16, #24, #27, Elective (select one); Total required = 3

Service Component: #01, Mandatory; Elective (select one, #18 is recommended); Total required = 2

01   Leadership Characteristics: You are a Leader What is leadership? What are effective leaders like? What are ineffective leaders like? How are leaders and managers different? How does one become an effective leader? What is the value of responsible management and cultivating support? Participants acquire a basic understanding of many leadership/management concepts and principles.

02   Understanding Freedom and Democracy The difference between democratic and authoritarian leadership and how each works in different circumstances will be explored. Can there be democracy without freedom? What is the constitutional meaning of freedom and how are individual freedoms limited by the common good? Is democracy tyranny of the majority?

03   Community Service: Opportunities and Responsibilities Participants engage in a dialogue to examine aspects of volunteer service to the community, including the University community, as a function of leadership. Needs of the University and surrounding communities are specifically examined as they relate to services in which participants and presenters are already involved.

04   Effective Communication Participants learn principles and techniques of effective communication within the context of the leader's and members' roles, e.g., psychological principles of communication, listening effectively, non-verbal behaviors, patterns of miscommunication, principles of upward and downward communication, understanding communication flow, and barriers to communication.

05   Group Process This module explores the basic concepts of group process. Participants learn about groups and their various characteristics and become knowledgeable about task dimensions of groups, group norms, and the impact of effective leaders in working groups.

06   Civic Responsibility This module introduces participants to their role as active and informed citizens. Topics for discussion include the rights and responsibilities of leaders who influence public policy decisions and governmental reform.

07   Conflict Resolution: Negotiating Differences This module familiarizes participants with sources of conflict and how differences can be resolved in an appropriate manner. Emphasized is the development of effective negotiation skills.

08   Personal Motivation The relationship between motivation, individual personality and leadership style is explored. Emphasis is directed toward the importance of understanding one's own motives, needs and priorities as they relate to effective leadership.

09   Cross-Cultural Awareness Participants enhance their awareness of cross-cultural differences; become more aware of their own cultural perceptions, values and behavior; and learn more appropriate cultural perceptions. This module also relates cross-cultural awareness to the essential characteristics of effective leadership for the next century.

10   Ethics and Leadership Participants explore scenarios designed to stimulate discussion of ethical questions facing leaders. Opportunities are provided to examine ethical decision making and problem solving.

11   Role Models and Risk Takers: Blueprints for Successful Leaders Participants examine factors that contribute to and nurture the leadership styles of selected notable individuals. The role of the leader as risk taker is explored.

12   How to Get Things Done: Time Management Participants learn the importance of personal organization, task priority, and certain interpersonal skills which enable them to maximize the effectiveness of their work time. The sources of time management problems will also be considered.

13   Setting Goals for Effective Leadership Participants learn about the value of goals and objectives for effective leadership. Discussion will focus on the process of developing goals that are relevant, challenging and appropriate.

14   Leadership Through Assertion Participants learn to think and act in ways that are clear, decisive and fair. Discussion will clarify passive, assertive and aggressive behaviors.

15   Effective Meetings This module familiarizes participants with those elements that combine to produce effective outcomes at organizational meetings. Included in this module are the fundamentals of parliamentary procedure and its use within the small group process. The importance of preparing for meetings, taking minutes and following through subsequent to meetings is also emphasized.

16   <u>Major Influences in the Political Process</u> Participants learn about the influence which the individual and groups may have within the political process. The functions of a lobby and lobbying at the national, state, and local levels are examined and explained.

17   <u>Managing Stress</u> Participants learn to recognize, to assess, and to reduce stress in their personal lives and in work groups for which they are responsible as leaders. In addition, participants discuss the types of decisions leaders face when their work group and/or individuals in their work group are under unpreventable stress.

18   <u>Human Relations</u> Participants learn about the importance of being sensitive to a work group. Discussion will focus on assuming an appropriate role--team player or team leader--within the work environment.

19   <u>Delegating Responsibility Effectively</u> This module explores the meaning of delegation, why it is appropriate to delegate, when to delegate, and the relationship between delegation and effective leadership.

20   <u>Effective Decision Making</u> Participants review the numerous ways leaders make effective decisions, including the use of intuition, brainstorming, consultation, external review and staff recommendation.

21   <u>Community Change: What a Leaders Needs to Know</u> Participants examine the institutional, technological and cultural processes related to community change. Emphasis is placed on leadership skills essential for responding to community change.

22   <u>Developing Self-Esteem</u> Participants learn the importance of increased self-confidence, self-respect and self-worth in their personal lives. As these qualities are developed, leaders are better able to take charge of their lives.

23   <u>Leadership and Public Speaking</u> Participants gain an understanding of the skills and confidence level necessary for speaking effectively. Discussion will include audience analysis, topic selection, speech outlines, appropriate language, visual aids and non-verbal communication.

24   <u>International Affairs: What a Leader Needs to Know</u> Participants explore the cultural and economic interdependence between advanced and emerging nations.

25   <u>Leading Your Peers</u> This module is designed for student leaders who are responsible for group or organization direction. Discussion will focus on gaining the respect and support of peers and developing a working relationship that supports enthusiasm and follow-through.

26   <u>Motivating Others</u> Participants explore the skills that effective leaders use to foster enthusiasm. Discussion focuses on the leader who inspires commitment and success.

27   <u>Law and Its Impact on Society</u> Participants gain a perspective on the nature and

complexity of judicial decision making and the role of law in an ordered society, how the law has evolved to its present state, and how it will continue to evolve.

28 Understanding the Organizational Climate This module familiarizes participants with the many facets of organizational climate and enhances their understanding of the way leaders may assess and shape the climate within their organizations.

29 Analyzing Public Perception This module provides participants with the opportunity to evaluate the significance of personal charisma, perceived competence, and public trust upon the leadership effectiveness of recent public figures.

30 Leadership Challenges for Women Participants examine their personal ideas regarding the unique leadership challenges that women encounter. The impact of race, gender, and socio-economic factors on women's personal and professional development will be examined.

31 The Leader as an Effective Interviewer This module focuses on ways leaders select people who will work effectively within the organization. Participants learn to define job specifications, determine priorities for qualifications, formulate appropriate questions and evaluate responses. Participants may also develop more effective interviewee skills.

32 The Art of Listening Participants examine effective listening skills often demonstrated by leaders. A discussion of both verbal and non-verbal messages will be included.

33 Leadership Opportunities on Campus This module focuses on campus opportunities to develop and enhance leadership skills. The benefits of co-curricular involvement in Student Government, student organizations and University committees will be discussed.

34 Image and Etiquette Participants develop a basic understanding of the fundamentals of professional image projected through etiquette and situational conduct. Appropriate conduct at meetings, interviews, receptions, and other social settings will be discussed.

35 Assess Your Leadership Skills This module provides participants with the opportunity to examine their current leadership traits and set goals for acquiring new leadership characteristics.

36 Leadership Challenges for Minorities This module will explore specific challenges faced by leaders from minority groups. Discussion will include the internal and external factors impacting minority leadership, goal setting and attainment, and the value of networking.

St. Norbert College
DePere, WI 54115

Richard Rankin
Vice President for Student Life
414/337-3055
Thomas F. Hartford
Director, Center for Leadership Development
414/337-4023
Lori Pollard
Assistant Director of Student Activities
414/337-3149

Center for Leadership Development

The Center for Leadership Development provides all students the opportunity to develop, expand, explore and experience leadership skills through workshops, seminars, college courses, sports, work, clubs, organizations, and other activities. Currently it is organized under the direction of the Vice President for Student Life with a limited staff supported by grants. A confidence course is being constructed and a leadership resource center is being developed. Brochures for all programs have been designed.

LEAD (Leadership Experience And Development) Program: This is voluntary for all students who want to learn more about themselves and others while learning leadership skills that will give them an edge on their peers upon graduation. It is a series of non-academic, non-credit seminars and workshops that supplement academic studies, work, internships, and various student opportunities with leadership, management, and human resource development concepts, theories, and experiences. Students may select and schedule in tailoring a program to their specific needs and desires. The ultimate goal is for students to progress through three distinct phases: <u>Learn</u> leadership skills; Gain <u>Experience</u> as a leader; <u>Share</u> skills and experiences with others.

Leadership certificates for various levels of achievement are awarded to students and an activity transcript will be provided upon graduation to certify all leadership roles and enrichment received through the program.

MINI (More Involvement - New Ideas) Program: It is designed to give on-campus leaders the basic skills to increase their effectiveness as a leader and the club's efficiency as a team. It is voluntary for all students serving in or elected to key leadership roles on the college campus. MINI is divided into an eight-hour core program focusing on leadership theory and styles, self-motivation, communications, and group dynamics and an optional program consisting of eight two-hour workshops of which two must be completed. MINI is a step toward leadership success and its workshops also count toward the LEAD program. Leadership certificates and plaques are awarded to organizations exceeding established standards of participation.

BOLD (Business Organization Leadership Development) Program: This is designed for businesses, community groups, and volunteer organizations interested in providing opportunities for their executives, supervisors, managers, and other employees to learn more about themselves and others while using leadership skills to improve the organization. The program can complement in-house business training activities and is available to all employees. More importantly, this program provides quality training for small businesses

220

and community organizations without a formal training program. BOLD is divided into workshops and seminars that may be conducted at the College, business, or other locations.

Special features of the Center for Leadership Development: Systemic approach integrating all college leadership opportunities; Open to all college students; Flexible scheduling (afternoons, evenings, and weekends); Non-academic, non-credit; Voluntary; Over 50 different workshops currently available with more being developed; Involves students as facilitators; Recognizes individual and group achievements; Multi-event Confidence Course located on the campus; Provides formal certification of all leadership activities for future employment through an activities transcript; Facilities available on-campus for large groups (townhouses, conference rooms, etc.).

The Future: Program Evaluation; Individual Assessments; Progress Review; High School Programs; Leadership Camp; Outdoor Leadership Program; Student Resource Center.

St. Olaf College
Northfield, MN 55057

Shannon M. Murphy
Director of Student Activities
507/663-3999

Leadership Effectiveness and Development (L.E.A.D.)

A leadership training and development program directed towards student leaders. The Division of Student Life has the responsibility for shaping and developing the program. The implementation of specific elements of the program is shared by a group of ten students who comprise the "L.E.A.D." (Leadership Effectiveness and Development) team.

GENERAL OBJECTIVE: To assess student leadership needs; to develop leadership programs and services that address these needs, with emphasis on balanced living and lifelong leadership skills; to develop campus resources and networks to enhance and promote development; to inform the student body of leadership opportunities and campus activities; to serve as a support system and resource to student leaders; to encourage and develop broader student participation in campus leadership positions and encourage a peer-mentor relationship between students; to encourage students and organizations to take ownership for the Leadership Development program; to involve faculty, staff and alumni in the Leadership Development program.

Structure of the L.E.A.D. Team: (1) Ten students are selected through a nomination, application, and interview process in the spring; they are committed to personal growth in the area of leadership and to the concept of leadership development. (2) Student background: sophomore and juniors: diverse co-curricular and academic involvement; mix of men and women; campus leadership experience. (3) One year commitment to L.E.A.D. team (May-May): weekly team meeting; committee assignments. (4) Two advisors: Director of Student Activities and the Assistant to the Director of Student Activities for Leadership Programs (a half-time position).

Training of the L.E.A.D. Team: National Collegiate Leadership Conference held in Shelby, Michigan in early August sponsored by the American Youth Foundation and ongoing individual skill and team development on campus.

Programs Developed and Sponsored by L.E.A.D.:

• Training and skills development programs for campus leaders:

Hall Council Officer Training-September; Student Senate Orientation-September; Fall Leadership series-October; A special constituency series focusing on leadership-January; Spring leadership series-March/April; One-time workshops/seminars for identified needs of campus organizations/student leaders; "Servant as Leader" seminar series led by St. Olaf College President.

• Developmental Leadership Courses:

Emerging Leaders - Twenty freshman students selected through a nomination and application process in a series of 9 leadership courses. Purposes are: to build a foundation for future leadership on campus; to raise awareness of skills needed to become an effective leader; to increase one's confidence and self-understanding; to develop leadership skills; to increase understanding and awareness of St. Olaf College, its personnel, and the leadership opportunities it provides; to encourage involvement in cocurricular activities that enhance leadership development.

Insights (Advanced Leadership Course) - Twenty sophomores, juniors, and seniors, selected through a nomination and application process and a course consisting of 7 advanced leadership classes. Purposes are: to identify ways in which leadership skills can be learned; to become knowledgeable of leadership theories and research that will enable participants to better understand the dynamics of leadership; to develop an understanding of and sensitivity towards settings and persons of diversity; to help students clarify and develop their own ethical orientation; to challenge participants to analyze the nature of leadership as observed in a variety of situations; thus identifying the behaviors essential for effective leadership; to provide a setting in which active student leaders can increase knowledge of themselves; to expand the participants' analytical and problem-solving skills.

• Other programs: Periodic Leadership newsletter - "L.E.A.D. the Way"; Student Leaders Recognition Reception - held in May; Publication of student leader resource guide; Assist with Fall "Activity Extravaganza" - student organization recruitment activity.

Stanford University
Public Service Center, P. O. Box Q, Stanford, CA 94309

Timothy K. Stanton
Assoc. Director
415/725-2859

You Can Make a Difference

Through the programs and support of the Public Service Center, Stanford students throughout the academic year and into the summer step off campus and enter a different type of learning environment. There are no lecture halls. The "classrooms" are in neighborhoods and communities--as close to home as East Palo Alto or as distant as New Delhi, India. These students are involved in voluntary service, where personal satisfaction and accomplishment are measured not by academic assessment but in the difference their involvement makes in other people's lives. For some, involvement with the Center marks the beginning of a public service career; for others, it is the start of a lifelong commitment to volunteerism. Some selected programs include the following:

The **Stanford Volunteer Network (SVN)**, organized and directed by students, is the link between student volunteers and the needs of the local community. The Network sponsors and develops group volunteer programs such as tutoring projects for children, food drives, work with the physically disabled and the elderly.

Each fall the Network sponsors <u>Reach Out Today</u>, a campus-wide one-day public service effort. Hundreds of Stanford students go into the community to help renovate community facilities, visit the elderly, host field days for children, and work with the needy. This one-day event serves as a catalyst for many students to become involved in public service activities on a continuing basis. In the spring, SVN sponsors the Stanford Carnival, which raises money for a student-initiated public service project.

Stanford-In-Government (SIG) enables students to participate in government and policy-making. For each of the past five summers more than 100 students have spent a summer working in Washington, D.C. with the support of this student-managed program. SIG sponsors four Fellows who work on special assignment in offices such as the Office of Technology Assessment, the House Judiciary and Rules Committee, and Office of the United States Trade Representative.

SIG has broadened, creating state-level internship programs such as SIG-In-Sacramento, and continues to develop fellowship opportunities in other state capitals. Throughout the academic year, SIG sponsors on-campus speakers programs featuring national policy-makers who address contemporary public interest issues.

The **Stanford International Development Organization (SIDO)** educates and involves students in issues of Third World development. SIDO sponsors educational programs and provides internship opportunities.

Fundraising for local self-help projects is a major SIDO activity. For example, SIDO supports a women's cooperative in El Salvador that constructed a school and pig farm cooperative for a refugee community. For the past several years, students and others have participated in Bike-Aid. Soliciting pledges, volunteers then pedal across the U.S. and Europe, raising money for the awareness about hunger and poverty in the United States and Third World countries. In 1987, 160 riders raised over $200,000.

SIDO, a founding member of the Overseas Development Network (a national student consortium) focuses on international development educational programs, working cooperatively with colleges throughout the nation to promote understanding of development issues.

In addition to student-directed public service programs, the Public Service Center offers a variety of University-supported fellowship, internship and volunteer programs.

An important part of the Center is the **Public Service Opportunities Clearinghouse**, a resource center where students can locate volunteer, internship and community-sponsored research opportunities at local, state, national and international organizations.

With more than 500 public service listings on **Odyssey**, the internship and research database accessible across campus, Clearinghouse staff help students match individual interests and talents with people and organizations needing help. Students can identify short-term, summer, or ongoing public service projects through the Clearinghouse.

The **John Gardner Public Service Fellowship Program**, a collaborative effort between Stanford University and the University of California, Berkeley, gives three outstanding graduating seniors from each campus a unique and invaluable opportunity to work directly with a distinguished mentor in a public service setting. Designed to encourage recent graduates to consider public service careers, Fellows receive an eleven-month grant and travel assistance. Fellows work on public policy issues and important social problems often drafting legislation, developing health policy, and researching economic development issues.

The **Public Service Summer Fellowship Program** allows students to implement their own ideas for solving human problems. Each year approx. 25 students receive fellowships based on the creativity and practicality of project proposals. With these funds, Fellows spend the summer putting their ideas into action, returning to campus in the fall to share their experiences.

Team, initiated by the Stanford Volunteer Network, is a recent expansion into athletic and recreational programs for children. Stanford students develop games and coach fourth through sixth graders in a variety of sports activities, giving the children structured recreational programs and a chance to play in competitive intramural sports events.

Once a year students conceptualize and organize the **You Can Make A Difference Conference**, a major event that brings together national figures to discuss contemporary public policy topics. Widely supported by the undergraduate and graduate schools, the Conference's aim is to expose students to public issues, increase awareness, and generate greater student initiative and involvement in public service activities.

BACKGROUND: The design and delivery of leadership programs is an area which has received considerable interest from various professionals over the years. In 1976, Commission IV of the American College Personnel Association formed a task force to explore the nature and delivery of leadership programs. The Leadership Task Force efforts resulted in the publication of <u>Student Leadership Programs in Higher Education</u> (Roberts, 1981) by ACPA. This book was the first to explore the concept of the deliberate design of comprehensive leadership programs in the college setting.

One of the greatest strengths of <u>Student Leadership Programs in Higher Education</u> was the delineation of the terms of training, education and development. This differentiation improves the design of a "Comprehensive Leadership Program." The point made was that unless these terms are defined to be distinct the leadership educator does not have a framework to help in planning and delivering broadly based programs which meet the needs of all student leaders. While the reader should refer to <u>Student Leadership Programs in Higher Education</u> for a full explanation of this framework, brief definitions will at least introduce the importance of clearly defining these words and the implication this has for program design:

> **Training** - "involves those activities designed to improve performance of the individual in the role presently occupied. A training activity is one which is concretely focused and is directed at helping the individual being trained to translate some newly learned skill, or piece of information, to a real and immediate situation." (Roberts, 1981, p. 19);

> **Education** - "consists of those activities designed to improve the overall leadership competence of the individual beyond the role presently occupied. Education takes the form of providing information or enhancing abilities which may be helpful to the individual in his/her present role; however, the ultimate purpose is to provide generalized theories, principles, and approaches which are relevant in a broader setting." (Roberts, 1981, pp. 21-22);

> **Development** - "involves those activities designed to provide an interactionist environment which encourages development in an ordered hierarchical sequence of increasing complexity." (Roberts, 1981, pp. 22) ". . .changing perceptions of the world and situations which a person encounters are assumed to take place in an environment where there is interaction with other people and with one's surroundings. The individual who reaches higher levels of developmental maturity is one who is able to more effectively and productively interact in a complex, diversified world." (Roberts, 1981, pp. 22-23)

One of the shortcomings of <u>Student Leadership Programs in Higher Education</u> was that it dealt with only those leadership programs created and initiated by student developmental educators. As interest in leadership programs has been seen more recently in the ranks of faculty, renewed interest and new conceptualizations of what is possible have emerged. This renewed study of leadership programs has, in fact, lead to the creation of an Inter-

Association Leadership Project which has attempted to draw together representatives from various student personnel professional associations in order to update and expand our current thinking about leadership programs. A partial result of this Inter-Association Project is the text which follows in this article. Project members have reviewed numerous drafts of this Model Program statement. The Model, completed in July 1989, represents taking the original conceptions in <u>Student Leadership Programs in Higher Education</u> and expanding them to embrace the broader interest in leadership programs expressed by the faculty and the broader community. The original formulators of this Model include: George Bettas, Washington State University; Patrick Brown, University of Vermont; Anthony Chambers, University of Missouri at St. Louis; Nance Lucas, Ohio University; Ann Morgan, Boston College; Tim McMahon, University of Iowa; Dennis Roberts, Lynchburg College; Ronald Slepitza, Creighton University; Craig Ullom, University of Miami.

INTRODUCTION: One of the central purposes of higher education has been the preparation of citizens for positions of leadership. Now, as then, this purpose remains an essential component of the educational mission. With the growing complexity of education, its increased tendency toward specialization, and the need for leaders to cope with change, leadership programs assume an even greater importance.

It is because of this perceived urgency in preparing leaders who can cope with the complexity and challenges of leadership that this model for leadership programs has evolved. Through a model which encompasses broad segments of both the higher learning community and the community at large, we in higher education can be better unified and empowered to work toward the critical mission of preparing informed, educated leaders and citizens for society and the world.

LEADERSHIP PROGRAM CORE BELIEFS: Any educational institution must define the broad purpose and direction of the leadership program through studying carefully the specific mission and purpose of that particular environment. Institutional environments are unique and the foundation of a leadership program is strongest when congruent with institutional values. Some essential beliefs of one's leadership program emerge through the integration of institutional values and other assumptions about the nature of leadership. Examples of such core beliefs include:

1. Leadership is demonstrated by those individuals designated as leaders and those who participate actively in the organization.
2. Leaders and active participants must be capable of making thoughtful, critical and informed decisions.
3. Leaders maintain, protect, and extend those individual freedoms that form the basis of participation in society.
4. Responsible leaders develop commitment in the membership to both the organization and to its broader role in society.
5. Leaders must possess both a realistic contemporary perspective and a hopeful vision for individuals and society for the future.
6. Leaders must be able to identify their own and other's strengths and weaknesses, and use this to the benefit of the organization and society.

7. Leaders must work within a new paradigm that includes a concept of global community, a commitment to values-based decisions, an understanding of community service and a concern for the common good.

UNDERLYING PRINCIPLES IN PROVIDING A COMPREHENSIVE LEADERSHIP PROGRAM: Beyond the basic mission and goals of the leadership program, certain planning and organizing principles assist in the successful development and implementation of a comprehensive leadership program:

1. A broad range of faculty, student affairs staff and students should be involved in the planning and delivery of the various components of the leadership programs.
2. The needs of the recipients of the leadership program should be assessed and considered carefully in the design of program offerings.
3. Leadership programs should be carefully evaluated on an ongoing basis. Areas which might be included are satisfaction, outcomes to participants, organizational productivity/effectiveness and overall contribution to the learning environment.
4. Leadership training, education and development have different purposes, which are important to a successful comprehensive leadership program. A comprehensive program continues to offer activities which represent each.
5. Multiple strategies for implementation should be used in order to respond to the diverse needs of recipients and the complexity of the multiple purposes of the leadership program.
6. The leadership program should be designed and directed to meet the needs of the various special populations which exist in the specific higher education institution. (Examples might include, but are not limited to blacks, hispanics, women, disabled and international students.)
7. The leadership program should advocate consistency between what is taught through the program and the process by which institutional decisions affecting students are made.

A UNION OF THOUGHT AND ACTION: To provide a comprehensive leadership program at any college or university requires the collaborative efforts of student affairs professionals and faculty.

This union will do much to satisfy the societal need for experienced, well-prepared and thoughtful leaders. Establishing a Leadership Studies program should include team teaching and a broad selection of courses relating concepts, skills, and theories to the practice of leadership. Such a program should recognize the importance of providing experiential opportunities on and off campus to help prepare students with the knowledge and experiences to cope with their present and future leadership roles. Opportunities within such a leadership studies program would be grouped under academic and experiential areas.

Academic:

Liberal Arts - This program area represents those classes currently offered in the liberal arts curriculum that relate directly to the concept of leadership and/or to the concepts that better prepare one for leading. Courses in disciplines such as philosophy, literature, logic, history, etc., provide a strong foundation for one who assumes leadership responsibilities.

As these courses are currently offered, the major program need is to inform students of particular courses that apply to the Leadership Studies program and encourage registration.

Applied Sciences - Within the social and behavioral sciences and related professional curricula (i.e., psychology, sociology, business, education, communication, etc.) exist a variety of courses that address a specific perspective or approach to leadership. Many social psychology courses examine the dynamics of a group and the impact of a group leader. Courses that focus on organizational behavior originate from the business college. These courses could be expanded to include courses that use biography and film as a means to examine how others represent leaders as well as what type of people become significant leaders. These opportunities would encourage creativity that crosses from academic department to academic department. These courses would also permit the addressing of contemporary societal issues (poverty, racism, sexism, etc.), international dimensions of leadership, and leadership in the public and private sector.

Experiential:

Campus Involvement - Involvement in the campus community can provide numerous additional experiences needed for significant growth and development. Reflection on these experiences can provide a richer understanding of the importance of leadership, as well as the knowledge of how one can be an effective leader. Many current leadership programs are centered in student affairs offices and include credit and non-credit programs. These classes, workshops, seminars, retreats, etc., are usually facilitated by student affairs professionals and paraprofessionals, and address the general area of understanding how theory becomes practice. Student organizations, the campus administrative system and "mentors" are but a few of the laboratories available to interested students. It is important to provide the opportunity to study one's own actions and learn from those experiences.

Community Service Involvement - All students involved in leadership programs should be encouraged to become involved in community service. As students serve those in need they enter into a mutually transforming process. In addition to meeting real community needs students discover opportunities for leadership and learn more about themselves. It is believed that service challenges students to incorporate integrity, justice, and care into their personal makeup and therefore their leadership style. The integration of the academic and the experiential (reflection and doing) significantly enriches the leadership opportunities for our students.

Outcomes Assessment and Program Evaluation - Comprehensive leadership programs have a responsibility to those they serve and to those who provide resources for their existence to clearly demonstrate their impact and effectiveness. While the ultimate benefit of program evaluation and outcomes assessment is better programs, evaluation and assessment are also useful in making decisions about future directions, justifying a program's existence, lending credibility, and responding to accountability demands. Although program evaluation and outcome assessment are closely related, the focus of each is different:
1. Program evaluation emphasizes the analysis of factors impacting the design and administration of the program's activities.

2. Outcomes assessment emphasizes an analysis of the degree to which student participants are affected by their involvement in the leadership program. The development of outcome assessments and program evaluation strategies are integral to the design and implementation of comprehensive leadership programs.

Leadership Program Content: A comprehensive leadership program should include numerous topics, among them the following:

1. The Concept of Leadership - Historical perspectives and evolution of leadership thought; Theoretical foundations of leadership; Philosophical dimensions; Values considerations and ethical issues; Cultural variations of leadership; Gender differences.

2. Personal Skill Development - Definition and exploration of personal leadership approaches; Developing an awareness and understanding of various leadership styles and approaches; Self-assessment and personal goal setting; Creativity development; Communication skill; Problem solving and decision making; Personal management issues (time, stress).

3. Leadership in Organizations - Group dynamics; Team building; Motivation; Organizational structures and functions; Task and resource management; Conflict management; Crises management.

4. Contemporary Leadership Issues - Leadership in the private sector (e.g., business, industry, etc.); Leadership in the public sector (e.g., government, politics, education, etc. on local, state, and national level); Societal problems (e.g., poverty, racism, sexism, economics, crime, etc.); International dimensions of leadership (e.g., nuclear arms, war and peace, relations with other countries, etc.); Evaluation and research assessing leadership concepts and behavior; Leadership in community service.

A Checklist for Implementing a Student Leadership Program: 1. Assemble a planning team - Invite faculty, student affairs staff, and students interested in and committed to the development of an interdisciplinary student leadership program. Senior faculty and chief administrators should be included on the planning team or in initial discussions in order to gain their support. 2. What kind of program is appropriate for your institution? - Conduct a campus wide needs assessment to generate ideas for a leadership program. Pay particular attention to the needs and concerns of specific student populations, i.e., women, ethnic and racial minorities. Use the "Student Leadership Program Model" statement as a guide in developing a mission statement for the leadership program. 3. What is currently happening in your institution? - Identify current academic and co-curricula leadership-related programs on the campus. Locate the gaps that exist between the mission statement and the types of activities currently being offered. 4. What are the resources available? - Consider institutional resources as well as those in the community and the region. Community-based leadership programs can offer many resources as well as businesses and other educational institutions.

5. Design the program - Based on the mission statement, develop programs that employ multiple strategies to address needs of the various target groups. These programs should supplement existing programs and maximize the resources that are available.

6. Assessment and evaluation - Determine how students are affected by their participation in the program. Evaluate the effectiveness of the program design in accomplishing the program's mission. Student leadership programs should be an integral part of our academic

and co-curricular offerings. By providing students with opportunities to learn about and practice leadership skills, we enhance the quality of life on our campuses and prepare students to assume future leadership roles in our society.

REFERENCES: Roberts, D. C. (editor) Student Leadership Programs in Higher Education, 1981, The American College Personnel Association.

For further information concerning this program contact Patrick Brown, Office of Student Activities, University of Vermont, Burlington, VT 05405-0040, Telephone 802/656-2060.

The National Society for Internships and Experiential Education   **Sally Migliore**
3509 Haworth Drive, Suite 207, Raleigh, NC 27609   Program Associate
919/787-3263

The National Society for Internships and Experiential Education (NSIEE), founded in 1971, is a professional association that brings together the many types of people involved in providing the diverse array of experiential learning opportunities for the exchange of ideas, professional support, training, research, state-of-the-art discussions, and help for institutions and programs.

Experiential education includes:
- all forms of active learning;
- internships;
- community and public service and learning;
- cooperative education;
- field studies;
- intercultural programs;
- leadership development;
- practicum experiences;
- experiential learning in the classroom;
- outdoor education.

NSIEE's goals are:
- to advocate for the use of experiential learning throughout the educational system and the larger community;
- to enhance the professional growth and leadership development of our members;
- to disseminate information on principles of good practice and on innovations in the field;
- to encourage the development and dissemination of research and theory related to experiential learning.

NSIEE offers the Experiential Education newsletter, national and regional conferences, publications, information and consulting services, a national talent bank and referral center, several interest groups, and a special set of services for employers and field sponsors.

NSIEE's membership is diverse. Its members represent public and private colleges and universities, internship programs, school systems, deans' offices, community service programs, academic departments (liberal arts, professional, and technical fields), high schools, cooperative education programs, state and local governments, museums, international programs, counselors, career planning and placement offices, community-based organizations, corporations, consulting firms, and interested individuals from all fields. The benefits of membership are: A one year subscription to the Experiential Education newsletter; Discounts on NSIEE publications, conference registration fees, consulting services.

The National Directory of Internships edited by Amy S. Butterworth and Sally A. Migliore. Complete descriptions of thousands of internship opportunities across the country for students from high school through graduate school and beyond. Also lists opportunities for young people and adults not enrolled in school. Openings in government, nonprofit organizations, and corporate settings. Divided by type of host organization. Contains indexes by field of interest, location, and name of organization.

NSIEE offers information and accessibility to an extensive list of publications, Occasional Papers, and Panel Resource Papers. One such book is Strengthening Experiential Education within Your Institution by Jane C. Kendall, John S. Duley, Thomas C. Little, Jane S. Permaul, and Sharon Rubin. It is a sourcebook for college and university faculty and administrators who want to help their institutions tap the full potential of experiential education. Includes chapters on integrating experiential learning into the institution's mission, curriculum, faculty roles, evaluation system, administrative and financial structures.

The University of Vermont   Patrick Brown
Office of Student Activities   Director of Student Activities
Burlington, VT 05405-0040   802/656-2060

Leadership Program

INTRODUCTION:

The University of Vermont and the Leadership Program recognize leadership training, education, and development as important and critical components of the educational experience of undergraduate students. To enrich the experiences available through campus and community involvement, the Leadership Program includes a diverse set of educational and reflective opportunities for participating students. These programs, detailed below, include credit classes, outreach to student organizations, focused program efforts for women and minorities, advisor support, community/volunteer leadership, and residential life programs. The leadership programming efforts of the University, although coordinated by the Student Activities Office, are supported campus-wide by student affairs and academic offices.

PROGRAM PROFILE[1]: Leadership Program Components in Developmental Stages

Implemented	Developing	Conceptual
Credit Classes	Activity Surveys	Research
Leader's Manual	Minority Students	Mentor Program
Advisory Committee	High School Conference	Faculty Involvement
Cat's Paw Newsletter	Advisor Support	Peer Training
Residential Life	Student Activities	Burlington Resources
Ldshp Committee	Committee	Campus Recognition
Emerging Leaders	Women in Ldshp/	Strategies
Workshops/Retreats	Nexus Conference	Student Organization
Campus Planning Model	Student Organization	Networking
Outdoor Leaders	Series	Involvement Day and
	EAGLE Program	Month
	Volunteer Leadership	Graduate Class
	Programs	Management
	Library Resources	Development Series
	Marketing Strategies	Leadership Studies
	Visiting Leader Program	Program

---

[1]The content and presentation of The University of Vermont Leadership Program differs sufficiently from what was included in Source Book '87 to merit its inclusion in the '90 edition. Attention should be directed primarily at their intent to emphasize the broad aspects and developing nature of a university leadership program.

SELECTED PROGRAM SUMMARY

Implemented - Programs with significant history that are consistently offered.
1) Credit Classes - The Introductory Class (2 credits) challenges students to apply theoretical and philosophical aspects of leadership to their organizations. The Advanced Seminar (2 credits) focuses on the examination of perceptions of leadership in organizational development beyond the University setting. 2) Leader's Manual - An annual publication distributed free to all student leaders and student organization advisors as a guide to the University, campus programming, and organizational development. 3) "The Cat's Paw" - A monthly newsletter sent to over 800 student leaders, advisors, student affairs staff, and university administrators to provide readers with information about campus events, leadership opportunities, and accomplishments of students and their organizations. 4) Emerging Leaders - Thirty freshmen selected to examine and explore leadership opportunities early in their college careers, meet monthly and are trained to become strong, active student leaders. 5) Outdoor Leaders - The nationally recognized outdoor emphasis available at the University of Vermont is built upon a cadre of competent, well-trained leaders who receive training in the many facets of outdoor leadership.

Developing - In various stages of implementation, all have been offered at least once, some in existence for a few years. 1) Leadership Library - A resource center located in the Student Activities Office available for students, staff, and faculty. Its resources include books, workbooks, video tapes, audio tapes, and an extensive collection of reprints and articles. 2) High School Leadership Conference - Providing leadership training for 50 area high school student leaders with university professional staff, graduate students, and undergraduate student leaders serving as group leaders for a day and a half residential program. The long-term goal is to expand the program to address the needs of high schools throughout the state. 3) Women in Leadership Program - A one-day conference that examines the role of women in the arena of leadership and its impacts on organizations and lifestyles. Programs and presentations by out-of-state and local leaders are coordinated by an active student coordinating committee. 4) Eagle Program - Based in a women's residence hall, designated for women, this program assists those interested by establishing a support group for exploring many potential areas of involvement. 5) Minority Student Program - Assistance with development of strategies to increase involvement and effectiveness of minority students in leadership positions on campus. 6) Activity Interest Surveys - All incoming freshmen respond to a survey requesting information concerning their areas of interest, which is sorted and distributed to student organizations for their use.

Conceptual - Areas beginning to be addressed or designed to be implemented within the next two years. 1) "Mentor" Program - To link current student leaders with local and regional contacts in a powerful, reflective relationship to provide opportunities to explore areas of leadership in the world beyond the academic. 2) Involvement Day/Month - Many qualities of effective leadership can be experienced within the educational setting. Efforts will be coordinated each September to increase the involvement of students in campus organizations and community volunteer activities. 3) Peer Training - As students participate in the leadership program and their skills develop they become valuable resources for their peers. The peer education program will create opportunities and strategies for student leaders to assist their peers. 4) <u>Research</u> - To answer the question of educational outcomes in current literature concerning leadership programs and with the strong history and breadth of the program, the time has come for research to be conducted on topics of leadership development at the University of Vermont. 5) <u>Campus Recognition</u> - To foster and encourage involvement a plan is underway to broaden recognition on both the formal and informal level. 6) <u>Faculty Outreach/Support</u> - Leadership programs extend beyond student affairs to academic units. Courses in business, political science, history, literature, and other liberal arts, along with the important role of organizational advisor, represent dimensions that need to be incorporated into a comprehensive program.

As many of the programs in the developing and conceptual categories are new, significant amounts of staff time are needed to create, develop and implement each program and each program requires financial support. Combining additional personnel and adequate consistent program funding would guarantee the growth of the University of Vermont's Leadership Program into a more effective and far-reaching campus program.

Currently the University of Vermont Leadership Program is funded via a tripartite Funding strategy. The University's general fund supports the program through funding the full-time coordinator's salary and fringe benefits, a graduate student stipend, percentages of professional and support staff time and some minimal operating funds for office support. Many of the programs are partially, or entirely, self-funded. There is always an attempt to have those participating pay for the programs, yet this has an impact on the numbers in attendance. The bulk of the program funds are supported through efforts of the Student Activities Office to raise funds for general program development through various "business" operations [a copy center, a sales desk area, and campus vending] on campus.

Leadership: Theories, Styles and Realities - EDHI 213 Meets twice weekly.
Instructors: **Russell Baumhover**, Coord. of Leadership Programs, **Lisa Falcone**, Coord. of Greek Affairs & **Barry Bram**, Graduate Asst. for Leadership Programs.

COURSE DESCRIPTION: An introduction to the dynamics of working groups and the impact leadership can have on the effectiveness and success of these groups. It provides the student with the opportunity to link directly the concepts and theories discussed in class to everyday functioning of student organizations. This is accomplished through lectures, case studies, discussions, group experiences, media, and assignments. The goals are: To assist students in learning more about themselves and the way they function in groups; To introduce theories of leadership and group development; To challenge students to develop and strengthen their skills and abilities as leaders; To examine the practical application of leadership theory to the everyday functions of organizations; To challenge students to examine the role and responsibilities of leadership in society.

CLASS SCHEDULE

Class
Meetings

1 - Introduction; What is a leader?
2 - Team Building
3 - Group Process
4 - Group Development
5 - Leadership Style I
6 - No Class
7 - Leadership Style II
8 - Leadership Style III
9 - Communication; Leadership Paper
Due
10 - No Class
11 - Assessment, Goal Setting, Evaluation
12 - Motivation and Delegation
13 - Power and Authority

14 - Problem Solving and Decision
Making
15 - Conflict Resolution; Group
Observation Memo Due
16 - Guest Speaker - David Kearns
(tentative)
17 - Presentations
18 - Presentations
19 - Ethics
20 - Ethics
21 - No Class
22 - Leadership and Responsibility
23 - Leadership and Responsibility

ASSIGNMENTS: Attendance, Class Participation, Discussion of Readings - 20%. Learning takes place in classroom discussions, projects, and exercises. Therefore, attendance and participation are expected. Each week, students discuss the readings in small groups and apply them to everyday organizations. **Leadership Definition/Style Paper** - 20% - Due class meeting 9. In a 4-6 page paper, students will respond to the question, "What is a leader?" They will also be asked to analyze their own leadership style. **Group Observation** - 20% - Due class meeting 15. Students will serve as a consultant to a student organization by observing an organizational meeting and assessing the group's strengths and weaknesses. They will send their observations to the group's president in a two-page memo. **Group Project** - 15% - Class meeting 17 and 18. Students will research a campus issue and present their findings to the class. **Final Examination** - 25% - A paper synthesizing learning in the course.

Advanced Seminar in Leadership - EDHI 214

For those students who have taken EDHI 213 and are interested in furthering their studies regarding leadership, **EDHI 214 Advanced Seminar in Leadership** examines many areas relating leadership to the broader society. Topics covered in the past have included: the culture of leadership, change, appreciating differences, and others.

University of California - Davis
Davis, CA 95616

Leadership Institute - A Proposal

Stephanie Beardsley
Director, Residence Halls
Student Housing Office
916/752-2491

(Ed. note) In response to a charge to design a process to enable the Davis campus to assist students in developing much needed leadership skills in a more systematic fashion than in the past, the following proposal was devised by a workgroup committee. A list of current leadership opportunities is referred to as Attachment A. More details of these existing programs were described in Source Book '87. This proposal is included to assist those currently planning new or expanded leadership programs.

PREMISES OF THE PROPOSAL: Premises of the planned Davis campus' leadership development model: 1) There are numerous, outstanding opportunities for leadership development that currently exist on campus. The model should build upon rather than duplicate these existing programs. 2) Leadership development is a process rather than a specific outcome or product, and, therefore, cannot be conceptualized in a singular program fashion. Any campus development program should be designed to offer as many participants as possible opportunities to engage in this process of development, and should have multiple entry points and means of involvement. 3) There is no single, most effective leader, leadership style, or leadership training process. Thus, the design of the leadership development model should include components for enhanced self-insight as well as skill building, experience, feedback, recognition, and individual choice and circumstance. 4) The model designed should encourage interaction among all participants, but with particular emphasis on enhancing student to student contact.

The committee members utilized a portion of their planning time to identify key leadership development opportunities and programs already in existence on campus (Attachment A). The purpose of this exercise was to have a better understanding of the full array of opportunities, to insure that each committee member had the same base of information, to identify those programs where expansion or reconfiguration might be possible, and to determine what gaps might exist.

The committee used brainstorming as the vehicle for generating a long list of ideas, possibilities, and concerns. The purpose of this exercise was to quickly bring forward any and all topics for consideration in this project. Through this highly interactive process, several themes emerged which ultimately focused discussion and recommended plans. A general list of all ideas is attached to this report (Attachment B).

The final phase of the committee's planning meeting included consolidating and fine-tuning agreed upon ideas, and determining a timeline for implementation of those ideas.

GENERAL RECOMMENDATIONS: The committee recommends that a strategic, three-year process begin immediately leading to the creation of a "Leadership Institute" program. Critical features of this Institute would include:

1.   The implementation of an integrated developmental transcript system providing

students who participate in the Institute with formal, University acknowledgement for his/her accomplishments. This acknowledgement could take many forms, but recognition at commencement and a yet-to-be-designed involvement transcript appear to be most promising. Other possibilities include formal notation on the official transcript or a Work-Learn Internship notation. A set of standards or criteria for the receipt of this acknowledgement would be created and students' satisfaction of these would be tracked.

2. The offerings included as part of the Institute would satisfy five important ingredients in leadership development:

    1) acquisition of important facts, knowledge, concepts and theories;
    2) learning effective attitudes and behaviors through observation and interaction with role models;
    3) opportunities for supervised role-playing and practice;
    4) transferability of skills and knowledge to real-life situations;
    5) assessment and reinforcement of effectiveness.

    An array of opportunities within each of these five general categories would be available within the Institute so that the students could choose a variety of ways to meet the criteria for the transcript.

3. Students would apply and be selected for inclusion in the Institute. Once fully operational, students from all class levels could be involved in various programs included in the Institute, and could remain active in the process from one year to another. A system of tracking student involvement in various aspects of the Institute would be created.

4. Most of the existing programs offered on campus that support leadership development would satisfy some part of the criteria. For example, participation in an extended job-training program within Student Affairs might meet one or more of the yet-to-be established criteria. In general, these training programs would not require alteration.

5. Additional programs might need to be developed in order to fully attend to the five categories listed above. For example, the committee thinks that the offering of an academic course on issues, theories and concepts of leadership, with directed study and reading, is a crucial component that must be added if the Institute is to be comprehensive and coherent. Other examples might include the creation of a campus-wide student leadership assessment center; specialized programs with other forms of self-assessment; an interactive, outdoor group experience program; the institution of a "Day in the Life of...." program whereby students become the Vice Chancellor, Dean, etc., for a day; the creation of new internship possibilities for students with government, education and business leaders; and the creation of a student-to-student mentorship program.

The committee views the Institute to be analogous to establishing a "core curriculum" through the use of selected electives. The process should be flexible and attend to individual differences and needs, but contain internal integrity and congruity. There is potential to create a sense of belonging and investment among participants, both to the institution as well as to one another, by virtue of some shared experiences, by the sense of being "special," and by experiencing commitment on the part of the University to their growth and development.

Attached is a possible strategy for the full realization of the Institute. Any and all suggestions are open to revision, but the committee is confident that the plans represent attainable goals.

ATTACHMENT A: Partial List of Current Leadership Opportunities

HOUSING: Fall Leadership Conference for student volunteers (200+); Assessment Center (volunteer participation, 30-50/year); Resident Advisor Training; Community-based programs on life skills (4-5/floor/qtr; 600-1000 programs/year)

GREEK SYSTEM: 30 peer rush counselors; 40 hrs. training; Fall orientation for fraternity/sorority presidents (40); Leadership training workshops for Greek Councils (22); Leadership life skills program (selected); J-Com leadership training, ongoing (11); Education 160 (20/qtr.)

STUDENT ACTIVITIES/RELATIONS: Leadership Conference, Winter Qtr. (150); Leadership Skills Programs (e.g., Women in Leadership); Speakers Network; Leadership Task Force

ASUCD: Fall Retreat; Leadership Development Programs (2 qtrs.); On-job training

ADVISORS:
STEP, Learning Skills Center;
PAC, EOP/SAA (10 positions); Spring Training; Serve as STEP advisors; On-job training
    with counselors;
HOUSE Staff; 60 volunteer; Ongoing training and workshops;
HEALTH CENTER; DRInC; Peer Counselors in Sexuality; Health Advocates;
ROTC;
SUMMER ADVISING; Spring quarter retreat; weekly training;
ACADEMIC PEER ADVISORS/FIRST RESORT ADVISORS; Fall training;
MISCELLANEOUS; Black Leadership Conference; Chicago Leadership Conference; Asian Pacific Coalition; Colleagues in Educational Opportunity; Chancellor's Ambassadors.

ATTACHMENT B: Strategic Implementation of Leadership Institute

Year One:
1. Write job description, hire intern to coordinate the Institute.
2. Identify initial group of student participants.
3. Prepare a publication for students on current leadership opportunities on campus.
4. Plan and implement an outdoor, interactive team building activity.
5. Institute a "Day in the life of..." (e.g., Vice Chancellor, Dean).
6. Plan and implement a Leadership Skills Assessment Center for general student population or develop a program session utilizing an assessment instrument (i.e., Strong-Campbell II).
7. Plan and begin a marketing campaign to all interested/involved parties.
8. Plan and conduct a number of life skills/leadership programs to be offered during the year. Utilize the Leadership Task Force.
9. Plan the tracking system for student participants.
10. Identify those leadership activities which would qualify for "credit" in the Institute. This could include volunteer and paid positions, on and off campus.
11. Establish the standards/criteria for receiving the "transcript."
12. Plan and implement a Leadership Conference for Winter; content could model anticipated curriculum for course.
13. Develop an evaluation tool for the program.
14. Coordinate with CAL, ASUCD and other groups to connect special opportunities with students participating in the Institute; if possible, create special seminars, session, etc., with speakers or after special activities.
15. Host a special orientation/team building session for participants in November.

Year Two:
1. Continue the activities from Year 1.
2. Offer the assessment program not offered during year 1 (#6).
3. Review local and state government leadership internships for inclusion in the program; encourage the creation of new or expansive internships.
4. Draft language for the goals statement of the Student Affairs unit which includes a commitment for leadership development.
5. Develop a mission statement, goals and possible curricular outline for course on leadership carrying academic credit. Begin to discuss this possibility with key members of academic administration.
6. Work with appropriate academic departments to offer 198/199 courses in Leadership Skills.
7. Offer formal recognition to those completing the Institute, including commencement acknowledgement.

Year Three:
1. Continue activities from year 1 and 2.
2. Offer Leadership Class for academic credit.
3. Plan and implement first phases of student-to-student mentorship program.

University of Colorado at Boulder
Campus Box 7, Boulder, CO 80309

Student Leadership Institute

Kathleen Novak
Program Director
303/492-8342

MISSION: To identify and nurture leadership with a commitment to business and community development in Colorado.

PROGRAM OBJECTIVES: Expose students to basic concepts in areas of leadership and organizational development; Provide opportunities to observe leaders in action and find role models helpful to future growth; to allow students to hear, see perceive, and understand those dimensions of leadership that cannot be put into words; Expose students to the real, imperfect, and "untidy" world; Develop and improve necessary skills in areas such as communication, group dynamics, team building, goal setting, planning, problem solving, conflict management, and other related areas; Enhance knowledge and understanding of the self and how students relate to others; Enhance knowledge and understanding of the complexity, dynamics, issues, operations, and realities of today's society and institutions; Develop students' ability to integrate these tasks and make applications to current and future leadership positions; Provide opportunities for students to test their judgments under pressure, and in challenging situations; Provide opportunities for students to exercise responsibility and to try out skills required for leadership; Provide opportunities to test and sharpen their intuitive gifts and to judge their impact on others.

The Student Leadership Institute is a two-year leadership development program. Sixty new students are selected each year and receive a $500 scholarship each semester they are in the program. They are enrolled in a three credit academic course designed to develop their leadership potential.

What kinds of students are eligible for SLI? Students interested in applying need not have a background in student government or other traditional leadership activities. SLI seeks individuals with diverse backgrounds and interests. Although selection is based partially on academic achievement, emphasis is placed on active involvement in school and/or community activities, as well as initiative, self-confidence, open-mindedness, communication skills, and willingness to take on responsibility. The program selects students whose fields of study range from history and drama to engineering and business.

In the Freshman Year students are introduced to the concept of leadership and to the issues facing present and future leaders. They attend weekly lectures featuring various community and state leaders, seminars at a variety of businesses, organizations, and institutions, and weekly ten-member group recitations led by former students of the program.

Sophomore Year: Students take a more active role in the development of their leadership potential attending lectures similar to the first year series, but on a monthly basis, recitations, community service projects and "The Walkabout," a semester long internship created to provide opportunity for "hands on" learning.

Each year SLI holds two retreats (a fall orientation weekend and a winter cross-country ski

242

trip), which provide students with an excellent opportunity to get to know one another in an informal setting.   Additional social activities help to foster the cohesiveness felt by students.

Students earn three credit hours each semester they are in the program. The six credit hours earned during the freshman year are accepted by all colleges and schools within the university as elective credit.   Acceptance of credit earned beyond the freshman year is dependent upon approval from the student's college or school.

READINGS, as well as films, are drawn from a wide range of studies and disciplines: political science, philosophy, organizational development, psychology, sociology, management theory, history, literature, etc. Books used include, but are not limited to the following: The Tao of Leadership, John Heider; Megatrends, John Naisbitt; Inside the Third World, Paul Harrison; Our Town, Thornton Wilder; The One Minute Manager, Ken Blanchard; Slapstick, Kurt Vonnegut; The Fountainhead, Ayn Rand; The Closing of the American Mind, Allan Bloom.

ASSIGNMENTS: Heavy emphasis is placed on written analysis and oral presentations. The following is required each semester; 3 short essays discussing various speakers; 3 three to five page papers dealing with each unit; 1 final paper focusing on any one of a number of topics presented during the entire semester; several group and individual oral presentations.

University of Colorado at Boulder
Presidents Leadership Class
400 Willard Hall, Campus Box 147, Boulder, CO 80309-0147

Adam J. Goodman
Executive Director
303/492-8342

The Presidents Leadership Class, a program of the Student Leadership Institute, is an undergraduate experiential academic and scholarship program designed to foster individual leadership and community service potential in some of the nation's most gifted students.

PLC is the premier program of the Student Leadership Institute, a Colorado non-profit agency. The program, in its 17th year, is unique to CU-Boulder and the state. Over 400 high school seniors apply each year and are selected as PLC scholars on the basis of demonstrated academic excellence, leadership potential, and community service. Acceptance into the program, limited to 60 new students each year, is one of the highest honors that can be bestowed upon entering freshmen at CU-Boulder. In class, these scholars are exposed to Colorado and national leaders through weekly lectures, seminars, projects, and internships in the fields of business, education, government, sciences, and the arts.

Through these activities, scholars gain a deep understanding of the problems facing the state, and their responsibilities as members of society. Scholars also receive a $1,000 annual scholarship and academic credit, up to four semesters.

Over 250 businesses and individuals throughout the state sponsor the PLC programs with their time, expertise, and financial support. The curriculum is guided by a 30 member Board of Trustees composed of senior officers representing the state's largest corporations.

Students interested in applying for the program need not have a background in student government, nor are they required to have experience in traditional leadership roles. PLC seeks individuals with diverse backgrounds and interests. Although selection is based in part on academic achievement and participation in extracurricular activities, emphasis is placed on individual initiative, self-confidence, open-mindedness, communication skills, and willingness to undertake responsibility. In addition, the program selects students whose fields of study range from history and psychology to engineering and fine arts.

The first two years of PLC provide scholars with an introduction to the leaders, businesses, and institutions that comprise the Colorado community. The final semester provides them with an opportunity to work closely with a Colorado leader on a specific project of substance.

Freshman Year: The first-year program is divided into three areas: a lecture series, seminars, and recitations. The weekly lecture series features community leaders from across the State including past speakers such as Governor Roy Romer; former Governor Richard Lamm; William Coors, Chairman of the Board, Adolph Coors Company and Delmont A. Davis, President of the Ball Corporation. Students also attend 8 of over 30 on-site seminars throughout Colorado which are designed to show the inner workings of industries, agencies, and institutions. Seminars are given by organizations such as Hewlett Packard, United Bank of Denver, Denver Center for the Performing Arts, and St. Joseph's Hospital. Finally, each scholar participates with their peers in a 10-member weekly recitation group led by Class Advisors (CA's) who are graduates of the program. In their recitations scholars take part in a variety of special activities, discuss books, and express their ideas through written work. In addition, each scholar and recitation section performs a community service project.

Sophomore Year: As sophomores, scholars take responsibility for much of their own education. Through the use of contract learning with an emphasis on personal challenge, the students complete two different critical analysis units which focus on societal institutions such as business, religion or government. A group and individual project designed to both aid the community and provide an educational challenge is also required. Scholars complete the year with a Walkabout, an internship involving about 15 hours a week of "hands on" learning, at places such as the Colorado State Legislature, the Denver Nuggets, and the Children's Museum of Denver.

The PLC program extends far beyond the traditional undergraduate classroom learning experience. In addition, each year PLC holds two retreats, a fall orientation weekend and a cross-country ski trip, to provide scholars with an opportunity to really get to know each other. Additional social activities also help the class form a cohesive group. During the two years scholars are together, they develop strong friendships with their classmates, some of CU's most interesting and active students.

Admission: Colorado residents may obtain nomination forms from high school counselors or from the Student Leadership Institute office. Nonresidents should also contact the Institute directly. Applications must be received by the Institute no later than February 1 of each year. After a review of the applications, interview panels for approximately 120 in-state students are held throughout Colorado. Nonresident interviews are conducted over the phone. Acceptance into the program is announced in April of each year and is considered an honor for both the nominated scholar and the high school.

University of Hawaii at Hilo
Office of Student Services, Hilo, HI 96720-4091

Manu Meyer
HLDP Coordinator
808/961-9413

Hawaiian Leadership Development Program

The Hawaiian Leadership Development Program recruits talented Native Hawaiians and facilitates their academic and leadership development, assisting them to attend and complete post secondary programs. It trains them to develop their leadership potential and increases the number of Hawaiian leaders in professional fields and the community.

Activities are designed to develop each participant's potential. Participants enroll in courses to facilitate personal, academic, cultural and leadership growth. (Classes are offered in Human Development, Hawaiian Language and Hawaiian Leadership.) Structured out-of-class activities augment program goals through scheduled study times, tutoring, peer counseling, mentor-student relationships and leadership experiences. Students facilitate meetings, plan exhibits, work on community projects, help with the Leadership Conference, attend off-island workshops, learning leadership skills through on-the-job internship programs.

Students are Hawaiians with proven academic ability and potential leadership ability. They develop their leadership skills and understand their cultural background to serve the Hawaiian community. They are assisted by faculty of Hawaiian ancestry to explore diverse areas of interest to choose an academic major and life goal to realize their fullest potential. Advisors are the Committee of Faculty of Hawaiian Ancestry at the University of Hawaii, Hilo Campus.

OBJECTIVES: Recruitment Criteria: Non-Remedial; Leadership potential; Part-Hawaiian/Hawaiian students at UH Hilo or incoming students.

Retention Components: Mentorship; Human Development Course and Hawaiian Language 101; Big Brother/Big Sister; Identification of student's needs; Faculty advising; Hikes, Pa'ina, weekly meetings.

Leadership Development Opportunities Components: Leadership Course; Internships; Guest Speakers; School related activities such as Leadership Conference, Campus Tour Facilitators, Recruitment, Orientation; Community related activities such as Special Olympics, Super Kids, Career Conference, Summer Project.

The Hawaiian Leadership Development Program is based on the following assumptions: 1.There IS potential in us all and it CAN be nurtured. 2. Hawaiians have a well-spring of potential. 3. Hawaiian students with leadership potential should be given opportunities to develop this facet of their person. 4. Leadership Development should not be a 'hit or miss' situation, but a clear, nurturing and vital step in the developmental phase of students.

Consensus Definition of Effective Hawaiian Leadership: Effective Hawaiian leaders remain true to their culture, use their mana to accomplish their peoples' goals of excellence and empower their people in contemporary society. They must be aggressive in the Western world to protect Hawaiian peoples' rights, values, traditions and 'aina.

Common Characteristics of Effective Hawaiian Leadership Today: Ability to persuade and motivate; Sacrifice personal gains for benefit of the whole; Sensitive to the needs of the group/people; Respect group/people; Must embrace Hawaiian culture; Develop a common purpose for the group/people; Facilitate group to work together toward common purpose; Has broad based information; Able to communicate effectively with people.

Hawaiian Leadership Development Program: Developing Your Potential

<u>Week</u>   (Topics, Ideas, New Vocabulary, etc...)
  1   **Orientation to course objectives** (Synergy) Koa
         Expectations, Journals, Workshops, Career Library, Study Skills, Participation, Attendance and EACH OTHER!
  2   **Awakening the Present** (Genjokoan) Kuh'o
         "Why are you here at UHH," "What is available?" Choice, Responsibility, Confusion, Commitment = Work Ethic
  3   **Awakening the Self** (Om-Namah-Shivaya) Kaona
         Who are we? The Self-Triangle, Values Clarification, Stereotypes, The Sabotage of our Self Esteem, Essence vs. False Personality
  4   **Awakening the Communication** (Wu-Wei) Ho'omanawanui
         I-Messages, Hooking-On, NLP, Dale Carnegie, Ho'oponopono, Active Listening, Body Language
  5   **Awakening the Physical** (Endorfins) Pa'ahana
         Learning through our bodies, principles of exercise, Myth and Facts, Juggling, Autogenic Relaxation, Yoga
  6   **Awakening the Clown** (Mah-Pen-Lai) **and Child** (Play!) Le'ale'a Cosmic Humor, Your Funny File, The ability to laugh and play, Trust, Acceptance, Joy, Secrets, Fantasy, Curiosity
  7   **Awakening the Senses** (Maya) Mauli ola
         Watching, Listening, Feeling, Music, Tasting, Touching
  8   **Awakening the Intellect** (Cogito Ergo Sum) Na'auao
         Brain Potential, Montessori, Studying Habits, Bucky Fuller
  9   **Awakening the Heart** (Sentio Ergo Sum) Aloha
         Relationships, Love, Reciprocity, Dialogue, Risk, I and Thou
  10   **Awakening the Mind** (Konjo) Kela
         Visualization, Abundance, Affirmation, Laws of the Universe
  11   **Awakening the Spirit** (Amor Fati) Ho'omana
         Maya, Shunyata, Bhakti, Karma, Wu-Wei, Existential and Personal Search, Unanswered Questions, Death
  12   **Awakening the Leader** (Drala) Alaka'i
         Effective Leadership, Path as Goal = Process as Content, Goal Setting, Consequence, Action vs. Expectations, Problem Solving
  13-15 **Awakening our Creativity** (A'Ole I Pau Ku'u Loa)
         Individual Presentations: "How I Develop My Potential"
         Exam, Closure, Pa'ina

247

University of Minnesota
Student Organization Development Center
340 Coffman Memorial Union
300 Washington Ave., S.E., Minneapolis, MN 55455

Kathleen Rice
Kirk Millhone
612/624-5101

Student Leadership Program

Future plans are to develop a comprehensive leadership program concerned not only with issues of management, but also with leadership. Current and new programs will incorporate several thematic approaches: Utilize a model of preparation, experience, and thoughtful reflection and application; Challenge and support students as they struggle with responsibilities of leadership including an understanding of, and an involvement in, both the university and outside communities to experience and appreciate the gifts of cultures other than their own; Work with students to develop leadership programs for women and black students; Incorporate learnings into their own style of leadership.

Two full time professionals coordinate and/or provide support and training for students assisted by one full time secretary. Funding and budgetary details are available and may be obtained by contacting Kathleen Rice.

Leadership and Service Recognition Coordinators are a committee of students and staff.

The purpose is to express appreciation to students who have made contributions to the University and/or Twin Cities communities, and to make the University community more aware of the significant impact students have on and off campus. Each year, 1/2 of 1% of the student population at the University of Minnesota is recognized for their outstanding contributions of leadership and service to the University or Twin Cities communities. Awardees are invited to attend an Award Reception and Dinner, sponsored by the University President and Vice President for Student Development.

A committee of staff and students plans the event and completes the entire award nomination and selection process and includes representatives from student culture centers, the Office of Community Service Activities, Residence Life, Greek organizations, international students, sports clubs, athletics, orientation, and the Offices of the President and Alumni Affairs.

University faculty, staff, administrators, and students nominate undergraduate or graduate students whom they feel have made a significant contribution to the campus or community. Nominees are asked to apply* for one of approximately 150 President's Leadership and Service Awards. Applications are reviewed by the student and staff committee; those selected are invited to attend the Award Reception and Dinner in May. One woman and one man are selected to receive the Zander Award, for outstanding contributions of leadership and service. University Regents, Vice Presidents, Deans, and Student Development Staff are invited to attend the event as well. The President traditionally serves as the guest speaker.

*Application forms are designed but not included here.

Emerging Leadership Development Program
Instructors: Kirk J. Millhone and selected University Professionals

Program objectives are fourfold: a) development of self-confidence; b) familiarization with simple leadership and management theory; c) familiarization of the resources and support systems which exist on campus for student leaders; and d) development of simple management skills.

The program, Emerge, lasts for six weeks, meeting as a group once a week, usually in the afternoon. It is for students who have little or no experience in leadership positions who are interested in learning more about leadership through campus or community involvement.

Emerge participants are also matched with an upperclass mentor, who has experience and has been effective in leadership positions on campus or in the community. Mentors are chosen based on recommendations by faculty, staff and community professionals, an interview with the program coordinator, information provided on their Mentor Application Form*, and a good match with a participating student.

Participants are given full control over topics to be covered in the program, placing them in an active decision-making process, while also forcing them to think about and discuss what is most needed for their development as someone in a leadership position. Topics in the past have included: What is Leadership? Creative Problem Solving; Persuasion and Influence; Motivating Others; Stress Management for Leaders; a Challenge/Confidence Course.

Emerge is a non-credit personal development opportunity so there are no assignments and no grading. Selection for participants is made on a first come first to participate basis. The first 30 students with a filled out application* and a $10 registration fee are in the program.

*Forms are designed but not included here.

Annual Edwin O. Siggelkow Leadership Retreat
Instructors: Selected University and Community Professionals

The program objectives are five-fold: a) provide an opportunity for student leaders from different arenas to learn together and get to know each other; b) provide an opportunity for advanced students of leadership to think through, plan and execute a leadership development experience for their peers; c) familiarize student leaders with the resources and support systems existing on campus; d) provide an opportunity for the development of management skills; and e) provide for discussion and contemplation about the issues of being a leader.

Founded in 1975 to revive leadership interaction between key members of the University community and students from the five coordinate campuses, it was named for Mr. Siggelkow, Director of Unions and Coordinator of the Student Activities Center who died in 1975. He was recognized as the best Director of Unions in the country. The retreat is held from late afternoon on a Friday until early afternoon on Sunday, usually in the spring. Scholarships to defer most of the cost to attend are given by many University programs including: the Alumni Association, the Foundation, Colleges, Schools, some Departments, some Student Organizations and College Programs for their students. Last year all 124 students attending were supported by scholarships.

Registration in 1988 cost $60. This covered all but 10% of the total cost which was subsidized by the Office of Student Development. Goals were as follows: To focus on small group interaction and interpersonal communication between students; To build a strong sense of community among student leaders; To provide the opportunity for personal growth in leadership development; To cultivate leadership potential within all student participants and motivate them to action; To recognize that leadership is diverse--with two equally important sides to every issue.

Programming included: A cultural exchange hosted by the Minnesota International Student Association and workshops on the following topics: Persuasion; Team-Building; Stress Management; Alcohol Awareness; Motivating Others; Gender Issues; Building Diverse Relationships; Building Friendships; Networking; Effective Meetings; Personal Motivation; Risk Taking; Ethical Leadership; Interpersonal Communication.

Each year six to 12 students volunteer to conceptualize, plan and make Siggelkow a reality. This offers an advanced leadership development experience for students who have gone through other developmental programs and now turn to passing on their skills and insights.

Leadership/Management Development Workshops
Instructors: Selected University Professionals

The program objectives are: a) take leadership/management learning opportunities into the organizations who have requested them; b) provide interactive learning opportunities to meet the logistic and content needs of the requesting organizations; c) provide individual and organizational development opportunities to members of student organizations.

Workshops can be requested by any currently registered student organization and are presented at no cost providing the organization is currently registered, has given two weeks notice, and meets with the presenter to discuss how the workshop can be adapted to meet the specific needs of the organization.

Workshops on the following topics have been standardized and outlined with presenter's guide and handouts already prepared: Recruitment; Leadership Transition; Getting Involved; Creativity; Fund Raising; Leadership; Dealing with Difficult Situations; Effective

Meetings (group and leader versions); Retention; Delegating; Gender Issues; Effective Listening; Team Building; Followership; Organizational Development Series including: Organizational Purpose, Goal Setting, and Planning; Individual Development Series including: Personal Motivation, Personal Goal Setting, Time Management Skills, and Personal Discipline.

Workshops can be customized to address a specific problem or need. Topics presented in the past include: Creative Programming, Train the Trainer, Group Facilitation Skills, Assertive Communication, Academic Motivation, Communication Style, Conflict Resolution, Creative Problem Solving, Decision Making, Ethical Leadership, Ice Breakers, Impromptu Speaking, Myers-Briggs Type Indicator and Leadership, Parliamentary Procedures, Persuasion, Power, Problem Solving, Stress Management for Leaders, and Trust.

Organizational retreats can also be designed. Help is available to plan a structure with realistic goals and present a majority of the events planned or present the entire retreat.

Excel Leadership Program
Instructors: K. Rice, campus and community leaders, former Excel participants

The purpose is to: 1) challenge students to define further their personal philosophy of leadership and determine how it can be incorporated into all aspects of their daily lives; 2) provide them with a support network of student and community leaders who can assist them in fulfilling their leadership roles with their student organizations; 3) supplement their development of management skills.

Each spring, fifty students who hold leadership positions in various student organizations are selected to participate in this program during the following fall and winter quarters. There are two components: 1) participation in weekly leadership seminars, and 2) weekly meetings with their campus or community mentor. Students do not receive credit for participation.

The two hour weekly seminars enable students to broaden their perspectives of leadership, discuss with their peers issues related to student leadership, and learn from experienced leaders who serve as guest facilitators. Topics for the seminar are determined during the fall retreat. These have included: personal goal setting; group development; conflict; building community; appreciating differences; multicultural perspectives of leadership; change; power; organizational culture; ethical leadership; etc.

Fifty campus and community mentors from various professional backgrounds are matched with a student. In weekly meetings, the student and mentor discuss anything from career aspirations to the challenges of leadership, personal hobbies, family issues, or community involvement.

A luncheon where students and mentors first meet kicks off the program in September.

The students attend a retreat at the beginning of each quarter, and mentors are invited to come for lunch. Students and mentors participate in one of five community service projects on a Saturday.

A reception for mentors and students concludes the program in early March. Many mentors and students continue to meet long after the conclusion of the program. Forms for student and mentor application are designed but not included here.

Excel Program; Seminar Syllabus
Wed. and Thurs., 2:00 - 4:00 p.m.

"Leaders are guided by vision for a better world for all, s/he is clear in this vision and works for its implementation by guiding, facilitating, empowering, inspiring, and entrusting others to do their best in accomplishing the goal." Helen Astin, educator.

Week

1   Overview of Seminar. What is Leadership Part II
2   Defining Personal and Organizational Mission and Goals
3   Introduction to Leadership. Theory and Followership
4   Appreciating Differences
5   Appreciating Differences Part II
6   Group Development, Process, Norms, and Values
7   Resolving Conflict
8   Building Community
9   A Global Exploration of Leadership

Excel Program; Seminar Syllabus - Winter Quarter, 1989
All seminars meet from 2:15 - 4:15 p.m.

Week

1   A Seventh View of Leadership. Bob Terry, Humphrey Institute Reflective Leadership Program
2   Winter retreat
3   Facilitating Change in Organizations, Kathleen Rice
1-4 Observe Professional Organizational Meetings
5   Organizational Culture, Decision Making and Group Dynamics (as they relate to the meetings you observed). June Perkins, MSA Advisor and SODC Consultant Dianna Edwards, former Excel student.
6   Personal and Organizational Power. Carol Kerner, Sr. V.P. for Communications, IDS Financial Services, Inc.
7   Ethical Leadership. George Shapiro, Professor, Speech Communications
8   Volunteering, Leadership, and Ethics. Barb Lee, Program Coordinator, UYMCA
9   Saturday, Community Projects for Mentors and Students
10   Multicultural Perspectives of Leadership. Juan Moreno, CMU Programming Office,

Bea Swanson, Loaves and Fishes
11   The Personal Challenges of Leadership. Excel students
12   Where to take Excel from here? Excel students
13   Final Reception for Mentors and Students

Excel Seminar Guidelines

To ensure that the weekly seminars will be challenging, thought-provoking, valuable, and fun for all, the following guidelines are recommended.

- Seminars begin at 2:00 promptly, and conclude at 4:00 p.m.
- If you are unable to attend a seminar, please contact Kathleen Rice at 624-5101. Many discussions and class projects will be planned, based on the number of students in the seminar.
- If you need to miss more than two seminars a quarter, we will need to discuss your commitment to the program.
- To capitalize on the creativity, expertise, and diversity of our presenters and the seminar participants, we will utilize a format which examines differences, explores alternate views, and stimulates discussion and counterpoint.
- Articulating your thoughts and ideas is encouraged and valued, as is careful listening to the ideas of others.
- Appropriate use of humor is encouraged.
- Gender inclusive language is expected.
- Timely feedback (either positive or constructive) for the presenter, other Excel participants, or Kathleen Rice is welcome and encouraged.
- The unique manner in which we each learn is respected.
- Taking individual responsibility for yourself, your ideas, and your own learning is expected.
- Each participant is expected to contribute to the learning of the group as a whole.

Adapted from "Seven Principles for Good Practice in Undergraduate Education," The Wingspread Journal.

University of New Hampshire
126 Memorial Union Building
Durham, NH 03824

Anne Lawing
Assoc. Dir., Student Affairs
603/862-1001

Emerging Leader Program
Coordinators: selected faculty, staff, and student leaders make up the UNH Leadership
Education Committee

The Emerging Leader Program provides a comprehensive multi-year experience whereby
students learn major theories in leadership and management, then apply the theories to
their positions in campus organizations. Acceptance to the ELP allows students with little
or no prior leadership experience to explore, in-depth, a variety of their own developmental
issues concerning interpersonal effectiveness, and practice acquired leadership and
management skills that are taught by University faculty and staff.

GOALS: To assist students in their search for and selection of available leadership
opportunities; To provide leadership mentors to help students develop their interpersonal
skills; To assess students' experiences and relate them to current leadership theories and
practices; To develop a leadership pool within the student body.

OBJECTIVES: Identify University and community leaders who will further the goals and
enhance the effectiveness of the ELP. Possible activities include teaching a seminar, serving
as a mentor, and providing information about leadership opportunities; Develop a
Leadership Resume that documents students' experiences; Develop a network of contacts
around the University community.

DEFINITIONS: "Leadership is the process of persuasion and example by which an
individual . . . induces a group to take action that is in accord with the leader's purpose or
the shared purposes of all." (Gardner, 1987); Students also learn management skills as a
result of their leadership positions; this, too, is recognized and nurtured in the Emerging
Leader Program. The working definition of management is where students "preside over
the processes by which the organization functions, allocates resources, and makes the best
use of people." (Gardner, 1987).

Tasks that Leaders are Expected to Perform: The ELP recognizes that there is a multitude
of ways in which to study leadership. For the sake of simplicity, the committee targets
specific behaviors that should be learned in order for students to successfully begin or
continue their process of becoming leaders. These behaviors are taught as skills that enable
one to successfully accomplish a set of tasks that are necessary. The tasks are oriented
towards leadership (influencing others) and management (maintenance of an organization).
The tasks are as follows: For a leader:
  a) envisioning goals;
  b) affirming values;
  c) motivating constituents;
  d) providing optimism and realism;
  e) serving as a symbol, and;
  f) representing constituents.

254

For a manager:

    a) planning and priority setting;
    b) organizing/evaluating/creating procedures;
    c) decision making/agenda setting, and;
    d) conflict resolution. (Gardner, 1987).

Structure: Thirty students are selected each year to participate. Most have little or no leadership experience at UNH when they begin. Once they are selected, they are expected to join and actively participate in a campus or community group, and to continue to be involved with a group for as long as they are a member of the ELP. In the first year, during the first six weeks of each semester, the group meets once per week with a member of the faculty, staff, or local business community to discuss issues related to one of the major tasks expected of leaders/managers. The presenter is selected on the basis of his/her expertise with the particular task to be discussed. During the last half of each semester, each LEC member takes a sub-group of students and meets with them to connect their experiences in campus groups with current leadership/management theories. S/he also reviews each Leadership Resume to verify seminars attended and experiences acquired.

The second year experience includes a credited course entitled Skills For Working Together (Hamilton and Moore, 1986) that teaches individual and group communications skills. Experiences for the third and fourth years are yet to be developed.

University of North Carolina at Chapel Hill
Office of the Vice Chancellor for Student Affairs
Chapel Hill, NC 27599-5100

Cynthia A. Wolf
Director
919/966-4041

North Carolina Fellows Program and Leadership Development

The North Carolina Fellows Program at the University of North Carolina at Chapel Hill is one of three such programs in the State. Founded in 1968 this four year Leadership Development Program is designed to accelerate and support the development of highly motivated young people with exceptional leadership potential into effective leaders with a strong sense of responsibility to those whom they serve.

The program is founded on two premises: (1) that persons with exceptional leadership abilities can be identified at an early age, and (2) that the personal development and leadership capacity of such young people can be significantly enriched and encouraged by identifying them as leaders and providing them with special development opportunities.

PROGRAM GOALS: The North Carolina Fellows Program at UNC-CH has a strong developmental focus. It is designed to foster intellectual, moral, personal and social development. With this emphasis, the program challenges each student to define leadership and to find ways for enhancing leadership style, skill and potential. Each spring semester, all freshmen are invited to apply to the N.C. Fellows Program. Applications are screened and approximately 70 candidates are interviewed. From these, approximately 40 applicants are chosen for final interviews. Of these finalists, approximately 20 are selected to become N.C. Fellows. This selection process is coordinated by the Program Director and involves UNC faculty and staff, current Fellows, alumni Fellows and local community leaders. Selection is based on motivation for leadership ability, and commitment to the N.C. Fellows Program.

The Program offers participants the opportunity to: increase their self-knowledge and maturity; be exposed to different types of leaders and leadership styles; analyze the nature of leadership and leadership needs in a variety of situations; gain practical understanding of leadership roles; appreciate the importance of service as a necessary ingredient of responsible and effective leadership; be involved in a mentor relationship; benefit from the unique sense of community the Program inspires.

PROGRAM REQUIREMENTS:

Freshman Year: Freshman Retreat Weekend focuses on self-awareness and examination of one's present style of leadership.
Sophomore Year: Three Credit Seminar entitled "Special Studies 90: Leadership Seminar" taught during Fall Semester only, focuses on leadership theories and philosophies.
Junior Year: Junior Year Retreat focuses on personal value systems within the context of leadership. Juniors are required to spend time with community members different from themselves and to evaluate value similarities and differences.
Senior Year: Retreat Weekend: Focus on the ethics of leadership, the issue of transition into the working world, and an examination of one's changes in leadership styles.

256

In addition to events specific to a particular class, all N.C. Fellows are required to participate in the following events: <u>Internship:</u> a structured internship usually full-time during the summer between junior and senior years. <u>Monthly Dinners with Community Leaders:</u> each year. <u>Selection of future Fellows:</u> each year.

PROGRAM ACTIVITIES: N.C. Fellows participate in a number of additional program activities: Group Service Projects for the University and/or local community; Abbreviated training programs at the Center for Creative Leadership in Greensboro; Exchange Retreat with members of the Fellows Programs at N.C. State and Davidson; Carolina Contact Program coordinated with the UNC-CH Admissions Office.

INTERNSHIPS:

The ideal internship provides, with Program assistance, a personal model for development as well as practical exposure to leadership problems and strategies. The organization providing the internship often pays the intern a stipend or salary adequate to cover living expenses; in some instances the Program can make funds available to students whose organization does not provide funding. Internship sites have included: American Repertory Theatre Company, Inc., Cambridge, MA; Coalition for Battered Women, Durham, NC; Comite' Nacional pro Ciegoes y Sordomudas, Guatemala, Central America; NC Center for Public Policy Research, Inc., Raleigh, NC; Organization of American States, Washington, DC.

Special Studies 90: Leadership Seminar
Taught by: Bill Balthrop of Speech Communication

Special Studies 90 is a Seminar in Leadership for sophomore class members of the North Carolina Fellows Program. Its goals are (1) to explore the meaning of leadership and its exercise in different situations, including the acquisition and use of influence in a wide range of social situations; (2) to explore different styles and forms of leadership--what variables exist, what differences do they make in leadership effectiveness, and how can leaders adapt to them; (3) to examine the responsibilities associated with leadership--the questions of followership and loyalty, service and ethical considerations, among others; (4) to become aware of and develop skills in effective leadership; and (5) to reflect upon one's own views of leadership, one's skills, and to plan ways of enhancing those leadership attributes.

To move toward the fulfillment of these goals, the course will work to develop knowledge of "theoretical" aspects of leadership, including recent research, and will seek to integrate this knowledge with practical application through simulations, role plays, exercises, and seminar discussions.

The only required text will be a packet of reading materials. Additional case materials and occasional readings will also be handed out in class. These readings are designed both to inform and provoke. They do not contain the "right" answer so much as to provide

257

alternatives and grounds for discussions. Differing views have been included for topics. While seminar sessions will not "go over" readings, they are a valuable resource material and will add sophistication to analysis and discussion.

ASSIGNMENTS AND GRADING POLICIES: This seminar, graded on a "contract" basis, considers your goals and time commitments to determine the grade. Assignments will be evaluated as <u>not acceptable</u> (for instance, a description of "what happened"), <u>acceptable</u> (a description of "what happened" with analysis which incorporates a theoretically grounded perspective), and <u>highly acceptable</u> (description of events, analysis of them, incorporation of reading materials, and your evaluation of those events).

1. <u>A Profile/Analysis of a Leader, or the Role of Leadership in a Critical Event</u>--This paper should explore an individual who serves as a leader within the community, or an instance of how leadership succeeded or failed in an event of importance, also within the community. Preferably, this should be someone with whom you can discuss her or his style of leadership in person. Alternatively, if you select an event to analyze, you should be able to have direct contact with some of the participants. Some issues you might consider are power relationships, leadership style, areas of responsibility, importance and motivation for service, ethical choices made, and so on. The paper, approx. ten pages, should also include your assessment and explanation of these issues in addition to descriptive material.

2. <u>A Leadership Journal</u>--A journal, in whatever form you believe appropriate, that includes accounts of leadership-followership behavior that you encounter during the semester. You may include examples of both "effective" and "ineffective" leadership. Due in mid-October (just to check on how you're doing) and the last class period.

3. <u>Class Analysis Papers</u>--Relatively short papers (3-5 pages) that explore aspects of particular interest to you from class exercises, simulations, discussions, and so on. These papers are more valuable for students when focused upon one or two themes which are then explored in some depth, rather than trying to cover the entire range of events. Due throughout the semester as topics arise that you wish to explore.

4. <u>A Leadership "Projection" Paper</u>--This paper will explore the demands facing leaders in your chosen area of career interest during the next decade or so; and development of a "plan"--as best you can--of how you will prepare yourself for coping with those demands. This will require a candid, almost brutally honest assessment of your understanding of leadership, your strengths and relative weaknesses, and the relationship of these to the demands (both difficulties and opportunities) that you foresee for your area. Finally, it requires a "road map" of how you will prepare yourself for those challenges. Approx. 10 pages, due December 1.

All assignments, with the exception of the Journal, must be typewritten or produced on a computer. Each of you will contract for the grade you wish to receive, and contracts must be signed and returned to Dr. Balthrop not later than October 1. You may exceed the requirements for a grade contracted for, but will not receive a higher grade unless you renegotiate the contract grade by November 19. If you do not meet the required grade on any given assignment, you will have three weeks from the time the assignment was due initially to rework it and turn it in. You may continue to rework the assignment without penalty until it reaches the required grade, so long as it takes place within the three week period. The only exception is the Leadership "Projection" Paper, which must have all revisions completed by December 15.

GRADE REQUIREMENTS:

For Grade of "A": Attend all classes except two (absences include excused absences except for extremely unusual circumstances). Complete the Profile/Analysis Paper, including descriptive material integrated with conceptual material, evaluations of leader/leadership exhibited, and justifications for those evaluations. Must receive grade of "highly acceptable." Complete the Leadership "Projection" Paper, receiving grade of "highly acceptable." Complete three "Class Analysis Papers," receiving grade of "highly acceptable." Complete eight entries in the Leadership Journal.

For Grade of "B": Attend all classes except two. Complete the Profile/Analysis Paper, receiving grade of "highly acceptable." Complete the Leadership "Projection" Paper, receiving grade of "highly acceptable." Complete two "Class Analysis Papers," receiving grades of "acceptable." Complete five entries in the Leadership Journal.

For Grade of "C": Attend all classes except three. Complete the Profile/Analysis Paper, receiving grade of "acceptable." Complete the Leadership "Projection" Paper, receiving grade of "acceptable." Complete one "Class Analysis Paper," receiving grade of "acceptable." Complete three entries in the Leadership Journal.

SCHEDULE OF CLASS MEETINGS AND ASSIGNMENTS

Sessions	Assignment
1	Introduction and Orientation to the Course
2 & 3	What Constitutes "Leadership" and "A Leader"?: The Importance of Influence, Power and Leadership Styles [Exercise: Four problem-solving groups with leaders "assigned" to illustrate authoritarian, democratic, social, and laissez-faire styles of leadership. Discussion of group task and maintenance factors and of satisfaction of group members.] Readings: Sashkin and Lassey, "Theories of Leadership: A Review of Useful Research"; Sashkin and Lassey, "Dimensions of Leadership"; Yukl, "Power and Leadership Effectiveness"
4	A Day for Practical Concerns: Time Management and Wellness
5 & 6	The Assumptions of Transformational Leadership; Establishing a Supportive Communication Environment and Developing Skills in Active Listening Readings: Heller and Van Til, "Leadership and Followership: Some Summary Propositions"; Whetton and Cameron, "Supportive Communication"; McCaskey, "The Hidden Messages Managers Send"; Nenlo, "Have You Tried Listening?" [Exercise: Role-simulation where one person in a supervisory situation must interact with another in a subordinate position. Both are on student committee,

both see the other as responsible for their difficulties, and both anticipate seeking President of the Union.   Discussion following on supportive communication and listening.]

7	Understanding and Being Effective in Group Situations Readings: Wood, "Problem-Solving Group Communication"; Prince, "How to be a Better Meeting Chairman"; Myers, "Type and Teamwork."
8	Coping with Conflict: Winning, But Not Necessarily Through Intimidation Readings: Whetton and Cameron, "Interpersonal Conflict Management" [Exercise places small groups within a conflict situation requiring creative problem-solving and adoption of a "win-win" conflict resolution style.]
9	Dealing With Broader Issues: The Culture of Organizations and the Organization of Cultures; Readings: Hunt, "The Role of Leadership in the Construction of Reality"; Smircich and Morgan, "Leadership: The Management of Meaning"
10	Class Discussion on "Political Leadership"
11	Leadership and Questions of Prejudice Readings: The New Republic, "The Jeweler's Dilemma"; Jackson, "Racism: Why Is It Still With Us In the 1980s?"; Smith, "Cultural and Historical Perspectives in Counseling Blacks"; Seldon, "On Being Color-Blind"; Tinney, "Interconnections"
12	Leadership and Questions of Prejudice, cont.
13	Leadership and the Question of "Ethics" [Discussion of minority business owner asked to support economic boycott--similar to one he/she led several years earlier in another state--that will have severe repercussions for his/her business and the minority employees who work for him/her. Should he/she participate? Why?]
14	Leadership and the Question of "Service"

Leadership Matters . . . Program

This program is designed to increase the effectiveness of leaders and members of the 250+ recognized student organizations. Its goals are: working with student leaders to recognize the leadership potential within their organizations; training students in establishing and maintaining efficiently functioning groups; encouraging and assisting students to use resource materials to solve organizational problems and to learn new leadership skills.

Program components include: leadership skills training workshops; a resource library; a monthly newsletter; consultation services (professional staff and peers).

Peer Leadership Consultants (PLCs): Five to eight students are trained to work with student organizations, addressing leadership concerns and organizational development. PLCs advise officers, prepare and present workshops and provide research materials and referrals.

University of North Carolina at Chapel Hill   **Cynthia Wolf**

Emerging Leaders Program

This new program is being tested with a selected group of emerging leaders to prepare them for effective campus involvement and help them identify their leadership styles, develop skills, and take advantage of opportunities and gain confidence. Whether currently a leader or emerging as one, students are encouraged to be actively involved in student organizations and take advantage of leadership training opportunities.

Delegates Program

To help strengthen the leadership in and the organizational effectiveness of recognized student organizations, a structured, semester-long leadership training and organizational development program for leaders and members of recognized student organizations.

GOALS: To train students in organizational management skills, such as motivating group members, fund raising, and decision making; to provide experiential applications of workshop content in the form of exercises, small group discussion, and interactive participation; to focus on and address specific concerns of members of represented student organizations. The Delegates Program is open to all students, faculty and staff of the University affiliated with recognized student organizations.

University of Richmond
The Jepson School of Leadership Studies
Richmond, VA 23173

Zeddie Bowen
Vice President and Provost
804/289-8153

The University of Richmond is currently in the process of establishing the Jepson School of Leadership Studies. The School, endowed generously by Mr. and Mrs. Robert S. Jepson, will provide an opportunity for undergraduate students to earn a degree in leadership studies, the first of its kind in the U.S. The School will combine education about and for leadership (innovative teaching methods will be employed and interdisciplinary courses will be encouraged). The educational program will be developed over time by the School's faculty and staff, with the help of national experts, the University's current faculty, and the director (whose appointment is expected shortly).

The Jepson School will offer the B.A. degree; students will also be able to minor in Leadership Studies and courses will be available to the general student population. The School will enroll 80 students as majors, forty in each of the junior and senior classes; the first junior majors are anticipated to begin in the fall of 1992.

Also planned are: an extensive co-curricular program; a Leadership Forum (a series of symposia, lectures, debates, etc.) focusing on national and global concerns; a series of non-credit workshops, seminars, and directed field experiences; research and publication; and continuing education. Additionally, the program in its many components will be assessed and tracked.

Described below are several current and ongoing courses and programs at the University of Richmond.

Leadership Seminar
Janet Kotler
B School 126 / 804/289-8679

When you start to read about leadership, the same words appear over again: power, self-knowledge, conflict, risk, energy, vision, context, influence, teamwork, strategies, change, authority, ethics, styles. They all raise significant questions worth pondering at length.

This seminar provides opportunities to see leadership--in several kinds of organizations--and develop it in yourselves. The focus will be on <u>seeing leadership</u> and <u>doing leadership</u>.

Seeing leadership implies observing it in action as broadly as possible--on campus, locally, and nationally. It implies thinking about effective leadership in particular situations, and trying to understand some elements of leadership common to many contexts. **Doing leadership** implies, first, knowing your own capabilities, strengths, limitations, desires. It implies confronting, personally, risk, change, power, ethical decisions, and cultivating a style, a character, a vision, a sense of self as leader.

We will ask ourselves some questions: What is leadership? Why is it our concern? What are the elements of successful leadership? Are certain styles of leadership particular to men? To women? What do we do about that? What effective strategies might exist for organizational change?

I bring to the course strong interests in political science and history (my undergraduate majors) and business (I teach in the Business School)--the readings will reflect these interests to a degree. Ordinarily, I teach courses in writing and speaking. You will each bring expertise and experience to our work together. This is a seminar, not a lecture course. Its success depends on sharing and support. We will learn together and teach each other, and have fun.

THE WORK: I am not a person who undertakes anything without overdoing it; consequently, the course may be overloaded in spots, but we'll deal with that as we come to it.

In general terms, the **work** will involve:

1. Quite a lot of **reading**. You are to buy Warren Bennis & Burt Nanus, Leaders: The Strategies for Taking Charge, Harper & Row, 1985--about $7, and Contemporary Issues in Leadership, edited by Rosenbach & Taylor, slightly more. You also need to hand me $5 in cold cash to defray the cost of the vast number of handouts you'll be reading. While you're in the bookstore, buy a rather large three-ring binder for holding them, and a notebook that can serve as a journal.

You are each responsible for reading one book on the outside reading list (attached) and sharing its content with the rest of us. I strongly suggest that you buy that book.

2. A series (about five) of short (three to four pages) **papers**, which I call "talking point papers."

3. **Field experience** as a volunteer with a social change agency in Richmond. I believe that one of the best ways to learn about leadership is to see it operating. Further, I believe that the crucible of social change, rather than money-making or social activities, is the best place to watch leadership happening. Consequently, you will volunteer a minimum of two hours a week for 10-12 weeks with a social change agency, which you can arrange (I'll help) through the Volunteer Action Committee on campus.

(Yes, I thought of that. I am aware that the field experience requirement could be seen by a person with a tendency toward depression as a healthy drain on your time. While I hope--and expect--that you will come to see it in other terms, I am not so far gone that I don't anticipate rebellion here. Therefore, I have--except for the first and last couple of weeks--considerably shortened the time we will meet as a group. I hope that helps.)

4. **Participation** as an observer/leader in some campus group. I am assuming that is something you're already doing. You will be expected to keep a log of your participation in this group and of your field experience.

5. **Practice** in leading the seminar discussions.

6. **Knowing** what's going on in the country. To this end, you need to read a good newspaper (the <u>Washington Post</u> or the <u>New York Times</u>) every day, listen to NPR's "All Things Considered" (5:00-6:30 p.m.) or "Morning Edition" (around dawn; I wouldn't know), and/or watch the MacNeil Lehrer Report (Channel 23, the Sesame Street channel, 7:00-8:00 p.m.; repeated on Channel 57 at 10:00 p.m.).

I plan mostly to listen to what you say and to read what you write.

EVALUATION: Since the seminar method relies wholly on aggressive and informed participation by everyone, roughly 40% of the credit for the course is based on the quality of that participation. Obviously, my grading of your participation is subjective, but these criteria will guide me: Do you have something intelligent to say? Does your participation grow out of your reading and experience or does it seem to be off-the-cuff? Have you pushed your participation to the limit (but not over it), given your own personality and abilities?

The Talking Point Papers are intended to prepare you for seminar discussions. They can take various directions--such as tackling related or unrelated points suggested to you by the reading, making expository arguments, pursuing apparent inconsistencies, or exploring perplexing ideas encountered in the reading or field experience. <u>A series of empty abstract sentences</u> ("Machiavelli presents many sound ideas that I feel apply to leaders in today's society"; "The ability to recognize the need for change is a great asset to a leader.") <u>will simply not do</u>. Your papers need to have a <u>point</u>, easily discernible. To write a successful paper, sound like who you are--a <u>person</u>.

My criteria for grading written work will be the extent to which the paper grows from your own experience and thought, the significance of what you write, and the extent to which the writing is well-crafted and graceful. This is college.

All papers are to be <u>typed</u>, <u>double-spaced</u>. Please put your names <u>lightly</u>, at the <u>bottom</u>, on the <u>back</u> of the last page.

From time to time I will collect your journals. Journal entries should <u>briefly</u> chronicle your field experience and your participation in a campus group.

OUTSIDE READING LIST: Saul Alinsky, <u>Rules for Radicals</u>; David S. Broder, <u>Changing of the Guard: Power and Leadership in America</u> (1980); C. D. B. Bryan, <u>Friendly Fire</u> (1976); J. M. Burns, <u>Roosevelt: The Lion and the Fox</u> (1956); Robert Caro, <u>The Power Broker: Robert Moses and the Fall of New York</u> (1975); Thomas R. Dye, <u>Who's Running America?</u>; E. H. Erikson, <u>Gandhi's Truth: On the Origins of Militant Nonviolence</u> (1970); Carol Gilligan, <u>In a Different Voice: Psychological Theory and Women's Development</u> (1982); Fred Greenstein, <u>The Hidden-hand Presidency: Eisenhower as Leader</u> (1982); David Halberstam, <u>The Reckoning</u> (1986); <u>The Best and the Brightest</u> (1983); <u>The Powers That Be</u> (1979); Alex Haley, ed., <u>The Autobiography of Malcolm X</u>; Sarah Hardesty and

Nehama Jacobs, <u>Success and Betrayal, The Crisis of Women in Corporate America</u> (1986); Trudy Heller, <u>Women and Men as Leaders</u> (1982); Seymour Hersh, <u>The Price of Power: Kissinger in the Nixon White House</u> (1983); Sylvia Ann Hewlett, <u>A Lesser Life: The Myth of Women's Liberation in America</u> (1986); Aileen Jacobson; <u>Women in Charge: Dilemmas of Women in Authority</u> (1985); Sy Kahn, <u>How People Get Power</u>; Rosabeth Moss Kanter, <u>The Change Masters</u> (1983), <u>Men and Women of the Corporation</u> (1977); Barbara Kellerman, <u>Political Leadership</u> (1987); John Kotter, <u>The Leadership Factor</u> (1988); Arthur Levine, <u>When Dreams and Heroes Died</u> (1980); J. Lipman-Blumen, <u>Gender Roles and Power</u> (1984); Marilyn Loden, <u>Feminine Leadership, or How to Succeed in Business Without Being One of the Boys</u> (1985); N. Machiavelli, <u>The Prince</u> and <u>The Discourses</u> (c. 1514); Patricia McBroom, <u>The Third Sex: The New Professional Woman</u> (1986); Charles Murray, <u>Losing Ground: American Social Policy</u> (1984); Ralph Nader, <u>The Big Boys</u> (1986); Richard Neustadt, <u>Presidential Power: The Politics of Leadership from FDR to Carter</u> (1980); Stephen Oates, <u>Let the Trumpet Sound: The Life of Martin Luther King, Jr.</u>; T. J. Peters and R. H. Waterman, <u>In Search of Excellence</u> (1982); Bette Ann Stead, <u>Women in Management</u> (1985); Tom Wolfe, <u>The Right Stuff</u> (1979).

SCHEDULE

Week One: **Introduction**
Session 1   Introduction to Course. <u>Choose</u>: 2 books from the reading list (1st choice & alternate) by week 2.
Week Two: **Plunging In**
Session 1   Starpower 1.
Session 2   Starpower 2. <u>Write</u>: Talking Point Paper 1 (Due Week 3).
Week Three: **Leadership: What <u>Is</u> It?**
Session 1   Discussion of Starpower. <u>Make</u>: definite arrangements for field experience. Form (FE) due Week 4. <u>Read</u>: B&N, 1-18; R&T, 31-39, 42-60, 305-316, 318-325; Hollander handout for discussion.
Session 2   Discussion: What is Leadership?
Week Four: **You As A Leader (Self-Assessment)**
Session 1   Discussion (with Jane Hopkins): "What Makes a Leader?" <u>Read</u>: B&N, 19-86; R&T, 255-269, 271-280, 281-288; handouts. <u>Write</u>: Personal Inventory.
Week Five: **The Organizational Context of Leadership**
Session 1   Discussion (with John Roush): Leadership at UR. <u>Read</u>: B&N, 87-151; handouts - Deal & Kennedy, Kotter, Hollander.
Session 2   No class. <u>Write</u>: Inventory of your organization. Due Week 6.
Week Six: **Styles of Leadership**
Session 1   No class. <u>Read</u>: R&T, 75-123; handouts - Hollander, Loden, Christiansen, Adams & Yoder. <u>Write</u>: TPP 2 due Week 7.
Session 2   Discussion (with Stephanie Micas): Masculine/feminine Leadership Styles.

Week Seven:	**Leading and Following**
Session 1	Exercise. <u>Read</u>: B&N, 152-186; R&T, 138-143; 144-161; 192-206; 223-229; Hollander handout.
Session 2	Discussion of Exercise.
Week Eight:	**Leadership for What?**
Session 1	Discussion (with David Dorsey): Leadership and Social Change. <u>Read</u>: B&N, 187-229; handouts - Hollander, Grob; Bush, Dukakis, & Jackson speeches.
Session 2	No class. <u>Write</u>: TPP 3 due Week 9.
Week Nine:	**Leadership for What?**
Session 1	Discussion: What Makes Leading Worth It?
Session 2	No class. <u>Read</u>: Hamilton, Lewis, Tucker, Burns, & Steinem handouts for Week 10.
Week Ten:	**Political Leadership**
Session 1	Discussion: Leadership in the 1988 Elections.
Week Eleven:	**Personal Perspectives on Leadership**
Session 1	Individual Presentations. <u>Write</u>: TPP 4 due Week 14.
Week Twelve:	**Personal Perspectives**
Session 1	Individual Presentations
Week Thirteen:	**Personal Perspectives**
Session 1	Individual Presentations
Week Fourteen:	**Are You Being Educated for Leadership?**
Session 1	Deans Cliff Poole (BS) and Sheldon Wettack (A&S). <u>Read</u>: R&T, 305-325; Kotter handouts.
Week Fifteen:	**Looking Back at Leadership**
Session 1	Evaluation

WILL - Women Involved in Living and Learning
Stephanie Micas, 804/289-8472

The Women Involved in Living and Learning (WILL) program focuses on <u>leadership</u> development and gender issues through curricular and co-curricular experiences. The program is distinctive in that it is designed not only to help identify interests, skills, and talents, but also to help apply them.

WILL courses and seminars are on topics ranging from self-awareness, gender stereotyping, and life planning, to women in the Western and other cultural traditions. It is a series of skills development workshops which focus on such topics as leadership styles, decision making, goals clarification, assertiveness training, resume writing, job interviewing, job search skills, and personal growth.

WILL internships enable students to practice acquired skills and explore the world of work. They are required in the third year of the program. WILL is a progressive learning experience, with each new component carefully drawing upon the previous program component. Participants experience certain courses in each year of the program as well as take part in and plan co-curricular programs for themselves and for other students through outreach programming.

<u>Year 1</u>: The selection process proceeds through nomination (faculty, staff, self), completion of application requirements, and review by a faculty screening committee in the Fall. Approximately 30 new WILL students are selected on the basis of interest in the program's goals, high school academic and co-curricular records, and a personal statement focusing on the student's definition of leadership and concept of her role as a leader.

New WILL students are tapped by upperclass students and honored with a welcoming reception attended by faculty and upperclass WILL students.

Women's Studies Program
Suzanne Jones
804/289-8307

Sociology 220: Sociology of Women. An exploration of the physical, psychological, and social development of women with emphasis on confronting one's own identity and determining future directions. 3 sem. hrs. credit.

<u>Year 2</u>: **English 230: Women in Literature.** Modern woman's search for identity and struggle for self-realization through a study of selected figures from nineteenth and twentieth century literature. 3 sem. hrs. credit.

Women's Studies 302: Women and the Law. Traditional and contemporary relationship of women to the law. Includes the study of legal history and of factors bearing on women's legal status. 3 sem. hrs. credit.

<u>Year 3</u>: **Women's Studies 398: Life Planning Seminar.** An exploration of career planning and/or post graduate work. Includes Myers-Briggs survey, career search, resume writing, and internship development with a corporation, state agency, or non-profit organization. 3 sem. hrs. credit.

Women's Studies 388: Internship. Work experience with a major corporation, state agency or non-profit organization. Internships are served under the joint supervision of a faculty member and an agency project director. 3-6 sem. hrs. credit.

Community Internship Opportunities (sample listing): Virginia Museum, Maymont Foundation, City Parks & Recreation, Greater Richmond Chamber of Commerce, Virginia General Assembly, Legal Aid Society, Valentine Museum, YWCA, United Way, Chesterfield County Municipal Government, Senate Finance Committee

<u>Year 4</u>: **Interdisciplinary Studies 340: Leadership: Development of Personal Style.** A course that combines some theoretical understanding of leadership and its problems with practical experience and development of skills. 3 sem. hrs. credit.

Leadership Opportunities Coordinated by the Richmond College Dean's Office that are available to <u>UR Undergraduates</u>.

1.   Student Government Leadership Workshop

During the first week of April, the newly elected student government leaders for the three undergraduate student governments and the presidents/chairs of other major student organizations are invited to attend a two-day workshop conducted at an off-campus site. Generally there are twenty-five students in attendance. Eight to ten University administrators who work closely with student leaders also are invited to attend. During the workshop a series of facilitators examine such topics as leadership styles, effective communication, motivating your organization, planning models, conducting meetings, and the University's decision-making structure. Many of the presentations are experiential in nature. One of the major goals is for the student leaders to get to know one another as well as some key administrators. Participants have the opportunity to experience new management strategies and to identify some concerns/issues on which their organization might focus.

2.   Emerging Leaders Workshop

During February, each student organization is invited to send four students who are new to their leadership position or who may be leaders in the future to the Emerging Leaders Workshop. The workshop is sponsored by Omicron Delta Kappa. There generally are fifty to seventy students in attendance. During the six-hour workshop, students hear presentations on such subjects as leadership styles, motivation, effective communication and resolving typical organization concerns. Student members of Omicron Delta Kappa serve as facilitators for some of the workshop components, while "professionals" assume responsibility for other components. Participants have the opportunity to meet other young leaders, to identify some campus resources who might be able to assist them in the future and to begin to understand how critical the involvement of an organization's members is to the success of the project.

Leadership Opportunities Coordinated by the Richmond College Dean's Office that are available to Richmond College Students only.

1.   Spinning Your Web

Thirty-four freshman men are selected to participate in an eleven-event, eight-week program conducted during the first eight weeks of the fall semester. The participants live on the same floor in Freeman Hall. The individual programs focus either on opportunities for student involvement at the University or on the participant's understanding himself better. An example of the first category would be a panel discussion directed to the question of joining a social fraternity; an example of the latter would be participants completing the MBTI followed by the analysis of the results in a group format. The Dean's Office staff identifies particularly able students to incorporate into the college's committee and task force structure.

2.   Orientation Counselors

Thirty-eight men, including three upperclass co-chairs, are chosen each spring to serve as Orientation Counselors for New Student Orientation for the following fall. Orientation Counselors participate in a two-day training experience conducted by the Dean's Office and supported by other University staff members. Orientation Counselors receive instruction in academic advising, personal counseling, problem solving and referral techniques, as well as on how to implement specific Orientation activities.

3.   Honor Council/Judicial Council

All members of these two councils participate in a two-day workshop that takes place early in the fall semester. The workshop focuses on such issues as consensus decision making, confidentiality, standards of guilt, sanctions and their consequences, and a review of the statute appropriate to the organization.

Leadership Opportunities Coordinated by the Richmond College Dean's Office and open to Richmond College, E. Claiborne Robins School of Business men and T. C. Williams School of Law men.

1.   Head Resident and Resident Assistant Positions in the Residence Halls

Our staff supervises the work of thirty-three head residents and resident assistants. All student staff must complete a seven-week, two-hour per week resident assistant course and a week of pre-fall semester training before assuming the staff position.

2.   Hall Presidents

Eight men are selected to serve as presidents of their hall. They complete a one-day workshop on the "how to's" of programming and chairing a Hall Council. All Hall Council members complete a three-hour workshop on programming.

University of San Diego
University Center/Alcala Park, San Diego, CA 92110

Thomas J. Cosgrove
Associate Dean of Students
619/260-4589

"Leadership Development at the University of San Diego: A Four-Year Plan."
Excerpts from a paper by Cosgrove

We do not believe that leadership can be achieved overnight, in a weekend workshop, via a single course, or by supplying students with a few, quick-fix management techniques. We certainly do not believe that holding a position automatically makes a student a leader. We believe that leadership is a complex phenomenon, inescapably connected to a person's overall human development. Leadership, therefore, relates directly to a person's sense of identity and to his/her sense of purpose or mission in life. For these reasons, we have developed a four-year model of leadership development grounded in the research on college student development as well as in the interdisciplinary research on leadership development.

The assumptions underlying the University of San Diego's approach to leadership development are the following: 1. Leadership is a complex phenomenon. 2. It can be learned. 3. To gain an understanding of what leadership is, the concept needs to be addressed from a variety of perspectives including the historical, political, sociological, psychological, and business and management. This program has been developed with full awareness that each of these disciplines has approached the subject and has made significant contributions to it. 4. Leadership is different from management, explored long before management theory existed which traces its origins to the late 1920s. Aristotle talked about leadership. As management theory became popularized and preeminent in the 1970s, the two tended to be equated. They should not be and are not in this program. 5. Both management skills and leadership are teachable, but leadership--because it is more complex and more personal--requires different strategies for its development in persons and a longer period of time than is required to teach management skills. 6. Leaders do not exist unless there are followers (or members of a group); therefore, teaching membership skills is important. 7. Leaders do not always need to assume the leadership role. They make room for others to lead. 8. Leadership involves the use of power resources to meet the leader's own needs as well as the needs and wants of followers. If leaders are not meeting the needs and wants of followers, then they are engaged in power wielding and not leadership. 9. Leadership is developmental; true leaders develop other leaders. A corollary to this assumption is that leaders, therefore, are conscious of their leadership. Leaders are consciously competent. 10. Leadership involves vision, values, and purpose, and so is fundamentally ethical.

The goals of the University of San Diego's leadership development program are three-fold: Cognitive, behavioral, and attitudinal.
A.   Cognitive: Students will come to an understanding of leadership concepts enabling them to articulate, for example, the differences between leadership and management; they will understand the benefits of followership and membership or the importance of followership and membership skills; they will be able to identify the contributions of various disciplines to the study of leadership. The cognitive goal will be achieved by: 1) Classes in the Emerging Leader Program; 2) Leadership seminars offered to all students; 3) Leadership retreats and workshops; 4) Classes in the leadership

minor (for those who choose this option).

B.   Behavioral: Teaching students "to do" leadership by seeking changes in behavior in the following ways:
   1)   Students in the Emerging Leader Program are required to join an organization.
   2)   Each class in the Emerging Leader Program is designed to include an experiential component; students will "try on" different leadership behaviors.
   3)   Following freshman year, students are encouraged to continue involvement in student organizations and "contract" with an advisor to receive feedback on their leadership behavior.
   4)   Once students have had some experience in student organizations, they are challenged to run for elected office either in the organization or in the Associated Student Government.
   5)   Students are challenged to demonstrate leadership skills, and if they meet the minimum criteria, may be invited to serve as part of a consulting team to work with student organizations.
   6)   Students who have completed the process may design workshops and presentations.
   7)   Students will have the opportunity to get involved in the national professional associations (NACA, ACU-I and others).

C.   Attitudinal: Students will develop a commitment to leadership both on campus and in the society which they enter upon graduation as follows:
   1)   In classes and seminars, students will be challenged to reconsider some of their assumptions about leadership.
   2)   In personal advising relationships, students will be challenged to reflect on their attitudes and position regarding leadership.
   3)   For those who choose the leadership minor as an option, the "Leadership Seminar" is designed as a capstone course which will serve to integrate all of the student's previous learning about leadership.
   4)   Students in the USD's Leadership Program will be challenged to develop and write their own philosophy of leadership.

THE FOUR-YEAR PLAN: A TWO-TRACK SYSTEM

USD's School of Education offers a leadership minor. Because of this unique option available to students, USD's Leadership Development Program has two fundamental tracks (a credit and a non-credit). Both begin with an introductory, non-credit course available to all freshmen called the Emerging Leader Program.

The Emerging Leader Program

The Emerging Leader Program consists of 18 two-hour sessions offered once a week from September through April, taught by members of the Student Affairs Professional Staff. Enrollment is limited to 100. The class will be broken up into five sections each, facilitated by a member of the professional staff. Periodically, the Emerging Leader group will come together to share the learning in that setting.

The Emerging Leader Program is designed to:

1) Gather together freshman students with previous leadership experience who would like to continue with that experience as well as students without previous leadership experience who are now interested in acquiring it.

2) To have these students meet one another and provide them with an opportunity to share their goals.

3) To acquaint students with various resources on campus that afford them the opportunity for leadership development.

4) To develop in those students fundamental skills and ability that will increase their personal effectiveness.

5) To teach these students to be effective members of groups to which they belong. Students in the Emerging Leader class will be required to join a student organization and be challenged to practice skills learned in class sessions in that organization.

6) To increase these students' sense of identity and competence.

The theory base for the emerging leader program and its methodology may be obtained by writing to Thomas Cosgrove.

The Academic Credit Track: The Leadership Minor - About mid-point in the Emerging Leader Program, students will be given a presentation about USD's leadership minor. This academic program is an opportunity for students to continue their leadership development in a systematic way and for college credit. For students who choose this option, the sequence will be as follows:

Following the Emerging Leader Program which teaches them personal competency skills and membership skills, Education 16, Leadership in Organizations, offered in their sophomore year, teaches them how to apply those individual skills to groups from a leader position. Like the Emerging Leader Program, this class includes the requirement that the student be a member of an organization. Students in this class would be challenged to increase their level of responsibility within an organization, perhaps by becoming a chairperson or a member of the executive board of that organization.

In the junior year the student enrolls in Education 150, Leadership in Groups. This class builds on the content of the previous two classes and will teach students how to become process consultants in organizations or how to help leaders in groups to operate more effectively. Continuing with the experiential components consistent throughout the program, during the junior year the student in a leadership minor will also be expected to complete an internship (Education 352) which consists of a supervised experience in a leadership position on campus. This requirement challenges students in the program to enter into the political process and get themselves elected to or appointed to a position of responsibility within a campus organization. The supervision of this experience will be by members of the Student Affairs Professional Staff. Finally, during the senior year the student attends a leadership seminar, Education 151, which is the capstone course of the program, designed to facilitate a student's integration of previous knowledge base and experience base and to help them develop a personal philosophy of leadership.

As part of the leadership minor, the student must also complete six additional units (or two classes) from a list of approved electives offered in various departments, reflecting our belief in the importance of an interdisciplinary approach to a thorough understanding of leadership.

The Non-Credit Track - Students in the Emerging Leader Program who do not elect the academic credit track will be encouraged to follow the following sequence in order to continue their personal leadership development:

Sophomore year: Students will be challenged to seek increased levels of responsibility within organizations of which they are already members, by becoming a chairperson or member of the executive board. Students will also be encouraged to attend a series of seminars offered by members of the Student Affairs Professional Staff and attach themselves to a mentor with whom they will contract to get feedback on their leadership performance.

Junior Year: Students will be challenged to take on positions of primary leadership. Examples are: AS elected positions; RA (Resident Assistant), University Center position with supervisory responsibilities. Students continue to take advantage of leadership seminars and workshops which are offered by members of Student Affairs Professional Staff. Students get involved in one of several professional associations (NACA, ACU-I, others).

Senior Year: Students become part of consulting team and help other leaders and student organizations to increase their effectiveness. Students in major leadership positions develop some systems to ensure that their vision for the organization(s) is maintained and continued. Students write personal philosophy of leadership and secure feedback on that statement from their mentor, advisor, and other established leaders both on and off campus. Students attend series of discussions offered by the Student Affairs Staff for established leaders.

The University of San Diego's Leadership Development Program is not without history. What is new is a comprehensive, four-year, multi-dimensional approach. Because of the comprehensiveness of its scope, its thorough grounding in the interdisciplinary research on leadership, and its theory to practice emphasis, USD's Leadership Development Program is on the cutting edge of what is happening in leadership development across the nation. Therefore systematic short-term and longitudinal research on the program is being initiated.

University of San Diego   **Thomas J. Cosgrove**

Leadership in Organizations - EDAD 60
School of Education

(This is the foundational course for Leadership minor.)

TEXTS: Yukl, Gary A., (1981). Leadership in Organizations. Englewood Cliffs: Prentice-Hall Inc.; Bennis, W. and Nanus, Lee, (1985). Leaders. New York: Harper and Row.

EXPECTATIONS AND REQUIREMENTS: 1. Because this class will be experiential and discussion-oriented, attendance is expected. Furthermore, students will be expected to come to class having completed the reading assignments and prepared to discuss the material. Active participation in class activities is also expected. 2. There will be a mid-term and final exam. These exams will focus primarily on theoretical constructs and readings. 3. For grading purposes, the following is the point distribution:

1) Class preparation and participation	25 pts
2) Mid-term exam	15 pts
3) Final exam	20 pts
4) Application paper	10 pts
5) Theoretical paper	15 pts
6) Class presentation	15 pts
	100 pts

MAJOR ASSIGNMENTS:

Group Observation Report: With a focus on one specific leadership or management behavior discussed in class (list to be furnished), 1) Select an organization to observe; 2) Attend and observe at least three meetings of that organization; 3) Write a 3-5 page paper answering the following three questions: (a) What did you observe relative to the issue on which you were focusing? (b) How did you evaluate leader and member behavior in the group? (c) If you were the leader of the organization in what ways would you have behaved differently?

Theoretical Paper: Leadership can be approached from many perspectives: historical, psychological, political, sociological, ethical, biographical, and the point of view of specific groups, e.g., women and minorities. In this paper select and present one of these approaches to leadership. Included in the paper should be: 1) Methodology used in this approach; 2) Principal findings; 3) Evaluation of this particular approach to leadership. The paper should be 7-10 pages in length and include a minimum of 5 references.

Public Presentation: Bennis and Nanus describe four leadership strategies. Your group is to take one strategy and prepare a public presentation such as might be given to a Board of Directors of a major corporation. The presentation should be professional in nature and make use of audio visuals. The presentation should include: 1) at least two examples of the strategy in action; 2) a minimum of 5 specific behaviors leaders can engage in to implement this strategy.

CLASS SESSIONS

Session	Topic	Assignment
1	Overview of Course; Introductions; Expectations	
2	Introduction to Leadership as a Discipline. What is Leadership? A Discussion	Yukl, XI-9; Bennis & Nanus, pp. 1-18
3	Approaches to Leadership: Historical Review	Bennis & Nanus, pp. 19-86
4	Trait Theories of Leadership - Part I: Assessing Your Own Traits	Yukl, pp. 67-77
5	Trait Theories of Leadership - Part II: Traits versus Qualities Associated with Leadership	Yukl, pp. 77-92
6	Methods of Observation	Yukl, pp. 92-113
7	Goal Setting	Yukl, pp. 113-131
8	Communication	Bennis & Nanus, pp. 110-151
9	Formal and Informal Organizations	Yukl, pp. 201-220
10	Delegation	Yukl, pp. 220-231
11	Group Decision Making	Yukl, pp. 233-267
12	Perspectives on Organizations: Background Assumptions and Theories-in-Use	Handout
13	MID-TERM	
14	Situational Leadership Theory, Part 1	Yukl, pp. 132-153
15	Situational Leadership Theory, Part 2	Yukl, pp. 153-169
16	Politics and Leadership (Group Observation Report Due)	Handouts
17	Power, Authority & Influence, Part 1	Yukl, pp. 10-37
18	Power, Authority & Influence, Part 2	Yukl, pp. 38-66
19	Ethics & Leadership	Handouts
20	Interdisciplinary Approaches to Leadership	Yukl, pp. 268-290
21	Women in Leadership	Handouts
22	Vision and Leadership	Bennis & Nanus, pp. 87-109
23	Transformational Leadership (Theoretical Paper Due)	Bennis & Nanus, pp. 152-186, 215-229
24	Managing Yourself	Handouts + Bennis & Nanus, pp. 187-214
25	Class Presentations	Presentation Preparation
26	Class Presentations	Presentation Preparation
27	Where Do We Go From Here?	Review for Final
28	FINAL EXAM 2-4 p.m.	

University of South Carolina
Campus Box 85128, Columbia, SC 29205

Novella Fortner
Asst. Dean of Student Life
803/777-5780

Leadership Training Programs

PROGRAM OBJECTIVES: Leadership Training Programs at the University of South Carolina are designed to enhance the quality of student involvement and aid in the personal and leadership skill development of each student. The program is comprehensive in nature, utilizing faculty and staff expertise in providing developmental opportunities in a broad variety of mediums with a goal of responding to the diverse needs of various student populations. The program is administered through the Department of Student Life/Division of Student Affairs and coordinated by a full-time staff member in the Campus Activities Center. This collaborative effort supports four main components of the Leadership Program at the University of South Carolina: A) Resources, B) Training/-Organizational Development, C) Mentoring/Individual Training and Development, and D) Leadership Recognition. Outline below is a brief description of each component.

RESOURCES:

Leadership Training Lab: Located within the Campus Activities Center, the Lab provides individuals the opportunity to explore leadership topics and gather resources to assist in all leadership situations. The Lab contains the following plus more: Resource Files, a Leadership Library, a Viewing Room, Periodicals, and a Leadership Training Handout Series.

Leadership Advisory Committee: Comprised of faculty, staff and students, the Advisory Committee meets monthly to assist in providing direction for the design and implementation of the program. Members of the Committee are selected to represent areas throughout the University who are coordinating aspects of leadership development for students. The student members of the committee are leaders who have participated in portions of leadership programs. Evaluation and assessment of leadership programs is a central purpose of the Advisory Committee.

Student Organization Advisors: A faculty or staff member serves as an advisor to each of 240 student organizations. Advisors are utilized as a communication link to student leaders and/or potential leaders in their groups. Additionally, the Leadership Training Program provides developmental opportunities through publications, workshops and seminars for the leadership development of individual advisors.

Faculty/Staff/Graduate Assistants: It would not be possible to provide a comprehensive leadership program without the assistance of faculty, staff and graduate students. These individuals provide workshops and serve as mentors, general resources and facilitators to portions of the program. Without this support, the impact of the overall program would be greatly limited.

ORGANIZATION DEVELOPMENT:

Leadership Training Network: The Network provides workshops for organizational development. Skilled consultants offer workshops on topics ranging from budget development to time management, some tailored for an individual group. Members of the Division of Student Affairs and faculty members are recruited to serve as workshop presenters in their areas of personal expertise. Graduate students are recruited as consultants and trained in a specific area. Inexperienced graduate students are paired with a faculty or staff expert. The Network offers workshops throughout the semester for general attendance by any student, faculty or staff member.

Consultation Services: The Leadership Office provides assistance to all organization leaders and advisors on organizational planning or concerns. Officer training, organizational retreats, conferences or seminars are areas in which the staff may assist a group. Diversity of training methods are individualized for each group.

Greek Leadership Training: The Greek Life staff advise student leaders in the design and development of semester long training workshops as well as an annual retreat for newly elected chapter presidents and Sorority and Fraternity Council officers.

MENTORING/INDIVIDUAL TRAINING AND DEVELOPMENT:

Emerging Leader Program: A six week class offered each semester to fifty freshman students as an intentional approach to personal and leadership skill development for those aspiring to be collegiate leaders. Objectives include: development of basic leadership skills and behaviors, integration of emerging leaders into active participants in campus life, development of awareness of available campus resources to assist student leaders and organizations, and provision of a foundation of basic skills, knowledge and resources for future student leadership on campus. The class consists of six one and a half hour developmental modules based upon personal and leadership skill development topics. Modules are taught by faculty and staff members; a staff member from the Leadership Office serves as the group leader through all the sessions. Established student leaders (those who have participated in advanced Leadership Training Programs) lead icebreaker exercises at the beginning of each class. Attendance requires participation in at least four complete sessions. Lead On! is the required textbook. Class members are provided a course binder for information. The class ends with a certificate ceremony for the class members, and faculty, staff and student leaders who have assisted with the class.

Student Leadership Training Conference: A one day conference for emerging leaders, established leaders and staff members who are interested in developing various leadership skills and gaining information offers concurrent tracks of workshop sessions in the areas of Greek Life, general organization development, programming skills, personal leadership skills, special population leadership skills (women, minority, Greek) and advisor workshops. A morning and luncheon speaker address various leadership issues; the day concludes with an afternoon mingle of like student leaders (i.e., residence hall leaders, student government leaders, programming leaders, etc.). The conference is held annually the first Saturday in

February. Institutions throughout the Southern region are invited to participate. A typical conference makeup includes approximately 525 students and staff from thirty institutions of higher education.

LEAD Conference (Leadership Enrichment and Development): Held each spring at the conclusion of final exams, top student leaders and key administrators meet to set goals for the upcoming school year. Sixty-five students and twenty-five staff participate in this overnight program held out of town. Key administrators such as the President of the University, Dean of Student Life and the Vice President of Student Affairs are active speakers and workshops facilitators during LEAD. Attendance is competitive. Forty slots are preselected by nature of a student leadership position (i.e., Editor of the Newspaper, Student Body Officer, Governing Officer of Greek, Residence Hall or International Students, etc.). The remaining twenty-five slots are filled through an application process. The goals of the Conference are 1) to provide the opportunity to network with primary student leaders and key administrators formally and informally, 2) to concentrate on personal skill development and a team approach to common campus challenges in workshops and large/small group sessions, and 3) to share information on goals and objectives of individual student organizations in an effort to work toward common campus life goals.

Leadership Class: A three hour credit course in leadership development available through the College of Education taught by members of the Student Affairs Staff, offers flexibility for individual design such as for Residence Hall Assistants, Student Orientation Leaders or student leaders in general. Course syllabus and readings vary according to the class focus.

Peer Educators: Peer to peer training has proven to be one of the most effective modes of learning. Peer educator programs at Carolina include: Student Orientation Leaders, MAPS (Minority Assistance Peer Counselors), Residence Assistants/Residence Hall Directors, CARA's (Columbia Area Resident Assistants) and Alcohol Program Peer Educator. The students who serve in these leadership positions are important role models for others and are provided with ongoing assessment, training, and development of their personal leadership skills.

LEADERSHIP RECOGNITION:

Hall of Leaders: The Division of Student Affairs and Leadership Training Programs recognize fourteen core student organizations that are called upon throughout the year to serve as modes of communication, University ambassadors, special event hosts or simply as sounding boards for new policies and programs. Additional requests and responsibilities are given to the leadership of these groups. Each organization annually selects a member who has served in a significant leadership role with regard to the organization's overall purpose to be named a Hall of Leader recipient. The fourteen students who are named to the Hall of Leaders each year have significantly contributed to the overall quality of campus life. Recipients' names are engraved on a permanent plaque in the student union.

Caroliniana Award: This award was established with the intent to award students who have not been previously honored through normal means, but who have been the tireless, behind the scenes workers every student organization or activity needs. Their outstanding work relates to the betterment of the Carolina community through co-curricular activities. Award recipients are chosen through a nomination by a faculty or staff member and formal application process. This annual recognition is awarded to multiple students to emphasize the importance and appreciation of a leader who is also a follower and supporter. Recipients' names are engraved on a permanent plaque in the student union.

Advisors: Advisors of the registered student organizations at Carolina are recognized for their time and talent shared with student groups during a reception in the spring. Certificates of appreciation are presented to each advisor by the President of Inter-Club Council and the Vice President of Student Affairs. Special ribbons are given to advisors and student leaders to note their special status on campus and are worn throughout Honors and Awards Week. During the reception, the Caroliniana Awards and the Hall of Leaders Awards are announced.

University of Wisconsin
University Center, Stevens Point, WI 54481

Julie M. Gross
Asst. Dir., Student Development
715/346-4343

Emerging Leader Program

The UWSP Emerging Leader Program allows freshmen to develop their leadership talents and discover their own special strengths and limitations through interaction with other emerging leaders and university staff. They will learn to appreciate the influence they can have on others and the strategies that recognized leaders use to be successful. It is designed for new freshmen leaders (100) from varied backgrounds challenging participants to broaden their perspectives on themselves, their environment and their view of the world. Topics emphasize how to be an effective group member and participant.

GOALS: The Emerging Leader Program encourages participants to learn practical skills to help them succeed in college, participate actively in campus life, develop leadership potential to take on leadership roles at UWSP, learn practical leadership skills for personal development, meet other freshmen leaders, and get to know key people and resources.

FORMAT: Intended to be challenging yet stressless, the program consists of eight two-hour weekly evening sessions held over a two-semester period using a variety of educational tools and techniques to link leadership theory and practice. These include: small group interaction, lectures, discussion and presentation; participants are expected to take active roles in discussion and debate and serve as resources to other participants. Sessions are taught by the Student Life staff and others. During fall semester participants must join a campus organization to apply and test learned leadership concepts.

The Emerging Leader program will use the following agenda: General Announcements and Information; Guest Lecturer/Speaker; Small Group Discussion.

First Semester covers: Introduction to Emerging Leader Program; Group Dynamics; Personal Leadership Style Development; Goal Setting, Planning, Implementation, Follow Through.

Second Semester covers: Balancing Academics and Involvement; Effective Communication; Values Clarification/Ethics; Conclusion/Certificate Presentation Ceremony.

Leadership: The Personal Dimension - Communication 349 Sect. 2

PURPOSE: To identify, practice and improve leadership skills; To increase self-awareness through regular feedback on performance during the program; To stimulate further personal growth.

MAJOR GOALS: Gain a better understanding of leadership and management and the difference between the two; Understand personal strengths and weaknesses; Develop new leadership styles and behavior; Learn how to present ideas in a powerful engaging way; Define personal goals more clearly.

PROGRAM TOPICS:

Sessions

1	The Essence of Leadership: Your Key to Personal Power
2, 3, 4	Success Seminar--Camp Luther
5	Unveiling the Mystery: Ten Dominant Characteristics of an Effective Leader
6	Four Master Keys to Power: New Psychology of Leadership
7	Leadership Panel Discussion: Corporate Leadership--CEOs of Sentry, Inc. and Consolidated Papers, Inc. (at Sentry Headquarters)
8	The Visionary Leader: How to Create a Vision of the Future
9	Commitment Through Communication: How to Inspire followers With Your Vision
10	Dynamic Positioning: How to Gain Mass Support for Your Dream
11	Leadership Panel Discussion: Civic Leadership--Federal, State and Local Government Leaders (at City Hall)
12	Management of Self: How to Lead Others Through Self-Mastery and Example
13	Learning Environment: How to Get the Most Out of Your Followers
14	Management of Change: How to Create A Climate for Your Vision to Take Root
15	Leadership Panel Discussion: Leadership in Higher Education--The Chancellor and His Cabinet
16	Final Transformation: Your Vision Becomes Reality
17	Personal Dimension Final

TEXT: Bennis, W. and Nanus, B. (1985). Leaders: The Strategies For Taking Charge. New York: Harper and Row. Assignments of textual readings will be scheduled.

Seminars will be taught by members of the Student Life professional staff and selected members of the University Community.

ATTENDANCE: Attend your classes regularly. We do not have a system of permitted "cuts." If you take part in an off-campus authorized trip, make arrangements in advance with the Personal Dimension Instructor. If you are absent from classes because of emergencies, etc., your Personal Dimension Instructors will help you make up the work.

SPECIAL REQUIREMENTS: Students are asked to seek increased levels of responsibility within organizations of which they are already members, i.e., becoming a chairperson or member of an executive board of an organization. Participants must attend Success Seminar--a two-day weekend leadership retreat at the beginning of the course.

FORMAT: 6:30 - 6:40 p.m. General Announcements and Information; 6:40 - 8:00 p.m. Guest Lecturer/Speaker; 8:00 - 9:00 p.m. Small Group Discussion to be led by Student Life staff facilitators.

Section C
PROGRAMS FOR PROFESSIONALS AND PROFESSIONAL SCHOOLS

The awareness of the need in their fields for leaders and the demonstration of leadership behavior throughout business, industry, government, the military and education has increased steadily for some years. Programs to prepare and train leaders and managers have proliferated at a great rate. In this section are examples of programs designed and offered by colleges and schools within universities as well as those offered by independent research and training organizations and consulting groups. Some are focused on the educational preparation for teaching and supervising; others are designed primarily for honing skills and inspiring those who have the qualifications and willingness to assume greater responsibility and leadership roles.

The programs selected as samples include: integrated curricular plans; programs that are taught on-job-site as well as those in "retreat"; internships that are coordinated with classroom learning; varying levels of education and training based on more or little experience; those that recognize and encourage persons already out in the field and those intended for persons who want to learn more about themselves as potential leaders and as prospects for promotion. The length of time devoted to programs, the sequencing of the curriculum, the format of the learning mode, the ages and educational levels of students vary enormously. However, wherever they are offered these leadership programs are usually intense and carefully structured and considered as serious and expensive undertakings by those who enroll.

PROGRAMS FOR PROFESSIONALS AND PROFESSIONAL SCHOOLS

TABLE OF CONTENTS

Bellarmine College
Bellarmine Institute for Leadership Development
Newburg Road, Louisville, KY 40205

Diane T. Bennett
Executive Director
502/452-8161

Leadership Education

PURPOSE AND OBJECTIVES: Promoting the continued development of leadership among committed career teachers, kindergarten through grade 12--this is the purpose of Leadership Education, a program sponsored by Bellarmine College. Designed for teachers in this metropolitan area, Leadership Education will provide a probing study of community challenges that may best be addressed by educators, business and industry. Leadership Education will select individuals who have already demonstrated leadership capability in work and civic activity, are devoted to social progress and have the energy to devote to greater community involvement.

Leadership Education will: Identify key teachers who have demonstrated leadership qualities and concern for education and the metropolitan community; Provide a carefully designed educational program to familiarize these participants with the area's opportunities, needs, problems and resources; Establish an effective dialogue and peer relationship among participants as a common ground for communication; Provide the opportunity for a rapport between participants and individuals currently in leadership positions in the metropolitan community.

Several members of the 1985 class of Leadership Louisville understood the need to train teachers to be leaders and developed the concept of Leadership Education. Leadership Education is a program designed to enhance and promote leadership qualities and skills in elementary and secondary teachers. It is modeled on the Leadership Louisville program and sponsored by Bellarmine College. All local educational systems are represented-- public, private, and parochial. There are thirty-five members in each class. A carefully selected advisory board serves this project.

Adults as Learners: Leadership Education is, first of all, an educational program for adults and the "learners" and "teachers" are a very special breed. The body of theory and practice that specifically addresses this situation emphasizes the importance of viewing adults as self-directed individuals ready to learn whatever is required to cope more adequately with life's problems. This poses a set of assumptions and roles far different from that of traditional learning environments.

Learners: We can safely make these general assumptions about the adult learners in Leadership Education: They _are_ self-directed. They have a distinguished record of academic achievement and career development, of community involvement and family nurturance. They have demonstrated characteristics of independence for years. Expect them to express the same self-directedness in Leadership Education. They bring a vast experiential base to the program. While they are learners in this class, they represent a rich resource base and are eager to share with their peers. Their orientation to the learning opportunities Leadership Education provides will be highly problem centered--they want solutions to current problems in Louisville and they want them fast. They are highly motivated as individuals; but, because of their unique backgrounds and experiences, group motivation may be difficult to achieve and maintain. They face tremendous daily demands and time constraints and will probably not meet your deadlines or do the "homework" you design.

The Teachers: Actually, we are well advised to abandon our traditional concept of teacher and adopt the more appropriate role of facilitator of learning. As facilitator, you will: Explore the year's theme and program concepts; Study the learning needs and interests expressed by new class members; Select committee members who have the expertise and resources needed to design and execute a problem or issue centered day; Design a program day that celebrates inquiry, exploration, and experiences rather than morning-to-evening canned lectures.

The Learning Climate: If Leadership Education's coming year is to become a venture that celebrates inquiry and discovery, we must establish a climate that supports these activities. Five elements will build this climate: Mutual respect for our varied interests, experiences, creativity, lifestyles, and learning needs. Mutual trust for open and honest expression of our motives and biases. Freedom to participate actively in questioning, probing, responding without concern for peer ridicule or media coverage. Clarity about our roles as learners in an adventure of mutual inquiry. Warmth in our growing relationship.

SELECTION DAY PLANNING COMMITTEE: Committees--objects of ridicule; bodies of achievement. The Leadership Education staff offers these few suggestions and caveats (based on our experience with volunteer groups) for selection and successful work of planning committees.

Selection: As chairperson of a day committee, you are responsible for naming the full group. Select persons particularly interested in your topic. Choose persons who bring needed expertise and resources. Keep your planning committee small for the sake of efficient decision making and quick action. Confirm all committee appointments with the program director as soon as possible. The program director and members of Leadership Education Alumni Association will serve on your committee as consultants.

Organization: Begin your work right away with concise, clear agendas and meeting schedules. Be specific in member responsibilities and assignments. Establish firm reporting patterns to the director. Develop a planning time line with built-in "space" knowing that Murphy's Law will hold true. Include the Program Director and LEAA alumni in your planning meetings.

A carefully constructed calendar for staff planning timelines and activities is made available to Program Planners in a manual that includes much of the preceding text and checklists for their use.

Leadership Education is designed as an issue or problem oriented program. The year's focus is established by the general theme and each program day explores issues relating to

286

that theme. For example, **"Teachers as Change-Agents--Moving from the Theoretical to the Practical"** is the 1988-89 theme. Eight program days will address these topics: Community Leadership and Teachers; The Changing Nature of our Community; Arts and Leisure; Economic Development; Human Needs and Services; Politics, Government, and the Media; Social Justice; How Teachers Fit In.

After exploring the concepts of the entire program with the Program Coordinator, your first step is the identification of local issues of pressing concern to the incoming class. Your own expertise and that of other committee members should provide a broad scope of issues relevant to our study. Your second step, then, presents this dilemma: Is it better to scan many issues or to study one or two in greater depth? Evaluations of previous years indicate the latter. Then, third, clarify your specific objectives in planning the program day. Objectives provide the goal toward which your efforts are directed. Without them, your work tends to be aimless, burdensome, confusing.

These are the stuff from which successful program days are designed. A few brief words about each:

RESOURCES: Louisville is extremely generous to this program, both in commitment of personnel and through corporate and private philanthropy. Identify your resource needs very early; the staff may have ideas to help you.

STRATEGIES: How many methods or techniques are available to support your issue exploration? Be creative! Be a master teacher! Remember how tiring speakers can become? Involve as many senses as possible in the day for greatest learning!

SITES: Adults require carefully planned facilities--room arrangements, seating, lighting, climate control, A-V support, restrooms, break and dining areas, parking areas, and a place to smoke away from our "public breathing space." Some sites are free to Leadership Education; others available at a modest rental; the rest we tend to avoid. The staff can help you with this.

SCHEDULES: The planning line we suggest in this handbook puts you to work early with a July meeting for sharing plans to avoid overlaps, and to make early modifications in your plans. Our best counsel is this: <u>don't</u> <u>wait</u> <u>until</u> <u>the</u> <u>last</u> <u>minute</u> <u>to</u> <u>pull</u> <u>this</u> <u>together</u>. The detail work involved in planning a day is incredible!

STUDY MATERIALS: Carefully choose current materials that specifically relate to the day's program. You may select your own; you may choose to explore the data bases available to us through the Courier-Journal and Louisville Times Reference Services; or you may design ACTION ASSIGNMENTS as homework.

TRANSPORTATION: Buses are efficient if the entire group must travel to a distant site. The staff arranges this service at your request. Private cars are good for short moves and walking is outstanding.

PARKING: The bane of our existence, particularly for some downtown sites, is parking. Consider this carefully in site selection.

AGENDA: A model agenda is included. Plan for numerous drafts on somebody's word processor before the final copy is ready for printing.

LEADERSHIP EDUCATION CALENDAR

Sept.   Opening Retreat
Oct.   The Changing Nature of Our Community
Nov.   Arts and Leisure
Dec.   Economic Development
Jan.   Human Needs and Services
Feb.   Politics, Government, and the Media
Mar.   Social Justice
Apr.   Closing Retreat

TUITION AND FUNDING: Leadership Education is completely underwritten by corporate gifts and foundation grants, individuals selected may enjoy this non-credit educational opportunity tuition free. The value of one membership, however, is approximately $1,200. Apart from this monetary consideration, participants will find great intrinsic value in this non-credit program which offers community-based study rarely found in traditional curricula. The Leadership Education design follows closely the Leadership Louisville model.

APPLICATION: Leadership Education is open only to elementary, middle and secondary career teachers who believe they have demonstrated strong leadership qualities in education and in civic activities. Admission will be highly competitive, however. Persons who are not selected upon the first application are encouraged to reapply. To receive application materials and information, please contact your school principal or the Program Director at Bellarmine College.

ATTENDANCE: Commitment to regular attendance at all retreats and program day meetings is imperative. Class participants are expected to attend all these functions full-time except in the case of extreme emergency or illness.

Individuals who cannot attend the opening retreat, which is considered vital to the initiation of the year's program, will be expected to withdraw from the class early enough to permit another applicant to participate.

PROGRAM: Leadership Education may be compared with graduate-level study in terms of participants' time, commitment and intensity of study. Programming will include these components: Opening and closing retreats; Six day-long seminars; Forum discussions with local leaders; Study assignments; Experiential learning opportunities.

Case Western Reserve University
Mandel Center for Nonprofit Organizations
2035 Abington Road, Cleveland, OH 44106

Dennis Young
Director
216/368-2275

The mission of the Mandel Center is: To foster effective management, leadership, and governance of nonprofit organizations, in human services, the fine and performing arts, culture, education, community development, religion, and other areas through instruction, research, and related academic activities.

The Mandel Center for Nonprofit Organizations is a university-wide center for education and research on nonprofit organizations, co-sponsored by three graduate schools of Case Western Reserve University--the Mandel School of Applied Social Sciences, the Weatherhead School of Management, and the School of Law. In addition to the Certificate Program, the Center offers a Masters Degree in Nonprofit Organizations, executive education programs, research colloquia, conferences, and publications which periodically address topical issues and disseminate results of the Center's wide-ranging research programs.

The Certificate in Nonprofit Management is administered by the Mandel Center and is taught by an interdisciplinary program faculty drawn from the three sponsoring professional schools as well as the humanities and social science faculties of the university.

The Certificate Program in Nonprofit Management is designed specifically for practicing managers of nonprofit organizations who aspire to top executive positions.   These individuals seek state-of-the-art knowledge in critical areas of management methodology and the operating environment of the nonprofit sector.

Students in the Certificate Program hold responsible positions in their organizations, or may be lifelong volunteers seeking to begin paid careers in the nonprofit sector. Many hold advanced degrees in their professional fields. All are recognized for their potential for top management and leadership.

Intensive courses in nonprofit management and the nonprofit sector are selected to meet the particular needs of the student. It takes approximately one year to complete the program on a part-time basis. Classes held on the campus of Case Western Reserve University are offered on weekends and evenings to accommodate working students. Scholarships are available on a matching basis with employers or other sources. Admissions criteria include evidence of satisfactory undergraduate work and ability to master graduate level coursework, evidence of potential for leadership and top-level management of nonprofit organizations, and experience and familiarity with nonprofit organizations.

Students who satisfactorily complete the Certificate Program and meet other qualifications can receive credit for their coursework towards the Masters Degree in Nonprofit Organizations (MNO). The MNO is offered jointly by the Mandel School of Applied Social Sciences and the Weatherhead School of Management, and administered by the Mandel Center.

The Master of Nonprofit Organizations is designed to educate managers and leaders of

289

nonprofit organizations as rigorously as managers for business or government are now educated in schools of business or schools of public administration--but with an important difference. The MNO has been specially designed for the nonprofit manager and leader. Its curriculum recognizes the special concerns of nonprofit organizations in a variety of areas including: Management of volunteers and professional workers; Resource development and fundraising; Governance by volunteer boards of trustees; Management of multiple sources and types of funds; A unique legal and regulatory framework; Special values of service, community, and charity; The entrepreneurial character of nonprofit leadership; Special ethical and moral issues; Measurement of performance without a profit criterion.

The MNO curriculum covers much of the same territory as curricula for business or governmental managers and leaders. Financial management, human resources management, marketing and entrepreneurship, and research and analysis methods are emphasized, but the applications and focus are on the nonprofit manager and leaders. In addition, the MNO includes special areas of study including the law of nonprofits and historical and social scientific background on the nonprofit sector which provide a broad foundation and set of guiding principles for managers and leaders operating in the nonprofit arena.

THE PROGRAM: 45 credit hours; 17 months full-time or 24 months part-time; Classes held on the campus of Case Western Reserve University on weekends, evenings, and 5-day intensive residency periods to accommodate working students; Scholarships available on a matching basis with employers or other sources; Admissions criteria include satisfactory completion of a baccalaureate degree and GMAT scores, evidence of potential for leadership and top-level management of nonprofit organizations, experience and familiarity with nonprofit organizations.

THE CURRICULUM: Introduction to the Nonprofit Sector; Ethics, Professionalism and Leadership; Quantitative Methods for Nonprofit Organizations; Economics for Nonprofit Organizations; Financial Accounting and Reporting; Financial Management; Marketing Management; Management of Information, Systems and Operations; Law of Nonprofit Organizations; Organizations and Management; Management of Human Resources; Practicums on: Organizational Effectiveness, Governance and Management of Change, Strategic Planning.

Center for Creative Leadership
5000 Laurinda Dr., P.O. Box P-1
Greensboro, NC 27402-1660
919/288-7210
13 S. Tejon, Suite 500, P.O. Box 1559
Colorado, Springs, CO 80901
719/633-3891
4250 Executive Square, Suite 600
La Jolla, CA 92037
619/453-4774

Programs offered outside the U.S. are described
in the International Perspectives section.

The Center for Creative Leadership is a nonprofit educational institution founded in 1970 in Greensboro, North Carolina. It also operates branches in Colorado Springs, Colorado and San Diego, California, and licenses programs to executive training institutions worldwide.

The Center's three tenets are **research, training, and publication.** It concentrates on five areas of study: Executive Leadership; Leadership Technologies; Innovation and Creativity; Education and Nonprofit Sector; Leadership Development. Each of these areas has a research group and an applications group. Through research, effective management models are developed and are then described in published materials and used as guides in training and development programs. By turning ideas into action, the Center provides accessible research, applicable training, and practical publications.

LEADERSHIP DEVELOPMENT PROGRAM - A Six-Day Program

Purpose: To identify, practice, and improve leadership skills; To increase self-awareness through regular feedback on performance during the program; To develop measurable goals that can be achieved after the program; To stimulate further personal and career growth.

Major Goals of the Program: A better understanding of personal strengths and weaknesses; Discovery of how others see one's leadership behavior; Improved skill in giving feedback to subordinates on their performance; Development of new leadership styles and behavior; Increased effectiveness in meetings; More clearly defined personal goals; Increased confidence for leadership.

Program Topics

Assessment--personal feedback on leadership abilities, attitudes, and shortcomings.

The Creative Leadership Process--The Center's model of how leaders translate their vision of the future into action and empowerment.

Factors in Executive Success--a description of the Center's research on the differences and similarities between successful executives and those who derail.

Performance Development--leading through the encouragement of potential in others.

Decision Making--how and when to involve others in decision making.

Utilizing Group Resources--how to work more effectively with groups.

Principles of Feedback--how to give feedback that is useful and motivating.

Peer Feedback--small-group sessions where participants give and receive specific feedback on their leadership behavior.

Staff Feedback--a private, confidential 2-1/2 hour session discussing the results of assessment and testing.

Goal Setting and Planning--the climax of the week; insights and program experiences are used to set achievable goals for further self-directed development.

Special Features--questionnaires provide extensive feedback on how one is perceived by subordinates, peers, and superiors.

Who Should Attend: Anyone in a position of leading others, from mid-level managers to executives.

Available at the following locations: In Berkhamsted, England, **Ashridge Management College**, Telephone 44-44284-3491 or 44-44284-2311. Fee: £2,900 plus 15% VAT (subject to change). In College Park, MD, **The University of Maryland**, Telephone 301/985-7206. Fee: $3,200.00. In Colorado Springs, CO, **Center for Creative Leadership**, Telephone 919/288-7210 in Greensboro (non-smoking sessions). Fee: $3,500.00 (Alumni Program $1,750.00). In Greensboro, NC, **Center for Creative Leadership**, Telephone 919/288-7210. Fee: $3,200.00. In Hartford, CT, **Hartford Graduate Center**, Telephone 800/433-4723. Fee: $3,200.00. In Mt. Eliza, Australia, **Mt. Eliza Australian Management College**, Telephone 03-787-4211. Fee: $3,750.00 Australian. In Mexico City, Mexico, **Tecnologia Administrativa Moderna** (TEAM), S.C. (conducted in Spanish), Telephone 512/493-1452 in San Antonio. Fee: $2,200.00 plus 15% VAT. In Minneapolis, MN, **Personnel Decisions, Inc.**, Telephone 612/339-0927 or 800/633-4410. Fee: $3,200.00. In St. Petersburg, FL, **Eckerd College,** Telephone 813/864-8213. Fee: $3,200.00. In San Antonio, TX, **Center for Creative Leadership** (assessment and feedback portions available in Spanish on request), Telephone 919/288-7210 in Greensboro. Fee $3,200.00. In San Diego, CA, **Center for Creative Leadership**, Telephone 919/288-7210 in Greensboro. Fee $3,200.00.
Alumni program available in Colorado Springs, CO for those who attended the Colorado Springs and Greensboro, NC programs.

MANAGING FOR COMMITMENT - A Three-Day Program

This program draws on key elements from the **Leadership Development Program.**

Purpose: To develop areas critical to effective management: building teams, developing people, and giving constructive feedback.

Major Goals of the Program: Increased understanding of the role and the managerial behaviors which lead to high levels of commitment and productivity in the work group; Increased understanding of one's potential strengths and weaknesses and the impact they produce; Increased managerial effectiveness through greater confidence and skill in the ability to choose and implement the most effective managerial behaviors for various types of situations; Increased commitment and performance from groups--teams, task forces, committees--by developing a greater understanding of group process and the roles of the leader.

Program Topics

The Manager as an Effective Leader--a model for gaining productivity through commitment rather than control; examines how values and behaviors can build commitment and develop teamwork.

The Role of the Manager in Producing Decisions--a look at when and how to involve subordinates in decision making, how perceived power and personality play their part, and a model for making the process more rational and effective.

Performance Development--a model for building individual and group confidence and capability, and for obtaining the greatest productivity for the least managerial effort.

Interpersonal Awareness and Effectiveness--understanding how treatment of others can impact performance and how feedback and other techniques can improve interpersonal relations and performance.

Setting Goals for Development--applying program content to personal, family, community, and career goals.

Special Features--receiving confidential information provided by subordinates back home; discussing assessments and course content, and applying both to "back home" situations; and setting new goals and opportunities for follow up by a staff member.

Who Should Attend: First-level to middle-level managers, project and task force leaders from all sectors who would like to improve their effectiveness in working with others. This program is especially well suited for people with technical backgrounds who are moving into managerial roles. Program Fee: $1,500.00.

For information: Martha Bennett - 919/545-2815.

LOOKING GLASS, INC.® - A management simulation of a day in the life of top management.

The Looking Glass simulation is a powerful aid in helping managers assess their management styles and improve their skills. After running a simulated company for a normal day, participants examine their leadership and decision-making styles and receive feedback on their actions and choices. Looking Glass recreates a day of complexity and difficult decisions. At the outset, no goals or strategies are given. There is no compelling vision of the future. The participants supply all of this. As they grapple with the issues, participants produce a wealth of information about themselves. All of this is being quietly observed by trainers and by one's peers. Over and over, Looking Glass has succeeded in capturing the normal work habits of managers. One who makes quick decisions on the job will usually make hasty decisions in the simulation. A manager who is a poor delegator will usually fail to delegate well at Looking Glass. Looking Glass can dramatically increase

the impact of an existing management development program or can be used as a component of a new program.
For information: Jo-Anne Hand - 919/545-2814.

Looking Glass, Inc.® - University Edition

The University Edition of Looking Glass provides professors and their undergraduate or graduate students a richly textured simulation for studying managerial and organizational behavior.

Students learn about the pace, pressure, ambiguity, variety, and complexity of managerial work. They experience firsthand issues covered in organizational behavior and management courses such as communications, motivation, leadership, and decision making. They also learn about themselves in a managerial context, gaining experience with long-range planning, delegating responsibility, and dealing with subordinates.

Because it is specifically designed for full-time students enrolled in degree-granting programs, this edition may be purchased only by faculty teaching these students in colleges and universities. Included in each set of the University Edition is an administrator's guide, a participant's guide, annual reports, in-baskets, and selected readings for participants. The price for 20 students is $195.00 plus $10.00 shipping and handling.
For information: Jo-Anne Hand - 919/545-2814.

WORKSHOP IN ORGANIZATIONAL ACTION

Purpose: To give managers an opportunity for self-assessment and development.

Major Goals of the Program: Assessment of managerial strengths and weaknesses by participating in Looking Glass, Inc.®--a realistic simulation of organizational life. More knowledge of the process of management and how to make it work effectively. Greater confidence by learning to overcome blocks to effectiveness. A plan for continued managerial development.

Program Topics
    The Looking Glass Simulation--a day in the life of the top management team of a medium-sized corporation; recreates the pressure, problems, and fast pace of real management.
    Post-Simulation Debriefings--an analysis and assessment of actions taken, results achieved, and individual and group performance during Looking Glass.
    Controlling the Job--coping with the complexities of management.
    Dealing with Problems--navigating the "sea of troubles" confronting managers daily.
    Networks--activating networks for results; preventing networks from breaking down.
    Agenda Setting--setting priorities "on the run."

Managerial Success Factors--taking advantage of "key learning events" in your career based on the results of a two-year study of successful vs. "derailed" managers.

Action Planning--setting realistic goals for further managerial development.

Managerial Skills Assessment--using **SKILLSCOPE®**, an instrument that assesses managerial strengths, participants compare feedback from their Looking Glass experience with information from back-home co-workers; they also compare self-perceptions to the perceptions of others and identify areas for improvement.

Who Should Attend: Middle- and upper-level managers from the private and public sector, project managers and staff members who want to understand better the line manager's job.

Program Fee: $2,500.00
For information: Pat Wegner - 919/545-2812.

BENCHMARKS^{SM}: Developmental Reference Points for Managers and Executives (A new instrument)

Benchmarks^{SM} is a questionnaire of 170 items which assesses a wide range of characteristics. From arrogance to patience, from compassion to toughness, from sense of humor to handling pressure--the profile captures a varied, complex world of management behaviors. Unlike other rating instruments, Benchmarks^{SM} measures how a manager develops, including managerial values, perspectives and skills. This instrument also helps find potentially derailing managers and suggests ways for managers to build on their strengths through challenging work assignments.

Benchmarks^{SM} is based on six years of research on executive development. It measures values and perspectives as well as managerial skills; It measures competencies that managers develop during their career as opposed to innate characteristics and it measures the inclination to do things and the ability to do them. It helps managers predict their development future in terms of what it takes to become successful.

To take Benchmarks^{SM}, managers rate themselves in various areas of their managerial life. They are also rated by their peers, superiors, and subordinates. This feedback shows managers how their perceptions of themselves compare to those held by their co-workers. The Center offers a two-day Train-the-Trainer program for human resource professionals who wish to administer Benchmarks^{SM} within their organization.
For information: Jo-Anne Hand - 919/545-2814.

POSITIONING FOR LEADERSHIP: Developing Career Perspectives (A new program)

Positioning for Leadership is a two-day workshop that gives managers an opportunity to assess their strengths and weaknesses and gain new perspectives on their careers. Structured around the Center's newest feedback instrument, BENCHMARKS^{SM}, this program helps managers weigh their career aspirations in terms of their values system. Presentations on important findings from the Center's research on executive learning, growth and change are also part of the program. From this consolidation of research, feedback and intrapersonal examination, managers learn to: identify the skills and perspectives they need to improve in their present jobs and to better position themselves for future leadership roles. They also identify specific jobs and developmental events that sharpened their skills and perspectives and determine how their values influence their career choices; Finally, they determine their derailment potential and implement a plan to avoid derailing.

Program Fee: $1,000.00 (for the 2-day workshop); $2,495.00 (for the 4-day trainer certification program)

This workshop is designed for line managers interested in enhancing and developing their careers. Human resource professionals may also take a training course to offer Positioning for Leadership within their organizations.
For information: Jo-Anne Hand - 919/545-2814.

RADMIS - A project management simulation set in a technical environment

RADMIS is an intense computer-based simulation that puts participants into the thicket of project management and provides an assessment of their management and decision styles. It also lets them see clearly how other team members see them. RADMIS realistically captures the behavioral complexities of a project management situation. As a member of a product development team, participants manage a project from the planning stage through completion. Teams must develop a plan that fits the organizational strategy, and implement the project plan in the face of tight resources, governmental controls, and changing market conditions.

During the simulation activities and behaviors are observed, recorded, and video-taped by trainers. Following the simulation, trainers lead the teams through an analysis of their project activities. Teams which do not establish a clear direction for the project cannot meet their targets; managers who cannot negotiate and agree on decisions find their team faltering in times of critical decision making. As managers examine their behavior in RADMIS, they extract lessons about management that apply specifically to themselves. They come away from the program ready to improve their on-the-job decision making and team interactions.

296

RADMIS can be used as a two-day stand-alone program or as part of an existing program. For information: Jo-Anne Hand - 919/545-2814.

TARGETED INNOVATION

Purpose: To provide managers the latest, most practical tools of the trade for stimulating an environment where creativity and innovation can flourish. The focus is on the application of creativity to real problems.

Major Goals of the Program: Participants acquire usable, creative solutions to problems by learning to apply proven innovative problem-solving techniques in an organization. They learn easier and more effective implementation of innovative solutions through the Targeted Innovation (TI) Model, which demonstrates how to evaluate and get action on creative ideas and to generate greater creativity in one's organization by learning how to remove the barriers and provide the stimulus to creativity. Participants receive direct experience and practice by working during the program with actual clients on tough problems.

Program Topics:
  Building and Using a Creative Team--the key to effective group problem solving.
  From Idea Generation to Idea Evaluation--tools for successful creativity and innovation.
  Targeted Innovation Model--a diagnostic method to focus on problem solving.
  Organizational Environments--environment stimulus and barriers to creativity.
  Managing Change--the process to successfully complete the loop from idea to action.

Who Should attend: Managers and idea people seeking a warmer reception for new ideas or a better structure to get at problems. Those who benefit are problem solvers in industry, government, education, and volunteer agencies, and those who train others in the technologies of solving problems.
For information: Pat Wegner - 919/545-2812.

EXECUTIVE CHOICES for EDUCATIONAL LEADERSHIP (EXCEL)

This highly interactive simulation is designed for school administrators who would like to improve school operations. The simulation lasts seven hours and is structured around twenty-five participants in a range of positions, from superintendent to assistant principal. Each person sets priorities, makes decisions, networks and solves problems. The program also includes debriefing sessions where these activities are analyzed and evaluated. Each participant then takes home and uses the information that he or she learned about leadership styles, interpersonal skills, and decision making. The cumulative effect of the EXCEL experience is that participants anticipate evolving issues and become more capable in dealing with issues and events in their own organizations.

HUMAN SERVICES ADMINISTRATOR PROGRAM

Purpose: To help human services administrators assess their own strengths as leaders, and to develop a strategic direction for their agencies.

Major Goals of the Program: Participants identify and improve the leadership skills they need to succeed in the public sector. Human services administrators better understand their strengths and weaknesses as administrators and learn to promote further self and organization development through goal setting. They also create and solidify a lasting resource network, and develop an atmosphere for mutual consultation.

Program Topics

    Assessment--feedback through activities and instrumentation on specific leadership behaviors, perceptions, strengths, and areas for improvement.

    Performance Development--examines a model for developing improved leadership skills.

    Decision Making--how and when to involve others in the decision-making process.

    Goal Setting--planning to implement the skills and knowledge "back home."

    Leadership in the Community--examines a leader's role as a community advocate for human services.

    Strategic Planning--a model for plan design and implementation.

    Individual Case Studies--drawing on the expertise and experience of others.

    Innovation and Creativity--examined from the perspective of the individual, work team, and the organization.

    Organizational Behavior--provides four "frames" through which to view organizations.

Who Should Apply: This course is tailored to directors of nonprofit (public or private) organizations that provide a service to the community or some segment of the community. For information: Karen McNeil-Miller - 288-7120, ext. 2656.

Center for Leadership Development   **Madeleine Green**
The American Council on Education (ACE)   Vice President & Director
One Dupont Circle, Washington, DC 20036-1193   202/939-9420

ACE Fellows Program

The ACE Fellows Program (AFP) provides the opportunity for 30 selected women and men to: Gain a campus-wide point of view by serving a full academic year in a mentor/intern relationship with a college or university president or vice president; Learn new administrative skills through seminars and practical experience; Understand higher education in national and regional contexts by talking to national leaders and visiting campuses. Since 1965 the Program has helped over 900 men and women gain expertise and perspective for assuming leadership roles in higher education. Fellows also participate in three week-long seminars designed to sharpen their administrative skills and enhance their awareness of campus and national issues. The Fellows Program is the only professional development program in higher education at the national level to provide on-the-job learning for an extended period.

Fellows have opportunities to learn to: Understand budgeting and financial procedures; Formulate financial and academic plans; Understand complexities of collective bargaining; Become familiar with faculty personnel issues and financial aid; Lead curriculum planning and evaluation activities; Become aware of the implications of national higher education issues for their institution. They gain from: Experience in helping to deal with problems that chief campus leaders typically face; An understanding of the decisions chief executive and academic officers must make; A national network of colleagues for sources of ideas and successful practices.

Fellows serve as interns either on their home campuses or at host campuses. The president and chief academic officer serve as Mentors; other senior administrative officers may also serve as Mentors. The successful Fellowship year combines observation and active participation in institutional administration. Fellows should have complete access to all aspects of the institutional decision-making process and take on projects and assignments to enhance their expertise and understanding that benefit the institution. They should attend key decision-making meetings, serve as executive assistants to the chief executive or chief academic officer, work on projects such as revising faculty handbooks, developing early retirement policies, conducting admissions and retention studies, and chairing search committees, and write position papers and speeches.

Experience shows that the host campus option is preferable. Assignments are arranged in consultation with the nominator, the Fellow, ACE staff members and cooperating campuses. The needs of the Fellow and the characteristics of the host institution are weighed carefully in the selection of host institutions. Fellows are encouraged to interview in person with officials at potential host colleges and universities.

Three national Fellows Seminars are high points of the Fellowship year. Conducted in September, December, and May, these five-day sessions use role playing, problem solving workshops, discussions, and lectures to help Fellows understand and deal with central issues in higher education. Free flowing dialogues among Fellows, Mentors, experts, and national leaders provide unique learning experiences. Seminar topics are organized around five central themes: financial management and planning, academic management and planning, personal and interpersonal dimensions of administration, leadership, and external forces affecting higher education. Topics range from federal policies affecting higher education to theories of management and leadership, from legal issues to opportunities for personal and professional growth.

Fellows are encouraged to visit other campuses to broaden their perspective on their own institutions and on higher education in general. Former Fellows agree that these visits are invaluable. Fellows also organize regional seminars where current and former Fellows meet to talk about selected aspects of higher education administration allowing study of a cross-section of institutions, meetings with higher education leaders, and in-depth discussions on topics.

An intensive, high quality program such as the Fellows Program inevitably requires a financial commitment by colleges, universities, and ACE. It is an investment in human resources for the future and in all of postsecondary education. The nominating institution is responsible for interview expenses and continuation of the Fellow's salary and benefits during the Fellowship year. Institutions sponsoring home Fellows or receiving host Fellows pay their Fellow's expenses for three national seminars. The total cost of these seminars is estimated at $6,000 to $8,500. Institutions provide a travel stipend of at least $2,500, which permits Fellows to visit other campuses and attend regional meetings. Host institutions may choose to cover the Fellow's commuting or moving costs, but are not required to do so. Total costs can be estimated at $8,500 to $11,000.

Institutions that are not ACE members are eligible to participate in the Program for a tuition fee of $1,700. This fee is in addition to other Program costs. Many ACE memberships cost less than $1,000; thus, membership dues are often less than tuition. ACE member institutions receive up-to-date information on issues and solutions to problems in higher education through policy briefs and journal reports. They have access to expert consultants who can assist campuses with specific issues, and an annual meeting where they share their interests with colleagues. Through its government relations staff, ACE insures that higher education's interests are represented on Capitol Hill.

Dallas Theological Seminary
Center for Christian Leadership
3909 Swiss Avenue, Dallas, TX 76204

William D. Lawrence
Executive Director
214/841-3515

Dynamics of Leadership 1001

The Center for Christian Leadership is both an idea center and training center for three major target groups: 1) students on campus, 2) alumni, pastors, and other vocational Christian workers, and 3) laymen in leadership roles in their church, in Christian organizations, or who are interested in utilizing certain aspects of a Christian philosophy of leadership in their workplace. Its leadership development philosophy emphasizes developing character and vision; training for basic leadership skills to communicate, strategize and carry out the vision; and equipping others to grow as leaders. The work of the Center for students involves two courses (1001 is described below), personalized training of student leaders, and several leadership development projects conducted jointly with the Dean of Student Services.

Dynamics of Leadership 1001 is an elective course for students interested in personal leadership development and training others. Other courses in the seminary include sections that discuss the leader in the role of pastor, lay leader, church administrator, educator, Christian organization executive, or father/husband and mother/wife. This course augments these courses by helping each student see broader issues common to each of these potential leadership roles, and develop personal leadership characteristics contributing to their life plan. The course is not confined to leadership issues traditionally discussed under management and administration, covered in a required course within the normal four-year curriculum. Instead, areas such as personal assessment, creativity, vision, and life planning are highlighted. Principles of leadership are drawn from current writing in the field as well as Biblical models. Strategies for leadership are primarily drawn from Bennis and Nanus, Leaders (Harper & Row, 1985).

OBJECTIVES: Upon completion, 1) Be able to give a definition of, a biblical basis for, and characteristics of Christian leadership, citing key scriptural support; 2) Make a commitment to pursue a lifetime of Christian leadership and make a plan to accomplish it; 3) Gain a working knowledge of significant secular material on leadership which has application to the Christian leader; 4) List key skills needed for leadership and plan to strengthen those areas.

TEXTS: Bennis, Warren and Burt, Nanus. Leaders: Strategies for Taking Charge. New York: Harper & Row, 1985; Sanders, J. Oswald. Spiritual Leadership. Chicago: Moody Press, 1980; Smith, Fred. Learning to Lead. Waco: Word Books, 1985; Blanchard, Kenneth, with Patricia and Drea Zigarmi. Leadership and the One-Minute Manager. West Caldwell, NJ: William Morrow Publ. Co., 1985; Haggai, John. Lead On! Waco: Word Books, 1985; Hersey, Paul. The Situational Leader. New York: Warner Books, 1985.

REQUIREMENTS: Complete daily assignments; Read required texts and a biography of a significant leader (past or present, Christian or non-Christian) summarizing keys to his/her leadership in a short paper; Do <u>two</u> of the following; 1) Observe a leader for two working days and write a paper discussing observations, evaluations, and conclusions, or 2) Lead a group in a task and write a summary of your task, experiences, observations, and lessons learned, or 3) Write a paper giving an overview of the key passages of Scripture which inform Christian leadership. What are the major issues in Scripture regarding leadership? How does it differ from other leadership models? How does Scripture affect leadership in the arena to which you are called?; Develop a plan of action for your personal development as a Christian leader. The format for this project is up to you, but it should include the following: a. A personal diary of your thoughts and lessons learned during the course (three entries per week); b. A description of yourself: gifts, talents, strengths, weaknesses, calling; c. A statement of your personal vision; d. Goals for development toward that vision. I do not expect this to be a finalized work, but rather the first step in a life-long process.

GRADING: Daily Assignments, 25%; Reading, 10%; Biography, 10%; Project, 25%; Personal Action Plan, 30%

SCHEDULE:

Sessions

1   Introduction: Aims. Requirements. Process.

The Philosophy of Leadership
2   Moses as Leader
3   Nehemiah as Leader
4   Jesus as Leader - The Servant Leader
5   Jesus as Leader - Training through Discipleship
6   Paul as Leader
7   Summarizing Principles - Models of Leaders

The Process of Leadership
8   Definition and Myths of Leadership
9   Characteristics of Leadership
10 Obstacles/Barriers/Frustrations to Leadership
11 Decision Making and Leadership
12 Styles of Leadership
13 Styles of Leadership

Sessions

14 Strategies for Taking Charge--Vision
15   "   "   "   "--Communication
16   "   "   "   "--Positioning
17   "   "   "   "--Self-Management
18 Motivation in leadership
19 Mentoring/Modeling in Leadership

The Problems of Leadership
20 Spiritual Dimensions of Leadership
21 Roles Leaders Play
22 The Place of Power in Leadership
23 Handling Stress and Failure
24 Developing Leadership Teams
25 Leadership Training
26 Leadership Training
27 Creativity--Avoiding Institutional Dry Rot
28 Resources and Summary--Three Challenges

Harvard University
Gutman Library, Appian Way, Cambridge, MA 02138

Sharon A. McDade
Director, IEM
617/495-2655

Institute for Educational Management

___

The twentieth annual session of Harvard University's Institute for Educational Management gathered together educational leaders from across the United States and several foreign countries to analyze and explore issues and trends in the management of higher education.

This rigorous program, with a comprehensive curriculum focused on leadership and management skills, serves senior level administrators. The curriculum is enhanced by a series of prominent speakers and intellectually challenging discussions on topics of concern to college and university administrators. The program faculty are chosen specifically for their blend of practical experience in the field and their teaching ability.

Since IEM was founded in 1970, more than 1900 administrators from over 500 institutions representing 52 states and territories and many other nations have attended the program. Most participants serve at the president, vice-president or dean level of responsibility. The depth and wealth of experience these participants bring to the classroom is of major value to all attending.

The Graduate School of Education has a continuing commitment to the professional development of the alumni of IEM that goes well beyond the Institute. IEM Alumni Workshops on current topics in higher education are held regularly, and alumni from across the years attend, refresh their management skills, see their classmates, and meet new colleagues who participated in IEM in other years.

This is a four week summer program with a comprehensive fee of $6,500 including tuition, room, board, and all materials.

CURRICULUM: The challenges facing presidents and senior administrators in colleges and universities have become substantially more demanding and diverse. In a world of rapid change and high uncertainty, they must be able to respond effectively to four major questions: 1. Where are we? (What are the major trends and forces in the environment that we need to understand and anticipate?) 2. Where are we trying to go? (What are our basic goals and strategic directions? Where do we hope to lead our institution?) 3. What do we need to get there? (How do we obtain or develop the financial, institutional and human resources that we need?) 4. How do we manage the implementation process to ensure effectiveness and high performance? These questions define four major challenges facing everyone who seeks to provide leadership in higher education.

Monitoring the Environment: The mandate of higher education is a very old one, but one that changes significantly with shifts in the larger social context. Colleges and universities have become less insulated and more interdependent with other major institutions. Demography, economic trends, government actions, and legal developments all play a powerful role in affecting educational management.

303

Setting Directions: Senior executives are responsible for charting the institution's course. They need to set goals, develop strategies, and articulate values that provide the institution with a sense of purpose and direction.

Marshalling Resources and Support: In an era of tight resources and increasing pressures for accountability, few administrators need to be reminded of the importance of putting together the particular combination of resources and support that an institution requires to accomplish its mission. Colleges and universities need to attract students and faculty, develop sources of financial support, and maintain the support of key constituencies (such as governing boards, alumni, state and federal government, and foundations).

Managing Implementation: Without effective management, even the right goals and abundant resources provide no guarantee of success. How do we move from goals and policy to action? How do we make sure that "decisions" are really implemented? How do we build information and control systems to ensure that we know what is happening in our institution?

The IEM curriculum is organized to address these four challenges. Courses in strategic planning and marketing address the problems of setting directions in a complex, changing environment. Courses in human resource management and labor relations address critical problems of building an institution's human resources and managing them effectively.

Courses in law and politics, among others, address major features of the environment that affect higher education. Units on advancement and leadership address central issues of building the support and resources needed to carry on the work of colleges and universities. Courses in financial management and decision analysis develop critical administrative skills and sensitivities.

Management Development Program (MDP)

Harvard's Management Development Program (MDP) prepares men and women for responsible management and leadership. It explores significant issues and effective solutions. The program is designed for individuals who manage major enterprises within the college or university--those with significant levels of administrative responsibility and whose future responsibilities will demand increased knowledge and skills. MDP's goal is to prepare these administrators to develop resourceful solutions to the problems they are likely to encounter as they grow with their institutions.

The MDP curriculum is carefully planned by a faculty group that includes Harvard professors and outstanding practitioners. But much of the learning comes from the informal discussion among the 95 participants in MDP each summer. To ensure that the dialogue among participants is rich and provocative, MDP intentionally includes representatives of a broad range of administrative positions in higher education.

Participants are likely to hold such titles as chairperson, director, associate dean, dean, assistant or associate vice president. The Admissions Committee also seeks diversity in institution type, location, participant ethnic background, and gender.

MDP is housed at the Harvard Graduate School of Education. It is sponsored by the Institute for Educational Management, which for more than twenty years has provided leadership training for senior officers of higher education institutions and organizations. Many of the same faculty who teach in IEM also teach in MDP. Although each program is geared to the needs of its particular group of participants, they share an educational philosophy that emphasizes a strong link between theory and practice.

The Management Development Program runs for two weeks each summer. The comprehensive fee of $3,250 includes tuition, room, board, and all program materials.

CURRICULUM: The curriculum of the Management Development Program seeks to accomplish two main objectives: to broaden each participant's management perspectives and leadership skills; to help participants understand the unique role and mission of their institution, so that management skills can be applied in the service of institutional goals.

The curriculum focuses on the interconnected themes of Leadership and Management as they affect and relate to the higher education enterprise.

Cultural Diversity in Higher Education begins with the understanding that colleges and universities will become more culturally diverse as new ethnic groups enter the ranks of students, faculty, and administrators. What can today's administrators do to better utilize the contributions these groups can make to higher education?

Decision Making examines the problems of risk and uncertainty that often make decision making difficult, and presents tools to help administrators make better choices.

Faculty Personnel Policy and Administration explores the unique role of faculty within a college. What are the relationships between faculty and the academy? What are the appropriate roles of tenure, academic freedom, and faculty governance?

Financial Management takes a managerial perspective on budgeting and planning. What budgeting strategies are likely to be most effective for my office? What constitutes an effective measure of success? What factors will influence the allocation of an institution's financial resources?

Human Resource Management focuses on the human side of academic administration. What are more effective ways to build and maintain the skills and capacities of the people who are at the heart of the academic enterprise?

Law and Higher Education surveys major legal issues affecting higher education and provides background information to aid administrators in making better informed decisions from a legal perspective.

Leadership and Organization encourages participants to explore the following questions: What is leadership? What are the characteristics of leadership in academic organizations? What can I do to become more effective in moving my institution forward?

Leadership Issues in Higher Education assesses the creative leadership opportunities as higher education institutions face key issues such as assessment and evaluation and retention.

Small Group Leadership investigates the dynamics of small groups and provides a laboratory setting for the improvement of small group leadership skills.

The MDP curriculum emphasizes the effective implementation and execution of administrative decisions in colleges and universities. Much of the curriculum is based on case studies--a teaching method pioneered at Harvard--so that classes are lively and involving. But classes are only one facet of the dialogue that provides MDP's intellectual richness. Conversations over meals, daily meetings of small discussion groups, coffee breaks and late evening discussions represent some of the many opportunities, both formal and informal, for participants and faculty to learn from one another.

Detailed information describing curricula and syllabi and copies of application forms of various sorts can be obtained by writing or calling the Institute Office.

**Pratt Institute Center for Community
and Environmental Development**
379 DeKalb Ave., 2nd Floor
Steuben Hall, Brooklyn, NY 11205

Rex L. Curry
Pratt Architectural Collaborative
Associate Director
718/636-3486

Pratt Community Economic Development Internship

Ed. Note: This is a fully accredited workshop program taught over an eight month period that describes the way in which an internship program can be used successfully to develop leaders in a specialized field.

PHILOSOPHY: The Internship program in its fourth year emphasizes a commitment to the highest quality of adult education and training. As professionals in the field of housing and community economic development, Interns will be expected to develop self-directed learning skills to achieve clearly stated learning objectives and have the opportunity for individual emphasis in specialized areas.

A learning plan is written by each Intern entering the program at the first workshop and is revised throughout the year. Revision identifies and monitors the accomplishment of individual goals enabling Intern and staff to design supplemental or remedial activity, where appropriate. Interns are expected to exercise initiative in setting and meeting their own goals. The experience, knowledge and skill of each Intern is a major resource for the program, supplementing the extensive expertise of faculty and staff. Workshop activities and practicum format create a community of learners in a specialized area, fostering exchange of skills among peers.

REQUIREMENTS: The program is designed specifically for managers or directors of nonprofit, community-based economic development organizations currently planning or implementing housing and economic development activities, as well as personnel of agencies that work with such groups. The manager may be the chief staff person (executive director) of the organization or the director of the division or unit of the organization responsible for community economic development. If the applicant is not the top staff person, the program requires the following conditions: (1) a considerable degree of delegated authority and autonomy in the direction of project development, and management of the people responsible for economic development projects in the organization; and (2) the executive director and/or board of directors must understand the Internship program requirements, and be committed to supporting the applicant in completing them.

Directors whose organizations are only considering whether or not to become involved in housing or community economic development will benefit from the program, but may not have the opportunity to apply the knowledge and skills taught in actual projects. It is preferable, but not required, that applicants be actively planning or implementing a housing or community economic development project. The immediate use of learning in real world situations is emphasized in the educational design of the program.

In addition to attendance at workshops, applicants should consider whether they will be able to devote several hours to learning activities for the full duration of the program. Successful completion requires an investment of time beyond required workshops. The schedule identifies days away from the office required of all Interns.

WORKSHOP CURRICULUM: Thirty-six days of instruction conducted in six workshop sessions over 38 calendar days scheduled. Instructional material is integrated into five core components of the curriculum and two concentrations of advanced material. Core curriculum consists of six major subjects: Community Economic Development Strategy; Accounting; Business Development; Real Estate Development; Organizational Management and Effectiveness; Integrative Workshop.

Management & Organizational Effectiveness and the Integrative Workshop are described here because they emphasize leadership development. For information about other content areas contact Rex Curry.

The management curriculum is designed to increase the capacity of participants to diagnose management issues or problems in their organizations and to identify appropriate interventions and resources to address those issues. The sequence is divided into core offerings and a series of mini-courses on specific topics based on the needs assessment conducted during the first workshop. During the first workshop, each Intern also has the option to begin a management assessment of his/her organization to assist in evaluating the organization's community economic development strategy in relation to its management needs.

Course Topics: Basic Managerial Skills; Assessing Organization Needs; Leadership and Small Group Dynamics; Methods of Organizational Change; Executive Time Management; Board Development; Goal Planning; Negotiating Skills.

The Integrative Workshop is designed to facilitate the ability of Interns to utilize the skills developed in Organizational Management, Real Estate, Business Development and related sessions; to enhance the application of community economic development skills within the Internship, the Intern's organization, and their communities. As an open forum it enables peer to peer communication, information sharing, and the application of newly acquired skills within the organizational and community settings of Interns.

Course Topics: Maximizing the Workshop Environment; Socio-Political Context of CED; Workshop Integration and Feedback; Cognitive, Affective and Skill Development; Intern Presentations and Community Meetings; Work Obligations and the Practicum.

PRACTICUM ASSIGNMENTS: Practicum periods between each workshop are an integral part of the educational program of the Internship, during which Interns apply concepts and skills learned in the workshop to the daily work of their organizations. Three major practicum assignments are given as guides, and the Internship provides support to the Interns during practicum periods.

During the first each Intern completes a written assessment of his/her organization and the conditions within which the organization sets goals and develops a strategic plan. From the organizational analysis, faculty guide each Intern to pursue a plan to improve individual management skills. In the second practicum Interns refine the overall strategic plan of their organizations (or guide the process of writing such a plan if one does not exist). Throughout each of the subsequent practicum periods, Interns will be required to complete a series of assignments related to the planning and financing of a development project. Pratt Center staff will be available to assist.

Interns with undergraduate degrees will be eligible to earn thirty graduate credits from Pratt Institute's Graduate Department of City and Regional Planning (DCRP). The total program cost is $13,500 per Intern. Special funding for this training reduces this cost to $3,500, including lodging, meals, and all curriculum materials.

Roche Biomedical Laboratories, Inc.   **Jerry R. Tolley**
A Subsidiary of Hoffman-La Roche Inc.   Ass't. Vice Pres., Training & Recruitment
231 Maple Avenue, Burlington, NC 27216   919/229-1127

Circle of Excellence Executive Development Program

PROGRAM DESCRIPTION: The RBL Circle of Excellence Executive Development Program is designed to provide selected employees the opportunity to participate in an executive training program. The curriculum will center around the RBL culture and philosophy, problem-solving techniques, decision-making processes, leadership styles and leadership development, communications skills, team building, goal setting, corporate finance, management skills, and other pertinent topics. In all, there will be over 90 hours of instruction. Students are given the opportunity to evaluate faculty who are selected outside presenters.

PURPOSE: To provide selected RBL employees the opportunities to learn more about the corporation in general and to develop a wide range of managerial and leadership skills.

ATTENDANCE AND PARTICIPATION: Attendance is required. Only under extreme emergency circumstances should participants miss class. Because much of the learning taking place will be as a result of interaction with faculty and discussion with other class participants, it is essential that class attendance and participation be mandatory. Class will begin promptly at the designated time. Only under emergency circumstances should participants dismiss themselves from class. This not only disrupts the class, but shows a lack of courtesy for the speaker.

COURSE CONTENT: The General Management Process: The basic objectives of this module are to present an integrated view of the management process, to identify the organic, universal functions of management, to survey the basic knowledge, skills and tools important to manager's success, and to lay a foundation for more detailed study. Specific areas covered are the functions of planning, organizing and controlling with specific overviews of problem solving, decision making, organization and leadership, human relation and motivation, and communications. The presentation of materials is supported by readings, lectures, class discussions, and case studies.

Reading: Management by Griffin; Critical Incidents In Management by Champion and James

Activities: Case studies as presented in Griffin and Champion

Leadership/Team Building: The basic objectives of this module are to define leadership, review the basic theories, models, traits, and styles of leadership, outline the history of leadership from Socrates to the present, differentiate between managing and leading; to review the concept of leadership as it relates to team building, discuss the nature of team building as it relates to group dynamics and present an overall analysis of group leadership development.

Reading: Leadership and the One Minute Manager by Blanchard and Assoc.; In Search

310

of Excellence by Peters and Waterman; Leaders by Bennis

Activities: "Situation Leadership" - individual activity; "Selecting Members of Your Team" - group activity; "NASA" - individual and group leadership styles activity; "Blake-Mouton" - personal inventory; "The Passion for Excellence" - video; "The Desert Interlude" - individual and group leadership styles activity; "Strength Development Inventory" - personal inventory; "Mr. Roberts" - case study in leadership; "Bridge Over the River Kwai" - case study in leadership.

Problem Solving/Decision Making: The basic objectives of this module are to present varying approaches in making decisions and solving problems, to define problems and opportunities more precisely, review methods for involving others in the decision-making process, define alternative solutions to problems/opportunities and gathering data and to outline approaches for evaluating alternatives and selecting those which appear to be most likely to satisfy important decision requirements.

Readings: Management by Griffin; Critical Incidents In Management by Champion and James; "How Senior Managers Think" by Daniel Isenberg; "Deciding About Decisions" by Thomas R. Horton

Activities: "Analyzing My Individual Decision-making Style"; "Preparation of Personal Case Study" (prepared by each participant); "Case Studies"; "Defining the Problem/Opportunity"; "Defining the Problem Clearly"; "Determining the Involvement of Others in the Decision-making Process"; "Generating Alternatives"; "Evaluating Alternatives"; "Implementing the Decision"; "Murder One" - Individual and group decision-making activity

Human Relations/Motivation: The basic objectives of this module are to present the overall nature of motivation and human relations, review the historical perspective of motivation and human relations, and to outline the dynamics of the overall group process in our rapidly changing society.

Reading: Management by Griffin

Activities: "Leadership Effectiveness and Adaptability Description" - personality inventory; "An Exercise in Human Development and Motivation"; "Genesis Secundus" - individual and group activity; "The Caine Mutiny" - a case study on human relations and leadership; "How to Diagnose Group Problems"; "Conflict - Climate Index"; "Conflict Style Questionnaire"; "Professional Burnout Index

The Roche Biomedical Corporate Culture: The basic objectives of this module are to define corporate culture, present a historical perspective of corporate culture in the United States, review the various elements of culture, discuss an emerging Roche Biomedical Laboratories, Inc. corporate culture, and specifically identify six areas through the use of the "HRI Normative Systems Indicator" that individual RBL managers may wish to target for improvements.

<u>Reading</u>: "Confronting the Shadow Organization - How to Detect and Defeat Negative Norms" by Allen and Pilnick

<u>Activities</u>: "The HRI Normative Systems Indicator"

The Fundamentals of Finance and Accounting for the Non-Financial Executive: The basic objectives of this module are to review the basics fundamentals of finance and accounting as they relate to the RBL statistical method, the basic financial statement concept, the elements of expense report, and the capital budgeting process.

<u>Activities</u>: "An Introduction to the RBL Financial System" - video

Executive Presentation Skills Workshop: The basic objectives of this module are to set communication goals to achieve results, organize ideas and information for clarity, maintain audience attention and interest, develop ideas with support for understanding and impact, develop an effective vocal style and delivery, become aware of appearance and body behavior, and to learn to deal with the problem of nervousness.

<u>Activities</u>: Class size in this all day module is limited to six participants. During the workshop each attendee will make three different presentations of varying lengths. All presentations are videoed and critiqued by attendee(s) and instructor.

The RBL Mentor Program: The basic objective of this program is to give participants the opportunity to build a mentor relationship with a selected officer. Class participants are paired with a mentor who will teach, counsel, coach, and serve as a confidant.

<u>Reading</u>: "Much Ado About Mentors" by Gerard Roche

The Responsibilities of the Mentor: Set aside at least one hour per week for your protege; Help your protege learn more about the organization and your position and responsibilities in it; Give your protege an opportunity to get to know you both as a professional and as a person; Provide opportunities for your protege to see you in action in real situations. These could include departmental meeting, conference calls, presentations, and discussions with colleagues, etc.; To the degree that it is comfortable for you, share your personal philosophy of leadership with your protege.

The Responsibilities of the Protege: Meet with your mentor for at least one hour a week; Take full responsibility for making arrangement to meet with your mentor. Set firm appointment times, and keep appointments; Learn about your mentor's department and your mentor's responsibilities within the organization; Be observant. Ask questions, take the initiative. Take the responsibility for learning; Communicate that you are fully committed to achieving the goal of the company; Seek advice from your mentor through intelligent thoughtful questions (good mentors want to feel their efforts are not wasted); Be sure to know what you want to do and where you want to go and that you are committed to getting there.

Texas Foundation for the Improvement of Local Government
1020 Southwest Tower, Austin, TX 78701

Gary Watkins
Executive Director
512/478-6601

The Public Executive Institute V: Shaping A Professional Renaissance*

The program will discuss the public executive as a person as well as a leader, examining new perspectives about healthy living; new directions in improving organizational structure, group dynamics, internal and external communications, employee motivation, problem solving, planning, and public image. Program leaders will be innovators whose ideas for transformation and transfusion in public sector management have attracted national attention.

CURRICULUM: This is an intensive eight-day executive development program which blends lectures, case studies, audio/visual presentations and open discussion between presenters and public sector leaders.

The daily program schedule is demanding. A typical day begins at 7:30 a.m. for breakfast to reflect on concepts--methods learned in previous day, discuss the work for the day and explore related issues. Curriculum presentations begin at 8:30 a.m. Following lunch, which participants and presenters will usually have together, there will be afternoon sessions until 4:30 p.m. Some free evenings, but most will be devoted to presentations on specific topics by special invited experts from across the country.

ADMISSION: The Public Executive Institute is intended to be especially valuable to public officials with major policy and managerial responsibilities. The curriculum is designed for key decision makers from medium and larger size cities, as well as from state and county levels of government, and special district organizations. Applications are welcome from non-profit organizations that deliver public services.

A maximum of 40 participants will be accepted. In the selection process consideration will be given to the applicant's position, job experience and evidence of his or her readiness to benefit from the disciplined inquiry that the Institute offers and ability to contribute to the experience of other participants. Every attempt will be made to achieve a balance among participants on the basis of size and type of government, geographic region, and diversity of professional background.

The program fee is $1,500.

---

*Presented by Texas Municipal League and the Lyndon B. Johnson School of Public Affairs, The University of Texas, Austin. Affiliated Co-sponsors - Texas City Management Association and the Texas Foundation for the Improvement of Government.

313

The National Outdoor Leadership School focuses on using the outdoors as the medium to teach wilderness, educational and environmental leadership. The objective of the curriculum is to prepare students to assume leadership positions in the wilderness, and lead their own expeditions. NOLS' goal is to provide them the tools to make this possible.

SCHOOL PROFILE:

Over the past 25 years, the National Outdoor Leadership School (NOLS) has taught wilderness skills, conservation, and outdoor leadership to more than 27,000 students. NOLS is a non-profit educational organization, incorporated as a licensed private school with international headquarters based in Lander, Wyoming; with six branch schools located in Wyoming, Alaska, Washington, Mexico, Kenya and South America. The school offers 38 different types of outdoor courses year-round, from 13 to 95 days, in wilderness areas worldwide for students from ages 14 to 75. Most NOLS courses are eligible for college credit. As a recognized leader in wilderness skills education, NOLS holds conferences and seminars on wilderness related educational topics, conducts research, and produces publications on environmental conservation, wilderness skills and leadership.

Founded in 1965 by Paul Petzoldt, a recognized outdoor leader and world-class mountaineer, NOLS was conceived from the idea that fledgling programs such as Colorado Outward Bound were hampered by a lack of qualified leaders. In response Petzoldt developed an educational organization to train outdoor leaders who could instruct future wilderness users to be responsible, knowledgeable and safe in the backcountry. Since its inception, NOLS has expanded its mission to assume a leadership role among outdoor educational programs. NOLS seeks to educate the public of the value of wild lands and to provide knowledge, skills and experiences for safe recreational use and conservation of wilderness areas.

CURRICULUM: NOLS courses are extended expeditions, 2 weeks to 3 months in length, to some of the plant's most remote wilderness areas. Every course includes NOLS' core curriculum:

1. **Safety and Judgment** Basic first aid, safety and accident prevention, hazard evaluation, heat/cold-related injury prevention and treatment, rescue techniques, emergency procedures.
2. **Leadership and Expedition Dynamics** Small group expeditions, human psychology, "leader of the day" opportunities, leadership styles, expedition planning, outdoor teaching techniques.
3. **Minimum Impact Camping and Resource Protection** Campsite selection, shelter, stove use and care, fire-building, sanitation and waste disposal.
4. **Environmental Awareness** Ecosystems, flora and fauna identification, geology, weather, anthropology, astronomy, history, foreign languages, cultural exchanges.
5. **Outdoor Living Skills** Cooking and baking, nutrition and rations, climate control, high altitude physiology, equipment care and selection.

6. **Travel Techniques** Energy conservation, map-reading and compass use, time control plans, route-finding and navigation, backpacking, kayaking, horse packing, sailing, fishing, telemark skiing, caving, climbing.
7. **Public Service** Local and regional environmental priorities, multiple use theory and practice, land management issues and wilderness ethics.

Outdoor leadership skills and judgment are taught in the immediate classroom of the wilderness and reinforced through firsthand experiences. Leadership training is taught in a real environment, in real weather; it nets real results. Practical demonstration of skills in an unforced, real world setting ensures that students learn by doing.

"What I hear, I forget; what I see, I remember; what I do, I know." This Chinese proverb mirrors NOLS' teaching philosophy. NOLS believes the best wilderness education comes through experience. By explaining, demonstrating and immediately practicing new skills, NOLS gives students responsibility; in the backcountry, the relationship between action and result is vivid and gratifying. Student successes and mistakes are equally important to learning judgment and leadership.

Course participants are actively involved and gradually take charge of day to day decision making. They become comfortable with assuming responsibility when leading their peers. Individually and as a team, students become increasingly adept at route-finding, camping without damaging the land, coping with the weather, taking care of each other. NOLS outdoor "classrooms" change as student skills grow. Experience teaches judgment about the safest route, the capabilities of partners, the likelihood of hazards. Out of dealing with challenges grows leadership.

Leadership Tools Used by NOLS: Feedback; Evaluations; Coaching; Expedition Behavior (Students are taught personal and group accountability for their actions); Technical & Interpersonal Skills; Role models (NOLS instructors and students provide a visible model of leadership); Commitment; Experience (Judgment opportunities are provided to practice leadership styles through "leader of the day" situations, small group expeditions, and expedition planning).

Outdoor leadership includes the ability to adapt to difficult conditions, to keep tentmates laughing, to cook a gourmet meal (by wilderness standards) at the end of a long day. NOLS believes the best leader is the person who exercises the common sense and good judgment to help everyone travel safely and enjoyably through any terrain in all situations.

The University of Tennessee
711 E. Andy Holt Tower, Knoxville, TN 37996-0174

Sara Phillips
Director, Personnel Services
615/974-2243

Institute for Leadership Effectiveness

PURPOSE: Annually, The University of Tennessee sponsors an Institute for Leadership Effectiveness, to recognize, reward, and encourage superior performance on the part of University administrators. The Institute brings together representatives from every part of the University, including the academic campuses at Knoxville, Chattanooga and Martin, a medical school in Memphis and a medical center in Knoxville, the Institute of Agriculture, the Space Institute at Tullahoma, the Institute for Public Service and Continuing Education, and the System Administration.

OBJECTIVES: It is designed to help participants: Gain insight into their communication and leadership styles, helping them to choose appropriate courses of action in their jobs; Identify and discuss problems or issues related to the future direction of higher education and the decisions that must be made in a changing environment; Meet with colleagues from different institutions who share a concern for leadership within higher education; Recognize their potential to make a difference in the outcomes and successes of their institution; Share in taking responsibility for and fulfilling the University's mission.

The Leadership Institute is conducted over a five-day period at an off-campus resort. Participants are involved in group discussions, experiential activities, case studies, and self-assessment opportunities. Small group work is an integral part of the experience, with each group of ten participants facilitated by two training staff members. Participants receive feedback and glean information from a variety of areas related to their leadership roles:

- Personal Communication Style
- Self-awareness
- Organizational Dynamics
- Campus Culture

- Power Issues
- Group Development
- Conflict Management
- Networking

Each year, approximately forty participants from both academic and non-academic positions of leadership are chosen and invited to attend the Institute. This increases the understanding of roles between academic and non-academic personnel. Participants are nominated to attend the Institute by the Vice Presidents and Chancellors of their respective campuses and units and are chosen based upon their past accomplishments and promise of continued leadership within higher education.

Also, each year, representatives from The University of Tennessee's sister system, the State Board of Regents, are invited to participate. This process improves communications and strengthens the bond between institutions of higher education within the State.

Participants leave the Institute with a greater awareness of their leadership styles, their methods of communication, and their ways of handling conflict. They obtain in-depth, current information on political and budgetary issues affecting their institutions. Through experiential activities, they have had practice in developing techniques which will increase their effectiveness as group leaders.

Since the Institute's setting is informal and conducive to networking, the varied backgrounds and responsibilities of the participants help them assimilate and clarify the overall mission of the University and each of its parts.

The Leadership Institute is coordinated through the Office of Personnel Services; the training staff is composed of former participants who share a strong commitment to the Institute and its success. The staff uses a cyclical process to continually refine the program content. In addition to their normally assigned responsibilities, the training staff meets several times per year to plan, organize and assess the Institute program and to focus on special topics related to advanced leadership training and group facilitation skills.

While the thrust of the Institute is very much directed toward public higher education in the State of Tennessee, The University of Tennessee accepts a limited number of participants from other institutions of higher education, particularly those who may be considering the implementation of a similar program.

OVERVIEW: The Institute encompasses the following broad areas:
1. Self-Assessment of Personal Leadership Characteristics
2. Introduction to Group Process
3. Managing Conflict
4. Simulation Exercise on How Organizations Function
5. Power
6. Networking
7. Campus Culture

The Institute also provides several social events and opportunities to have fun at a pleasant location in the Tennessee mountains. The purpose of the Institute is both to strengthen and enhance present leadership skills and characteristics as well as reward participants for past accomplishments as a developing academic leader.

The program includes a detailed schedule of events, forms for filling out self-assessments, questionnaires for evaluations of the program, descriptions of various training methods used, trainers' information materials and action planning worksheets. Further information can be obtained by contacting Sara Phillips as noted in heading of program.

U.S. Coast Guard Academy
Superintendent (cld), New London, CT 06320

Rex J. Blake
Chief
Leadership Development Program
203/444-8279

The Coast Guard Academy's Leadership Program

The smallest of the five Federal Service Academies, the Coast Guard Academy fills much the same function as the others. Its graduates receive a bachelor of science degree as well as a commission as an officer in the Coast Guard. Class attendance is mandatory, as is participation in either intercollegiate or intramural athletics.

Cadets pursue a B.S. in one of seven majors while at the same time performing duties as members of the Cadet Regiment. Their performance of these duties is evaluated by classmates, cadets senior to them and commissioned company officers. The curriculum, which is highly technical, has little room for choice. Nor do the summers represent a respite: the cadets spend their summers attending professional training and several weeks each of their first two summers aboard the Coast Guard's sail training vessel, _Eagle_. As the crew of that ship, they fill, in turn, the roles of supervised and supervisor and have an opportunity for practical application of technical skills that have been introduced in the classroom.

Throughout their four years at the Academy, the cadets receive evaluations in parallel military and academic systems. Cadets who graduate have mastered the skills needed to balance competing demands under great pressure. In appearance and bearing they have a common stature that is unmistakable. Yet, they are certainly not the same. In acceptance of the regulations and underlying values and in their degree of mastery of professional and academic subjects there is wide variation. Approximately one-half of the cadets who enter graduate. Following graduation every new Ensign is assigned to duty aboard a ship for two years. All will pursue qualification as Officers of the Deck (OOD's) who, as the Captain's surrogate for four hour "watches," are responsible for every aspect of the ship's mission. All will serve as first line managers supervising two to twenty people. While the primary mission of vessels may differ, all junior officers aboard ships perform similar roles. Since the Coast Guard officer, at least initially, is a generalist, the first two years of service can be considered a common apprenticeship. It is during this apprenticeship period that the efficacy of our training programs is judged.

Rationale for developing a formal leadership program

Most graduates are rated as successful by their first commanding officer; most are subsequently promoted as fully qualified. Yet, a study undertaken by the Coast Guard during the early eighties suggested that the complete picture of the graduates' job success was more complex. The findings indicated that while the Ensigns were well prepared for the technical aspects of their jobs--as navigators, engineers--they were much less proficient in their supervisory roles.

Coupled with that feedback were our own informal observations of the cadets in the regiment. The behaviors exhibited by cadets supervising other cadets was not what most would characterize as effective supervision, management or leadership. Generally, senior cadets displayed openly antagonistic behaviors towards subordinates who were required to

318

act respectfully, politely, and deferentially toward their seniors. It seemed that the prevailing Academy environment fostered the acquisition of behaviors/habits that were detrimental to effective senior-subordinate relations. To be effective supervisors in the fleet, our graduates would have to un-learn some of these habits following graduation.

Objectives of the program

In 1986, we undertook the development of a comprehensive leadership development program. The goal of the program was to provide support to the cadets as they practiced more effective leadership behaviors in the supervisory roles they enact at the Academy. The curriculum progresses from conceptual exploration of the roles of leaders and managers to the introduction and supervised application of discrete supervisory skills.

Earlier efforts at formal leadership education at the Coast Guard Academy were sporadic. When leadership classes had been conducted, they usually consisted of relatively unfocused seminar-style discussion in informal gatherings. Such discussions were usually conducted outside the usual workday--early in the morning or late at night. The constraints imposed by (1) an already enormous core curriculum and (2) the relative inflexibility necessitated by the need to retain ABET accreditation for the engineering curricula made the accommodation of a more extensive/ambitious leadership program unlikely.

The program that emerged, and is presented here, necessitated tradeoffs with other curriculum elements. It is not an optimal design but it is one that works here with the constraints of the existing curriculum and resources. The result is an interdisciplinary hybrid combining in-the-classroom and out-of-the-classroom learning that spans the full four years of the Academy experience. Its elements are conducted by faculty and staff from throughout the Academy community, and it takes advantage of the opportunities for practical application afforded by the barracks "laboratory."

FOURTH CLASS YEAR (Freshman Year) The first year's activities provide an orientation to the Academy and the Coast Guard organization encompassing some of the less tangible aspects of the Coast Guard culture, including the unique customs, traditions, and language of the service. Included is material on human behavior--how humans behave individually, in groups, and in the special groups called organizations. Taken together, the courses help the students understand their current and potential role in the organization, make informed career decisions, and prepare for upcoming leadership courses.

A History of the U.S. Coast Guard - Department of Humanities The course's objective is to help the students to understand how the modern Coast Guard evolved into its present form and to appreciate the unique accomplishments and culture of the Service.

Orientation to the Modern Coast Guard - Cadet Administrative Division The course follows the Coast Guard History lecture series and provides an overview of the Coast Guard organization and missions as they exist today. Unlike the other military services, the Coast Guard has an active peacetime mission--or rather, many of them.

Foundations of Human Behavior - Department of Humanities

TEXTS: <u>Understanding Psychology</u>, Robert S. Feldman, 1989; <u>Psychological Research: An Introduction</u>, Arthur J. Bachrach, 1981; <u>Theories of Adolescence</u>, Rolf E. Muuss, 1988; <u>Organizational Behavior: Readings and Exercises</u>, John W. Newstrom and Keith Davis, 1989.

OBJECTIVES: This course contributes to the development of the student's ability to think critically about the world and the way it works; it is a fundamental building block in the process of general education. Educated persons must be able to reflect upon themselves, their behavior and their place in the world. Psychology--the science of human behavior-- is one way to learn about people. This course surveys what psychologists know about human behavior with a special emphasis on behavior in organizations. Along the way students will learn about the methods psychologists use in their systematic search for the principles that govern human behavior.

Additionally, an understanding of human behavior is the foundation of effective leadership. Since graduates of the Coast Guard Academy will all be leaders, there is practical value in mastering the content of this course. This course also opens the door to future courses that will further develop the foundations of effective leadership.

After successful completion of this course, students will be able to: Demonstrate a basic understanding of the methods used to study human behavior; Identify, describe and discuss the basic building blocks of human behavior; Apply relevant psychological principles to the analysis and discussion of their own and others' behavior in organizations; Develop strategies for effective membership in organizations.

COURSE DESCRIPTION/FORMAT. This course is first about people and ultimately about the way people come together to form effective organizations. The course begins with a survey of the basic building blocks of human behavior--the brain and nervous system, sensation and perception, learning, memory, cognition, motivation and emotion. It moves on to examine the development of personality and what happens when people have difficulty functioning effectively in society. Next, the student's attention is turned to the principles that govern the behavior of people in informal and formal groups and, finally, to the ways in which individuals interact in organizations, addressing issues such as becoming a member, employee motivation and loyalty, conflict, and performance evaluation.

Classes will generally be conducted as lectures with ample opportunity for cadets to ask questions. In addition to the lectures, there will be 14 two-hour "lab" sessions during which cadets will conduct behavioral experiments and participate in experiential exercises.

COURSE REQUIREMENTS:

<u>Class Participation</u>: Grade will be based primarily on participation in Lab sessions and active participation in class question and answer sessions. Participation is based upon the following: (1) Assigned reading and your ability to ask relevant questions and answer basic

questions concerning the reading material; (2) Talking in class will not earn a high mark for participation; but, silence will earn less. Comments, objections, questions, observations, etc. which indicate that you are thinking about the material will earn you the greatest credit; (3) A large number of brief and longer in-class exercises.

Exams: Two exams on readings and lecture material during first half of the course to demonstrate familiarity with the basic elements of human behavior. A comprehensive Final Exam will be given covering lecture material and the application of that material to the discussion of behavior in organizations. Students with an overall pre-final grade of 95% will be exempt from the final.

Papers: Two personal application papers (4-6 pages) will be assigned during the second half of the course to relate the material discussed in class to everyday experience.

Grades: Grades for the course will be calculated as follows: Two exams (15% each), 30%; Lab Reports, 5%; Personal Application Papers (15% each), 30%; Class/Lab Participation, 10%; Final Exam, 25%.

Topics: Introduction / Study Skills; Physiological Foundations; Sensation and Perception; Learning, Memory and Thinking; Motivation and Emotion; Development; Personality; Abnormal Behavior; Making Social Judgments; Relationships; The Organization: Structure, Culture, and Goals; Taking a role as a member; Satisfaction and Performance; Teamwork; Resolving Conflicts; Tough Choices.

THIRD CLASS YEAR (Sophomore Year) **Introduction to Leadership - Interdisciplinary**

TEXTS: Military Leadership: In Pursuit of Excellence, R. L. Taylor and W. E. Rosenbach (Eds.), 1984; Leadership in Organizations, G. A. Yukl, 1981.

OBJECTIVES: The course progresses from the consideration of the concept of leadership as discussed in the literature, to the observation, analysis, and evaluation of leadership as displayed by leaders in the "real world" and the development of self-awareness of potential strengths and weaknesses in the cadets' own roles as leaders.

COURSE DESCRIPTION/FORMAT: The class meets once a week for 50 minutes for the entire year, averages 20 students and is conducted as a seminar. Instructors will be drawn from the Department of Economics and Management, the Department of Humanities, and the Cadet Administration Division.

Fall Semester. Students explore the basic literature in leadership--philosophical, historical, and scientific. They are exposed, in the course of assigned readings and classroom discussions, to the variety of opinions about the definition of leadership, what constitutes effective leadership, and the overall complexity of the concept. They have an opportunity to assess the overall validity of the concept as they look at prominent leaders in the world.

Topics: Leadership as a college course; Definitions of leadership; Development of modern concepts of leadership trait approach, situational leadership, contingency models, transactional leadership; Related terms: interpersonal influence, power, authority, accountability, credibility, legitimacy; Popular conceptions of leadership; Myth of reality: attribution of leadership as a factor in success of a group; Roles of leaders in politics, organizations, the military; Leadership as an interpersonal phenomenon; Leadership as strategic management and decision making; Leaders as symbols; Leadership and management; Leadership and headship; Formal and informal leaders; Leadership in military and civilian organizations; Naval leadership; Coast Guard leadership; Military leadership philosophy; Ethics in military leadership; Followers and followership: impact of the followers' behavior, reciprocal influence processes; Charismatic leadership; Selection and development of leaders.

Course Requirements:

Journal. Each student is required to keep a "journal" for the class. Each week, after completing the readings, the students use the journal to reflect on the content of the assignment for 15-20 minutes. The students bring the journal to class. At the beginning the instructor poses a question to the group. During the first ten minutes of class, students write their individual responses to the question in the journal, using the readings for support. Journals are collected at random intervals during the semester (at least three times), reviewed by the instructor, and returned. They are collected a final time at the end of the semester and assigned a grade.

Biographies. A five-page essay on a leader of the student's choice. May be anyone of interest to them who has been recognized on either an international, national, state, or local level, contemporary, historical, political, military, or a leader in any other field.

The essay will include: Basic facts. Birth and death; where, when, under what circumstances. Education. Social background. Economic background. Any unusual factors in life. Nature of leadership. Context or circumstances. Style. Change over time. Sources of power or influence. Strengths and weaknesses. Contemporary public assessment of the leader's effectiveness in the leader's day. History's judgment of the leader's effectiveness (for historical figures). Each student will also conduct a five to ten minute presentation/discussion on the subject of his/her paper during the last three class meetings of the semester.

Calculation of grades: Journal, 40%; Biography, 30%; Class participation, 30%.

Spring Semester. Students will analyze situations in their daily exposure to others acting as leaders/supervisors to identify effective and ineffective interpersonal behaviors. They also will begin to evaluate their own abilities and tendencies, strengths and weaknesses as potential leaders. Finally, based on their observations during the semester, each student will draft a "self-development contract" detailing specific goals and action steps for their own leadership development to be implemented during the next year's leadership experiences.

Topics:

The person. Temperament and individual differences. Personality and interpersonal relations; how personality may effect interpersonal behavior in a leadership role. Stereotypes. Prejudice and discrimination. Sex differences. Self-assessment: FIRO-B.

The situation. Observing the behaviors of leaders. Situational theories of leadership effectiveness (Hersey-Blanchard, Fiedler). Observing the situation. Self-assessment: LEAD-self.

Decision making. Decision making in a hierarchical organization; constraints on decisions. Ethical decision making. Values and decision making. Group think. Decision-making styles; systematic biases due to temperament. Self-assessment: Myers-Briggs Type Indicator (MBTI).

Power. Sources of power. Power and leader effectiveness. Developing bases of power and influence. Interviews with faculty/staff/local officers; power and influence at the Academy.

Course Requirements:

Journals. As in the fall semester, students will maintain a "journal." However, the nature of the entries in the journal will be somewhat different. Instead of commenting on the readings, each week the student will be asked to identify, describe, and analyze a particular incident that occurred in the barracks. The journal becomes a commentary and analysis of "critical incidents" of leadership in the barracks. Students will write a brief (two or three page) narrative report of an incident in which effective (or ineffective) leadership was displayed/demonstrated. The report will be in two parts: 1) Specifically describe the conditions and behaviors involved. The narrative should include the positions, but not the names, of the people involved, the events leading up to the incident, the incident itself, and what happened after the incident. 2) Analysis. Thoroughly analyze the situation and the behaviors of those involved in the context of the ideas/theories presented in the readings and discussed in class. Students will be selected to present these in class throughout the semester.

Self-development contract. The final assignment of the semester is an action plan for their own leadership development, integrating classroom learnings, their observations of other leaders during the year, and their own self-insight into a series of objectives, goals, and actions for their own development.

During the final class period, each student will prepare a "contract" detailing individual goals and objectives to further his or her own leadership development. It will take into account the concepts presented in the course as well as the student's own assessment of his or her level of development. The contract will be reviewed by the instructor who will work with the student to ensure the goals are specific, relevant, and achievable. The contract will be passed on to the summer platoon officers and waterfront supervisors and, eventually, to the company officer. The contract will guide the student's activities during the second class leadership applications.

Calculation of grades: Journal: "critical incidents," 60%; Class participation, 40%.

During their second year, students also choose one of four electives in social science. Each of these courses builds on the Foundations of Human Behavior course. While these courses are offered in different disciplines, they share a common theme in the study and development of effective leadership. The four courses are:

Great European Statesmen of the 19th and 20th Centuries - Department of Humanities
A study of four prominent European statesmen of the 19th and 20th Centuries.

Shapers of 20th Century American Diplomacy - Department of Humanities A study of the lives of four prominent 20th Century American statesmen who contributed significantly to the development and implementation of American foreign policy. The course will also include an assessment of the achievements and failures of the statesmen, the degree of consistency and change in policy and the extent to which their policy and diplomacy was moralistic and realistic.

Group Dynamics and the Development of Effective Teams - Department of Economics and Management Through study and experience the course will examine the functioning of informal and formal groups including issues such as group formation, influence, trust and cohesiveness. Particular emphasis will be given to strategies for the assessment of working teams and their development.

Introduction to Counseling Skills - Interdisciplinary This course will first create a framework for thinking about those who help and those who are in need of help in living their lives at work and in the broader community. Particular attention will be paid to the relationship between and the respective roles of managers, employees and professional counselors with respect to dealing with behavioral and emotional problems. The course will then focus on skill development--problem exploration and clarification, developing new perspectives and setting goals and taking action.

SECOND CLASS SUMMER (between Sophomore and Junior Year)

Supervisory Skills - Interdisciplinary

Objectives: The program objectives include the introduction, development, and practice of a basic set of supervisory skills--telling people what you expect them to do, teaching them how to do it, monitoring their performance of the task, providing feedback and consequences for their performance, and moving on to new tasks/goals when the trainees had mastered more basic tasks.

Course Description/Format: Conducted during the summer, the class meets for one week. Five eight-hour days yield a 40-hour program.

The class is organized to introduce and provide for the practice of discrete skills. A skill is introduced in lecture together with the rationale and context for its effective application. The skill is modeled for the students, either by the instructor or using a videotape of another's performance. Each student practices the skill and receives feedback on his or her performance.

Videotapes are used extensively to provide objective feedback to the students on their level of skill development. In the counseling/interviewing segment of the course, for example, classroom demonstrations and practice are followed by individual role playing of a one-on-one counseling scenario. Each student has the opportunity to counsel and to be counseled. The role playing is videotaped and replayed for the cadet. Cadets receive feedback from their classmates, the instructor, and the videotape itself.

The component skills are presented/developed individually in modules. The modules are presented sequentially during the week, describing the requisite skills for the series of steps a supervisor might follow when taking over a new work group. The capstone event of the week illustrates how the various pieces of the model would "fit" together to describe the complete process of supervision.

The topics that comprise the course are: Introducing yourself; Conveying expectations to group/individuals; Maintaining and enhancing the morale and self-esteem of subordinates; Effective teaching and training; Giving orders and instructions; Communication and listening skills; Counseling/interviewing; Performance management; Monitoring performance; Diagnosing performance problems; Remediation; Providing feedback; Consequences of performance: natural and artificial; Growth: setting new goals; Overview and integration: the process of supervision.

Leadership Application I - Cadet Administrative Division

For a period of two to three weeks, third year cadets are placed in supervisory roles over first year cadets at the Academy and aboard the sail training vessel _Eagle_. In this role, the upper class cadets are responsible for the initial orientation and training of the incoming class. They are expected to use the experience as an opportunity to practice the skills taught in the classroom in what amounts to a leadership laboratory.

Cadets are guided by commissioned faculty and staff members during this phase of the program. The faculty members provide encouragement, monitor performance, and provide feedback as the cadets work to effectively apply the skills taught during the classroom phase of the program. During the two to three weeks of program, one faculty member supervises some six cadets as they, in turn, work with some 60 first year cadets. The faculty members have daily meetings with the cadets.

Throughout the program, a clear connection is made between the effective application of the supervisory skills and the cadets' success in the program; the behaviors taught in the earlier classroom sessions have been incorporated into a performance report consisting of behaviorally anchored rating scales. Their grade for the summer consists of the marks on

325

that report.

SECOND CLASS YEAR (Junior Year) **Leadership Consultation/Leadership Application II - Cadet Administrative Division**

The active supervisory role of the second class cadets over the fourth class continues through the summer into the academic year. The second class cadets refine their supervisory skills with supervision/feedback/remediation by Company Officers (during the year, a commissioned officer is assigned full time to each "company" of some 110 cadets). As in the summer, the supervisory skills are incorporated into the cadet's performance reports.

Additionally, there are regular, structured supervisory sessions with the company officers. Topics addressed during these sessions include reinforcement/refinement of the basic skills introduced during the summer, skill building in new areas (like team building and problem solving), and the application of skills to specific problems encountered by cadet leaders at the Academy. The course makes extensive use of situations actually occurring in the barracks as well as case study scenarios and role plays illustrative of typical situations.

Fall Semester. The topics covered include: 1. Expectations. The leader's role; accountability for the morale and performance of subordinates; developing subordinates; setting goals for subordinates. 2. Goal setting: Group. Evaluate the success or effectiveness of the summer program; debrief summer leadership experiences; extent to which objectives were fulfilled; measures of success; morale; enthusiasm, performance. 3. Goal setting: Individual. Feedback of summer performance evaluations. Assessment by subordinates, peers, seniors, self. Identify areas that were easy/difficult, successful/unsuccessful. Evaluate extent to which goals established at the end of spring semester (in the self-development contract) were met. Develop individual goals/targets for further skill development. 4. Team building. Creating a sense of community, esprit de corps; cooperation and competition; factors effecting the performance of the group. 5. Facilitating performance and morale. Sustaining performance and morale; enforcing the regulations; balancing challenge and support. 6. Problem solving. Force-field analysis; identifying obstacles to performance and morale; driving and restraining forces; developing an action plan; mid-course correction to original goals. 7. Assessing performance. Performance evaluation; preparing effective performance reports. 8. Interviewing and counseling skills. Listening skills; counseling subordinates on military, academic performance; developing subordinates. 9. Emerging problems. Frustration; disobedience from subordinates; hostility from subordinates; grudging compliance.

Spring Semester. The topics covered include: 1. Revising, setting goals. Assess progress toward goals, individually and as a group. 2. Conflict management. Conflict resolution; with peers; with subordinates; with seniors; mediation; negotiation. 3. Feedback on perceptions of leadership effectiveness; administration of LEAD-Other. 4. Emerging problems. Sexual harassment; sexual behavior; sexual attraction; issues of morality; alcohol use/abuse; enabling behavior; discrimination/prejudice; fraternization; group norms/peer pressure; stress; academic performance.

FIRST CLASS SUMMER (between Junior and Senior Year) **Orientation to the role of Junior Officers - Cadet Administrative Division**

During their final summer at the Academy, cadets spend some thirteen weeks assigned to a Coast Guard Cutter. They are assigned singly or in groups of two or three. While there, they fill the role of junior officers, performing many of the duties and jobs that make up that role. They are integrated into the ship's crew, participating in various inport and underway activities. The ships evaluate the cadets' performance of duties as they would that of a junior officer--their performance on duty (as the Commanding Officer's surrogate for daily watches) and their completion of various administrative tasks. While they have only limited supervisory authority and responsibility, they nevertheless have the opportunity to observe the other members of the crew--how jobs are assigned, monitored, how performance is evaluated, how morale and discipline are maintained (and the consequences when either one is not). They observe things done well, and things not done so well.

FIRST CLASS YEAR (Senior Year) **The Division Officer - Department of Professional Development**

Building on previous summer programs and courses in Leadership and Nautical Science, the course focuses on the cadets' final preparation for their first duty assignment as junior officers aboard a Coast Guard Cutter. Classroom instruction focuses on the administrative and supervisory aspects of the Division Officer's duties. It includes the application of leadership skills and techniques to shipboard situations (with extensive use of case study scenarios and role plays; cadets offer their own experience from the summer to expand/provide some variations on the situations described in the role plays).

Leadership Application III - Cadet Administrative Division

The cadets return to the Academy at the end of the summer to fill roles that approximate that of junior officers. Assigned to leadership positions in the cadet regiment, they work directly for the Commandant of Cadets and the Company Officers to direct and coordinate all the activities of a student body of some 900 cadets. They establish policies, enforce regulations, publish schedules, govern committees, and captain sports teams. They are assigned more important projects, and are expected to use their experience to successfully complete routine tasks without supervision. They are held accountable for the welfare of the junior members of corps of cadets. As during their prior three years, the cadets continue to balance these responsibilities with the equally pressing demands of completing an undergraduate education. Although there are no formal classroom sessions, extensive one-on-one contact with Company Officers is the rule. As in the previous year, these meetings provide an opportunity for encouragement, feedback, and remediation.

United States Military Academy
Dept. of Behavioral Science & Leadership
West Point, NY 10996

Howard Prince
Professor & Dept. Head
914/938-3206

West Point Fellowship in Leader Development

PROGRAM DESCRIPTION: The West Point Fellowship in Leader Development is a post-graduate academic program designed to prepare Army officers for service as company tactical officers at the U.S. Military Academy. It is taught and administered by the faculty and staff of the U.S. Military Academy.

The graduate students come from all Army sources of commissioning and from many different branches of the Army. They are selected by the Commandant of Cadets based on military and academic criteria. Students must have outstanding records of military service that show high potential for leadership and command at higher levels of the Army. They must also show academic potential based on the Graduate Record Examination and their undergraduate record.

The curriculum was developed based on a formal needs assessment and a job analysis of the role of the company tactical officer at the Military Academy. Data for the job analysis came from interviews with serving company tactical officers, their supervisors, others involved in leader development, and official documents. The company tactical officer is the person most centrally involved in cadet leader development. Tactical officers integrate information from all of the Military Academy's developmental programs including intellectual, military, physical, and moral. They are feedback agents--coaches and counselors--as well as teachers. They are responsible for establishing an environment that is not only consistent with the developmental goals set by the Military Academy but which also contributes directly to cadet development as a leadership laboratory, providing direct experience and the opportunity to learn by observing others.

The curriculum is a multi-disciplinary one, drawing on both the behavioral sciences and the humanities. Education objectives derived from the major role requirements of the company tactical officer position guided the selection and development of courses to be taught in the graduate program. The program has a professional emphasis because it prepares officers for professional practice as leader developers, not just at the Military Academy but also during their later service as leaders and commanders in the field Army. The program also is designed to develop more general education objectives such as analysis, problem solving, communications, investigation, critical thinking, synthesis, and design. Indirectly the program should develop such affective outcomes as commitment to learning, curiosity, enthusiasm, and self-confidence. Although the courses are very applied because the end is professional practice, applications are rooted in a sound body of theory and research-based knowledge. The program provides the graduate student with experiences that lead to the effective translation of knowledge into action. Students will write extensively and will frequently present and defend their ideas in small seminar discussions or formal presentations. They will be assigned to lead seminar meetings to increase communications skills and foster mastery of integrated frameworks. In addition to critical analysis of scientific literature, written work will emphasize the design of products that are useful in the professional practice such as an organizational assessment questionnaire, a group development plan, or a class to be taught to cadets by the company tactical officer. The graduate program consists of 14 courses taken during three terms over one calendar year. Each course is 3.0 credit hours. There is neither a thesis requirement nor a comprehensive examination. Grades are assigned using the letters A, B, C, D, F. The plan is to offer the Master of Arts in Leader Development to students who successfully complete the program.

EDUCATION OBJECTIVES:
A. Develop Individual Cadets To Be Leaders Of Character: Analyze & explain individual performance; Plan, supervise, & evaluate developmental programs; Design, conduct, evaluate, & revise individual & group learning experiences; Apply performance appraisal techniques; Apply counseling techniques; Communicate effectively.

B. Create A Developmental Environment In The Cadet Company: Understand the role of the USMA in developing leaders of character for the Army throughout its history; Explain the effects of group and organizational phenomena on cadet development; Design & supervise entry & continuing socialization programs for an organization; Apply concepts of group development to enhance individual cadet development; Apply assessment techniques to evaluate the effects of group and organizational phenomena on cadet development; Lead organizations through change; Integrate organizational systems to enhance cadet development.

THE ACADEMIC PROGRAM:
Summer Term: PL 500, Foundations of Military Leadership; EN 600, From Idea to Action: Communications for Effective Leading; PY 600, Applied Ethics and the Military Profession; PL 650, Organizational Socialization
Fall Term: PL 587, Counseling for Leaders; PL 600, Motivation Theory and Practice; PL 610, Leadership and Group Development; PL 651, Individual Development; HI 600, The American Military and the USMA Experience
Spring Term: PL 620 Learning and Teaching for Leaders; PL 630, Systems Leadership; PL 640, Leading Organizations Through Change; PL 649, Leadership Theory and Development; PL 652, Individual and Organizational Assessment

COURSE DESCRIPTIONS:

EN 600   From Idea to Action: Communications for Effective Leading
3 Credit Hours   Summer Term

Scope: A graduate seminar concerned with the practical application of communications theory, this course gives particular attention to symbol, word, invention, design, and audience. By examining writers as diverse as Aristotle and Jung, Augustine and Wheelwright, Kosinski and Hermogenes, students will come to recognize the universal applicability of certain theories of communication, the inappropriateness of others, and the especial value of a few to the process of leadership development. This seminar also addresses the role and influence of the print and broadcast media in the contemporary workplace; further, it considers several techniques students themselves might use to ensure

329

that what they communicate to media representatives and what they intend to communicate to them are, in fact, one and the same. The course emphasizes ways to translate ideas into action--effectively, quickly, economically--within a high-pressure environment increasingly made public by mass communications.

Lessons: 16 @ 150 mins.

Special Requirements: Each week students lead a seminar discussion. They also complete one written study of 4000-5000 words focusing on the practical application of a topic suggested by the primary or supplemental course reading. At the last seminar meeting students formally present oral summaries of their written projects.

PL 500 Military Leadership
3.0 Credit Hours   Summer Term

Scope: This graduate-level course is an academic, multi-disciplinary study of organizational leadership involving theory and application. The content of the course provides the theoretical prerequisites for further study of leadership and leader development. Graduate students will investigate the impact of direct leadership on individual motivation and group processes using leadership theories and skills. They will also consider the effect of indirect leadership on subordinates' performance using theories of organizational systems, professionalism and ethics. These theories are applied in the analysis of military leadership situations.

Lessons: 16 @ 180 mins.

Special Requirements: One individual and two group projects requiring the analysis of a complex organization. One group oral presentation which requires the diagnosis of a situation and the application of systems and direct measures to enhance organizational effectiveness.

PL 650 Organizational Socialization and Culture
3.0 Credit Hours   Summer Term

Scope: Competent organizational leadership demands a thorough understanding of socialization, the process whereby people learn the values, attitudes, and behaviors expected of members of a given culture. The leader additionally must be able to design and implement such a process to achieve the organizational purpose and goals. Since organizational culture serves as the blueprint for living in the organization, that is, the culture defines those salient values, attitudes, and behaviors, the organizational leader must also be able to both analyze and evaluate the existing culture and change it as required. This course is specifically designed to help you achieve these competencies. We will first develop a scientifically based analytical framework for the study of organizational socialization and culture. We will then apply this framework as we investigate research-based studies of actual organizations, to include the USMA. Finally, you will have the opportunity to apply your newly acquired knowledge and skills as you complete a group project studying either Cadet Basic Training or Cadet Field Training and an individual design project dealing with a regular-letter cadet company.

Lessons: 17 @ 120 mins., 5 field trips to cadet summer training.
Special Requirements:
1.   Group project to describe, analyze and evaluate the existing culture and the socialization programs used during Cadet Basic Training or Cadet Field Training. Oral presentation and short written summary.
2.   Individual project to design a plan for analyzing and evaluating the culture and socialization program in your company, and describing and defending the culture and socialization program you will attempt to create. Written report and oral defense before a panel of officers.
3.   Four, one-page precis of assigned books.
4.   Group discussion leader of assigned articles and readings, several times during the term.

PY 600 Applied Ethics and the Military Profession
3.0 Credit Hours   Summer Term

Scope: PY 600, a seminar course, provides an opportunity and a framework for systematically analyzing moral issues that arise in the context of military activity. The course is designed to promote the understanding of the role of ethics in formulating military policy, training, decision making, and operations. Ethics constitutes a subdivision of the discipline of philosophy concerned with principles of right conduct and good character. As an academic discipline, ethics includes the study of the nature and language of moral discourse, but PY 600 focuses on another aspect: applying moral principles to specific spheres of activity, in this case the activities of military professionals. After an initial examination of traditional ethical theories, seminar members will study readings that address military ethics, conduct in war, and specific cases involving demanding situations that require moral judgment. The seminar readings and discussion will help prepare officers for their responsibilities as developers of moral character and for their continued development as military professionals. Seminar members will engage in Socratic dialogue, prepare a course paper, and complete a term end examination.
Lessons: 32 @ 75 mins.
Special Requirements: One course paper of 1500-2000 words.

HI 600 The American Military Experience and the United States Military Academy
3.0 Credit Hours   Fall Term

Scope: This colloquium employs seminar discussion of important works to examine the American military experience and the profession of arms. It will focus on themes of American military history from the colonial period to the present day. During this time the United States Army and the United States Military Academy have adapted to the security needs of the growing Republic and an interdependent world. Students will do oral and written projects about these issues and important features of the West Point experience such as the Fourth Class System, the Honor Code and System, the Academy Education, and the disciplinary system.

Lessons: 15 @ 180 mins.
Special Requirements: A research paper of 3,500 words. Presentation and defense of paper before a committee of faculty and fellow students. Students will serve as discussion leaders for class meetings.

PL 587 Counseling for Leaders
3.0 Credit Hours   Fall Term

Scope: This course introduces the student to the fundamentals of counseling. It focuses on the practical applications of counseling principles and techniques. Using the vehicle of videotaping, the course emphasizes personal, performance, and career counseling to help prepare students to further develop their counseling skills as part of the leader role. Emphasis is placed on students understanding basic counseling concepts, applying them in the development of their own counseling skills, and developing subordinate leaders' counseling skills through evaluation and feedback of counseling sessions. The course covers the counseling process and the dynamics of the interpersonal relationship within that process. Leadership skills learned include attending, active listening, goal setting, developing action programs, assertiveness training, and crisis intervention counseling. Evaluations are both written and behavioral with heavy emphasis on practicing counseling skills.
Lessons: 40 @ 55 mins.
Special Requirements: Students prepare a paper (1800 words) that requires a self-assessment of the counseling skills demonstrated in the first two behavioral partial reviews. Students will also evaluate and provide feedback to subordinate leaders conducting counseling sessions.

PL 600 Motivation Theory and Practice
3.0 Credit Hours   Fall Term

Scope: This course focuses on the scientific study of human motivation in organizational settings. It surveys motivation theories and associated research. Special emphasis is devoted to the application of theories to organizational leadership situations. The course provides the opportunity to design a program intended to initiate, direct, and sustain individual performance in organizations. Specific topics include: assumptions which underlie the study of motivation, need theories, goal setting, job enrichment, job redesign, and expectancy theories.
Lessons: 40 @ 55 mins.
Special Requirement: Course project (5000 words) which requires the student to design a program to enhance cadet performance in a cadet company. This project must incorporate motivational theories and models examined during classroom attendances.

PL 610 Leadership and Group Development
3.0 Credit Hours   Fall Term

332

Scope: This course is designed to improve the student's understanding of human behavior in small group settings. Students' efforts are directed toward understanding small group dynamics concepts, applying these concepts to real group settings, and developing subordinate leaders in the application of small group theories and concepts. Course content includes group structural characteristics, such as roles, norms, inter-member relations, power, tasks, and physical and personal environment. Emphasis is placed on the stages of group development. Students use acquired knowledge to account for group performance, intra- and intergroup conflict, conformity, deviancy, cohesiveness, problem solving, and decision making. The study of these phenomena is conducted from the leader's perspective, with the primary focus on the manner in which a leader can improve subordinate satisfaction, group productivity, and performance. The course is particularly relevant for further professional development in that students gain a comprehensive understanding of the dynamics of small group interaction and learn techniques that can be used to influence group effectiveness.

Lessons: 40 @ 55 mins.

Special Requirements: Course project presented as a paper (2500-3000 words) requiring the application of small group dynamics. Students will be required to design a plan to foster and enhance the group development of the First Class in a cadet company during the first six weeks.

PL 651 Individual Development
3.0 Credit Hours   Fall Term

Scope: In this course students will examine the theory and research on individual development, with specific emphasis on adolescence and early adulthood. The course begins with a review of the major theoretical and methodological issues in developmental psychology. Next, students study several illustrative theories of development, including the work of Freud, Erikson, Piaget, Kohlberg, and Levinson. The course then focuses specifically on college student development, placing emphasis on personality, intellectual, moral-ethical, social, and career development. Students consider the application of theory and research findings to the design of developmental experiences at West Point.

Lessons: 16 @ 150 mins.

Special Requirements: A seminar presentation reviewing the relevant literature on one dimension of college student development. A term paper (5000 words) applying course concepts to the design of developmental programs at West Point.

PL 620 Learning and Teaching for Leaders
3.0 Credit Hours   Spring Term

Scope: In this course, students will develop their teaching skills and will formulate a conceptual basis for their instructional practices as Army officers. The course is oriented toward the psychological theories of learning and their application to the design, delivery, and evaluation of education and training experiences. Students will review the major theories of human learning and instruction, with balanced treatment given to behavioristic,

333

humanistic, and cognitive perspectives. Instructional design emphasizes a systems approach to planning and conducting teaching.

Lessons: 16 @ 150 mins.

Special Requirements: A series of short papers reviewing the major theoretical approaches to learning and instruction. A course practicum in which the students design, deliver, and evaluate learning experiences for cadets (e.g., performance appraisal, counseling, human sexuality, honor). A small project in which the students evaluate and recommend improvements to another person's teaching.

PL 630 Systems Leadership
3.0 Credit Hours   Spring Term

Scope: This course studies the structure and design of contemporary organizations from both a theoretical and an applied perspective. The classical works in organizational theory provide the foundation for the analysis of organizations. The study of contemporary organizations begins with the concept of organizations as systems, the relationship of organizations to the environment, and the identification of organizational goals. In addition, the impact of technology, size, power, decision making, and type of organization will be considered. This course helps graduate students gain new insights into the leadership process within organizations in general, with an emphasis on the military in particular. Classroom exercises are designed to provide an enriched understanding of the tools of analysis of scientific organizational study.

Lessons: 40 @ 55 mins.

Special Requirement: A 5,000 word paper that presents an open-systems analysis of the cadet company within the context of USCC and the USMA. This paper must include an in-depth examination of the relevant contextual factors and their relationship to contemporary theories of organizational design.

PL 640 Leading Organizations Through Change
3.0 Credit Hours   Spring Term

Scope: Change is a common feature of any organization; in the Army we have experienced changes in our weapons, TOEs, support systems and personnel systems. We will continue to see change in a wide variety of areas. This course is designed to enhance the students' ability as an organizational leader by developing a comprehensive understanding of this common feature of organizational life. The course will cover what the leader should know about change, and will concentrate on developing specific leader actions that can assist the leader in the conduct of both planned and unplanned change. Knowledge of the sources of change, the dynamics of the change process, the sources of resistance to change, and the leader actions available for planned and unplanned change will help each student better understand leadership processes within organizations. Students will have the opportunity to refine skills and apply knowledge involved in organizational change through the analysis of organizational change cases from the USMA, the field Army, the JCS, and the civilian world.

334

Lessons: 40 @ 55 mins.
Special Requirement: This course has a major writing requirement of 5000 words. This paper will apply organizational change models to planned and unplanned change within a cadet company, from the point of view of a tactical officer.

PL 649 Leadership Theory and Development
3.0 Credit Hours   Spring Term

Scope: This course presents a survey of theories and research in the area of leadership, with special emphasis on studies of leadership effectiveness and organizational performance. The course seeks to provide the student with an in-depth understanding of the theories, controversies, and research in the area of leadership. Students will analyze and evaluate the major theories and models of leadership effectiveness and learn to apply them in organizational settings. The focus is on the organizational leader with emphasis on self-assessment and self-development as well as the development of subordinate leaders and effective subunits/teams. The concepts of commitment, goal setting, and participation are also addressed as they impact on organizational effectiveness.
Lessons: 40 @ 55 mins.
Special Requirements: Students will be required to prepare presentations to critically discuss and evaluate theories of leadership. Presentations will emphasize a critical examination of the empirical support of certain leadership theories and the research they generated. Course project which leads to the creation of a personal leadership handbook tailored to the Tactical Officer role as leader and leader developer (3000 words).

PL 652 Individual and Organizational Assessment
3.0 Credit Hours   Spring Term

Scope: This course focuses on the theory and methods of individual and organizational assessment. It enables students to design, implement, and evaluate assessment programs in organizational settings. Heavy emphasis is placed on understanding reliability and validity issues in testing and assessment. Individual assessment includes an overview of contemporary psychological measurement of interests, abilities, and attributes and an in-depth look at performance appraisal methodology emphasizing performance factors, attribution biases, person perception, measurement, interpretation, and feedback. Organizational assessment focuses on how leaders monitor and evaluate the functioning of major subsystems in an organization that relate to the developmental behavior of individuals and organizational goals. In a practical sense, the course is designed to help students improve their knowledge of assessment techniques, develop their own assessment skills, and evaluate organizational subsystems.
Lessons: 40 @ 55 mins.
Special Requirement: A course goal paper of 3000 words that requires the design of an assessment program for evaluating some organizational behavior issue, e.g., organizational climate, developmental programs, interpersonal relations, support systems.

University of Denver
College of Systems Science
2327 East Evans Ave., Denver, CO 80208

Hal W. Hendrick
Dean
303/871-4250

Master of Science in Systems Management

The goal of this college is to prepare graduate students for positions of responsibility in industry and government by offering a stimulating academic program to stretch the creative ability of each student. The college offers a graduate degree of Master of Science in Systems Management (MSSM) as evidence of satisfactory preparation for continuing growth and responsibility in systems management. The degree is internationally recognized for academic leadership, quality and the success of its graduates. Furthermore, the worldwide system for delivery of professional education at the graduate level that the University of Denver (DU) has assumed from the University of Southern California (USC) is the standard by which other off-campus programs have been judged.

The College of Systems Science also offers continuing professional programs and is planning related degree programs to further enhance the contribution of our students to the world.

CURRICULUM: The primary objective is to develop the ability of students to anticipate, recognize and solve problems, optimize human capabilities and performance, utilize and effectively allocate resources, and apply systems management theory in management situations. The core provides knowledge about the theories and principles of systems, and a basic set of tools for managerial analysis and decision making. The structure and content of the University of Denver's MSSM program is interdisciplinary. Courses within each area of the program are equivalent in the sense that, while their subject matter may vary, their emphasis remains on the systems way of thinking. Course content at each of the study centers is closely monitored by campus academic departments to assure continuity with that offered on the main campus. The MSSM curriculum is administered by the Director of the Systems Management Program. Faculty teaching and research interests parallel the following three academic areas comprising the program:

Human Factors: The human factors component of the curriculum is responsible for the human factors engineering and applied behavioral courses offered in the MSSM degree. These courses stress the effective management of human resources in the design, operation and maintenance of systems. Human-made systems are increasingly complex and technologically sophisticated. The capabilities and limitations of people to function productively, safely, and with a high quality of life in these environments is an increasing concern. For these reasons, the design of systems for human use, along with the selection, placement and management of people, is a specialized and significant task in systems management. The human factors curriculum integrates a systems approach with data and theoretical constructs from the behavioral, social, life and system sciences. Through its research and teaching the department ensures that systems are designed and managed in ways that are compatible with the characteristics, capabilities, and needs of people.

Systems Technology: Technology is integral to systems thinking, the process of management, and the relationship of organizations to society. Its influence is pervasive and

336

transcends traditional academic, managerial, and organizational boundaries. The systems science program recognizes the crucial role of technology as an inherent attribute of management in the following ways: (1) Technology influences the development and application of tools available to managers to assist in the process of management, (2) Technological advances have a major influence upon the way organizations organize to do business. Recent gains in information systems and communications have, for instance, accelerated the trend toward decentralization and the reduction of layers of middle management within numerous organizations, (3) Technological evolution is a major force in the pace and direction of new product and process design and development, (4) Entirely new industrial systems and managerial requirements have evolved from the application and commercialization of technology. Thus, the systems management curriculum addresses the effective use of technology as a managerial tool, the management of systems in technology dependent environments, and the development and management of large, complex systems. Curriculum content covers concepts, tools, and techniques. Included are the theory and application of the scientific method, modeling and simulation, artificial intelligence and expert systems, decision analysis, cybernetics, information systems, decision science, operations research, and the quantitative social sciences.

Systems Management: The systems management component of the curriculum addresses the basic management needs for MSSM degree students. The curriculum reflects the need of today's systems managers to operate in an environment characterized by rapid change, exponential growth, increasing complexity, and technological sophistication. Such systems are found in manufacturing, process and service industries, construction, computers, aerospace, public works, government, education and many other areas. Managing such systems involves the necessary premise that the entire system must be considered as a whole, with particular emphasis on system interfaces interrelations. The objective of the systems management component is to provide managers with the knowledge and skills to manage complex systems development and operations, high technology, innovation and the acquisition process.

The Program: A total of 36 units, including 27 units of core courses and 9 units of an option (emphasis in a particular subject or a general option), are required for the MSSM degree. No more than 12 units of graduate work taken in special or provisional status may be applied toward the master's degree. The program has three general requirements: a general core, a three-course option, and a thesis/capstone experience.

Candidates applying for the MSSM program must have (1) a baccalaureate degree or its equivalent from a regionally accredited college or university; (2) an acceptable grade point average (GPA) computed for the final 60 semester units of undergraduate work; (3) satisfactory scores on the verbal and quantitative portions of the General Test of the Graduate Record Examination (GRE).

University of Georgia
Dept. of Human Resource Development
Division of Instructional Services
Athens, GA 30602

Vickie Stout
Dept. Head
404/542-3451

National Leadership Institute in Adult & Continuing Education

---

The National Leadership Institute addresses our need for professionals committed to being future leaders. Comprehensive in design and approach to leadership development, this year-long program consists of three leadership focuses: individual leadership, organizational leadership, and leadership in the field of adult and continuing education. Colleagues selected to participate will: Interact with leadership experts; Communicate with their peers via a computer network; Enjoy three visits to the Georgia Center, a comprehensive university-based residential adult learning center; Study, think and reflect with other future leaders; Contract for a self-designed learning project in the Personal Adult Learning Laboratory; Learn innovative ways to conceptualize and practice leadership. Combining developmental assignments, three intense on-site focuses, and alumni activities provides fertile ground for leadership cultivation.

The steering committee of the Institute will select fifty participants from a national pool of nominations contingent upon recognizable leadership potential representing the entire field including educators from continuing higher education, business, industry, government, and professional associations. Emerging leaders are defined as individuals with demonstrated leadership capacity committed to cultivating their own leadership potential and a sense of responsibility for a successful future.

LEARNING GOALS AND OBJECTIVES: Following is a list of the broad learning goals and objectives for the Institute based on the discussions of the Steering Committee to be used to help speakers focus their presentations. Objectives will become more specific and extensive after deliberation with speakers and presenters.

FOCUS I The Individual as Leader July 12-16, 1989
This focus is designed to:
- Equip participants with an orientation to leadership development theory and research;
- Have participants design an operational framework for recognizing and applying their own strengths as a leader;
- Provide participants the opportunity to experience leadership and teamwork through an Outdoor Executive Adventure.

Participant Introductions
Goal: To become familiar with one another's names, place of employment, and position held.

Objectives: To learn the names of all of the participants; To link names with faces, places of employment, positions held, and areas of special interest.

338

<u>Special Features:</u> Some type of activity will be planned and conducted to facilitate the participants getting to know one another, e.g., a booklet with pictures and bio sketches of each participant distributed prior to the start of the program.

Orientation
<u>Goal:</u> To give the participants an overview of the entire National Leadership Institute in Adult & Continuing Education.

<u>Objectives:</u> Share the vision that led to the development of the Institute, its philosophy and the schedule, logistics, and requirements of the program.

What Do the "Experts" Say? An in-depth overview of research on leadership
<u>Goal:</u> To familiarize the participants with relevant theories and research in the field of leadership development.

<u>Objectives:</u> Overview of research on leadership; discussion of outstanding theories on leadership development; relationship of research and theory to their own frame of reference.

Executive Adventure
<u>Goal:</u> To provide an outdoor based experiential teambuilding experience.

<u>Objectives:</u> To develop closer class ties and relationships; improve communications among participants; stimulate cooperation among participants; develop an awareness of how their individual style affects others.

The Individual as an Innovative Leader
<u>Goal:</u> Inspire participants (keynote address) to be all that they can be as leaders.

<u>Objectives:</u> Discuss: What it means to be an innovative leader in today's world; the importance of self-renewal for leaders; individuality and leadership; practical ideas on being innovative leaders.

Leadership Strategies for the Emerging Leader
<u>Goal:</u> To provide strategies for implementing ideas generated by the keynote speaker.

<u>Objective:</u> Provide: activities to encourage participants to internalize what they heard from the keynote speaker; opportunities in small group setting to apply keynote remarks on leadership to personal, organizational, and community life.

Exploring Your Own Philosophy and Style as a Leader
<u>Goal:</u> To recognize one's philosophies of leadership and discover one's leadership style.

<u>Objectives:</u> Develop an activity that will allow participants to share leadership philosophies with one another; use some type of leadership style inventory to provide participants with accurate feedback on their leadership styles.

Vision and Individual Leadership: Can one person really make a difference?
Goal: To stress the importance of individual vision in leadership.

Objectives: Discuss what it means to be visionary; share one's own experiences as an individual and a leader; discuss holistic leadership.

Being an Ethical Leader
Goal: To discuss the importance of ethics in leadership.

Objectives: Define ethics; discuss what it means to be an ethical leader; identify an individual sense of professional ethics in the field of Adult and Continuing Education.

Becoming a Reflective Practitioner
Goal: To provide the framework to make explicit the knowledge that is imbedded in participants' practice.

Objectives: Define reflection-in-action; discuss importance of reflection-in-action for leaders; provide participants with the opportunity to reflect on their knowledge as practitioners; integrate the concepts of leadership, ethics, and responsible professional practice; develop from this integration an individual theory-in-action.

Transition to Organizational Leadership
Goal: To prepare the participants to begin to focus on being leaders in their organizations.

Objectives: Discuss the difference between individual and organizational leadership; provide some background on assessing and analyzing organizations; discuss transition assignments.

FOCUS II - Organizational Leadership November 7-10, 1989

This focus is designed to:
- Give participants a deeper understanding of the concepts and applications of organizational leadership.
- Provide participants with an understanding of managing organizational culture and change.
- Develop within participants the ability to think and manage strategically in organizations.

Assessing, Analyzing and Building Organizational Culture
Goal: To provide participants with the skills necessary to assess, analyze and develop organizational cultures.

Objectives: Review transition assignments; develop an activity that will allow participants to use assessment and analysis skills; discuss organizational culture and the impact that it has on organizations.

Dealing with Diversity and Change in Organizations
Goal: To expose participants to information regarding diversity and change in organizations.

Objectives: Discuss importance of diversity in organizations; discuss impact of change in organizations and how leaders can be effective change agents; provide an activity to encourage participants to apply concepts of diversity and change.

Strategic Planning
Goal: To provide a teleconference on strategic planning in organizations.

Objectives: (Georgia Center) Explain the teleconference process; allow time for questions from participants.

Objectives: (Dr. Simerly) Discuss steps to strategic planning; discuss implications of strategic planning; questions and answers.

Operationalizing Strategic Planning
Goal: To provide participants with a framework and example of implementing strategic planning.

Objectives: Discuss impact of strategic planning at the Georgia Center; discuss implications for other organizations; provide an exercise or activity that will encourage participants to begin to apply the strategic planning model to their own organizations.

Empowerment and Power in Organizations
Goal: To give participants a clear understanding of the importance of power and empowerment in organizations.

Objectives: Review information on power and empowerment; provide an activity that will allow participants to recognize the difference between the responsible use of power and empowering others (including client groups, staff, etc.); have participants develop a plan of action for their own organizations.

Critical Issues Facing Adult and Continuing Educators
Goal: To highlight for participants some of the primary issues that they, as leaders in the field, will be dealing with.

Objectives: Briefly discuss the main issues that have surfaced in the recent past; discuss primary problems that seem to be looming in the future; discuss the implications for the leaders of the future.

Transition to Leadership in the Field of Adult and Continuing Education
Goal: To encourage participants to think of themselves as leaders in the field and to prepare them for the transition assignments.

<u>Objectives:</u>   Develop from the discussion of "critical issues" a personal agenda for influencing the field of professional practice in adult and continuing education;   discuss consequences of exerting leadership and strategic management;   prepare participants for writing "I've Been Thinking" pieces.

FOCUS III - Leadership in the Field of Adult & Continuing Education
February 8-11, 1990

This focus is designed to:
  · Inspire participants to develop and use critical thinking skills in their practice.
  · Allow participants to build and strengthen the bridge between theory and practice.
  · Have participants create a vision for the future of the field of adult and continuing education.

What Does it Mean to be a Leader in Our Field?
<u>Goal:</u> To process the transition assignments that the participants completed and to tie them into the topics to be covered in Focus III.

<u>Objectives:</u> Share and discuss "I've Been Thinking" pieces; develop a strategy to exert your influence to bring about the change mentioned in your transition activity; tie discussion into the issues to be discussed the next day.

Leadership: A Futurist's Perspective
<u>Goal:</u> An overview of future trends to expect in our field.

<u>Objectives:</u> Discuss the trends of the future; discuss the impact of these trends on the future leaders; give recommendations for preparing to deal effectively with these issues.

Leading the Way: The Future of Adult and Continuing Education
<u>Goal:</u> To emphasize for participants the need in the field for strong leaders and provide them with practical ideas for using their leadership abilities.

<u>Objectives:</u> Discuss the critical need in the field for leadership; discuss what it means to be a leader in our field today and what will be required in the future; give ideas about implementing leadership skills in the field; consider ways in which higher education, business and industry, and professional associations might work cooperatively to enhance the profession.

The Scope of Our Field: The Problems and The Benefits
<u>Goal:</u> To provide an interactive panel that represents the scope of our field in order to discuss both the problems and benefits raised by its breadth and depth.

<u>Objectives:</u> Have each panel member address specific questions posed by the moderator based on the problems and benefits from their own perspective; discuss the implications of these problems and benefits for the future of our field; allow time for questions and

answers.

Legal Concerns Facing Adult and Continuing Educators
Goal: To expose participants to the legal implications of their practice and possible concerns for the future leaders in our field.

Objectives: Discuss primary legal issues; discuss the possible issues facing leaders in the near future; give suggestions for dealing with these issues proactively.

Strengthening the Bridge Between Theory and Practice
Goal: To discuss the importance of research providing a bridge between theory and practice.

Objectives: Discuss the strengths of good research, the implications of research for effective practice, the importance of practitioners being involved in research.

Research Issues and Interest
Goal: To allow participants some time to meet with faculty in small groups to discuss research currently being conducted in the field of adult and continuing education and explore with participants their own research interests.

Objectives: Provide a small group setting that allows for casual dialogue between participants and faculty; discuss current and future research interests.

Integrating Leadership and Change: A commitment to self, others, and the field
Goal: To provide participants with a model of leadership that allows them to prepare for change and to continue to develop as leaders.

Objectives: Discuss change and the implications for leaders; provide activities that will encourage participants to develop a comprehensive plan of leadership action; review what participants have learned from the Institute; provide opportunity for them to plan for thorough implementation of new learnings; develop with participants plans for their continued growth and development.

Closing
Goal: To provide closure for the participants of the Institute.

Objectives: Evaluate the Institute; assess the impact of the Institute on participants; have participants develop appropriate plans for themselves as alumni.

University of Michigan
School of Business Administration
Executive Education Center, Ann Arbor, MI 48109-1234

Ann Walton
Dir., Executive Education
313/763-6402

Leadership Programs offered by Michigan Business School's Organizational Behavior and Human Resource Management Faculty

---

Advanced Human Resource Executive Program

A two-week program designed to meet the needs of senior-level executives with organization-wide responsibility for human resource management--individuals who are increasingly called upon to play a leadership role in the strategic management of their organizations.

The program aims to help senior human resource executives develop their transformational leadership roles. It will provide state-of-the-art concepts and technologies in strategy formulation and implementation--with emphasis on the role of selection, reward, appraisal, and development systems--to drive strategic change and overall organization performance.

Schedule:
#A901 April 22-27, 1990 (Week I)
Clinic: June 19, 1990
#A903 October 14-19, 1990 (Week II)
Program Fee: $7,000 includes tuition, books and instructional materials, accommodations and meals. For information: Ron Bendersky - 313/763-3154.

Management of Managers

OBJECTIVE: To give the manager of other managers a sound foundation of interpersonal, administrative and conceptual skills for a positive impact on the organization and its people. Skills that increase productivity in dealing with all levels of management are explored.

UNIQUE FEATURES: The Management of Managers program is structured to develop a well-rounded approach to management by exploring a full range of skills used by successful managers. An integral part of the course includes an individual survey completed by each participant and managers with whom they work. The feedback provided by the survey is vital to the understanding of each individual manager's performance. To complete the survey analysis, program registrations must be received 5 weeks prior to the start of the course.

WHO SHOULD ATTEND: Senior mid-level managers whose success depends upon working with managers or a professional staff. This seminar is most beneficial for mid-level managers with more than eight years of management experience where skills in working with people are critical.

INTRODUCTION: The most successful companies in today's business world are those that believe people are of significant importance--both within the organization and within the marketplace. The Management of Managers program, offered since 1967, focuses on "people related skills." By bringing together an experienced management faculty and selected executives representing a diversity of experiences and knowledge, the program generates an atmosphere for new managerial perspectives and the exchange of ideas. The format encompasses interactive lectures, group discussions, self-evaluation instruments, and case studies.

OUTLINE:
Managing Human Resources (Clan): Building the management team; The development of groups; The importance of providing feedback.

Managing in a Competitive Environment (Market): Bargaining, negotiating, and managing conflict; Using power and influence; Establishing a motivational climate.

Managing Organizational Process (Hierarchy): Human resources as a competitive advantage; Appraising and improving performance; Acculturating employees and developing subordinates.

Managing Innovation and Transformation (Adhocracy): Creative problem solving; Managing the change process; Setting the entrepreneurial climate.

Action Planning: Self-assessment and feedback from subordinates; Identifying key organizational and managerial strengths; Implementing action plans.

BENEFITS OF ATTENDANCE: Build upon managerial strengths by increasing self-awareness; Enhance management career and potential for promotion; Improve ability to work effectively with all levels of managers and personality types; Develop staff into a dynamic management team; Establish a motivational climate that increases productivity; Discover how to utilize human resources as a competitive advantage; Manage creatively in a dynamic environment; Expand entrepreneurial thinking; Develop management style that gets results--even with "difficult-to-manage" staff members; Create action plans for image enhancement and become the best manager you can be; Gain insight into your perception as a manager; Increase your negotiating skills; Change win/lose situations into win/win; Handle conflict promptly; Gain a perception of your power bases.

Faculty Director: Kim Cameron, Associate Professor of Organizational Behavior and Human Resource Management, The Michigan Business School, The University of Michigan

Fee: $3,250 includes tuition, living accommodations, meals, instructional materials. For information: Lucy Chin, Assoc. Director - 313/763-4395.

Management II: A Mid-Management Development Program

OBJECTIVE: To sharpen the ability of mid-level managers to manage themselves and their subordinates more effectively by developing their skills in self-assessment, decision making, communication, creative thinking, problem solving, and motivation.

WHO SHOULD ATTEND: Mid-level managers who are responsible for planning and directing daily operations of an organizational unit. Participants are managers with a range of 2 to 8 years of management experience.

INTRODUCTION: The Management II program, offered since 1974, centers on developing a manager's "people skills" both in self and in subordinates. Starting with an introspective examination of the manager's individual style, the program moves to the group process and the manager's role in leading a productive organization. Under the professional direction of experienced seminar leaders, the program serves as a forum for an active interchange of ideas and a sharing of experiences among the participants. The format consists of interactive lectures, self-evaluation instruments, team exercises, and case studies.

UNIQUE FEATURES: What qualities does an effective leader possess? Which of these qualities do you have? To discover the answer, each participant completes a self-evaluation instrument that provides insight into their individual leadership style. Private consulting sessions with the program's faculty are then available on an individual basis to provide participants specific answers and recommendations to their unique situations.

OUTLINE:
Leadership and Management Styles: The mismanagement of organizations; Your management style and its impact; Characteristics of effective leaders.

The Power of Working Together: Group process and team productivity; Key elements of excellence in leadership: Establishing priorities, Setting objectives, Organization and strategies.

Interpersonal Communications: Understanding barriers to communication; Identifying the traits of excellent communicators; Opening lines of communication.

Creative Thinking and Problem Solving: Stimulating the thinking process; Overcoming self-imposed barriers; Mental imaging to discover untapped potential.

Delegating For Results: Identifying common delegation barriers; Developing a delegation system; Building in follow-up methods that work.

Setting the Motivational Climate: Factors affecting employee motivation; Identifying motivational problems; Techniques for motivating employees.

BENEFITS OF ATTENDANCE: Gain insight into your individual management style. Enhance your capabilities for a more influential role in your organization; Sharpen your communication skills and broaden your understanding of changing employment relationships; Identify the "turn-ons" and "turn-offs" of motivation: What causes people to feel satisfied or dissatisfied with their work?; Open your mind to fresh solutions for stale problems. This program is an opportunity for you to step back and review your approach to management; Discover what is and isn't important to those people that you manage. For example, individuals that are perceived as effective managers by others share a common personality trait; Improve your ability to plan and organize in order to achieve strategic goals, and to avoid being consumed by one crisis after another. Use your time more efficiently; Discover which tasks should and should not be delegated; Develop the ability to communicate your ideas clearly and effectively; Enhance your management career and your potential for promotion; Establish a productive, motivational climate by setting realistic goals, being supportive, and using the one technique that truly gets things accomplished: listening; Interact and gain insight with other management professionals from around the country.

Fee: $2,950 includes tuition, living accommodations, meals, books and instructional materials. For information: Lucy Chin - 313/763-4395.

The Michigan Leadership Program (Program under development)

The core objective of The Michigan Leadership Program is to facilitate the development of leadership among senior executives and their employees. This program will enable senior executives to clarify and re-define their own leadership perspective, to articulate a leadership vision for their organization, and to develop a leadership mindset. To this end, the course will target the characteristics of successful leadership, the latest research on the impact of leadership on organizations, and the attributes of an effective vision statement, rather than focusing on the traditional general management functions.

Designed for senior executives in major national and international organizations, this week-long program will be organized in the following way: One month before the program, an in-depth qualitative analysis of both the individual and the relevant organizational unit will be conducted. Meaningful data feedback focused on individual and organizational strengths and weaknesses, values and cultures, challenges and opportunities, will be provided during the program.

This course includes the presentation of leadership theories and roles, explores underlying values, is faculty-intensive, provides a forum for the development and interchange of leadership concepts, is geared to the individual participant's unique situation, and addresses career issues and organizational challenges.

The core faculty will consist of five Michigan faculty members: Kim Cameron, Bob Quinn, Noel Tichy, Dick Daft, and Karl Weick who will interact intensely with each other and the participants throughout the course. The program will contain perspectives from a variety of disciplines including cognitive psychology, organizational behavior, philosophy, communications, social psychology, sociology, political science, and human resource management. For information: Lucy Chin - 313/763-4395.

University of Virginia
Center for Public Service
2015 Ivy Road, Charlottesville, VA 22903-1795

Linda C. Winner
804/924-3396

Senior Executive Institute

The Senior Executive Institute (SEI) is an annual, two week intensive training program designed for senior local government executives and managers of business and nonprofit organizations who work with local governments. The fee is $2100.

The curriculum of SEI emphasizes four main areas: political and economic environment; behavior within organizations; the manager as leader; applied leadership skills.

Topics include executive health, creativity, understanding human behavior within organizations, organizational development models, motivation, ethics, conflict management, leadership and team development, and the political environment.

There is a special emphasis on small learning teams. SEI encourages health and physical fitness by offering an optional exercise program and a comprehensive fitness evaluation. Alumni return each year for two days of courses and camaraderie.

Section D
PROGRAMS FOR COMMUNITY LEADERSHIP

In these programs the central focus is improving the lot of those who live in a given area. Whether the programs are intended for rural revitalization or urban rejuvenation, whether the population is large or small, whether the cultural life is sophisticated or impoverished, the worthiness of careful and sensitive planning is invaluable. In a democratic society, the cultural, economic, and social differences within a community make all problems more complex. The selection and training of leaders for a community and the setting of goals and priorities to improve the quality of life for those who live there is neither simple nor straightforward. Also, communities differ so greatly one from the other that models that are effective in one place do not apply in another. Some issues that must be grappled with are similar in both rural and urban areas while others differ because of location or demographic factors. It appears that the best way to proceed is to study the needs, divide the issues and problems into components that can be handled, apply methods that have worked elsewhere, and proceed to improve conditions and fulfill explicit needs without losing sight of the overall vision.

Examples or brief accounts of plans and programs for tackling the problems of community leadership include: courses designed to effect the social change process for leaders and followers; ways of assisting and developing volunteers, paid employees and elected officials; workshops and seminars for clarifying issues and establishing operational methods for those who have assumed responsibility of leadership and those who wish to do so; evaluation of the impact of experiments and trials in communities; a description of efforts to form a network to improve management of state and local government; and the way in which a university and a community can interact. In all instances dedication and commitment to betterment is evident, and the many facets of leadership selection and development are required.

PROGRAMS FOR COMMUNITY LEADERSHIP

TABLE OF CONTENTS

Carnegie-Mellon University
School of Urban and Public Affairs
Pittsburgh, PA 15213

Donald C. Stone
Director
412/268-2179

Coalition to Improve Management in State and Local Government

---

MISSION: To consider ways of overcoming the deterioration in and respect for government and the public service. Denigration of the civil servants and citizen apathy, reflected in the low percentage of citizens who vote, are contributing factors. Other factors are the declining responsibility of political parties, failure of the Congress and the President to work constructively, impairment of federal administration by several layers of short-term political appointees, and publicized improprieties. The result has been declining confidence in democratic, responsible, and effective government, notably at the national level.

OBJECTIVES, ORGANIZATION, PROGRAM: The purpose of the Coalition is to help states, counties, and cities to develop the executive capability to cope simultaneously with rapid economic and social change, reduced federal grant money, and increased service demands.

The states and their constituent counties and cities differ widely in their executive and managerial competencies. All need specially tailored programs to improve administration, productivity, quality of services, and intergovernmental and intersector cooperation.

Coalition strategy. The Coalition has developed a seven-point strategy based on successful efforts of the best administered governments. High priority is placed on intergovernmental and intersector cooperation since all three levels of government and the nonprofit and business sectors have an important role in most functions.

1. Initiate or strengthen and give continuous visibility to a program to achieve excellence in all aspects of administration, e.g., management, organization, productivity and quality of services, at least cost. Build a climate that supports creativity and risk taking.
2. Appoint a highly qualified management and productivity director with appropriate staff to help plan and implement such a program; utilize borrowed personnel, task groups, loaned executives, consultants, and other competent sources of expertise.
3. Appoint executives with leadership and managerial talents to head departments, agencies, and public authorities and charge them with initiating and implementing management improvement programs within their organizations. They are the key to better operations at lower cost.
4. Enlist the executive's policy and administrative staff to work as a team with the management improvement staff and the line departments in carrying out government-wide projects.
5. Foster leadership and management which involves supervisors and employees (including unions) in improving administration and operations, and give credit to those who propose and implement better methods.
6. Develop policies and processes to strengthen state and local intergovernmental cooperation and make more effective use of nonprofit organizations and private enterprise in providing and paying for public facilities and services.
7. Utilize various media to highlight the goals and accomplishments of an aggressive

management improvement program and to strengthen public confidence in government.

Any government that gives these interrelated initiatives high priority will develop the capacity to deal with almost any problem.

Implementation. The Coalition in association with its cooperating organizations:
1. Publishes management guides for states, counties, and cities on optional ways to implement the seven-point strategy;
2. Fosters use of guides; provides information on successful application; stockpiles materials; keeps officials informed through communications and direct contact;
3. Organizes and participates in conferences, workshops, and executive development programs on applying Coalition strategy and improving performance;
4. Provides on-site consultation with city, county, and state governments on ways to strengthen executive management and apply strategy to specific situations;
5. Develops networks for disseminating materials and promoting interchange.

Management guides. The following have been issued or scheduled:
1. The Governor's Management Improvement Program (January 1986);
2. Planning the State's Administrative Management in Gubernatorial Transitions (November 1986);
3. The County Executive's Management and Productivity Program (March 1987);
4. Similar guides for mayors and city administrators;
5. Planning transitions of mayors and county executives;
6. Increasing local government capabilities for intergovernmental cooperation;
7. A guide for states on organizing state-local and interstate cooperation;
8. Orchestrating the governor's executive policy and management team and processes;
9. Cooperation among the governmental, nonprofit, business, and civic sectors in planning, monitoring, and paying for human services;
10. State organization for economic development which involves local governments as well as the business and voluntary sectors as partners;
11. Improving organization and management of public authorities and enterprises.

Administration. The support services provided by Carnegie-Mellon University and the Director's venue as Distinguished Public Service Professor led to an arrangement for the Coalition to be headquartered in the School of Urban and Public Affairs. Policies, management guides, and other program elements are worked out with Coalition cooperating organizations with many inputs by state and local officials. Funds are provided by individuals and foundations. Program costs are small since many services are voluntary.

Cooperating Organizations:

Academy for State and Local Government
Advisory Commission on Intergovernmental Relations
American Society for Public Administration
National Civic League

Council of State Community Affairs
Council of State Governments
Council of State Policy and Planning Agencies
Government Finance Officers Association
International City Management Association
International Personnel Management Association
National Academy of Public Administration
National Association of Counties
National Association of Regional Councils
National Association of Schools of Public Affairs and Administration
National Association of State Budget Officers
National Conference of State Legislatures
National Governors' Association
National League of Cities
Office of Management and Budget, Executive Office of the President
U. S. Conference of Mayors
U. S. General Accounting Office

Institute for Conservation Leadership
1400 Sixteenth St., N.W., Washington, DC 20036-2266

Dianne Russell
Ass't. Director
202/797-6656

Leadership Workshops for the Conservation/Environment Community

---

The Institute is a non-profit joint effort of the conservation and environmental community. We provide training, consulting services and follow-up so that local leaders can answer these questions:

- What is leadership? Where do leaders come from and how can they be developed?
- What keeps a conservation organization healthy, growing and effective?
- How do I plan my group's future and build a stronger organization for the long haul?

PROGRAM SUMMARY

GOAL: Through training and research, to increase the number and effectiveness of volunteer conservation leaders and their organizations.

OBJECTIVES: To organize and conduct training for individual volunteers to develop and increase their leadership skills and abilities; To organize and conduct conferences with governing boards of conservation groups to improve their organization's ability to attract, utilize and develop additional voluntary leadership; To organize state networks of conservation organizations (and their leaders) toward effective cooperation on issues of common concern; To conduct evaluation and publish Institute findings as to effective methods of volunteer training and leadership development.

PROGRAMS:

Individual Training - Six day, small group training sessions to emphasize communication, facilitation and skill development as well as alternative learning and operational styles.

Board Training - Organizational self-assessments of the existing "habitat" for leadership development, problem identification and objective setting to establish improvement.

Network Development - Statewide conferences of existing leaders facilitated by the Institute as an outside agency to develop common areas for action and to increase communication and cooperation among all elements of the conservation community.

Custom Services - Training sessions designed to meet specific needs of participating organizations including long-range planning, constituency development, citizen participation and issue prioritization.

Research and Evaluation - Using pre-session and post-session data, computerized for analysis, to build a base which will allow informed modification of Institute programs as well as conclusions as to effectiveness of varied training methods.

PROCESS: By developing a corps of trained facilitators across the country available on weekends for part time work it will be possible to service organizations and states with training programs at a fraction of the cost for professional consultants. Institute staff will be minimized, thus allowing participating national organizations to fund the administrative costs of the Institute on a shared basis. Organizations receiving service will be expected to fund the actual cost of the trainer and travel (not expected to exceed $600) in order to assure their commitment to the process. Individuals receiving training will similarly be expected to cover the actual costs of their subsistence, travel and training albeit it is expected that most will be sponsored, to some degree, by their organization. The Institute is seeking, and will assist local organizations in seeking, grants to subsidize costs for all training programs. Eventually the Institute expects to develop an ability to provide these programs to organizations outside the USA. The possibility also exists for additional service to provide training and facilitation for citizen education and mobilization on issues of importance to the participating organizations. Nonparticipating organizations will be able to utilize the Institute at rates which will allow recovery of administrative costs as well as overhead. These services will allow minimization of the dues paid by the participating organizations.

Individual Training Summary

GOAL: To train individual volunteer leaders in subjects and skills which will develop and increase their leadership capabilities on behalf of conservation. In addition, the training will encourage these leaders to assist and mentor others.

OBJECTIVES: To observe, understand and manage relationships when working with other people, taking into account different individual styles and personalities; To improve communication skills, listening and speaking, particularly while training others; To instill into practice the six principles of successful volunteer organizations; To practice giving and receiving evaluation; To introduce planning skills applicable to educational goals, financial/organizational development and political action programs; To equip leaders with the skills to manage and integrate organizational and volunteer development goals into all aspects of their group's program.

PROCESS: A six day, Sunday through Saturday, residential training session in the Washington, DC area will permit the intensive training and practice necessary to reach the objectives. Fifteen experienced leaders nominated by participating organizations will be invited to participate in each session.

Using a combination of guided seminars, group discussion and practical exercises, the participants will be exposed to an integrated curriculum which will use, to the maximum extent possible, their own experiences as the teaching vehicles. Simultaneously, they will be expected to practice and improve their abilities to recognize and respond to varying personality styles.

Extensive questionnaire data will be collected both prior to and after the session for evaluation purposes. Attendees will be asked to identify achievable personal objectives for applying learned principles and sharing this training with others afterwards. The Institute will follow up with these individuals for evaluation purposes as well as to reinforce the training.

ADMINISTRATION: A nomination period will be announced approximately four months ahead of the scheduled session. Based on the response, spaces will be assigned as equitably as possible. A short waiting list will be maintained with preference given for the following session. Nominating organizations are requested to assure the availability of their nominees for the training.

Food, lodging and transportation will be the responsibility of the individual, or their sponsoring organization. If scholarship funds can be found they will be available on application and will be used to assist transportation. The Institute will make every effort to keep participant costs minimized by its choice of facility.

Training will be coordinated and managed by Institute staff with extensive use of staff from participating organizations.

GENERAL CONSIDERATIONS: The point of the training is to multiply the number and quality of capable leaders within the community. Training materials developed by the Institute will be available to back up the graduates.

The key parameter for candidate selection will be the prospect of each individual playing a catalytic role in developing future leaders for conservation. These experienced leaders will be able to directly apply the learning from the training session to organizational work at hand.

Board Conference Summary

GOAL: To improve organizational ability to attract, utilize and develop additional voluntary leadership.

OBJECTIVES: To communicate the six principles of successful voluntary organizations to the members of the organization's Board of Directors; To lead the Board of Directors in an honest assessment of their organization's performance and observance of these principles; To assist in the establishment of specific objectives to increase performance and institutionalize the principles; To follow up on performance.

PROCESS: This twelve hour, weekend conference has been the key ingredient in the National Wildlife Federation's Leadership Development Program over the last nine years. It has demonstrated its ability to spark organizational improvement along with far higher levels of voluntary participation. Using the decision-making body (unless over 20 people) the conference leader first introduces each principle and then invites the participants to look critically at their organization's current activity. When a consensus is reached, the group moves on to successive principles. On Sunday, the problem statements from Saturday are reviewed, prioritized, and solutions are sought that individuals will take responsibility to see are implemented. These typically range from preparing proposals for bylaws changes to instituting a committee system. The focus is on defining specific objectives for achievement, due dates and clear, volunteered responsibility.

At best, the conference ends at lunch on Sunday with every participant committed to not only his or her specific obligations, but to the overall improvement of the entire organization's ability to attract, empower and utilize volunteers.

ADMINISTRATION: Board conferences will be scheduled on a first come, first served basis. Three months of advance time is recommended. Close to full attendance by the Board is highly desirable if the conference is to bear significant fruit. These conferences will normally be led by a contract trainer from the Institute who resides close to the conference site. The trainer will normally brief the organization's president on Friday evening. A retreat setting is highly desirable. The full weekend (Saturday AM to early Sunday PM) will be necessary (concurrent Board meetings are discouraged). The receiving organization will be responsible for making all site arrangements as well as furnishing the Institute, within 30 days of the conference, a mailing list of the invited participants and directions to the site. Appropriate group recreation on Saturday night is recommended. Costs for the conference will include travel and per diem for the trainer as well as a $400 consultant fee. For nonparticipating organizations an additional administration fee will be necessary. The Institute expects to have available a list of local foundations and a generic grant application to help defray these costs.

GENERAL CONSIDERATIONS: Any voluntary organization which is committed to improving its ability to draw and develop additional volunteer resources can benefit from this conference. Because its format is open, different aspects can be emphasized to match the need of the receiving organization. The key emphasis of the conference is that the trainer helps the participants to see where their problems lie and to develop their own solutions. This assures individual ownership, the key to performance.

Network Conference Summary

GOAL: To organize state networks of conservation organizations (and their leaders) toward effective cooperation on issues of common concern.

OBJECTIVES: To identify a set of specific issues within the state towards which all attending organizations can agree to take common and concerted action; To begin action planning towards success on these issues; To significantly increase the level of communication between existing conservation leaders and their organizations within the state and establish an informal network for more systematic communication.

PROCESS: The invitation list should include all the conservation groups within the state who are actively involved in conservation issues, local, regional and state-wide. The invitees will be advised that they are invited as leaders of their organizations (and encouraged to bring others) but that no binding commitments will be made at the conference. Using pre-conference questionnaires the attendees will be presented a draft ranking of the group's perception of issues within the state. Through facilitated discussions, these will be evaluated, ranked, and by consensus, decisions made as to which can be worked on together, and how. Additionally, a high level of social interaction will be organized to assure that the participants have adequate time and opportunity to interact with those with whom they are unfamiliar. Using a two day, weekend format (with optional Friday night), Saturday's discussion will focus on issue selection, with Sunday morning devoted to action planning on each issue. Action agendas will be shared with the whole group and subsequently distributed by the Institute.

ADMINISTRATION: The host organization will be responsible for furnishing the Institute with the list of invitees as well as making the arrangements (but not paying the costs) for housing and food. Attendees will be charged their pro rata share of these as well as other incidental costs on site. Tracking these expenses and conducting registration will be the host's responsibility. An accounting of these charges will be a useful handout for the registrants. The site should be, to the maximum degree possible, one which allows costs to participants to be minimized. An attractive retreat location will be helpful. The Institute will mail invitations and questionnaires as well as tabulating responses, planning and conducting the meeting. Post-conference evaluations will be conducted by the Institute but post-conference action will be the responsibility of the participants and their organizations. While the intent is to conduct similar conferences in each state to foster evaluation, local conditions may necessitate some modification. This should be discussed by Institute and the host organization.

GENERAL CONSIDERATIONS: While organizing the administrative arrangements is not a major job, hopefully the host organization will be able to devote sufficient skilled help to it. In large part, the host organization can exercise a significant leadership role both in, and as a result of, the conference. The quality of the preparation will tell the participants a great deal about the quality of the host organization.

Customized Services Summary

GOAL: To provide leadership development and grassroots educational services to participating organizations as may respond to their needs.

OBJECTIVES: For participating organizations, to train at the local level on issues and development of constituencies; To provide training and facilitation in advanced aspects of using volunteers such as: committee development, local organization and issue prioritization; To design and facilitate long-range planning for local, regional and state conservation organization; To design volunteer training programs for conservation organizations.

PROCESS: Voter education, constituency development, citizen participation and other outreach aspects of foundation and governmental grants pose staffing problems to many conservation organizations. Having a joint training institution will permit much of this work to be accomplished by skilled trainers at minimal cost and maximum effectiveness. Additionally, no long-term staffing commitments need to be made. Many local and state organizations are well developed and vital but need to take new initiatives towards further development. The Institute staff has experience with this and other developmental conferences. The use of an independent facilitator can often spur progress impossible through existing leadership. Particularly for the well developed voluntary organization, the long-range planning process must be integrated into regular operations. An impartial consulting capability to assist this is available through the Institute. Atypical organizations, or those with specific problems, may need custom designed approaches to exploit their unique opportunities. The Institute staff, together with available contract trainers, will design and conduct conference formats and outcomes to fit specific situations.

ADMINISTRATION: Participating organizations are invited to discuss unique training opportunities or special problem situations with the Institute staff. As with Board of Directors conferences, these will be available at cost. Nonparticipating organizations are similarly invited for consultation. Fees charged will include administrative surcharges to allow the Institute to recover full costs.

GENERAL CONSIDERATIONS: The most useful step in planning special events of these kinds will be for the sponsoring organization to identify, as specifically as possible, the objectives they wish to be achieved. This will form the basis for evaluation and allow the Institute staff to focus on the outcome sought. Evaluation results will be made available to the sponsoring organization.

The Project for Executive Excellence

Leadership for the 90s is co-sponsored by The Mershon Center and The Jefferson Center for Learning and the Arts and funded by the Columbus Foundation.

The Mershon Center is The Ohio State University's center for research and education on national security and public policy with an interest in understanding the skills involved in being an effective public leader. The Jefferson Center for Learning and the Arts (JCLA) is a campus of not-for-profit organizations in the arts, education and human services located in downtown Columbus; the JCLA member organizations are housed in late 19th century buildings that together comprise the Jefferson Neighborhood Historic District.

Seminar leaders of the project are: Peg Hermann, a research scientist at The Mershon Center and associate professor of political science at The Ohio State University. Her research, writing and teaching focus on the psychological and political dimensions of leadership. She consults regularly with community and government groups on topics related to leadership development; and Donn F. Vickers, the executive director of The Jefferson Center for Learning and the Arts and organizing director of The Thurber House. His consulting work is in organizational planning and staff development with a focus in higher education, the arts, human services and religion.

Over 600 professionals serve as chief executive officers in the not-for-profit organizations of metropolitan Columbus. In the arts, education, health, human services, mental health and community organizations these executives more than anyone else determine the health of this richly diverse institutional sector that is so crucial to the character and quality of life of the city. Leadership for the 90s is designed for these top executives. It is focused on professional development and well being intended to promote professional stature and competence equal to the vital role not-for-profit organizations play in this community.

New Executives: Establishing Leadership Effectiveness

You're "new" if you've been in your present job two years or less. Whatever your age, your present organization honeymoon has not fully given way to habit and relationships have yet to become routinized. It's a good time to work on your leadership behaviors, styles and competencies. The seminars will focus on ways of assessing the culture of your organizations, identifying a central focus for your own professional activity, establishing time and work patterns appropriate to your setting, creating a positive working relationship with your board and dealing with issues related to inherited staff. Other leadership questions that the participants identify as important to them will receive attention. Five one-half day sessions 12:15 - 4:00, lunch provided. Registration 15. Opportunities for private consultation available. Fee, $300.00.

Mid-Career Executives: Renewing Leadership Effectiveness

You are "mid-career" if you have been working in a top leadership position for six years or more. You may be toward the end of your first position, well into your second or what might be your last before retirement. In any case, you have developed patterns of leadership and established some ways of running an organization. More importantly, you now are open to looking freshly at your usual way of conducting business. These consultations will focus on assessment, renewal and change for leaders: evaluating your own leadership style and ability, exploring your next job (maybe your next career) and developing ways for you to make changes in your relationship to your board, in the way you spend your professional time, in the positioning of your organization in the community, in the key programs and functions of your agency, in the use of full or part-time staff and volunteers. Additional change-related issues will be addressed as identified by the group. Five one-half day sessions 12:15 - 4:00, lunch provided (spaced throughout year). Registration 15. Opportunities for individual discussion available. Fee, $300.

Executive Roundtable: Confronting the Leadership Issues of the 90s

Twelve not-for-profit executives gather with a similar number of private sector CEOs for conversation with well-known national figures on leadership issues key to the decade of the 90s. Format will include presentation and opportunity for group discussion. First guest will be Richard Lyman, formerly President of Stanford University, head of the Rockefeller Foundation, and president of the board of the Independent Sector. This roundtable series is designed to promote lively interchange between for-profit and not-for-profit chief executives. From 12:00 until 2:00 with lunch provided. The initial meeting is February 8; additional sessions to be scheduled in May and September. Registration 24. Because of the rare opportunity for not-for-profit and for-profit CEOs to meet as intellectual colleagues, this series is by invitation only. Participants are asked to apply. Final selections are made to ensure a diverse representation of sectors, race, gender and age. Early registrants have priority. Fee, $320.

National Center for Nonprofit Boards
Ste. 340, 1225 19th St., N.W. Washington, DC 20036

Larry H. Slesinger
Deputy Director
202/452-6262

MISSION: The purpose of the National Center for Nonprofit Boards (NCNB) is to improve the effectiveness of nonprofit organizations by strengthening their boards of directors.

ORIGIN: The National Center for Nonprofit Boards, which began operations in 1988, was formed by Independent Sector (IS), a nonprofit coalition of 650 corporations, foundations, and private voluntary organizations concerned with philanthropy and voluntary action, and by the Association of Governing Boards of Universities and Colleges (AGB), a nonprofit organization of 1,100 boards of postsecondary education. NCNB's advisory board is composed of individuals with experience governing or managing a wide variety of nonprofit organizations.

SERVICES OFFERED: 1. NCNB operates a clearinghouse for information about nonprofit boards; 2. NCNB publishes papers, books, and other material on governing nonprofit organizations; 3. NCNB helps organizations design and conduct tailored training programs, workshops, and conferences for board members and chief executives.

ORGANIZATIONS SERVED: NCNB services are designed for governing boards and chief executives of organizations such as social service agencies, arts and cultural organizations, community groups, environmental agencies, research institutes, health care organizations, educational institutions, advocacy groups, international organizations, and religious institutions. NCNB works with national, state, and local organizations.

STAFF: NCNB carries out its board development activities with a full-time staff of three and the assistance of many knowledgeable consultants. The executive director is Nancy R. Axelrod, who previously was vice president of programs and public policy of the Association of Governing Boards of Universities and Colleges. The deputy director is Larry H. Slesinger, formerly a program officer at the Markle Foundation. Valeria W. Moore is NCNB's administrative assistant.

FINANCIAL SUPPORT: NCNB is supported by a major grant from the W. K. Kellogg Foundation, and has also obtained grants from the William and Flora Hewlett Foundation, the Rockefeller Brothers Fund, the Warner-Lambert Foundation, the Exxon Fund for Management Assistance of the New York Community Trust, the Beatrice Foundation, and the Mobil Foundation. NCNB will finance its activities from these and other grants from private and corporate foundations concerned with the effectiveness of nonprofit organizations; and from income generated from the sale of its publications and fees from its training programs, conferences, and workshops.

FOR ADDITIONAL INFORMATION: The National Center for Nonprofit Boards maintains a mailing list, and will add the name and address of anyone interested in learning more about NCNB's information clearinghouse, training programs, or publications. Also, a list of NCNB publications is available.

Northeast Regional Center for Rural Development
104 Weaver Bldg., The PA State Univ., Univ. Park, PA 16802

Daryl K. Heasley
Director
814/863-4656

Leadership for Social Change - Rural Sociology 305

Exploration, analysis, understanding, and application of leadership skills and concepts in groups, organizations and communities. Prerequisites: 6 credits in Social or Behavioral Science (or equivalent experience). If in doubt, contact instructors.

COURSE OBJECTIVES: 1. To understand and be able to diagnose the leadership style of self and styles of others in small group, organizational, and community settings; 2. To understand and be able to use sociological principles applied to leadership in small groups, organizations, institutions, and communities; 3. To learn and be able to use leadership strategies, techniques, and principles in order to promote effective group action based upon group need; 4. To improve individual competence as a member, volunteer leader and professional in the social change process; To be able to communicate the first four course objectives through oral communications (large and small group discussions, educational simulations, small group techniques) and written communications (two short papers and two essay examinations).

SCOPE AND APPLICATION: Students participate in helping to set specific goals for the course. Discussion groups, short--individual--small group--total class exercises, simulations, role playing and the use of films and case studies are among the methods used in applying principles to practice. Writing styles as well as substantive material of the concepts are also used in applying principles to practice. Specific topical areas include: What is known about leadership--the science and the art? What is known about leadership/membership styles relationships--how to diagnose, evaluate, and improve? What leadership roles are required in groups and how are these determined? How can the effectiveness of a group or a leader be improved? What processes are effective in bringing about change in groups and communities?

EVALUATION OF STUDENT WORK: 20% - class participation. **Note:** Due to the nature of this class, **active** participation is required in order to receive a passing grade. 10% - A short paper (3-5 pages), properly referenced, that identifies your leadership style. The paper is **due** when listed on the syllabus. 15% - A paper (6-12 pages), properly referenced, that identifies, diagnoses, and evaluates your leadership/membership styles in this class. It will also list ways you feel you could have improved. The paper will be **due** 5 class periods before the last day of class. In order to efficiently and effectively discharge the roles and responsibilities of leadership, leaders must be proficient in oral and written communication skills. Individual conferences and class times in R. Soc. 305 are devoted to the development of both of these skills. For each of the two short papers designed to improve the students' writing skills students will (1) submit a typed rough draft by the dates indicated on the syllabus (papers will be referenced and formatted according to styles attached); (2) meet with the instructor to discuss this draft; and (3) revise this draft for final submission within about a week. Students will schedule an individual conference following both papers to discuss ways of improving their written expressions. Thus, there will be a total of four submissions. Rough drafts will not be graded, and all first submissions will be considered rough drafts (unless they are of solid "A" quality). An "A" paper from a previous semester for each of these assignments will be reproduced and distributed as a "model" for students. **Both** papers will be graded for substance and writing style. Comments appropriate to **both areas** will be attached to the papers. 10% - participation in the community-based simulation--Libertyville, USA. 45% - two essay exams during the course. The examination will be graded for substance and writing style. Comments appropriate to both will be written on the exam booklet by the instructor. The period immediately following each of the essay examinations will be devoted to a general discussion of both the substantive content and the ways of improving general writing problems that surfaced. The best student examples of written answers for each question will be shared with the other students.

READINGS AND REFERENCES: Students are expected to read all assignments in articles distributed in class and in the texts. Required: 3-volume handbook set; resource book of readings, exercises, diagnostic forms, etc.; Supplementary readings on special topics will be assigned or suggested for each topic.

COURSE OUTLINE: (Reading assignments are not included here since they are in volumes available to those students who take the course. Further information concerning them should be directed to Daryl K. Heasley.)

Sessions

1	Class Orientation--introductions, requirements--exercises--"housekeeping details"
2	"Housekeeping details" cont. Why study leadership?
3	Leadership theories--state of the science--of the art; Styles of leadership
4	Styles of membership
5	Self-diagnosis of leadership style/membership style. Myers-Briggs Short Form --Personality Style. Short paper--Your leadership styles (rough draft)
6	Individual Motivation
7,8	Meeting management, agenda building, and parliamentary procedure for common use. Short paper due--final draft
9	Group roles. Conferences to be scheduled with instructors to discuss other than "A" papers--substantively and writing styles
10	Analyzing group effectiveness
11	Communication Networks. Laos Simulation
12	Written Course/instructor feedback. Exam review time
13	First exam--essay--bring a Bluebook (8-12 pp.)
14	Discussion of examination--substantive and writing areas. Interpersonal relationships
15,16	Communication skills, listening-influencing
17	Community power and leadership
18	Identifying community leaders
19	Change agent roles. Community change and resistance to change
20	Change strategies
21	Adoption-diffusion of ideas. Social action model to effect changes
22	Written Course/instructor feedback. Exam review time. Second paper due

(rough draft). Bring Libertyville/Impact Information Sheet

23   Second exam--essay--bring a Bluebook

24   Discussion of examination--Substantive and writing areas. Orientation to an assignment of Libertyville, USA, roles

25   Libertyville, USA--Week I. Conferences to be scheduled with instructor to discuss other than "A" papers--substantively and writing styles. Second paper due--final draft

26   Discussion of Week I and preparation for Week II

27   Libertyville, USA--Week II

28   Discussion of Week II and preparation for Week III

29   Libertyville, USA--Week III

30   Discussion of Libertyville. Summary of course. Formal course evaluation

---

Leadership Development - Rural Sociology 505

Exploration, understanding, and application of leadership roles, strategies, and principles in group and community settings.

PREREQUISITES: R. Soc. 305 and 6 credits in social or behavioral sciences or equivalent.

FOCUS: Students who are professionally employed as or anticipate employment as change agents and who are in need of advanced leadership concepts in order to perform their roles effectively and satisfyingly to themselves, members of their work group, and their communities will be the focus of this course. These key concepts will be provided through exploring and applying them to real-life situations.

INSTRUCTIONAL OBJECTIVES: a. To explore, understand, and be able to apply effectively and satisfyingly leadership roles, functions, and styles in small groups, organizational, or institutional and community settings. b. To explore, understand, and be able to apply effectively and satisfying leadership strategies and principles applied to effective group action. c. To improve individual competence as a member, volunteer leader and/or professional in the social change process as a result of accomplishing objectives a and b.

EVALUATION OF STUDENT WORK: Based on class participation and individual learning contracts.

Note: The Directory of Statewide Rural and Agricultural Leadership edited by Daryl K. Heasley is impressive in its scope of leadership development programs funded with start-up money by the W. K. Kellogg Foundation at Battle Creek, Michigan. Leadership development programs are spread across the entire United States and one province of Canada. Some states have been more successful than others; some programs resemble each other, but there are differences in their concerns over issues and their methods of presentation. Information concerning them can be sought by contacting Daryl K. Heasley.

United States Department of Agriculture
Extension Service
3428 South Bldg., Washington, DC 20250

John A. Michael
Evaluation Specialist
202/475-4557

The National Impact Study of Leadership Development in Extension (NISLDE)
This is reprinted from a draft of an executive summary of a book in press.

PURPOSE AND SCOPE: To examine the development of leadership among persons participating in Extension's instructional programs. Reviewing the aims, methods, clientele, resources, and related features of leadership development work, the study's scope is limited to an examination of inputs. It probes issues relating to the management of leadership development work as well as practice.

AUSPICES: NISLDE was sponsored by the Extension Service, U.S. Department of Agriculture, with additional support coming from Washington State University's Cooperative Extension and Department of Rural Sociology and other Cooperative Extension Services nationwide. The Extension Accountability and Evaluation Council in 1983 authorized this and four other national impact studies. Principal investigators include Drs. John A. Michael, Study Director, ES-USDA, M. Chris Paxson and Robert E. Howell, Washington State University.

METHOD: Data come from questionnaires mailed in February 1986 to a nationally representative cross-section of Extension administrators and educators. Ancillary evidence, largely anecdotal, comes from completed questionnaires, semistructured interviews, field observations, EMIS (Extension Management Information System), and secondary sources.

FINDINGS: Since no standard definition of leadership development exists, many conceptions prevail among Extension staff members, as shown by interviews, questionnaires, and field observations.

The study defines leadership development as <u>the nurturing of competencies for influencing people's thoughts, feelings and behavior</u>. Included are competencies (skills, knowledge, attitudes, and behaviors) for influencing oneself as well as others. To specify their nature, the leadership development competencies being taught by Extension staff were enumerated through interviews, observation, and a review of educational materials provided by Extension staff. Well over 100 competencies were grouped into the first 13 categories of the following scheme:

Solving Problems	Understanding Leadership
Directing Projects or Activities	Understanding Society
Forming and Working with Groups	Understanding Social Change
Planning for Group Action	Arbitrating
Managing Meetings	Developing Resources
Communicating Effectively	Developing Followership
Developing Proficiency in Teaching	Changing Behavior
Mobilizing for Group Action	Clarifying Attitudes
Understanding and Developing Oneself	Creativity
Understanding Financial Matters	Other

To measure the type and extent of leadership development work with clientele, the study surveyed Extension staff about the frequency with which they tried to develop the specific competencies included in the first 13 categories during 1985. (A detailed list of leadership competencies appears in the technical report.) Additional competencies volunteered during the survey were grouped into the remaining seven categories.

Most Extension staff tried to develop a wide array of leadership competencies among clientele in 1985. With categories arrayed above in terms of their relative frequency, each of the first 13 categories was attempted at least once during 1985 by between 68% to 86% of the staff, with the modal staff member attempting all 13. The last seven categories were attempted by fewer than 5% of the staff. Staff tend to emphasize competence in "doing" over "understanding."

The average staff member spent seven hours a week to develop leadership among clientele, i.e., 15% of a 50-hour work week, according to the survey data. This represents over 2,600 staff years for the Cooperative Extension System.

At least three-quarters of the staff used each of the following teaching methods; advising, providing experience, group instruction, and role modeling. Multiple methods were the rule; combinations with advising were most popular. Of six educational practices studies, staff members averaged four. The greater the number of methods and practices staff used, the more time they spent on leadership development work.

Staff tried to enhance the leadership competencies of 13.7 million persons in 1985, averaging a median of 200 clientele per staff member. Seventeen percent of the staff reached 79% of the clientele. They spent an estimated six hours with each client on average during 1985 developing leadership, where clientele of "representative" examples of leadership development work are concerned (see below), spread out over a 12-month period. "Representative" work consists of the activities that survey respondents described as best representing their work during 1985 in developing the leadership skills of clientele. Analysis reveals that "representative" work is not statistically representative of all leadership development work attempted during 1985. At best, data on "representative" work are suggestive of the total picture.

Staff tended to target their "representative" leadership development efforts to clientele between the ages of 35 to 64, those in lower-middle-income groups ($10,000 to $34,999), and females, in disproportion to their numbers in the U.S. population. Established leaders were more often targeted than emerging leaders or other adults and youth (42% vs. 27% and 31% respectively).

Staff targeted racial and ethnic groups in rough proportion to their numbers in the general population. This was largely because of the efforts of a few staff: while a majority (53%) reached no black clientele in their "representative" work, 5% accounted for roughly two-fifths of all black clientele targeted for leadership development.

Staff members reached a median of eight organizations in 1985 for leadership development work. Of the nine types of organizations examined, staff most frequently tried to develop leadership among persons affiliated with a farm, ranch, or agriculture-related business (35% tried at least once a month).

Thirty percent of Extension staff see leadership development among clientele as a primary responsibility; 54% see it as a secondary responsibility. Three-fifths of Extension staff tried to develop leadership among clientele while teaching agronomy, nutrition, or some other non-leadership subject. For them, the development of leadership is often a means to other ends.

Extension personnel tended to feel more responsibility for leadership development work when it was included in their plan of work, position description, and as a criterion in performance appraisal; and when they believed their supervisors expected such work. Proportionately more personnel assumed responsibility for developing leadership than might be predicted on the basis of such inducements, the survey reveals, particularly in the agricultural and natural resources programs. This points up the lack of organizational inducements for developing leadership while teaching non-leadership subjects.

Support for leadership development that staff received from Extension, apart from their own salary, was help and encouragement from agents (80%), state program leaders (76%), and specialists (71%), followed by counseling and encouragement from supervisors (70%). Most useful was financial assistance (so judged by 64% of those receiving it), followed by help from agents (60%), clientele (59%), and specialists (56%). Least useful was leadership development research (38%), followed by encouragement from state program leaders (40%) and supervisors (44%).

The most common form of support from outside Extension (reaching 80% of staff) was help and encouragement from clientele. Clientele provided additional time (reaching 63% of staff), refreshments (44%), additional funds (36%), facilities (34%), equipment (26%), and educational materials (21%). More than 100,000 organizations supported Extension's leadership development work during 1985, with facility use, financial support, and staff time being the most common forms of support. The average staff member received support for leadership development work from eight organizations in addition to Extension.

Most staff received support from volunteers for leadership development work. Over a third of a million persons volunteered for Extension's leadership development work in 1985, averaging a median of 22 volunteers per staff member.

Supervisors reported giving their staff a wide variety of supports for leadership development work on an infrequent basis. Supervisors who felt able to judge the quality of leadership development work tended to support leadership development work more than their peers who did not feel able to judge.

Extension personnel most often tried to develop leadership among clientele with characteristics similar to their own. This tendency was observed for gender, race and ethnic background, and age. For example, white staff members estimated an average of 88% of the clientele to their "representative" work were white; black staff members estimated an average of 57% of their leadership development clientele were black; and the other staff members estimated that 48% of their leadership development clientele were among the other racial and ethnic minorities.

Staff attitudes and qualifications are more strongly correlated with the number of hours spent on leadership development than demographic traits and ties to Extension or community.

RECOMMENDATIONS

1.   Policy.   Extension should state the relevance of leadership development work for accomplishing the organization's goals.   Extension needs to state the purpose of its leadership development work in a way that inspires common language and understanding.

2.   Procedure.   Extension should establish procedures enabling staff members to conduct and manage leadership development in a manner commensurate with policy and level of commitment.   This can be accomplished through organizational structure, educational practices, accountability procedures, deployment of resources, and personnel practices.

3.   Linkages.   Extension should strengthen the research and knowledge base of its leadership development education.   Ties within land-grant institutions and beyond are a prerequisite to quality, research-based leadership development work.

University of Georgia
Carl Vinson Institute of Government
Georgia Center, Athens, GA 30602

Hal Holtz
Administrator, Governmental Training Division
404/542-1328

The Leadership Institute for Georgia Municipal Elected Officials

Every municipal organization in Georgia, whether it is an individual city or the Georgia Municipal Association, must have outstanding leadership at the top. Mayors and councilmembers must be skilled in both the world of politics and the practice of policy formulation. Meeting the municipal leadership challenge requires stronger analytic skills, better strategic planning, improved communications, and a stronger bottom line orientation from key elected officials. The Georgia Municipal Association, in cooperation with the University of Georgia's Carl Vinson Institute of Government, Georgia Center for Continuing Education and J.W. Fanning Community Leadership Development Center, established The Leadership Institute for Georgia Municipal Elected Officials to serve as the focal point for the leadership development of municipal elected officials. The Leadership Institute serves the same purpose for cities as a good executive development program would provide for a major corporation. It is an opportunity that GMA and the University of Georgia offer for elected officials to better prepare themselves to meet the challenges of public leadership.

PROGRAM: The Leadership Institute examines three aspects of local government leadership.

Individual Leadership: Includes an overview of what it takes for an individual to be a leader. Current trends that have an impact on local government are explored. Each person's leadership style is assessed and a discussion of the helpful and hindering aspects of each style provides personal awareness as well as an appreciative understanding of the style of others.

Council/Commission Leadership: Looks at each individual's responsibility for taking initiative and exercising leadership as a contributing member of the council/commission. Participants explore skills related to consensus building and managing situations where there is diversity of opinion, disagreement and conflict. There is an opportunity to develop means for assessing council or commission effectiveness and for establishing a more cohesive city team.

Community Leadership: Building and maintaining community partnerships and coalitions is emphasized. Participants also examine the broader issue of governance within a statewide context in order to more effectively represent their community and the GMA on policy issues affecting local governments in Georgia.

The Leadership Institute's approach is grounded in practicality, but brings in basic concepts of management, behavioral science and political science. The program instructors are selected on the basis of their knowledge of the subject area and their ability to communicate that aspect of leadership to participants. Program materials, including a specially designed Leadership Development notebook, were carefully designed to supplement classroom learning.

370

Interaction and an exchange of ideas with other elected officials is one of the most valuable aspects of the Leadership Institute. In a setting removed from the daily pressures of public office there is time to reflect, to listen, to share and to learn.

The program begins on Wednesday evening with a dinner and an orientation. Sessions begin each morning at eight and end at three. There is a closing luncheon at noon on Saturday. The conference center at Callaway Gardens provides a comfortable and convenient setting conducive to professional development. There are planned meals to allow participants to continue their discussions and enjoy getting to know one another better.

SPOUSE'S PROGRAM: Because serving as an elected official often involves the entire family, special seminars are held each day from nine to noon for the spouses of the participants. This provides an opportunity for spouses to share common problems and solutions and to get to know one another. Examples of programs include: "Living With a Public Official--and the Public," "Balancing the Pressures of Career and Family," "Understanding Your Leadership Style" and "Look the Part."

COST: Each participant is required to pay a $300 registration fee and to be responsible for their housing costs (approximately $300). The registration fee covers the cost of meals for the participant and his or her spouse and the refreshment breaks for the Institute and spouse's program. Program costs are covered currently by the Georgia Soft Drink Association.

Leadership DHR of Georgia
Vivian Ashley

Leadership DHR (Department of Human Resources) is a year-long educational and leadership program developed through a collaborative effort between The University of Georgia, the Georgia State Merit System, and the Department of Human Resources. This year's program has emphasized change, growth and discovery.

PURPOSE: To enhance the Department's ability to meet the challenges of the future by developing leaders who have an understanding of the opportunities and problems of the State of Georgia and a commitment to addressing the diversity of human service needs throughout the state.

GOALS: 1. To expand our capacity to more effectively respond to human services issues facing our state; 2. To identify and explore the major political, social and economic issues that will impact human services during the next decade and to enable DHR to respond more effectively; 3. To share creative management models (a "toolbox") to enhance our ability to provide leadership in ways that are consistent with DHR's mission, values and philosophy; 4. To build relationships between existing and emerging DHR leaders and other community leaders; 5. To foster the development of networks that are committed to solving human services problems throughout Georgia.

LEARNING OBJECTIVES: 1. Human Service Environment - Participants will demonstrate an understanding of the current and future social, political, and economic environment that impacts on human service issues at the state and local level. 2. Leadership - Participants will demonstrate an understanding of leadership concepts, have opportunities for self-assessment, and determine their responsibility to provide leadership within the Department of Human Resources; 3. Organizational Mission - Participants will demonstrate an understanding of the philosophy, mission, values, and goals of the Department of Human Resources. 4. Networking - Participants will have opportunities to develop ties of comradeship and mutual support within the group.

Participants in Leadership DHR represent a geographic and ethnic mix of leaders in the human services field. Sixty participants are chosen each year. The program, at four sessions a year, develops state leaders who have a deeper understanding of human services issues--how they impact Georgia's political, economic, and social realities. The program also seeks to strengthen participants' commitment to improving human services throughout Georgia.

Janet Bittner, deputy commissioner of DHR, explaining the program's purpose, said, "Government has leaders, but we need to do more to nurture them and to build relationships between them and other community leaders." Frank Wilkinson, director of the Training and Organization Development Division for the Merit System of Georgia (a partner to Leadership DHR), said, "Leadership DHR is an excellent example of the integration of a human resource development program with the strategic objectives of an organization."

In its third year, Leadership DHR consists of four weekend meetings to provide support and encouragement to participants. The program focuses on leadership skills, exploration of critical issues, trend analysis, goal setting, and managing changes. Topics from the 1989 program included: Building a Leadership Foundation, Managing Issues Within a Culturally Diverse Workplace, Vision and Empowerment, and The Change Process.

State and national leaders are carefully selected and oriented to the special nature of this program. William Winter, former governor of Mississippi, in a speech during one of the 1988 sessions, urged Leadership DHR participants to take responsibility for creating the understanding and momentum to change the way things are. He encouraged the leaders to "educate themselves and most importantly, to educate others about what needs to be done to alleviate suffering and help people to attain a decent standard of health and well-being."

According to Terrell Slayton, assistant to the commissioner of DHR and co-facilitator of the group, participation in the program is not tied to a person's position but rather to potential for growth and creative leadership. "Leadership DHR nurtures and challenges leaders to create a more effective human services delivery system for the citizens of our state. But this is also a program for individual growth and change, for reflection and self-discovery," he said.

Along with Slayton, Vivian Ashley of the Georgia Certified Public Manager Program of The University of Georgia serves as a co-facilitator of the Leadership DHR program. She believes the program is an excellent example of innovation and collaboration in state government. "Leadership DHR could be used by other states as a model for investing limited and scarce resources in the development of state government leaders," Ashley said.

University of Wisconsin
Dept. of Continuing & Vocational Education
225 North Mills St., Rm. 276, Madison, WI 53706

Boyd E. Rossing
608/262-5930

The **Wisconsin Community Leadership Development** program **(WCLD)** is designed to attract people who are actively involved in community volunteer organizations and service agencies. The program goal is to provide opportunities for selected participants to expand their understanding about how the community works, how people effectively work together around community concerns, and ways in which leaders and others influence community decisions.

The WCLD program is conducted through two types of activities: workshops and seminars. Several workshop series are carried on throughout the year in the participants' own community. Each of these series involves twelve (12) sessions including one held in the state capital, Madison. A second program activity is a two and a half day seminar which acts as an advanced learning opportunity for thirty participants selected from the workshop series. The seminar cycle involves quarterly meetings which includes one session to be held in a southern community and another to be held in the national capital, Washington, D.C.

WCLD--Workshop Content Overview

Leadership Knowledge and Skills Content
(1) Community leadership--Explore; What is community; What is leadership--Styles and Experiences (2) Self-Awareness--Personal and History (3) Interpersonal communications (4) Group dynamics (5) Community development processes and principles
(6) Community problem analysis and solving processes--Information gathering; Decision making; Strategic and action planning; Influencing public decisions (7) Public policy analysis (8) Management and use of conflict (9) Coalition formation

Community Needs Assessment and Problem Identification
(1) Needs assessment models (2) Nominal group process use

Experience and Explore Community Needs and Problems
(1) Community problem-solving teams--Real world experiences (2) Further study of selected community needs and problems--Current situation; Hard data (information); Feelings about situation; Community resources both Public and Volunteer; Community response; Present actions; Needed actions; Resource access and limitations; Action prospectus; Forces supportive of change, Barriers to improvement, Action plans

WCLD--Workshop Content Sequence

1. Participant introductions; Expectations; Introduction of syllabus; Workshop series goals; What is community?; What are leadership styles and experiences?; Self-awareness exercise.
2. Group local history; Coalition formation; Introduction to nominal group process; Community need and problem identification exercise.
3. Community development principles and process; Interpersonal communications.

4. Community need and problem analysis; Information gathering; "Puzzle: Approaches to Problem Solving" exercise; "The Cave" exercise; Introduction to a problem-solving process.

5. Public policy analysis; Problem-solving team formation; Identification of resource persons to address community needs and problems.

6. Influencing community changes; Other community leaders' experiences; Management and use of conflict.

7. through 10. Problem-solving teams: progress reports; In-depth exploration of selected community needs and problems.

11. State capital session.

12. Workshop wrap-up; Problem-solving teams: substantive reports; Introduction to seminar cycle; Where do we go from here?

Wisconsin Community Leadership Program
Seminar Planning Guidelines

GOALS AND OBJECTIVES: The Wisconsin Community Leadership Program (WCL) seeks to expand leadership opportunities and effectiveness for people of color. Persons targeted for participation include Blacks (Afro-Americans), Hispanics (Latinos), and Indians (Native Americans).

The learning objectives of WCLP are to: Expand participants' perspectives about community problems, their ability to analyze and understand these problems, and ways to gain access to and influence decision-making processes at various local, state, and national levels; Help participants gain knowledge about community structures, how and where decisions are made in both public and private sectors at the local, national, and global levels, and ways to increase citizen involvement in community affairs; Build community leaders' capacity to work effectively within their immediate reference group, with groups in the broader community that share common concerns, and among similar groups at the national level; Help participants examine their respective cultural concepts related to leadership, develop an appreciation for cultural diversity, and an understanding about community leadership and values as they relate to the practice of leadership.

PROGRAM: The program pursues its goals and objectives through two primary components: a workshop series and a seminar cycle. Workshop series are organized around either the concerns of a single ethnic group or are composed of multicultural groups from the community. The workshop series focus on building group cohesion and leadership commitment, strengthening leadership knowledge and skills, identifying community needs and exploring solutions to selected community problems.

Following completion of a workshop series participants are invited and selected to participate in a seminar cycle. Participants from diverse ethnic backgrounds are drawn from the workshop series to make up the seminar group. Enrollment in each seminar group is limited to 30. Seminars occur every 3 months over a 2-year period. They typically last 2 - 2 1/2 days and are scheduled in varied locations. In addition to Wisconsin seminars the series includes a session in another state and a session in Washington, D.C. The seminars in Cycle I focus on 1) increasing understanding of the similarities and differences in needs and experiences of different ethnic groups, 2) building linkages between ethnic groups, 3) increasing understanding of problems, perspectives and opportunities in high priority topical areas: e.g., education, family, economic development, health care delivery, and 4) further strengthening leadership and relevant social change.

Seminar Planning Process and Product For each seminar a qualified person, with expertise on the topic and on design of intensive adult education activities will be invited to serve as chair of the planning process. When possible the chair will be selected from UW-System faculty. The chair will then lead a planning process which creates a complete design for the seminar to include location, objectives, topics, activities, resource people, and other specifics related to the conduct of an excellent learning experience.

Seminar Objectives To provide a guideline for designing the seminar, attention should be given to considering and selecting objectives that state the desirable learnings to be fostered. A set of 2-5 central objectives will integrate the seminar and provide a guideline for selecting specific activities.

Seminar Elements Each seminar focuses on a selected topical area within which some mix of the following will usually yield the most effective seminar: 1. Information and analysis of the status and trends of selected conditions that pose important problems for members of each ethnic group in (and in the world outside) their communities. 2. Examples of real community action initiatives that are addressing important problems and perspectives of leaders, others acting to solve such problems. 3. Opportunities for participants to analyze conditions and develop solutions using effective group processes. 4. Appropriate leader skill and solidarity building experiences and application opportunities. 5. 1-4 designed in ways that increase understanding and appreciation of similarities and differences of needs, experiences and resources across diverse ethnic groups.

Resource People Qualified person(s) should be identified and recruited to moderate, present or otherwise insure that each segment of the seminar is effectively conducted. Resource people representing ethnic backgrounds of all participant groups should be involved, to demonstrate leadership models and to insure sensitivity to the perspectives of each group. Qualified resource people of other ethnic backgrounds (white) can also make valuable contributions and are included to build broader understandings of wider world perspectives. Seminar planners should also consider opportunities for involving WCL participants as session moderators or in other leadership roles during the seminar.

Seminar Methods A mix of educational methods is usually most effective to sustain interest, and meet individual needs. Methods might include presentations followed by discussion, panels, case studies, problem solving workshops, participant roundtables, analysis of films, self and group assessment activities, field trips and others. The overall design should ensure ample time for participants to share and discuss information, ideas, and implications among themselves and with resource people.

Seminar Design Specifics

Wisconsin seminars begin late Thursday afternoon and continue through Saturday noon. Length of out-of-state seminars is expected to be longer and is to be determined. WCL has budgeted $1200 to cover costs for resource people's travel/meals and honoraria (where appropriate) for each Wisconsin seminar. Additional funds are set aside to cover costs for participant travel/meals/lodging. Honoraria will usually be limited to $100 for efforts contributing to a half day or less. Honoraria above $100 will be authorized only in special cases where a key resource person would otherwise not be available. When possible, resource people will be asked to donate their time as a public service without honoraria.

The seminar chair ensures that resource people are properly contacted and oriented prior to taking part in a seminar. The chair should also ensure that letters of appreciation are sent to resource people following the seminar. Resource people should be encouraged to identify appropriate hand-outs, other educational material. Materials to be used at a given seminar, if furnished to WCL staff 3 weeks in advance, will be copied and assembled for distribution. In some cases it will be useful to participants to complete an assignment before the seminar. Such assignments might include: 1) advance reading; 2) interviews of appropriate people; 3) selected visits/observations; 4) other. Advance notification and instructions on the requested activity should be furnished to participants with sufficient lead time (min. 3 weeks).

WCL staff will arrange for a written evaluation of each seminar. Time for a discussion of seminar strengths and weaknesses may be scheduled by seminar planners at appropriate times during the seminar. WCL staff should coordinate with the seminar planning chair to ensure the written evaluation addresses important concerns. A Planning Checkpoint schedule is designed and available for those interested.

Wisconsin Family Community Leadership

Wisconsin Family Community Leadership (WFCL) gets people involved in community affairs by teaching leadership, public affairs, and more. WFCL helps people work together to address the problems and issues that families face today by teaching them to: understand issues affecting families; understanding how public policy is formed and changed; develop leadership skills; and learn how to educate others in the community. WFCL trains volunteers to be master (certified) teachers who then teach and conduct community service and public policy education programs.

WFCL is a new program in Wisconsin that builds upon many of the concepts and resource materials developed in the Family Community Leadership (FCL) program. FCL, established in six western states, has been the force behind positive changes brought about in hundreds of communities by strengthening the personal abilities of thousands.

FCL regional and state institutes and conferences provide training for FCL master teachers and Extension agents who participate as teams (one agent, one volunteer). At institutes participants will learn about: Issue analysis; Public policy; Leadership; Group process; Teaching others; Working with volunteers. Participants will have the opportunity to hear dynamic speakers on current family trends and issues, practice new skills and develop plans for future programs in their home counties.

There is no charge for the training. In return for their training participants contract to pay back twelve eight-hour days developing and conducting local programs. The twelve days include some preparation, but the majority of this time will be spent in community education and teaching. An Extension agent must identify an Extension Homemaker who wants to work with that agent as a county team member. Or an Extension Homemaker who wants to participate must find an Extension agent who will pair up to form a team. Teams are asked to make preliminary plans as to the kinds of program(s) they want to implement after receiving training at the institute.

WFCL is co-sponsored by the Wisconsin Extension Homemaker Council and the Family Living Education program area of the University of Wisconsin-Extension. Support for the program has been provided by the W. K. Kellogg Foundation. More information is available by calling Robert Young, WFCL Coordinator, 428 Lowell Hall, 610 Langdon Street, Madison WI 53703, telephone (608) 262-7886.

A copy of a 100-page study of the Impact of Wisconsin Cooperative Extension Service Programs on Leaders and the Organizations and Communities They Serve, by Boyd E. Rossing (1987), is available by contacting him.

Leadership in Community Programs - CAVE 605

PURPOSE: To understand and apply key concepts and skills that contribute to the development and exercise of leadership in community settings, the course provides a foundation for community-based continuing, vocational and recreational educators to identify, evaluate and develop community leaders, and work with them to carry out a community leadership role.

OBJECTIVES: To help learners: 1. comprehend leadership dynamics in community settings; 2. know how to identify, study and evaluate leadership in communities; 3. understand and be able to apply basic individual, group and community leadership concepts/theories/skills to real community leadership situations; 4. recognize leadership capacities and potentials in themselves and others and understand how leadership is developed.

APPROACH: Class sessions will include a mix of lectures, group discussion, group exercises, group presentations and invited presentations. A key activity will be a group/individual out-of-class community leadership study project (see below).

Community Leadership Study Project:

Group Portion: Class members will work within a small group to carry out and report on an analysis of leadership in a selected community setting. Within the framework of an overall group study each individual will carry out specific chosen assignment(s) (see Individual Portion). The group will present a summary of their total study to the full class.

Individual Portion: The individual part of the community study will provide an opportunity for each class member to examine a real leadership situation and to analyze the situation in terms of leadership concepts. Each class member will be responsible for arranging his or her project within the context of the group assignment. A written analysis of the project will be prepared. The time invested in direct contact with the leadership situation should be from 6 to 10 hours.

Readings: Two bound readers with items from a variety of sources and library resources.

Evaluation of Performance: The learning/performance expectations for the course and their associated grade weight ranges as follows: 1. Complete assigned readings (0); 2. Attend and participate in class (0) (Grade adjusted for non-attendance); 3. Community Leadership Study a. Individual Products (1) Interview Summary, 10, (2) Community Leadership Study Report, 20-40; b. Group Presentation/Report, 10-20; 4. Other Learning (choose 1 to 3 of following): a. Course Test, 10-30; (1) In Class Short Answer Test OR (2) Take Home Essay Test; b. Special Interest Report (required for graduate students), 10-40; c. Extra Credit (see instructor).

You can select the weighting to be used for each category for grade purposes. Weights must be selected in multiples of 10 within the ranges designated above. The total to equal 100. A sheet specifying grade assignments and grade weights will be completed by March 1. It is expected that paper(s) submitted for the class will be typed and will be proofed and corrected for spelling, grammar, etc. Papers with significant grammar/spelling problems will be returned for re-submission.

Community Leadership Study - I: This project will provide an opportunity to explore and observe directly leadership in a community setting and to analyze the experience in terms of concepts from the literature. The project will provide an opportunity to experience group development, participation and leadership within the class. Each class member will participate in a small group formed according to a community setting of interest (e.g., Geographic: village, town, neighborhood, city, county; Issue Based; Common Background, etc.) which all group members can visit periodically during the semester. Members of the group will then assume responsibility for carrying out the following tasks: 1. Collecting and summarizing a few basic facts about the community (e.g., population, economic/social characteristics, etc.); 2. Identifying community leaders (e.g., power structure) and major community issues/concerns. (Each group member will interview two selected community leaders.) 3. Identifying and selecting a set of community organizations, programs, projects and related groups that provide community service or seek to change the community. Each group member will then arrange to observe members of community organizations/groups in action on 2 occasions.

The community study conducted by the group will provide information for two products:

Individual Product: Each group member will prepare a report that includes the following:
1. Summary of interviews you conducted, e.g., Person interviewed, why selected; Date, location of interview; Information/ideas presented in interview, Your interpretation/evaluation of key themes, patterns in interviewee's leadership knowledge and behavior; Discussion of interview in relation to class literature;
2. Summary of your community group observations: e.g., Nature of organization, group and why selected; Dates, locations of observations; Observation procedures you used; Description of key observations, evidence; Your interpretation/evaluation of observations to identify selected patterns, strengths and weaknesses in the way group/leader(s) function (e.g., participation, communication, leadership style, decision making, conflict resolution, etc; If possible, contrast observed interviewer behavior with leadership impressions from interview; Discussion of observations in relation to class literature.
3. Discussion of the insights you have gained (from your interviews and group observations, from inputs of other group members and from basic community facts) regarding who participates, what issues are addressed and how community members function (particularly with regard to your program/issue interest) in this community setting. Draw on class literature in your discussion. Your individual report should be from 8-12 pages long.

Group Product: Each group will plan and conduct a class session which helps the class understand: 1. The nature of the community the group studied; 2. The key community leaders in that community; 3. Major community issues/concerns/programs; 4. Some of the leadership strategies/dynamics/results of groups operating in the community; 5. Conclusions regarding the state of leadership in the community (who participates, what they address and how they function, strengths, limits and needs for improvement or change).

The group presentation should involve most or all group members. A presentation that is active and creative is encouraged, e.g., demonstration, role play, simulation, etc. Active involvement of the class in portions of the presentation is also welcome, if it contributes to the goals of the presentation. A 2-3 page group report summarizing main points should accompany the presentation (handed out in class).

Community Study II - Community Interviews

Each group member will conduct at least 2 interviews. Program/Issue Leader Interview: Select at least one person in the study community who is of interest to you. Arrange and conduct an interview that includes: introduction - purpose; identification of leader's program/issue concerns/goals.

Interview Procedure: Identify the topics or questions you wish to discuss prior to the interview. Use them as a guide to direct the flow of the interview. Be conscious of time so that you include the most important topics without overextending your stay. Make brief notes during the interview and more complete notes soon afterward. Consider using a tape recorder if it will not disturb the interviewee.

Community Study III - Community Group Observations

Each group member will conduct at least 2 group observations.

1. <u>Program/Issue Group</u>. Select at least 1 group, organization, agency, etc. in the study community that addresses the concern of interest to you (preferably a group in which one of your interviewers participates). Identify time(s) and place(s) when the group or a committee of the group will meet and arrange to sit in on a meeting. During the meeting observe <u>some</u> of the following (pay particular attention to interviewee's behavior): physical setting and its effects; group climate, developmental stage; issues/topics addressed and decisions made/not made; communications; leadership and decision-making style(s); conflict management; formal activities (within meeting) versus informal activities (pre, post, breaks, etc.); other significant events/behavior.
2. <u>General/Related Group</u>. Select at least 1 other group (either general governmental or other community group) whose activities <u>have a bearing</u> on the program group in 1. (In lieu of observing a general/related group you can observe the program/issue group twice.) Identify time(s) and place(s) when the group will meet and arrange to sit in on a meeting.
3. <u>Observation Procedure</u>. Identify the aspects you wish to observe prior to the meeting. Use them as a guide during your observation. Make brief notes of your observations during the meeting. Make more complete notes soon afterward. In your follow-up notes, include: descriptions of observed aspects; your reactions/findings in the situation; your interpretations/explanations of what happened.

CLASS SCHEDULE

<u>Schedule Topics</u>: Readings are assigned in keeping with topics noted.

<u>Session</u>	
1	Introductions/Course Overview
2,3,4	Communities & Community Leadership
5,6	Community Leadership Study Groups
7	Cancelled Class - Study Group Time
8,9,10,11	Leadership Theory
12	Study Group Time
13,14	Groups and Leadership
15,16	Spring Break
17,18,19	Key Group Leadership Tasks/Skills/Styles
20,21	Community Organizations and Leadership
22,23,24,25	Leadership for Community Participation and Change
26	Study Group Time
27,28,29,30	Group Presentations
31,32	Community Leadership Development

Volunteer Consulting Group, Inc.
24 West 40th Street, New York, NY 10018

Brooke W. Mahoney
Director
212/869-0800

The Volunteer Consulting Group, Inc. (VCG), founded in 1968 by the Harvard Business School Club of Greater N.Y., is a non-profit organization whose programs focus on strengthening the governing ability of non-profit Boards of Directors. A fundamental mission is bringing exceptional business executives into service as Trustees, enhancing the managerial strength of the Board. Organizational assignments assist Boards with operational and process issues: recruitment strategies, design of committee structures, development of policies for increased operational efficiency, etc. VCG's education programs teach voluntary leadership about their roles and governance responsibilities. As a primary center for non-profit Boards in the NY, NJ and CT area, VCG is focusing on leadership development--seeking to augment corporate involvement in volunteer leadership roles.

To provide its direct services most effectively, the VCG in recent years has developed a series of programs, among them the Board Recruitment Program, the Board Management Consultation Program, the Seminar Program and the Curriculum Development Program. Through these programs and others which may evolve, VCG serves the non-profit sector, recruiting volunteers, training boards and senior management to use the governance process effectively and educating potentially valuable trustees.

Recently, VCG received a grant from the Lilly Endowment to conduct a national research endeavor, examining extant training programs focused on "in-service, voluntary leadership: Directors and Trustees." The purpose is to better understand the nature and accessibility of these programs and to provide the Lilly Endowment with a significant report of activity in this area of interest for evaluation and future research. The Discovery Phase of the research will include compiling information on types of training offered, teaching methods and materials used, target audience etc., within seven sectors: Health, Education, Culture, Advocacy, Community Service, Social Services and Religion. A goal is to enhance communication and collaborative efforts in this important field of continuing adult education.

Sponsored, supported and hosted by a diverse and impressive group of corporations and foundations in New York City, the program has produced a variety of teaching materials for use in the annual public program and other forums conducted by the organization. Assistance is generally focused on structural issues--the organization of a board, committee definition and mandates, effective management of individual trustees, board/staff relations and long-range planning for both governance and operational components.

Although its focus has broadened over the last two decades, the central interest of the Volunteer Consulting Group has never wavered from the serving of community interests and the improvement of quality of life.

As a third decade of service begins, the mission continues: to bring organizational skills and managerial expertise to the non-profit community to enhance their governance and management and to improve the services and products they create.

382

Section E
PROGRAMS WITH AN INTERNATIONAL PERSPECTIVE

To assume leadership in today's world it is imperative to be internationally and interculturally concerned. Whether one is preparing for a responsible life in business, industry, government service, academe, the military, the helping professions, or the various functions of community and organizations, it is essential to know a great deal about those who do not share our traditions, our values, our manners, our language, our customs and our practices. In the broadest sense, using educational terms, this is what we should mean when we talk about "going back to the basics." Insularity and self-interested actions, especially on a global scale, are recognized as being non-productive.

In this section are examples of programs being offered outside the United States. Fortunately, many of the descriptions of courses and programs found in the other sections have components that emphasize the importance of being constantly aware of a world outside our borders that are culturally and traditionally different from what we encounter on a daily basis. We apologize not for the quality of the programs in Section E, but for the small number. We can expect that this is the beginning of a movement that will influence and expand our thinking about international matters so that it will be natural and not unusual to incorporate their diverse and creative subject matter and modes of thought into our own concepts about leadership theory, research and practice.

Some of these programs are offered in other countries by centers and academic institutions based in the United States. We read a good deal now about the training centers conducted by major industries all over the world to develop leadership and management in those places where they have satellite operations. Some programs are wholly conceived, designed, and implemented by their own institutions. It becomes clear almost at once that the terms "leadership" and "management" are used differently from what we are accustomed. Also, the terms "creativity" and "innovation" are words integrated into their leadership curricular descriptions. It can be hoped that where cultural differences continue to separate people this accent on leadership development will stimulate greater cooperation and communication.

PROGRAMS WITH AN INTERNATIONAL PERSPECTIVE

TABLE OF CONTENTS

Bocconi University
Via Bocconi, 8, 20136 Milan, Italy

Severino Salvemini
39 2 8384.6625

International Teachers Programme

The International Teachers Programme is an intensive, six-week, residential, professional development programme, held annually for management educators from Universities, Schools of Management, Colleges of Advanced Education or Training Centers, whether these are sponsored by governments, private agencies or companies. It provides a unique opportunity for sharing and comparing teaching experiences in an international and challenging environment. It is conducted in English.

This twenty-year-old course, founded by Harvard Business School, teaches international instructors up-to-date didactic methods for teaching innovative management concepts. Contributions are made by the schools which belong to the International Schools of Business Management (ISBM) consortium. The programme reinforces traditional values and goals: an international setting; further development of individual teaching skills; experiments applying the latest information technologies; and an overview of management disciplines within an interfunctional framework. The programme incorporates minor pedagogical sessions about the course design and teacher's dramatization; the utilization of a "classroom of the future" (a special classroom, equipped with the most current computing facilities); a special room dedicated to presenting the participants' institutions, emphasizing the international network and giving the participants the occasion to exploit all the potential opportunities for transferring teaching and research experiences from one country to another.

During its existence the programme has changed a great deal. However, one aspect of the philosophy of ITP has been maintained and that is the belief that management teachers' abilities should be built on sharing experiences in an international context. And this helps participants to develop a better understanding of the implication of globalization. Every effort is made to ensure that there is an even distribution of participants from different parts of the world. The world-wide arena on which ITP is based is one factor that contributes to ITP's position of prestige among international programmes. This value is returned to the participant who is willing to share and work with foreign colleagues. Spending a lengthy and intensive period living and working with an international group provides many ways of learning about national and cross-cultural issues.

The ideal participant is a young management educator (working in an academy or in the management education department of an organization), who wants to develop his/her own potential through further knowledge of management topics and improved teaching technology skills.

ITP is a programme for all teachers/trainers of management, whatever discipline they teach.

In keeping with the above mentioned changes, ITP has been specifically designed to achieve the following objectives: 1) Make management educators conscious of the implications that internationalization processes have on today's business world. In addition to an international faculty and an international class, ITP is preparing special seminars taught by managers, entrepreneurs and consultants devoted to this topic. 2) Teach participants how to exploit the enormous resource <u>information technology</u> presents. This does not mean ITP will teach programming in traditional or new computer languages. ITP relies on high-level applications which can be used effectively by non-computer specialists. The focus of the programme is on the pedagogical applications of software, not on its technique. 3)T o provide participants with an opportunity to increase their wide knowledge of management through daily collaboration with foreign colleagues of other disciplines. The <u>cross-fertilization</u> coming from a better understanding of interfunctional issues is a great means for the professional development of management educators.

The faculty stays, lives and works with participants during the programme to guarantee the high quality of the pedagogical relationship between participants and teachers.

The Programme Framework

	Objective	Teaching Methods
Week 1 Opening Course	offer a common base of general management knowledge	lectures, cases small group work use of PCs
Week 2 Globalization Module	understand the implications of internationalization	lectures, cases exercises simulations
Week 3 Area Seminars	update both content and process knowledge, provide cross-fertilization of ideas	lectures small group work seminars
Week 4 Pedagogical Seminars	reflect on the teaching process	role playing simulations group dynamics exercises lectures
Week 5 Electives	discuss main topics in today's business environment	lectures, cases small group work
Week 6 Practice Teaching Workshop	experiment individual teaching styles	simulations use of PCs

Center for Creative Leadership
Programs Offered Outside the U.S.

Center for Creative Leadership
5000 Laurinda Dr., P.O. Box P-1
Greensboro, NC 27402-1660
919/288-7210
13 S. Tejon, Suite 500, P.O. Box 1559
Colorado, Springs, CO 80901
719/633-3891
4250 Executive Square, Suite 600
La Jolla, CA 92037
619/453-4774

International Perspectives

INTERNATIONAL PROGRAMS

Our interest in cross-cultural leadership and management has resulted in major growth in our international network. We are welcoming an increasing number of participants from multi-national organizations, and we are creating links with training and development organizations around the world.

For several years, the **Leadership Development Program** (LDP) has been available in Spanish in Mexico City. In Great Britain, the Ashridge Management College continues to offer LDP for a predominantly British and European audience. In 1988, the Mt. Eliza Australian Management College began offering LDP as a regular public program at their beautiful facility in Mt. Eliza, Victoria.

A special Leadership Development Program for international managers will be conducted in San Antonio, Texas, December 2-7, 1990. This program is designed to bring together managers who currently have international experience in a country other than their home country or expect to have in the near future. With special emphasis on managing across cultures, participants will have the rare opportunity to build international networks, look at negotiations issues, and establish relationships with peers who manage from a different perspective.

Another successful program, **Looking Glass, Inc.®**, has proven its capability of holding up a mirror to executives in a highly realistic simulation of life in a medium-sized American corporation. As Looking Glass reaches its 10th anniversary, its applicability and adaptability to international management issues has become more and more evident.

Two organizations have sought permission to use Looking Glass in the European market. They are The Cambridge Management Centre in the United Kingdom and Sigma in Oxford, England. The result is Looking Glass PLC, a successful and established variant of the original.

Last year two groups of consultants in France began a collaboration on the translation of Looking Glass into the French language. Public demonstrations of Looking Glass S.A. are now available in both Paris and Lyon, France.

387

Our newest Looking Glass licensee is the New Zealand College of Management in Wellington, New Zealand, which will be offering both Looking Glass, Inc.® and the Workshop in Organizational Action.

Within the last few years the Center has had staff exchanges with Ashridge, and exchange staff visits from The Netherlands Organization for Applied Scientific Research (TNO) and the Scandinavian Airlines System. Our **RADMIS** simulation has become a scheduled part of the programs of TNO.

In February 1989 we saw the first run of **Targeted Innovation** in Japanese. We are especially proud of the links which have been formed between the Japan Management Association (JMA) and our Innovation and Creativity area. We are also proud of our ties with the Niagara Institute, Niagara-on-the-Lake, Ontario; TEAM, Mexico City, Mexico; and C.A.P.I.C., Paris, France, as they continue to successfully conduct our **Working With Others** program.

Excellence in Leadership - A meeting of Scandinavian and American executives in a highly participative program of self-assessment and learning

What happens when 10 European managers are put together with 10 North American managers and are told to run a corporation?

When that corporation is Looking Glass, Inc.® more than just inter-cultural issues are surfaced--participants get to focus on their personal management styles as well as the unique leadership challenges of their own organizations.

Add to this experience a chance to explore the topic of self-managing work teams, as well as time for personal goal setting, and you have the outline of our unique adaptation of the Workshop in Organizational Action: **Excellence in Leadership.**

Any North American manager interested in getting a wider perspective on the issue of self-managing work teams, a clearer view of his or her own management style, and the cross-cultural experience of sharing a week with 10 high-level, English-speaking Scandinavian managers must enroll in this course.

Only one session of **Excellence in Leadership** is scheduled for 1990. The date is April 22-27, 1990; the class will be held in Greensboro and the fee is U.S. $2,800.00 for North American participants. The Scandinavian participants are being selected by IFL-NILA.

Information on how to enroll and more detail on the course can be obtained from William Shea in Greensboro (919/545-2811) or from Per Valebjorg at IFL-NILA in Norway (02-46 58 42).

WORKING WITH OTHERS: A MANAGEMENT PROCESS

The original version of the **Managing for Commitment** program (**Working With Others: A Management Process**) has been licensed to other organizations by the Center and is available at the following locations.

Mexico City, Mexico
TECNOLOGIA ADMINISTRATIVA MODERNA
(TEAM), S.C. [conducted in Spanish]
(Telephone 512/493-1452)
Program Fee: $900.00 plus 15% VAT

Niagara-on-the-Lake, Ontario
THE NIAGARA INSTITUTE
(Telephone 416/468-4271)
Program Fee: $1,050.00 for members, $1,300.00 for non-members

NOTE: This program can also be delivered on a contract basis either by the Center for Creative Leadership or the licensed organizations above, as well as by the following: **Mt. Eliza Australian Management College**, Kunyung Road, Mt. Eliza, 3930, Australia (phone 03-787 4211), **Personnel Decisions, Inc.**, 2000 Plaza VII, 45 S. Seventh Street, Minneapolis, MN 55402 (phone 612/339-0927 or 800/633-4410), and **C.A.P.I.C.**, 18 Rue Volney, 75002 Paris, France (phone 42-61-03-27).

Czechoslovak Academy of Sciences
Institute of Philosophy and Sociology
Jilska 1, 110 00 Prague 1, Czechoslovakia

Ondrej K. Landa
Senior Research Specialist
2319115

Innovation Management, Creativity and Problem-Solving Methods for Corporate Entrepreneurs: A 5-day learning/training and implementation/action residential program

---

PURPOSE: An intensive action learning program with necessary theoretical and methodological support. Based on creative problem solving and inventive activities in the domain of selected in-company management innovation projects.

OBJECTIVES: To enhance awareness of participants' potentialities, to demonstrate mechanisms of selected barriers of creative thinking and ways to overcome them, to provide insight in the structure of one's creative potential; To foster creative attitudes of participants, to demonstrate innovative potential of stimulated and guided creativity, both individual and collective; To provide intensive training in various methods and techniques of creative problem solving, and to test the applicability of these methods to real-life innovation problems; To provide operational understanding of basic theoretical concepts which underlie mechanisms, principles and methods of creative problem solving; To generate ideas for creative solution of selected innovation problems, to provide stimuli for organizational learning and important management meta-innovations.

1. <u>Diagnostic Component</u>: a) Specific knowledge test, "Innovative Management and Problem-Solving Methods" (16 multiple-choice items); b) Creative thinking items (Guilford and Torrance type). Personal creativity tests: c) "Are You Creative?" d) "Structure of Your Creative Potential" and e) Decision-making and risk-taking exercise (concise business game, "Production Management for Volatile Market").

2. <u>Theoretical Component (Specific Content)</u>:

Innovation Management: a) Intensification of development processes in the society and structural changes in goals, functions, content, mechanism, forms, and methods of business management; b) Global character of change processes--the challenge of innovative management; c) Permanent proactive innovation and creative change as an integral part of corporate life; demands on executive and managerial behavior; d) Innovative management--its crucial role in releasing and fostering creative potential of the company; e) Dual nature of innovative management--managing ideas and supporting entrepreneurship and creativity of employees; f) Innovations as complex technological, economic, organizational and social processes; socio-political nature of innovations and organizational change; g) Organizational, administrative, and socio-cultural barriers to innovation; h) Change management and strategies of promotion of innovative ideas and projects in rigid organizations; i) Social impacts of new technologies; prognostic assessment of social effects of technological innovations.

Creativity: j) Nature of human creativity. Features of creative solution to innovation problems. Bisociative character of creative act; k) Creative process, specific features and demands of its individual stages, organization and management of creative processes;

390

l) Personality of creative manager, prerequisites and possibilities of enhancement of creative potential; m) Subjective barriers of creative thinking and behavior (motivational and attitudinal, perception and cognition, intellectual and methodological, emotional, expression and communication); n) Laws and mechanisms of creative thinking. Dual nature of creative thinking, its modalities. Phantasy and logic in inventive activities. Principles of stimulation of creative thinking.

Creative Problem Solving and Its Methodology: o) Concept and morphology of problems in management. De-composition of complex problems--explanation problems, forecasting, invention, decision/optimization, implementation. Demands on methodology and organization of specific problem-solving processes; p) System of creative problem-solving methods and techniques; q) Invention problems, basic methodological concepts of their creative solution: r) Direct stimulation of creative ideation (brainstorming/brainwriting type techniques); s) Techniques based on analogy and metaphor; t) Morphological techniques; u) Methodological foundations of management forecasting, Delphi method, scenarios; v) Stochastic aspects of managerial problem solving, risk assessment and risk management; w) Decision making in complex problem situations. Basic techniques of heuristic optimization - decision analysis, decision trees; x) Organization and management of innovation processes and creative activities.

3. Methodological Component - Applied Training in Creativity and Problem-Solving Methods and Techniques:

a) Creative collaboration technique ("creativity workshop"); b) Brainstorming; c) Brainwriting; d) Idea card-sorting technique; e) Forced relationships, superposition; f) Synectic discussion; g) Ideation morphology; h) Delphi method; i) Expert assessment and scaling; j) Scenario method; k) Decision analysis, decision trees; l) Risk assessment; m) Cognitive maps; n) Force field analysis.

4. Applied Problem Solving and Innovative Action Component:

Case: Automation and data processing/computer equipment producer

a) Forecast of long-term social impacts of technological innovation in microelectronics, especially in computer technologies (brainwriting and Delphi method); b) New business opportunities in changing socio-economic environment (brainstorming session); c) Management and administrative barriers to creativity and innovation within the company --development of an expert assessment system (idea card technique, expert assessment, scaling); d) Innovative measures for release and enhancement of employees' creative potential and entrepreneurship in the company (remote stimuli, forced relationships); e) New features of information systems for innovation management (synectic discussion); f) Morphology of data processing systems for special uses (morphological analysis); g) Innovation and business strategy in turbulent environment--microelectronic components (scenario method, decision analysis).

PROGRAM SCENARIO:

1st day: 1) Opening of the program. Information about philosophy, goals, specific content, organization and methods of the program, about its demands on participants and tutors (25 minutes); 2) Individual knowledge test (1a - 35 minutes); 3) Innovation management--basic theoretical concepts (2a to 2e - 20 minutes); 4) Analysis of the problem-solving activities profile of program participants (30 minutes); 5) Training program's data processing system--instruction for interactive computer-assisted problem solving and idea generation activities (15 minutes); 6) Subjective barriers to creativity and their overcoming --creativity exercises, demonstration of barriers of creative thinking (1b, 2m - 30 minutes); 7) Personality questionnaire, "Are you creative?" (1c - 40 minutes); 8) Creativity and creative problem solving--basic theoretical and methodological concepts (2j, 2k, 2n, 2x - 50 minutes); 9) Social impacts of new technologies and their prognostic assessment--introductory presentation (2i - 30 minutes); 10) Prevision of long-term social aspects, impacts and effects of technological innovation in microelectronics, especially in computer technologies--brainstorming session, 1st round of expert forecast (4a - 50 minutes).

2nd day morning: 1) Theoretical and methodological foundations of innovation management and creative problem solving--feedback and analysis of knowledge test results (45 minutes); 2) Morphology of complex management problems; basic principles and methods of their solution--an overview (2o, 2p - 30 minutes); 3) Invention problems--basic methodological concepts (2q - 30 minutes); 4) Brainstorming--introductory instruction (2r - 30 minutes); 5) New business opportunities in data processing technologies in changing socio-economic environment--brainstorming session, discussion of generated ideas (4b - 80 minutes).

2nd day afternoon: 1) Organizational, administrative and socio-cultural barriers to innovations--introductory presentation and discussion (2g - 20 minutes); 2) Management and administrative barriers to creativity and innovation within the (electronics) company --idea generation: card technique (4c - 50 minutes); 3) Function of analogies and metaphors in stimulation of creative thinking (2s-I - 20 minutes); 4) Measures for release and enhancement of creative potential and entrepreneurship within the company--idea generation based on random stimuli and forced relationships technique (4d - 40 minutes); 5) Morphological method and its application in stimulation of idea generation processes (2t - 20 minutes); 6) Morphology of data processing systems for special uses (4f - 60 minutes).

3rd day morning: 1) Barriers to creativity and entrepreneurship in the (electronics) company - expert assessment and scaling of items formulated previously (4c) by the participants (4c-II - 60 minutes); 2) Synectics--introductory presentation and methodological instruction (2s-II - 50 minutes); 3) Information system for innovation management--synectic discussion (4e - 90 minutes).

3rd day afternoon: 1) Managerial forecasting and its methodology: Delphi method--introductory presentation and methodological instruction (2u - 30 minutes); 2) Long-term forecast of social aspects, impacts and effects of technological innovation in microelectronics/computer technologies--Delphi method, 2nd round (4a - 50 minutes); 3) Risk in management--I: risk assessment for decision making--introductory presentation, decision-making exercise/business game, feedback, analysis and discussion of results (2v, 1e - 125 minutes).

3rd day evening: Creative process in various human activities. Studying the mechanisms of creative idea generation in managerial problem solving by analysis of creativity in art (M. Escher)--discussion over slides presentation (2j, 2k, 2n - 120 minutes).

4th day morning: 1) Delphi forecast of long-term social impacts of technological innovation in microelectronics and computer technologies - 3rd round (4a - 45 minutes); 2) Scenarios and relevance trees for dynamic forecasting problems--demonstration and methodological instruction (2u - 40 minutes); 3) Model of innovation and business strategy in turbulent environment--scenario and relevance tree for selected microelectronics components (2u, 4g - 130 minutes).

4th day afternoon: 1) Decision making in complex situations; basic principles and methods of heuristic optimization: decision analysis, decision trees. Risk assessment and expected utility in decision analysis--introductory presentation, demonstration, methodological instruction (2v, 2w - 40 minutes); 2) Innovation and business strategy in turbulent environment: selected microelectronics components--decision tree for strategy scenarios (2u to 2w, 4g - 90 minutes); 3) Matrix form of risk assessment--demonstration with ensuing sophisticated evaluation of alternative innovation and business strategies (2v, 4g - 70 minutes).

5th day morning: 1) Closing seminar--Resultative part: presentation and discussion of results of self-assessment creativity questionnaires (1c, 1d) and of group idea generation, problem-solving activities (4a, 4b, 4c, 4d), distribution of feedback print-outs (90 minutes); 2) Change management and strategies of promotion of innovation ideas and projects in rigid organizational environment--creative collaboration technique supported by force field analysis and conceptual mapping (2h - 90 minutes); 3) Participant evaluation of the program, suggestions for improvement, closing statements of organizers and program leader (20 minutes).

Manchester Business School
Booth Street West, Manchester M15 6PB, England

Alan Pearson
Dir., R&D Research Unit
Mrs. B. Rigby
Administrator

Creative Leadership for R&D Managers

The **Manchester Business School,** in conjunction with the **Center for Creative Leadership,** North Carolina, has designed a special workshop on Creative Leadership for R&D Managers. It is aimed at managers in business and government research laboratories, and for those who train R&D managers. It is also valuable for taskforce and project leaders.

This week-long interactive programme is designed to enable participants to learn more about themselves and their interactions with others in the organisation. It is a people-oriented programme designed to demonstrate how to exercise control and to lead groups without stifling individual initiatives and motivation.

The focus throughout the seminar will be on actions that a research team leader can take to help manage people and projects better. Actions that are fully within the typical span of control of such a research team leader and which will lead to more effective performance.

Intensive participative sessions, in-depth discussions, and informal exchange of ideas create an environment that encourages interaction--not only with the training staff, but also with counterparts from other companies in science and technology based industries.

The approach is practical. It focuses on real-life cases, as well as on issues and problems drawn from participants' own experiences. A number of simple questionnaires are used to identify important characteristics of individual and group behaviour. An exercise using video feedback is used to demonstrate the ways in which a group can be more effectively managed.

PROGRAMME DESIGN: A recurring problem for all R&D managers is how to lead and control their staffs without stifling innovation. They must be people oriented to maintain effective control over the innovative process. This seminar will explore leadership issues as they apply to managers and project leaders in R&D organisations.

At the end of this seminar you will have learned:

- What your basic leadership style is.
- What your style of creativity is and how to increase your innovative ability.
- How to adapt your decision-making style to specific situations to help ensure quality, acceptance, and timeliness.
- How to use group dynamics to tap the knowledge and creativity of your group.
- How feedback can help you manage your people.
- How to integrate leadership styles and planning techniques.
- How microcomputer technology can help in R&D decision making.
- What factors influence the performance of teams.
- How to set goals for implementing some of the concepts you learn in the workshop.

394

The Management-Symposium for Women

The Management-Symposium for Women is a forum for women from different generations, of different nationalities and in different areas of activity where they can discuss the problems arising from these societal changes.

The Association Management-Symposium for Women, in accordance with its objectives, would like to contribute to this important process by securing the viability of this Symposium.

The 5th Management-Symposium for Women was held in Zurich, from September 22 to 26, 1989.

The Association Management-Symposium for Women was founded in 1988, with the purpose of promoting and training female executives. Aware of the fact that neither society nor the business community can afford any longer to forego the potential of women, a number of business women and men have felt motivated to support this important Symposium and secure its future.

The financial means are procured by membership fees as well as contributions in the form of patronage and/or sponsorship. There are three categories of membership:

1.   Individual, for those who identify with the objectives of the Association and who want to contribute to the advancement of female executives.

2.   Collective, for associations and organizations that support the objectives of the Association and are willing to recommend the Symposium to their members.

3.   Corporate, for all corporations that support the Association with a minimum annual contribution of SFr. 3'000.- (SFr. 1'000.- for companies with less than 500 employees) and express their additional support of the Association's objectives by promoting their female executives.

Norwegian Center for Leadership Development
Drammensveien 37, 0271 Oslo 2, Norway

Per Groholt
Partner
(02) 561790

How to Combine Leadership Roles and Creativity

During the last few years, I have attempted to evolve a leadership role concept based on situational leadership and creative problem-solving models. I would like to share with you how I currently see creative problem-solving methods becoming an integrated part of the leadership process.

My purpose is to focus more on creativity in leadership with a model consisting of three basic elements: leadership processes, creative problem solving and leadership roles.

Before describing the leadership roles, I need to say a few words about what I mean.

In my search for a possible general definition I have found the work of Professor Erik Johnsen at the Copenhagen Business School of interest. He claims that leadership is goal-oriented, problem-solving cooperation. Goal orientation is the development and setting of objectives and problem solving is thinking and searching for solutions. The key operative concept is cooperation, but it is limited to goal-oriented and problem-solving activities.

Leadership is enacted through leadership roles and all employees manage to the extent that they actively take part in goal-oriented, problem-solving cooperation. For my purposes, this is a functional definition of leadership and is independent of the formal title a person may have in an organization.

Leadership Processes

In my definition the key word is cooperation, which means that people are interacting.

People have a leadership role when carrying out goal-oriented, problem-solving activities which involve interaction. The core of the leadership process is to combine task and people activities. This may be illustrated in the X-model.

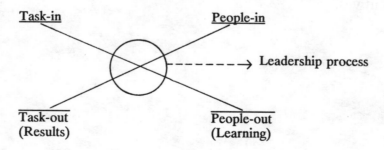

Good leadership is the effective combination of tasks and people to produce optimum results and learning. Based on this view, independent task and people leadership is not leadership. However, enacting simultaneous task and people interaction is leadership. There are several reasons for this:

- You get better solutions by simultaneously solving task and people relations.
- There may be conflict between the task content and the interests of people.
- Personal relations cannot be analyzed by task oriented methods.
- The terminologies for task and people aspects are different.

Creative Problem Solving

A general method for creative problem solving is the Osborne/Parnes model--the CPS model. This model illustrates the basic elements of creative problem solving with its five phases, each split into phases of divergent and convergent thinking.

The divergent, open, non-evaluative process is essential in any creative activity, and produces new ideas. Through a convergent, closed, evaluative process the usefulness of the new ideas is analyzed. Creativity may now be defined as new and useful solutions.

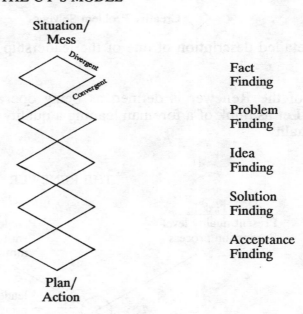

THE C P S MODEL

An Integrated Model

The four leadership roles, the X-model, and the creative problem-solving model may now be combined in one integrated model.

GOAL/SITUATION

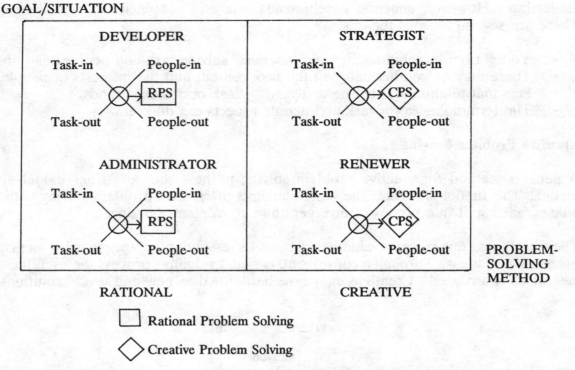

RATIONAL   CREATIVE

☐ Rational Problem Solving

◇ Creative Problem Solving

A more detailed description of one of the leadership roles will help clarify the integrated model.

The role of the Renewer is defined as being operative using creative problem-solving methods. Let us think of a foreman leading a quality circle with the purpose of improving product quality.

THE RENEWER

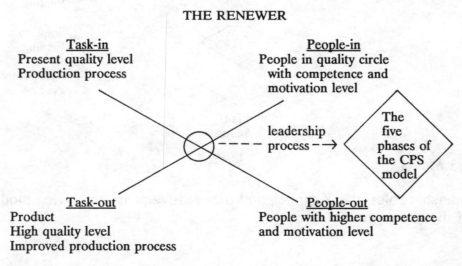

The CPS model is used in the leadership process and the core of this process is to combine task and people. This may be illustrated as follows:

The X-model of task and people is included in each of the five problem-solving phases. In the creative problem-solving process the foreman is combining task and people in a simultaneous creative process. To solve the problem he must establish an open, positive, and risk-taking atmosphere in the quality circle group. The role of the Strategist includes all the elements of the Renewer role. The Renewer in the same way includes all elements of the Administrator, but adds the divergent problem-solving activity. The Strategist is in a development situation. He is at the same time a creator, executer, philosopher and politician. His concern is the future and wholeness. The basic elements of the X and CPS models are the same.

Concluding Remarks: This Integrated Model is based on the following assumptions. 1. A functional definition of leadership (and not one based upon formal status). 2. The roles are inclusive. The simplest role is the Administrator. The Strategist includes all other roles. 3. The core of the leadership process is the simultaneous integration of task and people. 4. Creativity is completely dependent on the same simultaneous, integrative process as in leadership. Based on these four assumptions I have described a tentative approach which combines leadership roles and creativity.

It is important to bring creativity into the world of management to re-evaluate the traditional concept of leadership based on general principles and formal status. I have put forward an alternative paradigm--the need for every person/company to develop their own experience-based theory of leadership--a theory continually changing through organizational learning. To achieve this, creativity in leadership thinking and process is paramount.

The Impact of A Visioning Process   Marjorie Parker
Preview of a Case Study   Partner and Chairman of the Board

The increasing number of articles in management and business journals on the subject of visionary leadership give evidence that creating visions of the future is a process awakening more and more interest among institutions of all kinds. This is also the case in Norway. We have noted, however, that most of the literature is limited to discussing how important visions are, and less about the thinking processes that can be used when going about developing visions. Today in Norway many leaders and management groups do indeed articulate visions, but neither the process nor the vision itself has necessarily led to empowerment of the entire organization and quantifiable results over time.

The Norwegian Center for Leadership Development has received funds from the Norwegian Council for Scientific and Industrial Research to document methodologies used in a major industrial plant in which the management, union leaders, and employees were developing the content of the organizational vision and plans for implementation. Results thus far are extraordinarily promising, providing considerable learning which we would like to share.

Creative technologies, intuition, imagery and the use of metaphor are among the processes used in the development of this company's vision. These are processes which the Center has been using for a number of years in value clarification, strategy and culture interventions as well as leadership development programmes. In Norway we have, however, as of March 1989, only this one company as an example of total employee participation in a visioning process. Should any reader be familiar with comparable case projects or studies in the U. S., we would appreciate very much being informed. The documentation we are undertaking here should be available by January 1990.

Philosophy and Leadership: Marjorie Parker
A 3-Day Seminar for Business Managers

1. Objective: To apply various positions in the history of philosophy and the history of ideas in general to problems of business management.
2. Main Thesis: A business manager faces today some of the basic problems dealt with in the classical philosophical systems.
3. Main common problems:
   - The problem of creating a unity out of a manifold (Plato, Aristotle, Christianity, Spinoza, Confucianism).
   - The problem of health as a problem creating an harmonious relation between managers and employers in a company and between the company and its environment (Hippocrates, Galen, Antonowski).
   - The problem of creating democracy within a company (the political philosophers of the social contract theory (Rousseau, Locke, Mill, Marx).
   - The problem of creating a valid moral system within the company. Can knowledge be morally significant (Socrates, Spinoza, Kant, Bentham, Confucius).
   - The problem of increasing the self-knowledge and the social competence within a company. The logic of emotions. The changing of attitudes (Socrates, Spinoza, Heidegger).
   - The problem of communication. The company as a "communicative" unit. The communication between the company and the market/environment. An individual as a social unit. The significance of the notion of lifeworld (Marx, Heidegger, Habermas).
   - The problem of sex roles and difference in attitude and behavior between man and woman (Plato, Descartes, Rousseau, Mill, Marx/Engels, Simone de Beauvoir, Adrienne Rich et al.)
   - The significance of history in shaping the identity of an individual and a company (Marx, Dilthey, Heidegger).
   - The impact of modern mass culture on the problems of leadership. The fragmentation of the individual. The "counterforces" to creating a "unity out of a manifold" (Harrington, Lash, Allan Bloom).
   - The problem of creating a creative and visionary leadership (vision in political

philosophy and theology. The notion of creativity (Socrates, Spinoza, Heidegger, Habermas).
- The significance of <u>religious and philosophical thought</u> for the work ethics (Christianity, Confucianism).
- The manager's instrument: The revival of the <u>rhetorical tradition</u> (Cicero, Tertullian).
- The art of communicating a message and of getting people to talk to each other.

4. The role of <u>architecture</u> for the social climate in a company (Chr. Norberg-Shulz, Thomas Thiis-Evensen).
5. The role of <u>music</u> for the social climate in a company (i.e., Plato, Jon Roar Bjorkvold).
6. <u>Theory and Practice</u>
An attempt to instantiate the theoretical viewpoints by describing some modern companies:
- a brief <u>history of the trade and the business man</u> and their religious and philosophical background in the various cultures.
- How to <u>reorganize an imperium</u>. (The Roman Empire under Augustus. Similarities with a company.)
- A Norwegian <u>furniture company</u>. <u>HAG</u>-company and its application of slogans and rituals.
- <u>Swedish Volvo</u>: Significance of religious folk's culture and strong leaders.
- The Norwegian <u>Silicon Valley</u>: <u>Horten</u> electronic industries.
- The <u>force of reorganization</u>: a Norwegian cordeales and his history.
- The <u>democratic culture</u> in the old banking system (Sparebankene) and their orientation towards the local community.
- An East-Asian Company: <u>Samsung</u> an Daewoo Corporation and the role of <u>Confucianist ethics</u>. The ethics of duty, of cooperation between social classes and of a life-long education.

Philosophy and Leadership:
A Three-Day Course for Higher Level Managers

<u>Main topics</u>

1. Recent changes in the philosophy of leadership and business culture. Some perspectives.
2. Philosophy of leadership and business culture in antiquity.
3. Philosophy of leadership and business culture in modern times.
4. Some case studies of ancient and modern societies and companies, illustrating different models of leadership and culture.
5. On rhetoric. The art of dialogical leadership.
6. The significance of music and architecture in leadership training.

The course has been arranged twice, in 1986 and 1987, for top level managers. The course was divided into five main sessions (of four hours), two evening sessions (of two hours) and an opening and concluding session. The main session consisted of lectures in sequences of 20-30 min., short discussions in plenum and group discussions.

Royal Roads Military College   **Atholl Malcolm**
Dept. of Military Leadership & Applied Psychology   Head
FMO Victoria, B.C. V0S 1B0 Canada   380-4550

Applied Military Psychology and Leadership Education

The Department of Military Leadership and Applied Psychology at Royal Roads Military College in Canada is responsible for the B.S. degree in Applied Military Psychology and Leadership Education.

The Applied Military Psychology program is designed to meet the need of the Canadian Forces for leaders trained in behavioural sciences. It focuses on developing an understanding of human behaviour and cognitive processes from a physiological perspective.

The foregoing areas of study will provide the foundations for the study of topics in Applied Military Psychology. In part, these topics include: the effects of sustained operation, an examination of fear, courage, transmeridional deployment and psychological warfare. In addition the program focuses on the study of leadership and its integration into the area of Applied Military Psychology. Students in the Honours program will also study psychological measurement, and will complete a research project of direct relevance to the Canadian Forces in an area of Applied Military Psychology.

On graduation students will have completed an educational program relevant to their future careers while simultaneously meeting the requirements for graduate studies in psychology at other institutions.

All students from all degree programs take the following leadership programs:

Military Leadership and Applied Psychology - RR111
Psychology of the Individual - Part 1

An introduction of those areas of human development and behaviour relevant to future leaders' needs and interests commencing with an exposure to the fundamental topics and elementary psychological vocabulary necessary for the understanding of the rationale of individual differences. These topics are then related to certain developmental and social psychological concepts with a view to understanding human behaviour in situations where there is a requirement to influence the behaviour of others. To this end, elementary topics of perception, learning, motivation, intelligence, personality, adjustment, and maturation will be related to concepts of social structure, individual socialization, attitude formation, and interpersonal processes.

Military Leadership and Applied Psychology - RR212
Social Psychology

The basic objective is to introduce and acquaint the student with the broad field of social psychology. The course is designed to provide a fundamental understanding of human social behaviour. Emphasis is placed on the types and degrees of social influences on individuals by groups. An awareness of the dynamic components of social behaviour will contribute to the development of effective leadership and management principles and help the student to prepare for a career as a military officer. Topics will be selected from social perception, norms, attitudes and persuasion, conformity, obedience, groups and group behaviour, aggression, violence and conflict, and social power. In addition, professional officer development and leadership theories and approaches will be presented.

Military Leadership and Applied Psychology - RR311
Leadership and Management Theories and Techniques

This course is designed to familiarize students with leadership theories and techniques as well as the basic management skills required of military leaders. It also aims at developing elementary skills in interviewing and in the analysis of group phenomena. Exercises deal with group dynamics, the leadership process, human relations, supervisory skills, communication and non-directive interviewing, problem analysis, conflict management and decision making.

Military Leadership and Applied Psychology - RR402
Professional and Ethical Issues

This course is designed to provide students with an opportunity to develop an awareness and understanding of some of the issues, concerns, challenges they will have to face and deal with as military officers. Proceeding from a comprehensive review of military professionalism and ethics, the course examines some of the ethical dilemmas which must be confronted by the military officer. Ethical decision making, assessing the ethical climate, institutional pressures, ethical codes and the role of the military personnel system in supporting the military ethos are topics studied in detail. Leadership challenges posed by the nature of continuous operations as well as contemporary issues in military leadership are examined. Organizational leadership, development and change and the attainment of institutional excellence are studied. Finally, an understanding of advanced communication skills is provided through the medium of a media workshop.

References: Taylor & Rosenbach, <u>Military Leadership: In Pursuit of Excellence</u>; Wakin, <u>War, Morality and the Military Profession</u>; Rosenbach & Taylor, <u>Contemporary Issues in Leadership</u>.

The offerings of the Department of Military Leadership and Applied Psychology are many and similar to those offered by departments of psychology in other institutions of higher education. A complete description of courses and more detailed syllabi of those described above may be obtained by writing or phoning Dr. Atholl Malcolm.

Section F
PROGRAMS FOR PRE-COLLEGE STUDENTS

There are probably many more leadership programs for students in elementary and secondary schools than are publicized. Just as the survey conducted in 1985 to discover what was going on in leadership studies in higher education stimulated activity as well as awareness, a survey of pre-college educational institutions might have the same effect. However, the sampling we have in this Source Book was the result of interest and request for information asked of the editors by contributors during the last several years.

In some of the examples, the programs have been fashioned on those offered in higher education. However, others originated in secondary or elementary schools or for K-12 students and may present models ready for adaptation for younger or older persons. They range from peer leadership training to week-long summer residential programs, to a national program that projects out to individual schools for its effect, to workshop models, to selection of students with high potential for leadership, and to generalized curricular change. Unquestionably, it is never too soon to start a sound and research-based program to excite persons to improve themselves and accept major responsibilities, so more and more emphasis at earlier educational levels should be the way to go.

PROGRAMS FOR PRE-COLLEGE STUDENTS

TABLE OF CONTENTS

American Youth Foundation
1315 Ann Avenue, St. Louis, MO 63104

National Leadership Conferences

Robert S. MacArthur
President
314/772-8626

The purpose of the American Youth Foundation is to develop adults who will achieve their best, lead balanced lives and serve others. AYF is a non-sectarian, not-for-profit organization incorporated in Missouri, Michigan, and New Hampshire.

Intensive ten-day programs for high school juniors and seniors and entering college freshmen, the AYF's National Leadership Conferences (NLC) provide a distinctive forum for young people to develop personal effectiveness and leadership skills. NLCs are conferences held in camp settings at Miniwanca on the shores of Lake Michigan and Merrowvista in the Ossipee Mountains of New Hampshire. Participants are sponsored by schools, churches, and civic groups and come from every state and many countries.

ASSUMPTIONS: Leadership ability derives from the interplay of heredity and environment. Young people can be taught skills that will enable them to manage their personal lives effectively and make positive contributions to the larger community. In the years ahead the world young people will inherit will be characterized by increasing: stress on individuals and families; diversity of races, cultures, nationalities, and religions; conflict among groups; destruction of the environment; technological advances that can be used for good or ill.

CURRICULUM: The AYF's focus on leadership includes twelve core themes that are organized into four areas of emphasis.

A. Knowing and Valuing Myself: 1. Understanding Myself as a Unique Individual: What are my basic values and what are their sources? How do I recognize and express my feelings? How do I learn? How do I deal with conflict? Is my life in balance? What are my visions and goals for the future?

B. Learning to be More Effective as an Individual: 2. Developing Mental Capacities: Gathering, analyzing, and applying information; Planning; Solving problems; Managing conflict; Taking prudent risks; Making commitments and keeping them. 3. Maintaining Physical Health and Wellness: Practicing fitness as a balance of nutrition, rest and regular exercise; Understanding the interdependence of the mind and body; Using chemicals responsibly. 4. Improving Personal Communication Skills: Developing active listening skills; Learning to give and receive feedback; Expressing ideas and feelings clearly; Understanding non-verbal communication; Improving writing skills; Practicing the skills of public speaking. 5. Developing Spiritual Insights: Developing spirituality as part of balanced personal growth; Understanding the impact of religious experience on culture; Understanding the role of symbols, rituals, and ceremonies in community life; Exploring basic ideals of Judaism, Christianity, Islam, and other world religions.

C. Understanding a Changing World: 6. Valuing Differences and Creating Inclusive Communities: Understanding and appreciating the changing roles of women and men;

405

Understanding and appreciating those from different races, cultures, nationalities, and religions; Understanding and appreciating those from different generations.
7. Understanding the Consequences of our Impacts on the Environment: Pollution; Consumption of non-renewable resources. 8. Understanding Some Implications of Advancing Technology: Impacts on the environment; Communications and media; Bio-medical research; Leisure and play.

D. Improving Skills for Leadership in a Changing World: 9. Leading and Following in Small Groups: Recognizing tasks related to efficiency and productivity; Developing personal satisfaction and the quality of interactions among group members; Practicing the principles of feedback; Modeling various forms of decision making; Understanding stages of group development. 10. Effecting Change in Organizations: Understanding an organization's culture and values; Creating a vision for the future; Planning and implementing; Developing consensus and constituency support; Understanding influence and power; Managing conflict effectively. 11. Understanding and Applying Principles for Action (Ethics): Identifying values; Understanding stages of moral development; Understanding major ethical systems; Exploring dilemmas for individuals and leaders. 12. Practicing Responsible Citizenship: Accepting responsibility for membership in communities; Seeking a balance between our rights as individuals and our obligations as citizens in a democracy; Performing community service.

National Collegiate Leadership Conference

The conference uses a variety of modes to cover the topics described above, including lecturettes, leadership inventories, simulations, challenge courses, guest speakers, recreational activities, community service, and quiet times. The National Leadership Conference is staffed by volunteers from education, business, and the professions. The NLC Leader's Resource Guide is published as a reference for the conference curriculum.

The American Youth Foundation's National Collegiate Leadership Conference (NCLC) is an intensive six-day program that brings together teams of ten student leaders and two faculty/staff members from diverse colleges and universities. Colleges choose campus leaders according to their institutional program objectives. During the NCLC the team develops an Action Plan for making a difference on campus the following academic year.

OUTCOMES:

1. To develop individual leadership abilities, including self-awareness, critical thinking, communications skills, and balanced living for personal health.

2. To increase the understanding of group process, including organizational theory and development, with a focus on the skills most valuable to campus leaders.

3. To provide the opportunity for team-building for each participating college or university, including the creation of an Action Plan for the following academic year.

4. To provide a national forum for members of diverse institutions to exchange ideas and develop solutions to common problems.

5. To explore selected dilemmas in leadership and determine possible responses based on writing in philosophy, religion, and moral development.

6. To provide peer training and support for participating college advisors.

7. To increase the visionary capability of individuals and teams, including the ability to define and evaluate those powerful goals that motivate individuals and groups.

CURRICULUM:

To accomplish these outcomes, the core faculty offers a set of workshops, seminars, and activities in four areas.

Self-Knowledge and Personal Effectiveness: Myers-Briggs and C-Zone Instruments; Self-Evaluation of Balanced Living; Motivation; The Learning Journal.

Team Building: Group Dynamics; Communication; Team Challenge Course; Valuing Diversity; Responsibility to Self and Others.

Organizational Skills: Organizational Culture; Leadership vs. Management; Power; Conflict Management; Ethics; Delegation.

The Plan of Action: Visions, Purpose, and Reality; Framework for Planning; Development of Individual College Team Action Plans.

In addition to these formal sessions the daily schedule provides a balance of time for physical activity and recreation, solitude, social interaction, and spiritual reflection.

Note: The Program at St. Olaf College (see Section B) directed by Shannon M. Murphy is an example of a campus program in Leadership Effectiveness that depends on American Youth Foundation team training.

Culver Educational Foundation
Box 145, Culver, IN 46511

John Thompson
Chairman, Department of Leadership
219/842-8320

Culver Department of Leadership

Leadership always has been a theme at Culver Academies. Since 1894 cadets have practiced it in a military structure in Culver Military Academy (CMA), while young women have experienced it in a prefectorial system of dorm committees in Culver Girls' Academy (CGA), founded in 1971. Recently, however, a new dimension has been added to the leadership experience at Culver.

Responding to a concern that experience alone is not enough to teach the difficult lessons of leadership, Culver created in 1986 a Department of Leadership which offers a curriculum of formal instruction in leadership values and skills. Following are the "core" courses which cadets and girls take during the first semester of each year they attend Culver.

Leadership I: Orientation introduces all new students to some important aspects of life at the Academy with the aim of helping them develop a sense of purpose early in their Culver careers. Leadership I covers Culver's history and traditions, its philosophy of education, its leadership structures, its standards of conduct, and its Honor Code. Leadership I, a one-semester course, may be thought of more as an exercise in followership than in leadership. It examines some basic fundamentals of leadership, but it is more concerned with an examination of Culver as an institution in which students will learn, grow, and develop a variety of skills--not the least of which are those skills which make for effective leadership here at Culver and beyond.

Meeting twice a week, the course is taught by an interdisciplinary group of faculty and administrators from across campus. Serving as teacher's assistants are a group of senior students who were selected on the basis of their potential for serving as positive role models, teachers, and mentors in the classroom. The text is published by Culver.

In **Leadership II: Values and Leadership**, students examine the values involved in effective citizenship and leadership. The values are represented by the Culver Code of Conduct, which was developed in 1986 as a statement of students' responsibilities at Culver. The Code goes further than that. It is a statement of what is required of all of us who wish to contribute to the groups with whom we live--whether the groups be our circles of friends, our families, our colleagues, or our fellow citizens. It is as much a Code of Citizenship or a Code of Leadership as it is a Code of Conduct. Through use of readings, films, and role-playing activities, students and instructors progress through the Code of Conduct line by line over the course of the semester. Also involved in the course are a community project which each class develops for itself and an individual project in which each student examines a particular line of the Code and presents an oral interpretation of values involved in the line. The text is published by Culver.

Leadership III: Skills for Life and Leadership introduces students to specific skills involved in effective leadership. The course deals with communication, group dynamics, decision-making, goal setting, time management, conflict resolution, motivation, listening, leadership styles, and ethics. As a course requirement all students give a speech analyzing a leader faced with an ethical dilemma. The text is NASSP's <u>Skills for Leaders</u> by Gray and Pfeiffer, along with a text published by Culver.

Leadership IV: Leaders and Leadership Styles considers methods of analyzing leadership styles--task vs. people, autocratic vs. democratic, manager vs. leader--and takes a critical look at leaders in history and current events. The purpose of the course is to encourage students to apply what others have discovered about leadership to their own experiences in working with groups of people.

The course begins with an overview of leadership research with a focus on the phenomenon of leadership style, which may be defined as the patterns of leader behaviors--their words and actions--as perceived by others. As a follow-up, students will complete an inventory which gives an indication of their own personality patterns so that they may begin to understand their strengths and areas for improvement in dealing with others. The texts are <u>Leaders: The Strategies for Taking Charge</u> by Bennis and Nanus; <u>Leadership Papers</u> #1, 3, and 4, by Gardner; and a text published by Culver. The course also takes a look at various 20th century leaders--to include Winston Churchill, Adolf Hitler, Franklin D. Roosevelt, Mahatma Gandhi, and John F. Kennedy--as examples of contrasting leadership styles.

As a course requirement all students will give oral presentations in which they describe their personal leadership styles and lessons learned from the variety of styles studied in the course.

Women in Leadership

Women in Leadership, a required course for first year young women, introduces some important choices they will face in their teenage years and beyond. Topics covered in the course include values, goal setting, decision making, assertiveness, family planning, career planning, women leaders, and women's leadership qualities. The topics are presented in the text for the course, <u>Choices: A Teen Woman's Journal for Self-awareness and Personal Planning</u>, by Bingham, Edmonson, and Stryker. The course is designed to present leadership and personal development topics of specific interest to Culver's young women while cadets are enrolled in the military science program during the second semester of the school year. It meets twice a week (Mon/Thur or Tues/Fri) in the Founders Room of the Memorial Library.

The course involves assigned readings, discussion, guest speakers, and videos. During the second quarter, students select a topic of interest to them related to women or women in leadership. They develop the topic into a presentation for the rest of the class.

Women in Leadership is taught by male/female faculty teams assisted by Culver girls enrolled in Leadership Practicum, an elective offered by the Department of Leadership.

COURSE OBJECTIVES: 1. To introduce a variety of choices young women face in today's society. 2. To sharpen skills in critical thinking and making decisions. 3. To consider personal values and priorities. 4. To recognize qualities women possess which make for effective leadership. 5. To consider issues in family planning. 6. To consider issues in career planning. 7. To discover positive role models in terms of women leaders. 8. To sharpen library research skills. 9. To develop skills in oral presentation.

LEADERSHIP ELECTIVES:

These courses are designed for students with special leadership interests. The courses are open to both cadets and girls. They will meet twice a week. Students will earn a letter grade with a weight of two (2). A cadet choosing to take an elective will take it along with his second-semester JROTC course.

Ethical Leadership: The purpose is to investigate ethical theories, moral knowledge and the meaning of correct and incorrect moral choices. Also, students will discuss contemporary issues involving ethical choices, and they will be encouraged to develop their own system of ethical principles and a moral strategy of leadership. The course will involve outside reading, class discussion, films, and possibly a guest speaker or two. Students will be asked to keep a journal and write a paper describing their personal system of ethical decision making. Prerequisite: Leadership III, all 12th graders.

Psychology of Leadership: This course is designed to acquaint students with basic issues of psychology. Special emphasis will be placed on the major theoretical perspectives in psychology and how each perspective is helpful to a person working with a group as its leader. Resources will be articles, novels, and films. The course format will be lecture and roundtable-type class discussion. Students will have short quizzes, a semester exam, and a project. The course will challenge students to question how they view themselves and their relationships with their peers, family, and society. Prerequisite: Leadership III, all 12th graders.

Peer Leadership: This course is designed to help students develop skills which will enable them, as peer helpers or leaders, to give other students individual attention for specific needs and concerns. The class will consider various communication styles and how these affect interaction with others. Skill-building will be offered in such areas as active listening, question-asking, communicating regarding sensitive issues, and giving feedback. Decision-making and problem-solving abilities will be enhanced through class exercises and assignments. Students will use a journal to help them evaluate progress. The text will be Real Friends by Barbara B. Varenhorst. Prerequisite: Leadership II.

Peer Tutoring: The purpose of this course is to allow students an opportunity to share their expertise, their knowledge, and their concern for others within the setting of the Academic Skills Center. Students will develop abilities to offer assistance in skill-related reading, writing, and studying. Eventually, the course may be a prerequisite for participation in the ASC's Peer Tutor Program. Prerequisite: Leadership II, 10th and 11th graders in good academic standing may apply.

Leadership Practicum: Students taking this course will be assigned to a Women in Leadership class meeting twice a week, where they will serve as a Teacher's Assistant. They will assist the instructors in supervising students in individual and group studies, teach several topics themselves, take on the supervision of one group project, and keep a journal of personal reflections on their experiences in class. The purpose is to sharpen skills in working with people in an academic setting. Prerequisite: Leadership II, junior and senior girls may apply.

Duke University
Box 40077, Durham, NC 27706-0077

Robert Sawyer
Director, TIP Program
919/684-3847

Talent Identification Program (TIP)

The Duke University Talent Identification Program is one of four regional Talent Search programs in the United States. The other three are located at The Johns Hopkins University, Northwestern University, and the University of Denver. Each conducts an annual search for academically gifted junior high school students using the Scholastic Aptitude Test (SAT) of The American College Testing Assessment (ACT). In order to avoid duplication of effort, each program incorporates a particular group of states as its Talent Search region. Each also administers educational programs for academically gifted students. These programs are independent of one another, but admission to all is based on SAT or ACT scores, and Talent Search participants from one region may apply for the academic programs of another. The Duke program is described:

The Talent Identification Program at Duke University, Durham, North Carolina.

The Summer Residential Program offers intensive, fast-paced courses in the humanities, social sciences, natural sciences, mathematics, and computer science. Students enroll in a single class during a three-week session and generally complete the equivalent of a year of high school or a semester of college-level work. Classes meet six hours per day Monday through Friday and three hours on Saturday. Typical class size is 12-20. The instructors are a talented and diverse group that includes members of university faculties, teachers from outstanding secondary schools, and advanced graduate and undergraduate students experienced in teaching academically talented students. All classes also have teaching assistants with expertise in their fields. Most classroom and residential facilities are located on the East Campus of Duke University. Three courses are offered each term at Duke's Marine Lab in Beaufort, North Carolina.

Criteria:

The Summer Residential Program is designed for students entering grades 8 through 11. Students who are juniors and those sophomores who have received an A or B in a TIP college-credit class should seriously consider the Precollege Program. The eligibility criteria for all courses are based primarily on scores attained on one of the two major college entrance examinations, the Scholastic Aptitude Test (SAT) or the American College Testing Assessment (ACT). For courses with a significant writing component, students submitting SAT scores must also earn appropriate scores on the Test of Standard Written English (TSWE).

412

COURSES

Term I

Chemistry
Chinese I
Economics: Microeconomics
French I
International Relations
German I
Japanese I
Latin I
Number Theory
Precalculus Math
Writing I

Term I at Marine Lab

Animal Behavior
Astronomy
Biology: Marine Focus

Term I College Credit

Computer Science
Logic
Psychology
Statistics

Term II

American History: Fads and
    Fading Dreams: 1919-1941
Ancient Greek
Biology: Structural Focus
Computer Science
French I
Japanese I
Latin I
Musical Masterpieces
Number Theory
People and Power
Philosophy
Physics

Precalculus Math
Russian I
Writing I (The Practice of Natural Science;
               The Practice of Social Science;
               The Practice of Literature
Writing and Literary Experience

Term II at Marine Lab

Advanced Precalculus: Functions
Biology: Marine Focus
Economics: Macroeconomics

People and Power Writing II   **TIP Second Session 1989**
                                                          Instructors, Bill Johnson/Scott McEathron

This course is simultaneously an exploration of the dynamics of leadership and a writing
workshop. The course is structured so as to provide images of leadership styles and tools
for the evaluation of such styles of leadership. The writing component of the course is
designed to encourage students to use these images and tools to focus individual thinking
and to enable the class to appropriate them for the construction of a cooperative project.

People and Power is an advanced writing course addressing the issues of leadership. The thematic concerns of the course are the lives, experiences and influences of significant men and women who have emerged as leaders in a variety of settings. The written components of the course encourage students to experiment with a number of rhetorical modes.

The course is divided into three weekly segments. During the first week, the students are introduced to a wide range of leadership styles. They examine the characteristics of influential individuals through literary, biographical and cinematic sources. During the course's second week, students study the relationship between individuals and their communities. Readings for this segment of the course are drawn from philosophy, psychology and sociology. The final week of the course focuses on leadership and social change. Students research, write and present a culminating project on an individual whose leadership has made a significant impact upon the human community.

TEXTS: Robert Bolt, <u>A Man for All Seasons</u>; Sigmund Freud, <u>Group Psychology and the Analysis of the Ego</u>; Niccolo Machiavelli, <u>The Prince</u>; Duplicated selections distributed throughout the term.

<u>Student Responsibilities</u>: 1. Keep up with assigned readings. 2. Participate in class discussions. 3. Work cooperatively on group tasks. 4. Submit written assignments when due. 5. Maintain a journal of the course experience. 6. Contribute to the creation of class project.

<u>Schedule of Topics</u>

Week One:	Images of Leadership in Literature and Film and an Introduction to the Writing Process. 1. <u>Patton</u> and <u>TAPS</u>. 2. <u>The Miracle Worker</u>. 3. <u>A Man for All Seasons</u>; 4. Women in the <u>Hebrew Scriptures</u>: <u>Ruth</u>. Selections from Phyllis Trible's <u>God and the Rhetoric of Sexuality</u>, <u>Places in the Heart</u> 5. <u>Lord of the Flies</u>
Week Two:	The Emergence of the Individual and the Dynamics of the Group 1. Freud on group psychology: <u>The Wave</u>. 2. Community Models which delimit the individual; the individual and history. Selections from Braudel, Fish, Hegel and Marx. 3. Machiavelli on the exercise of individual power: <u>Citizen Kane.</u> 4. Gender issues in the decision-making process: <u>The Color Purple</u>. Selections from Carol Gilligan's <u>In a Different Voice</u>.
Week Three:	Leaders as Agents of Social Change. 1. Martin Luther King, Jr. and the politics of vision. 2. Rhetoric: Principles and strategy. 3. St. Francis and the politics of gratuitous action. 4. Class project: making the case for significant leaders. 5. Leadership in action: retrospect and prospect.

<u>Major writing exercises</u>

Week One: Narrative essay: personal reflection on a leadership situation.
Week Two: Analytical essay: response to the critical theories offered through the
                 week's readings/lectures.
Week Three: Persuasive essay: argumentative writing for group project with special
                 attention to oral presentation and the process of revision.

Commuter Program

The Commuter Program provides an enrichment experience on weekends for students who
live near enough to Duke to commute. Its purpose is to present a high-level introduction
to a variety of topics and issues. It is not intended to provide high-school or college credit.
The Commuter Program is open to all junior high- and senior high-school students who
have participated in TIP's Talent Search--no minimum SAT or ACT score. An example of
a weekend of study in one course is cited below.

People and Power: Commuter Course, Weekend

"People and Power" is a writing course centered on the topics of leadership and the
relationship between the individual and the community. Friday evening the group is
introduced to the course and views the film "Taps." Saturday morning the film is discussed
and some models of individual and group psychology are introduced. The students spend
the remainder of Saturday's class time thinking about, organizing, and writing a critical
response to "Taps," focusing on the issue of leadership. During the afternoon, each student
has the opportunity to meet at least twice with one of the two instructors to discuss their
writing on an individual basis.

Saturday evening the students view another film, "Places in the Heart," and the first portion
of Sunday morning is spent discussing the film in relation to the essay by Carol Gilligan
that the students had read and written about before arriving for the weekend. For the
remainder of the morning, the students work on a narrative essay in which they discuss
some aspect of leadership as it pertains to their personal experience. On Sunday afternoon
the students, in individual consultation with one or both of the instructors, revise their
choice of one of the three essays they had written for the course, including the piece they
had written before the weekend.

TEXTS

Freud: <u>Group Psychology and the Analysis of the Ego</u> (selections)
Gilligan: <u>In a Different Voice</u> (selections)
"Places in the Heart" (film); "Taps" (film)

National Association of Secondary School Principals
Division of Student Activities
1904 Association Drive, Reston, VA 22091

Rocco Marano
Assoc. Director
703/860-0200

National Leadership Training Centers

National Leadership Training Centers are five and six-day educational workshops sponsored by the NASSP Division of Student Activities for student leaders in middle level and senior high school. Each site is a camp-style setting. The curriculum focuses on communication skills, project planning, meeting skills, leadership development, and organizational techniques.

The NLTCs are designed to provide delegates with an opportunity to acquire leadership skills and experience personal growth which will enable them to serve successfully in their position of leadership. The following skill areas are addressed at each training center.

Goal Setting: Importance of goals; Techniques; Long and short-term goals; Personal and organizational goals.

Organization: Planning and conducting an effective meeting; Project planning and development; Member roles and responsibilities; Personal and group time management; Planning an activities calendar.

Group Process: Team building; Roles in groups; Cooperation/competition balance between individual and group efforts; Behavior observation and understanding; Conflict management skills.

Problem Solving and Decision Making: Problems and identification of cause; Leadership --styles of leadership, situational leadership; Needs analysis; Brainstorming; Problem-solving methods; Implementation of solutions; Individual and group decision making.

Evaluation: Techniques/process of evaluation; Evaluation for growth; Personal, group, and goal evaluation.

Communication: Verbal and nonverbal communication skills; Effective listening; Interpersonal and group communications.

Self-Awareness: Self-esteem; Personal motivation.

These programs are designed for the middle level and high school student leader who participates in student council, speech, debate, National Honor Society, or cheerleading, or who will assume a leadership position in the future. Delegates from schools that are affiliated with the Division of Student Activities will receive a reduced registration fee rate. **All programs are for students only** with the exception of the adviser program at Jumonville. Each school may send **five delegates** to the same NLTC site. Students who have previously attended an NLTC may not return to the same site. Because of the nature of this leadership program, advisers or observers may not participate in the program at sites other than Jumonville.

The registration fee is $175 per delegate for schools that have affiliated with the NASSP Division of Student Activities. Schools that are non-affiliates can participate in the program for $225 per delegate. This payment includes lodging, meals, leadership materials, and training. It does not include transportation to the site or personal spending money.

Specific questions regarding the NLTC Programs should be directed to the Division of Student Activities as noted above. A curriculum notebook has been prepared for use at the center which is detailed and includes a section on "Leadership: What is it?"

PROGRAM DESCRIPTION: The Princeton Center for Leadership Training was formed by Dr. Sharon Rose Powell to provide training services to public and private secondary schools and nonprofit community organizations interested in leadership development.

A specific focus of the Center's work is helping schools establish Peer Leadership Training Programs. These programs are designed to help freshmen adjust to their new environment by providing support from upperclass students who learn about leadership and group dynamics in an intensive training course as part of their regular high school curriculum.

Sponsored by the National Executive Service Corps in New York, Dr. Powell, who served as director of the Peer Leadership Training Program at Princeton High School (N.J.) and as director of the Peer Leadership Training Program at Princeton Day School (N.J.), introduced the Peer Leadership model in urban high schools in 1985. The program is now successfully operating in sixteen urban high schools in New Jersey, New York and Connecticut, with a significant roster of sponsors. Through individual consultations Dr. Powell has assisted more than fifty additional public and private high schools in establishing Peer Leadership programs. The Center has also provided training and development assistance to a variety of national and regional service organizations.

A Primary Prevention Program for High Schools
The training in leadership and problem-solving skills and the opportunity to be positive role-models, which the Princeton Peer Leadership Project provides, empowers students and frees them from the social pressures that can interfere with their effectiveness in school and, later, in the workforce. The Princeton Peer Leadership Project is designed to help freshmen adjust to their new environment by providing support from upperclass students who learn about leadership and group dynamics in a comprehensive training course as part of their regular high school curriculum. The model includes extensive training for faculty who in turn work with senior peer leaders. Seniors run weekly in-school meetings with freshmen as well as special events like all-day retreats, large group social activities, and parent-student discussions.

The model includes the following components:
- Two years of training for faculty designated to run the program, including a 5-day conference, 2 one-day workshops, and on-site consultations.
- Attendance for faculty and peer leaders at the Urban-Suburban Peer Leadership Conference in Princeton each year.
- The Center's newsletter, "Peer Group Connection," published three times a year and distributed to all faculty and senior peer leaders.
- A three-day retreat for peer leaders and a leadership course for credit run by faculty advisors from each school.
- Weekly in-school meetings for freshmen, two parent nights, all-day retreat for freshmen, evening social events run by peer leaders, supervised by faculty advisors.

ETS Evaluation

In 1987-88, Educational Testing Service evaluated the Princeton Peer Leadership Project in three New Jersey urban high schools: Passaic, Plainfield, and Trenton. The results are exciting. In general, all participating students, current and former participants, whether peer leaders or first year students, and whether this year's or last year's participants gave the program high marks. A large majority of students reported: that they would participate in the program again if they could (82.3% current PLP; 95.2% former PLP; 100% current peer leaders); that they felt the program was very beneficial to students (71.7% current PLP; 88.0% former PLP; 81.8% peer leaders; and that they expected to use the skills they acquired after graduating from high school (79.6% current PLP; 79.8% former PLP; 100% peer leaders). ETS concluded that freshmen randomly selected to be in the program are absent less often, have fewer discipline problems, and achieve higher math and English grades than students who were not in the program. For a report of the evaluation (Feb. '89) call and ask for "An Evaluation of the Peer Leadership Program: An Examination of Students' Attitudes, Behavior and Performance," Hannaway and Senior.

The Effects on Students

For freshmen, Peer Leadership provides a sense of belonging to a close-knit group which includes respected upperclassmen. It provides them with a time and place each week during school when students listen, share, and support one another. A freshman stated, "Some upperclassmen put high school down and make freshmen feel low. The peer leaders make us feel good. It makes me want to do better."

Senior peer leaders take a rigorous course that gives them responsibility for a group of 12-15 freshmen. They learn critical thinking skills and techniques for leading groups effectively. They learn how to identify a problem and how to develop alternative solutions. They discuss a variety of relationships: teacher-student, boy-girl, parent-child, and they learn how people affect one another. One 1988 peer leader said, "I cannot imagine senior year without this program. It is the most exciting part of my school day."

The Effect on Schools

The faculty speak of how they have felt completely rejuvenated through the program and how their new understanding of group dynamics has affected their lives. Their teaching is better, and they have improved relationships with students and their colleagues. A faculty member noted, "With Peer Group I know I will never experience teacher burnout."

Principals report that after the introduction of the Princeton Peer Leadership Project students show greater respect for each other and school property. The emphasis on being good citizens strengthens the entire school community. One principal wrote, "I am in awe of the power of your program." For a full description of the program, see Sharon Rose Powell, Peer Group Handbook (mimeo); Sharon Rose Powell, "An Assessment of a Peer-Led Training Project," unpublished Ed.D. dissertation, Graduate School of Education, Rutgers University, 1983.

University of Southern Mississippi
The Center for Gifted Studies
Southern Station Box 8207, Hattiesburg, MS 29406-8207

Frances A. Karnes
Director
601/266-5236

Leadership Studies Program

The Leadership Studies Program is designed to fulfill the societal need for future leaders. The one-week summer residential program is a systematic, comprehensive approach for training average to superior students in grades six through eleven with leadership potential. The major goal gives the students the opportunity to acquire concepts and skills necessary for leadership and apply them to real life situations to achieve optimum growth in leadership development.

The program focuses on nine areas necessary for leadership development as derived from the literature on adult leadership training: fundamentals of leadership; written and speech communication; group dynamics; problem solving; values clarification; personal skills; decision making; and planning. The Leadership Skills Inventory has been designed to assess strengths and weaknesses in the nine areas. The self-rating, self-scoring aspect of the inventory allows the student to determine skills already acquired and those needed to be learned. The inventory is diagnostic and prescriptive in nature. After the student plots his or her scores on the Leadership Skills Inventory Profile Sheet, needed areas of training are graphically apparent.

Once the student has determined the areas of need, the teacher selects the appropriate activities from the Leadership Skills Inventory Activities Manual. It is not necessary to cover all the activities; time may instead be concentrated in the areas that need the most improvement. Nor is it necessary to use the activities in the exact order they are listed in the manual. However, if the order of the activities is changed, then care must be taken that materials from a previous activity are not required for the completion of the current activity.

The curriculum structure is diagnostic/prescriptive. Activities are student-centered rather than totally teacher-directed. Many activities utilize group discussion and simulation as a basis for learning. Students and teachers share in the interaction and become partners in the learning process.

A "Plan for Leadership" is developed by each student after all training activities are completed using a format similar to ones utilized in business, industry, and government. Components of the plan include: general statement of the goal; objectives; activities to meet objectives; time-lines; resource persons; evaluation. Plans may be implemented in the school, community, or religious affiliation.

Leadership II is an extension of the program with Leadership I as prerequisite. It focuses on situational leadership, assertiveness training, and other intensive areas of study to further develop leadership potential. Leadership III is an extension of the program with Leadership II as prerequisite. Training includes legal aspects of leadership, responsibilities of various positions of leadership, developing personal power, and leadership for the future. Guest speakers, films, and simulations are used to supplement all training.

420

The Leadership Studies Program has served young leaders from many states. All students in grades 6-11 who wish to develop and enhance their leadership ability and who are nominated by school personnel are invited to apply.

REFERENCES:

Karnes, F. A., & Chauvin, J. C. (1985). <u>Leadership Skills Development Program: Leadership Skills Inventory; Administration Manual and Manual of Leadership Activities</u>. East Aurora, NY: Disseminators of Knowledge, Publishers.

BIBLIOGRAPHY CONTENTS

INTRODUCTION TO THE BIBLIOGRAPHY

The following pages contain a broad diversity of books, articles, reports, texts, and reference materials related to the topic of leadership and leadership education. Just as there is great variety in the leadership courses and programs found in this Sourcebook, there is a corresponding variety in the bibliographic resources that are included herein. There are biographies, histories, training handbooks, political tracts, psychological studies, program reports, management texts, readings in group process, sociological investigations, popular works, classic fiction--and more.

The references in the *Books* and *Articles* sections of the bibliography are listed alphabetically by author. To find books on a particular topic or subject, use the comprehensive index at the back of the Sourcebook.

The boundaries of the subject of leadership are fuzzy. The subject is too broad and diffuse to be easily structured; it cuts across disciplines with writings that include pedantic armchair meanderings, narrowly-focused research, and thoughtful multi-disciplinary tomes, and the literature is growing rapidly. The substantive content of leadership is, in Karl Weick's words, constantly "twigging"--adding new branches to accommodate new research thrusts and learnings. A bibliography on leadership can never be complete. No matter how much is included there will always be more material that could be stuffed into the "leadership" category. Our objective for this bibliography was not to compile a list that was comprehensive (impossible) or tightly focused (of limited use), but rather to provide a pragmatic tool, with enough substance and variety to contain references useful in a diversity of courses, programs and other learning arenas.

The sources of material selected for inclusion in this bibliography include Sourcebook contributors, reference lists contributed by participants in leadership education conferences, exhaustive computer literature searches, recent bibliographies, the Center for Creative Leadership (CCL) Library's resource collection, and suggestions by CCL staff and colleagues.

All of the references are annotated. Some of the annotations are from non-CCL sources, and thus will have some stylistic variety. Use the annotations as pointers to material to select for review, not as definitive summaries of the item's content, nor as an unqualified recommendation of quality.

Readers who are just getting under way in setting up a leadership education course or program, or who are looking for new learning tools and training methods to buttress an existing course, should examine the *Reference and Resource Materials* section of the bibliography. Included in this section are a number of "methods" books on leadership development, group work, and individual growth. Also found in this section are books on simulations in leadership education, a review of instruments used to assess leadership, books useful as course texts, case studies of existing courses and programs, surveys exploring various facets of leadership education and development, and a number of bibliographies, source books and reviews that will enable you to tap additional readings and resources.

BOOKS

Adams, J., & Yoder, J. D. (1985). *Effective leadership for women and men.* Norwood, NJ: Ablex.

Adams and Yoder provide information they hope will help the military and other organizations to better utilize leadership talents of women. They provide a review of leadership theories and then discuss findings from "Project Athena," a comparative study of male and female leaders at West Point.

Alinsky, S. (1972). *Rules for radicals.* New York: Random House.

Alinsky draws on his extensive experience as an organizer of community groups to define areas of emphasis for potential activists and sets forth a method he believes is most successful in effecting social reform. Alinsky weights arguments on means and ends, examines the use of words in influencing peoples, and describes tactics he found viable and that can be employed to change society.

Argyris, C. (1976). *Increasing leadership effectiveness.* New York: Wiley.

A description and analysis of a learning seminar designed to teach top-level executives over a long period how to modify their approach to the world--shifting from emphases on control, winning, and rationality, to concern for valid information, free and informed choices, and expression of feeling. Argyris links his theory of "double loop learning" to the concept of leadership effectiveness.

Astin, A. W., & Scherrei, R. A. (1980). *Maximizing leadership effectiveness: Impact of administrative style on faculty & students.* San Francisco: Jossey-Bass.

The purpose of this study was to determine how an institution's particular style of management and administration affect faculty and students. Astin explores the outcome of administration on the quality of education by assessing its impact on the institution. Profiles of senior academic officers, descriptions of administrative styles, impact of leadership on faculty and students, implications for practice, and proposals for changes in college administration are discussed.

Badaracco, J. L., Jr., & Ellsworth, R. R. (1989). *Leadership and the quest for integrity.* Boston, MA: Harvard Business School Press.

This book poses the question, "How do managers deal with the messy realities and trade-offs of today's business world?" Intending to challenge traditional beliefs about leadership, the authors conducted lengthy interviews with the CEOs of Citicorp, Du Pont, Johnson & Johnson, Colgate-Palmolive and other major companies. Their experiences provide insight into how managers can juggle their responsibilities to the organization with their personal beliefs, their behavior, and their vision for the future of the organization. It is the consistency with which they balance their visions, intentions, and actions that equals integrity. This consistency, claim the authors, is the truest path to leadership.

Bailey, T. A. (1980). *The pugnacious presidents: White House warriors on parade.* New York: Free Press.

Bailey presents a novel approach to American history. This is a study of the basic militancy of each Chief Executive, of what might be termed his "pugnacity index" as disclosed in foreign and domestic crisis.

Baldridge, J. V., Curtis, D. V., Ecker, G., & Riley, G. L. (1978). *Policy making and effective leadership: A national study of academic management*. San Francisco: Jossey-Bass.

The decision and governance processes of colleges and universities are explored in this study. It is a description of the major developments in academic management and governance, including the role of faculty, the styles of administrative leadership, the functions of policy-making bodies, the efforts towards unionization, and control by state systems. A variety of research techniques were used including surveys, analysis of historical documents, interviews, case studies, etc.

Barber, C. J., & Strauss, G. H. (1982). *Leadership: The dynamics of success*. Greenwood, SC: Attic Press.

This book is organized into the general topics of individual processes, group processes, and organizational effectiveness, repackaging basic social psychology as if it had direct relevance to organizations. Barber and Strauss' book contains standard social psychology with plausible conjectures about how it might affect settings quite different from those in which its adequacy was first demonstrated.

Barber, J. D. (1977). *Presidential character: Predicting performance in the White House*. Englewood Cliffs, NJ: Prentice-Hall.

A study suggesting that discernable traits in personality of a candidate or an incumbent president forecast his conduct in office. Barber defines four tendencies or directions of behavior by which a President or aspirant to the position can be adjudged. Barber analyzes Presidents from Theodore Roosevelt to Richard Nixon, appraising each man's character, world views, and style on the basis of childhood experiences and adult conduct both in office and in private life.

Barnard, C. (1968). *The functions of an executive: Thirtieth anniversary edition*. Boston: Harvard University Press.

Path-breaking book on the analysis of business organizations and the functions of the executives in them. Barnard presents his theory of cooperative behavior in the formal and informal organization. Barnard takes that which has been developed at the level of theory and abstraction and puts it in the perspective of the practicing executive.

Bass, B. M. (1985). *Leadership and performance beyond expectations*. New York: Free Press.

Discusses the role of the transformational or charismatic leader--who these leaders are, how they get results, and why their leadership often exceeds all expectable limits. Bass attempts to close the gap between the work of social and organizational psychologists, whose focus has been on small groups and institutional settings, and that of political scientists and psychohistorians, who have done most of the important studies of world-class leaders.

Beal, G. M., Bollen, J. M., & Raudabaugh, J. N. (1962). *Leadership and dynamic group action*. Ames, IA: Iowa State University Press.

Three experts in group dynamics present their experienced techniques for improving leadership, both on the job and in community activities. The book is divided into three parts--Group Interactions, Group Techniques, and Evaluation. The authors hope to "make leadership more realistic and more attainable to the group member who wishes to improve his human relations skills and assume greater responsibilities."

Bellah, R. N., Madsen, R., Sullivan, W. M., Swidler, A., & Tipton, S. M. (1985). *Habits of the heart: Individualism and commitment in American life*. New York: Harper & Row Publishers.

Based on a five-year study of various white, middle-class American communities, this book explores the traditions Americans use to make sense of themselves and their society, and presents the conflict between individualism and the need for community.

Bennis, W. G. (1976). *The unconscious conspiracy: Why leaders can't lead*. New York: AMACOM.

This book provides commentary seeking to distinguish true leadership from mere managing, and to show the difference. The assumption is made that all leaders face basically the same problems. The problems grow more complex as the leader's own authority and autonomy grow more circumscribed by events and forces beyond control. The commentaries raise many questions to stimulate today's leaders to pose further questions in a search for the right answers.

Bennis, W. G. (1989). *Why leaders can't lead: The unconscious conspiracy continues*. San Francisco, CA: Jossey-Bass.

"What prevents leaders from taking charge and making changes?" Bennis writes here about the dark side of leadership, especially the problems a leader encounters in attempting to take charge of an organization. He believes we are presently lacking any true leaders. By the author's definition true leaders embody six important virtues: integrity, dedication, magnanimity, humility, openness and creativity. Not since the 1960s have we been inspired by public figures who have the "X factor--the leader who knows what we want and what we need before we do and expresses these unspoken dreams for us in everything he or she says or does."

Bennis, W. G., & Nanus, B. (1985). *Leaders: The strategies for taking charge*. New York: Harper & Row.

This book projects the belief that leadership is the pivotal force behind successful organizations. To create vital and viable organizations, leadership is necessary. Leadership will then help mobilize the organization toward a new vision of what the organization can be. This leader is one who commits people to action, who converts followers into leaders, and who may convert leaders into agents of change. This concept is called "transformative leadership."

Berkley, G. E. (1971). *The administrative revolution: Notes on the passing of organizational man*. Englewood Cliffs, NJ: Prentice-Hall.

The emphasis of this book is on social and organizational change. Berkley feels that the "system" is adjusting to new situations and new values reasonably well. Organizations and bureaucracies, public and private, here and abroad, "are finding themselves more and more in step with the social forces of their time and are becoming more and more disposed to making their procedures and goals consistent with those of the community in which they exist."

Betz, D. (1981). *Cultivating leadership: An approach*. Lanham, MD: University Press of America.

This book is for the individuals involved in the process of becoming a leader. The manner in which an individual proceeds to develop his/her talents--an odyssey of self-discovery--is utilized in the general discussion. The characteristics and modes of leadership, culture and leadership, the mystique of charisma, leadership in a free society, ideas for individual fulfillment, practice of leadership, and the education and cultivation of leadership are explored.

Birnbaum, R. (1988). *How colleges work: The cybernetics of academic organization & leadership*. San Francisco, CA: Jossey-Bass.

The author's purpose is to provide new thoughts about university and college leadership. In an effort to shed light on the primary dimensions of every university and college, Birnbaum has studied four models: bureaucratic, political, organized anarchy, and collegial. He describes why systems of organization which consider all four aspects are necessary in higher education. In an effort to synthesize these four dimensions, Birnbaum has integrated the best parts of each model into a new model of organization. He illustrates how this model can help academic leaders understand the nature of colleges as organizations, which in turn will enhance their leadership abilities.

Blanchard, K., & Johnson, S. (1982). *The one minute manager*. New York: William Morrow.

A brief presentation of how people produce valuable results and feel good about themselves, and the organization and the other people with whom they work. The book is a simple compilation of what many have taught concerning how people work best with others.

Blau, P. M. (1964). *Exchange and power in social life*. New York: Wiley.

Presents an argument which analyzes the social processes that govern the relations between individuals and groups and their importance for understanding the complex social structures of modern communities and societies. The author attempts to link the study of small groups and broad theories of society by deriving the social processes found in complex structures from simpler processes in small groups and interpersonal relationships.

Bleedorn, B. D. B. (1988). *Creative leadership for a global future: Studies and speculations*. New York: Peter Lang.

This book is apparently an elaboration of a doctoral study designed to elicit the perceptions of educators, students and business leaders regarding the identification of talents critical to effective leadership in the advancing global age. The author's goal was to see whether existing educational programs were in fact attempting to develop the leadership talents needed for our new and changing world.

Bogue, E. G. (1985). *The enemies of leadership: Lessons for leaders in education*. Bloomington, Indiana: Phi Delta Kappa Educational Foundation.

This book centers on the theme that leadership is an art form whose effectiveness is improved by the mastery of leadership and management research and by the display of personal integrity. The book tries to provide the operational answer to the question, "What exactly do we mean when we say that leadership is effective or ineffective?

Boles, H. W., & Davenport, J. A. (1984). *Introduction to educational leadership*. Lanham, MD: University Press of America.

The text deals with questions related to school administration and the development of leaders. The authors have made a conscious effort to show how the behavioral and social sciences contribute to the growth of school administration.

Boone, L. E., & Bowen, D. D. (1987). *The great writings in management and organizational behavior*. 2nd ed. New York: Random House.

An anthology of seminal essays written by individuals whose works have become the cornerstones for contemporary management and organizational theory. From pioneers Weber, Fayol and Follet, to second generation contributors Mayo, Barnard and Maslow, the text is chronological and gives the reader a historical point of reference. Part 3, "The paradigm creators" includes McGregor's "The human side of enterprise," "One more time: How do you motivate employees" by Herzberg, and Likert's "An integrating principle and an overview." The final section, "Major Current Contributions," includes essays by McClelland, Vroom and Schein.

Boyatzis, R. E. (1982). *The competent manager: A model for effective performance*. New York: Wiley.

The purpose of this study was to determine which characteristics of managers are related to effective performance in a variety of management jobs in a variety of organizations. An additional purpose was to investigate how managerial competencies affect each other and relate to other aspects of management jobs.

Bradford, D. L., & Cohen, A. R. (1984). *Managing for excellence: The guide to developing high performance in contemporary organizations*. New York: Wiley.

This book is aimed at managers who are interested in a model of management that the authors contend can move the manager's department "to a state of excellence." Utilizing their own observations along with gleanings from the management literature, Bradford and Cohen developed a model of leadership. To hone it, they applied their concepts in middle management workshops totaling over 200 participants.

Broder, D. S. (1980). *Changing of the guard: Power and leadership in America*. New York: Simon & Schuster.

This work evolved from a series of extensive interviews with this country's generation of political leaders--those born between 1930-1955. Broder shares the views and experiences of this group as well as offering his own thoughts on the men and women who will soon receive "custody of the nation's leadership."

Bruce, J. S. (1986). *The intuitive pragmatists, conversations with chief executive officers*. Greensboro, NC: Center for Creative Leadership, Special Report.

  This study presents the observations and conclusions-in-retrospect of a group of CEOs concerning what was important about their jobs. The report examines how a leader transforms an organization. The study was not intended to look at the results of what these CEOs did, but rather to look at the process by which they went about doing it.

Bullitt, S. (1977). *To be a politician*. New Haven, CT: Yale University Press.

  Initial publication was in 1959. Some additional chapters have been added: abstract and theoretical issues involved in seeking political candidacy for election. Bullitt muses about life and politics, and attempts to relate it to his running for office.

Burdin, J. L. (Ed.). (1989). *School leadership: A contemporary reader*. Newbury Park, CA: Sage.

  Selected articles from recent issues of Educational Administration Quarterly are presented here to provide an overview of school management and organization in the U.S. Four major topics of concern to leaders in education are covered. Chapters 1-5 discuss the characteristics and patterns of the society in which leaders lead. Chapters 6-10 describe the cultures and theories of power in which leaders lead educational organizations. Chapters 11-18 examine action theories and issues clarification to help leaders lead more effectively. Chapters 19-20 look forward to visions of the future of educational leadership. End notes follow each chapter.

Burns, J. M. (1978). *Leadership*. New York: Harper & Row.

  The "dynamic reciprocity" theme is presented in a highly readable volume of leadership analysis. History, biographies, and a socio-psychological approach combine to provide a highly innovative study of the elements of leadership. Teaching and learning leadership are discussed in narrative format. This book could well be used as a follow-up text to the study of leadership theory.

Burns, J. M. (1972). *Uncommon sense*. New York: Harper & Row.

  Burns' treatise asserts that the domestic and foreign policy troubles he identifies as confronting the U.S. are rooted in the habits of those that preserve outmoded myths and shibboleths which blind citizens and Presidents alike to the necessity for creative governmental change. The central argument of the book concerns means and ends, an examination of the capacity of the nation to define its fundamental values and to transform them into guides to action.

Burns, J. M. (1956). *Roosevelt: The lion and the fox*. San Diego, CA: Harcourt Brace Jovanovich.

  Highly readable, two volume biography (Vol. 2 "Roosevelt: Soldier of Freedom"). Burns describes the 32nd President as a man of "no fixed convictions about methods and policies" whose chief tenet was "Improvise."

Bursk, E. C., & Blodgett, T. B. (1971). *Developing executive leaders*. Boston: Harvard University Press.

This is the fourth and final volume of articles selected from the Harvard Business Review for the series in business administration. It brings together sixteen articles concerned with improving administrative competence while broadening the manager's viewpoint.

Campbell, C. (1986). *Managing the presidency: Carter, Reagan, and the search for executive harmony*. Pittsburgh, PA: University of Pittsburgh Press.

Argues that too many studies of the U.S. executives have focused on personalities and styles without adequately taking into account the president's relationship to his advisers and the machinery of the office. Campbell describes the institutional development of the presidency in recent years with particular emphasis on the Carter and Reagan administrations. Campbell draws on interviews with nearly two hundred officials, including senior members of the White House staff.

Caro, R. (1975). *The power broker: Robert Moses and the fall of New York*. New York: Random House.

This book reveals singular public service, achievements, foresight, and egotism of Robert Moses, and attacks the type of urban planning that Moses personified. The author contends Moses' planning was dehumanizing, insensitive toward the poor and minority groups, more concerned with parks and parkways than people, which paved the way for much of today's urban ills.

Caro, R. A. (1984). *The years of Lyndon Johnson: The path to power*. New York: Random House.

The first of a three-volume biography of Lyndon Baines Johnson, the thirty-sixth President of the United States. This volume begins with Johnson's boyhood and concludes with his defeat in his first race for the Senate in 1941. "The more one thus follows his life, the more apparent it becomes that alongside the thread of achievement running through it runs another thread, as dark as the other is bright, and as fraught with consequences for history."

Carroll, S. J., & Tosi, H. L. (1977). *Organizational behavior*. Chicago: St. Clair Press.

This book is about the human problems of management. It focuses on people and organizations, and the many ways these interact to result in varying levels of organizational effectiveness. This book is a prescriptive book; that is, written about what the authors think is the best way to manage different kinds of people in different kinds of organizations.

Caskey, F. (1988). *Leadership style and team process: A comparison of the managerial grid and situational leadership*. St. Paul, MN: University of Minnesota, Dept. of Vocational and Technical Education (ERIC Document No. ED 296162).

This monograph identifies literature on human systems developed from the primary constructs of "task" and of "maintenance" or "relationship." It reviews definitions of leadership and team process and the use of the primary constructs in leadership literature. The report systematically reviews and compares two frameworks developed on the balance of task and maintenance or relationship--the "Managerial Grid" and "Situational Leadership." Each review includes an overview and sections on purpose, constructs with anticipated results, validity, recent writings and critique. The report concludes with a summary, a chart comparison of Managerial Grid and Situational Leadership frameworks, and extensive references.

Chaffee, E. E., & Tierney, W. C. (1988). *Collegiate culture & leadership strategies*. New York: Macmillan Publishing Co.

This text is based primarily upon interviews conducted with over 400 academic administrators from a cross section of schools--small rural colleges to major research universities. Seven case studies are presented to provide researchers and administrators with documented information about the complex dynamics of culture and leadership. The authors consider three key issues: 1) How culture is important in shaping the organizational life of colleges & universities; 2) how academic leaders match decision-making strategies to their organizational cultures; and 3) how executives can develop strategies to address issues in their organizations. Four appendices provide documents, surveys, interviews and tables.

Champion, J. M., & James, J. H. (1989). *Critical incidents in management: Decision and policy issues*. 6th ed. Homewood, IL: Richard C. Irwin.

Designed as an instructional and educational tool for "students in all stages of professional development," this book has application for educators involved in traditional classroom courses as well as management training and executive leadership personnel. The book is comprised of fifty incidents which illustrate the variety of issues facing today's management. The situations take place in various settings including business, government, health care and education. The first forty incidents include: 1) description of the incident, 2) critiques written by academicians, 3) observations made by the authors of the book, 4) discussion items and 5) suggested readings. The last 10 incidents are without critiques.

Clark, K. E., & Clark, M. B. (Eds.). (1990). *Measures of Leadership*. West Orange, NJ: Leadership Library of America.

An introduction to a wide variety of measures of leadership, with detailed information on their characteristics and their validity. The book includes 29 research reports from well-known contributors to the study of leadership; they describe leaders' abilities, personalities, and behaviors. Includes an introduction that summarizes and interprets the findings, and a report of the proceedings of the conference on which the book is based. Written for general readership.

Clemens, J. K., & Mayer, D. F. (1987). *The classic touch: Lessons in leadership from Homer to Hemingway*. Homewood, IL: Dow Jones-Irwin.

This book taps the collective wisdom found in the classic works of Western philosophy, history, biography and drama and applies it to the problems of modern managers and leaders. It addresses such issues as how to build a team and keep it together, how to manage an acquisition once it's in place, how to eliminate daily distractions and how to better trust your intuition.

Clemmer, J., & McNeil, A. (1988). *The V.I.P. strategy*. Toronto: Key Porter Books.

The book is designed for practicing executives and managers who are interested in improving their executive ability and organizational performance. Grounded in popular management theory, Clemmer and McNeil define leadership as "a set of actions for dealing with people-related issues." Four leadership elements that exist in every organization are examined: vision, values, environment and behavior. The authors observe that the only way to change elements of leadership is through the acquisition of skills defined as personal, coaching, team and cultural. They provide examples of individuals who have been successful and offer suggestions on how one can develop these skills.

Cleveland, H. (1972). *The future executive: A guide for tomorrow's managers*. New York: Harper & Row.

Addresses aspirants to positions of responsibility in government, business, or the professions. Succinctly outlines the attributes necessary for the successful executive. Cleveland draws on his extensive experience to set forth the ramifications of the argument that the future will see the emergence of public, parapublic, and private systems organized along consensual or collective terms of increasing complexity.

Cleveland, H. (1985). *The knowledge executive: Leadership in an information society*. New York: Dutton.

Builds on the premise that more than half of all work now done in the United States is information work. Discusses the differences between information and other kinds of resources. Says that, "tomorrow's leaders will be those with a taste for paradox, a talent for organizational ambiguity, and the capacity to hold new and dissimilar ideas comfortably in the managerial mind."

Cohen, M. D., & March, J. G. (1986). *Leadership and ambiguity* 2nd ed. Boston, MA: Harvard Business School Press.

Examines some general ideas about leadership and ambiguity in the context of the American college president. The 2nd edition adds short commentaries, plus brief empirical addenda to the chapters on presidential activities and careers--also an essay on administrative leadership.

Conger, J. A., Kanungo, R. N., & Associates (1988). *Charismatic leadership: The elusive factor in organizational effectiveness*. San Francisco, CA: Jossey-Bass.

This work is a gathering of thoughts and research by experts from various fields: organizational development, management, psychology, and sociology. The rationale: to provide a broad analysis of the concept of charismatic leadership. The variety of contributors included attempt to bring clarity to the problems and differences in understanding the meaning of charismatic leadership. What is it? How does it develop? How might it be cultivated? The authors argue that charismatic leadership can be trained. They offer training approaches as well as provide a questionnaire which can be used to identify individuals, in any setting, with the potential for charismatic leadership.

Connor, P. E., & Lake, L. K. (1988). *Managing organizational change*. New York: Praeger.
   The authors have written this book to help us understand change management. Throughout its ten chapters, the results of extensive research are presented. The book describes how organizational change, though destabilizing and somewhat scary, can be managed with positive outcome. The first chapters discuss how the need for change is usually recognized by foresight of events, or by reaction to surprises. Later chapters illustrate how to proceed with organizational change and how to navigate change effectively. The final chapters discuss the ethical issues involved in organizational change. A selected bibliography, list of tables, figures and questionnaires, plus an index to the text are included.

Cornwall-Jones, A. T. (1985). *Education for leadership: The international administrative staff colleges, 1948-1984*. Boston: Routledge and Kegan Paul.
   This book is concerned with the issues the author encountered in helping others who, in Australia, Pakistan, the Philippines and Ghana, wished to make some use of the ideas for which Henley College then stood; and, in the process, to contribute to an understanding of these staff colleges and their original aims.

Cribbin, J. J. (1972). *Effective managerial leadership*. New York: American Management Association.
   This book was written in response to requests of line managers for realistic guidelines that they can translate into appropriate behavior in their workaday situations. Aimed at the manager who must achieve objectives despite the distractions and irritations of an existence in the corporate "zoo."

Cribbin, J. J. (1982). *Leadership: Strategies for organizational effectiveness*. New York: AMACOM.
   This book seeks to help you improve your leadership competence, based on examining some of the more significant research findings, reflecting on how different leaders have coped with a variety of situations, and formulating a leadership development program custom-tailored to you and your milieu.

Cronin, T. E. (1980). *The state of the presidency*. Boston: Little, Brown.
   Cronin views leadership by a "good ol' boy" (Jimmy Carter) as somewhat of a good thing, but has included his ideas about electoral reform and presidential checks and balances.

Crosby, P. B. (1987). *Running things: The art of making things happen*. New York: New American Library.
   Philip Crosby asks the simple but difficult question: "What is the purpose of an organization?" From the largest multinational corporations to the smallest of volunteer groups, the answer is always the same --- "To help people have lives." Although he is certain there are people who are born leaders, his concern in this book is for the rest of us who find ourselves in charge of something that requires an objective and the

involvement of people. Based upon imaginary characters, Mr. Crosby draws out situations and individuals who have taken on the task of leading and shows how they have adapted the skills of handling and doing while winning commitment from the people involved.

Cuban, L. (1988). *The managerial imperative and the practice of leadership in schools.* Albany, NY: State University of New York Press.

This author examines how the role of the teacher and school administrator has diverged over the recent decades. The gap in the relationship between the activities of each has also contributed to a loss of understanding of their roles in the task of improving what happens in the classroom and throughout schools. In reaction, a somewhat adversarial relationship has developed between teacher and administrator. This author seeks to develop new understandings and to reaffirm the common purposes that exist between these two groups. The author has anchored his premise in professional research, historical studies, and through personal experiences as educator and school administrator.

Czudnowski, M. M. (Ed.). (1982). *Does who governs matter?* DeKalb, IL: Northern Illinois University Press.

Contains essays drawn from a 1981 conference at Northern Illinois University commemorating the centennial of Gaetano Mosca. Most of the elites discussed consist of public officeholders in various nation-states. The social backgrounds, the career patterns, and some of the political attitudes of these elites are examined. Contains a variety of worldviews and intellectual strategies.

Czudnowski, M. M. (1983). *Political elites and social change: Studies of elite roles and attitudes.* DeKalb: Northern Illinois University Press.

Part of a two-volume set ("Does Who Governs Matter?") containing 22 essays drawn from a 1981 conference at Northern Illinois University commemorating the centennial of Gaetano Mosca. The elites discussed in these volumes consist of public officeholders in various nation-states. What is learned about political leaders in these essays has mostly to do with their social backgrounds and with changes therein over time, their career patterns, and some of their political attitudes.

De Gaulle, C. (1975). *The edge of the sword.* 2nd ed. Westport, CN: Greenwood Press.

This book is essentially a selection of essays in which De Gaulle presents his personal philosophy regarding the meaning of leadership, World War II and France's role in the war's history. These elements are woven together by discussions of character, prestige, military doctrine, the conduct of war, and politics and the soldier. The historical insights De Gaulle offers here carry greater meaning for his having lived through so many of the important events he discusses.

Dennison, B., & Shenton, K. (1987). *Challenges in educational management: Principles in practice.* New York: Nicholas Publishing.

The primary objective of this book is to look at the management skills and qualities of school staff and examine the ways in which these can be fully developed. To accomplish this the authors have attempted a comprehensive survey of management thinking as it applies to schools. The emphasis is on problem solving. Four objectives are extensively discussed: 1) attributes and skills associated with effective management can be learned; 2) an understanding of the learning methods is essential in acquiring these skills; 3) effectiveness of managers is influenced by insights about themselves and their work; and 4) information gained by learning about management and interpersonal skills can improve performance.

Doig, J. W. (1987). *Leadership and innovation: A biographical perspective on entrepreneurs in government*. Baltimore, MD: Johns Hopkins University Press.

This book is about men and women who have held top positions in public organizations. From these positions, each individual made a mark on the world, an innovative change, having an influence on what his or her office did, and how. In brief, they fashioned formal authority into effective influence. Using a biographical approach, the authors have selected a number of extraordinary government leaders. Profiles include: "David Lilienthal and the Tennessee Valley Authority," "Admiral Hyman Rickover: Technological entrepreneurship in the U.S. Navy," "The politics of art: Nancy Hanks and the National Endowment for the Arts."

Drucker, P. F. (1989). *The new realities: In government and politics, in economics and business, in society and world view.* New York: Harper & Row.

Drucker presents a synthesized and compelling view of the social, political and economic realities which are currently impacting the heart of many of our social institutions. He analyzes the functions of government, a transnational economy, shifting knowledge base, arms and the economy and other timely concerns. In Drucker's words, "this book does not focus on what to do tomorrow. It focuses on what to do 'today' in contemplation of tomorrow."

Drucker, P. F. (1982). *The changing world of the executive.* New York: Times Books.

This book provides insights into, and an understanding of, the world of the executive. It also provides a useful "executive agenda" to stimulate both thought and action. The book should be read with this overriding question in mind: "How can I, and we in my organization, use this idea or these insights to perform more effectively, to do a better job, and above all, to welcome and accommodate the new and the different."

Drucker, P. F. (1969). *The effective executive.* New York: Harper & Row.

A presentation of the findings based on a systematic study of what effective executives do that the rest do not do, and what they do not do that the rest tend to do. Findings show that effectiveness can be learned, and also, that it must be learned. This book presents in simple form the elements of this practice.

Durrenmatt, F., & Bowles, P., translator (1956). *The visit: A tragi-comedy.* New York: Grove Press.

Originally titled in German, "Der Besuch der Alten Dame," this particular translation adheres strictly to the playwright's original German script. The action of the play is set in the small town of Guellen, "somewhere in Central Eastern Europe." An aging, very wealthy heiress, Claire Zachanassian, returns after being away for many years. Upon the offer of her millions, she quickly turns Guellen, which has been financially poor, into a boom town. However, she has attached a treacherous string to her generosity. She embroils the town leadership in her plot of murder. From these elements the playwright constructs a multi-leveled play, which is at once a moving tragedy and a black comedy.

Dye, T. R. (1983). *Who's running America?: The Reagan years*. 3rd ed. Englewood Cliffs, NJ: Prentice-Hall.

Focuses on the decision-making power of persons in corporate, government, and public interest institutions. Biographical and structural data are presented and analyzed to substantiate Dye's assertion of interaction between private and public elites regarding national decision making.

Dye, T. R. (1986). *Who's running America?: The conservative years*. 4th ed. Englewood Cliffs, NJ: Prentice-Hall.

Revised edition of "Who's running America?: The Reagan years."

Dyer, F. C., & Dyer, J. M. (1965). *Bureaucracy vs. creativity: The dilemma of modern leadership*. Baltimore, MD: University of Miami Press.

This book addresses the problems of leadership, creativity, bureaucracy, progress, and efficiency. It is designed for readers who already have had practical experiences with, or who are engaged in, theoretical studies of modern organizations. Definitions of terms, analysis of what is taking place and what will probably take place, and guidelines on which to base decisions about measures that promise to increase or constrain bureaucracy or creativity are provided.

Engstrom, T. W., & Mackenzie, R. A. (1988). *Managing your time: Practical guidelines on the effective use of time*. Rev. ed. Grand Rapids, MI: Zondervan.

Touted as "a practical guide for chronic procrastinators and those bogged down in the swamps of daily trivia," the guidelines offered here are for the person who is committed to developing the skills of managing activities at work--actually in their whole life--with the little time they have at hand. The authors tell how to establish and refine personal and professional goals, and how to develop short and long range objectives. They note that being organized and directed does not squelch spontaneity or creativity; effective time management clears the path for just such impulses to flourish.

Erikson, E. H. (1970). *Gandhi's truth: On the origins of militant nonviolence*. New York: Norton.

Erickson reveals that what has always been thought of as a relatively minor episode in Gandhi's life--the Abmedabad Mill strike of 1918 and Gandhi's first fast--was, in fact, an event of crucial importance in his rise as a natural leader and as the originator of militant nonviolence.

Fiedler, F. E. (1967). *A theory of leadership effectiveness*. New York: McGraw-Hill.

This book presents a theory of leadership effectiveness which takes account of the leader's personality as well as the situational factors in the leadership situation. This theory attempts to specify, in more precise terms, the conditions under which one leadership style or another will be more conducive to group effectiveness. The book summarizes the results of a 15-year program of research on leadership and a theory of leadership effectiveness and integrates the findings.

Fiedler, F. E., & Garcia, J. E. (1987). *New approaches to effective leadership: cognitive resources and organizational performance.* New York: John Wiley & Sons.

The authors have paid close attention to the function of the leader and the effectiveness with which the group performs its assigned task. Four important concepts are examined: the leader, the group, the organization, and leadership effectiveness. The contingency and cognitive resource models used throughout are the major instruments by which the leader's personality, intellectual abilities, and directive behavior are measured. Included in the text are the characteristics of fourteen studies used in the models, plus a complete list of references.

Fiedler, F. E., & Chemers, M. M. (1977). *Improving leadership effectiveness: The leader match concept.* 2nd ed. New York: Wiley.

Tells how to identify your leadership style and to match it with the situation in which you perform best. Offers guidelines on how to change a situation to strengthen your leadership effectiveness.

Fisher, J. L., & Tack, M. W. (Eds.). (1988). *Leaders on leadership: The college presidency.* San Francisco, CA: Jossey-Bass.

Asked to speak from their own unique perspective, eighteen college presidents have consented to write about the characteristics which promote effective, successful leadership. Writing from such institutions as Notre Dame University, Johns Hopkins University, Boston University and the University of California, each of these past and present leaders writes from his/her personal perspective about the energy, commitment, vision, courage and personal style demanded of their position. Compiled to function as a sourcebook providing valuable insights about the highest ranks of leadership in educational administration, this text offers a view of the problems and issues from leaders' desktops.

Fisher, R., & Ury, W. (1981). *Getting to yes.* Boston: Houghton Mifflin.

This book is about the method of principled negotiation. Descriptions of the problems that arise in using standard strategies of positional bargaining, the four principles of this method of negotiation, and questions concerning the method. Principled negotiation represents an all-purpose strategy.

Folkertsma, M. J., Jr. (1988). *Ideology and leadership.* Englewood Cliffs, NJ: Prentice-Hall.

From four modern political ideologies--American Liberalism, Marxism, Fascism and Islamic Fundamentalism the author has selected seven political leaders who exemplify and embody the essence of each of these ideologies. The leaders surveyed include: James Madison, Franklin D. Roosevelt, Martin Luther King, Jr., Joseph Stalin, Mao Zedong, Adolf Hitler and Ruhollah Khomeini. It is the author's goal to "explain what these leaders believe, how they acted upon their beliefs, what difference it made to their country and, where relevant, to the world about them."

Forisha, B. L., & Goldman, B. H. (1981). *Outsiders on the inside: Women and organizations.* Englewood Cliffs, NJ: Prentice-Hall, Inc.

In this collection of essays, the unique and complex aspects of woman in the workplace are viewed from a sociological and psychological perspective. The text is organized according to four thematic sections: "The setting: Are women different from men"; "Reflections of power: Utilizing the difference"; "Search for support: Surviving in the workplace"; and, "Integrating work and love: Women, work and relationships." Barbara Goldman, Rosabeth Moss Kanter, Helen Graves, Mary Rowe, and Marilynn Rosenthal are among the book's contributors.

Fox, W. M. (1987). *Effective group problem solving: How to broaden participation, improve decision making, and increase commitment to action.* San Francisco, CA: Jossey-Bass.

The author has examined the ways in which one can achieve by using participative problem solving in the work group, committee, or volunteer group. The many achievements of participation-based programs in industry are described, with gentle reminders to others of the difficulties they may encounter if they fail to understand and learn from such model programs. The Improved Nominal Group Technique is presented. This process consists of research-based guidelines that minimize or eliminate the many problems found in conventional group procedures. As a follow-up and review, the appendix includes a test of the concepts of the INGT.

Freeman, D. S. (1942). *Lee's lieutenants.* (Vols. 1-3). New York: Scribner.

A three-volume study of the Confederate commanders who served with and under General Robert E. Lee in the Civil War. "The necessary qualities of high military command manifestly are military imagination, initiative, resourcefulness, boldness coupled with a grasp of practicality, ability to elicit the best of men, and the more personal qualities of character, endurance, courage and nervous control."

Friedman, S. D. (Ed.). (1986). *Leadership succession.* New Brunswick, NJ: Transaction Books.

Succession systems in large corporations are the topic of this examination. The questions posed are: As the position of CEO is so critical, should there be a formal process by which to prepare successors in advance of the CEO's leavetaking? Should potential successors be sought from without the organization to provide a fresh outlook, or should a successor be moved up from within the organization to assure continued commitment to the company's purposes? Answers are offered throughout a series of articles in this text. The various authors have strong views as to the best approach for leadership succession, and in some cases they provide data and research to support their positions.

Frost, P. J., Mitchell, V. F., & Nord, W. R. (1986). *Organizational reality--reports from the firing line.* 3rd ed. Glenview, IL: Scott, Foresman.

An anthology of articles on current management and the picture of many aspects of what people perceive to be the reality of organizations: staffing, making it, images, being different, alignments and realignments, compulsion to perform, control and resistance, humor, hazards, courage, leadership, rises and falls, and organizational effectiveness.

Gabarro, J. J. (1987). *The dynamics of taking charge.* Boston, MA: Harvard Business School Press.

For the new manager, the elements involved in managing an organization, office, department or special project are explored here. The author has distilled the factors which he suggests make a difference to the new manager in any job situation. The stages of taking charge are also pointed out. The organizational and interpersonal work of taking charge are detailed with the new manager in mind. The final chapter addresses the pitfalls and stumbling blocks that may occur in the process of taking charge, and highlights ways to enhance the process. Appendices offer research studies and information on research methodology and design.

Gardner, J. W. (1964). *Self-renewal.* New York: Harper & Row.

The author brings together the topics of moral decay and renewal, and the individual's capacity for lifelong learning. Gardner feels that unless we attend to the requirements of renewal, aging institutions and organizations will eventually bring our civilization to ruin. A call to foster versatile, innovative and self-renewing men and women, who share a vision of something worth saving.

Gardner, J. W. (1978). *Morale.* New York: Norton.

Hope, but not blind optimism, is applauded by the founder of Common Cause and former secretary of Health Education and Welfare, in an essay on the attitudes and values in contemporary society. Offers encouraging thoughts on renewing belief in ourselves.

Gardner, J. W. (1989). *On Leadership.* New York: The Free Press.

John Gardner has put together his series of leadership papers with some additional material to produce a book that explores the multifaceted nature of leadership. The strength of the book is his ability to explicate this complexity while keeping the reader's attention with enlightening anecdotes and a studied optimism. Commenting on leadership development Gardner states, "Fortunately, the development of leaders is possible on a scale far beyond anything we have ever attempted. . . The reservoir of unused human talent and energy is vast, and learning to tap that reservoir more effectively is one of the exciting tasks ahead for mankind."

Garner, L. H., Jr. (1989). *Leadership in human services: How to articulate and implement a vision to achieve results.* San Francisco, CA: Jossey-Bass.

This book addresses the unique demands imposed on leaders working in the field of human services. Drawing on case studies and based on the principles of "result-oriented management," the author outlines how human services practitioners must learn to articulate a vision and then translate their vision into specific objectives.

Garreau, J. (1981). *Nine nations of North America*. Boston: Houghton Mifflin.

The author argues that the disparity within traditional geographic borders of resources, styles of living, and employment make these boundaries ridiculous. More feasible divisions, such as the Foundry (industrial North East), Bread-basket (Midwest), Dixie, and Mexamerica, are suggested with this history and social and economic development concisely imparted as documentation of each area's uniqueness and wholeness.

Gaventa, J. (1980). *Power and powerlessness: Quiescence and rebellion in an Appalachian Valley*. Champaign, IL: University of Illinois Press.

Systematic research on the history of coal and people in the Appalachian valley. Raises question of why the local people haven't put up greater and more frequent resistance to King Coal. The documentation includes the periods of powerful rank-and-file resistance that swept through the valley.

Geneen, H. S., & Moscow, A. (1984). *Managing*. New York: Doubleday.

The author offers his principles of good business management based on his experience as chief executive of ITT. His belief that peak experiences of ordinary, normal people create leaders in business and elsewhere are described along with the fascinating, demanding, and creative processes of management. Topics include: Theory G on Management, how to run a business, leadership, acquisitions and growth, entrepreneurial spirit, and the board of directors.

Gilbert, B. (1983). *Westering man: The life of Joseph Walker*. New York: Atheneum.

A history of the frontier and pioneer life of Joseph Reddeford Walker (1798-1876). Walker was characterized as exceptional for his physical prowess, intellect, talents and because of a consistent pattern of decent, principled behavior which men of great strength and self-confidence can sustain--an example of what a Frontier Hero could and should be.

Gilmore, T. N. (1988). *Making a leadership change: How organizations and leaders can handle leadership transitions effectively*. San Francisco, CA: Jossey-Bass.

The author provides tips on how managers and executives in new positions can quickly take charge. He offers insights on dealing with "the inheritance" left behind by former leaders, and illustrates, for new leaders, how to avoid being caught up in the daily operating routine before having a chance to explore new directions. The ways to bridge lines of communication with existing staff while delegating responsibility, as well as building an effective team and winning its commitment, are outlined. Gilmore also covers the topic of conducting a search for a new leader. The appendix provides a biographical interview sample.

Glasman, N. S. (1986). *Evaluation-based leadership: School administration in contemporary perspective*. Ithaca, NY: State University of New York Press.

This book moves school leaders and decision-makers toward a new model of operation rooted in evaluation. Through his analysis Glasman integrates important theoretical research and practical considerations with a special emphasis on the role of the school principal as one whose work can enhance student achievements.

Golding, W. (1962). *The lord of the flies*. New York: Putnam.

A parable about the breakdown of civilized restraints under extreme circumstance. A nuclear war forces the evacuation of children from Britain. One airplane filled with prep-school boys is wrecked on an uninhabited island. All adults on board are killed; only the boys remain alive. What ensues is the boys' attempt to create a society according to their sense of order based on a combination of their education and character.

Gouldner, A. W. (1965). *Studies in leadership: Leadership and democratic action*. New York: Russell and Russell.

An anthology dealing with the analysis of leadership, made by social scientists promising help to people engaged in democratic action. The book is an effort to provide some understanding of leadership behavior. The book is divided into five parts: types of leaders, leadership and its group settings, authoritarian and democratic leaders, the ethics and techniques of leadership, and affirmations and resolutions.

Graubard, S. P., & Holton, G. (1962). *Excellence and leadership in a democracy*. New York: Columbia University.

A collection of essays addressing the problem of encouraging high standards of leadership in a democracy and to consolidate current thinking on the subject. The book tells us something about the relations between the President and Congress, about admission to American universities, and about trends in scientific research.

Greenleaf, R. K. (1977). *Servant leadership: A journey into the nature of legitimate power and greatness*. New York: Paulist Press.

A constructive and critical examination of leadership and the perversions of leadership in major spheres of American life, including the crucial sphere of the responsibility (and irresponsibility) of boards of trustees. The book develops the concept of the servant-leader and deals with the structure and mode of government that will favor optimal performance of our many institutions as servants of society. The book gives biographical models of two great servant leaders.

Greenstein, F. I. (1982). *The hidden-hand presidency: Eisenhower as leader*. New York: Basic Books.

Analysis of Eisenhower's policies and strategies. Greenstein establishes that the president practiced "public vagueness" and "private precision." Eisenhower purposely projected the image of being a politically benign, folksy leader who reigned but did not rule, so as to publicly accent the head-of-state role of the president, thus garnering public support. Greenstein draws together the lessons that contemporary and future presidents can learn from Eisenhower's style.

Greenstein, F. I. (Ed.). (1988). *Leadership in the modern presidency*. Cambridge, MA: Harvard University Press.

The author acknowledges two premises which underlie the leadership of the nine presidents that have held office during the past 56 years. First, presidents influence public policy and second, the impact of their presidency is a function of their personal leadership qualities. In Chapters 1 through 9, scholars on each of the presidents from F.D.R through Reagan provide insight into the nature of each president's leadership qualities and discuss the impact these qualities have had on policy-making decisions. Drawing on the material presented for each president, Greenstein concludes with his own analysis and observations on modern presidential leadership.

Guest, R. H., Hersey, P., & Blanchard, K. (1986). *Organizational change through effective leadership*. 2nd ed. Englewood Cliffs, NJ: Prentice-Hall.

This book deals with how managers cope with the inevitable barrage of changes that confront them daily in attempting to keep their organizations viable and current. Using a real life plant as a case study, this book follows the plant from disintegration through rebuilding.

Guthrie, E., & Miller, W. S. (1981). *Process politics: A guide for group leaders*. San Diego, CA: University Associates.

Process politics believes groups can change while incorporating the needs of personal fulfillment and individual accomplishment. Self-awareness and group effectiveness are the main focus of this volume. Some applicable "maintenance checks " are included in the appendix.

Halberstam, D. (1983). *The best and the brightest*. New York: Penguin.

A study of the people who filled Cabinet and other high government positions in the administration of John F. Kennedy--'the best and the brightest'--and the questioning of why so many of their decisions and policies were later to be proved so wrong.

Halberstam, D. (1979). *The powers that be: Time, CBS, Washington Post, New York Times*. New York: Alfred A. Knopf.

The subject is the growing influence of the media on American political life. The author examines five great corporations (CBS, LA Times, Time, Washington Post, NY Times).

Harris, P. R. (1989). *High performance leadership: Strategies for maximum career productivity*. Glenview, IL: Scott, Foresman and Company.

The author is both a top management consultant and a behavioral psychologist who has studied, in great detail, the skills that managers must have or will have to develop in order to create a high performance work environment. These important skills include: effective communicating, handling organizational change, an understanding of human behavior and performance, and a commitment to lifelong learning. Each skill is studied and illustrated to show the possibilities for developing peak performance in others. Questionnaires and inventories are provided as aids for data collection. An appendix of resources with a directory of organizations, plus a bibliography, offer further sources of information.

Harvey, J. B. (1988). *The Abilene paradox and other meditations on management.* Lexington, MA: Lexington Books.

Here, through a series of essays, Dr. Harvey contemplates the organizational behaviors in business life which unintentionally set up obstacles to success, growth, and innovation. The title essay, "The Abilene Paradox," illustrates how people in organizations take part in projects or assignments in which there is unspoken agreement that an idea won't work, and yet they proceed to pour valuable time, effort and money into it. Harvey's parables about human behavior in organizations are insightful and engaging.

Heider, J. (1985). *The Tao of Leadership.* Atlanta, GA: Humanics New Age.

Primarily an adaptation of the Chinese classic tome of wisdom, "Tao Te Ching," by Lao Tzu, Heider has found a new application for this work. As a teacher and trainer of group leaders, Heider has taken the principles set down in the "Tao", and applied them to the leadership process. Based upon the same structure as the "Tao," each page is the author's version of the meaning of Lao Tzu's own words. This text is meant to provide inspiration and a path to the higher intentions of leadership for those who lead, in whatever context, whether family or group, church or school, business or military, political or administrative.

Hein, E. C., & Nicholson, M. J. (1986). *Contemporary leadership behavior: Selected readings.* 2nd ed. Boston: Little Brown.

Written for practicing professional nurses, the forty-eight articles included in this work--all written by known leaders in the field of nursing--delve into the origins of professional nursing, with an accent on the use of leadership in clinical practice. The intention is to help nurses cultivate and hone their leadership skills. The book starts with a section on the culture of nursing. Subsequent readings identify needed leadership skills: power, assertiveness, mentoring, and more. Later sections offer thoughts on the future, especially the technological, economic, and social changes that will affect the nursing profession during the coming twenty-five years.

Heller, T. (1986). *Leaders and followers: Challenges for the future.* JAI Press.

Discusses the concepts and dynamics of leadership and followership. Reviews the concept of participative leadership and the changing environment of leadership.

Hellriegel, D., & Slocum, J. W., Jr. (1979). *Organizational behavior.* St. Paul, MN: West Publishing.

An in-depth examination of organizational behavior should be required by all who teach or facilitate leadership development. This book provides a solid base from which the understanding of organizations can arise. A good resource book for staff, yet the lengthy nature of the book limits its use beyond that group.

Hersey, P., & Blanchard, K. H. (1988). *Management of organizational behavior: Utilizing human resources.* 5th ed. Englewood Cliffs, NJ: Prentice-Hall.

A highly readable book about organizational behavior that provides a thorough study of the applied behavioral sciences. This fifth edition builds on the situational leadership thrust of earlier editions, and integrates this with concepts from "One-Minute Managing." The authors seek to help managers cultivate effective organizations by helping them understand why people act as they do, by improving their accuracy in understanding, analyzing and improving their own and other's behavior, and by making use of their ideas in social, family, and work environments.

Herzberg, F. (1966). *Work and the nature of man.* New York: Thomas Y. Crowell.

Third book in a trilogy concerning job attitudes. It represents an elaboration of the "motivation-hygiene" theory of job satisfaction initially formulated by Herzberg in his second book. Provides a summary of more experimental data resulting from replications of his initial study.

Herzberg, F., Mausner, B., & Snyderman, B. B. (1959). *The motivation to work.* New York: Wiley.

This book reports the findings from a study of job motivation. The analysis and interpretations of the authors suggest that a breakthrough may well have been made to provide new insights into the nature and method of operation of job attitudes. The presentation of this study is in clear and simple language. The book presents an interesting and potentially important hypothesis of the nature of job motivation and its effects.

Hitt, W. D. (1988). *The leader-manager: Guidelines for action.* Columbus, OH: Battelle Press.

This is about the practical actions for any leader-manager who aspires to be more effective. The author's approach is based upon the premise that all managers have a "certain amount" of leadership potential and that this potential can be more fully developed. The focus is upon assessing where you happen to be along the leadership continuum and then using the plan of action designed here to develop your attributes. Hitt suggests that, "with concerted effort over about a two-year period. . . an individual manager should be able to improve his or her position."

Hodgkinson, C. (1983). *The philosophy of leadership.* New York: St. Martin's.

A companion to Hodgkinson's "Towards a Philosophy of Administration." He argues that leadership is essentially a philosophical activity that must deal with values because they "impinge upon every phase of the administrative process." The relationship of administration and leadership is one of identity.

Hoferek, M. J. (1986). *Going forth: Woman's leadership issues for women in higher education & physical education.* Princeton, NJ: Princeton Bk. Co.

The concern of this work is the issue of women and their potential for effective leadership, especially in the field of higher education. The author attempts to provide workable strategies for women to reach their potential within college communities. Dr. Hoferek seeks to answer important questions of the leadership process for women: "How do social and cultural expectations shape the roles that women take in academia?" "How can women leap over the obstacles and hurdles into the realms of academic leadership?" Within this brief study the author has compiled convincing data and research to help women chart successful career paths toward rewarding positions of leadership in their chosen fields of higher education.

Hollander, E. P. (1978). *Leadership dynamics: A practical guide to effective relationships*. New York: Free Press.

The contents deal with defining and approaching leadership, authority and followership, social changes and exchange leadership effectiveness and functions in organizations, and a summary chapter on leadership dynamics. The main focus of the book is on leader-follower relations and is an appropriate resource for those interested in the leadership process.

Hunt, J. G., & Larson, L. L. (Eds.). (1979). *Crosscurrents in leadership*. Carbondale, IL: Southern Illinois University Press.

This book examines the variety of leadership approaches that are characteristic of the field today. Vol. 5 in the Leadership Symposia Series originated in 1971. This series covers the content of biennial symposia held at Southern Illinois University. These symposia were established to provide in-depth consideration of current and future leadership directions and to provide an interdisciplinary perspective for the scholarly study of leadership.

Hunt, J. G., & Larson, L. L. (Eds.). (1974). *Contingency approaches to leadership*. Carbondale, IL: Southern Illinois University Press.

In this second leadership symposium volume, 16 outstanding scholars in the field of administrative sciences review and discuss recent contingency approaches to leadership. Extensively illustrated with tables, graphs, and sample scale items.

Hunt, J. G., Baliga, B. R., Dachler, H. P., & Schriesheim, C. A. (1988). *Emerging leadership vistas*. Lexington, MA: Lexington Books; D. C. Heath and Company.

This review of leadership research covers the various, and sometimes controversial, perspectives of researchers across the subject. The research examined here attempts to find answers to "What is meant by leadership?" Beginning in Pt. 1, the first four chapters examine the concept of charismatic leadership. The focus is on how this form of leadership shapes individual motivation and behavior. In Pt. 2, three chapters measure the activities of leadership within the organization. Examples are shown of how leadership runs deep within the functioning of the organization. Pt. 3 reviews the theories of leadership research. The concluding chapters look at some overlooked research, plus new, emerging findings.

Hunt, J. G., Sekaran, U., & Schriesheim, C. A. (Eds.). (1982). *Leadership: Beyond establishment views*. Volume VI. Carbondale, IL: Southern Illinois University Press.

This book is volume 6 of the Leadership Symposia Series originating in 1971. This series covers the content of biennial symposia held at Southern Illinois University. This volume joins the earlier ones in charting the state of the field. This series was established to provide in-depth consideration of current and future leadership directions and to provide an interdisciplinary perspective for the scholarly study of leadership.

Hunter, F. (1959). *Top leadership, U.S.A.* Chapel Hill, NC: University of North Carolina Press.

    This series of studies is an array of logical statements compounded of research abstractions. The exploration of the hypothesis that a power structure exists in concretely definable terms at the national level of affairs was a theoretical statement that guided the research in part. Actual visits with national leaders, observations of them and analysis of their statements and behavior in relation to each other guided the research presented.

Iacocca, L., & Novak, W. (1984). *Iacocca: An autobiography.* New York: Bantam Books.

    An account of Lee Iacocca's life in leadership from his 32 years with Ford Motor Company, to his taking over the helm of Chrysler. The book is filled with personal reflections on his experiences and view of corporate and national leadership.

Ijiri, Y., & Khun, R. L. (Eds.). (1988). *New directions in creative and innovative management.* Cambridge, MA: Ballinger Publishing Co.

    Experts in management and organizational innovation explore domains and methods in creative and innovative management. They cover such topics as, 1) creative management and contemporary society; 2) public policy applications of innovative management; and 3) behavioral science as applied to organizational innovation.

Jacobs, J. (1984). *Cities and the wealth of nations: Principles of economic life.* New York: Random House.

    Treatise on the rise and fall of urban economies--aims to provide reasons for these dramatic economic curves and the resulting social upheaval they produce. The author points up the fallibility and failures of macroeconomics and supplies her own original interpretation of what really causes economies to thrive and expand.

Jacobs, T. O. (1971). *Leadership and exchange in formal organizations.* Alexandria, VA: Human Resources Research Organization.

    The purpose of this book is to review and reinterpret the existing literature on leadership, power--and influence processes in general--in order to arrive at a more general approach to understanding them. The focus is on influence processes in formal organizations. The research was conducted under a contract performed by the Human Resources Research Organization for the Office of Naval Research.

Janis, I. L. (1982). *Groupthink: Psychological studies of policy decisions and fiascoes.* 2nd ed. Boston, MA: Houghton Mifflin.

    The author examines five events from WWII to Watergate which turned into major fiascoes for five American presidents: F.D.R. (being unprepared for the attack on Pearl Harbor); Harry Truman (the invasion of N. Korea); J.F.K. (the Bay of Pigs invasion); L.B.J. (escalation of the Vietnam War); and Richard Nixon (the Watergate cover-up). By a close examination of the group process which led to the course of action taken for each of these events, the question Mr. Janis seeks to answer is: "How could such bright, shrewd leaders and their advisors arrive at such poor decisions?" The author has developed a convincing and controversial set of dynamics to explain group decision-making strategies, and how they can fail.

Janis, I. L. (1989). *Crucial decisions: Leadership in policymaking and crisis management.* New York: The Free Press, Division of Macmillan, Inc.

This leading authority on decision making has published an extensive analysis of how leaders can avoid making fatal policy decisions. Taken from research studies of top-level decision makers in business, government, and military leadership positions, Janis illustrates how when specific steps of information appraisal, verification, and planning are employed, possible failure is virtually eliminated. The author also shows how leaders can keep possible threats and crises in the organization at bay. Lists and profiles of characteristics and practices which will promote effective decision making for managers of all levels of policymaking are included.

Jensen, M. (1987). *Women who want to be boss.* Garden City, NY: Doubleday and Co.

The author explores here the traits of women who have attained success as executives. The unwritten rules of moving up in the organization are well defined. The important skill of developing allies and promoters on the job is also emphasized. Helpful ways to develop a management style which is genuine yet convincing are offered in the profiles of the women interviewed. Issues that drive successful managers are adapted to the unique approach women may find they bring to handling their power and position in business situations. Most of the information presented is distilled through interviews with women working at various levels of management, from the entry-level manager to company president.

Johnston, J. S., Jr. et al. (1986). *Educating managers: Executive effectiveness through liberal learning.* San Francisco, CA: Jossey-Bass.

This book draws on extensive research and management studies to provide business professionals with a clear picture of the special qualities liberally educated managers offer--such as strong management, decision-making, and problem-analysis capabilities, as well as creativity. The book offers administrators and faculty guidance on effectively integrating business education with liberal learning.

Joiner, C. W. (1987). *Leadership for change.* Cambridge, MA: Ballinger Publishing Company.

Drawing on his own experiences with the auto industry and as head of Mead Imaging, Joiner's book is a thoughtful amalgam of theory and experience, logic and practice. It is designed to provide a framework for planning and leading individuals through the step-by-step process that builds a competitive organization. Some of the key ingredients for successful change include: building a top management team; selecting a strategic issue; identifying one key change; and establishing strong personnel support systems.

Jones, B. D., Bachelor, L. W., & Wilson, C. (1986). *The sustaining hand: Community leadership.* Lawrence, KS: University Press of Kansas.

The urban drama, assembly plants in Michigan are primarily used as the vehicle for the examination of the role of the multi-national industrial corporation in decision making in the local community. The effect of auto production on the city and the consequences of changes in production and how an even greater consequence of change may affect patterns in the communities.

Josefowitz, N. (1980). *Paths to power: A woman's guide from first job to top executive.* Reading, MA: Addison-Wesley.

A self-help guide for women managers that provides a multitude of practical suggestions on how to get ahead in the male-dominated business world. Josefowitz offers a variety of personal insights on how women can help themselves and other members of their sex at various stages of the career cycle.

Jouvenel, B. de (1949). *On power: Its nature and the history of its growth.* New York: The Viking Press.

This is a classic work on the origins of power and the history of its development. Divided into what the author terms as books, each section delves into a particular aspect of the use and meaning of power. Book I examines the origins of civil obedience as well as the growth of sovereignty as a divine and political right. Subsequent sections study the notions of the power of command in time of warfare and explore the use of power in controlling social order. Later sections discuss how power may appear to change through revolution and new government when in fact its essential nature remains constant. The issue of limited vs. unlimited power, as in the choice between liberty or security, is discussed.

Kanter, R. M. (1983). *The change masters: Innovation for productivity in the American corporation.* New York: Simon & Schuster.

A thorough and scholarly, but readable, book on the way organizational cultures affect innovation.

Kanter, R. M. (1977). *Men and women of the corporation.* New York: Basic Books.

Through a detailed tour of a firm called "Industrial Supply Corporation," Kanter demonstrates how the careers and self-images of the managers, professionals, and executives, and also those of the secretaries, wives of managers, and the women looking for a way up, are determined by the distribution and exercise of power. Her theory of the effects of power and powerlessness within corporate structures explains why people behave as they do at work.

Kaplan, R. E., Drath, W. H., & Kofodimos, J. R. (1985). *High hurdles: The challenge of executive self-development.* Technical Report 25. Greensboro, NC: Center for Creative Leadership.

The authors of this 40-page report conducted a study to explore self-development, and the particular challenges to its path faced by executives. The report explores the premise that executives, unlike most professionals throughout an organization, tend to be exempt from coming to terms with their limitations, and are further shielded from self-examination by staffs who shy away from opportunities to offer useful criticism. A combination of forty executives, and experts on executives, were extensively interviewed. After careful analysis of over 400 pages of transcripts, distinct patterns emerged in what executives found to be difficult about their positions, and whether or not they attempted personal change.

Kearns, D. (1976). *Lyndon Johnson and the American dream*. New York: New American Library.

Kearns has taken her observations and what LBJ told her during their years together as part of the White House Fellows Program, and distilled them into an anecdotal-analytical picture of his personality and his accumulation of power and how it was put to use in light of the nature of political power in general and the changing character of U.S. government since the 1930s.

Keegan, J. (1987). *The mask of command*. New York: Viking.

Historian Keegan recognizes "the leader of men in warfare can show himself to his followers only through a mask, but a mask made in such form as will mark him to men of his time and place as the leader they want and need." It is the intent of the author to penetrate behind the mask. The following leaders are discussed: "Alexander the Great and heroic leadership"; "Wellington: The anti-hero"; "Grant and unheroic leadership"; and "False heroic: Hitler as supreme commander." He concludes with a provocative "Post-heroic: Command in the nuclear world."

Kellerman, B. (Ed.). (1984). *Leadership: Multidisciplinary perspectives*. Englewood Cliffs, NJ: Prentice-Hall.

This book represents cooperative work in Leadership Studies. It provides a comprehensive range of perspectives on the interactions between those labeled leaders and those labeled followers. It serves as both an introduction to the subject and as a forum for related ideas that may be expected to stimulate more advanced discussion and study. The volume consists of a series of original essays by scholars from different disciplines, each considering leadership issues.

Kellerman, B. (Ed.). (1986). *Political leadership*. Pittsburgh, PA: University of Pittsburgh Press.

This is a source book for the study of political leadership. All of the essays address some aspect of leadership, yet among the authors are philosophers, psychologists, sociologists, political scientists, historians, mythologists, literary figures, activists, and public officials. The collection is particularly rich in work in political psychology, work that explicitly connects political life to the psychology of individuals and groups.

Kellerman, B., & Rubin, J. Z. (Eds.). (1988). *Leadership and negotiation in the middle east*. New York: Praeger.

Published in cooperation with the Society for the Psychological Study of Social Issues, this book consists of a series of thought provoking essays which examine "the nature of that Middle East crisis and the possibilities for compromise, negotiation, and resolution through the personalities and perspectives of national leaders of governments or organizations whose interests were strongly affected by the crisis." The following leaders are discussed: Bashir Gemayal, Menachem Begin, Yasser Arafat, Hafez Al-Assad, King Fahd, King Khaled, Leonid Brezhnev and Ronald Reagan.

Kennedy, D. M., & Parrish, M. E., General editors (1986). *Power and responsibility: Case studies*. San Diego, CA: Harcourt Brace Jovanovich.

The essays in this volume seek to illuminate factors of the complex relationship between leaders and all those followers. The aim is to explain more than simplify the personality traits of several leaders or the techniques of power-wielding. Examines nine case studies of the pursuit and exercise of power in modern America.

Kets de Vries, M. F. R. (1989). *Prisoners of leadership*. New York: John Wiley & Sons.

Kets de Vries explores the inner world of the leader, probing into the psychoanalytical side of leadership behavior. Using a "psychobiographical" approach and drawing on case illustrations and studies of leaders in action, his book examines leadership success and failure at the psychic level. "I want the reader to understand that the leader's task is paradoxical: at one level the leader appeals to the rational capacities of the followers, while at another his or her message is aimed directly at their unconscious."

Kidder, T. (1982). *The soul of a new machine*. New York: Avon.

The story of how a team of computer engineers at Data General Corporation designed and built a powerful new minicomputer.

King, M. L., Jr. (1964). *Why we can't wait*. New York: Harper & Row.

An inside account of the non-violent movement for civil rights which achieved its greatest victory to date with the Negro demonstration in Birmingham in the summer of 1963. Rejecting both planned gradualism and unplanned spontaneity, King here reveals himself as a master-strategist in conducting civil rights demonstrations.

Kokopeli, B., & Lakey, G. (1978). *Leadership for change: Toward a feminist model*. Philadelphia: New Society.

This small book (32 pages) talks about the differences between developing leaders and developing leadership. Starting with the perspective that most leadership has been "patriarchal" with the final responsibility vested in one person, the authors develop the thesis that a different kind of leadership is both possible and desirable. This new mode is called shared leadership, and the emphasis is on distributing the function of leadership throughout the group, rather than relying on a single person as leader. Included are a model of shared leadership and a brief chapter on tactics for achieving shared leadership.

Kolb, D. A., Rubin, I. M., & McIntyre, J. M. (1984). *Organizational psychology: An experiential approach to organizational behavior*. 4th ed. Englewood Cliffs, NJ: Prentice-Hall.

This book is intended as a source of primary material in organizational psychology for the student of management at all three levels--undergraduate, graduate, and in-service. A representative collection of the works of those who have contributed to our understanding of human behavior in groups and organizations. The book tries to portray a balanced view of the field of organizational psychology, including basic ideas and concepts, new approaches, and emerging perspectives.

Korda, M. (1976). *Power: How to get it, how to use it*. New York: Ballantine Books.

    As Korda sees it, life is a series of power plays--from office politics to bargaining with the clerk in a fruit stand. Consequently, he offers guidance in understanding power and developing methods for assuming and exerting it.

Kotter, J. P. (1982). *The general managers*. New York: Free Press.

    This book seeks to report and discuss the implications of a study of a group of executives in generalist or general-management jobs. Conducted between 1976-1981, this investigation employed multiple methods to look in depth at 15 general managers from nine different corporations spread out across the U.S.

Kotter, J. P. (1988). *The leadership factor*. New York, NY: Free Press.

    In a very precise and direct manner the components which allow effective leadership to occur are presented. This book covers such factors as: "Why Effective Leadership is Increasingly Important Today," and, within today's corporate world, what does effective leadership really mean to business outcomes, profits and products. Companies which have shown superior leadership are presented to illustrate the elements present in real situations which promote the growth of effective leadership. The appendix offers an "Executive Resources Questionnaire" helpful to those who may be curious to know where their business falls in the effective leadership spectrum.

Kouzes, J. M., & Posner, B. Z. (1987). *The leadership challenge: How to get extraordinary things done in organizations*. San Francisco, CA: Jossey-Bass.

    Designed for executives, managers and nonmanagers, authors Kouzes and Posner challenge conventional practices of management teaching and leadership effectiveness. Distinguishing management from leadership, they assert "leadership begins where management ends, where the systems of rewards and punishments, control and scrutiny, give way to innovation, individual character, and the courage of conviction." They provide a series of chapters based on leadership practices (knowing, inspiring, enabling and modeling) that can serve as a foundation for developing the reader's own leadership capabilities.

Kraus, R. G. (1985). *Recreation leadership today*. Glenview, IL: Scott, Foresman.

    This book presents an up-to-date analysis of the role of leisure-service professionals in terms of direct program involvement. It has many references drawn from the current literature, and from manuals, guidelines, and other materials submitted by recreation and park agencies throughout the United States and Canada, which describe current leadership practices in the 1980s.

Kraus, W. A. (1980). *Collaboration in organizations: Alternatives to hierarchy*. New York: Human Sciences.

    Kraus advances a series of normative arguments for transforming our organizational structures from competitive/hierarchical bureaucracies into cooperative/horizontal types.

Lansing, A. (1976). *Endurance*. New York: Avon.

    The account of Sir Ernest Shackleton's Imperial Trans-Antarctic Expedition of 1915.

"For scientific leadership give me Scott; for swift and efficient travel, Amundsen; but when you are in a hopeless situation, when there seems no way out, get down on your knees and pray for Shackleton."

Levine, A. (1980). *When dreams and heroes died: A portrait of today's college student*. San Francisco: Jossey-Bass.

This volume discusses the results of three Carnegie surveys: parallel studies of thousands of students and faculty in 1969 and 1976 and a smaller sample in 1978 as well as a 1978 interview study at 26 institutions by the author. Summarizes the surveys and suggests that student characteristics since 1900 alternate between periods in which community interest and self-interest predominate, thus reflecting the national mood.

Levinson, H. (1981). *Executive*. Cambridge, MA: Harvard University.

Levinson states that without effective leadership, neither businesses, communities, nor social groups can accomplish anything. Leaders must be prepared to understand their contemporary role and to act accordingly. This book is designed to foster such understanding--to help senior executives learn more about their role from a psychological point of view and to help them meet the expectations of their organization and the public.

Levinson, H. (1973). *The great jackass fallacy*. Cambridge, MA: Harvard University Graduate School of Business Administration.

The title of this book stems from the so-called "carrot-and-stick" philosophy of management. Levinson believes that only (or primarily) jackasses respond to crush a program of motivation. Levinson substitutes the satisfaction of employees' and managers' psychological need, which he groups under love, hate, dependency and self-esteem.

Levinson, H., & Rosenthal, S. (1984). *CEO: Corporate leadership in action*. New York: Basic Books.

Levinson and Rosenthal demonstrate leadership personified through six well-known leaders in established American organizations. Chief executives such as Wriston of Citicorp, McGregor of AMAX, Inc., and Watson of IBM were interviewed along with their colleagues. Each of these CEOs led his organization in new directions while preserving the organization's strong identity. An excellent treatise in organizational leadership.

Likert, R. (1961). *New patterns of management*. New York: McGraw-Hill.

This book is intended for persons concerned with the problems of organizing human resources and activity. It is written especially for those who are actively engaged in management and supervision and for students of administration and organization. It presents a theory of organization based on the management principles and practices of managers who are achieving the best results in American business and government. It also draws upon research of volunteer organizations.

Likert, R., & Likert, J. G. (1976). *New ways of managing conflict.* NY: McGraw-Hill Book Company.

The authors have written a highly detailed text on the methodology, principles and step-by-step procedures for managing social conflict within organizations--referred to as "System 4." The basic strategy to the Likert method is to substitute the "win-lose" approach to a "win-win" philosophy. The text provides administrators in business, government, education and community groups a clearly detailed presentation on how to reduce internal and external conflict. This book will have special relevance for social science educators and students.

Lilienthal, D. E. (1967). *Management: A humanist art.* New York: Columbia University.

This book is a collection of three lectures presented at the Carnegie Institute of Technology. The lectures are concerned with some aspects of business or public administration; the relationships between business and government, management and labor; or a subject related to themes of preserving economic freedom, human liberty, and the strengthening of individual enterprise.

Lindsey, E. H., Homes, V., & McCall, M. W., Jr. (1987). *Key events in executives' lives.* Technical Report No. 32. Greensboro, NC: Center for Creative Leadership.

This report is designed for those individuals who are concerned with the development of executive talent. Drawing on information gathered from over 191 successful executives from 6 major corporations, this book systematically examines the key events and pivotal experiences which have contributed to these individuals, "high potential" designation.

Lipman-Blumen, J. (1984). *Gender roles and power.* Englewood Cliffs, NJ: Prentice-Hall.

Lipman-Blumen, well known for her research on women, is especially concerned in her book with the etiology of gender differences. The early part of the book examines how ideologies maintain gender inequality, while the latter portion evaluates women's progress from the perspective of our social institutions. A section is devoted to the gender ideologies of ancient civilizations as reflected in mythological and biblical transmissions.

Little, M., & Haley, A. (1965). *The autobiography of Malcolm X.* New York: Grove Press.

Malcolm X describes the brutalities suffered by his family and himself, but also includes an equal measure of commentary about his own degeneracy and two conversions.

Lombardo, M. M. (1978). *Looking at leadership: Some neglected issues.* Technical Report No. 6. Greensboro, NC: Center for Creative Leadership.

This paper reviews some of what is known about leadership, focusing on the data collected about the nature of managerial work. Three dimensions are presented as useful in understanding managerial performance: complexity/simplicity, use of structures, and use of power. A typology is suggested to provide a way of studying leaders through observing how their activities relate to effectiveness in the use of these dimensions.

Lombardo, M. M., & McCall, M. W., Jr. (1981). *Leaders on line: Observations from a simulation of managerial work*. Technical Report No. 18. Greensboro, NC: Center for Creative Leadership.

Leadership makes the most sense when viewed in its environmental and organizational context. This premise forms the basis for the design of a complex simulation for use in this research. This paper addresses issues of measurement, focusing on major organizational problems as the unit of analysis; the impact of different external environments on managerial behavior; the role of coupling and decoupling strategies in managerial action.

Lombardo, M. M. (1986). *Values in action: The meaning of executive vignettes*. Technical Report Number 28. Greensboro, NC: Center for Creative Leadership.

The premise of this paper is that organizational and individual values are cemented not only through grand events, but also through small ones. These vignettes or episodes are vividly remembered even decades later. This paper attempts to show that these vignettes collectively have major significance for organizations, and what they signify needs to be managed to enhance individual and organizational effectiveness.

Losoncy, L. (1985). *The motivating leader*. Englewood Cliffs, NJ: Prentice-Hall.

Enthusiasm, inspiration, and encouragement define the motivating leader. The author has created a program which pinpoints the most effective strategies for cultivating commitment and enthusiasm in others. Eight goals described throughout this text illustrate how much can be accomplished by winning people over to their work and to the organization. Included are personality inventories which direct you to the chapters you most need to read. End-of-chapter summaries draw out the significant points of putting these concepts into action. The writing style is engaging and vital.

Low, A. (1982). *Zen and creative management*. New York: Jove.

Describes how organizations operate and what is happening to people in this age of de-individuation, and how Zen can be practiced at work.

Loye, D. (1977). *The leadership passion*. San Francisco: Jossey-Bass.

This book surveys 180 years of thought and research bearing on the relationships between ideology in the individual and social leadership and management styles. Variables receiving major attention include liberalism-conservatism, risk taking, alienation, anomie, extremism, activism, Machiavellianism, locus of control, as well as leader-follower, parent-child, and age generational relationships. Findings support new models of ideological functioning.

Lukes, S. (1975). *Power: A radical review*. Atlantic Highlands, NJ: Humanities Press International.

Lukes presents what he terms a three-dimensional model of power which, among other things, adds to the model the concepts of "real interests" and "latent" conflict. This study is of the less visible dimensions of power.

Luthans, F., Hodgetts, R. M., & Rosenkrantz, S. A. (1988). *Real managers*. Cambridge, MA: Ballinger Publishing Company.

    Chock full of insightful observations, this book lays out the factors which make "real managers." Following an introductory chapter, the authors investigate what real managers do, then next discuss what successful real managers do. Included are discussions of the networking, human resources management, and communication activities of managers. The authors conclude with a chapter on how their findings fit into current management thinking. In this concluding chapter, the author discusses how his findings fit into current management thinking. Suggested further readings, plus references and an index, are provided.

Maccoby, M. (1981). *The leader: A new face for American management*. New York: Ballantine.

    Leaders come in many forms and are called many things. This book gives a brief review of leadership today, but focuses on the lives and career paths of six leaders. A good book for advanced study and group discussion. The range presented includes an assistant secretary to a congressman to a chief executive officer to a plant manager.

Maccoby, M. (1976). *The gamesman: The new corporate leaders*. New York: Simon & Schuster.

    A nonfiction paperback that holds your attention like a novel if you know anything or care to know anything about the political life of modern corporations.

Machiavelli, N. (1952). *The prince*. New York: New American Library.

    A leadership classic of value to everyone who is likely to work with or for manipulative leaders or be tempted to become one.

MacKinnon, D. W. (1978). *In search of human effectiveness*. Buffalo, NY: Creative Education Foundation.

    This publication brings together Dr. Donald W. MacKinnon's vast background in the nature and nurture of creativity. This volume is a collection of papers that focus on the understanding and nurturing of the creative potential in individuals. The articles included come from a variety of diverse sources. The major theme of the research and writing is a concern to find ways to help people become as fully functioning as possible.

Maier, N. R. F. (1963). *Problem-solving discussions and conferences: Leadership methods & skills*. New York: McGraw-Hill.

    This book deals with research on improving the effectiveness of a leader's performance in group problem solving and decision making. This volume integrates these studies with earlier research on problem solving and frustration. The principles of group behavior that are used by leaders and how they may serve to improve meetings is the subject of this book.

Manchester, W. (1983). *The last lion: Winston Spencer Churchill*. Boston: Little, Brown.

    Working with diaries, memoranda, government documents, the private correspondence of Churchill and others, interviews with Churchill's surviving colleagues and members of his family, the author provides a narrative re-creating the past and private life of Churchill. This is the first of a two-volume biography.

Manchester, W. (1978). *American Caesar: Douglas MacArthur, 1880-1964*. Boston: Little, Brown.

A biography of the General of the Army, Douglas MacArthur. "He was a great thundering paradox of a man, noble and ignoble, inspiring and outrageous, arrogant and shy, the best of men and the worst of men, the most protean, most ridiculous, and most sublime."

Mansfield, H. C., Jr. (1980). *Machiavelli's new modes and order: A study of the "discourses on Livy."* Ithaca, NY: Cornell University Press.

Mansfield discloses and explicates things that Machiavelli thought prudent to conceal and camouflage, and highlights Machiavelli's clever conspiratorial, philosophical, and humorous strategy.   In exploring the extent of Machiavelli's intention and his responsibility for modernity, Mansfield demonstrates "how the control of things not previously or usually thought political is represented in his discussion of political things."

Manz, C. C., & Sims, H. P., Jr. (1989). *Superleadership: Leading others to lead themselves.* New York: Prentice-Hall.

With this work Manz and Sims challenge the traditional authority-based concept of management theory. Building on Manz's earlier concept of "self-leadership," which posits that the highest performance comes from those who lead themselves, the "superleader" is seen as one who teaches others to lead themselves. Written for the practicing manager, the book provides behavioral and cognitive strategies to facilitate this goal. Eisenhower, William McKnight, Joe Paterno and Ruth Randall are profiled as individuals embodying the spirit of the superleader ideal.

March, J. G., & Weissinger-Baylon, R. (1986). *Ambiguity & command: Organizational perspective*. Marshfield, MA: Pitman Publishing Inc.

This book is about military decision making under conditions of ambiguity, situations where objective, technology, or experience are unclear, and where solutions and problems are joined together. The intent is to explore whether theories of decision making under ambiguity, developed through observations of nonmilitary organizations, might contribute to understanding and improving some aspects of command decision making in the navy.

Marcus, S. (1974). *Minding the store*. Boston: Little, Brown.

In addition to a smooth sales pitch for his successful and luxurious merchandising enterprise (Neiman-Marcus), Marcus portrays humor, and a cultivated and relaxed sense of self. Marcus' somewhat unorthodox political and social attitudes and details of expertise in store management give this biography its interest.

McCall, Jr., M. W. & Lombardo, M. M. (1983). *Off the track: Why and how successful executives get derailed*. Technical Report Number 21. Greensboro, NC: Center for Creative Leadership.

A report of a study conducted by the Center for Creative Leadership of those who were once quite successful top executives, who later derailed. The results have been organized to answer four questions: Why were those who derailed so successful in the first place? What events brought their weaknesses to the surface? Why did they derail? How did they differ from those who remained successful? The study was based on interviews of Fortune 500 corporation executives.

McCall, M. W., Jr. (1977). *Leaders and leadership: Of substance and shadow*. Technical Report Number 2. Greensboro, NC: Center for Creative Leadership.

This paper examines some of the problems with the accumulated research on leadership, reviews some studies of managerial work that stimulate new ways of thinking about leadership in organizations, and suggests some directions that might improve our understanding of the topic.

McCall, M. W., Jr., & Lombardo, M. M. (Eds.). (1978). *Leadership: Where else can we go?* Durham, NC: Duke University.

A series of readings compiled at the Center for Creative Leadership provides a different perspective to stimulate more creative thoughts about the future of leadership study. Alternative conceptual frameworks, new variables, and alternative methodologies are offered.

McCall, M. W., Jr., Lombardo, M. M., & Morrison, A. M. (1988). *The lessons of experience: How successful executives develop on the job*. Lexington, MA: D. C. Heath and Co.

"Where do successful business leaders come from?" "How do they learn the skills that propel them to the top of their companies?" In pursuit of answers, these authors sought out top executives across the U.S. and asked them about the work experiences which had had the greatest influence on the direction of their careers. By examining these career profiles and evaluating them in a systematic manner against current research in the fields of learning and human motivation, the authors reveal surprising answers to what actually shapes the managerial lives of individuals with executive leadership potential.

McCaskey, M. B. (1982). *The executive challenge: Managing change and ambiguity*. Marshfield, MA: Pitman.

This book offers timely suggestions and practical help for managers facing change and ambiguity. Its discussions of mapping, of the stress of ambiguity, of forces that favor or block creativity, of qualities of the creative person--including courage, humility, toleration of disorder, use of intuition, integration of opposites in the personality--all are valuable to the manager in gaining insight.

McClelland, D. C. (1979). *Power: The inner experience*. New York: Irvington.

The author is primarily concerned with major personal and national motives, such as the need for Power, the need for Achievement, and the need for Affiliation, as they are revealed in personal and group fantasies. Using modern techniques of measurement, the author tests and validates the theory of psychosexual and psychosocial development. Detailed findings are provided. National motivational characteristics are explored as to where they fit in a psychosocial power drive.

McFarland, A. S. (1969). *Power and leadership in pluralist systems*. Stanford, CA: Stanford University Press.

    This book creatively synthesizes all relevant works on the nature of power in pluralist systems including such diverse works as Dahl's "Who Governs?" (1961), K. Mannheim's "Ideology and Utopia" (1936), and Easton's "The Political System" (1953). An analysis of the differing approaches to problem solving in the political arena.

McFeely, W. S. (1981). *Grant: A biography*. New York: Norton.

    A biography of Ulysses S. Grant, Union Army Commander and eighteenth President of the United States. "It is, finally, a story of the quest of an ordinary American man in the mid-nineteenth century to make his mark. Grant failed as a peacetime army officer, a farmer, a minor businessman, a store clerk--and still he wanted to be taken into account."

McGregor, D. (1966). *Leadership and motivation: Essays*. Cambridge, MA: MIT (Edited by W. G. Bennis, et al.).

    A collections of essays by McGregor, covering the various periods in his career: Industrial Relations days at M.I.T., Antioch College presidency days, and then his return as Sloan Professor to M.I.T.'s Sloan School of Management. Essays reflect McGregor's ability to change an entire concept of organizational man and to replace it with a theory that stressed man's potentials, emphasized man's growth, and elevated man's role in industrial society.

Mills, C. W. (1956). *The power elite*. New York: Oxford University Press.

    The power elite is composed of men whose positions enable them to transcend the ordinary environments of ordinary men and women; they are in positions to make decisions having major consequences. This book studies these hierarchies of state and corporation and army which constitute the means of power, which offer us the sociological key to an understanding of the role of the higher circles in America.

Mintzberg, H. (1973). *The nature of managerial work*. New York: Harper & Row.

    Dr. Mintzberg has sought to identify the whole range of relationships comprising the manager's world in the contemporary organization, and as a result his conclusions have great worth in a world dependent of leadership skills. An identification of the behavioral skills combined with an overview of how managers manage is presented. Characteristics of managerial work, work roles, variation in work, science and the manager's job, and future of managerial work are topics covered.

Mitchell, T. R. (1982). *People in organizations: An introduction to organizational behavior*. New York: McGraw-Hill.

    This book focuses mainly on the individual and group levels of analysis, and frequently and consistently reminds the reader of the impact of environment on behavior. The author states that he intends to provide a survey of the field of organizational behavior that reflects current research and that does so in a highly readable fashion.

Morgan, G. (1988). *Riding the waves of change: Developing managerial competencies for a turbulent world.* San Francisco, CA: Jossey-Bass.

Gareth Morgan argues that it is not enough to look at what organizations and managers are doing well, but rather, it's critical to see how managerial skills can enhance one's ability to anticipate change. The competent manager needs to have one foot in tomorrow's business. He defines the ways managers can look for what is changing in new technologies, market conditions, management trends, and in employees' values and expectations. Morgan sets out a program for cultivating a "proactive mindset" to managing.

Morgenthau, H. J., & Hein, D. (1983). *Essays on Lincoln's faith and politics.* (Vol. 4). Lanham, MD: University Press of America.

Morgenthau approached Lincoln's view of ethics and religion from the vantage point of the political scientist and historian. Hein has approached the study of Lincoln's faith as a theologian and religious historian. Lincoln's religious and political ethics represented the core values in the American political tradition.

Morrison, A., White, R. P., Van Velsor, E., & the Center for Creative Leadership (1987). *Breaking the glass ceiling: Can women reach the top of America's largest corporations?* Reading, MA: Addison-Wesley.

Although women run many smaller companies in America, the top of the largest companies is different. These women run into the glass ceiling, a transparent barrier at the highest level, that only a handful have been able to break. Based on a three-year study of women executives in America's largest manufacturing and service companies, this book examines the factors that determine success or derailment in the corporate environment.

Morrison, M. K. C. (1987). *Black political mobilization, leadership power and mass behavior.* Albany, NY: State University of New York Press.

The term "Black political mobilization" describes the political victories of Black Americans in the South. The author returned to Mississippi to examine the many advances in Black electoral involvement in the years after the passage of the Voting Rights Act of 1965. The book focuses on three rural Mississippi towns. The towns are agricultural and poor, with populations around 2000 and significant Afro-American voting majorities. Influenced by the civil rights era of the 60s, they have elected Black mayors since the early 70s. An excellent example of minority electoral politics, this region has become a rich environment for a new class of Black leaders.

Murphy, J., & Hallinger, P. (1987). *Approaches to administrative training in education.* Albany, NY: State University of New York Press.

This book is directed at a variety of audiences: leadership academies, students of educational administration, professors, staff developers, practitioners, policymakers, and staff members of principal centers. Practical information is provided on a wide selection of training programs. Presenting a diversity of training models, the authors have attempted to build upon what has been learned in the past by placing these models into an historical perspective. Those involved in implementing and developing administrative training programs throughout the sphere of educational administration should find this text of special interest.

Murray, C. (1984). *Losing ground: American social policy*. New York: Basic Books.

Murray strongly indicts American social policy in this heavily documented and densely written analysis. His central argument is that the "Great Society" programs have been disastrous to the poor, especially the poor blacks. Their failures, he contends, have stemmed from ignoring basic principles.

Naisbitt, J. (1984). *Megatrends: Ten new directions transforming our lives*. New York: Warner.

This book is about a new American society that is not yet fully evolved. This book focuses on the megatrends or broad outline that define the new society. Trends tell you the direction in which the country is moving. This book describes the environment in which to consider the decisions of life: what to study; the right job path; where to live; where to invest money; whether to start a business, join a union, or run for public office. Offers a context to assess today's events.

Napier, R. W., & Gershenfeld, M. K. (1981). *Groups: Theory and experience*. 2nd ed. Boston: Houghton Mifflin.

This book focuses on group dynamics. Theory, concepts, and data are presented in chapters dealing with such themes as perception, group norms, leadership, and problem solving. At the end of each chapter several group exercises are described in sufficient detail to be implemented.

Natemeyer, W. E. (1978). *Classics of organizational behavior*. Oak Park, IL: Moore.

As stated in the title, this volume is a classic. From Maslow on motivation to Hersey and Blanchard on the life-cycle theory, this book is a foundational presentation of organizational behavior. The 32 individual essays/articles are some of those we see over and over again. It is nice to have them all in one volume.

National Commission on Excellence in Educational Administration (1987). *Leaders for America's schools*. Tempe, AZ: The University Council for Educational Administration.

The focus of this report is the improvement of educational leadership. Contents include: significant recommendations; a vision of school leadership; what public schools, professional organizations, universities, state policymakers, federal policymakers, and the private sector should do; and concluding remarks.

Neustadt, R. (1980). *Presidential power: The politics of leadership from FDR to Carter*. New York: Wiley.

This is not a book about the Presidency as an organization, or as legal powers, or as precedents or as procedure. The purpose here is to explore the power problem of the man inside the White House. . . It is a problem common to Prime Ministers and Premiers, and to dictators, however styled, and to those Kings who rule as well as reign. It is a problem also for heads of private 'governments,' for corporation presidents, trade union leaders, churchmen.

Neustadt, R., et al. (1986). *Thinking in time*. New York: Free Press.

This is a book about time and high-level political actions, but it is not a book on time management. The authors' focus is time past, and they offer stories and suggest tools with the hope that they can illustrate ". . . how to use experience, whether remote or recent, in the process of deciding what to do today about the prospect for tomorrow."

Newman, A. S. (1981). *Follow me: The human element in leadership*. Novato, CA: Presidio Press.

Written from the perspective of military command and leadership, the author writes about aspects of managing people. Based upon recollections, anecdotes, and incidents over the forty-plus years of leadership within the U.S. Army, Major General Newman explains what he considers to be three primary aspects of motivating people: 1) "Command Presence." 2) "Command Techniques."3) "Command in Battle." Convincing others to follow is a skill which this author believes dates back to mankind's earliest beginnings. These colorful stories not only offer interesting history, they serve to illustrate how commanders are effective in directing their followers, while encouraging their independent thought and action.

O'Connell, B. (1976). *Effective leadership in voluntary organizations: How to make the greatest use of citizen service and influence*. New York: Association Press.

The viewpoints in this book constitute some guidelines for making voluntary organizations effective instruments for citizen service and influence. Topics include: getting organized, the role of the president, volunteers and staff, recruiting the right staff, training and holding a good staff, constructive planning, board of directors and committees, fund raisers, communications, budgeting, involvement of minorities, dealing with controversy, and evaluating results.

Oates, S. B. (1983). *Let the trumpet sound: The life of Martin Luther King, Jr.* New York: New American Library.

It is a magnificent recreation of his life--of a boy dominated by the minister father who "ruled his home like a fierce Old Testament patriarch"; of a young scholar passionately caught up in the teachings of Thoreau and Gandhi; a man driven by his vision of racial equality. Stephen Oates portrays the forces that shaped "a very human man"--parental, cultural, spiritual, and intellectual--and of the force he became at a crucial moment in American history.

Odiorne, G. S. (1987). *The human side of management: Management by integration and self-control*. Lexington, MA: Lexington Books.

In light of the transition in our economy from industrial-goods producing to information producing, managers increasingly find themselves concerned with the motivation of a work force that is well educated and highly talented. These "knowledge workers" require ongoing intrinsic incentives to commit to the organization's mission. The author aims to show managers how they can act as the integrators of their staffs. Throughout the book's fourteen chapters, each component of managing, from hiring, training, development, appraisal and mentoring to firing can be approached to cultivate the talents and strengths of one's staff, while achieving the mission and goals of the

462

larger organization.

Olmsted, M. S., & Hare, A. P. (1978). *The small group*. New York: Random House.

This study has two aims--first, to serve as an introduction to an area of interest in sociology and psychology, and second, to organize and interpret a body of ideas and research. The study of small groups seemed to stand in considerable need of organization and interpretation, which provided the basis for this book.

Ott, J. S. (1989). *The organizational culture perspective*. Chicago, IL: The Dorsey Press.

This is a careful examination of the procedural difficulties and concerns in defining an organizational culture. Dr. Ott pinpoints where the organizational culture viewpoint fits into organization theory, and why it differs from the other aspects of human organization. Dr. Ott also provides a description of the uses, procedures, concepts, language, and theories of organizational culture. An historical analysis on the growth of organizational culture perspective is combined with viewpoints drawn from cultural anthropology, sociology, and ethnoarcheology. In addition to an extensive bibliography, charts, tables, and a subject index are included with the text.

Ouchi, W. (1981). *Theory Z*. Reading, MA: Addison-Wesley.

Ouchi shows how American corporations can meet the Japanese challenge with a highly effective management style that promises to transform business in the 1980s. Theory Z management takes the best of Japanese business techniques and adapts them to the unique corporate environment of the United States. The book goes behind the scenes at several U.S. corporations making the Theory Z change and shows step-by-step how the transition works. Corporate philosophies are examined.

Owen, H. (1987). *Spirit: Transformation and development in organizations*. Potomac, MD: Abbott Publishing.

This is a book about "Spirit," and how it changes and develops in organizations. Pt. I: Chapters 1-6 lay the groundwork for Mr. Harrison's thesis that spirit plays as important a role within an organization as its leadership. Pt. II: Chapter 7 describes the need for someone to be the facilitator to the process of infusing the organization with spirit. Pt. III: Chapters 8-10 build the theory and practice of organizational spirit upon concrete findings extracted from three case studies: The Internal Revenue Service, The Eastern Virginia Medical Authority, and The Norfolk, Virginia Water Management Authority. Moral: Spirit = Meaning. A selected bibliography is provided following the text.

Paige, G. D. (1972). *Political leadership*. New York: Free Press.

A book of readings plus an accompanying monograph and bibliography to help establish the study of political leadership as a special subject of inquiry in world colleges and universities or in other places where independent scientific thought is possible. The book suggests the outlines of what such a field could be like and illustrates some of the foundations for it that are already available. The book is in 5 parts, each focusing upon an aspect of political leadership.

Pascale, R. T., & Athos, A. G. (1982). *The art of Japanese management: Applications for American executives*. New York: Warner Books.

Presents findings and opinions on how Japanese business management differs from ours, and how it can be advantageously applied in reversing the "steady deterioration in our industrial standing." Dissecting Japan's Matsushita Electric Co. and ITT as two profoundly unlike models of industrial management perceptions, beliefs, assumptions, style and skills, the authors draw into their analysis key Japanese and American cultural premises.

Pearce, W. B., & Cronen, V. E. (1980). *Communication, action, and meaning: The creation of social realities*. New York: Praeger.

The authors feel communication either as a process or an entity can "best be studied as a process of creating and managing social reality rather than as a technique for describing objective reality." The authors focus upon the historical development of philosophical logic systems that either explicitly or implicitly describe this function of language.

Perlman, B., Gueths, J., & Weber, D. A. (1988). *The academic intrapreneur: Strategy, innovation, & management in higher education*. New York: Praeger.

As defined in this book, intrapreneurship is entrepreneurship turned inward; it is the new venture within an organization. The authors have investigated how it works in the academic community. They begin with an overview of the concept of intrapreneurship and its process, then go on to describe the intrapreneurial world. Later chapters examine a model of intrapreneurship and delve further into the meaning and use of intrapreneurship to the growth of organizations. The book concludes with a look at the future possibilities for intrapreneurship. An extensive index and bibliography are included.

Peters, T. (1987). *Thriving on chaos: Handbook for a management revolution*. New York: Alfred A. Knopf.

Thomas Peters, well known lecturer and author of *In Search of Excellence*, stirs the waters of the status quo calling for revolution in American management. According to Peters, his book "challenges everything we thought we knew about managing, and often challenges over a hundred years of American tradition." Peters recognizes "chaos" as an inherent element in any competitive situation. Chaos must be addressed and dealt with "proactively" if American business and industry want to remain key players in the global marketplace. Peters prescribes what changes are necessary for positive results.

Peters, T. J., & Waterman, R. H., Jr. (1982). *In search of excellence: Lessons from America's best-run companies*. New York: Harper & Row.

Thomas Peters is a frequent speaker at business conferences and seminars telling American management how to lead effectively. Peters and Waterman studied 43 successful American companies and found eight basic principles shared by all of them. The Wall Street Journal called it "Exuberant and absorbing--one of those rare books on management that are both consistently thought-provoking and fun to read."

Petrullo, L., & Bass, B. M. (1961). *Leadership and interpersonal behavior*. New York: Holt, Rinehart & Winston.

   This volume represents an introduction to a way of examining the leadership process. The text is based on a symposium of the Office of Naval Research, and is an anthology of the various reports. The book deals with systematic experimental developments in the field of leadership research. Topics include: current psychological theories of leadership and interpersonal behavior, in the small group and in the large organization.

Prewitt, K., & Stone, A. (1973). *The ruling elites: Elite theory, power, and American democracy*. New York: Harper & Row.

   Brief examination of elite theory. Presents both a philosophical and historical summary of the elitist position.

Ritti, R. R., & Funkhouser, G. R. (1987). *The ropes to skip & the ropes to know: The inner life of an organization.* 3rd ed. New York: John Wiley & Sons.

   How an individual operates and fulfills his role within an organization is the topic. From subordinate, to manager, to executive, the authors use characterizations to illustrate how each of us learn "the ropes," or the internal protocol of an organization. This protocol is not found written in the staff procedures manual, or listed within the history of the company. The ways of survival and success in any organization are discovered in the ability to read the invisible definitions to which it subscribes. Each company, or business, or office has its own rituals. These rituals make each business distinctive. The authors invite responses and criticisms. Additional suggested readings follow the text.

Robbins, S. P. (1979). *Organizational behavior*. Englewood Cliffs, NJ: Prentice-Hall.

   Organizational behavior is dissected into the individual, the group, and the organization in this book. Values, personality, perception, communication, and dynamics are but a few of the pertinent chapter titles. A strong resource for staff, this book provides easy-to-find information on all organizational behavior subjects.

Rosenbach, W. E., & Taylor, R. L. (Eds.). (1984). *Contemporary issues in leadership*. Boulder, CO: Westview.

   Purpose of this book is to describe the phenomenon of leadership and to identify what it is that makes a person an effective leader. Articles cover an inter-disciplinary overview of the key issues in leadership at different organizational levels from a variety of perspectives.

Rothberg, D. L. (1981). *Insecurity and success in organizational life: The psychodynamics of leaders and managers*. New York: Praeger.

   This study of the psychology of leadership among 330 business and military elites seeks to better understand what drives organizational leaders to pursue power and success. Each of the four leadership types--rational, existential, administrative, and entrepreneurial--are explored. The book discusses the complex relationships that exist between personality and the attainment of success, and then identifies and systematizes the distinguishing psychological characteristics.

Roy, R. H. (1977). *The cultures of management*. Baltimore, MD: Johns Hopkins University.
    A study of management cultures in four principal areas: organization, technology, quantitative methods, and behavior, based on the author's lifetime of experience as educator, business executive, labor arbitrator, and consultant. A book full of practical wisdom on the top-management job, replete with aphorisms, and good chapter summaries.

Ruch, R. S., & Goodman, R. (1983). *Image at the top: Crisis and renaissance in corporate leadership*. New York: Free Press.
    The answers to reviving the American corporation and healing the costly rift between business and labor, according to the authors, lies with top corporate officers who must learn how to communicate openly and willingly with employees, the media, and the public.

Rustow, D. A. (1970). *Philosophers & kings: Studies in leadership*. New York: George Braziller.
    Includes essays on James, Mill, Newton, and William James, as well as essays on more explicitly political leaders. This collection seeks to explore the phenomenon of leadership. The approaches vary from historical analysis of the leader and his times to psychological analysis of the leader and his followers to theoretical analysis of leadership demands inherent in certain political movements. There are also essays dealing with conceptual approaches to leadership.

Sarason, S. (1972). *The creation of settings and the future societies*. San Francisco: Jossey-Bass.
    The primary purpose of this book is to investigate a "setting" (any instance when two or more people come together in new and sustained relationships to achieve certain goals). This definition is meant to include a continuum of social phenomena which ranges from marriage to revolution.

Sawhill, I. V. (Ed.). (1988). *Challenge to leadership: Economic and social issues for the next decade*. Washington, DC: The Urban Institute Press.
    "What kind of nation do we want to be?" is the crux of a thought-provoking discussion of the important social and economic issues facing the U.S. As the U.S. enters the final decade of the 20th century, four key issues will demand effective moral and political leadership: America's economic and political position in the world; each generation's responsibility to the next; the necessary limits of individual freedom in a large, interdependent society such as ours; the continuing obligations of those who have for those who do not. The consensus seems to be that the leadership decisions that are made tomorrow and in the near future will determine what kind of nation we will live within during the 21st century.

Sayles, L. R. (1989). *Leadership: Managing in real organizations*. New York, NY: McGraw-Hill Book Company.
    While many aspiring managers and business school graduates develop an understanding of the goals of management and their outcomes within the dynamics of

an organization, the "how" of pursuing goals and outcomes is often the stumbling block for managers. The author provides a detailed examination of managing in the real world. He points out the intricate navigational skills required in managing within assigned areas of responsibility, as well as the negotiating skills needed for working with other divisions of an organization which may indirectly contribute to one's success or failure.

Schaller, L. E. (1986). *Getting things done: Concepts and skills for leaders*. Nashville, TN: Abingdon Press.

Although based upon a framework of leadership within the church organization, this book is written for all managers. The author discusses the factors which comprise influential, effective leaders. How leaders use their skills to organize and direct individuals and groups to "get things done" is explained by a series of premises which the author poses. These include: "Effective leaders are both willing to lead and also know how to organize for action." "Effective leaders recognize and affirm the value of coalition, know how to enlist others, and are also willing and able to function comfortably and creatively with committees." "Leaders are proactive; they find time and opportunity to initiate new ways."

Schein, E. (1985). *Organizational culture and leadership*. San Francisco: Jossey-Bass.

Purpose of this book--to clarify the concept of "organizational culture" and to show how the problems of organizational leadership and organizational culture are intertwined. Organizational culture can aid or hinder organizational effectiveness, and leadership is the fundamental process by which organizational cultures are formed and change is explored.

Schiffer, I. (1973). *Charisma: A psychoanalytic look at mass society*. New York: Free Press.

Focuses on the psychological ingredients, especially the unconscious forces that allegedly create the conditions for the emergence of the charismatic leader. Schiffer wants to emphasize the part that the individual psychology of the masses plays in creating leaders rather than the specific abilities of the leaders themselves.

Schlesinger, A. M., Jr. (1985). *Robert Kennedy and his times*. 2nd ed. New York: Ballantine.

Historian Schlesinger writes as an admirer and friend of Robert Kennedy in this massive biography. Granted free access to the Kennedy family papers and other documents, the author combines a thorough review of Kennedy's public career with a more intimate record of his private life.

Schull, B. D. (1975). *How to be an effective group leader*. Chicago: Nelson Hall.

Attempts to identify the components of group leadership and to simplify the process of becoming a successful group leader through the identification of attributes, qualities and characteristics of effective leadership, each of which have been loci of research emphasis in leadership.

Schutz, W. (1977). *Leaders of schools: FIRO theory applied to administrators*. La Jolla, CA: University Associates.

   This study provides the outlines of a theory of administrative personnel, and the directions for the selection and training of institutional managers--directions that are substantially tied to a logical, theoretical system and that have a clear, pragmatic payoff for those who confront selection decisions.

Scott, R. F. (1923). *Scott's last expedition: Captain Scott's own story*. Philadelphia: Transatlantic.

   The personal journals of Captain Robert Falcon Scott on his 1910-1912 expedition to the South Pole. "Had we lived, I should have had a tale to tell of the hardihood, endurance, and courage of my companions which would have stirred the heart of every Englishman."

Selznick, P. (1983). *Leadership in administration: A sociological interpretation*. Berkeley, CA: University of California Press.

   Leadership in Administration has become a classic in the art of executive leadership. His reminder that the true exercise of leadership transcends a concern with mere efficiency is even more appropriate in today's era of quasi-scientific thought about organization.

Sessoms, H. D., & Stevenson, J. L. (1981). *Leadership and group dynamics in recreation services*. Boston: Allyn & Bacon.

   This book is a text and training manual for students wishing to apply group dynamics techniques to recreation service environments. It consists of ten chapters: Introduction, The Nature and Art of Leadership, The Nature and Function of Groups, Forces Affecting the Functioning of Groups, Small Group Techniques, Large Group Techniques, Group Problems, Leadership Development, Supervision and Consultation, and Evaluation.

Shakeshaft, C. (1987). *Women in educational administration*. Newbury Park, CA: Sage Publications, Inc.

   In response to the large amount of literature about administrators and the business of school administration, Shakeshaft prepared this book which addresses the special issues and concerns of women as they pursue leadership positions throughout the ranks of higher education. The author attempts to answer such key questions as, "Where are the women managers?" and, "How can we remove the barriers to women's advancement into school administration?" The appendix of the text offers strategies for enlarging women's access to administrative positions. The author also strongly advocates training programs concentrated solely for women in educational administration.

Sheehy, G. (1988). *Character: America's search for leadership*. New York, NY: William Morrow and Company.

   Well known for her previous works, "Passages" and "Pathfinders," Gail Sheehy profiles the top political figures of our recent past and on the current scene. In an effort to reveal the elements of leadership and character which propel one to the top, Sheehy has chosen such men as Jesse Jackson, Bob Dole, Gary Hart, Mike Dukakis and President Bush. Each individual's profile is here presented in a clear, if not always flattering, light. As the author puts it, "Readers should feel the same cold slap of insight, awakening them from conventional thinking, that I feel each time I study the character of a leader as it has developed."

Silk, L., & Silk, M. (1981). *The American establishment*. New York: Avon.

The Establishment as the third important force in American society--following democracy and capitalism--is the subject of this study of the U.S. power structure. What the Establishment is, how it operates, and the powerful role it plays in U.S. history today are examined in mini-histories of what the authors believe to be the nation's most influential organizations.

Simonton, D. K. (1987). *Why presidents succeed: A political psychology of leadership*. New Haven, CT: Yale University Press.

This book examines the four standards of presidential success: success in presidential elections, popularity in the polls, performance in the White House, and presidential greatness. As a political psychologist, the author looks at the presidency and the appearance of personal qualities that may contribute to effective leadership. Such factors as attitudes, intelligence, childhood experiences, age, environment, motivation, and cognitive style are measured in winning an election, acting as commander-in-chief, and carrying out legislative programs. The author's use of empirical methods to analyze the relationships of traits to effective leadership lend credibility to his conclusions.

Smith, P. B., & Peterson, M. F. (1988). *Leadership, organizations, and culture: An event management model*. London: Sage Publication Ltd.

The authors have designed their own research model to show that being able to read the culture of an organization is central in all types of leadership functions. With the expansion of multinational corporations, this ability has become increasingly crucial to corporate survival. Chapters 1-4 focus on an historical analysis of leadership research, beginning with studies in the 1940s, up to contemporary research. Chapters 5-7 present the author's research model. Chapters 8-10 develop this model further by discussing its 3-tiered perspective. The final chapter contrasts the author's model with five other models analyzed in the book. A thorough bibliography, plus an index, follow the text.

Srivastva, S. (Ed.). (1988). *Executive integrity: The search for high human values in organizational life*. San Francisco, CA: Jossey-Bass.

Twelve leading scholars in the field of organizational behavior examine the role integrity plays or could play in contemporary organizational thinking and decision making. From Michael Maccoby's inventive "Integrity: A fictional dialogue," to the empirically based "Reciprocal integrity: Creating conditions that encourage personal and organizational integrity," by Chris Argysis and Donald Schon, this collection of original essays should appeal to academics, executives, students and individuals concerned about ethical thinking in the corporate environment.

Stewart, R. (1976). *Contrasts in management: A study of different types of managers' jobs, their demands and choices.* New York: McGraw-Hill.

This book addresses primarily those who have to select and train managers, and to those who seek to evaluate their jobs. It also addresses any manager who is interested in the nature of his job, in trying to do it better by understanding the choices that it offers him, or in seeking to plan his career. The contrasts between managers' jobs is also addressed.

Stogdill, R., & Coons, A. E. (1957). *Leader behavior: Its description and measurement.* Columbus, OH: Ohio State University College of Administrative Science.

This book describes the procedures involved in the development of a research tool, the Leader Behavior Description Questionnaire; the successive revisions and adaptations of the questionnaire; and summaries of the results of its use in a variety of organizational settings. This is part of the Leadership Series in Ohio Studies in Personnel published by the Bureau of Business Research.

Tannenbaum, R., Weschler, I. R., & Massarik, F. (1961). *Leadership and organization: A behavioral science approach.* New York: McGraw-Hill. (Reissued by Garland Publishing, New York, in 1987).

This book represents a selected collection of the writings of members of the Human Relations Research Group of the Institute of Industrial Relations at UCLA. The writings are followed by independent distinguished experts in management theory, group psychotherapy and psychology, and sociology.

Taylor, R. L., & Rosenbach, W. E. (Eds.). (1984). *Military leadership: In pursuit of excellence.* Boulder, CO: Westview Press.

Taylor and Rosenbach have been military leaders and have taught military leadership. Their motivation in assembling this selection of readings was to make a contribution to the development of the concept of leadership in the military.

Taylor, R. L., & Rosenbach, W. E. (Eds.). (1989). *Leadership: Challenges for today's managers.* New York: Nichols Publishing.

This book is comprised of twenty-two articles written by nationally recognized authorities on management. The book is aimed at practicing managers "who are doing leadership or aspire to be leaders." From John W. Gardner's "The Antileadership Vaccine," found in Part 1, to Bernard Bass' "Leadership: Good, better, best," the reader is provided a variety of thought-provoking essays. The purpose of the book is to stimulate thought and to help provide a framework for understanding the multifaceted nature of executive leadership.

Terrill, R. (1980). *Mao: A biography.* New York: Harper & Row.

A biography of the late Chinese leader, imbued with Terrill's familiarity with and respect for Chinese culture. The author shows how Mao identified his own suppression as a boy under an unrelenting, dictatorial father with the suppression of the peasants, and consequently forged strength and lessons useful in his complex future.

Thompson, K. W. (Ed.). (1983). *Ten presidents and the press*. Lanham, MD: University Press of America.

   The present volume brings together the work of leading presidential interpreters and scholars who met for extended discussions at the Miller Center. It contains presentations and discussions on ten presidents and their relations with the press: Woodrow Wilson, Franklin D. Roosevelt, Harry S. Truman, Dwight D. Eisenhower, John F. Kennedy, Lyndon B. Johnson, Richard M. Nixon, Gerald Ford, Jimmy Carter, and Ronald Reagan.

Thompson, K. W. (Ed.). (1985). *Essays on leadership: Comparative insights*. Lanham, MD: University Press of America.

   Six studies of important world leaders, including Winston Churchill, Dwight Eisenhower, and Adlai Stevenson, are presented. Their direction has had a lasting effect, especially on leadership in the Cold War. Each essay looks at the background, philosophy, and charisma of these very different leaders from across the world. The purpose is to draw out principles of leadership by focusing on the political practices of these statesmen. A thoughtful reflection, and a review of the historical facts dominate these essays.

Tichy, N. (1986). *Transformational Leader*. New York: Wiley.

   "This book probes into the practical issues facing the leaders of the fundamental changes needed in American industry. The answers to persistent and massive competitive pressure are found in the experience of leading-edge firms and outstanding managers. The stories are brought to life and the underlying patterns revealed. Relevant and timely for all general managers."

Tucker, R. C. (1981). *Politics as leadership: The Paul Anthony Brick lectures*. (11th series). Columbia, MO: University of Missouri.

   Originally a series of lectures delivered in 1980. The book examines the traditional way political scientists and political philosophers have viewed the nature of politics, specifically the view that politics is an exercise of power.

Vaill, P. B. (1989). *Managing as a performing art: New ideas for a world of chaotic change*. San Francisco, CA: Jossey-Bass.

   Vaill's most recent publication is intended for practicing managers who want a fresh look at organizations and how to manage them. The book's two concurrent themes are introduced in the title. First "performing art" is Vaill's metaphor representing "dynamism, fluidity, extraordinary complexity and fundamental personalness of all organizational action." The second concept of "chaotic change" describes "a system of problems or instabilities," which Vaill sees present in today's corporate environment. These two themes are brought together in a series of chapters meant to challenge and stimulate the reader to new levels of management innovation and effectiveness.

Van Fleet, D. D., & Yukl, G. A. (1986). *Military leadership: An organizational behavior perspective*. Greenwich, CT: JAI Press.

   Concepts and research from organizational behavior are employed in an effort to further our understanding of military leadership. In addition, a more complex framework for the study of leadership is presented and its utility illustrated through actual experiences of research based on military samples--from general to specific.

Vroom, V. H., & Yetton, P. W. (1975). *Leadership and decision making*. Pittsburgh, PA: University of Pittsburgh.

This book is written for scholars, researchers, managers or administrators who share an interest in leadership, decision making, and organizational behavior. Central to all the research reported in this book is the role of situational differences as determinants of the choice of a decision process. A summary of the major findings and how they relate to other approaches in the study of leadership is provided.

Vroom, V. H., & Jago, A. G. (1988). *The new leadership: Managing participation in organizations*. Englewood Cliffs, NJ: Prentice-Hall.

The significance of the power sharing of leaders with their constituents and staff members, and its impact upon cultivating participation and influence in organizations is measurable, say the authors. Intended for use by several different audiences, the book presents a model for measuring situational leadership. Chapters 2 through 4, and 8 through 12 are of particular interest to managers. Academic readers will want to look closely at chapters 6 through 12. Leadership trainers will find chapters 6 and 8 through 13 useful. Appendices expand upon the meaning of measurements and definitions. The bibliography provides 105 references to related literature.

Wall, J. A. (1986). *Bosses*. Lexington, MA: Lexington Books.

The author writes about those managers, men and women, who are first-line leaders, not about boardroom executives and middle managers who may never "walk the floor" with their employees. These leaders occupy the "hands-on" positions that feel the pressure from the top and bottom as well as from peers. They are the buffer between customers, employees, and upper management. The nature of their daily routine is unpredictable. Their days are packed with many brief and varied obstacles to overcome. The people interviewed for this book cover a diverse selection of occupations, from assembly-line supervisor, air controller manager, and research director, to heart transplant surgeon.

Walton, C. C. (1988). *The moral manager*. Cambridge, MA: Ballinger.

How does the ethical manager tackle the hard questions that decision makers must ask? "If knowing what's right doesn't necessarily mean doing what's right, how is virtue instilled in managerial development?" "How can we keep vital those organizational values that brought success in the first place?" The author brings to this work two original features that make this book useful. An ethics quiz at the start of each chapter encourages readers to challenge their own belief systems while they feel the pressure of ethical dilemmas. In addition, scenarios found throughout the book draw out the often conflicting values managers must weigh in their work.

Walton, R. E. (1987). *Managing conflict: Interpersonal dialogue and third-party roles.* 2nd ed. Reading, MA: Addison-Wesley.

Conflict resolution is an important managing skill necessary at all levels of management. The author has developed an outline for diagnosing continuing conflicts and offers several options for resolving them. Methods and concepts are presented here that can be applied to various types of conflict, including both interpersonal and intersystem. Topics span fundamental steps of managing conflict, skills for facilitating open dialogue, and third-party advantages of consultants. Examples of conflict resolution are provided through three case studies and through a presentation of an international workshop on the dialogue of conflict over border disputes and intergroup conflict.

Warren, R. P. (1960). *All the kings men.* New York: Random House.

This work was originally a novel and later adapted as a play. The events take place in an un-named state of the deep South. The setting is a building site for the dedication of a new hospital. The plot revolves around the rise of a man named Willie Stark. He is looked upon as a hero of his community, having risen out of poverty to become the political leader in his state and region. A man known for getting things done, he builds new roads, bridges, and buildings. Underlying these concrete achievements, though, is deceit, manipulation, and corruption. Through the descriptions provided by the role of the narrator, Jack Burden, a community learns of their leader's moral crimes.

Wecter, D. (1972). *The hero in America: A chronicle of hero-worship.* New York: Charles Scribner's Sons.

With this 1941 book, Dixon Wecter was the first historian to undertake the task of examining the impact of the known political, military, and celebrated leaders/heroes of American history. He asks the question: "How do Americans choose their heroes?" Throughout its eighteen chapters, Wecter examines the public personalities who have come to represent the symbols of government, our national ideals, and what is best about being "American." This is a classic presentation of our past leaders. Detailed profiles cover the pilgrim founders to the architect of the New Deal. An extensive bibliography and thorough index are included.

Weisbord, M. R. (1987). *Productive workplaces: Organizing and managing for dignity, meaning and community.* San Francisco, CA: Jossey-Bass.

In this excellent work the author offers fresh thinking and new approaches to making businesses and organizations more effective, satisfying and rewarding environments for employees. Weisbord revisits the histories and theories of organizational development, with his new interpretations. In later chapters he examines the application of these theories through case study profiles. Finally he presents new applied theories, thoroughly documenting their operation. His intention is to move beyond the intellectual developments of current organizational theory toward developing new humanistic solutions to real organizational problems.

Welch, M. (1980). *Networking: The great new way for women to get ahead.* San Diego: Harcourt Brace Jovanovich.

The author describes a way for ambitious women to develop their own networks on a local or national scale.

Westin, A. F., & Aram, J. D. (1988). *Management dilemmas: Cases in social, legal and technological change.* Cambridge, MA: Ballinger Publishing.

Authors Westin and Aram address the social, legal and technological changes which confront modern management decision making. They present twelve factually based case studies including such contemporary issues as: Medical ethics and business decisions; Sexual discrimination and the corporate culture; Reproductive risk and EEO; Employee protest vs. employee loyalty; Testing employees for substance abuse; Due process in a non-union firm; and Big brother in the automated office. The book is intended to expose the reader to a range of questions facing organizations, to assist in developing diagnostic skills and to present the management change processes that are now confronting large corporations.

Williams, T. H. (1969). *Huey Long.* New York: Knopf.

Biography of a Louisiana governor and U.S. Senator and a study of southern and national politics. Williams maintains that Long in the beginning reached for power in order to do good and that "finally the means and the end became so entwined in his mind that he could not distinguish between them, could not tell whether he wanted power as a method or for its own sake." Based on nearly 300 interviews, manuscripts, documents, newspapers, periodicals, and secondary sources.

Willner, A. R. (1984). *The spellbinders: Charismatic political leadership--A theory.* New Haven, CT: Yale University Press.

The author has attempted to unravel and explain the spells exerted by political leaders who have succeeded in inspiring, swaying, or seducing multitudes and holding their minds and emotions in control. This work was originally begun in 1964 as a comparative study of the leadership strategies of Sukarno, Nasser, and Nkrumah. Weber's concept of political charisma is used as the general theme relating these three leaders.

Wilson, M. (1981). *Survival skills for managers.* Boulder, CO: Volunteer Management Associates.

This book is a statement about people and what happens to them in today's technocratic, hierarchical organizations. This book deals with both the responsibility and opportunity of being entrusted with leadership in today's organizations. The author deals with the problem of nurturing creative pragmatists who can and will make our organizations more humane.

Wofford, H. (1980). *Of Kennedys and kings: Making sense of the Sixties.* New York: Farrar, Straus and Giroux.

Wofford combines memoirs and narrative in this book, mingling others' opinions with his own to give balanced assessments of men and events. Wofford is positive about the accomplishments of the decade and remains committed to public service and responsible political action.

Yates, D. (1985). *Politics of management*. San Francisco, CA: Jossey-Bass.

Yates proposes a model of organizational management based on political process, to include bureaucratic politics and conflict management. He presents the distinctions between public and private management, but covers the commonalities as well. Has much to say to those who see management as a scientific methodology.

Yukl, G. A. (1989). *Leadership in organizations*. 2nd ed. Englewood Cliffs, NJ: Prentice-Hall.

The focus of this text is on managerial leadership in organizations. The book presents a broad survey of theory and research on leadership in formal organizations, as reflected in the following chapter titles: The nature of leadership; Sources of power and influence; Power, influence tactics, and leadership effectiveness; Nature of managerial work; Effective leadership behavior; Managerial traits and skills; etc. The book is designed for managers, administrators and could also be used as a text for undergraduate and graduate courses in leadership or managerial effectiveness.

Zaleznik, A. (1989). *The managerial mystique*. New York: Harper & Row, Publishers.

Zaleznik asserts that business has developed a managerial mystique which emphasizes order, efficiency and predictability, which has given rise to the importance of form, rather than the substance of business. He admonishes today's business schools and MBA programs, asserting they are preparing their students to fit a mold and they are not preparing them for leadership roles. He explains why this is so and illustrates how business needs leaders who are visionary and willing to challenge the status quo.

Zaleznik, A., & Kets de Vries, M. F. R. (1975). *Power and the corporate mind*. Boston: Houghton Mifflin.

The basis for this book is the clinical perspective of psychoanalysis. It continues the work begun with earlier publications and leads the way to further communications on the psychodynamics of leadership and organizations. The author contends that understanding how leaders accumulate and use power is a special and continuing requirement of a democratic society.

ARTICLES

Abshire, D. M. (1983). The leadership debate. *Washington Quarterly*, 6(1), 29-31.

     Four leadership articles in this issue are reviewed. The authors agree that there is a lack of innovative leadership in America. Often the techniques of management ignore the relationship between close personal ties and effective leadership. The debate over whether formal education is the answer to producing more innovative leaders will continue until leadership roles are more closely defined.

Adair, J. E. (1983, June). The building blocks for good leadership. *International Management*, pp. 38-47.

     Adair is promoting the idea that while there are some natural leaders, many more must be taught leadership skills. The skills needed for leadership traits can grow out of basic human qualities. Qualities he suggests developing are: integrity, leadership by example, willingness to go out in front, and some creative imagination. A ranking of attributes by top level management is included in the article.

Adams, J. (1984). Women at West Point: A three-year perspective. *Sex Roles, 11*, 525-541.

     A longitudinal study compared male and female cadets during the first three years of coeducation at West Point. Results showed relative similarity on comparisons of personality variables, but some differences in attitudes towards the rights and roles of women in society.

Ashour, A. S., & Johns, G. (1983). Leader influence through operant principles: A theoretical and methodological framework. *Human Relations, 36*, 603-626.

     Literature on learning and leadership is reviewed. This article discusses a leader's influence on subordinate motivation and behavior acquisition. Operant theory is used to explain leader influence. Suggestions for research in the leader reinforcement are discussed.

Atwater, L. E. (1988). The relative importance of situational and individual variables in predicting leader behavior: The surprising impact of subordinate trust. *Group & Organization Studies, 13*, 290-310.

     Drawing on earlier studies, Atwater's research assesses "the relative influence of personality traits of leaders, job characteristics, expectations of supervisors and subordinates, and trust and loyalty upward upon leader behavior." Examining 98 triads, composed of a first-line supervisor, the supervisor's immediate supervisor, and one or two subordinates, the research revealed subordinates' levels of trust and loyalty toward leaders were predictive of supportive leader behavior while personality traits were predictive of demanding leader behavior. The importance and positive results of developing an atmosphere of trust and loyalty are examined.

Barnes, D. F. (1978). Charisma and religious leadership: An historical analysis. *Journal for the Scientific Study of Religion, 17*, 1-18.

     A theory of charismatic leadership is proposed which explores conditions under which charismatic leadership emerges. Leaders arise in periods of social change when new religious beliefs may be formalized. Biographies of fifteen charismatic leaders are included in this article.

Bass, B. M., Waldman, D. A., Avolio, B. J., & Bebb, M. (1987). Transformational leadership and the falling dominoes effect. *Group & Organization Studies, 12,* 73-87.

This investigation examined the practice of transformational leadership (TL) at two levels of management in a New Zealand government agency. TL was defined as the extent to which a manager is seen as charismatic, as treating each subordinate as an individual, and as intellectually stimulating. Implications were drawn concerning the importance of developing TL abilities at upper levels of management to enhance the likelihood of such leadership at lower levels.

Bauer, B. G., & Anderson, W. P. (1985). Leadership enhancement: The Chancellor's leadership class. *Journal for Specialists in Group Work, 10*(1), 14-18.

Presents a model detailing issues to be considered when developing a structured group experience to enhance leadership skills in college students. Issues include time constraints, deciding on topics, and individualizing topics.

Bavelas, A. (1960). Leadership: Man and function. *Administrative Science Quarterly, 4,* 491-498.

Differences between the personal quality of leadership and leadership as an "organization function" are discussed. Current leadership models are reviewed. Types of leadership coinciding to the emotional tone of the organization are put into model form. The trend in leadership is to rely less on a specific individual's abilities and more on research and analysis. Leaders are now stereotyped as individuals who interact with a panel of experts for consultation.

Bennis, W. G. (1984). The four competencies of leadership. *Training and Development Journal, 38*(8), 14-19.

Bennis interviewed 90 outstanding leaders and their subordinates, with the intention of learning what makes real leaders (as opposed to effective managers) tick. After five years of research and thought, he identified four competencies common to all 90 leaders.

Bennis, W. G. (1982, May 31). Leadership transforms vision into action. *Industry Week,* pp. 54-56.

The author describes transformative power--the essence of what it originally meant to be a leader. He views CEOs as leaders, not managers, who possess the following characteristics: vision, communication and alignment, persistence, consistency, focus, empowerment and organizational learnings. He continues by stressing the vision a leader has must leave room for creativity, for there is where the art form of leadership exists.

Bennis, W. G. (1982). The artform of leadership. *Training and Development Journal, 36*(4), 44-46.

A study was conducted on 90 CEOs to provide information on effective leadership. All CEOs possessed the following in varying degrees: vision, capacity to communicate vision, persistence, consistency, focus and empowerment.

Bennis, W. G., & Jones, J. E. (1980). John E. Jones interviews Warren Bennis on leadership and power. *Group & Organization Studies, 5,* 18-34.

Through the lively dialogue between Jones and Bennis, Bennis points towards planning for this decade as he provides a number of prognostications with regards to leadership and power.

Bisesi, M. (1983). SMR forum: Strategies for successful leadership in changing times. *Sloan Management Review, 25*(1), 61-64.

The author discusses the importance of leadership in times of social change. He suggests that a successful leader must both view his organization as part of the total system and recognize the importance of people within the organization. Suggestions are given to enhance leadership ability.

Blake, R. R., & Mouton, J. S. (1982). Theory and research for developing a science of leadership. *Journal of Applied Behavioral Science, 18,* 275-291.

This article explores the two theories of leadership: the Contingency Model and the one most effective style. Both theories are discussed and the authors believe in the idea of there being one best theory of leadership.

Blumenson, M. (1972). The many faces of George S. Patton, Jr. *Harmon Memorial Lectures in Military History, 14,* 1-27.

The author attempts to look at the many facets of George S. Patton, Jr.'s life, including both his private and public life. Patton was well read in history, well trained and dedicated to his profession. All these characteristics have made Patton an effective leader.

Bolin, F. S. (1989). Empowering leadership. *Teachers College Record, 91*(1), 81-96.

The author argues that "teacher empowerment requires investing in teachers the right to participate in the determination of school goals and policies and the right to exercise professional judgment about the content of the curriculum and means of instruction." The article describes what kind of school leadership is required to accomplish such a goal.

Bradford, D. L., & Cohen, A. R. (1984). The postheroic leader. *Training and Development Journal, 38*(1), pp. 40-49.

A new style of management/leadership called The Manager-as-Developer follows the thought that a manager must first believe in a concept and then act in the creation of a team of key subordinates who are jointly responsible with the manager for the department's success. At the same time the manager works to develop management responsibility in subordinates, he or she must help develop the subordinate's abilities to share management of the unit's performance.

Brechtel, J. B., et al. (1982). Leaders in high schools? *Community and Junior College Journal, 52*(7), 29-30.

Delgado Community College's leadership training seminar was offered to 40 high school students. The seminar identified student leadership styles and worked on students' team-building, organizational and planning skills. Offers guidelines for setting up similar programs.

Britton, V., & Elmore, P. B. (1979). Developing leadership skills in women students. *NASPA Journal, 16*(3), 10-14.

    This study was designed to determine if a leadership and self-development workshop for women could change the participants' attitudes toward leadership and individual issues which are identified with the concerns of women. The workshops differed from traditional leadership training in its emphasis on self-development for women.

Bryson, J., & Kelley, G. (1978). A political perspective on leadership emergence, stability, and change in organizational networks. *Academy of Management Review, 3*(4), 713-723.

    A political approach to leadership in organizational networks is presented. From a review primarily of the political science and public administration literatures, a theoretical perspective is developed suggesting individual, processual, structural, and environmental variables affecting leadership emergence, stability, and change. A list of hypotheses describe much of the political dynamics of organizational leadership.

Burke, W. W. (1980, November). Leadership: Is there one best approach? *Management Review*, pp. 54-56.

    Recent research on leadership is reviewed. The leader's job is to provide direction as well as to be considerate to his subordinate's needs. According to the author, the most effective leader is one who uses participatory management.

Burns, J. M. (1980, July/August). Political leadership in America. *Center Magazine*, pp. 10-18.

    Burns is interested in the relationship between values reduced to purpose, on the one hand, and intended social change, on the other. Leadership can be crucial in bringing about intended social change. He explores political leadership and political conflict by interviewing a number of professors of Political Science and Sociology, directors of institutions and other prominent leaders.

Burns, J. M. (1977). Wellsprings of political leadership. *American Political Science Review, 71*, 266-275.

    This paper, presented as the Presidential Address at the American Political Science Association meeting in Chicago, in September, 1975, is an exploration of sources of leadership that lie in areas that are to some degree outside the traditional boundaries of political science. It is excerpted and summarized from a larger work in progress.

Butler, D. C. (1979). Improving management practices through leadership training. *Public Personnel Management, 8*, 134-136.

    With more and more responsibility being given to city governments and at the same time more and more budget cuts, Bowling Green has come up with a training program to teach city administrators the team management concept.

Carew, D. K., Parisi-Carew, E., & Blanchard, K. H. (1986). Group development and situational leadership: A model for managing groups. *Training and Development Journal*, *40*(6), 46-50.
> Reviews the concepts of situational leadership and group development and functioning and combines them into a single leadership model, with the premise that there is no one best leadership style for all situations.

Christie, R. (1970, November). The Machiavellis among us. *Psychology Today*, pp. 82-86.
> Various experiments were conducted to determine an individual's level of Machiavellianism. Characteristics of both high and low Machiavellian individuals are given. A true Machiavellian is not concerned with morality, is cool and detached from other people, and is more concerned with the means than the ends.

Clark, K. E. (1985, March). Teaching undergraduates to be leaders. *American Association of Higher Education Bulletin*, pp. 11-14.
> This article explores the current situation in the education process of developing leaders. Research and workshops conducted at the Center for Creative Leadership are described, along with several important course offerings at various colleges and universities. Calls "for colleges to challenge students to develop their capabilities to the fullest, to learn how organizations function and can be led, and to understand the necessity for accommodating the interest of others. . ."

Cronin, T. E. (1984). Thinking and learning about leadership. *Presidential Studies Quarterly*, *14*, 22-34.
> The author discusses his ideas on leadership and education of leadership. Leadership qualities and characteristics are examined.

Csoka, L. S. (1974).   A relationship between leader intelligence and leader rated effectiveness. *Journal of Applied Psychology*, *59*, 43-47.
> A leader with high intelligence contributed to group performance if the leader had a low Least Preferred Coworker score (LPC) and experienced the favorable situations of a supportive group atmosphere, high levels of experience, and strong position power. Less intelligent leaders under low group atmosphere, low levels of experience, and weak position power performed better than highly intelligent leaders. Intelligence and experience contribute to group performance.

Culberton, J. A. (1983). Leadership horizons in education. *Educational Administration Quarterly*, *19*, 273-296.
> Our culture has changed into an information society. This article discusses the impact of the information society on education, particularly on educational leaders. School leaders have to be able to do such things as purpose setting, program adaptation and using new electronic media effectively while maintaining their own self-awareness.

Curtis, B., Smith, R. E., & Smoll, F. L. (1979). Scrutinizing the skipper: A study of leadership behaviors in the dugout. *Journal of Applied Psychology*, *64*, 391-400.
> The Coaching Behavior Assessment System was used by trained observers to

classify the behaviors of coaches toward their players into 12 categories. Samples of 51 and 31 coaches in a boys' baseball program were observed during the 1976 and 1977 seasons, respectively. Players were interviewed at the end of the season concerning perceptions of their coach's behavior and attitudes toward their experience.

Davidson, H. J. (1977). The top of the world is flat. *Harvard Business Review, 55*(2), 89-99.
    "Things fall apart, the centre cannot hold"--this description of disintegration by W.B. Yeats is applied here to the American way of life. The death of the family and social and economic decline signal that a peak has been passed. How will this end? Where are the leaders to restore the "something of value" needed in American lives?

Davis, K. E. (1982). The status of black leadership: Implications for black followers in the 1980s. *Journal of Applied Behavioral Science, 18*, 309-322.
    The author discusses the Black leadership movement of the 1980s. Black leadership is limited by: widespread presence of threats, the issues and the lack of financial support. Great strides have been made in the Black movement, however the movement seems to be focusing on economic rights and employment opportunities.

Davis, T. R. V., & Luthans, F. (1984). Defining and researching leadership as a behavioral construct: An idiographic approach. *Journal of Applied Behavioral Science, 20*, 237-251.
    The authors first discuss the problem of defining leadership, suggesting three minimal criteria. The authors then stress the importance of considering environmental influences on the leadership process and suggest an idiographic approach to researching leadership under such theoretic assumptions for leadership. The rest of the article presents a demonstration study for this approach.

DeJulio, S. S., Larson, K., Dever, E. L., & Paulman, R. (1981). The measurement of leadership potential in college students. *Journal of College Student Personnel, 22*, 207-213.
    This study administered a leadership scale, the Leadership Opinion Questionnaire, to college leaders and nonleaders of both sexes. Results suggest its potential usefulness in the selection and training of students for campus leadership roles.

Deluga, R. J. (1988). Relationship of transformational and transactional leadership with employee influencing strategies. *Group and Organization Studies, 13*, 456-467.
    This study attempted to assess the relative effectiveness of transformational versus transactional leadership. The transformational pattern, in which manager and employees mutually negotiate and accept a common goal, was shown to generate a more stable work relationship and to enhance productivity.

DeMause, L. (1984). The making of a fearful leader: Where's the rest of me? *Journal of Psychohistory, 12*(1), 5-21.
    This chapter was taken from Reagan's America by Lloyd DeMause. It deals with Reagan's personal anxieties and how those anxieties have affected his politics. This chapter evaluates Reagan's phobias and explains why he developed phobias. The author states the reason for Reagan's success in 1980 was not so much his abilities but his promises to us that psychologically dealt with the same inner turmoils that Americans

were experiencing during that time.

Denmark, F. L. (1977). Styles of leadership. *Psychology of Women Quarterly*, 2(2), 99-113.
    The issue of what kinds of leaders emerge in what kinds of groups is examined.
The focus of groups is on women--the kinds of women leaders that emerge, the styles of
leadership utilized by women in contrast to those utilized by men, and the effects these
kinds of leadership have on group behavior. The reasons for the shortage of women in
leadership positions are outlined.

Ekpo-Ufot, A. (1979). A course in leadership and human relations. *Journal of European
Industrial Training*, 3(4), 21-24.
    Describes a management training course in leadership and human relations at the
University of Lagos (Nigeria). Includes the initial participant questionnaire on home
organizations' goals, psychological testing, assignments, study group interaction, lectures,
games, feedback and evaluation. The course objective is to develop effective leadership
skills and attitudes toward organizational human relations.

Ellis, R. J. (1983, March). Organizational leadership in turbulent times. *Management
Review*, pp. 59-61.
    In turbulent times a manager must be able to stimulate problem-solving activities
to generate as many innovative ideas as possible. Three aspects of an organization may
help stimulate new ideas: "free atmosphere," a "supportive environment," and a "loose
structure." Ideas not only must be stimulated, but also supported through the use of
reinforcement or disapproval and the manipulation of the organization and information
flow.

Elsner, P. A. (1984). Meeting the challenges with new leadership development programs.
New Directions for Community Colleges, 12(2), 33-40.
    Explores assumptions about the nature of leadership, change and the future with
a view toward identifying realistic organizational activities that community college leaders
can undertake.

Ernst, R. J. (1982). Women in higher education leadership positions - It doesn't happen
by accident. *Journal of the College and University Personnel Association*, 33(2), 19-22.
    Most leadership roles in education are filled by men. The author gives
suggestions to women to improve their chances of becoming an educational leader as
well as explaining how institutions would benefit by having more women on staff.

Erwin, T. D., & Marcus-Mendoza, S. T. (1988). Motivation and students' participation in
leadership and group activities. *Journal of College Student Development*, 29(4), 356-361.
    This article studies the activities and leadership status of entering freshman
students. Using Kuhl's motivational theory, the research focuses on the correspondence
of action versus state orientation.

Fernald, L. S., Jr. (1988). The underlying relationship between creativity, innovation and
entrepreneurship. *Journal of Creative Behavior*, 22(3), 196-202.

The author identifies the creative, innovative and entrepreneurial characteristics found in common in the lives of 7 individuals who exemplify these important attributes. Individuals identified are: Stanford Ovhinsky, Steven Wozniak, Wally Amos, Helen Smith, Jerome Lemelson, Bob Gundlach and Wilson Greatbatch.

Fiedler, F. (1971). Validation and extension of the contingency model of leadership effectiveness: A review of empirical findings. *Psychological Bulletin, 76*, 128-148.

This paper reviews studies which tested and extended the contingency model of leadership effectiveness. The model predicted a curvilinear relationship such that leaders with low least preferred co-worker (LPC) scores ("task-oriented") would perform more effectively in very favorable and unfavorable situations, while high LPC leaders ("relationship-oriented") would perform more effectively in situations intermediate in favorableness.

Fiedler, F. E. (1981). Leadership effectiveness. *American Behavioral Scientist, 24*, 619-632.

Current leadership theories are reviewed. Fiedler finds that current theories ignore the importance of a leader's knowledge, ability to solve problems and to make judgments to effective leadership. The author believes that a person will respond to a situation in a way which is compatible with the individual's personality. The effects of stress on performance is also discussed.

Fiedler, F. E. (1987, September). When to lead, when to stand back. *Psychology Today, 21*, 26-27.

Fiedler's terse article highlights current research in the area of directive versus nondirective leadership theory. He asserts that leadership intelligence does not guarantee leadership effectiveness and evidence suggests neither directive nor nondirective leadership is more effective.

Freedman, A., & Freedman, P. E. (1982). Mass line leadership: Another view of Mao's China. *American Psychologist, 37*, 103-105.

Argues that in his analysis of mass leadership in China, J. Barlow presents a one-sided and highly misleading portrait of Mao's China. Barlow overlooks the fact that small study groups and other organs of participation in the People's Republic of China operate within a context of coercion that conditions the individual's behavior. Mao's use of physical punishment and outright terror are discussed.

Gardner, J. W. (1965). The antileadership vaccine. *Carnegie Corporation of New York, Annual Report*.

There are many leaders in our society. The author discusses what he calls an "antileadership vaccine," meaning that a larger number of young people are being steered away from leadership roles. The process begins in society itself. Individuals do not envision themselves as individuals but rather as an anonymous member in a mass of people. Stereotypes of leaders enhance the unattractiveness of leadership positions. The necessity of leaders in our society is discussed.

Gardner, J. W. (1987). Leaders and followers. *Liberal Education, 73*(2), 4-8.

    Gardner describes the interaction that takes place between leaders and their constituents. He discusses the failures of followership. He believes that 90% of leadership can be taught, while the other 10% is comprised of exceptional energy, stamina and other undefined qualities.

Gardner, J. W. (1987). Leadership: The role of community colleges in developing the nation's young potential leaders. *Community, Technical and Junior College Journal, 57*(5), 16-21.

    Gardner recognizes diversity in leadership styles and describes basic qualities which contribute to effective leadership. He makes recommendations for developing community college leadership programs based on three components: the school supports broad liberal arts education, encourages student participation in group activities and gives students opportunities to lead.

Goodwin, D. K. (1978, October). True leadership. *Psychology Today*, pp. 46-58, 110.

    The author interviews James MacGregor Burns about his theories on leadership. Burns believes that we must study the development of leaders and followers to understand the concept of leadership. He feels that "leadership and followership lie in the vast pool of human wants, and the transformation of those wants into social aspiration, collective expectations and political demand." Leaders of today tend to be charismatic and superficial, partly because of media influence.

Graeff, C. L. (1983). The situational leadership theory: A critical view. *Academy of Management Review, 8*, 285-291.

    Theoretical issues undermining the robustness of the situational leadership theory and the utility of its prescriptive model are discussed. More specifically, conceptual ambiguity associated with the mechanics of applying the concept of job-relevant maturity and other problems with the normative model are seen as seriously limiting its pragmatic utility. In addition, problems with the LEAD instrument are identified and discussed.

Gregory, R. A., & Britt, S. K. (1987, Summer). What the good ones do: Characteristics of promising leadership development programs. *Campus Activities Programming*, pp. 33-35.

    Reports the result of a survey conducted by the Center for Creative Leadership of the leadership education efforts of over 1300 higher education institutions nationwide. The study showed almost 500 leadership programs offered by the nation's colleges and universities. The survey revealed the variety of programs offered. From the results of the survey the authors delineate the components of "good" leadership development programs.

Hayes, J. L. (1981, May). Preparing future leaders. *Management Review*, pp. 2-3.

    The key to developing new leaders is the chance for young people to have jobs in which they can practice the skills learned in college. In order to be a successful leader in the year 2005, leaders must be able to handle all media effectively. The key to management is practice.

Heider, J. (1982). The leader who knows how things happen. *Journal of Humanistic Psychology*, 22(3), 33-39.

   The author presents 12 chapters of Lao Tzu's sixth century B. C. Chinese text, Tao Te Ching, on how to rule a kingdom.

Hersey, P., & Blanchard, K. H. (1979). Life cycle theory of leadership. *Training and Development Journal*, 33(6), 94-100.

   Previous research on leadership models is reviewed. A theory called the "life cycle" has been developed. This theory emphasizes the follower rather than the leader. It involves four stages, moving the followers through various stages of maturity. The "life cycle" theory believes as the followers' maturity increases, leader behavior requires less structure and less emotional support.

Hill, N. C., & Ritchie, J. B. (1977). The effect of self-esteem on leadership and achievement: A paradigm and a review. *Group & Organization Studies*, 2, 491-503.

   Studies on leadership have experienced distinct evolutionary cycles typical of much of social science research. This paradigm is utilized to describe a variety of investigations that suggest that self-esteem is a significant variable in individual productive functioning and leadership effectiveness. This literature is reviewed, focusing on superior-subordinate interactions.

Hofstede, G. (1980). Motivation, leadership, and organizations: Do American theories apply abroad? *Organizational Dynamics*, 9(1), 42-63.

   It is important to remember that management theories developed and studied in one country may be of little use in other countries, due to differences in culture. National culture has been divided into four dimensions: power distance, uncertainty avoidance, individualism-collectivism, and masculinity-femininity. Differences in employee motivation, attitudes, management styles and organizational structures between countries can be traced to differences in mental programming.

Hogan, J. C. (1978). Personological dynamics of leadership. *Journal of Research in Personality*, 12, 390-395.

   Fifty members of a university football team were given the California Psychological Inventory (CPI) to determine what personality traits characterize leaders. Subjects were given leadership scores. Leaders were found to possess high scores on CPI scales of dominance, self-acceptance and responsibility. The coaches' leadership ratings were correlated with scores on the leadership regression equation. Stable personality traits characterizing leaders is supported.

Hollander, E. P., & Yoder, J. (1980). Some issues in comparing women and men as leaders. *Basic and Applied Social Psychology*, 1, 267-280.

   Reactions of followers to both male and female leaders were studied. Factors such as the nature of the group task and attitudes of both leaders and followers toward the sexes contributed the reactions noted. Leadership role, style, and situational characteristics all influence leader behavior. Further studies are needed to examine the behavior of women and men in groups.

House, R. J., & Mitchell, T. R. (1974). Path-goal theory of leadership. *Journal of Contemporary Business*, *3*(4), 81-94.

    An integrated body of conjecture by students of leadership, referred to as the "Path-Goal Theory of Leadership," is currently emerging. This article attempts to describe the theoretical framework for understanding the effect of leadership behavior on subordinate satisfaction and motivation.

Howard, A., & Wilson, J. A. (1982). Leadership in a declining work ethic. *California Management Review*, *24*(4), 33-46.

    AT&T conducted its second longitudinal study of managers in 1970. Results from the 1970 study were compared with results from a 1950 study. The 1970 survey indicates that baby boomers are less motivated toward success, less optimistic and less committed to corporate life. A historical look into why this transformation has taken place as well as the future directions of corporate life are explored.

Hunter, J. E., Hunter, R. F., & Lopis, J. E. (1979). A causal analysis of attitudes toward leadership training in a classroom setting. *Human Relations*, *32*, 889-907.

    This research article presents an analysis of the interrelationships of various student attitudes in a leadership training program.

Hynes, K., Feldhusen, J. F., & Richardson, W. B. (1978). Application of a three-stage model of instruction to youth leadership training. *Journal of Applied Psychology*, *63*(5), 623-628.

    This study examined the cognitive, behavioral, and attitudinal effects of a three-stage leadership training program consisting of 12 instructional units administered to high school vocational education students. Results of the one-way analysis of variance indicated that leadership training was effective in improving leadership knowledge as measured by a mastery test. Additional results and measurements of the Ideal Leader Behavior Description Questionnaire are discussed.

Jago, A. G. (1982). Leadership: Perspectives in theory and research. *Management Science*, *28*, 315-336.

    Reviews prominent trends in leadership research and constructs a typology based on the themes in the research. Argues that existing research has covered only a part of the wide domain of leadership phenomena.

James, D. C. (1982). Command crisis: MacArthur and the Korean War. *Harmon Memorial Lectures in Military History*, *24*, 1-16.

    The controversy surrounding the dismissal of MacArthur by Truman is explored.

Johnson, D. P. (1979). Dilemmas of charismatic leadership: The case of the People's Temple. *Sociological Analysis*, *40*, 315-323.

    A proposed model of charismatic leadership is used to interpret the power of Jim Jones' People's Temple which ended in a mass suicide in Jonestown, Guyana. Charismatic leaders are constantly seeking ways in which to reinforce their power: additional recruitment, providing benefits to members, delegating authority, giving up worldly possessions for the good of all, and creation of rituals. However, these strategies may also serve to undermine the leader's power.

Jones, J. D. (1979). Alternative methods of assisting students in developing leadership skills. *NASPA Journal, 17*(2), 49-57.

   Reports results of a national survey on methods used to develop leadership skills.

Kanter, R. M. (1982). Dilemmas of managing participation. *Organizational Dynamics, 10*(2), 5-27.

   Kanter discusses six sets of dilemmas that must be resolved to ensure that participating teams work effectively for the organization: dilemmas around initiation, structure, issue, choice, teamwork links between teams and their environment, and evaluation/continuation.

Kelly, C. M. (1987). The interrelationship of ethics and power in today's organizations. *Organizational Dynamics, 16*(1), 4-18.

   The focus of this article is on Kelly's analysis of the "Destructive Achiever." The "destructive achiever has the charisma of a leader, but lacks his operational values, this achiever's net effect on the long-term welfare of the organization is negative." The author identifies three types of Destructive Achievers, and discusses their influence and negative impact on an organization. Kelly concludes that leaders should be sensitive to counterproductive behaviors. Dialogue, values discussion and active participation within the organization are required.

Kerr, S. (1977). Substitutes for leadership: Some implications for organizational design. *Organization and Administrative Sciences, 8*(1), 135-146.

   Kerr utilizes a sociological perspective to establish the wide variety of characteristics (individual, task, and organizational) influencing leadership strategies.

Kerr, S., & Jermier, J. M. (1978). Substitutes for leadership: Their meaning and measurement. *Organizational Behavior and Human Performance, 22*, 375-403.

   Current leadership theories and models are reviewed. This article stresses that some leadership styles can be effective, regardless of the situation. A number of substitutes for "leadership" can be found to give guidance and promote good feelings within an organization.

Kets de Vries, M. F. R. (1989). Leaders who self-destruct: The causes and cures. *Organizational Dynamics, 17*(4), 5-17.

   The author identifies three psychological forces (transference, fear of success and isolation from reality) which may occur when an individual assumes a position of leadership. Aggressive behavior, paranoid reaction, depression and substance abuse are among the stress reactions discussed. To prevent the occurrence of harmful reactions, the author suggests 1) executives learn to identify potential signs of trouble, 2) board members take an active role in noting warning signs and 3) executive training programs provide nonthreatening environments for individuals to discuss their working experiences.

Kormanski, C. (1982). Leadership strategies for managing conflict. *Journal for Specialists in Group Work*, 7, 112-118.

      Discusses the impact of conflict in small group development theory. Conflict is a positive, normally occurring behavior. Presents leadership strategies involving withdrawal, suppression, integration, compromise, and power. Examples of situational contingencies in group therapy are presented along with a rationale for strategy selection and intervention.

Kotter, J. P. (1978). Power, success, and organizational effectiveness. *Organizational Dynamics*, 6(3), 26-40.

      Kotter describes power in organizations: how people acquire and manage power; why success in some jobs depends on power-oriented behavior, but in other jobs does not; how and why successful power-oriented behavior can work for or against the overall interests of the organization.

Lantis, M. (1987). Two important roles in organizations and communities. *Human Organization*, 46(3), 189-199.

      The author discusses the anthropologist's role in providing research in the area of the relation between leader and follower. The author argues that the literature has come primarily from social psychology, applied psychology and political science. She feels the anthropologist can make an important contribution in this area and that the time has come for anthropologists "to delve further into this subject." She identifies the usefulness of this research as it relates to contemporary organizations and community programs.

Latham, G. P., Cummings, L. L., & Mitchell, T. R. (1981). Behavioral strategies to improve productivity. *Organizational Dynamics*, 9(3), 4-23.

      Inevitably, employee performance problems create productivity problems. Strategies for dealing with both involve defining performance behaviorally, training managers to reduce rating errors, setting specific goals, and offering positive consequences for performance improvement.

Latham, G. P., & Yukl, G. A. (1975). A review of research on the application of goal setting in organizations. *Academy of Management Journal*, 18, 824-845.

      Research on goal setting is reviewed in order to evaluate Locke's theory of goal setting and to determine the practical feasibility of this technique for increasing employee motivation and performance. An attempt is made to identify limiting conditions, moderator variables, and promising directions for future research.

Lewis, R. G., & Gingerich, W. (1980). Leadership characteristics: Views of Indian and non-Indian students. *Social Casework: The Journal of Contemporary Social Work*.

      The findings of a study of the attitudes that American Indian and non-Indian students have about leadership indicate that the Indian students see leadership roles very differently than the non-Indians. The Indian students believe that the kind of person a leader is is more important than skills or knowledge.

Lindsay, B. (1988). A lamp for Diogenes: Leadership giftedness and moral education. *Roeper Review*, *11*(1), 8-11.

> The recognition of moral education as an important component of the total curriculum for gifted students is discussed. The author addresses the tensions and paradoxes of defining and implementing such a program.

Lippitt, G. (1983). Leadership: A performing art in a complex society. *Training and Development Journal*, *37*(3), 72.

> A brief article dealing with complexities for the modern leader. The author contends that different leaders and different kinds of leadership may be needed periodically throughout an organization's lifespan. He chooses four methods that can be applied in directing activities of humans: Force, Paternalism, Bargain, and Mutual means.

Lippitt, G. L. (1987). Entrepreneurial leadership: A performing art. *Journal of Creative Behavior*, *21*, 264-270.

> According to the author entrepreneurial leadership as an art means "orchestrating the totality of the enterprise with energy, self-confidence, persistence and learning capabilities." Lippitt identifies 6 behavioral characteristics of the entrepreneurial leader: risk taking, divergent thinking, sharp focus, personal responsibility, economic orientation and learning from experience. Practical guidelines for self-development are provided.

Lippitt, R. (1982). The changing leader-follower relationships of the 1980s. *Journal of Applied Behavioral Science*, *18*, 395-403.

> The author identifies several trends of change that seem to have particular relevance for the relationships between leaders and followers, examining some of the changing role requirements and competency challenges for leaders and followers and for their interactions.

Lombardo, M. M. (1982). How do leaders get to lead? *Issues & Observations*, *2*(1), 1-4.

> The opportunity to exercise skills and latent capabilities is the crucial factor in the development of leaders. Some practical suggestions for ways to create opportunities for more managers are presented.

Lombardo, M. M., & McCall, M. W., Jr. (1983). Great truths that may not be. *Issues & Observations*, *3*(1), 1-4.

> This is an overview of part of a major Center research project on how executives learn, grow, and change throughout their careers.

Lombardo, M. M., & McCall, M. W., Jr. (1983, March). Management homilies: Do they hold up under close examination? *Management Review*, pp. 52-55.

> One hundred and nine executives were interviewed to determine how executives learn and change through their careers. From interviews it was found that successful leaders do make big mistakes and possess a combination of toughness and basic values; both good and bad role models are important to executive development; and diversity in types of experiences rather than diversity in jobs or increased responsibility provide

well-rounded managers.

Manz, C. C. (1986). Self-leadership: Toward an expanded theory of self-influence processes in organizations. *Academy of Management Review*, *11*, 585-600.

       Manz offers the premise that the central control mechanisms within organizations are self-control systems. He outlines strategies commonly used by individuals to manage both boring tasks and intrinsically satisfying tasks. Strategies for self-leadership practice are given.

Manz, C. C., & Sims, H. P., Jr. (1984). Searching for the 'unleader': Organizational member views on leading self-managed groups. *Human Relations*, *37*, 409-424.

       The increasing adoption of the self-managed work group approach in organizations has created a puzzling paradox for leadership practice: How does one lead those that are supposed to lead themselves? Employee views at several organizational levels within a production plant that uses a self-managed work system are presented.

Manz, C. C., & Sims, H. P., Jr. (1981-82). Social learning theory: The role of modeling in the exercise of leadership. *Journal of Organizational Behavior Management*, *3*(4), 55-63.

       This paper explores learning through modeling as it relates to the exercise of leadership. The paper distinguishes between modeling as a natural learning occurrence versus a planned effort to change behavior. The emphasis is on the issue of how appointed leaders can utilize models to influence employee behavior. Research results and implications for managerial leadership are discussed.

Marsick, V. J., & Cederholm, L. (1988). Developing leadership in international managers - an urgent challenge! *Columbia Journal of World Business*, *23*(4), 3-11.

       Managers working in the international marketplace are challenged with new ways of leading, decision-making and doing business. In light of these demands, the authors draw on a model developed by a Swedish research institute to describe the principles and advantages of "Action Learning." This article "introduces both theory and experience with Action Learning as a means to develop transformational leaders in the global market." The authors cite evidence that Action Learning has shown to be an effective and viable model for developing international managers.

Maxcy, S., Jr., & Liberty, L. (1983). Should education leaders be humanistic? *Journal of Thought*, *9*, 101-106.

       This article calls for "humanistic leadership" in education. Although no clear definition has been identified, it would be enough to say that humanistic leadership would involve leading in a truly human and feeling way while keeping in mind the value of historic and classical learning.

McCall, M. W., Jr. (1980). Conjecturing about creative leaders. *Journal of Creative Behavior*, *14*, 225-234.

       Creativity is seen today as a deviant response by the leader in order to solve some problem. The author sees creative leaders as crafty, contrary, grouchy, dangerous, feisty, inconsistent, evangelistic, prejudiced and spineless. The creative leader tries to create new ideas and evaluate them.

McCall, M. W., Jr., & Lombardo, M. M. (1983, February). What makes a top executive? *Psychology Today*, pp. 26-31.

     This article looked at reasons why executives were derailed: inability to adapt to new boss, overdependence on mentor, inability to think strategically, and failure to staff effectively. The authors further compare the behavioral differences between the arrivers (people who make it to the top) and the derailers.

McCarthy, M. J., & Sarthory, J. A. (1978). The ethical dimension of educational leadership: The administrator as a moral agent. *Journal of Thought*, *13*, 8-13.

     The author discusses the idea that an effective leader must be able to act as a moral agent to persuade others to follow the leader's moral point of view. The leader must be able to articulate his view and only during "moral dispute" can conflict over ethical dimensions be resolved.

McWhinney, W. (1984). Alternative realities: Their impact on change and leadership. *Journal of Humanistic Psychology*, *24*(4), 7-38.

     The different ways people experience reality result in their having distinctly different attitudes toward change. Understanding these different concepts contributes to new understanding of resistance to change and the modes of leadership. A description of four alternative realities and a pencil-and-paper instrument are used to assess the reality concepts people use. "A scenario in four languages," a hypothetical case, elucidates the ways in which managers react.

Meier, A. (1965). On the role of Martin Luther King. *New Politics*, *4*, 52-59.

     Martin Luther King's combination of militancy and conservatism led to his great success. King, better than anyone else, could articulate the desires of the Negroes both to the Negroes and to White America. This along with King's ability to hold the center position between conservative and radical groups made King an effective leader.

Miller, W. C. (1984). Can leaders be developed? *Training*, *21*(6), 86.

     Describes the author's feelings about today's need for more leadership skills. He states differences between leading and management functions. Several goals for more effective leadership are discussed and comparisons of daily responsibilities between managers and leaders are drawn. Some of the skills effective leaders must learn are listed and explained.

Miner, J. B. (1982). The uncertain future of the leadership concept: Revisions and clarifications. *Journal of Applied Behavioral Science*, *18*, 293-307.

     Leadership was developed in a study of small groups and focused on the emergence of a leader. Today we are focused on the functions of organizations and we are finding that our current model of leadership is no longer useful. The author suggests alternative areas of research in the leadership field.

Mink, O., Rogers, R., & Watkins, K. (1989). Creative leadership: Discovering paradoxes of innovation and risk. *Contemporary Educational Psychology, 14*, 228-240.

The research reported in this article attempts to explore the paradoxes inherent in the enactment of creative leadership in complex interpersonal situations. The situations in this study were difficult interpersonal interactions faced by public school superintendents. Detailed interviews with these superintendents showed that they most often attempted to deal with these situations as problems to be solved rather than as problems to be explored.

Mintzberg, H. (1975). The manager's job: Folklore and fact. *Harvard Business Review, 53*(4), 49-61.

The author examines the common misconceptions, myths, and rumors that dominate the average manager's thinking about his job. He bases his article on many recent studies and tries to define a set of usable and well-defined components for managers. The author feels managers play a complex, intertwined combination of interpersonal, informational, and decisional roles. He hopes to enable the manager to better understand his job.

Moore, K. M. (1982). The role of mentors in developing leaders for academe. *Educational Record, 63*, 23-27.

Discusses formalizing the mentor process by establishing mentor programs to aid the identification and development of promising administrators.

Morris, D. J. (1987). Innovation: The changing perception of leadership. *Performance and Instruction, 26*(1), 20-24.

Morris briefly outlines the history of leadership theory. He identifies some of the problems with these theories and builds an argument that it is necessary for today's successful leader to attain mastery of many jobs by building on knowledge, skills and attributes (KSA). He recommends the application of Theory W and its four-step approach to leadership development as an appropriate model for the implementation of organizational innovations and success.

Morris, T. D. (1984). Taking charge in Washington. *Harvard Business Review, 62*(4), 24-40.

The author discusses the leadership of McNamara, Staats and Califano while heading federal government positions. To be an effective federal manager one must bring "zest" for new career experiences, be able to make contributions quickly because of limited appointment, be an effective communicator, have strategies for attaining goals and develop long-range objectives.

Mueller, R. K. (1980). Leading-edge leadership. *Human Systems Management, 1*, 17-27.

With society changing at such a fast pace, leaders must be able to adapt quickly to new-form situations. Attributes of freer-form organizations are discussed. A triple framework (TISC, LRSQ & PISQ) is suggested for maintaining organizational management and providing guidance for leaders of the future.

Nanus, B. (1986). Leadership: Doing the right thing. *Bureaucrat, 15*(3), 9-12.

Explores the differences between leadership and management. Findings from interviews with 90 well-known leaders from business and the public sector led to the formulation of four major skills shared by effective leaders: a results orientation, articulating and communicating meaning, earning trust by taking stands and sticking to them, and knowing one's own strengths and weaknesses.

Neider, L. L., & Schriesheim, C. A. (1988). Making leadership effective: A three-stage model. *Journal of Management Development, 7*(5), 10-20.

    Building on existing leadership research, the authors introduce a three-phase diagnostic model of leadership effectiveness. The model is intended as a pragmatic and useful tool designed for practicing managers in assisting them assess and increase their effectiveness as leaders. Expectancy, path-goal theory and transactional perspectives are used to illustrate the model.

Newman, R. G. (1983). Thoughts on superstars of charisma: Pipers in our midst. *American Journal of Orthopsychiatry, 53*, 201-208.

    Discusses the effects of charisma in the use and misuse of power, using R. Browning's (1895) version of *The Pied Piper*. The interdependent relationship between a leader and his/her followers is explored, and the psychological implications of these forces for society and its institutions are addressed.

O'Ballance, E. (1981). IRA leadership problems. *Terrorism: An International Journal, 5*, 73-82.

    The development of leadership in the IRA is reviewed. Differences and reasons for splitting into the "officials" and the "provisionals" and the Irish National Liberation Army are discussed.

Passow, A. H. (1988). Styles of leadership training. . . and some more thoughts. *Gifted Child Today, 11*(6), 34-38.

    The first part of Passow's article addresses the need for developing a clear conception of leadership as it relates to university training. He outlines the areas for which leaders in the field of educating the gifted and talented need insight and understanding. The second portion of the article focuses on the process of training gifted students for leadership.

Peters, T. J. (1979). Leadership: Sad facts and silver linings. *Harvard Business Review, 57*(6), 164-172.

    A busy executive may be the most effective. This article discusses four sad facts about executives and their potential silver linings. The sad facts include: (a) Senior managers get only one option, (b) time is fragmented and issues are late, (c) bad news is normally hidden, and (d) major choices take months or years to emerge. Effective management lies in foresight and a shrewd sense of timing. Managers must use all their skills to solve problems of the organization.

Petrie, T. A., & Burton, B. (1980). Levels of leader development. *Educational Leadership, 37*, 628-631.

    Leadership is conceived of as a sequence of five levels of activity. The levels are analyzed to determine tasks associated with each level and the technologies available to help leaders acquire the necessary skills.

Plachy, R. J. (1981, September). Leading vs. managing: A guide to some crucial distinctions. *Management Review*, pp. 58-61.

It is impossible for an individual to be both a manager and a leader. The relationship between manager and leader is reciprocal, if an individual tries to be too much of one, the other will suffer. The individual who understands the distinction between leader and manager will have greater success in achieving the goals for either the individuals or the organization.

Posner, B. Z., & Kouzes, J. M. (1988). Relating leadership and credibility. *Psychological Reports*, *63*, 527-530.

Posner and Kouzes research reports a relationship between leadership and credibility. Their sample consisted of responses from 998 subordinates of 146 managers. Three dimensions of credibility (trustworthiness, expertise and dynamism) were correlated with the behaviorally based *Leadership Practice Inventory*. Five dimensions comprise the inventory: challenging the process, inspiring a shared vision, enabling others to act, modeling the way, and encouraging the heart.

Reed, B. G. (1983). Women leaders in small groups: Social-psychological perspectives and strategies. *Social Work with Groups*, *6*(3-4), 35-42.

Reviews research and theories concerning female leaders of small groups and identifies ways that female leaders can minimize negative reactions to their leadership and take advantage of opportunities to promote growth, learning, and new knowledge. Research shows that the gender of a group's leader clearly affects the group and that male and female group leaders behave similarly, but females are often perceived and reacted to differently (usually more negatively).

Reinharth, L. (1978). The missing ingredient in organization theory. *Advanced Management Journal*, *43*(1), 14-24.

This article shows how to pinpoint the "key leaders" in an organization and discusses what attributes key leaders in stable versus growth organizations should have. It affirms that key leadership is the crucial factor in giving or changing the direction of an organization.

Rejai, M., & Phillips, K. (1988). Loyalists and revolutionaires: Political elites in comparative perspective. *International Political Science Review*, *9*(2), 107-118.

Based on the examination of 50 well-known revolutionary and loyalist leaders, Rejai and Phillips reveal the results of their comparative analysis of these two political elite populations. Their study examines the historical, situational, social and psychological condition of these leaders. Questions raised include: Do the two groups differ in social background attributes, politicization patterns, situational encounters and psychological dynamics? The study identified cluster traits that applied to both populations. However, at a second level of analysis, traits and characteristics emerged which significantly separated the groups. The list of loyalists and revolutionary leaders is included.

Salancik, G. R., & Pfeffer, J. (1977). Who gets power--and how they hold on to it: A strategic-contingency model of power. *Organizational Dynamics*, *5*(3), 2-21.

> Power adheres to those who can cope with the critical problems of the organization. As such, power is not a dirty secret, but the secret of success. This article argues that traditional "political" power, far from being a dirty business, is one of the few mechanisms available for aligning an organization with its own reality.

Schwartz, B. (1983). George Washington and the Whig conception of heroic leadership. *American Sociological Review*, *48*, 18-33.

> The author discusses the transformation of George Washington from a military hero to a moral symbol and how his leadership demonstrated the Whig conception of heroic leadership. Leadership is discussed in the Republican tradition.

Sergiovanni, T. J. (1979). Is leadership the next great training robbery? *Educational Leadership*, *36*, 388-402.

> Critically examines the concept of leadership and the viability of leadership training.

Shoemaker, D. J., & Nix, H. L. (1972). A study of reputational community leaders using the concepts of exchange and coordinative positions. *Sociological Quarterly*, *13*, 516-524.

> The general purpose of this study was to investigate group and organizational affiliates of reputed community leaders in a rural community.

Simonton, D. K. (1988). Presidential style: Personality, biography, and performance. *Journal of Personality and Social Psychology*, *55*, 928-936.

> The author used biographical information on 39 U.S. presidents as a basis for assessments of presidential style by seven raters. Five basic style dimensions were delineated: interpersonal, charismatic, deliberative, creative, and neurotic. These styles were shown to be related to both objective and subjective indicators of presidential performance.

Sinetar, M. (1981). Developing leadership potential. *Personnel Journal*, *60*, 193-196.

> Selecting managers with high leadership quotients is only part of an organization's task. The other part--a developmental process--is not immediately actualized. Grooming managers for effective interpersonal functioning is a key adjunct to any selection process. The article defines leadership--the skills, traits, and behavior--and poses questions regarding teaching leadership. Also, leadership training criteria and selection and training of leaders is explored.

Singleton, T. M. (1978). Managerial motivation development: A study of college student leaders. *Academy of Management Journal*, *21*, 493-498.

> This study measured the results of a special managerial motivation development training course taught at Georgia State University during the spring quarter of 1975. The study was initiated to examine the impact of a formal managerial motivation training

program upon campus student leaders. The study attempts to measure the impact of the training upon the motive to manage of the training subjects.

Sisk, D. A. (1988). Leadership development for cross-cultural understanding. *Gifted Child Today, 11*(6), 31-33.

    The author expresses the need to prepare and educate students to meet the demands of a multicultural society. Drawing on this need, a 10-day program, with graduate and undergraduate students from 16 countries, was sponsored by the Agency for International Development and the National Council for International Visitors, coordinated by Creativity, Innovation and Leadership, University of South Florida. Kolb's learning cycle (concrete experience, reflective observation, abstract conceptualization and active experimentation) served as a model for conducting the seminar proceedings. This article observes the outcome and success of the seminar.

Smircich, L., & Morgan, G. (1982). Leadership: The management of meaning. *Journal of Applied Behavioral Science, 18,* 257-273.

    The basis of this paper focuses on understanding the phenomenon of leadership, not to improve the practice of leadership but as a means of understanding the phenomenon of organization. The authors' approach is to analyze leadership as a distinctive kind of social practice, present a case study of leadership in an organizational context, and analyze its consequences.

Smith, J. E. (1987, Summer). INROADS: Preparing minorities for corporate America. *Journal of College Admissions, 116,* 26-31.

    Describes the INROADS program which was set up to develop talented minority students in the ways of business and industry and to prepare them for leadership roles in the corporate world and in their communities. The article discusses various levels of the program: pre-college, college, and alumni, and includes an evaluation of the program by alumni.

Stockdale, J. B. (1983). Educating leaders. *Washington Quarterly, 6,* 49-52.

    The author suggests that a return to the basics of history and philosophy will provide today's leaders with the wisdom to solve everyday difficulties. The author further states that an effective leader should possess five traits. He should be a moralist, a jurist, a teacher, a steward and a philosopher. The author feels that "leadership traits can only be tested in a real life crisis."

Stogdill, R. H. (1974). Historical trends in leadership theory and research. *Journal of Contemporary Business, 3*(4), 1-17.

    A brief review by Stogdill of the history of and trends in leadership theory.

Stupak, R. J., Sargent, A. G., & Stupak, V. C. (1987). The androgynous manager. *New Management, 4*(4), 15-18.

    The authors cite five events that have challenged and created new attitudes in business: booming service economy, more women in the work force, need for new forms of leadership, concept of organization families, and new attitudes in management as expressed in Tom Peters' *In Search of Excellence*. For today's manager to become an effective leader requires a blending of masculine characteristics (dominance, independence, verbal behavior) with feminine characteristics (concern for relationships, paying attention to nonverbal behavior, mediating skills), which give rise to the authors' concept of the androgynous manager.

Sudanowicz, E. (1989). A field perspective on the PMI program. *The Bureaucrat*, *18*(1), 53-58.

Sponsored by the Office of Personnel Management, the Presidential Management Intern (PMI) program is a federally funded program aimed at selecting some 400 highly qualified master's degree graduates and placing them in federal career fields. This article gives an overview of the program, as well as addresses the motivational qualities and areas of personal commitment that are required for work in the public sector. The article is intended for graduate students, but should also be useful to educators working with student leaders interested in public service careers.

Tannenbaum, R., & Schmidt, W. H. (1973). How to choose a leadership pattern. *Harvard Business Review*, *51*(3), 162-175, 178-180.

A *Harvard Business Review* classic: appearing 15 years prior. For this publication the authors have added a commentary examining the nature of leadership from the perspective of the 1970s. The authors capture the main ideas involved in the question of how a manager should lead his organization.

Tetrault, L. A., Schriesheim, C. A., & Neider, L. L. (1988). Leadership training interventions: A review. *Organization Development Journal*, *6*(3), 77-83.

This article is a review of the five major leadership models used in leadership training interventions: Blake and Mouton's (1978) Managerial Grid; Hersey and Blanchard's (1977) Situational Leadership model; Leader Match concept by Fiedler, Chemers and Mahar (1976); Graen's Leader-Member Exchange; and Vroom & Yetton's Contingency model (1973). The authors discuss the degree of effectiveness these individual programs offer, as well as the drawbacks associated with these specific models. The larger question regarding the effectiveness of leadership training, in general, is addressed.

Thomas, A. B. (1988). Does leadership make a difference to organizational performance? *Administrative Science Quarterly*, *33*, 388-400.

With this article it is the author's aim to "resolve the leadership performance issue." Through a review of the main methodological criticisms directed at Liberson & O'Connor's (1972) major study on leadership and organizational performance, Thomas argues that "their implications for leadership performance issues have largely been misstated and some criticisms are unfounded." Further he asserts, "contrary to general opinion Liberson and O'Connor's study provides definite support for the individualist view of leadership and that its findings are wholly consistent with those of later studies that appear to have fielded opposite results."

Turcotte, W. E. (1983). Leadership vs. management. *Washington Quarterly*, *6*, 46-48.

The author believes a military executive must possess a combination of leadership qualities and effective management skills to solve today's military problems. He suggests ways to go about getting these skills.

Van Gelder, L. (1984, January). Carol Gilligan: Leader for a different kind of future. *Ms.*, pp. 37-40, 101.

An article focusing on Carol Gilligan, *Ms.* Woman of the Year. The challenges that stand between 1984 and the year 2000, and the survival that may depend on a revolution in values, are centered on one of the leaders of this revolution--Carol Gilligan. Gilligan's work reflects implications . . ."for a rather different kind of future--one in which humanity takes its cues not from Big Brother, but from sisters, mothers, and daughters."

Vanderslice, V. J. (1988). Separating leadership from leaders: An assessment of the effect of leader and follower roles in organizations. *Human Relations*, *41*, 677-696.

What are the distinctions between leadership and leadership functions? Can these functions be carried out by other members of the organization? What conditions are necessary to make a "leaderless" organization successful? These are some of the questions addressed in Vanderslice's comparison study which examines Moosewood Industries, a leaderless structured enterprise, and another company that has a flat structure. The conclusions of the study raise some basic questions for behavioral scientists regarding the definition of motivation, power and responsibility.

Vicere, A. A. (1987). Break the mold: Strategies for leadership. *Personnel Journal*, *66*, 17-73.

The author recognizes the importance of the human resources manager and provides a three-step development program aimed at moving a senior human resources executive into a position of leadership and influence. The following steps are outlined: Step 1, Assess strategic human resources leadership skills; Step 2, Develop a program of organizational integration, intended to rotate the individual through various staff and line management positions; Step 3, a program of staff development must be created once the individual has been exposed to the organization. The individual is now ready to develop a strategic human resources management department.

Vroom, V. A., & Jago, A. G. (1988). Managing participation: A critical dimension of leadership. *Journal of Management Development*, *7*(5), 32-42.

From foreign competition to new tax laws, major changes have altered the way in which corporations are structured and managers make decisions. In light of the vast changes that occurred in the past 15 years, the authors introduce a revised version of the V. A. Vroom and P. W. Yetton (1973) decision-making model. According to the authors the essential features of the training are unchanged, however the "concepts of the feasible set and rules are replaced by heuristics, and new decision trees replace those of the old model."

Wallace, D., & White, J. B. (1988). Building integrity in organizations. *New Management*, *6*(1), 30-35.

An audit of organizational ethics reveals common gaps between desired behavior and actual practice. The authors identify nine lessons which are considered the most important factors that determine an organization's climate of integrity. Also identified are seven commonly held assumptions that turn out to be dangerous myths.

Watson, C. M. (1983, Autumn). Leadership, management and the seven keys. *McKinsey Quarterly*, pp. 44-52.
Recent research has suggested that managers and leaders are basically different types. In terms of the McKinsey 7-S model, the typical manager is seen as overrelying on the "hard" S's (strategy, structure and systems), while the leader's mastery of the "soft" elements (style, skills, staff and shared values) helps to galvanize his organization into superior long-term performance. There is truth in the distinction, the author believes, but it is overdrawn.

Weiss, J. C. (1988). The D-R model of coleadership of groups. *Small Group Behavior*, *19*, 117-125.
This article is concerned with the coleadership of citizen groups, groups for teaching and training and work groups in general. The author has developed a model of coleadership referred to as the "D-R" model, which focuses on five overlapping processes: Develop/relationship; discuss/roles; divide/responsibility; defer/respect; and debrief/review. The model is intended to be used as a practical guide and is designed to improve group relationships.

Welte, C. E. (1978). Management and leadership. *Personnel Journal, 57*, 630-632.
Differences between both managership and leadership, as well as between style of leadership and leadership behavior, are discussed. These distinctions may provide guidelines for improvements in managerial and leadership performance.

Wilson, J. C. (1969). Leadership for change. *Personnel Administration, 32*(5), 4-7, 14-15.
Leadership and organization are keys to development. As society develops at an accelerated rate, demands on leadership will also increase. Innovators and creators are needed in this era of technological change. Education is the key to our future; we will require leaders with intellectual capacity beyond mere technical skills to solve our complicated problems.

Youngs, B. B. (1983). Identifying and developing prospective school leaders. *NASSP Bulletin, 67*(467), 98-106.
Describes a model for developing leadership potential in education using specialized assessment scales and one-to-one conferences.

Zaleznik, A. (1977). Managers and leaders: Are they different? *Harvard Business Review, 55*(3), 67-78.
The author examines the two basic positions of leadership: leaders and managers. He suggests that managers and leaders are basically two different types of people. Combined with different conditions which breed the different types, it is difficult for one person to be both.

REFERENCE AND RESOURCE MATERIALS

Leader Handbooks and Resources

Bates, M. M., & Johnson, C. D. (1972). *Group leadership: A manual for group counseling leaders*. Denver, CO: Love Publishing.

> The authors state that their main purpose is to present to the professional group leader the tools "which will enable him to activate group process in a way which insures that members have growth-producing experience."

Bradford, L. P. (1976). *Making meetings work: A guide for leaders and group members*. La Jolla, CA: University Associates.

> Dr. Bradford has distilled in this small volume a treasury of helpful ideas for those who find themselves in positions of leadership, or who want to be helpful members of the groups in which they participate. The author brings together practical suggestions of "what to do" with clear explanations of why certain kinds of behavior produce the results they do.

Egan, G. (1988). *Change-agent skills A: Assessing and designing excellence*. San Diego, CA: University Associates.

> A companion to *Change-Agent Skills B: Managing Innovation and Change*, this book has been developed for executives, trainers, managers, consultants, or any individual who may play a role in the assessment and design for planning within a business or organization. The author has created a model known as "Model A." When applied to assessing any or all dimensions of an organization--operations, personnel, facilities, marketing or resources--it provides a map pinpointing the weaknesses and strengths of present business functions. The results sift through in such a way that the key objectives of an organization's mission are given in a point-by-point outline useful for future planning.

Egan, G. (1988). *Change-agent skills B: Managing innovation and change*. San Diego, CA: University Associates.

> A companion to *Change-agent skills A: Assessing and designing excellence*, this volume offers a plan for stimulating innovation and change within an organization or business. The author has developed a model which incorporates three stages of the process of cultivating change and innovation. The stages are, 1) assessing the current scene--recognizing problems and blind spots; 2) the preferred scene--considering the spectrum of possibilities & translating ideas into a workable agenda; and 3) getting there--choosing strategies, formulating plans, and moving from transition to action.

English, C. B. (1987). The art of leading meetings. *American Journal of Occupational Therapy, 41*(5), 321-326.

> An effective manager must know when to hold a meeting and what leadership style is appropriate. Four types of meetings are discussed: staff, problem-solving or decision-making, combination, and creative. Leadership style, program planning and dealing with problem participants are examined.

500

Francis, D., & Young, D. (1979). *Improving work groups: A practical manual for team building*. San Diego, CA: University Associates.

   Based on the philosophy that a team management approach is an effective and positive way to improve organization, this handbook provides a step-by-step guide to help the reader acquire the skills needed for team building. The structure of the book is based on defining the team approach: surveying the reader's own group and describing the characteristics of successful teams. The last chapter is comprised of 46 projects to be used for enhancing and developing group skills.

Harrison, F. C. (Ed.). (1989). *Spirit of leadership: Inspiring quotations for leaders*. Germantown, TN: Leadership Education and Development.

   Poets, presidents and philosophers are but a few of the many individuals represented in this collection of quotations which address the multifaceted nature of leadership.

Kahn, S. (1982). *Organizing: A guide for grassroots leaders*. New York: McGraw-Hill.

   Kahn, organizer and musician, has written a straightforward "do-it-yourself" manual on grassroots organizing. The author examines leadership effectiveness, organizations, constituencies, meetings, strategies, communication styles, unions and politics.

Lawson, J. D., Griffin, L. J., & Donant, F. D. (1976). *Leadership is everybody's business*. San Luis Obispo, CA: Impact.

   This book is a practical guide for volunteer membership groups. It is divided into 3 parts: the preliminaries of leadership--being human, learning more about yourself and others, and group dynamics.

Lawson, L. G., Donant, F. D., & Lawson, J. D. (1982). *Lead on! A complete handbook for group leaders*. San Luis Obispo, CA: Impact.

   This book is an excellent step-by-step guide for leaders of volunteer groups. Twenty-four key leadership skills, from understanding your own leadership style and communicating effectively, to solving conflicts and developing new leaders, are addressed here in a clear, concise manner.

Nadler, L., & Nadler, Z. (1987). *The comprehensive guide to successful conferences and meetings*. San Francisco, CA: Jossey-Bass.

   An invaluable resource for anyone who must plan, organize, and conduct a meeting or conference. The elements involved in coordinating such an event are covered here in great detail. Such considerations include the design of the conference, handling related events and activities, site selection, meeting and function rooms, presenters and speakers, use of audio-visuals, food and beverage functions, arranging exhibitions, effective marketing, public relations, developing a budget, and preparing a participant program book. This guide unravels the complexities of managing a large-scale event, while providing a step-by-step plan to insure a successful and well-run conference.

Napier, R. W., & Gershenfeld, M. K. (1983). *Making groups work: A guide for group leaders*. Boston: Houghton Mifflin.

      A resource book to provide ways of thinking about groups and to supply the tools for developing what is termed a "design mentality," along with tapping those artistic and creative energies that separate the most successful group leaders from the rest. A text book to be used in a variety of programs and courses in educational institutions or other organizations dedicated to increasing skills in areas related to group processes.

Portnoy, R. A. (1986). *Leadership: What every leader should know about people*. Englewood Cliffs, NJ: Prentice-Hall.

      Each chapter targets an important element of leadership training, including training leaders to work with people, components of human behavior, emotional stability in leadership, basic communication skills, direction and policies, and case studies: their problems and solutions. Packed with illustrations and examples, the material is presented in a straightforward manner. Discussion topics and recommended readings are included with each chapter, and flow charts offer step-by-step direction.

Reddy, W. B., & Jamison, K. (1988). *Team building: Blueprints for productivity and satisfaction*. Alexandria, VA: NTL Institute for Applied Behavioral Science.

      In this comprehensive work 19 chapters address a wide range of team building issues. Written for the team builder and the manager, the material covered represents what has been currently written on the subject. The book has five sections: Part 1 provides the basic elements of team building; Part 2 explores a broader view of the theories of team building; Part 3 shows various applications for building teams; Part 4 illustrates how team building is a manageable activity; and Part 5 looks at the social issues involved in building teams. The final chapter includes biographical summaries of the twenty-three contributors to this text.

Thomas, G. L., & VerBurg, K. (1987). *Conducting public meetings*. Rev. ed. East Lansing, MI: Community Development Programs, Lifelong Education Programs.

      A straightforward easy-to-follow guide "designed to assist leaders and group members to run or participate in public meetings more effectively and efficiently." Topics discussed include Public meetings; Nature and variety; What to do before the meeting starts; The meeting gets underway; and Decision making and problem solving.

Training Resources, Guidebooks and Curricula

Arter, J. A. (1988). *Assessing leadership and managerial behavior: A consumer's guide*. Portland, OR: Northwest Regional Educational Laboratory (101 S.W. Main, Suite 500, 97204).

      This guide provides summaries and analyses of measures that relate to leadership and administrative skills. The author writes that, "it is intended to provide the information necessary for users to become more informed consumers of assessment tools which attempt to measure leadership." Included are reviews of over forty assessment tools, a brief analysis of the issues involved in assessing leadership, and how to select a measure of leadership. Some of the instruments discussed are specifically related to school leadership, but most are more general measures of leadership and management. Appendix E, a summary table of instruments, provides a good comparative overview of all the measures covered in the book.

Bard, R., Bell, C. R., Stephen, L., & Webster, L. (1987). *The trainer's professional development handbook*. San Francisco, CA: Jossey-Bass.

This handbook provides a reference work for the ongoing professional development of trainers in the field of human resource development. The learning techniques and resource materials described here are intended to fit within a variety of organizational settings, from small to large, and public to private. The text is divided into three parts: 1) a guide to help design your own professional development plan; 2) a comprehensive listing of materials and resources which promote professional development; and 3) an encyclopedia of important terms and significant contributors to the field of HRD. This work will be useful to both the novice and the experienced trainer seeking to chart their professional growth.

Craig, R. L. (et al.) (1987). *Training and development handbook*. 3rd ed. New York: McGraw-Hill.

Intended to be comprehensive in scope and in-depth in treatment, this handbook covers in its 49 chapters and five sections the many aspects of operating a training and development division within an organization. Highly useful for practitioners in HRD, this text provides detailed charts, tables, and analysis in the design, development and operation of a HRD service. It also includes useful chapters on leadership and communication training.

Dimock, H. G. (1986). *Groups: Leadership and group development*. San Diego, CA: University Associates, Inc.

An in-depth analysis of groups, and how and why they function as they do. Resource guide to: evaluating what's happening in a group, understanding the dynamics at work, assessing the weaknesses and strengths of alternative actions, increasing effectiveness of groups, and providing more growth and satisfaction for individual group members.

Heron, J. (1989). *The facilitator's handbook*. New York: Nichols Publishing.

As the author defines it, a facilitator is one who is less concerned with formal teaching than with eliciting active self-directed learning from participants, thus ". . . enabling them to take more responsibility for what they learn and how they learn it." Author Heron provides a model for facilitating experiential learning groups. Within his framework he surveys the many options available to facilitators for managing the learning process in groups.

Johnson, D. W., & Johnson, F. P. (1987). *Joining together: Group theory and group skills.* 3rd ed. Englewood Cliffs, NJ: Prentice-Hall.

      Group theory and group skills establish the framework of this book. Each chapter addresses a theoretical area, such as conflict, communication, and cohesion, while also providing exercises that apply each theory to a group situation. Many of the exercises have become standard in many leadership and counseling programs.

Jordon, D. (1989). A new vision for outdoor leadership theory. *Leisure Studies, 8*(1), 35-47.

      The author reviews and groups 12 models of leadership according to trait, behavioral, group and situational theories. Based on these theories, she develops an outdoor leadership model that encompasses the unique demands of outdoor recreation leadership.

Mayo, G. D., & Dubois, P. H. (1987). *The complete book of training: Theory, principles, and techniques.* San Diego, CA: University Associates.

      Training is a time consuming and costly activity for all businesses and institutions. The authors of this book present information to trainers which they say has proven through research to be effective. This includes, 1) a description of the many training techniques, formats, and aids that are presently available; 2) illustrations of how training can be improved through planned evaluation studies; and 3) a theoretical base for training which includes the results of applicable psychological research. The less commonly known results of research conducted by the military services have also been incorporated into the research review.

Moore, C. M. (1987). *Group techniques for idea building.* Newbury Park, CA: Sage.

      The author describes four different group techniques for idea building: Nominal Group Technique (NGT), Ideawriting, Delphi Technique, and Interpretive Structural Modeling (ISM). Explicit, useful descriptions of these four task-oriented group techniques are provided. The author further explains which techniques are best suited for a particular project. These techniques, especially designed for use by small groups focusing on specific decision-making or planning tasks, can be used in combination. This study explains how these group techniques may be linked together to promote the achievement of a group's goals.

Parnes, S. J. (1988). *Visionizing.* East Aurora, NY: D.O.K. Publishers.

      "This book is designed for those interested in encouraging and nurturing creative awareness, attitudes and accomplishments in themselves and others." The book is based on the Osborn-Parnes Creative Problem-solving process, and can be used as a workbook for individual study or group instruction.

Perrin, K. (Ed.). (1985). *National leadership training center: Leadership curriculum guide.* Reston, VA: National Association of Secondary School Principals.

      This curriculum guide is apparently designed to assist educators in the preparation and implementation of leadership training programs aimed at secondary school students. The guide is comprised of the following sections: Self-awareness; Leadership; Goal-setting; Communication; Organization; Group process; Problem solving; and

Evaluation. A variety of exercises which correspond to chapter topics are also included.

Pfeiffer, J. W., & Ballew, A. C. (1988-89). *UA training technologies*. San Diego: University Associates.

    This set consists of seven volumes covering the following topics: Using structured experiences in human resource development (HRD); Using instruments in HRD; Using lecturettes, theory, and models in HRD; Using role plays in HRD; Using case studies, simulations, and games in HRD; Design skills in HRD; and Presentation and evaluation skills in HRD. An index to all volumes is included.

Pfeiffer, J. W., & Jones, J. E. (Eds.). (1985). *Handbook of structured experiences for human relations training*. San Diego, CA: University Associates.

    A complementary series to the *Annuals*, this series now contains ten volumes, with the last volume published in 1985. Each contains structured experiences designed to promote varied learning experiences and to be useful in a variety of settings.

Pfeiffer, W. J. (Ed.). (1989). *The 1989 annual: Developing human resources*. San Diego, CA: University Associates.

    This series, formally called the *Annual Handbook for Group Facilitators*, has been issued each year since 1972 (often called the Pfeiffer and Jones books). The volumes contain current, nonoverlapping collections of structured experiences, instruments, lecturettes, professional development papers, and resources for trainers and consultants.

Pike, R. W. (1989). *Creative training techniques handbook: Tips, tactics & how-tos for delivering effective training*. Minneapolis, MN: Lakewood Books.

    This handbook is written by a trainer for trainers. The author is a successful trainer who now runs his own training and development business. He offers the techniques which have made his training models successful. The premise of his approach to training is that the most effective behavior-changing tools of training are those which demand the full involvement of the participant throughout the training program. With this in mind, the author shows, from planning to final day wrap-up, how to motivate and involve both the individual participants and participants as teams. The author also provides tips for optimizing training facilities, whether at a training center or at an off-site business location.

Rohnke, K. (Ed.). (1977). *Cowstails & cobras*. Hamilton, MA: Project Adventure.

    An outdoor educator's volume which can easily apply to numerous group situations. Rope courses and initiative games are the focus of this easy-to-use guide. Illustrations and photographs make it easy to understand the narrative directions. The *Blind Polygon* works wonders with a group of 40 student leaders!

Simonds, P. W. (1988). *A beginner's guide to leadership training programs*. Columbia, SC: NACA Educational Foundation. National Association for Campus Activities.

    This guide examines three important areas of student leadership training. It first presents a brief history of leadership theory and leadership training programs for higher education. Secondly, information is provided on what other colleges and universities have done in the past with leadership training programs. Last, a general guide is offered as a tool for the development of a variety of leadership training experiences for potential college student leaders. Exercises and training in decision making, problem solving, conflict resolution, consensus building and group building are included. This is an excellent beginner's manual to leadership development.

Smith, B. J., & Delahaye, B. L. (1987). *How to be an effective trainer: Skills for managers and new trainers*. 2nd ed. New York: John Wiley & Sons.

This second edition manual advertises itself as "a step-by-step, self-directed program you can use to train yourself to become a top-notch trainer." The twenty-six chapters are divided into six parts. From training techniques and planning aids, to managing the learning experience, each chapter focuses on a particular skill or topic. Most chapters include specific learning objectives, key concepts, plans to achieve objectives, a checklist for use as an on-the-site guide, and tests and exercises to check the understanding of each chapter. The authors are both instructors at the School of Management of the Queensland Institute of Technology in Brisbane, Australia.

Tubesing, N. L., & Tubesing, D. A. (Eds.). (1988). *Structured exercises in stress management: A whole person handbook for trainers, educators & group leaders, Vol. 4*. Duluth, MN: Whole Person Press.

The 36 designs offered in this volume are provided to help people apply what they've learned about stress management. The format of each exercise is structured to involve people in the learning process. To assist in their selection, the authors have grouped them into six broad categories: Icebreakers, Stress Assessments, Management Strategies, Skill Builders, Action Planning/Closure, and Group Energizers. Designed for easy use, each exercise description includes its time frame, materials needed, goals, group size, instructions, variations, and tips for group trainers. The authors encourage reproduction of the worksheets.

VanGundy, A. B. (1987). *Creative problem solving*. New York: Quorum Books.

An excellent resource for creativity trainers, this text facilitates the design and teaching of creative problem solving. Games, exercises, personal inventories, group and individual assessments are included to provide trainers with a wide range of models by which to structure workshops and test their effectiveness. These models and formats focus on using both rational and intuitive thinking skills in exploring and applying creativity to problem solving as well as to personal and professional goals, short-term objectives, and long-range planning.

Welsh, T. M., Johnson, S. P., Miller, L. K., & Merrill, M. H. (1989). A practical procedure for training meeting chairpersons. *Journal of Organizational Behavior Management, 10* (1), 151-166.

Based on their case study which compared the performance of two undergraduate chairperson trainees, the authors provide a practical approach for training chairpersons which is intended to improve chairperson performance and increased participant satisfaction.

Wood, J. T. (1977).   The leader's brief: Teaching an adaptive approach to leading. *Communication Education, 26,* 354-358.

      Presents an alternative method, the adaptive approach, of training leaders which focuses on the leader's ability to analyze the unique group members and situation and adapt his or her own behavior to meet the circumstantial requirements. Introduces the Leadership Brief as a technique for applying this approach.

Texts

Blimling, G. S., & Miltenberger, L. J. (1981). *The resident assistant: Working with college students in residence halls.* Dubuque, IA: Kendall/Hunt.

      Useful as a practical resource for students filling RA positions. Can serve as a text for credit course offerings that further legitimize the integration of the training-learning experience with the total educational experience of students attending colleges and universities. Help in achieving objectives in residence education by equipping RAs in various areas is addressed.

Campbell, D. P. (1984).   *If I'm in charge here, why is everybody laughing?* 2nd ed. Greensboro, NC: Center for Creative Leadership.

      This book examines a number of questions: How can leaders bring out the best in the people they work with? What are the best ways to overcome opposition? Why are friendships so special to people in charge? Campbell issues a call to take up the challenge of leadership, which can be demanding, enriching and exhilarating. This is a book full of useful tips for people who are in charge, who make things happen, and who want to have an impact on their world.

Cuming, P. (1981). *The power handbook.* Boston: CBI Publishing.

      This book examines the concept of power and its effect on organization. The six kinds of power and influence and manipulation are covered in direct, easy to understand chapters. A good book for lecture material, it also has various exercises and profiles to use with organizations or classes.

Gordon, T. (1977). *Leader effectiveness training.* New York: Bantam Books.

      This book can be used as a text for some leadership classes. It examines many of the components of leadership in an easy-to-read format and relies heavily on the concept of active listening.

Gray, J. W., & Pfeiffer, A. L. (1987). *Skills for leaders.* Reston, VA: National Association of Secondary School Principals.

      This book is designed for secondary school student leaders as a manual for enlarging on and developing leadership potential and skills. This straightforward guide is comprised of the following chapters: The challenge of leadership; Understanding communication; Understanding followers; Understanding yourself as a leader; and

Communication skills for leaders. This book could have broad application for educators, management trainers and human resources personnel who seek a concise and easy-to-follow introduction to leadership programming.

Shinn, G. (1986). *Leadership development*. 2nd ed. New York: McGraw-Hill.

      The audience for this book seems to be high school or community college students. The title is something of a misnomer, for most of the book emphasizes self-care and personal development. Many of the skills emphasized however are ones useful to the aspiring leader or manager. Representative section titles are, Personality Development, Personal Appearance, Developing Communication Skills, Memory, Creativity, Management and Leadership, and Employment.

Timpe, A. D. (1987). *Leadership: Volume 3 in Facts on File's series: The art & science of business management*. New York: Facts On File.

      This compendium provides access to a broad range of practical information, theory, and research associated with leadership ability and how to develop it. The variety of insights, experience and concepts presented offer many useful approaches for human resource planning. The sources represented in this volume cover a wide range of professional publications, including a number not readily available to most executives. And, for those wanting a more expanded discussion on a particular component, the bibliography is a valuable resource. This book is organized into six sections, including: Leadership--the effective traits; Perceptions of power and authority; Manager or leader?; and Leadership styles.

Williams, J. C. (1986). *Leadership quest*. McGregor, TX: Leadership Press.

      Presents four modules for the study of leadership: Leadership: a bias for action; Personal dimensions of leadership; Developing your leadership skills; and Resources and references.

Simulations, Games and Experiential Methods

Christopher, E. M., & Smith, L. E. (1987). *Leadership training through gaming*. New York: Nichols.

      Leadership skills are imperative for the successful manager. This book has been specifically written for those who use simulation and role play games for leadership training. Each chapter pinpoints certain games which have been shown to be most effective in drawing out the significant aspects of leadership qualities in its participants. By placing the various activities within both an international and theoretical context, the kind of learning experience they are likely to produce can be measured. The possible roadblocks and dead-ends in each simulation are also examined.

Fluegelman, A. (1976). *The new games book*. Garden City, NY: Doubleday.

      This is a standard group play resource. Numerous games illustrated in this book can be used as ice-breakers or initiatives. A good book to help you think about high or low activity games for large or small groups.

Greenblat, C. S. (1988). *Designing games and simulations: An illustrated handbook.* Newbury Park, CA: Sage.

This handbook will be invaluable to anyone involved with the design and model development of simulation and game formats. The author presents four case studies and provides examples of over 70 games and simulations. Practical advice is given on making decisions, setting objectives, constructing and modifying a model, preparing it as a product, designing the operator's manual, arranging for publication, and pre-testing. The approach of the manual is systematic and comprehensive. The author has distilled the complexity of model development, design, and application into one package. Extensive references, models, and a listing of periodicals and organizations are included.

Horn, R. E., & Cleaves, A. (Eds.). (1980). *The guide to simulations/games for education and training.* 4th ed. Beverly Hills, CA: Sage Publications.

This is a comprehensive reference source on simulations and games designed for educators and trainers. The guide contains only simulations and games that have specific educational purposes. Also included is a valuable collection of 24 essays evaluating and comparing simulations in various subject areas. The age level at which the simulation or game is aimed begins with the junior high level and up. Although somewhat dated now, this guide remains a useful resource.

Jones, K. (1989). *A sourcebook of management simulations.* New York: Nichols Publishing.

This sourcebook is comprised of 10 complete simulations. In Part 1 the author describes his rationale and provides detailed information on organizing the sessions. The 10 simulations are presented in Part 2. Each simulation is preceded by "facilitator's notes," which indicate the types of management skills to be exercised. Some of the skills covered include: decision making, planning, evaluation, strategy, interpersonal communication and interviewing.

Lewis, L. H. (Ed.). (1986). *Experiential and simulation techniques for teaching adults.* San Francisco: Jossey-Bass.

This compilation includes a number of original papers that explore and explain some of the uses of simulation and experiential methods in adult training and in the college classroom. Chapters include: "Developing managerial skills through realistic simulations"; "Intercultural simulation games: Removing cultural blinders"; and "Computer simulations come of age."

Lombardo, M. M., McCall, M. W., Jr., & DeVries, D. L. (1987). *Looking Glass, Inc.: University edition.* Greensboro, NC: Center for Creative Leadership.

This is a package containing all the materials necessary for conducting a simulation of managerial and organizational issues faced by a mid-sized U.S. company. It was designed to expose students to the pace, pressure and ambiguity of managerial work, and to have them experience first-hand the organizational challenges of communication, motivation, leadership and decision making. The simulation is available only for use with full-time students in degree-granting institutions.

Self-Development and Skill Training

Bliss, E. C. (1978). *Getting things done: The ABCs of time management.* New York: Bantam.

This book is designed to encourage people to make better use of their time and improve their efficiency at work. It is filled with suggestions on how to deal with a mixed bag of alphabetically arranged topics--correspondence, delegation, fear, interruptions, meetings, sleep and other topics.

Kroeger, O., & Thusen, J. M. (1988). *Type talk: Or how to determine your personality type and change your life.* New York, NY: Delacorte Press.

The authors have taken the previous work on personality identification, such as the Myers-Briggs Type Indicator (MBTI), and other work, such as Kiersey's *Please Understand Me,* and distilled the 16 personality type identifiers into a description of personality types easily understood and applied by anyone. This work is not written for professional evaluation of personality types, but rather its purpose is somewhat analogous to books about bird watching, with the focus here on "type watching."

Mandel, S. (1987). *Effective presentation skills.* Los Altos, CA: Crisp Publications.

Constructed to be direct, simple, and easy to apply, this short text is recommended for the novice public speaker and the reluctant public speaker. The author shows how to convert the fear associated with public speaking into energy which will contribute to a dynamic presentation. The seven sections of this text point out, step-by-step, how to assess your speaking skills, how to deal with anxiety, how to plan your presentation, how to organize, how to develop and use visual aids, how to prepare the presentation, and how to deliver it to your audience. A handy final review checklist is also provided.

Miller, S., Wackman, D. B., Nunally, E. W., & Miller, P. A. (1988). *Connecting with self and others.* Littleton, CO: Interpersonal Communication Programs.

To some degree we are always engaged in the "dance" of connecting or disconnecting with others. What makes this "dance" so engaging? Based on years of research and testing these authors present strategies, models and maps to clarify the time, energy, space, and choices which together form the actions we take in our relationships with others. The three-fold model of awareness, skills, and options in communicating and building relationships with others is set within a practical framework which shows the paths we travel in our various communication efforts.

Reviews, Bibliographies and Information Source Books

Bick, P. A. (1988). *Business ethics and responsibility: An information sourcebook.* Phoenix, AZ: Oryx Press.

This annotated bibliography covers a broad range of materials available on the topics of corporate social responsibility and business ethics. As no company or institution is exempt from social, political, and environmental issues facing communities, countries, and nations globally, it is imperative that organizations be well aware of their responsibility to maintaining ethical standards in their business practices. With this in mind, the author covers, by subject, material which addresses ethics in the areas of advertising, finance, management, marketing, accounting, and other areas.

Clay, K. (1988). *The school administrator's resource guide.* Phoenix, AZ: Oryx Press.

This annotated bibliography of resources will be of interest to school administrators and others in the field of education. Most of the information for this guide is drawn from extensive computer searches of such automated databases as the Educational Resources Information Center (ERIC), PsycINFO, Sociological Abstracts, and Social SciSearch. Items cited are primarily dated from 1982 to March, 1987. The guidebook is divided into nine chapters. A brief introduction helps to define each subject area. A few of the topics included are instructional leadership, staff development, supervision and evaluation, and administrative leadership.

Goehlert, R. (1982). *Political leadership.* Monticello, IL: Vance Bibliographies.

Part of the Public Administration Series that provides a bibliography on political leadership.

Hannah, M. E., & Midlarsky, E. (1981). *Toward an understanding of power and leadership in the young: A review.* San Rafael, CA: Select Press (P.O. Box 9838, 94912).

This paper presents a review of the literature regarding the antecedents (personal and situational characteristics), process and outcome in situations in which power and leadership are exercised. Methodological critiques of the existing literature (comprising over 130 references) are provided, as well as suggestions for future research.

Hare, A. P. (1976). *Handbook of small group research.* New York: Free Press.

Contains 15 chapters, as well as appendixes, indexes and a 323-page bibliography on small group research studies. The chapters fall into three basic categories: group process, structure interaction variables, and performance characteristics. This is primarily a reference resource which summarizes the major trends and findings on small groups from 1898 through 1974. Suitable for the serious reader interested in small group dynamics and leadership.

Heasley, D. K. (Ed.). (1989?). *Extension leadership development resources: U. S. and Canada bibliography.* University Park, PA: Pennsylvania State University. Northeast Regional Center for Rural Development.

This bibliography of resource materials was developed by a group that was formed at a 1986 conference on community leadership sponsored by the USDA Extension Service. Their goal was to put together a publication that would summarize the materials and resources for development that had been developed by local Extension Services throughout the U. S. and Canada. The book consists of responses by these agencies to a survey designed to gather specific data about each "leadership development resource" in use by these agencies; the information gathered includes title of the resource, audience, format, focus, author, availability and price.

Krug, S. E. (1987). *Psychware sourcebook, 1987-88*. 2nd ed. Kansas City, MO: Test Corporation of America.

In response to the growing field of computer-based assessment/scoring, this guidebook is the first in a series of guides to such computer-based products. It contains listings and descriptions of over 300 assessment products. A few of the topics covered by these products are: career and vocational, cognitive ability, interests and attitudes, motivation and needs, and structured interviews. Five indexes provide access to information about product title, product category, product application, service and supplier.

Leavitt, J. (1988). *Women in administration: An information sourcebook*. Phoenix, AZ: Oryx Press.

This expanded annotated bibliography covers the field. The author has arranged this listing into topics which span the broad range of concerns for women in leadership. Among the topics included are: Progress and Status of Women in Management; Mentors and Networking; Management Training for Women; Profiles of Women Managers; Career and Family; Women Bosses; Women as Directors; Obstacles; Comparisons of Men and Women Managers; Women Managers in Various Fields; Women Business Owners; and Women Entrepreneurs. An author, title, and subject index provide access to the sources listed. Additional sources of information listed include associations and directories.

Margerison, C. J., & Roden, S. (Eds.). (1987). *Management development bibliography*. Bradford, West Yorkshire, England: MCB University Press.

The editors have put together a bibliography of articles on or related to the topic of management development. A useful introduction reviews and summarizes each of the twelve categories of articles included. Within each of these introductions the authors provide a brief list of "key articles," and tell just what is included in the section. Unfortunately, the bibliography is not annotated, nor are the main sections further subdivided, so one must wade through long lists of citations to find specific subjects of interest.

McCauley, C. D. (1986). *Developmental experiences in managerial work: A literature review*. Greensboro, NC: Center for Creative Leadership, Technical Report Number 26.

As part of an ongoing research project on executive growth and learning, researchers at the Center for Creative Leadership interviewed successful executives about important events in their careers. The purpose of this paper is not to provide an extensive presentation of the CCL research, but to take a look at past research studies in the context of the CCL research.

Nejedlo, R. J., & Powell, J. A. (1982). *Mentoring and networking: An annotated bibliography*. Alexandria, VA: Association for Counselor Education and Supervision.
   The objective of this text is to provide a general annotated bibliography on mentoring and networking, primarily from the education literature.

Olmstead, J. A., & Galloway, D. R. (1980). *Management and supervisory training: A review and annotated bibliography*. Alexandria, VA: Human Resources Research Organization.
   Topics include the effectiveness of various training methods for improving knowledge and awareness, changing attitudes, skills, and improving on-the-job performance.

Pence, E., & Reed, N. (1983). *State-of-the-art in management development in the United States*. Ft. Belvoir, VA: Defense Systems Management College. Report. (NTIS order no. AD A130 583).
   The purpose of this report is to assess the state-of-the-art in contemporary American executive development and training and to highlight areas for application in the Department of Defense.

Peterson, M. W., & Mets, L. A. (1987). *Key resources on higher education governance, management, and leadership: A guide to the literature*. San Francisco, CA: Jossey-Bass.
   A valuable reference source for both scholars and practitioners, this new book is a complete overview of the most important literature on leadership, governance, and management in colleges and universities. In addition, a guide is provided to essential writings from the great body of literature on the three fundamental administrative functions of higher education, emphasizing how each of these areas is adapting to meet new demands. Complete bibliographic citations and evaluative annotations are included with all entries.

Phillips, N. R., Fetteroll, E., Nadler, L., & Nadler, Z. (Eds.). (1987). *The trainer's resource 1987: A comprehensive guide to packaged training programs*. 5th ed. Amherst, Massachusetts: Human Resource Development Press.
   This book offers a consolidated, single source to which you can go when looking for a packaged training program. It provides comparable data about what the packaged programs are, how they relate to your needs, what kinds of learning strategies are utilized, and the cost. Programs are clearly identified under subject categories in the table of contents, and the book provides indexes to subject, title and vendor of all packaged training programs.

Porter, L. W., & McKibbin, L. E. (1988). *Management education and development: Drift or thrust into the 21st Century?* New York: McGraw-Hill.
   Based upon interviews from an extensive sampling of respondents--students, faculty, curriculum coordinators, business owners, managers and corporate executives--the current direction of management education and development was examined in light of the changes anticipated in society over the next 30 years. The particular areas examined

were business education degree programs, student composition, faculty, special areas of research, and lifelong learning programs targeted for top level managers and executives.

Roberts, D. C. (1981). *Student leadership programs in higher education*. Carbondale, IL: ACPA Southern Illinois University Press.

  This book examines the rationale behind leadership development programs in higher education. Specific types of leadership programs and special population needs comprise the bulk of the book. The individually written chapters provide different perspectives while establishing key contact people in the field. This volume should be included in every leadership library.

Schneier, C. E., Beatty, R. W., & Baird, L. S. (Eds.). (1987). *The performance management sourcebook*. Amherst, MA: Human Resource Development Press.

  The authors of this sourcebook have consulted major corporations across the country in the design and format of this guide. They have attempted to provide in one volume the components which create performance management systems in business. It is intended as a tool for use in the development of policy manuals, operational guides, and orientation programs. In 12 sections, various topics and designs are examined: performance appraisal; performance management; planning, managing, and reviewing performance; developing performance testing methodologies, such as questionnaires, cases, and role plays. Tips and advice are also offered for working with external consultants on performance projects.

Stogdill, R. M., & Bass, B. M. (1981). *Stogdill's handbook of leadership: A survey of theory and research*. New York: Free Press.

  The chapters of this comprehensive work fall into eight major categories: introduction to leadership theory and research, the leader as person, power and legitimacy, leader-follower interaction, the antecedents and consequences of management and styles of leadership, situational aspects of leadership, special conditions, and applications and implications. This volume is suitable for the serious reader and those in search of an excellent reference work.

U.S. Army War College Library. (1987). *Senior level leadership and command: A selected bibliography*. Carlisle Barracks, PA: U.S. Army War College Library.

  A selected bibliography of books, documents and journal articles which address military leadership and command, compiled by the U.S. Army War College Library.

Vance, M. A. (1982). *Community leadership: A bibliography*. Monticello, IL: Vance Bibliographies.

  Part of the Public Administration Series, providing a bibliography on community leadership.

Program Descriptions and Case Studies

Follis, H., & Feldhusen, J. (1983). Design and evaluation of a summer academic leadership program. *Roeper Review, 6*(2), 92-94.

     The Purdue Academic Leadership Seminar is a two-week summer residential program for high school students emphasizing both academics and leadership training. This article describes the organization of the program, student selection procedures, staffing, and other aspects of the program.

Heasley, D. K. (Ed.). (1986). *Directory of state-wide rural and agricultural leadership programs*. University Park, PA: Pennsylvania State University Press.

     Describes current and earlier leadership programs jointly sponsored by the W. K. Kellogg Foundation and Cooperative Extension Service agencies. Also includes descriptions of twelve related programs not sponsored by the Kellogg Foundation.

Maher, R. (1984). Fostering student leadership: One school's approach. *Spectrum, 2*(4), 26-28.

     Describes a year-long leadership course at Lakeland High School (Shrub Oak, New York) initiated by students. Designed as part of the regular curriculum, the course begins with self-development and proceeds to community service projects.

Spitzberg, I. J., Jr. (1986). *Introduction to campus programs on leadership*. Washington, D.C.: Council for Liberal Learning of the Association of American Colleges, Luce Leadership Series.

     An examination of six campus-based leadership programs exemplifying the diversity of approaches found around the country. Highlights the opportunities and problems for those interested in starting leadership programs. Three categories of leadership programs are identified: cocurricular leadership development programs, academic courses (drawing mainly on social psychological and management studies), and liberal arts academic courses (humanities and social-science base).

Vega, J. E. (1987). *Hispanic leadership training project: Final report*. Trenton, NJ: New Jersey State Dept. of Higher Education. (ERIC Document Reproduction Service No. ED 298841).

     The Hispanic Leadership Fellows Program was a 3-year program supported by the Fund for the Improvement of Postsecondary Education, which sought to identify Hispanic college faculty and professionals who demonstrated the desire and potential to move into middle and top administrative positions in higher education. This article gives a thorough review of the program and also includes: the program handbook; a profile of Hispanic leadership fellows 1983-86, and Leadership Fellows Directory for 1983-84, 1984-85, and 1985-86.

Directories and Surveys

Billy, C. (Ed.). (1988). *Bricker's international directory: University executive programs.* 19th ed. Princeton, NJ: Petersons Guides.

   This directory is designed to help upper-level management and executives select management programs most appropriate to their needs. Especially worthy of comment is the index to programs by category and country. The programs are listed under subject headings such as General Management and Leadership and Organization. They are then arranged by geographical location. Each program profile is listed by the name of its host institution. The information given with each description includes program location, duration, profile of participants, subject matter, methods of instruction, calendar of sessions, tuition, faculty, facilities, special features, and the name of the official contact person.

Brown, P. (1986). *National leadership programs resource guide.* Burlington, VT: University of Vermont, The Leadership Task Force of Commission IV.

   The information in this guide was gathered from a resource survey mailed to over 450 institutions, including community colleges, colleges and universities. The first section provides a composite of programs offered at various institutions. The second section provides a contact person for each institution listed. The last section is an annotated listing of pertinent resources.

Gale Research Inc. (1989). 1990 Seminars directory. 2nd ed. Detroit, MI: Gale Research.

   This yearly guide is a comprehensive listing of approximately 10,000 seminars and workshops held in the United States and Canada. Although it covers a variety of topics, the seminars of most interest to readers of this source book will be found under the headings of Communications, Human Resource Management, Interpersonal Skills and Management. Information included for each seminar or workshop includes title, address, phone, description, location, cost, and (for some items) participant evaluations.

Kaye, B. L., & Scheele, A. M. (1975). Leadership training. *New Directions for Higher Education, 3*(3), 79-93.

   A survey of 60 programs to prepare women for leadership in business and education identifies two distinct types of skills training (lifebuilding skills, and technical and managerial skills) and offers ideas to institutions planning leadership programs. Six model programs are described and 24 are listed in the bibliography.

Northeast Regional Center for Rural Development (Date?). *Community leadership development: Implications for extension.* University Park, PA: Pennsylvania State University. Northeast Regional Center for Rural Development.

   The major objectives of this publication are to share the information gained from the survey on CES staff involved with community leadership (CL) efforts, to summarize recent national efforts that can be useful in developing and conducting CL programs, to summarize current leadership theory and literature, and to provide a directory of current leadership programs.

Radin, B. A. (1980). Leadership training for women in state and local government. *Public Personnel Management, 9,* 52-60.

      Fifty-five women in public administration responded to a survey and/or interviews to identify skills that would help their upward mobility and job effectiveness, detail on-the-job problems, describe training opportunities available to them, and describe the ideal training/development program.

Rich, P., & Garino, A. (1979). *Programs for training citizen leaders: A national survey.* St. Louis, MO: League of Women Voters. Citizens Information Resource Center.

      Various types of citizen training programs were surveyed by the staff of the St. Louis Leadership Program to determine the characteristics of a successful program. Findings covered purpose and philosophy, clients, program content, training techniques, funding, and evaluation.

Rossing, B. E. (1987). *Wisconsin CES Leadership Impact Study.* Madison, WI: University of Wisconsin Extension. (ERIC Document No. ED 300588).

      Report of a study on the impact of Wisconsin Cooperative Extension Service programs on leaders and the organizations and communities they serve. A total of 344 community leaders were selected, representing areas of the state where Extension had recently served. The survey results produced some the following conclusions: leaders assisted by Extension reflect positive changes in leadership skills; Extension rated as an important influence; Extension provides assistance and education regarded as important. Based on survey findings, recommendations are made for continued program planning and leadership training.

FILMS AND VIDEOS FOR LEADERSHIP EDUCATION

INTRODUCTION

The films and videos in the following pages represent a variety of disciplines, subject categories, stylistic treatments and historical periods. There are feature films, documentaries and docu-dramas, training films, and specialty films. Some discuss leadership from a behavioral science perspective. Others, especially the feature films, don't talk directly about leadership, but instead "show" it. The common thread among this variety is that every film is appropriate for developing or explicating some aspect of leadership--be that leader skills, the moral dimension of leadership, political leadership, theories of leader behavior, or personal growth.

A few of the films in this list are part of the Center for Creative Leadership collection and have been used in our programs. Others were identified by Frank Freeman and Tom Cronin when preparing a presentation for a Leadership Education Conference (LEC). Many were recommended by LEC participants and by respondents to a Center survey of leadership courses and programs in higher education. Still others were included on the basis of evaluative reviews.

Videos and films have a variety of uses in a classroom or training environment. Feature films (or selected segments if time is a problem) are often effective because of their visual quality and strong emotional impact--*Das Boot* and *A Man for All Seasons*, for example, present leadership dilemmas with a great deal of force. Video recordings of televised candidate debates can add a contemporary punch to studies of political leadership. Training films like *Meetings, Bloody Meetings*, *The Abilene Paradox*, and *Group Dynamics: Groupthink* can vitalize presentations on group process and problem-solving issues. Short personal-growth and motivational films like *You*, *Dreaming*, and *Desire to Win* set the stage for leadership development.

This is not a lengthy list; you may have used a film or video that is not included here. We welcome your recommendations for films or videos to include in the next edition of this Source Book.

Note that each film has a distributor code listed. The full name and address of each distributor mentioned may be found in this film distributor list. This address list is up-to-date as of December 1989, but be aware that distributors' names, addresses and phone numbers change frequently. If you cannot locate one of the items in this list, contact the audiovisual department of your college or public library for help. They will have the latest directories.

The final part of this section is a list of additional resources useful in identifying, locating and acquiring films and videos.

FILMS FOR LEADERSHIP EDUCATION

The Abilene Paradox (1985)
(Runtime: 27m   Format: 16mm/VT   Distributor: CRM)
   This film deals with the management of agreement in organizations. The theme is that mismanaged agreement is as dangerous to organizational effectiveness as excessive conflict because it can lead the organization toward inappropriate goals.

An Act of Congress (1979)
(Runtime: 52m   Format: 16mm/VT   Distributor: LCA)
   Traces the progress of a bill--the Clean Air Act of 1977--through committee, the House, and finally to enactment. Contrasts the leadership styles of Rep. Paul Rogers, supporter of strong clean air standards, and Rep. John Dingle, opponent of a strong bill.

Billy Budd (1962)
(Runtime: 125m   Format: 16mm/VT   Distributor: MGM/UA)
   In 1797 the sadistic master at arms of a British warship terrorizes the crew and is killed by young Billy Budd, who must hang for his unpremeditated crime. Beautifully photographed but poorly scripted attempt at the impossible: an allegory of good and evil more suited to opera or the printed page.

Bolero (1972)
(Runtime: 28m   Format: 16mm/VT   Distributor: PYRAMID)
   Lighting and creative camera work as dramatic as Ravel's music. Brief comments from soloists, concertmaster, and conductor Zubin Mehta give insight into the subtle leadership touches that make a truly great performance (by Los Angeles Philharmonic).

Breaker Morant (1979)
(Runtime: 107m   Format: 16mm/VT   Distributor: FILMS INC)
   Based on a true story, the film takes place when England was waging the Boer war in Africa. England court-martialed three Australian volunteer soldiers for murdering Boer prisoners, denying that the Aussies were acting under British orders.

The Bridge on the River Kwai (1957)
(Runtime: 161m   Format: 16mm/VT   Distributor: FILMS INC)
   In a World War II jungle POW camp, British prisoner Alec Guinness refuses to build a bridge for the enemy unless his officers supervise the work. After some grumbling the camp commander shrewdly relents, allowing Guinness to get his way while getting the bridge he wanted.

The Caine Mutiny (1954)
(Runtime: 125m   Format: 16mm/VT   Distributor: FILMS INC)
   An all-star cast enacts the drama of rebellion against unreasonable authority on the

combat vessel *Caine* in the Pacific during World War II. Humphrey Bogart stars as the paranoid captain in this superb film adapted from Wouk's prize-winning novel.

The Candidate (1972)
(Runtime: 110m   Format: 16mm/VT   Distributor: FILMS INC)
   Robert Redford performs as an idealistic lawyer whose ideals are steadily eroded when he runs for the U.S. Senate. Jeremy Larner, a speech writer for Senator Eugene McCarthy during his presidential campaign, wrote the screenplay.

A Case of Working Smarter, Not Harder (1982)
(Runtime: 15m   Format: 16mm/VT   Distributor: CRM)
   This case study provides a practical role model, a how-to lesson for supervisors and managers who are uncertain about how to delegate. It clarifies the distinction between delegation and dumping.

Churchill: Voice of a Lion (1978)
(Runtime: 24m   Format: 16mm/VT   Distributor: LCA)
   Presents the political life of Winston Churchill, with emphasis on the era of World War II. Identifies his traits and his techniques of leadership and presents excerpts from many of his speeches showing his bulldog temperament and his powerful use of words. Records his meetings with Roosevelt and Stalin.

Citizen Kane (1941)
(Runtime: 119m   Format: 16mm/VT   Distributor: FILMS INC)
   Considered by many to be a perfect film, if not the best American film of all time, Citizen Kane is truly a cinematic masterpiece. The emotion-paced story of Charles Foster Kane (based on the life of William Randolph Hearst), is told with ever-shifting perspective. Directing his own vital performance as well as members of the famous Mercury Players, Orson Welles created an enduring classic of leadership and power.

Command Decision (1949)
(Runtime: 111m   Format: 16mm/VT   Distributor: MGM/UA)
   The back-room boys--a general, his staff and his peers--debate the aerial bombardment of Germany. Plainly reproduced version of a determinedly serious play, with a remarkable cast.

Das Boot [The Boat] (1982)
(Runtime: 150m   Format: VT   Distributor: RCA COLUMBIA)
   A World War II drama about a German submarine crew. Reveals various faces of leadership and crew response in the midst of incredible tension and a literal fight for survival.

A Day Without Sunshine (1975)
(Runtime: 89m   Format: VT   Distributor: PBS VIDEO)
   A documentary, narrated by James Earl Jones, on the Florida citrus industry and the

plight of farm workers: low wages, malnutrition, disease, and poor living conditions.

The Democrat and the Dictator (1984)
(Runtime: 58m   Format: VT   Distributor: PBS VIDEO)
Bill Moyers examines the parallels between two charismatic leaders, Franklin Roosevelt and Adolph Hitler, both of whom came to national power in 1933 and died in 1945. Their presence and conflicting ideologies are revealed through their words and gestures captured on film.

Desire to Win (1983)
(Runtime: 13m   Format: 16mm/VT   Distributor: PRODUCERS INT)
A small-town marathon is the setting for this motivational film. The camera focuses on three participants who each define "winning" in their own terms. The narrator recalls scenes from childhood to emphasize the naturalness of achieving and risk taking.

Do You Believe in Miracles? (1980)
(Runtime: 24m   Format: 16mm/VT   Distributor: CORONET/MTI)
Most of this film is footage of the incredible and emotional victory of the U. S. Olympic Hockey team, with play-by-play descriptions. Includes reflection by coach and players on the role of leadership, team effort and determination.

Dreaming (1982)
(Runtime: 12m   Format: VT   Distributor: PRODUCERS INT)
Looks at the value of individuality within a corporate environment. It explores the risks and excitement of being yourself, of being more spontaneous, and suggests that we all have hidden potential waiting to be tapped.

Enterprise (1983)
(Runtime: 30m   Format: 16mm/VT   Distributor: LCA)
A series of 38 programs originally aired on PBS. Hosted by Eric Sevareid, this series explores the experiences of a variety of companies and their top executives as they face the risks and rewards of American business. These case studies combine high production value, lively story telling, and excellent profiles of a variety of business problems.

The Entrepreneurs: An American Adventure (1986)
(Runtime: 60m   Format: VT   Distributor: PBS VIDEO)
Features inventors, tough-minded tycoons, and other wizards of free enterprise in this series of six one-hour programs. The series, narrated by Robert Mitchum, contains archival photos, illustrations and historic film footage of the prototypes of products upon which industrial empires have been built.

Ethics in America (1988)
(Runtime: 60mm   Format: VT   Distributor: INTELLIMATION)
Produced by Fred Friendly, this series features nearly 100 panelists who tackle ethical issues involving loyalty, confidentiality, privacy, truthfulness, and personal ethics. Individual

titles are: *Do Unto Others; To Defend a Killer; Public Trust, Private Interests; Does Doctor Know Best?; Anatomy of a Corporate Takeover; Under Orders, Under Fire, Parts 1 & 2; Truth on Trial; The Human Experiment*; and *Politics, Privacy and the Press.*

Face to Face: Coaching for Improved Work Performance (1981)
(Runtime: 27m   Format: VT   Distributor: CALLY CURTIS)
This film dramatizes Fournies' book on the value of managing the behavior of others through the coaching process. Interspersed are the nine steps involved in coaching analysis and the five steps involved in the coaching discussion.

The Finest Hours (1964)
(Runtime: 116m   Format: VT   Distributor: PRISM)
This tribute to Sir Winston Churchill documents his rocky diplomatic career and his inspiring passionate leadership in World War II, recalling his words, humor, family life, and patriotic fervor. Narrated by Orson Welles.

Five Presidents on the Presidency (1973)
(Runtime: 24m   Format: 16mm/VT   Distributor: BFA)
Several topics are examined in excerpts from the filmed speeches of five presidents: presidential power, congressional relations, press relations, foreign policy, the president as politician, and the office in retrospect.

Focus on Decisions (197?)
(Runtime: 25m   Format: 16mm   Distributor: BNA)
A case study of an aircraft company facing some big decisions on expansion. Probes situational leadership and decision making.

Focus on Organization (197?)
(Runtime: 31m   Format: 16mm   Distributor: BNA)
A case study film that follows a woman manager through a year of confronting various organizational and operational problems in a commercial firm.

Focus on Results (197?)
(Runtime: 20m   Format: 16mm   Distributor: BNA)
A case study that looks at the planning and control problems facing a large multi-national company.

Gallipoli (1981)
(Runtime: 111m   Format: 16mm/VT   Distributor: FILMS INC)
The story of the ill-fated assault by Australian troops on the Turkish-held heights. Gallipoli is a place now mentioned in history books for the disaster that made Lord of the Admiralty Winston Churchill resign in disgrace.

Gandhi (1982)
(Runtime: 188m   Format: VT   Distributor: RCA/COLUMBIA)

Richard Attenborough's production and Ben Kingsley's award-winning performance highlight this dramatic account of the spiritual leader who inspired nonviolent resistance to British rule in India. The film follows Gandhi's life from his fight against racial inequality in South Africa to his unsuccessful attempts to unite Hindu and Muslim factions into an independent India.

General Della Rovere (1959)
(Runtime: 137m   Format: VT   Distributor: HOLLYWOOD HOME)
The central character, Vittorio Bardone, is a swindler and opportunist from Naples who follows the German and Fascist retreat when his city is occupied by Allied troops. Arrested for his crimes, he agrees to impersonate the recently killed General Della Rovere. He comes to believe in his role and to fight for the ideals of the Resistance.

Getting to Know Barbara (1988)
(Runtime: 16m   Format: VT   Distributor: CAROUSEL)
This segment from a 60 Minutes production features Barbara Proctor, who was described by Ronald Reagan as an embodiment of America's "spirit of enterprise." Describes this black woman's rise from ghetto impoverishment to her position as head of a multi-million dollar advertising agency.

Group Dynamics: Groupthink (1973)
(Runtime: 22m   Format: 16mm/VT   Distributor: CRM)
Analyzes, discusses, and illustrates the eight specific traits of group behavior isolated by Irving Janis. Graphically illustrates group pressure toward premature consensus.

Harvest of Shame (1960)
(Runtime: 53m   Format: 16mm/VT   Distributor: CRM)
Depicts the problems of the migrant farm worker. Analyzes factors contributing to the situation, and offers ways the conditions might be alleviated.

If I Can Do This I Can Do Anything (1986)
(Runtime: 30m   Format: 16mm/VT   Distributor: AEF)
The setting of this motivational film is the annual National Handicapped Skiing Championship, articulately hosted by Ted Kennedy, who himself lost a leg to cancer at 12. Disabled skiers from around the world participate in this event, under the same conditions and on the same slopes as world class skiers.

In Remembrance of Martin (1986)
(Runtime: 60m   Format: VT   Distributor: PBS VIDEO)
This remarkable documentary chronicles King's life through personal comments from family members, former classmates, close friends and advisors. Archival footage documents King's early civil rights efforts, including the *I Have a Dream* address on the steps of the Lincoln Memorial. Later events in King's life and a brief synopsis of key civil rights decisions of the 1950s and 1960s are also included.

In Search of Excellence (1985)
(Runtime: 90m   Format: VT   Distributor: PRODUCERS INT)
   Based on the best seller and featuring Tom Peters, this production emphasizes rising to individual excellence in business as well as in other spheres of life. Includes corporate examples of "excellence."

The Inside Track (1986)
(Runtime: 17m   Format: 16mm/VT   Distributor: CALLY CURTIS)
   Based upon a compilation of current writings and research, *The Inside Track* presents some of the common ways we hurt or help our own chances for happiness and success. Hosted by Meredith Baxter Birney and David Birney, the film walks us through common self-sabotaging habits, traits, and attitudes that limit our getting what we want out of life.

Joshua in a Box (1969)
(Runtime: 6m   Format: 16mm/VT   Distributor: CRM)
   Animated parable about freedom and control--and much else. A person imprisoned in a box eventually escapes--then becomes a box himself to control another creature.

Justice Black and the Bill of Rights (1969)
(Runtime: 32m   Format: 16mm   Distributor: BFA)
   Presents an interview with Associate Justice Hugo M. Black, often called the court's philosopher.

Le Grande Illusion (1937)
(Runtime: 111m   Format: 16mm   Distributor: ENCYCLO BRIT)
   A French anti-war film that is also an inspiring evocation of camaraderie and courage in the face of adversity.

Leaders of the 20th Century: Portraits in Power (1980)
(Runtime: 24m   Format: 16mm/VT   Distributor: LCA)
   A series of 26 films. Uses documentary footage to examine the use and misuse of power by a number of political figures of this century. The programs are available individually and include portraits of Churchill, DeGaulle, Adenauer, Kennedy, Franco, Roosevelt, Stalin, Gandhi, Hitler, Mao, and others.

The Leadership Alliance (1988)
(Runtime: 64mm   Format: 16mm/VT   Distributor: VIDEO PUB)
   Tom Peters explores the subject of successful leadership by visiting four organizations: General Motors Bay City components plant; Johnsonville Foods; Harley-Davidson's York motorcycle assembly plant; and the Julia B. Thayer High School. He explains successful leadership as a special kind of alliance between managers and workers that fully engages the talents and potential of everyone in the organization

Leadership Challenge (1989)
(Runtime: 26m   Format: VT   Distributor: CRM)

In 1987 James Kouzes and Barry Posner published a landmark book, *The Leadership Challenge: How to Get Extraordinary Things Done in Organizations*. This video is based on their findings and documents their premise that leadership can be found at all levels of the organization. It tells the stories of four manager/leaders from both the corporate and nonprofit sectors, and in the telling reveals the practices Kouzes and Posner believe are common to successful leaders: challenging the process, enabling others to act, modeling the way, inspiring a shared vision, and encouraging the heart.

The Leadership Edge (198?)
(Runtime: 18m   Format: VT   Distributor: SALENGER)
This video goes "behind the scenes" with seven high-performing managers, showing their individual leadership styles and ways of working with their group. The content of the video is its strong point--the scenes of "real" managers. However the direction and production are not high caliber. It has some abrupt transitions, and the voice-over narrations are too dramatic in tone.

Leadership: Style or Circumstance (1974)
(Runtime: 28m   Format: 16mm/VT   Distributor: CRM)
The relationship-oriented leader and the task-oriented leader are shown in action, and their methods and results compared. Includes live footage and animation.

Looking at Leadership (198?)
(Runtime: 175m   Format: VT   Distributor: NABW-EF)
A five-part series from the National Association of Bank Women. Each part includes a 35-minute videocassette focusing on a specific area of leadership, participant workbooks, and a leader's guide. Contains many interviews of women in executive leadership roles. Primarily aimed at leaders within the volunteer setting, but appropriate for anyone desiring to increase his/her leadership skills.

Machiavelli on Political Power
(Runtime: 28m   Format: 16mm/VT   Distributor: BARR)
A film that prompts managers to analyze their own leadership style and assess its effects on their company's most valuable resource--its people. Presented is a debate between Niccolo Machiavelli, author of "The Prince," and three other men representing more humanistic views of politics and human nature.

A Man for all Seasons (1966)
(Runtime: 120m   Format: 16mm/VT   Distributor: RCA COLUMBIA)
A biographical drama concerning sixteenth century Chancellor of England, Sir Thomas More, and his personal conflict with King Henry VIII. More chose to die rather than compromise his religious beliefs. An exquisitely rich portrayal that received several academy awards.

Martin Luther King, Jr.: From Montgomery to Memphis (1969)
(Runtime: 26m   Format: 16mm/VT   Distributor: BFA)

Surveys the career of Dr. Martin Luther King, Jr., and the anti-violent Civil Rights Movement under his leadership--from the 1955-56 bus boycott in Montgomery to his assassination in Memphis.

Meetings, Bloody Meetings (1976)
(Runtime: 30m   Format: 16mm/VT   Distributor: VIDEO ARTS)

Focuses on meetings that take too much of a manager's time and accomplish too little. Demonstrates, through whimsical drama, techniques for conducting meetings that are shorter and more productive.

Migrant (1970)
(Runtime: 53m   Format: 16mm/VT   Distributor: NBC)

This documentary of the plight of the migrant farm worker concentrates on conditions in Florida. Includes interviews with landlords, corporate growers and workers.

The Missiles of October (1975)
(Runtime: 155m   Format: 16mm/VT   Distributor: LCA)

A dramatic reenactment of the Cuban missile crisis of October 16, 1962. Follows the tensions and decisions faced by President Kennedy during the twelve-day period when the United States and the Soviet Union confronted each other with nuclear destruction.

More Bloody Meetings (1986)
(Runtime: 27m   Format: 16mm/VT   Distributor: VIDEO ARTS)

This is a companion film to *Meetings, Bloody Meetings*. Where the original film concentrated on the mechanics of meetings, this new film focuses on the human factor, including controlling aggression, keeping the group focused on the objective, and preventing dominant group members from overpowering the rest of the group.

New Leadership Styles: Toward Human and Economic Development (1978)
(Runtime: 26m   Format: 16mm/VT   Distributor: DOC ASSOC)

Michael Maccoby introduces two corporate heads who illustrate his idea of humanistic approaches to management. One of the companies is production oriented while the other is a service company. The president who is interviewed is very articulate in describing the humanistic organization. Both seem realistic about the limits of participative management.

A New Look at Motivation (1980)
(Runtime: 32m   Format: 16mm/VT   Distributor: CRM)

An examination by David McClelland of affiliation, power and achievement needs and their relationship to leadership and the social environment of the organization.

Nixon: Checkers to Watergate (1976)
(Runtime: 20m   Format: 16mm/VT   Distributor: PYRAMID)

From the heights of success to the depths of impending impeachment, this powerful visual survey highlights the triumphs and tragedies of Richard Nixon's life and career.

527

Norma Rae (1979)
(Runtime: 115m   Format: 16mm/VT   Distributor: FILMS INC)
Portrays the life of a textile worker whose life is changed by the arrival of a union organizer. Norma eventually joins his cause and begins to exert strong leadership in her plant.

Patton (1970)
(Runtime: 169m   Format: 16mm/VT   Distributor: FILMS INC)
A panoramic portrait of General Patton, the brilliant, unstable, and anachronistic World War II tactician.

The Peter Hill Puzzle (1975)
(Runtime: 32m   Format: 16mm/VT   Distributor: ENCYCLO BRIT)
A dramatization about a new corporate executive who attempts to overcome his predecessor's problems. A good portrayal of leadership style and situational variables.

Places in the Heart (1984)
(Runtime: 113m   Format: VT   Distributor: CBS/FOX)
The theme of emergent leadership characterizes this movie about a Texas widow and her extended family. Under her growing strength they work together to raise a successful cotton crop to save her farm during the depression.

Power (1986)
(Runtime: 111m   Format: VT   Distributor: KARL-LORIMAR)
A feature film with Gene Hackman and Richard Gere. Portrays the packaging of political candidates by media brokers. Characterization is sketchy, but the topic is compelling.

The Power Game (1988)
(Runtime: 4 x 60m   Format: VT   Distributor: PBS)
This four-part series attempts to reveal the way the federal government actually operates on a daily basis. It documents the way Congress, the presidency, the Pentagon, embassies and lobbying groups get and keep power. The four individual titles are *The Congress, The Pentagon, The Presidency,* and *The Unelected.*

Power Play (1978)
(Runtime: 109m   Format: VT   Distributor: MEDIA HOME)
A bloody, action film about idealistic reformers of corrupt governments who create even worse havoc than dictatorships. Peter O'Toole plays Colonel Zeller, a morally corrupt tank commander who joins forces with the rebels to overthrow the government, and who then performs atrocities in order to impede the *coup d'etat* leadership.

The Problem (1965)
(Runtime: 12m   Format: 16mm/VT   Distributor: FILMS INC)
A Czech animated puppet film about decision avoidance in bureaucracies. Questions the

nature of responsibility and man's reaction to it.

Productivity and the Self-Fulfilling Prophecy (1974)
(Runtime: 30m   Format: 16mm/VT   Distributor: CRM)
   From a bank failure to the achievement level of a child in school, circumstances are altered by expectation. Dr. Robert Rosenthal presents results of some of his 300 studies on the power of expectation in influencing human performance. This film takes one concept and explores it well, combining theory, philosophy, research and examples.

Running with Jesse (1989)
(Runtime: 60m   Format: VT   Distributor: PBS)
   From the PBS *Frontline* series, this video chronicles Jackson's presidential campaign through the eyes of reporters who accompanied him, his supporters and detractors. Assesses the hope and hype that accompanied the campaign of this Black presidential contender.

The Seduction of Joe Tynan (1979)
(Runtime: 104m   Format: VT   Distributor: MCA HOME)
   Alan Alda portrays a liberal New York senator pursuing his political career while grappling with domestic problems. The script is literate, and the individual performances of Alda, Meryl Streep and Barbara Harris are good, but the film is skimpy on drama.

Situational Leadership (1977)
(Runtime: 16m   Format: 16mm/VT   Distributor: UNIV ASSOC)
   Paul Hersey explains his situational leadership theory for assessing group maturity and then selecting a leadership style. This is a clear but unimaginative presentation of the situational leadership model.

Styles of Leadership (1981)
(Runtime: 26m   Format: VT   Distributor: ROUNDTABLE)
   Takes a common business problem regarding a new contract and shows how it might be handled by four different types of leaders. Presents the major characteristics of each leadership style--autocratic, democratic, manipulative, consultative--and compares their effects on subordinates.

Theory X and Theory Y: The Work of Douglas McGregor (1969)
(Runtime: 49m   Format: 16mm/VT   Distributor: BNA)
   A two-part series. Part 1, *Description of the Theory*, uses interviews and a brief vignette to compare the two styles of managing. Part 2, *Application of the Theory*, relates examples of Theory Y principles when applied to several management problems. McGregor's ideas are well presented without a lot of hype, but the film gets low marks for creativity.

Together: Volunteer-to-Volunteer Relationships (1989)
(Runtime: 38m   Format: VT   Distributor: ENERGIZE)
   This is a videotape for the volunteer leader which portrays, through a simulated

volunteer committee, the many issues involved in leading volunteer teams. A *Trainer's Guide* accompanies the video and includes recommendations on various ways to use the tape in training.

Triumph of the Will: The Arrival of Hitler (1974)
(Runtime: 13m   Format: 16mm   Distributor: FILMS INC)

Hitler's airplane soars through massive cloud formations en route to a party rally in Nuremburg. Cheering masses greet him at the airport and line the streets of Nuremburg as he rides past. The extract uses no voice-over commentary but appeals to the viewer's emotions through a powerful Wagnerian musical score and images that carry symbolic weight.

Twelve O'Clock High (1949)
(Runtime: 132m   Format: 16mm/VT   Distributor: FILMS INC)

A psychological drama that deals with the problems of an Air Force commander who must rebuild a bomber group whose shattered morale threatens the effectiveness of daylight bombing raids.

Up the Organization (1973)
(Runtime: 24m   Format: VT/16mm   Distributor: TIME LIFE)

Robert Townsend, who wrote the book *Up The Organization* that outraged the business world, gives his very personal views on such topics as the chief executive, personnel department, management consultants, computers, and the public relations department.

The Verdict (1982)
(Runtime: 129m   Format: 16mm/VT   Distributor: MGM/UA)

An explosive lawsuit presents an aging, small-time lawyer with a chance to redeem his once-promising career.

A Yen for Harmony (1977)
(Runtime: 26m   Format: 16mm/VT   Distributor: DOC ASSOC)

Investigates Japanese management methods that affect productivity in organizations, including participatory management, consensus decision making, and lifetime employment. The transplantation of these methods to Western society is also examined.

You (1980)
(Runtime: 4m   Format: 16mm/VT   Distributor: CALLY CURTIS)

Combining the thought-provoking narration of William Schallert with a series of fascinating and humorous scenes of a baby exploring a roomful of "treasure," the film encourages viewers to recapture the good qualities they had as children and put them to use today.

FILM AND VIDEO DISTRIBUTORS

AEF
American Educational Films
3807 Dickerson Road
Nashville, TN 37207
Phone: (800) 822-5678

BARR
Barr Films
12801 Schabarum Ave.
P.O. Box 7878
Irwindale, CA 91706-7878
Phone: (800) 234-7878

BFA
BFA Educational Media
468 Park Avenue South
New York, NY 10016
Phone: (800) 221-1274

BNA
BNA Communications, Inc.
9439 Key West Avenue
Rockville, MD 20850
Phone: (301) 948-0540

BOSUSTOW
Steven Bosustow Productions
2207 Colby Avenue
Los Angeles, CA 90064
Phone: (213) 478-0821

CALLY CURTIS
Cally Curtis
1111 North Las Palmas Avenue
Hollywood, CA 90038
Phone: (213) 467-1101

CAROUSEL
Carousel Films, Inc.
260 Fifth Avenue, Room 705
New York, NY 10001
Phone: (212) 683-1660

CBS/FOX VIDEO
1211 Avenue of the Americas
New York, NY 10036
Phone: (212) 819-3200

CORONET/MTI
Coronet/MTI Film & Video
108 Wilmot Road
Deerfield, IL 60015
Phone: (312) 940-1260

CRM
CRM Films
2233 Faraday
Carlsbad, CA 92008
Phone: (800) 421-0833

DOC ASSOC
Document Associates/Cinema Guild
1697 Broadway
Suite 802
New York, NY 10019
Phone: (212) 246-5522

ENCYCLO BRIT
Encyclopedia Britannica Educational
310 South Michigan Avenue
Chicago, IL 60604
Phone: (312) 337-7000

ENERGIZE
Energize Associates
5450 Wissahickon Avenue
Philadelphia, PA 19144
Phone: (215) 438-8342

FILMS INC
Films Incorporated
Film & Tape Division
5547 North Ravenswood Avenue
Chicago, IL 60640
Phone: (800) 323-4222, x44

INTELLIMATION
Intellimation
2040 Alameda Padre Serra
P.O. Box 4069
Santa Barbara, CA 93140
Phone: (800) 532-7637

KARL-LORIMAR
Karl-Lorimar Home Video
17942 Cowan Avenue
Irvine, CA 92714

LCA
Learning Corporation of America
108 Wilmot Road
Deerfield, IL 60015
Phone: (312) 940-1260

MCA HOME
MCA Home Video
70 Universal City Plaza
Universal City, CA 91608
Phone: (818) 777-4300

MGM/UA
MGM/UA Home Video, Inc.
10000 West Washington Blvd.
Culver City, CA 90232-2728
Phone: (213) 280-6000

MEDIA HOME
Media Home Entertainment, Inc.
5730 Buckingham Parkway
Culver City, CA 90230
Phone: (800) 421-4509

NABW-EF
National Assoc. of Bank Women
Educational Foundation
500 North Michigan Avenue
Chicago, IL 60611
Phone: (312) 661-1700

NBC
National Broadcasting Company
30 Rockefeller Plaza
New York, NY 10020
Phone: (212) 664-4444

NEM
National Educational Media
21601 Devonshire Street
Chatsworth, CA 91311
Phone: (818) 709-6009

PBS VIDEO
PBS Video
1320 Braddock Place
Alexandria, VA 22314
Phone: (800) 344-3337

PRISM
Prism
1875 Century Park East
Suite 1010
Los Angeles, CA 90067
Phone: (213) 277-3270

PRODUCERS INT
Producers International Corporation
3921 North Meridian Street
Indianapolis, IN 46208
Phone: (317) 924-5163

PYRAMID
Pyramid Film & Video
Box 1048
Santa Monica, CA 90406
Phone: (800) 421-2304

RCA COLUMBIA
RCA Columbia Pictures Home Video
3500 West Olive Avenue
Burbank, CA 91505
Phone: (818) 953-7900

ROUNDTABLE
Roundtable Films, Inc.
113 North San Vicente Blvd.
Beverly Hills, CA 90211
Phone: (800) 332-4444

SALENGER
Salenger Films
1635 12th Street
Santa Monica, CA 90404
Phone: (213) 450-1300

TIME LIFE
Time-Life Video
1271 Avenue of the Americas
New York, NY 10020
Phone: (212) 484-5940

UNIV ASSOC
University Associates
8517 Production Avenue
San Diego, CA 92121
Phone: (619) 578-5900

VIDEO ARTS
Video Arts Inc.
Northbrook Technical Center
4088 Commercial Avenue
Northbrook, IL 60062
Phone: (800) 553-0091

VIDEO PUB
Video Publishing House, Inc.
1011 East Touhy Avenue, Suite 580
Des Plaines, IL 60018
Phone: (800) 824-8889

REFERENCE SOURCES FOR FILM AND VIDEOTAPE

Published Sources

Educational Film-Video Locator (4th ed., 1990)
R. R. Bowker Co.
180 Avenue of the Americas
New York, NY 10036
Phone: (800) 521-8110

This is a compilation of film/video titles held by more than fifty major university film centers. Each film listed is briefly annotated and includes codes for the universities owning the film. Most university libraries and film centers will have this book on hand. Many of the university centers loan films to libraries and other organizations outside their region for a small rental fee.

Feature Films Available for Rental, Sale and Lease (8th ed., 1985) James L. Limbacher, editor
R. R. Bowker Co.
1180 Avenue of the Americas
New York, NY 10036
Phone: (800) 521-8110

A reference book containing a list of film companies and distributors for over 20,000 feature films and video cassettes in the United States and Canada.

Films Ex Libris: Literature in 16mm & Video (1980)
Salvatore J. Parlato
McFarland & Company
Box 611
Jefferson, NC 28640
Phone: (919) 246-4460

The Five Hundred Best British & Foreign Films to Buy, Rent or Videotape (1988)
National Board of Review of Motion Pictures
William Morrow & Company
105 Madison Avenue
New York, NY 10016
Phone: (212) 889-3050
       (800) 843-9389

Halliwell's Film and Video Guide (6th ed., 1989)
Charles Scribner
C/O Macmillan Publishing Co., Inc.
866 Third Avenue
New York, NY 10022
Phone: (212) 702-2000
        (800) 257-5755

Halliwell provides his own brief reviews on more that 10,000 feature films and videos. Though brief, these reviews provide a realistic perspective to the film producers' puffery.

Film and Video Finder (6th ed., 1985)
National Information Center for Educational Media
Division of Access Innovations
P. O. Box 40130
Albuquerque, NM 87196
Phone: (505) 265-3591

This is only one of NICEM's publications. They acquire and annotate information on nonprint media covering all levels of education and instruction, including college, professional, and adult education. Much of this information is available for computer searching through an on-line computer file (*AV Online* on DIALOG).

Leonard Maltin's TV Movies & Video Guide (1986)
Leonard Maltin
New American Library
1633 Broadway
New York, NY 10019
Phone: (201) 387-0600
        (800) 526-0275

Thompson-Mitchell and Associates (catalog)
3384 Peachtree Road
Atlanta, GA 30326
Phone: (404) 233-5435

This organization is a one-source distributor for a large number of training-film producers. Handles both sales and rental.

Video Source Book (11th ed., 1989)
Gale Research, Inc.
835 Penobscot Building
Detroit, MI 48226-4094
Phone: (800) 347-4253
         (313) 961-2242

Lists over 50,000 video program titles representing the combined contents of almost 1000 video catalogs.

Other Resources

University Film/Video Collections. Many colleges and universities have extensive video and film collections which are accessible to the general public for rental. They often have catalogs of other universities' collections as well.

Public Library Film Collections. Many of the medium to large public libraries have surprisingly good collections. Often larger public libraries will have public preview sessions of management and business films.

Video Rental Stores. This is a good source to get feature films to preview for possible course or classroom use.

RESOURCE PERSONS IN LEADERSHIP EDUCATION

INTRODUCTION

The individuals listed responded positively to an inquiry about their willingness to be available to others. The survey included contributors to this book, those who had been listed in previous editions, and a number of others known to the editors. Most are currently either teaching a leadership course, writing or doing research in the field, or directing a leadership program. Readers are encouraged to call on these Resource Persons to assist them in planning or improving programs. Also, many of them are available to run workshops, serve as speakers, panelists, or consultants. To locate resource persons by subject or interest area, see the master index at the back of the book. If the person is a contributor to this book, the page number of the course/program description is included.

Format

All entries (in alphabetic order by name) include full name, address and telephone number information. This data is current as of August 1989. The information generally states whether the person is teaching a course, directing a program, his/her focus of research, a sampling of publications, and the availability of the resource person to offer help, serve as a speaker, panelist or consultant.

State Index

Following the main listing is an index of these resource persons by state (with foreign listings following U.S. listings). The city of each resource person is also listed.

AGOR, WESTON H.

Professor, Masters in Public Administration Program, University of Texas at El Paso, El Paso, TX 79968
Phone: 915/747-5227
Course(s)/Program(s): Administrative Theory and Leadership, Brain Skill Management: How to Lead Productively.
Publications: Intuition in Organizations: Leading and Managing Productively (Ed.), Sage Publications.
Research in Progress: The role of intuition in leadership and creativity.
Resource Role: Panelist; attend conferences. Provide global network on intuition in leadership; promote and research the role of intuition in leadership and creativity; publish case illustrations of same.

ANDERSON, CAROL L.

Assoc. Director, Cooperative Extension, Cornell University N-130A MVR, Cooperative Extension, Ithaca, NY 14853-4401
Phone: 607/255-2245
Resource Role: Panelist; speaker; information sharing.

APPLEBY, R. NEAL

Director, Leadership Institute, Syracuse University, Schine Student Center, Syracuse, NY 13244-2070
Phone: 315/443-3729
Course(s)/Program(s): Seminar in Leadership; Syracuse University Leadership Institute.
Resource Role: Panelist; speaker; attend conferences; information sharing.

ARTMAN, RICHARD B.

Vice President, Student Affairs, Nebraska Wesleyan University, 5000 St. Paul Ave., Lincoln, NE 68504
Phone: 402/465-2153
Course(s)/Program(s): Creative Leadership (p. 63); Leadership Retreats for Undergraduate Students.
Resource Role: Panelist; speaker; attend conferences; information sharing.

BALLINGER, DAVID C.

Vice President, Academic Affairs, Cincinnati Technical College, 3520 Central Parkway, Cincinnati, OH 45223
Phone: 513/569-1421
Resource Role: Panelist; speaker; information sharing.

BARBER, ROBERT L.

Dir., Financial Services, Moses Cone Memorial Hospital, Greensboro, NC 27401-1020
Phone: 919/379-4005
Publications: Presently writing a classroom teaching aid on leadership.

BASS, BERNARD
Professor, School of Management, State University of New York at Binghamton, Binghamton, NY 13901
Phone: 607/777-3007
Computer Network Address or ID: BITNET: BG184@BINGVMA
Course(s)/Program(s): Center for Leadership Studies.
Publications: Leadership and Performance Beyond Expectations, Free Press, 1985.
Co-author: Handbook of Leadership, Free Press, 1990. Editor of the Leadership Quarterly.
Research in Progress: Field studies in transformational leadership.
Resource Role: Panelist; speaker; attend conferences; information sharing; welcome manuscripts for consideration for publication in Leadership Quarterly.

BEARDSLEY, STEPHANIE
Director of Residence Halls, University of California-Davis, 155 Student Housing-UCD, Davis, CA 95616
Phone: 916/752-2491
Course(s)/Program(s): Supervise entire residence hall system, which includes intentional educational efforts aimed at student and leadership development (p. 237).
Resource Role: Panelist; speaker; attend conferences; information sharing.

BEAVEN, MARY H.
College of Business Administration, Fairleigh Dickinson University, 1000 River Road, Teaneck, NJ 07666
Phone: 201/692-2154
Course(s)/Program(s): Power and Politics in Organizations.
Research in Progress: Transgression, Guilt, and Atonement as a Prelude to Transformational Leadership. Currently developing a program that will incorporate interpersonal, presentational, and leadership skills in our accounting curriculum. Some discussion about doing so for all of our undergraduate and graduate programs.
Resource Role: Panelist; speaker; attend conferences; information sharing.

BECK, ELLEN
Sinclair Community College, 444 West Third Street, Dayton, OH 45402
Phone: 513/226-2980
Course(s)/Program(s): Sinclair Ohio Fellows.
Resource Role: Attend conferences; information sharing.

BENAMATI, JACQUELINE D.
Vice President for Student Services, University of Bridgeport, 126 Park Avenue, Bridgeport, CT 06602
Phone: 203/576-4298
Resource Role: Panelist; speaker; attend conferences.

BENNETT, DIANE T.
Executive Director, Bellarmine Institute for Leadership Development, Bellarmine College, Newburg Rd., Louisville, KY 40205
Phone: 502/452-8161
Course(s)/Program(s): Leadership Education (p. 284), Public School Administrators Leadership Symposium.
Resource Role: Panelist; speaker; attend conferences; information sharing.

BEODEKER, BOB
Asst. Director, Student Activities, Southeast Missouri State University, 900 Normal, 2nd Floor, Cape Girardeau, MO 63701
Phone: 314/651-2953
Course(s)/Program(s): Leadership and Group Management (p. 65).
Resource Role: Panelist; speaker; attend conferences; information sharing.

BERTE, NEAL R.
President, Birmingham-Southern College, Box A-2, 800 8th Ave., West, Birmingham, AL 35254
Phone: 205/226-4620
Course(s)/Program(s): Leadership Birmingham, Birmingham Partnership. Both programs aimed at pairing leaders from the black community with leaders from the white community.
Research in Progress: Leadership as service.

BIRMINGHAM, CATHY
Asst. Director of Leadership Programs, Univ. of North Carolina-Wilmington, Univ. Union 212, Wilmington, NC 28403-3297
Phone: 919/395-3877
Course(s)/Program(s): The Leadership Center at UNC-Wilmington.
Resource Role: Panelist; attend conferences; information sharing.

BLACK, DONALD K.
Vice President, National Executive Service Corps, 257 Park Avenue South, New York, NY 10010
Phone: 212/529-6660
Course(s)/Program(s): Second Career Math/Science Teachers for Public High Schools.
Publications: Will be documenting above program over next 6 months.
Research in Progress: Feasibility study will be evaluated and, if successful, also disseminated.
Resource Role: Speaker; information sharing. NESC does extensive consulting regarding leadership with school systems for principals and administrative supervisory level people.

BLEZEK, ALLEN G.
Exec. Director, Nebraska LEAD Program, Nebraska Agri/Leadership Council,

University of Nebraska, 302 Agriculture Hall, Lincoln, NE 68583-0709
Phone: 402/472-2807
Course(s)/Program(s): Center for Leadership Development, Nebraska LEAD Program.
Resource Role: Panelist; speaker; attend conferences; information sharing.

BOATMAN, SARA A.
Director, Campus Activities & Programs, University of Nebraska, 200 Nebraska Union, Lincoln, NE 68588-0453
Phone: 402/472-2454
Course(s)/Program(s): Emerging Leader Program (p. 116); Campus Activities and Programs, Student Leadership Development Program.
Research in Progress: Influence of Emerging Leadership training on cognitive development; development of a leadership assessment and validation tool.
Resource Role: Panelist; speaker; attend conferences; information sharing on interdisciplinary efforts in leadership development. Currently working with business, agriculture and teachers' colleges in program development.

BOGUE, GRADY
Chancellor, Louisiana State University-Shreveport, 8515 Youree, Shreveport, LA 71115
Phone: 318/797-5200
Resource Role: Panelist; speaker; attend conferences; information sharing.

BOWEN, ZEDDIE
Provost, University of Richmond, Richmond, VA 23173
Phone: 804/289-8153
Course(s)/Program(s): Developing the first undergraduate School for Leadership Studies (p. 261).
Resource Role: Panelist; speaker; attend conferences; information sharing.

BREDENBERG, RICHARD
Professor Emeritus, Eckerd College, P.O. Box 12560, St. Petersburg, FL 33733
Phone: 813/864-8313
Course(s)/Program(s): Leadership Development Program.
Resource Role: Panelist; speaker; attend conferences.

BROWN, JOHN LOTT
President Emeritus, University of South Florida, Tampa, FL 33620
Phone: 813/974-2440
Course(s)/Program(s): Human Factors Design in Engineering.
Resource Role: Panelist; speaker; attend conferences; information sharing.

BROWN, MARTHA
Student Services, Creighton University, 2500 California St., Omaha, NE 68178
Phone: 402/280-2718

Course(s)/Program(s): Leadership: Theories, Styles, and Skills (p. 32); Creighton University Leadership Program.
Resource Role: Information sharing (regarding our campus-wide leadership programs).

BROWN, PATRICK
Director of Student Activities, The University of Vermont, Office of Student Activities, Burlington, VT 05405-0040
Phone: 802/656-0040
Course(s)/Program(s): Leadership: Theories, Styles & Realities, Advanced Seminar in Leadership; Leadership Program (p. 233).
Resource Role: Panelist; speaker; attend conferences; information sharing. Interested in campus leadership programs that blend the curricular and co-curricular efforts extending from the liberal arts to business classes to the applied sciences to student affairs classes to community service.

BROWN, RICHARD
P.O. Box 17059, Montgomery, AL 36193
Phone: 205/271-4334
Course(s)/Program(s): Performance Leadership. Provide leadership training programs as a consultant.
Resource Role: Panelist; speaker; attend conferences; information sharing.

BULL, BERNARD F.
Director of Student Teaching, Carson-Newman College, Box 1925, Jefferson City, TN 37760
Phone: 615/475-9061 x319
Course(s)/Program(s): Teacher as Leader (p. 23).
Resource Role: Panelist; speaker; attend conferences; information sharing.

BULL, KATHY CLEVELAND
Asst. Director, Univ. Student Center, North Carolina State University, Campus Box 7306, Raleigh, NC 27695-7306
Phone: 919/737-2452
Course(s)/Program(s): Student Leadership Center, Leadership Development Series (p. 195).
Resource Role: Panelist; speaker; attend conferences; information sharing. Helped create the new N.C. Leadership Consortium in Higher Education and would be happy to talk to those in higher education about what we plan to do with the Consortium.

CALIGURI, JOSEPH
Chair, Division of Educational Administration, University of Missouri, 5100 Rock Hill Road, Kansas City, MO 64110
Phone: 816/276-2716
Course(s)/Program(s): Leadership in Public Education (p. 114).
Publications: "Problem Solving Project Formats for Creative Approaches in

Evaluation," chapter in <u>Creative Ideas for Evaluation</u>, Kluwer Press, in press.
Resource Role: Information sharing.

CAPRA, FRAN
Assoc. Director, Executive Development, Southwestern Bell Corporation, One Bell Center, Rm. 38-L-02, St. Louis, MO 63101
Phone: 314/235-7075
Course(s)/Program(s): Southwestern Bell Corporation's External Executive Education Programs; External Executive Development.
Resource Role: Panelist; attend conferences; information sharing.

CHAMBERS, GLEN A.
Director, Student Life, Catonsville Community College, 800 South Rolling Rd., Catonsville, MD 21228
Phone: 301/455-4322
Course(s)/Program(s): Leadership in Small Groups; The Student Government Assn. "Leadership '89 Plan."
Resource Role: Panelist; speaker; attend conferences; information sharing.

CHRIST, JACK M.
Director, Leadership Studies Program, Ripon College, Box 248, Ripon, WI 54971
Phone: 414/748-8358
Course(s)/Program(s): Introduction to Leadership Studies, Biographical Studies, Leadership Roles and Processes, Independent Study; Leadership Studies Program (p. 205).
Publications: Wrote/produced/hosted "Leadership Skills and Values" (16 30-minute videotapes distributed by National Association of Secondary School Principals).
Resource Role: Panelist; speaker; attend conferences; information sharing. Developing curricular materials, particularly on videotape, for college and high school students.

CIENEK, RAYMOND P.
President, Human Dynamics, P.O. Box 7241, Greensboro, NC 27407
Phone: 919/854-0120
Publications: Currently mid-way through a new book on leadership potential development for mid-managers.
Resource Role: Panelist; speaker; information sharing.

COGNETTA, JOHN S.
Director, Student and Alumni Activities, DeAnza College, 25555 Hesperian Blvd., Hayward, CA 94545-5001
Phone: 415/786-6915
Research in Progress: Leadership styles.
Resource Role: Panelist; speaker; attend conferences; information sharing.

COLE, KATHERINE LEE
Executive Director, Princeton Center for Leadership Training, 92 Philip Drive, Princeton, NJ 08540
Phone: 609/924-0889
Course(s)/Program(s): Princeton Center for Leadership Training (p. 417).
Resource Role: Panelist; speaker; attend conferences; information sharing.

CONNER, ROSS F.
Assoc. Professor, Program in Social Ecology, University of California at Irvine, Irvine, CA 92717
Phone: 714/856-5575
Course(s)/Program(s): Leadership; Leadership Development.
Resource Role: Panelist; speaker; attend conferences; information sharing.

COPESTICK, KEVIN J.
Manager, Human Resources, Tampa Electric Company, P.O. Box 111, Tampa, FL 33601
Phone: 813/228-4343
Course(s)/Program(s): Previously taught and directed management development programs in Assessment Center operations, selection systems, performance analysis, and most recently, change management and organizational development.
Publications: "The Four Faces of Change: Successfully Managing Major Change." "Organizational Change: Managing the End And the Means," both in press.
Research in Progress: Effects of "change management" in large organizations; the pros/cons of the presence and absence of effective management. Leadership development: The identification of executive talent for the future. Interested in participating in the development of research and program curricula to prepare managers and executives for the nuances in leadership demands for the future. Have sufficient programs providing instruction on the science of management but too little emphasis on the art of leadership.
Resource Role: Panelist; speaker; attend conferences; information sharing.

COSGROVE, THOMAS J.
Assoc. Dean of Students, University of San Diego, University Center-Alcala Park, San Diego, CA 92110
Phone: 619/260-4589
Course(s)/Program(s): Leadership in Organizations; Emerging Leaders, Skill Builders for Managers and Leaders, Leadership Development at the University of San Diego: A Four Year Plan (p. 269).
Publications: "Cleaning Up Our Language About Leadership." Programming Magazine, August 1988. "The Politics of Student Leadership." Programming Magazine, August 1988.
Research in Progress: Following up on Emerging Leadership participants - 4 years.
Resource Role: Panelist; speaker; attend conferences; information sharing. Doctorate from U.S.D. is in Leadership Education. On Inter-Association Task Force on Leadership.

CRAFT, ROLF V.
Director, Ronald Reagan Scholarships, Eureka College, 300 College Ave., Eureka, IL 61530
Phone: 309/467-6413
Course(s)/Program(s): Entrepreneurship, Management; Ronald W. Reagan Scholarship Program.
Resource Role: Panelist; speaker; attend conferences; information sharing.

CRONIN, THOMAS E.
McHugh Professor of American Institutions and Leadership, The Colorado College, Colorado Springs, CO 80903
Phone: 719/475-1900
Course(s)/Program(s): Leadership & Governance: A Seminar (p. 85); Colorado College Leadership Project.
Publications: Currently writing a general book on leadership.
Resource Role: Panelist; speaker on Leadership in America, The Paradoxes of Leadership, Thinking and Learning About Leadership.

CROSS, WILLIAM M.
Assoc. Professor of Psychology, Onondaga Community College, Syracuse, NY 13215
Phone: 315/474-3762
Course(s)/Program(s): Psychology of Leadership and Work.
Research in Progress: The relationship of leadership development efforts in organizations and their effectiveness. Developing more socially desirable behavior in prisoners.
Resource Role: Panelist; speaker; attend conferences; information sharing.

CURRY, REX L.
Assoc. Director, Pratt Institute for Community and Environmental Development, 379 DeKalb Ave., 2nd Floor Steuben, Brooklyn, NY 11205
Phone: 718/636-3486
Course(s)/Program(s): Planning Studies, Community Planning; Pratt Community Economic Development Internship (p. 306).
Resource Role: Panelist; speaker; attend conferences; information sharing.

CURTIN, JOE
Management Assistants, 702 Washington St., #124, Marina del Rey, CA 90292
Phone: 213/827-2181
Course(s)/Program(s): Management Development in Leadership, Communication, and Motivation.
Publications: "A Reaction Theory of Leadership," University Microfilms International, Univ. of Michigan, Oct. 1986; "How to Improve an Organization's Total Communication Capability," The Net and the Fire, Los Angeles Organization Development Network, Aug. 1988; "Putting Self-Esteem First," Training & Development Journal, Oct. 1988; "Turning Around Your Company," (submitted for

publication).
Resource Role: Panelist; attend conferences; information sharing.

DANSEREAU, FRED
School of Management, State University of New York at Buffalo, 60 Groton Dr., Williamsville, NY 14221
Phone: 716/636-3236
Course(s)/Program(s): Leadership and Motivation (p. 81).
Publications: "Superior-Subordinate Communications," in <u>Handbook of Organizational Communications</u>, Sage, 1988.
Research in Progress: Longitudinal and multiple level studies of leadership in organizations.
Resource Role: Panelist; speaker; attend conferences; information sharing.

DAVIS, F. LEARY
Professor of Law, Campbell University School of Law, P.O. Box 158, Buies Creek, NC 27506
Phone: 919/893-4111
Computer Network Address or ID: ABANET: 1450
Course(s)/Program(s): Law Firm Planning.
Resource Role: Panelist; speaker; attend conferences; information sharing.

DECK, LINTON
Director, Education and Nonprofit Applications Group, Center for Creative Leadership, 5000 Laurinda Drive, P.O. Box P-1, Greensboro, NC 27402-1660
Phone: 919/288-7210
Course(s)/Program(s): Chief Executive Officer Leadership Development Program (Florida Superintendents).
Research in Progress: Field work with superintendents for development of a national video archive on the superintendency. Continue to work with educational leaders in school systems to enhance their practice of administration and leadership.

DECKER, LARRY E.
Assoc. Professor, University of Virginia, 405 Emmet St., Ruffner, Charlottesville, VA 22903
Phone: 804/924-0866
Course(s)/Program(s): Educational Leadership.
Publications: <u>Building Learning Communities: Community Leadership</u>.
Resource Role: Panelist; speaker; attend conferences; information sharing; leadership assessment and development for future educational leaders.

DEEGAN, JAMES E.
Dean of Special Programs, Eckerd College, P.O. Box 12560, St. Petersburg, FL 33733
Phone: 813/864-8213
Course(s)/Program(s): Leadership Development Program.
Resource Role: Panelist; speaker; attend conferences; information sharing.

DELUGA, RONALD
Assoc. Professor of Psychology, Bryant College, 450 Douglas Pike, Smithfield, RI 02917-1284
Phone: 401/232-6279
Course(s)/Program(s): Learning for Leadership (p. 17), Mentorship Program.
Publications: "The Relationship of Transformational and Transactional Leadership with Subordinate Influencing Behavior," Group and Organization Studies, 1988. "Employee Influence Strategies as Possible Stress Coping Mechanisms for Role Conflict and Ambiguity," Journal of Basic and Applied Social Psychology (in press), and others.
Research in Progress: Leader-Follower Influencing Dynamics; Interdisciplinary Approach; Self-Development of Participants.
Resource Role: Panelist; speaker; attend conferences; information sharing.

DEMUTH, CAROL
5747 South Utica, Tulsa, OK 74105
Phone: 918/749-2157
Research in Progress: An Analysis of Leadership Development in American Doctoral Higher Education Programs.
Resource Role: Panelist; attend conferences; information sharing.

DODSON, DAVID
Dean of Students, University of Puget Sound, 1500 North Warner, Tacoma, WA 98416-0662
Phone: 206/756-3360
Course(s)/Program(s): Community Service Seminar.
Publications: "The View from the Top" in Private Visions, Shared Dreams: Small College Student Affairs Work.
Research in Progress: In pursuit of model for student development, e.g., master-apprentice model as possible source for modification of mentor relationship.
Resource Role: Panelist; speaker; attend conferences; information sharing.

DRURY, JACK K.
Director, Wilderness Recreation Leadership, North Country Community College, P.O. Box 89, Saranac Lake, NY 12983
Phone: 518/891-2915 x254
Course(s)/Program(s): Wilderness Recreation Leadership Fall Practicum; Wilderness Recreation Leadership Program.
Publications: Wilderness Education Assn. Lesson Plan Manual.
Resource Role: Panelist; speaker; attend conferences; information sharing. Will share what we are doing in wilderness decision making and leadership training. WEA trains outdoor leaders. It also provides: leadership training, decision-making skills, and environmental ethics development.

EASTON, EDWARD
Director, Leadership Development, National Wildlife Federation, 1400 16th St., NW,

Washington, DC 20036-2266
Phone: 202/797-6823
Course(s)/Program(s): Institute for Conservation Leadership.
Publications: Column: Leadercraft.
Resource Role: Panelist; speaker; attend conferences; information sharing. Educate volunteers and staff in voluntary organizations.

FAIRHOLM, GIL W.
Dept. of Public Administration, Virginia Commonwealth University, P.O. Box 2031, Richmond, VA 23284
Phone: 804/367-1046
Course(s)/Program(s): Executive Leadership, Graduate Leadership Program (p. 124).
Publications: "Power Tactics," Personnel, 1985.
Research in Progress: Leadership excellence in state and local government.
Resource Role: Panelist; speaker; attend conferences.

FANELLI, RUSSELL
Assoc. Professor and Chairman, Management Dept., Western New England College, 1215 Wilbraham Rd., Springfield, MA 01119
Phone: 413/782-3111 x558
Course(s)/Program(s): Springfield Leadership Institute, Springfield Junior Leadership Institute.
Publications: "Corporate Culture as an Impediment to Employee Involvement," Work and Occupations, May 1989.
Resource Role: Panelist; speaker; attend conferences; information sharing.

FARSON, RICHARD
President, Western Behavioral Sciences Institute, 1150 Silverado Street, P.O. Box 2029, La Jolla, CA 92038-2029
Phone: 619/459-3811
Computer Network Address or ID: WBSINET: EIES350
Course(s)/Program(s): Management of the Absurd; International Executive Forum.
Publications: "The Electronic Classroom," New Management.
Research in Progress: Supervise a research institute devoted largely to studies of the social factors in computer communication.
Resource Role: Panelist; speaker; attend conferences; information sharing.

FEINBERG, RICHARD
Professor, Dept. of Consumer Science and Retailing, Purdue University, West Lafayette, IN 47907
Phone: 317/494-8301
Course(s)/Program(s): Leadership Strategies.
Publications: Leadership in Retail Executives.
Research in Progress: Leadership in Retail Executives.
Resource Role: Panelist; speaker; attend conferences; information sharing.

FENDT, PAUL F.
Dean, School of Continuing Studies, East Tennessee State University, Box 22270A, Johnson City, TN 37614
Phone: 615/929-4223
Research in Progress: Mostly dealing with leadership in adult education as a professional field. Focus on leadership in adult and continuing education.
Resource Role: Panelist; information sharing.

FERRIS, WILLIAM P.
Professor, Box 2082, Western New England College, 1215 Wilbraham Rd., Springfield, MA 01119
Phone: 413/782-1629
Course(s)/Program(s): A Humanistic Approach to Leadership and Management, Organizational Behavior.
Resource Role: Panelist; speaker; attend conferences; information sharing.

FILLINGER, ROBERT E.
Senior Program Associate, Ockenga Institute, Gordon-Conwell Theological Seminary, South Hamilton, MA 01982
Phone: 617/468-7111
Course(s)/Program(s): The Process of Change, Seminar in Leadership.
Resource Role: Panelist; attend conferences; information sharing.

FLETCHER, SHERRYL A.
Assistant Director of Undergraduate Admissions, University of Michigan, 1220 SAB, Ann Arbor, MI 48109
Phone: 313/764-7433
Course(s)/Program(s): State and regional alumni leadership training to recruit undergraduate students (p. 105).
Resource Role: Panelist; speaker; attend conferences; information sharing.

FORSBERG, THOMAS E.
Director, Student Activities, Brown University, P.O. Box 1930, Providence, RI 02912
Phone: 401/863-2341
Resource Role: Panelist; attend conferences; information sharing.

FORTNER, NOVELLA
Asst. Dean of Student Life, University of South Carolina, Department of Student Life, Columbia, SC 29208
Phone: 803/777-5780
Course(s)/Program(s): Leadership Training Programs (p. 275).
Research in Progress: Benefits of collegiate leadership training in post-graduate situations.
Resource Role: Panelist; speaker; information sharing.

FREMED, RESA

New England Counseling, 871 Ethan Allen Hwy., Ste. 102, Ridgefield, CT 06877
Phone: 203/431-4957
Course(s)/Program(s): New England Counseling - Management Training Workshops,
Leadership Training, Peer Leadership.
Resource Role: Panelist; information sharing.

GARDNER, KENT L.

Assoc. Vice President, Student Affairs, University of Texas at Arlington, UTA Box
L9348, Arlington, TX 76019
Phone: 817/273-2354
Course(s)/Program(s): Student Leadership Training.
Resource Role: Panelist; speaker.

GEAR, CURTIS E.

Community Development Specialist, University of Wisconsin, 535 Lowell Hall,
Madison, WI 53702
Phone: 608/263-7980
Course(s)/Program(s): Wisconsin Community Leadership Development.
Research in Progress: Leadership Effectiveness in Community Based Organizations.
Resource Role: Panelist; speaker; information sharing. Interested in community
leadership and needs of African Americans, Hispanics, Native Americans and
Southeast Asians.

GERBER, BARBARA W.

Professor of Counseling and Psychological Services, State Univ. of New York at
Oswego, 205 Mahar Hall, Oswego, NY 13126
Phone: 315/341-3282
Resource Role: Very much concerned about women in leadership.

GIULIANO, NEIL G.

Director of Constituent Relations, Arizona State University, Alumni Association,
Alumni Center, Tempe, AZ 85287-1004
Phone: 602/965-3566
Course(s)/Program(s): Personal Leadership Development; Insuring Tomorrow
(p. 141), National Leadership Network (a national leadership network program for
college & university students).
Resource Role: Panelist; speaker; attend conferences; information sharing.

GOODMAN, ADAM J.

Executive Director, Student Leadership Institute, University of Colorado at Boulder,
Campus Box 147, Boulder, CO 80309
Phone: 303/492-8342
Course(s)/Program(s): Development of student leadership and community service
for talented undergraduate students; Presidents Leadership Class (p. 243).
Resource Role: Panelist; speaker; attend conferences; information sharing; building

public/private partnerships in University settings to develop very talented undergraduates in leadership and community service.

GREEN, MADELEINE F.
Director, Center for Leadership Development, American Council on Education (ACE), One Dupont Plaza, Ste. 800, Washington, DC 20036
Phone: 202/939-9300
Course(s)/Program(s): ACE Fellows Program (p. 298); Center for Leadership Development offers programs for college presidents, department chairs.
Publications: Leaders for a New Era: Strategies for Higher Education, MacMillan, 1988.
Research in Progress: Careers of college presidents.
Resource Role: Panelist; speaker; attend conferences; information sharing.

GREEN, STEPHEN G.
Organizational Behavior and Human Resource Management, Krannert Graduate School of Management, Purdue University, West Lafayette, IN 47907
Phone: 317/494-6852
Computer Network Address or ID: BITNET: GREEN@PURCCVM
Course(s)/Program(s): Leadership, Managing to Lead.
Publications: Co-author: "A measure of psychological maturity," Group and Organization Studies, 13(2), 1988; "Psychological Maturity Measure," The 1988 Annual: Developing Human Resources, University Associates, 1988; "Chains of poor performance and supervisory control," Organizational Behavior and Human Decision Processes, 38, 1986; "Vertical Dyad Linkage: A longitudinal assessment of antecedents, measures, and consequences," Journal of Applied Psychology, 71(1), 1986; "Managerial control and discipline: Whips and chains," in R. Bostrom (Ed.), Communication Yearbook Eight, Sage, 1984; "Leadership and poor performance," in Hackman, Lawler, and Porter (Eds.), Perspectives on Behavior in Organizations (2nd Ed.), McGraw-Hill, 1983.
Research in Progress: Leadership in Self-Managing Teams; Leadership Roles in Innovation.
Resource Role: Panelist; speaker; attend conferences; information sharing.

GREENBERG, ELINOR M.
Project Leadership, 5700 South Quebec, Suite 102, Englewood, CO 80111
Phone: 303/773-3945
Course(s)/Program(s): Project Leadership: Men and Women of the Volunteer Board Room.
Publications: Co-author: Leading Effectively: Men and Women of the Volunteer Board Room; "Leadership," Journal of Jewish Communal Service, Fall 1988.
Research in Progress: Assessment of individual leadership. Gender differences.
Resource Role: Panelist; speaker; attend conferences; information sharing.

GUINTHER, PAULINE
California State University, Sacramento, 1945 Wingfield Way, Carmichael, CA 95608

Phone: 916/278-6192
Course(s)/Program(s): Leadership and Communication (p. 19); Senior Consultant for Information Management by Design.
Research in Progress: Consulting contracts.
Resource Role: Attend conferences; information sharing.

HAGERTY, JACK
Director, Rural Organizations and Services, Ontario Ministry of Agriculture, P.O. Box 1030, Guelph, Ontario, Canada, N1H 6N1
Phone: 519/821-1330
Resource Role: Director of a government (Provincial) branch involved in leadership development of rural people and organizations.

HALL, MARSHA PAUR
Director, Professional Leadership Program, School of Management, Rensselaer Polytechnic Institute, Troy, NY 12180
Phone: 518/276-6586
Course(s)/Program(s): Professional Leadership Program (p. 203).
Resource Role: Panelist; speaker; attend conferences; information sharing.

HAMMERSCHMIDT, PETER K.
Professor of Economics, Eckerd College, P.O. Box 12560, St. Petersburg, FL 33733
Phone: 813/864-8462
Course(s)/Program(s): Leadership Development, Leadership: The Human Side of Economics; Directing the planning stages of an Eckerd College Leadership Studies Program (ECLSP).
Publications: Working paper, "Women in Management: An Empirical Analysis."
Research in Progress: Analysis of male/female similarities and differences in management.
Resource Role: Panelist; speaker; attend conferences; information sharing.

HANDY, RAYMOND T.
Assoc. Professor, Tuskegee Institute, 2801 Azalea, P.O. Drawer KK, Tuskegee Institute, AL 36088
Phone: 205/727-0150
Course(s)/Program(s): Leadership Traits - Concepts of Leadership.
Resource Role: Panelist; speaker.

HANNA, NANCY
Coordinator, The Luce Leadership Program, The College of Wooster, Wooster, OH 44691
Phone: 216/263-2387
Course(s)/Program(s): The Luce Leadership Program.
Resource Role: Attend conferences.

HARRIS, PHILIP R.
President, Harris International, 2702 Costebelle Drive, La Jolla, CA 92037
Phone: 619/453-2271
Publications: <u>Culture Leadership</u>, <u>High Performance Leadership: Strategies for Maximum Productivity</u>, Scott, Foresman & Co., 1989.
Resource Role: Panelist; speaker; attend conferences.

HARRISON, CLIFFORD
Chairman, Business and Economics Dept., Concordia College, 901 S. 8th St., Moorhead, MN 56560
Phone: 218/299-3476
Course(s)/Program(s): Leadership - Business Admin. 462.
Research in Progress: Research in area businesses on ethics and values.
Resource Role: Panelist; speaker; attend conferences. Helped establish the Concordia Leadership Center and West Central Minnesota Leadership Program.

HARTFORD, THOMAS F.
Director, Center for Leadership Development, St. Norbert College, DePere, WI 54115
Phone: 414/337-4023
Course(s)/Program(s): Workshops for Leadership program (p. 219). Open to all college students, faculty, staff, families, and volunteer community. Leadership: Seminars, workshops, Confidence Course, Ropes Course.
Research in Progress: Tracking individuals and their success/failures in relation to those not in program and studying various confidence course events for difficulty, safety, and outcomes.
Resource Role: Speaker; attend conferences; information sharing. We have just been asked to develop an American Indian Leadership Camp for this summer by the State.

HARTLEY, ALEX
Director of Training, Coro Foundation, 609 South Grand Ave., Ste. 810, Los Angeles, CA 90017
Phone: 213/623-1234
Computer Network Address or ID: FIDONET: 1:102/373
Course(s)/Program(s): Coro Fellowship in Public Affairs.
Resource Role: Panelist; speaker; attend conferences; information sharing.

HARVEY, THOMAS R.
Chairman, Educational Management, University of LaVerne, 1950 Third St., LaVerne, CA 91750
Phone: 714/593-0471
Course(s)/Program(s): Strategic Planning, Change Strategies, Conflict Management.
Publications: <u>Checklist for Change</u>, Allyn and Bacon, Nov. 1989.
Research in Progress: Change strategies.

HARWOOD, PATRICIA C.
Dean, Westhampton College, University of Richmond, Richmond, VA 23173
Phone: 804/289-8468
Course(s)/Program(s): Women Involved in Living and Learning (WILL), a
leadership program for women which is curricular and co-curricular in nature (p. 26).
Research in Progress: Regarding the WILL program.
Resource Role: Panelist; speaker; attend conferences; information sharing.

HAWKINS, GERALD G.
Assoc. Vice Chancellor, North Carolina State University, Campus Box 7316, Raleigh,
NC 27695
Phone: 919/737-3151
Course(s)/Program(s): Leadership Theory; N.C. State University Fellows
Leadership Development Program (p. 189).
Research in Progress: Follow-up study of program participants over past 20 years.
Resource Role: Panelist; speaker; attend conferences; information sharing.

HEIFETZ, RONALD A.
Lecturer, J. F. Kennedy School of Govt., Harvard University, Cambridge, MA 02138
Phone: 617/495-7867
Course(s)/Program(s): Leadership and the Mobilization of Group Resources,
Research Seminar in Leadership (p. 40).
Publications: Co-author: "Teaching and Assessing Leadership Courses at the J.F.
Kennedy School of Government," Journal of Policy Analysis and Management,
Summer 1989.
Research in Progress: Prescriptive leadership theory and teaching. Develop better
theory and pedagogy; want to develop a program for leadership at the Kennedy
School that will serve as a resource for leadership education.
Resource Role: Panelist; speaker; information sharing.

HELLWEG, JULIE M.
Asst. Director, Student Development, University Center, University of Wisconsin,
Stevens Point, WI 54481
Phone: 715/346-4343
Course(s)/Program(s): Leadership: The Personal Dimension; UWSP Four Year
Leadership Series.
Resource Role: Panelist; speaker; attend conferences; information sharing.

HENDRICKS, HOWARD G.
Chairman, Center for Christian Leadership, Dallas Theological Seminary, 3909 Swiss
Ave., Dallas, TX 75228
Phone: 214/824-3094
Course(s)/Program(s): The Dynamics of Leadership, LEAD--Leadership Evaluation
And Development.

HERMAN, ROBERT D.
Professor, L.P. Cookingham Institute of Public Affairs, 5110 Cherry, Kansas City, MO 64110
Phone: 816/276-2894
Course(s)/Program(s): Management Issues in Nonprofit Organizations.
Publications: <u>Nonprofit Boards of Directors: Analyses and Applications</u>, Herman and Van Til (Eds.), Transaction, 1989.
Research in Progress: Leadership skills of nonprofit chief executives. Interested in advancing solid research on leadership.
Resource Role: Panelist; speaker; attend conferences; information sharing.

HODGES, JAMES A.
Professor of History, College of Wooster, Wooster, OH 44691
Phone: 216/263-2455
Course(s)/Program(s): F.D.R., The New Deal, World War II, and the Study of Presidential Leadership. Will soon offer introductory course with highlights of leadership study using biography.
Resource Role: Panelist; speaker; attend conferences; information sharing; interested in courses for undergraduates that approach leadership from multidisciplinary views.

HOFF, DEBBIE
Assistant Dean for Student Life, Muhlenberg College, Allentown, PA 18104
Phone: 215/821-3418
Course(s)/Program(s): Muhlenberg Institute for Leadership Education.
Resource Role: Panelist; information sharing.

HOLLANDER, EDWIN P.
Professor, Psychology Dept., Box 512, Baruch College of CUNY, 17 Lexington Ave., New York, NY 10010
Phone: 212/725-3201
Course(s)/Program(s): Organizational Psychology Doctoral Seminar.
Publications: "Leadership and Power" in G. Lindzey & E. Aronson (Eds.) <u>Handbook of Social Psychology</u>, 3rd ed., Random House, 1985. "Redirection in Leadership Research" in L. Atwater & R. Penn (Eds.) <u>Military Research: Traditions and Future Trends</u>. Annapolis, U.S. Naval Academy, 1989. Co-author: "Relational Features of Organizational Leadership and Followership" in K. E. Clark & M. B. Clark (Eds.) <u>Measures of Leadership</u>. Leadership Library of America, 1990.
Resource Role: Speaker; information sharing.

HOLLIDAY, VIVIAN L.
Professor, Classical Studies & History, College of Wooster, Wooster, OH 44691
Phone: 216/263-2488
Course(s)/Program(s): Participant in several discussions in Leadership Seminar; Leadership and Liberal Learning (p. 146).
Research in Progress: Looking at concepts of <u>arete</u> and <u>virtus</u> in Greek and Roman thought respectively and how they were translated into notions of leadership at

various points of time.
Resource Role: Information sharing.

HUBER, JODY L.
Student Activities Program Coordinator, University of Minnesota, Morris, Office of
Student Activities, Morris, MN 56267
Phone: 612/589-2211 x6080
Course(s)/Program(s): Student Leadership Program.
Resource Role: Attend conferences; information sharing.

ISAKSEN, SCOTT G.
Director, Center for Studies in Creativity, State University College at Buffalo, 1300
Elmwood Ave., Buffalo, NY 14222
Phone: 716/878-6223
Course(s)/Program(s): Creative Leadership through Effective Facilitation (p. 73).
Research in Progress: Examining cognitive and leadership styles and the creative
problem-solving strategies leaders employ. Particularly interested in the strong
conceptual connections seen between leadership and creativity.
Resource Role: Panelist; speaker; attend conferences; information sharing.

IVARIE, TED
Dean of Lumpkin College of Business, Eastern Illinois University, 109 Blair Hall,
Charleston, IL 61920
Phone: 217/581-3526
Resource Role: Panelist; speaker; attend conferences; information sharing.

JACOKES, LEE E.
Assoc. Professor of Psychology, Aquinas College, 1607 Robinson Rd., S.E., Grand
Rapids, MI 49506
Phone: 616/459-8281 x468
Course(s)/Program(s): Leadership.
Publications: Columnist for local business newspaper.
Resource Role: Panelist; speaker; attend conferences; information sharing.

JEGHELIAN, ALICE
Director of Professional Development, Boston College, McGuinn Hall 405, Chestnut
Hill, MA 02167
Phone: 617/552-3338
Course(s)/Program(s): Training and development programs for Boston College
employees.
Resource Role: Panelist; speaker; attend conferences; information sharing.

JENSEN, GWENDOLYN E.
Provost and Dean of the College, Marietta College, 215 Fifth St., Marietta, OH
45750-3031
Phone: 614/373-4643

Course(s)/Program(s): Conducting the Workshop for New Deans given by the Council of Independent Colleges (for the second year); have conducted other similar workshops.
Resource Role: Panelist; speaker; attend conferences; information sharing.

JERUS, ROBERT G.
Chairman, Division of Business Administration, Northwestern College, 3003 N. Snelling Ave., Roseville, MN 55113
Phone: 612/631-5357
Resource Role: Panelist; speaker; attend conferences; information sharing.

JORGENSEN, GERALD
Vice President, Student Development, Loras College, 1450 Alta Vista St., Dubuque, IA 52004-0178
Phone: 319/588-7104
Resource Role: Panelist; attend conferences; information sharing. Work primarily with higher education professionals and leaders of college student organizations as well as leadership teams of religious organizations and nonprofit organizations.

KELLERMAN, BARBARA
Dean of Graduate Studies and Research, Fairleigh Dickinson University, Teaneck, NJ 07666
Phone: 201/692-2095
Publications: Political Leadership: A Source Book (Ed.). Univ. of Pittsburgh Press, 1986.
Resource Role: Panelist; speaker; attend conferences; information sharing.

KERR, NANCY H.
Oglethorpe University, 4484 Peachtree Rd., NE, Atlanta, GA 30319
Phone: 404/261-1441
Course(s)/Program(s): Psychology of Leadership.
Resource Role: Attend conferences.

KINDLER, HERBERT
Professor of Management, Loyola Marymount University, Loyola Blvd. at West 80th St., Los Angeles, CA 90045
Phone: 213/459-6052
Course(s)/Program(s): Risk and Decision Making, Managing Disagreement and Stress.
Publications: Managing Disagreement Constructively, Crisp Publications. Risk Taking: A Guide to Decision Makers, Crisp Publications. Stress Training for Life, Nichols Publishing.
Research in Progress: Stress management, conflict management.
Resource Role: Speaker; information sharing; can provide training instruments and workbooks.

KING, SARA N.
Program Associate, Education and Nonprofit Sector, Center for Creative Leadership, 5000 Laurinda Drive, P.O. Box P-1, Greensboro, NC 27402-1660
Phone: 919/288-7210
Course(s)/Program(s): Programs for student leaders, higher education faculty and administrators, public education administrators, and human service administrators.
Resource Role: Speaker; information sharing; Serve as a clearinghouse for information on programs, courses, institutions, etc., which focus on leadership.

KRUGGEL, JOEL
Director, Leadership Development, Westmont College, 955 La Paz Rd., Santa Barbara, CA 93108
Phone: 805/969-3108
Course(s)/Program(s): Leadership Seminar (p. 128); Westmont College Leadership Development Program.
Research in Progress: Evaluating the impact of mentor relationships on leadership education in the undergraduate context: Use of adult mentors in leadership education; Use of peer reflection groups in leadership education.
Resource Role: Panelist; speaker; attend conferences; information sharing.

LAMBETH, THOMAS W.
Executive Director, Z. Smith Reynolds Foundation, Inc., 101 Reynolda Village, Winston-Salem, NC 27106-5199
Phone: 919/725-7541
Resource Role: Panelist; speaker; attend conferences; information sharing.

LAPIDES, JOSEPH
Adjunct Professor, Department of Psychology, University of Detroit, 4001 West McNichols, Detroit, MI 48221
Phone: 313/569-3219
Course(s)/Program(s): Psychology of Leadership and Supervision (p. 95); Coordinator Training Dynamics & Leadership Program.
Resource Role: Panelist; speaker; attend conferences.

LAWING, ANNE
Associate Director, Student Affairs, University of New Hampshire, 126 Memorial Union Bldg., Durham, NH 03824
Phone: 603/862-1001
Course(s)/Program(s): Emerging Leader Program (p. 253).
Research in Progress: Development of an instrument that will assess post-graduation impact of student leadership positions. The research project is being developed under Commission IV in ACPA.

LAWRENCE, WILLIAM D.
Center for Christian Leadership, Dallas Theological Seminary, 3909 Swiss Ave., Dallas, TX 75204

Phone: 214/841-3515
Course(s)/Program(s): Dynamics of Leadership (p. 300); Center for Christian Leadership.
Research in Progress: Character development, mentoring, gift assessment and development.
Resource Role: Panelist; speaker; attend conferences; information sharing.

LEEDY, MARIANNE V.
Assoc. Dean of Students, Goucher College, Dulaney Valley Rd., Towson, MD 21204
Phone: 301/337-6124
Course(s)/Program(s): Annual series of three seminars entitled Deans' Leadership, Presidential Leadership, and Trustees Leadership.

LINDSEY, RANDALL B.
Chairman, Division of Administration and Counseling, California State University, 5151 State University Drive, Los Angeles, CA 90032
Phone: 213/343-4250
Course(s)/Program(s): Leadership in Education, Educational Decision Making, Institutional Racism in U.S. Schools; Educational Administration and Counseling.
Research in Progress: Beginning a book on Leadership Training for Equity.
Resource Role: Panelist; attend conferences; information sharing.

LINSKY, MARTIN
John F. Kennedy School of Government, Harvard University, 79 John F. Kennedy St., Cambridge, MA 02138
Phone: 617/495-1163
Course(s)/Program(s): Political Leadership, To Be a Politician, Leadership, Politics & Democracy (p. 40).
Publications: Currently writing a book which examines, among other subjects, the exercise of leadership in a legislature.
Resource Role: Panelist; speaker; attend conferences; information sharing.

LOWANCE, SUSAN C.
Director, Smith Management Program, Smith College, Northhampton, MA 01063
Phone: 413/584-6660
Course(s)/Program(s): Smith Management Program.
Research in Progress: Women managers.
Resource Role: Panelist; attend conferences; information sharing.

LUCAS, NANCE
Assistant Dean of Students, Ohio University, 212 Cutler Hall, Athens, OH 45701
Phone: 614/593-2580
Course(s)/Program(s): Women and Leadership, Dynamics of Leadership; Chair, National InterAssociation Leadership Project.
Resource Role: Panelist; speaker; attend conferences; information sharing.

LUCE, HENRY, III
President, Henry Luce Foundation, Inc., 720 Fifth Ave., Ste. 504, New York, NY
10019
Phone: 212/489-7700
Course(s)/Program(s): Henry Luce Foundation Program in Leadership Studies.
Resource Role: Speaker.

LUZKOW, VIRGINIA
Director, Student Work Assistance Program, Marycrest College, 1607 West 12th St.,
Davenport, IA 52804
Phone: 319/326-9329
Resource Role: Panelist; speaker; attend conferences; information sharing.

LYNCH, CHARLES F.
Assoc. Vice Chancellor, Student Affairs, University of North Carolina, Charlotte, NC
28223
Phone: 919/547-2375
Course(s)/Program(s): Leadership Theory and the Dynamics of Group Process.
Resource Role: Panelist; speaker; attend conferences; information sharing; design and
implementation of student leadership programs.

MABEY, CHERYL L.
Director, Women's Leadership Program, Mount St. Mary's College, 12001 Chalon
Rd., Los Angeles, CA 90049
Phone: 213/476-2237
Course(s)/Program(s): Introduction to Leadership, Leadership Fieldwork,
Leadership Studies Seminar (p. 181); Women's Leadership Program.
Research in Progress: Assessing outcomes of program and leadership studies minor
on college students/alumnae. Interested in institutionalizing both teaching about
leadership as well as leadership development; particular focus on women's leadership
development; outreach to high school administrators and students.
Resource Role: Panelist; speaker; attend conferences; information sharing.

MAHONEY, BROOKE W.
Executive Director, Volunteer Consulting Group, Inc., 24 West 40th St., New York,
NY 10018
Phone: 212/869-0800
Course(s)/Program(s): Volunteer Consulting Group (p. 381).
Resource Role: Panelist; attend conferences; information sharing.

MALLOY, NANCY BUSHWICK
Associate for Leadership Development, Resources for the Future, 1616 P St., NW,
Washington, DC 20036
Phone: 202/328-5011
Course(s)/Program(s): National Leadership Development Program.
Resource Role: Panelist; speaker; attend conferences; information sharing.

MANLEY, T. ROGER
Dean, School of Management, Florida Institute of Technology, 150 W. University Blvd., Melbourne, FL 32901
Phone: 407/768-8000
Course(s)/Program(s): Leadership and Effective Management.
Resource Role: Panelist; speaker; attend conferences; information sharing; relating leadership with management of technology.

MARANO, ROCCO
Division of Student Activities, Nat'l. Assoc. of Secondary School Principals, 1904 Association Drive, Reston, VA 22091
Phone: 703/860-0200
Course(s)/Program(s): National Leadership Training Centers (p. 415).
Resource Role: Panelist; attend conferences; information sharing; training high school and middle level student leaders and their advisers.

MARINE, JAMES
Ass't. Dean/Professor, Higher Education, Ball State University, Muncie, IN 47306
Phone: 317/285-5036
Course(s)/Program(s): Leadership and Development of Student Organizations (p. 5).
Publications: The College Union's Role in Student Development, Bulletin of the Association of College Unions-International, February 1985.
Research in Progress: A comparative study to assess the outcomes of student participation in campus activities.
Resource Role: Panelist; speaker; attend conferences; information sharing; cooperate in the conduct of studies related to student leadership development.

MARKLEY, LARRY
Brown-Lupton Student Center, Texas Christian University, P.O. Box 32919, Fort Worth, TX 76129
Phone: 817/921-7927
Course(s)/Program(s): Leadership II; TCU Leadership Development Program.
Resource Role: Panelist; speaker; attend conferences; information sharing.

MASON, TISA
Director of Student Life, Christopher Newport College, 50 Shoe Lane, Newport News, VA 23606
Phone: 804/594-7260
Course(s)/Program(s): Student Leadership Institute program.
Resource Role: Panelist; attend conferences; information sharing.

MATTERN, CHRISTINE V.
Director, Organization Development and Training, R. J. Reynolds Tobacco Company, 401 North Main Street, Winston-Salem, NC 27102
Phone: 919/741-6910

Course(s)/Program(s): Management Development Program (2 weeks), Strategies for Effective Management (1 week). Twenty internal management/professional programs. Most touch on leadership skills in some way.
Resource Role: Panelist; speaker; attend conferences; information sharing.

MATUSAK, LARRAINE
Director, Kellogg National Fellowship Program, W. K. Kellogg Foundation, 400 North Ave., Battle Creek, MI 49017
Phone: 616/968-1611
Course(s)/Program(s): Kellogg National Fellowship Program.
Publications: FOCUS, Newsletter of Kellogg National Fellowship Program.
Resource Role: Panelist; speaker; information sharing.

McCAULEY, CYNTHIA
Director of Research, Education and Nonprofit Sector, Center for Creative Leadership, 5000 Laurinda Drive, P.O. Box P-1, Greensboro, NC 27402-1660
Phone: 919/288-7210
Research in Progress: Looking at psychological test data of college students identified as leaders. Mainly interested in expanding leadership research to include individuals identified as high potential leaders at a relatively young age.
Resource Role: Information sharing.

McCLUSKY, JOHN
Vice President, Academic Programs, The Washington Center, 514 10th St., NW, Suite 600, Washington, DC 20004
Phone: 202/624-8083
Course(s)/Program(s): Washington Center programs, involving 1500 college students/yr. from across the country.
Publications: Publications in Warren Bennis (Ed.), Planning of Change; Voluntary Action Leadership, APSA DEA News.
Resource Role: Panelist; speaker; attend conferences; information sharing.

McDADE, SHARON A.
Program Director, Institute for Educational Management, Harvard University, Cambridge, MA 02138
Phone: 617/495-2655
Course(s)/Program(s): Leadership Issues in Higher Education, Introduction to Leadership; Management Development Program & Institute for Educational Management (sponsored by Harvard University) (p. 302).
Publications: "Higher Education Leadership: Enhancing Skills through Professional Development Programs," ASHE-ERIC, Higher Education Report 5, 1987.
Research in Progress: Applying the "Lessons of Leadership" work of the Center for Creative Leadership to the development of leadership in higher education. Working with Kay Moore to trace higher education administrative careers.
Resource Role: Panelist; speaker; attend conferences; information sharing. My interest is in the development of leadership skills, particularly for higher education

administrators, and how the theory of leadership development can be better taught through ongoing professional development programs and activities. I ask how leaders can improve their skills and abilities to better serve their institutions and education.

McINTIRE, DAVID
Vice Chancellor for Student Development, Appalachian State University, Administration Bldg., Boone, NC 28608
Phone: 704/262-2060
Course(s)/Program(s): Advanced Leadership Development.
Resource Role: Panelist; speaker.

McKINZIE, KATHY
Associate Director of Career Services for Career Development, Converse College, 580 East Main Street, Spartanburg, SC 29301
Phone: 803/596-9027
Course(s)/Program(s): Assisting in coordinating Converse Leadership Program.
Resource Role: Panelist; attend conferences; information sharing.

McLEOD, REOLA
Program Director, American Leadership Forum, 1800 Grant St., Ste. 550, Denver, CO 80203
Phone: 303/863-9913
Course(s)/Program(s): Year-long leadership development program for community leaders and business executives in communities across the country (under the auspices of the American Leadership Forum).
Resource Role: Panelist; speaker; attend conferences; information sharing.

MEALY, LARRY
Director of Leadership Development, Taylor University, Office of Leadership Development, Upland, IN 46989
Phone: 317/998-5305
Course(s)/Program(s): Developmental Processes in Leadership; Student Leadership Program.
Resource Role: Panelist; speaker; attend conferences; information sharing.

MEDINGER, FRED
Director of Graduate Studies, College of Notre Dame, 4701 Charles St., Baltimore, MD 21210
Phone: 301/532-5317
Course(s)/Program(s): Master of Arts in Human Resources.
Resource Role: Panelist; speaker; attend conferences; information sharing.

MENDES, HAROLD C.
Military Leadership and Management, College Militaire Royal de Saint Jean, Saint Jean, Quebec, Canada J0J 1R0
Phone: 514/346-2131

Course(s)/Program(s): Career Development.
Publications: Group performance.
Research in Progress: Group performance.
Resource Role: Attend conferences; information sharing.

MEREDITH, SAM T.
Professor, Political Science, Blackburn College, Carlinville, IL 62626
Phone: 217/854-3231 x267
Course(s)/Program(s): Approaches to Political Leadership (p. 7), The Constructive Resolution of Conflict.
Research in Progress: Developing curriculum for using students' experiences (work, social, etc.) as part of the leadership education process. Developing role play simulations for use in undergraduate political science classes.
Resource Role: Panelist; attend conferences; information sharing.

METS, LISA A.
Asst. to the Vice President, Administration and Planning, Northwestern University, 633 Clark St., Crown 2-112, Evanston, IL 60208-1103
Phone: 312/491-4335
Computer Network Address or ID: BITNET: L_METS@NUACC. INTERNET: L_METS@NUACC.ACNS.NWU.EDU
Course(s)/Program(s): Looking at leadership education with an eye toward developing a program at Northwestern--to be initiated by the President.
Resource Role: Information sharing.

MEYER, MANU
HLDP Coordinator, University of Hawaii at Hilo, Hawaiian Leadership Development Program, Hilo, HI 96720-4091
Phone: 808/933-3413
Course(s)/Program(s): Hawaiian Leadership 294; Hawaiian Leadership Development Program (p. 245).
Research in Progress: Leadership development as it relates to ethnic minorities. The role of values in leadership development.
Resource Role: Panelist; speaker; attend conferences; information sharing.

MICHAEL, JOHN A.
Evaluation Specialist, U.S. Dept. of Agriculture, Extension Service, South Bldg., 14th & Independence, SW, #3428, Washington, DC 20250-0900
Phone: 202/475-4557
Publications: Popular report on study findings; More detailed technical report on major study, "Developing Leadership Skills Among Extension Clientele: An Evaluation of Inputs." Both in press.
Resource Role: Panelist; speaker; attend conferences; information sharing.

MILLER, MARY A.
Professor, Dept. of Nursing and Health, Metropolitan State College, 1006 11th St.,

Box 33, Denver, CO 80204
Phone: 303/556-3136
Course(s)/Program(s): Leadership (p. 50).
Resource Role: Attend conferences; information sharing.

MOORE, DAVID G.
President, Mott Community College, 1401 East Court St., Flint, MI 48502
Phone: 313/762-0453
Research in Progress: Organizational behavior, labor-management (especially faculty unions), renewal and restructuring.
Resource Role: Panelist; speaker; attend conferences; information sharing.

MORTON, DAVID L.
Employee Development and Education, Training and Development Dept., U.S. Postal Service, 475 L'Enfant Plaza, Washington, DC 20260-4352
Phone: 202/268-5756
Resource Role: Panelist; attend conferences; information sharing.

MORTON, T. BALLARD
Executive-in-Residence, University of Louisville, School of Business, Louisville, KY 40292
Phone: 502/588-5612
Course(s)/Program(s): Leadership (p. 103); Ten-week Program for Senior Executives.
Resource Role: Speaker; information sharing.

MULLENDORE, RICHARD
Assoc. Vice Chancellor, Student Affairs, University of North Carolina-Wilmington, 601 S. College Road, Wilmington, NC 28403-3297
Phone: 919/395-3089
Course(s)/Program(s): Student Leadership in Higher Education.
Resource Role: Panelist; speaker.

NELSON, EDWIN C.
President Emeritus, Chadron State College, 10th & Main St. - Crites 109, Chadron, NE 69337
Phone: 308/432-6259
Course(s)/Program(s): Summer workshop "Community Revitalization Through The Schools"; Occasionally "Creative Leadership"; Seminars, "Strengthening The Rural Community Through Effective Creative Leadership" (p. 25).
Research in Progress: Profiles of teachers in rural communities
Resource Role: Panelist; speaker; attend conferences; information sharing.

NEMEROWICZ, GLORIA
Dean, Arts and Sciences, Monmouth College, Cedar Ave., West Long Branch, NJ 07764

Phone: 201/571-3419
Course(s)/Program(s): Education for Leadership and Social Responsibility. Through a grant, we will be implementing a comprehensive program to prepare all of our students for roles of leadership and social responsibility.
Resource Role: Panelist; speaker; attend conferences; information sharing.

O'BRIEN, KATHLEEN A.
Assoc. Professor, Dept. of Business and Management, Alverno College, 3401 S. 39th St., Milwaukee, WI 53215
Phone: 414/382-6252
Course(s)/Program(s): Seminar - Women and Leadership (p. 136); Integrating leadership education throughout the curriculum.
Publications: Co-author "Effective Leadership: The Abilities of Women Managers and Executives," Potpourri, Junior League of Milwaukee. Co-author: ERIC monograph, "Developing a Professional Competence Model for Management Education, Nat'l. Inst. of Education, Res. Rpt. No. 10, Alverno Productions, 1982.
Research in Progress: Completed a research project, sponsored by NIE, on the competences of effective women managers in the Milwaukee area. Will update and follow-up on this research.
Resource Role: Panelist; speaker; attend conferences; information sharing.

OGILVIE, GREG
Comparative Oncology Unit, Colorado State University, 200 W. Drake, Fort Collins, CO 80523
Phone: 303/221-4535
Research in Progress: We are currently initiating a prospective research endeavor to evaluate leadership teaching and outcome. Developing program to enhance leadership skills of uniquely qualified freshmen college students.
Resource Role: Panelist; speaker; attend conferences; information sharing.

O'NEIL, EDWARD H.
Asst. Dean, School of Medicine, Duke University, 2016 Campus Dr., Durham, NC 27706
Phone: 919/684-3867
Course(s)/Program(s): Civic Life and Leadership.

PARIS, GRACE LAMACCHIA
Director, Leadership Development Program, Pace University, Choate House, Bedford Rd., Pleasantville, NY 10570
Phone: 914/741-3757
Course(s)/Program(s): Leadership Development Program.
Research in Progress: Conducting a longitudinal study of the program participants.
Resource Role: Panelist; speaker; information sharing.

PARNES, SIDNEY J.
Trustee Chairperson for Strategic Program Development, Creative Education

Foundation, 1050 Union Road, Buffalo, NY 14224
Phone: 716/675-3181
Course(s)/Program(s): Visionizing Workshop (Futures Creative Problem Solving); Creative Problem-Solving Workshop
Publications: <u>Visionizing: State-of-the-Art Processes for Encouraging Innovative Excellence</u>, 1988; <u>A Facilitating Style of Leadership</u>, 1985.
Research in Progress: Continuing research into the use of imagery processes in creative problem solving. Interested in connecting the knowledge about creativity to the field of leadership studies.
Resource Role: Panelist; speaker; attend conferences; information sharing.

PENNINGTON, WILLIAM D.
Director of Student Services, University Center of Tulsa, 700 North Greenwood Ave., Tulsa, OK 74106
Phone: 918/586-0730
Resource Role: Panelist; speaker; attend conferences.

PETTY, M. L.
Director of Student Development, Univ. of North Carolina, Asheville, One University Heights, Asheville, NC 28804
Phone: 704/251-6588
Course(s)/Program(s): The Leadership Course: Application and Theory.
Publications: "Personality Types, Learning Styles and Leadership Approaches of College Student Leaders," Student Services, Chapel Hill, Gen. Admin., 1988.
Research in Progress: Personality traits and learning styles of campus student leaders.
Resource Role: Panelist; speaker; attend conferences; information sharing.

PFEIFFER, ANGELA LAIRD
Assoc. Dean, College of Professional and Public Affairs, University of Arkansas-Little Rock, 2801 S. University, Little Rock, AR 72204
Phone: 501/569-3244
Publications: Co-author: <u>Skills for Leaders</u>, Nat'l. Assoc. of Secondary School Principals.
Research in Progress: Symbolic behavior of leaders. Role of leaders in creating, sustaining and changing culture.
Resource Role: Panelist; speaker; attend conferences; information sharing.

PHILLIPS, SARA
Director of Personnel, The University of Tennessee, 102 Alumni Hall, Knoxville, TN 37996-0612
Phone: 615/974-5151
Course(s)/Program(s): Institute for Leadership Effectiveness (p. 315).
Resource Role: Attend conferences; information sharing.

PIGG, KENNETH E.
University of Missouri, 209 Sociology Bldg., Columbia, MO 65211
Phone: 314/882-4350
Course(s)/Program(s): Leadership in Modern Society.
Publications: "EXCEL: Collaborative Research in Action," Sociological Practice.
Research in Progress: Study of local government officials in rural areas.
Resource Role: Panelist; speaker; attend conferences; information sharing. Interested in combining our State of Franklin simulation with Looking Glass to train community leaders.

PILCH, JUDITH T.
Assoc. Director, Office for Rural Education, Western Carolina University, Killian 223, Cullowhee, NC 28723
Phone: 704/227-7347
Course(s)/Program(s): Private Industry Council Youth Leadership Development Program, Legislators' Youth Leadership Development Program.
Resource Role: Panelist; speaker; attend conferences; information sharing; promoting the development of additional opportunities for Youth Leadership Development; development of a model for disadvantaged and minority youth who demonstrate academic and leadership potential.

PRENDERGAST, PATRICIA J.
Dean of Undergraduate Studies, North Adams State College, North Adams, MA 02147
Phone: 413/664-4511 x227
Resource Role: Panelist; speaker; information sharing.

PRESTON, JOANNE C.
Dept. of Psychology, University of Richmond, Richmond, VA 23173
Phone: 804/289-8130
Computer Network Address or ID: BITNET: PRESTONJO@URVAX
Publications: "Teaching Managers Leadership: An assessment of three training methods."
Research in Progress: Training, personality variables in leadership, and the antecedents of leadership on how these skills develop.
Resource Role: Panelist; speaker; attend conferences; information sharing.

PRINCE, HOWARD
Professor & Department Head, Dept. of Behavioral Science & Leadership, United States Military Academy, West Point, NY 10996
Phone: 914/938-3206
Course(s)/Program(s): PL300 Military Leadership, PL 486 Combat Leadership; Undergraduate major in leadership, M.A. program - West Point Fellowship in Leader Development (p. 327).
Resource Role: Panelist; speaker; attend conferences; information sharing.

RAAK, MARTHA
Director, Office of Continuing Education/Summer Session, Seton Hill College, Greensburg, PA 15601
Phone: 412/838-4208
Course(s)/Program(s): All Continuing Education programs and workshops.
Resource Role: Panelist; speaker; attend conferences; information sharing. Specialty - women's roles in leadership studies.

RAMSEY, MARY LOU
Chairman, Counseling and Personnel Services, Trenton State College, Trenton, NJ 08650-4700
Phone: 609/771-2119
Resource Role: Information sharing.

RATZ, JIM
Executive Director, The National Outdoor Leadership School, P.O. Box AA, Lander, WY 82520
Phone: 307/332-6973
Course(s)/Program(s): Catalogs, complete course descriptions, dates and costs of courses are available through the Admissions Office (p. 313).

REISCH, MICHAEL
Dept. of Social Work Education, San Francisco State University, 1600 Holloway Ave., San Francisco, CA 94132
Phone: 415/338-2715
Publications: Edited The Future of Nonprofit Management and the Human Services. Articles on organizational structure, minority participation in advocacy organizations; coalition building.
Research in Progress: On advocacy and political action groups, e.g., advocacy coalitions in the human services.
Resource Role: Panelist; speaker; attend conferences; information sharing.

REJAI, M. P.
Distinguished Professor, Dept. of Political Science, Miami University, Oxford, OH 45056
Phone: 513/529-4394
Course(s)/Program(s): Political Leadership (p. 57).
Publications: Co-author: Loyalists and Revolutionaries: Political Leaders Compared, 1988.
Research in Progress: American Presidents as Leaders.
Resource Role: Panelist; speaker; attend conferences; information sharing.

RENNEISEN, CHARLES M.
Vice Chancellor for Student Affairs, University of Tennessee-Chattanooga, 651 Vine St., Rm. 216, Chattanooga, TN 37403
Phone: 615/755-4534

Course(s)/Program(s): Creative Leadership.
Resource Role: Panelist; speaker; attend conferences; information sharing.

RHODES, MILTON
President, American Council for the Arts, 1285 Avenue of the Americas, New York, NY 10019
Phone: 212/245-4510
Resource Role: Panelist; speaker; attend conferences; information sharing.

RISSMEYER, PATRICIA A.
Dean of Students, Canisius College, 2001 Main Street, Buffalo, NY 14208
Phone: 716/888-2130
Course(s)/Program(s): Introduction to Leadership.
Resource Role: Panelist; speaker; attend conferences; information sharing; leadership issues particular to women.

RITTER, DEBORA A.
Asst. Director, Resident Student Development, University of South Carolina, 1215 Blossom St., Columbia, SC 29208
Phone: 803/777-4129
Course(s)/Program(s): Co-teaching graduate seminar - Leadership in Higher Education.
Resource Role: Speaker; attend conferences; information sharing.

ROBY, PAMELA
Professor, Sociology Dept., University of California-Santa Cruz, 203 Palo Verde Terrace, Santa Cruz, CA 95060
Phone: 408/459-2587
Course(s)/Program(s): Sociology of Leadership (p. 87).
Publications: "Union Stewards and Women's Employment Conditions," in C. Bose and G. Spitze (Eds.), Ingredients for Women's Employment Policy, SUNY Press, 1987.
Resource Role: Panelist; information sharing,

ROGERS, MANLEY E.
Scholarship Consultant, 3 Church St., Belfast, ME 04915
Phone: 207/338-4009
Course(s)/Program(s): A county Youth Leadership and Scholarship program for Rotary.
Resource Role: Panelist; speaker; attend conferences; information sharing. Helping others develop and run scholarship programs which encourage students and teachers to identify and improve leadership.

ROHRER, JOHN
Leader, Community Services, Cooperative Extension Service, Ohio State University, 2120 Fyffe Rd., Columbus, OH 43210

Phone: 614/292-8436
Course(s)/Program(s): Various Leadership Development Programs within context of Community Leadership. Focus is leadership for public officials and leadership for economic development.
Research in Progress: Assessment of leadership skills in community context.

ROSENBACH, WILLIAM E.
Professor & Chairman, Department of Management, Gettysburg College, Box 395, Gettysburg, PA 17325
Phone: 717/337-6646
Course(s)/Program(s): Organizational Behavior (large block devoted to leadership), Techniques of Leadership (graduate course for Univ. of Maryland); In capacity of Harold G. Evans Professorship in Eisenhower Leadership Studies, will begin developing a leadership program for Gettysburg College. Would like to explore and develop a network of "quality" co-curricular undergraduate programs for leadership development.
Publications: Co-author: Contemporary Issues in Leadership, 2nd ed., Westview Press, 1989; Leadership Challenges for Today's Managers, Nichols Publishing, 1989; "Transformational and Transactional Leadership of Business, Church, and Fire Service Executives," Best Paper Proceedings of the XXIV Congress of Psychology, Elsevier, Amsterdam, 1989.
Research in Progress: Transformational and transactional leadership behaviors of private and public sector executives.
Resource Role: Panelist; speaker; attend conferences; information sharing.

ROSSING, BOYD E.
Dept. of Continuing & Vocational Education, University of Wisconsin, 225 North Mills St., Rm. 276, Madison, WI 53706
Phone: 608/262-5930
Course(s)/Program(s): Leadership in Community Programs; Wisconsin Family Community Leadership Program (p. 373).
Publications: International Journal of Lifelong Education.
Research in Progress: Studies of informal leadership development from experience.
Resource Role: Panelist; attend conferences; information sharing.

SAND, LORI
Coordinator, Student Publications, Kirkwood Community College, 6301 Kirkwood Blvd., SW, Cedar Rapids, IA 52401
Phone: 319/398-4956
Course(s)/Program(s): Leadership Styles.
Resource Role: Panelist; attend conferences; information sharing.

SANDERSON, DONALD R.
Director of Student Activities, Oregon State University, MU East Activities Center, Corvallis, OR 97331
Phone: 503/754-2101

Course(s)/Program(s): Associated Students of Oregon State University Field Training; Student Organization Development Program.
Resource Role: Panelist; attend conferences; information sharing.

SAWYER, ROBERT
Professor, Duke University Talent Identification Program, Box 40077, Durham, NC 27706-0077
Phone: 919/684-3847
Course(s)/Program(s): Seminar on Gifted; Talent Identification Program (p. 411).
Resource Role: Panelist; speaker; attend conferences; information sharing. Interest is in potential leaders in the academically talented population.

SCHMUCK, RICHARD A.
Professor, DEPM/College of Education, University of Oregon, Eugene, OR 97403
Phone: 503/686-5171
Course(s)/Program(s): Management and Organization Development, Educational Leadership.
Publications: Handbook of Organization Development in Schools and Group Processes in the Classroom.
Research in Progress: Assessing to what extent the indicators of democratic participation are present in schools.
Resource Role: Panelist; speaker; attend conferences; information sharing.

SCHWAB, KENNETH L.
Executive Vice President, University of South Carolina, President's Office, Osborne Bldg., Columbia, SC 29205
Phone: 803/777-3101
Course(s)/Program(s): Leadership in Higher Education (p. 118).
Resource Role: Panelist; speaker; attend conferences; information sharing. Have built and used a ropes course as a part of leadership training.

SHIVELY, ROBERT W.
Professor, Babcock Graduate School of Management, Wake Forest University, Reynolda Station, P.O. Box 7368, Winston-Salem, NC 27109
Phone: 919/759-7671
Course(s)/Program(s): Executive Leadership (second year MBA Executive students), Leadership (half-semester course for full-time second year MBA students).
Resource Role: Panelist; speaker; information sharing.

SLESINGER, LARRY H.
Deputy Director, Nat'l. Center for Nonprofit Boards, Suite 340, 1225 19th St., NW, Washington, DC 20036
Phone: 202/452-6262
Course(s)/Program(s): Board development workshops; Nat'l. Center for Nonprofit Boards (p. 361).
Resource Role: Panelist; speaker; attend conferences; information sharing.

Resource Persons in Leadership Education

SMITH, KEITH L.
Assoc. Professor, Ohio State University, 2120 Fyffe Rd., Columbus, OH 43210
Phone: 614/292-6181
Course(s)/Program(s): Leadership in Agriculture.
Resource Role: Panelist; speaker; attend conferences; information sharing.

SNODGRASS, WILDER
Visiting Lecturer, Providence College, 1 Thorpe Ave., Portsmouth, RI 02871
Phone: 401/683-5260
Course(s)/Program(s): Leadership Development for Professionals.
Research in Progress: Research relating to relationship between leadership skills and student academic skills.
Resource Role: Panelist; speaker; attend conferrences; information sharing.

SNOW, DONALD
Director, Conservation Leadership Project, 328 S. Kootenai Rd., Stevensville, MT 59870
Phone: 406/777-5169
Course(s)/Program(s): Conservation Leadership Project.
Publications: A volume of nine essays on various aspects of leadership in the environmental field, written by prominent nongovernmental organizations and academic leaders, Island Press (in press).
Resource Role: Panelist; speaker; attend conferences; information sharing. Advising conservation areas, e.g., government agencies (state - federal), private philanthropy, environmental management departments of various corporations (e.g., forest products, mining, waste disposal firms, etc.).

SPENCER, GAYLE
Activities Advisor, University of Houston, University Center, Houston, TX 77204-3650
Phone: 713/749-1253
Course(s)/Program(s): Leadership Institute.
Resource Role: Panelist; speaker; attend conferences; information sharing.

SPITZBERG, IRVING J., JR.
President, The Knowledge Company, 9726 Admiralty Dr., Silver Spring, MD 20910
Phone: 202/298-0691
Research in Progress: Leadership in community context on campus.
Resource Role: Speaker; information sharing.

STANTON, TIMOTHY
Assoc. Director, Public Service Center, P.O. Box Box Q, Stanford, CA 94309
Phone: 415/725-2859
Computer Network Address or ID: BITNET: CR.TKS@STANFORD
Course(s)/Program(s): Policy Making and Problem Solving at the Local and Regional Level, Preparation for Internship Learning; Local Government Internship Program, You Can Make A Difference (p. 223).

Publications: <u>Experiential Education</u>; <u>New Directions in Student Services</u>, Jossey-Bass.
Resource Role: Panelist; speaker; attend conferences; information sharing. Interested in leadership for the public good--connecting leadership skills with ethical and socially responsible purposes.

STERNBERGH, WILLIAM W.
Director, CCL-San Diego, Center for Creative Leadership, 4275 Executive Square, Suite 620, La Jolla, CA 92037
Phone: 619/453-4774
Course(s)/Program(s): Center for Creative Leadership - San Diego.
Resource Role: Speaker; information sharing.

STEVENSON, JACK L.
Director, Honors Program, Clemson University, 532 Clemson House, Clemson, SC 29632
Phone: 803/656-4762
Course(s)/Program(s): Leadership and Group Dynamics.
Resource Role: Speaker.

ST. GERMAIN, PAT
Office of Activities and Organizations, State University of New York at Syracuse, 110 Bray Hall, Syracuse, NY 13210
Phone: 315/470-6658
Resource Role: Panelist; speaker; attend conferences; information sharing. Exploring significant events in the experience of women leaders in student affairs, and sharing these with women in graduate programs/entry level positions. Willing to present, co-author an article; especially interested in doing research on women's experiences in leadership.

STOLBOF, CECILE
Dean of Instruction, Rutgers University, 360 King Blvd., Rm. J302, Newark, NJ 07102
Phone: 201/648-5833
Resource Role: Speaker; attend conferences.

STRAUB, CYNTHIA A.
Director, Student Organization Development Center, University of Michigan, 2202 Michigan Union, Ann Arbor, MI 48109
Phone: 313/763-5900
Course(s)/Program(s): Introduction Leadership Development, Advanced Seminar in Leadership; Internship Program, Emerging Leader Program.

TAYLOR, GAIL
Director, Student Activities, Cypress College, 9200 Valley View St., Cypress, CA 90630
Phone: 714/826-3360
Resource Role: Attend conferences.

TAYLOR, ROBERT L.
Dean, School of Business, University of Louisville, Louisville, KY 40292
Phone: 502/588-6443
Computer Network Address or ID: BITNET: RLTAYL01-ULKYVM
Course(s)/Program(s): Introduction to Leadership, Leader Behaviors; The Effective Executive.
Publications: Leadership: Challenges for Today's Manager, Nichols/McGraw-Hill, 1989. Contemporary Issues in Leadership, Westview Press, 1989.
Resource Role: Panelist; speaker; attend conferences; information sharing; examining visionary leadership; self-knowledge as the key to leadership development.

TAYLOR, TIM
Minister of Education, McKinney Memorial Bible Church, 3901 South Hulen, Fort Worth, TX 76109
Phone: 817/921-5200
Course(s)/Program(s): Small Group Leadership.
Resource Role: Attend conferences.

THOMPSON, JOHN
Dept. of Leadership, Culver Educational Foundation, Box 145, Culver, IN 46511
Phone: 219/842-8320
Course(s)/Program(s): Values and Leadership, Skills for Life and Leadership, Leaders and Leadership Styles (p. 407).
Resource Role: Panelist; speaker; attend conferences; information sharing. Four years experience in leadership education at the high school level.

THOMPSON, KENNETH
Director, Miller Center, University of Virginia, P.O. Box 5707, Charlottesville, VA 22905
Phone: 804/924-7236
Course(s)/Program(s): Miller Center of Public Affairs.
Publications: Winston Churchill's World View. The Presidency and the Public Philosophy.
Research in Progress: History of the Cold War.
Resource Role: Speaker; information sharing. The Center's major focus is on the American presidency with leadership our foremost interest.

THOMPSON, WARREN K.
Dept. of Religion and Philosophy, Lebanon Valley College, Annville, PA 17003-0501
Phone: 717/867-6133

Course(s)/Program(s): Ethical Issues in Leadership
Research in Progress: Ethics and values in leadership
Resource Role: Panelist; speaker; attend conferences; information sharing.

TOLLEY, JERRY R.
Asst. Vice President-Training/Recruitment, Roche Biomedical Laboratories, Inc., P.O. Box 2230, Burlington, NC 27216-2230
Phone: 919/584-5171
Course(s)/Program(s): Developing Top Performers, When Opportunity Knocks, Circle of Excellence Executive Development Program (p. 309).
Resource Role: Panelist; speaker; attend conferences; information sharing.

TOTH, POWELL E.
Program Director, Educational Administration, West Virginia College of Graduate Studies, 737 Sullivan Hall, Institute, WV 25112
Phone: 304/766-2016
Course(s)/Program(s): Principles of Leadership; Center for the Study of Rural Appalachian Educational Administration.
Publications: "Creative Leadership" and "Creative Energy."
Research in Progress: Leader behavior as it relates to brain hemispherisity. Role of trust in leader effectiveness.
Resource Role: Panelist; speaker; attend conferences; information sharing.

TREVINO, CONSUELO
Student Development Specialist, University of Texas-Austin, Campus Activities Office, UNB 430, Austin, TX 78712
Phone: 512/471-3065
Course(s)/Program(s): Minority Student Leadership Issues, Developing Training Skills, taught by Melanie Wilson, CAO Staff Member. Leadership Board, coordinated by Melanie Wilson. Multicultural Program, coordinated by Consuelo Trevino.
Resource Role: Panelist; information sharing. Interest areas include multicultural programming and minority leadership issues.

VASQUEZ, GABRIEL
Student Life, Arizona State University, Tempe, AZ 85287-0512
Phone: 602/897-2853
Course(s)/Program(s): Personal Leadership Development; Leadership Scholarship Program, Leadership 2000 Program.
Resource Role: Panelist; speaker; attend conferences; information sharing.

WALLING, H. GRIFFIN
Director, Center for Lifelong Learning, State University of New York, Hawkins Hall 106, Plattsburgh, NY 12901
Phone: 518/564-2050
Course(s)/Program(s): Seminar in Administration and Leadership; M.A. Program in

Administration and Leadership.
Research in Progress: Preliminary research on "value added" skills obtained from leadership education.
Resource Role: Panelist; speaker; attend conferences; information sharing.

WARWICK, RON
Chairman, Educational Leadership Dept., National College of Education, 2840 Sheridan Rd., Evanston, IL 60201
Phone: 708/256-5150
Course(s)/Program(s): Leadership Communication Skills; Educational Leadership for School Administrators.
Resource Role: Panelist; speaker; attend conferences; information sharing.

WASILEWSKI, ANDREW
Director, University Center and Campus Activities, Northern Michigan University, Marquette, MI 49855
Phone: 906/227-2645
Course(s)/Program(s): Center for Excellence in Leadership and Personal Development.
Resource Role: Information sharing.

WATSON, CAROL D.
Assoc. Professor, School of Business, Rider College, Lawrenceville, NJ 08648-3099
Phone: 609/896-5069
Computer Network Address or ID: CWATSON@PILOT.NJIN.NET
Publications: "When A Woman Is The Boss: Dilemmas In Taking Charge" Group and Organization Studies, 1988.
Research in Progress: Examining determinants of leader ability to manage conflict in groups.
Resource Role: Panelist; attend conferences; information sharing.

WATSON, EUGENE R.
Professor, Educational Leadership Program, University of North Carolina, Peabody Hall, Chapel Hill, NC 27514
Phone: 919/966-1354
Course(s)/Program(s): Leadership Behavior and Organizational Change in Educational Settings.
Publications: Co-author: "Participation and Content in Community College Board Meetings," Community Junior College's Quarterly of Research and Practice, II, No. 4, 1987.
Resource Role: Panelist; speaker; information sharing; leadership of and by community college boards.

WELCH, DEBBIE
Director of Staff Development, Northern Colorado Board of Cooperative Educational Services, 830 S. Lincoln, Longmont, CO 80501

Phone: 303/772-4420
Course(s)/Program(s): Skills for Change Facilitators, Assessing School Culture, Adult Development and Self Esteem; Leadership Institute for Educators.
Resource Role: Panelist; speaker; attend conferences; information sharing.

WESSEL, DOUG
Dean, College of Education and HRD, Black Hills State University, 1200 University, Box 9004, Spearfish, SD 57783
Phone: 605/642-6550
Course(s)/Program(s): Leadership: Theory and Practice (p. 15).
Resource Role: Panelist; speaker; attend conferences; information sharing. Interested in interdisciplinary leadership education at the undergraduate level and post-graduate leadership development.

WHICKER, MARCIA L.
Professor, Public Administration, Virginia Commonwealth University, 816 W. Franklin St., Richmond, VA 23284
Phone: 804/257-1046
Publications: Public Sector Leadership, Univ. of Ala. Press, forthcoming. Co-author: When Presidents Are Great, Prentice-Hall, 1988.
Research in Progress: Test of Schlensinger's thesis of generational change.
Resource Role: Panelist; speaker; attend conferences; information sharing; would like to present ideas developed in Public Sector Leadership to broader audience. Book focuses on cycles and stages of societal level leadership resulting in expanded rights for disadvantaged groups.

WHITAKER, GORDON P.
Director, Master of Public Administration Program, #3265, University of North Carolina, Chapel Hill, NC 27599
Phone: 919/962-0426
Course(s)/Program(s): Urban Political Systems.
Resource Role: Panelist; speaker; attend conferences; information sharing.

WHITE, DONALD B.
Professor, Dept. of Horticulture Sciences, University of Minnesota, 456 Alderman Hall, St. Paul, MN 55108
Phone: 612/624-9206
Resource Role: Panelist; attend conferences; information sharing.

WHITE, JULIE BELLE
Director, M.A. in Organizational Leadership, College of St. Catherine, P.O. Box 4208, 2004 Randolph Ave., St. Paul, MN 55105
Phone: 612/690-6783
Course(s)/Program(s): Leadership and Ethics, Leadership Seminar, Leadership and Communication.
Publications: Co-author: "Building Integrity in Organizations," New Management,

Summer 1988.
Research in Progress: Model of leadership inclusive of women and female associated attributes; characteristics of organizational integrity.
Resource Role: Panelist; speaker; attend conferences; information sharing.

WHITNEY, CONSTANCE C.
President, Strategic Leadership Consulting, 10601 Wilshire Blvd., Los Angeles, CA 90024
Phone: 213/475-0977
Course(s)/Program(s): Leadership Seminar/Mt. St. Mary's College with Dr. Cheryl Mabey; Executive Director, Executive Education, Town Hall of California.
Resource Role: Panelist; speaker; attend conferences; information sharing.

WILLEN, CAROL
Cleveland Foundation, 1400 Hanna Bldg., Cleveland, OH 44115
Phone: 216/861-3810
Resource Role: Program officer for a community foundation. Area of specialization is higher education.

WILLIAMS, ALAN
Director of Guidance, Oakfield-Alabama School, 7001 Lewiston Rd., Oakfield, NY 14125
Phone: 716/948-5211
Course(s)/Program(s): Leadership seminars and a course for high school students.
Resource Role: Speaker; attend conferences.

WILSON, DOUGLAS
President, C.O.R.E., 260 Newport Center Drive, #250, Newport Beach, CA 92660
Phone: 714/640-8984
Course(s)/Program(s): What Works: Strategies for Managing Change.
Research in Progress: Successful change strategies--both in small business settings and large organizations such as SAS, AT&T, and Westinghouse Furniture Systems. Practical studies in how leaders get organizations moving to create significant change.
Resource Role: Panelist; speaker; attend conferences; information sharing.

WILSON, WILLIAM L.
Center for Leadership and Personnel Development, United States Military Academy, Building 720, West Point, NY 10996
Phone: 914/938-4723
Resource Role: Panelist; speaker; attend conferences; information sharing.

WINNER, LINDA
Center for Public Service, University of Virginia, 2015 Ivy Road, Charlottesville, VA 22903-1795
Phone: 804/924-3396
Course(s)/Program(s): Senior Executive Institute (p. 347); Leadership Development

Programs, Virginia Local Government Arrangement Assn.
Resource Role: Panelist; speaker; attend conferences; information sharing. Interested in research and writing related to leadership at state and local government management level.

WOLF, CYNTHIA A.

Director, North Carolina Fellows Program and Leadership Development, University of North Carolina at Chapel Hill, CB# 5100, 01 Steele Building, Chapel Hill, NC 27599-5100
Phone: 919/966-4041
Computer Network Address or ID: BITNET: CAWOLF@UNC
Course(s)/Program(s): Dynamics of Effective Leadership; N.C. Fellows Program and Leadership Development (p. 255).
Resource Role: Panelist; speaker; attend conferences; information sharing. Creating new programs (and staffing) to meet the needs of students; have been working with the "developmental" N.C. Fellows Program which works with the same students throughout their 4 years of college.

YOUNG, DENNIS

Director, Mandel Center for Nonprofit Organizations, Case Western Reserve University, 2035 Abington, Rd., Cleveland, OH 44106
Phone: 216/368-2275
Course(s)/Program(s): Economics for Nonprofit Management; Mandel Center for Nonprofit Organizations (p. 288).
Publications: Co-author: "Educating Managers of Nonprofit Organizations," 1988, and "Careers for Dreamers and Doers," 1989.
Research in Progress: Structure of national and international nonprofit associations.
Resource Role: Panelist; attend conferences; information sharing.

RESOURCE PERSONS IN LEADERSHIP EDUCATION

STATE INDEX

ALABAMA

Berte, Neal R. (Birmingham)
Brown, Richard (Montgomery)
Handy, Raymond T. (Tuskegee Institute)

ARIZONA

Giuliano, Neil G. (Tempe)
Vasquez, Gabriel (Tempe)

ARKANSAS

Pfeiffer, Angela Laird (Little Rock)

CALIFORNIA

Beardsley, Stephanie (Davis)
Cognetta, John S. (Hayward)
Conner, Ross F. (Irvine)
Cosgrove, Thomas J. (San Diego)
Curtin, Joe (Marina del Rey)
Farson, Richard (La Jolla)
Guinther, Pauline (Carmichael)
Harris, Philip R. (La Jolla)
Hartley, Alex (Los Angeles)
Harvey, Thomas R. (LaVerne)
Kindler, Herbert (Los Angeles)
Kruggel, Joel (Santa Barbara)
Lindsey, Randall B. (Los Angeles)
Mabey, Cheryl L. (Los Angeles)
Reisch, Michael (San Francisco)
Roby, Pamela (Santa Cruz)
Stanton, Timothy (Stanford)
Sternbergh, William W. (La Jolla)
Taylor, Gail (Cypress)
Whitney, Constance C. (Los Angeles)
Wilson, Douglas (Newport Beach)

COLORADO

Cronin, Thomas E. (Colorado Springs)
Goodman, Adam J. (Boulder)
Greenberg, Elinor M. (Englewood)
McLeod, Reola (Denver)
Miller, Mary A. (Denver)
Ogilvie, Greg (Fort Collins)
Welch, Debbie (Longmont)

CONNECTICUT

Benamati, Jacqueline D. (Bridgeport)
Fremed, Resa (Ridgefield)

DISTRICT OF COLUMBIA

Easton, Edward (Washington)
Green, Madeleine F. (Washington)
Malloy, Nancy Bushwick (Washington)
McClusky, John (Washington)
Michael, John A. (Washington)
Morton, David L. (Washington)
Slesinger, Larry H. (Washington)

FLORIDA

Bredenberg, Richard (St. Petersburg)
Brown, John Lott (Tampa)
Copestick, Kevin J. (Tampa)
Deegan, James E. (St. Petersburg)
Hammerschmidt, Peter (St. Petersburg)
Manley, T. Roger (Melbourne)

GEORGIA

Kerr, Nancy H. (Atlanta)

HAWAII

Meyer, Manu (Hilo)

ILLINOIS

Craft, Rolf V. (Eureka)
Ivarie, Ted (Charleston)
Meredith, Sam T. (Carlinville)
Mets, Lisa A. (Evanston)
Warwick, Ron (Evanston)

INDIANA

Feinberg, Richard (West Lafayette)
Green, Stephen G. (West Lafayette)
Marine, James (Muncie)
Mealy, Larry (Upland)
Thompson, John M. (Culver)

IOWA

Jorgensen, Gerald (Dubuque)
Luzkow, Virginia (Davenport)
Sand, Lori (Cedar Rapids)

KENTUCKY

Bennett, Diane T. (Louisville)
Morton, T. Ballard (Louisville)
Taylor, Robert L. (Louisville)

LOUISIANA

Bogue, Grady (Shreveport)

MAINE

Rogers, Manley E. (Belfast)

MARYLAND

Chambers, Glen A. (Catonsville)
Leedy, Marianne V. (Towson)
Medinger, Fred (Baltimore)
Spitzberg, Irving J., Jr. (Silver Spring)

MASSACHUSETTS

Fanelli, Russell (Springfield)
Ferris, William P. (Springfield)
Fillinger, Robert E. (South Hamilton)
Heifetz, Ronald A. (Cambridge)
Jeghelian, Alice (Chestnut Hill)
Linsky, Martin (Cambridge)
Lowance, Susan C. (Northhampton)
McDade, Sharon A. (Cambridge)
Prendergast, Patricia J. (North Adams)

MICHIGAN

Fletcher, Sherryl A. (Ann Arbor)
Jacokes, Lee E. (Grand Rapids)
Lapides, Joseph (Detroit)
Matusak, Larraine (Battle Creek)
Moore, David G. (Flint)
Straub, Cynthia A. (Ann Arbor)
Wasilewski, Andrew (Marquette)

MINNESOTA

Harrison, Clifford (Moorhead)
Huber, Jody L. (Morris)
Jerus, Robert G. (Roseville)
White, Donald B. (St. Paul)
White, Julie Belle (St. Paul)

MISSOURI

Beodeker, Bob (Cape Girardeau)
Caliguri, Joseph (Kansas City)

Missouri (Cont.)

Capra, Fran (St. Louis)
Herman, Robert D. (Kansas City)
Pigg, Kenneth E. (Columbia)

MONTANA

Snow, Donald (Stevensville)

NEBRASKA

Artman, Richard B. (Lincoln)
Blezek, Allen G. (Lincoln)
Boatman, Sara A. (Lincoln)
Brown, Martha (Omaha)
Nelson, Edwin C. (Chadron)

NEW HAMPSHIRE

Lawing, Anne (Durham)

NEW JERSEY

Beaven, Mary H. (Teaneck)
Cole, Katherine Lee (Princeton)
Kellerman, Barbara (Teaneck)
Nemerowicz, Gloria (West Long Branch)
Ramsey, Mary Lou (Trenton)
Stolbof, Cecile (Newark)
Watson, Carol D. (Lawrenceville)

NEW YORK

Anderson, Carol L. (Ithaca)
Appleby, R. Neal (Syracuse)
Bass, Bernard (Binghamton)
Black, Donald K. (New York)
Cross, William M. (Syracuse)
Curry, Rex L. (Brooklyn)
Dansereau, Fred (Williamsville)
Drury, Jack K. (Saranac Lake)

Gerber, Barbara W. (Oswego)
Hall, Marsha Paur (Troy)
Hollander, Edwin P. (New York)
Isaksen, Scott G. (Buffalo)
Luce, Henry, III (New York)
Mahoney, Brooke W. (New York)
Paris, Grace Lamacchia (Pleasantville)
Parnes, Sidney J. (Buffalo)
Prince, Howard (West Point)
Rhodes, Milton (New York)
Rissmeyer, Patricia A. (Buffalo)
St. Germain, Pat (Syracuse)
Walling, H. Griffin (Plattsburgh)
Williams, Alan (Oakfield)
Wilson, William L. (West Point)

NORTH CAROLINA

Barber, Robert L. (Greensboro)
Birmingham, Cathy (Wilmington)
Bull, Kathy Cleveland (Raleigh)
Cienek, Raymond P. (Greensboro)
Davis, F. Leary (Buies Creek)
Deck, Linton (Greensboro)
Hawkins, Gerald G. (Raleigh)
Lambeth, Thomas W. (Winston-Salem)
Legerton, Winifred R. (Greensboro)
Lynch, Charles F. (Charlotte)
Mattern, Christine V. (Winston-Salem)
McCauley, Cynthia D. (Greensboro)
McIntire, David (Boone)
Mullendore, Richard (Wilmington)
O'Neil, Edward H. (Durham)
Petty, M. L. (Asheville)
Pilch, Judith T. (Cullowhee)
Sawyer, Robert (Durham)
Shively, Robert W. (Winston-Salem)
Tolley, Jerry R. (Burlington)
Watson, Eugene R. (Chapel Hill)
Whitaker, Gordon P. (Chapel Hill)
Wolf, Cynthia A. (Chapel Hill)

OHIO

Ballinger, David C. (Cincinnati)
Beck, Ellen (Dayton)
Hanna, Nancy (Wooster)
Hodges, James A. (Wooster)
Holliday, Vivian L. (Wooster)
Jensen, Gwendolyn E. (Marietta)
Lucas, Nance (Athens)
Rejai, M. P. (Oxford)
Rohrer, John (Columbus)
Smith, Keith L. (Columbus)
Willen, Carol (Cleveland)
Young, Dennis (Cleveland)

OKLAHOMA

Demuth, Carol (Tulsa)
Pennington, William D. (Tulsa)

OREGON

Sanderson, Donald R. (Corvallis)
Schmuck, Richard A. (Eugene)

PENNSYLVANIA

Hoff, Debbie (Allentown)
Raak, Martha (Greensburg)
Rosenbach, William E. (Gettysburg)
Thompson, Warren K. (Annville)

RHODE ISLAND

Deluga, Ronald (Smithfield)
Forsberg, Thomas E. (Providence)

SOUTH CAROLINA

Fortner, Novella (Columbia)
McKinzie, Kathy (Spartanburg)
Ritter, Debora A. (Columbia)

Schwab, Kenneth L. (Columbia)
Stevenson, Jack L. (Clemson)

SOUTH DAKOTA

Wessel, Doug (Spearfish)

TENNESSEE

Bull, Bernard F. (Jefferson City)
Fendt, Paul F. (Johnson City)
Phillips, Sara (Knoxville)
Renneisen, Charles M. (Chattanooga)

TEXAS

Agor, Weston H. (El Paso)
Gardner, Kent L. (Arlington)
Hendricks, Howard G. (Dallas)
Lawrence, William D. (Dallas)
Markley, Larry (Fort Worth)
Spencer, Gayle (Houston)
Taylor, Tim (Fort Worth)
Trevino, Consuelo (Austin)

VERMONT

Brown, Patrick (Burlington)

VIRGINIA

Bowen, Zeddie (Richmond)
Decker, Larry E. (Charlottesville)
Fairholm, Gil W. (Richmond)
Harwood, Patricia C. (Richmond)
Marano, Rocco (Reston)
Mason, Tisa (Newport News)
Preston, Joanne C. (Richmond)
Thompson, Kenneth (Charlottesville)
Whicker, Marcia L. (Richmond)
Winner, Linda (Charlottesville)

WASHINGTON

Dodson, David (Tacoma)

WEST VIRGINIA

Toth, Powell E. (Institute)

WISCONSIN

Christ, Jack M. (Ripon)
Gear, Curtis E. (Madison)
Hartford, Thomas F. (DePere)
Hellweg, Julie M. (Stevens Point)
O'Brien, Kathleen A. (Milwaukee)
Rossing, Boyd E. (Madison)

WYOMING

Ratz, Jim (Lander)

CANADA

Hagerty, Jack (Guelph, Ontario)
Mendes, Harold C. (St. Jean, Quebec)

RESOURCE ORGANIZATIONS IN LEADERSHIP EDUCATION

INTRODUCTION

Many organizations throughout the United States and elsewhere profess an interest or involvement in leadership. However, only a few of these are actively involved in either leadership research or the sharing of leadership information and resources. The organizations included in the following list do seem to have an active involvement in leadership studies or leadership education, often with an expressed interest in sharing their knowledge with scholars and the community of leadership educators. In addition to research organizations and associations, this section now includes a small number of foundations who provide seed money, program support or fellowships for leadership development efforts.

There may be some organizations actively involved in leadership research or information gathering that we have overlooked. If you are aware of an organization that focuses on leadership studies and/or resource sharing, please let us know so that we may include it in the next edition of this Source Book.

AMERICAN CENTER FOR INTERNATIONAL LEADERSHIP
522 Franklin Street, Columbus, OH 47201
Phone: (812) 376-3456

Target goal is to promote the exchange of ideas and the growth of mutual respect and understanding between potential U.S. leaders (ages 23-40) and potential leaders in other countries (communist and non-communist). Has a 300-volume library of cross-cultural and leadership development materials; sponsors a speakers' bureau. **Publications:** *International Leadership* (quarterly); brochures and program description.

AMERICAN HUMANICS
4601 Madison Avenue, Kansas City, MO 64112
Phone: (816) 561-6415

Has 1500 members (individuals, corporations, foundations) and a staff of 24. Members support work in preparing young people for professional leadership in youth agencies. A major thrust is support and leadership for co-curricular programs on 15 campuses. Also sponsors field trips, workshops, and career counseling services. **Publications:** *Humanics News* (quarterly); brochures.

THE BUSH FOUNDATION
332 Minnesota Street, St. Paul, MN 55101
Phone: (612) 227-0891

Operates the Bush Leadership Fellows Program in MN, ND, SD, and western WI. **Publications:** Annual report, Application guidelines, Program policy statement. Write Humphrey Doermann, President, for additional information.

CATALYST
250 Park Avenue South, New York, NY 10003
Phone: (212) 777-8900

A research and advisory organization, Catalyst helps corporations foster the career and leadership development of women. It works on issues resulting from women's massive entry into the work force--issues such as child care, relocation, parental leave, and barriers to women's progress in corporations. It helps organizations locate qualified women for board directorships. The Catalyst Information Center is a major national clearinghouse for information on the career and leadership development of women. The Center's collection features books, periodicals, studies, and vertical files on various topics ranging from mentoring to flexible benefits.
Publications: *Perspective on Current Corporate Issues*; research reports; other.

588

CENTER FOR THE NEW LEADERSHIP

2641 Mann Court, Falls Church, VA 22046
Phone: (703) 573-1217

Members are individuals interested in voluntarism, leadership, and the future. This organization seeks to identify and work with America's "new leaders"--those whose skills, knowledge and values are directed toward helping people manage change in today's world. Maintains a clearinghouse and resource center on leadership, social innovations, and opportunities for citizen activism. **Publications:** *New Leader Bulletin* (quarterly).

CENTER FOR CREATIVE LEADERSHIP

5000 Laurinda Drive, P.O. Box P-1, Greensboro, NC 27402-1660
Phone: (919) 288-7210

A nonprofit educational institution founded in 1970 in Greensboro, North Carolina. Its mission is to encourage and develop creative leadership and effective management for the good of society overall. With a staff of 190, it accomplishes this mission through research, training, and publication--with emphasis on the widespread, innovative application of the behavioral sciences to the challenges facing the leaders of today and tomorrow. Through research it develops models of managerial practice; through training programs it applies these models as guides for assessment and development. **Publications:** *Issues & Observations* (quarterly), technical reports, special reports, proceedings, source books, audio and video tapes, and directories of programs and products.

CENTER FOR EFFECTIVE ORGANIZATIONS

Bridge Hall 400, University of Southern California, Los Angeles, CA 90089-1421
Phone: (213) 743-8765

Conducts research, training programs, and workshops on issues of organizational effectiveness involving design and management of human systems. Areas of interest include leadership, labor/management relations, organization development and design, career development, job design, and others. Research results published in professional journals. **Publications:** Report series; Annual report.

CENTER FOR LEADERSHIP DEVELOPMENT

American Council on Education, One Du Pont Circle, 8th Floor, Washington, DC 20036
Phone: (202) 939-9420

Provides professional development seminars on decision making and academic leadership for leaders in higher education. Programs are conducted for presidents, vice presidents, academic deans, and other senior administrators. Programs use speakers, seminars, case studies, simulations, and small group discussions covering concerns and issues in academic leadership.

CONFERENCE BOARD
845 Third Avenue, New York, NY 10022
Phone: (212) 759-0900

Independent nonprofit research organization with a staff of 350, formerly known as National Industrial Conference Board. Supported by more than 4000 subscribing members including business and industrial concerns, universities, libraries, trade associations, labor unions, government agencies, and nonprofit organizations. Areas of interest include economics, management and organization. Collects and analyzes strategic business data, provides forums for business leaders to exchange information, and supplies factual information through its publications, conferences, and information service. Maintains a Canadian affiliate, Conference Board in Canada, located in Ottawa.

CREATIVE EDUCATION FOUNDATION
1015 Union Road, Buffalo, NY 14224
Phone: (716) 675-3181

Encourages and stimulates creativity in learning and decision making through tools, publications and training. Has a library of 2500 volumes and 1500 doctoral dissertations on microfiche. Runs the semiannual Creative Problem Solving Institute. **Publications:** *Creativity in Action* (monthly); *Journal of Creative Behavior* (quarterly); other.

EDUCATIONAL LEADERSHIP PROGRAM
109 East 89th Street, New York, NY 10128
Phone: (212) 534-2904

Created in 1984 as a special program of the Christian A. Johnson Endeavor Foundation, the Educational Leadership Program conducts its own programs, sponsors research, and offers consultation to institutions and organizations. It provides academic leaders in both schools and colleges with continuing opportunities to renew their vision and to reflect upon their institution's mission and value to society. In addition to week-long seminars, the program also sponsors papers and research projects on leadership themes.

HITACHI FOUNDATION
1509 22nd St., N.W., Washington, DC 20037
Phone: (202) 457-0588

Grants include those emphasizing leadership skills for individuals and community groups. Total grants amount in last reported year was $707,095. Write Felicia B. Lynch, V.P. of Programs.

IC² INSTITUTE

University of Texas at Austin, 2815 San Gabriel, Austin, TX 78705
Phone: (512) 478-4081

This institute is a major research center for the study of innovation, creativity and capital. Key research and study concentrations include creative and innovative management, the management of technology, measuring the state of society, and the evaluation of attitudes and opinions on key issues. **Publications:** *Centers of Creativity, Innovation and Leadership*; monographs; policy papers; research articles; books.

INDEPENDENT SECTOR

1828 L Street, N.W., Washington, DC 20036
Phone: (202) 223-8100

Its 650 members include corporations, foundations, and national voluntary organizations; associates are professionals of local, state, and regional organizations, and individuals who are active volunteer leaders. Goals are: to "preserve and enhance our national tradition of giving, volunteering and not-for-profit initiative"; to educate the public about the role of the independent nonprofit sector; and to conduct research on the independent nonprofit sector and its usefulness to society. **Publications:** Annual report; *Memo to Members*.

INSTITUTE FOR CASE DEVELOPMENT AND RESEARCH

Simmons College, Graduate School of Management, 409 Commonwealth Avenue, Boston, MA 02215
Phone: (617) 536-8390

Develops and distributes case studies on issues and problems confronting women in management in a variety of fields. Areas addressed include career planning and development, minority women in management, and day care. Maintains a collection of materials on management. **Publications:** *Bibliography of Cases on Women in Management* (revised annually).

INSTITUTE FOR EDUCATIONAL LEADERSHIP

1001 Connecticut Ave, N.W., Suite 310, Washington, DC 20036
Phone: (202) 822-8405

Coordinates programs at national, state, and local levels that are designed to support and enhance the capabilities of educators and policy makers. Acts as educational forum for information exchange among government, nonprofit, and business sectors. Sponsors the Washington policy seminars designed to assist education leaders by providing training in federal policy processes. **Publications:** Triennial newsletter; policy reports.

INTERNATIONAL LEADERSHIP CENTER
1600 Two Turtle Creek Village, Dallas, TX 75219
Phone: (214) 526-2953

Working to build a network of leaders. Sponsors the International Business Fellows Program for U. S. Business Leaders, and the Leadership America Program, a summer-long program for college-age students which seeks to develop their leadership skills through leadership development programs, outdoor leadership training, seminars, and internships.

W. K. KELLOGG FOUNDATION
400 North Ave., Battle Creek, MI 49017-3398
Phone: (616) 968-1611

Aid limited to programs concerned with application of existing knowledge rather than research. Current funding priorities include projects designed to improve human well-being, which includes broadening the leadership capacity of individuals. Total giving amount in last fiscal year was $105 million. **Publications:** Annual report, informational brochure, newsletter. Write to Nancy A. Sims, Executive Assistant-Programming.

LILLY ENDOWMENT INC.
P.O. Box 88068, Indianapolis, IN 46208
Phone: (317) 924-5471

Support for religion, education, and community development, with special concentration on programs that benefit youth, develop leadership, and help develop state of the art fund-raising to make nonprofit organizations become more self-sustaining. Total giving in 1988 was over $79 million. **Publications:** Annual report, informational brochure, program policy statement, application guidelines. Write John M. Mutz, President.

MERSHON CENTER
Ohio State University, 199 West 10th Avenue, Columbus, OH 43210
Phone: (614) 292-1681

As part of an ongoing interest in citizenship education, the Mershon Center has launched a new program, *Preparing Youth for Leadership in a Global Age,* to explore how America develops the leadership capability of its youth. They have completed a nationwide survey of leadership development programs for young people, and will host conferences on leadership development. **Publications:** *Directory of Youth Leadership Programs* (in press).

CHARLES STEWART MOTT FOUNDATION
1200 Mott Foundation Building, Flint, MI 48502-1851
Phone: (313) 238-5651

Supports community improvement through grants for, among other programs, training in and improving practices of leadership. Mott is a pioneer in community education concept. Total giving in 1988 was $23.8 million. Write to Judy Samelson, Director of Communications.

NASSP DIVISION OF STUDENT ACTIVITIES
National Association of Secondary School Principals, 1904 Association Drive, Reston, VA 22091
Phone: (703) 476-5432

Resource center for materials relating to leadership and leadership training at the secondary school level. Develops and distributes leadership training resources and guides for secondary school use. **Publications:** *Leadership for Student Activities* (monthly).

PUBLIC LEADERSHIP EDUCATION NETWORK
2001 O Street, N.W., Washington, DC 20036
Phone: (202) 872-1585

Members are twelve women's colleges working together to educate women for public leadership positions. Sponsors annual seminars and public policy internships. **Publications:** *PLEN Newsletter* (semiannual); *Learning to Lead*; *Wingspread Report: Educating Women for Leadership*.

SOCIETY FOR NONPROFIT ORGANIZATIONS
6314 Odana Road, Suite 1, Madison, WI 53719
Phone: (608) 274-9777

Members are leaders, board members, volunteers, and others who serve nonprofit organizations. Purpose is to provide a forum for the exchange of information, knowledge, and ideas on strengthening and increasing productivity within nonprofit organizations and among their leaders. Provides education and training programs; maintains resource center with materials on the operation of nonprofit organizations; offers professional support services. Sponsors Nonprofit Leadership Institute. **Publications:** *Nonprofit World* (bimonthly); occasional publications on nonprofit leadership and management.

WILDERNESS EDUCATION ASSOCIATION
20 Winona Avenue, Box 89, Saranac Lake, NY 12983
Phone: (518) 891-2915

Trains and certifies outdoor leaders, working in affiliation with 20 colleges and universities. Its National Standard Program for Outdoor Leadership Certification provides standards for outdoor leadership training. **Publications:** Newsletter (quarterly).

WOMEN IN GOVERNMENT RELATIONS LEADER FOUNDATION
6728 Old McLean Village Drive, McLean, VA 22101
Phone: (703) 556-9228

Purpose is to provide women with career opportunities in the field of business and government relations through leadership, education, advancement, development, endowment, and research. Sponsors projects to enhance corporate management skills and increase knowledge. Provides resources, techniques, methods, information, and training opportunities not otherwise available to women. Has a central resource base of career development programs related to business/government relations; sponsors internship programs and career seminars.